EISENSTEIN ON PAPER

Thames & Hudson would like to thank Kino Klassika Foundation for their invaluable support in making this edition happen.

KINO KLASSIKA

EISENSTEIN ON PAPER

GRAPHIC WORKS BY THE MASTER OF FILM

NAUM KLEIMAN

foreword by
MARTIN SCORSESE

547 illustrations

Thames & Hudson

РГАЛИ

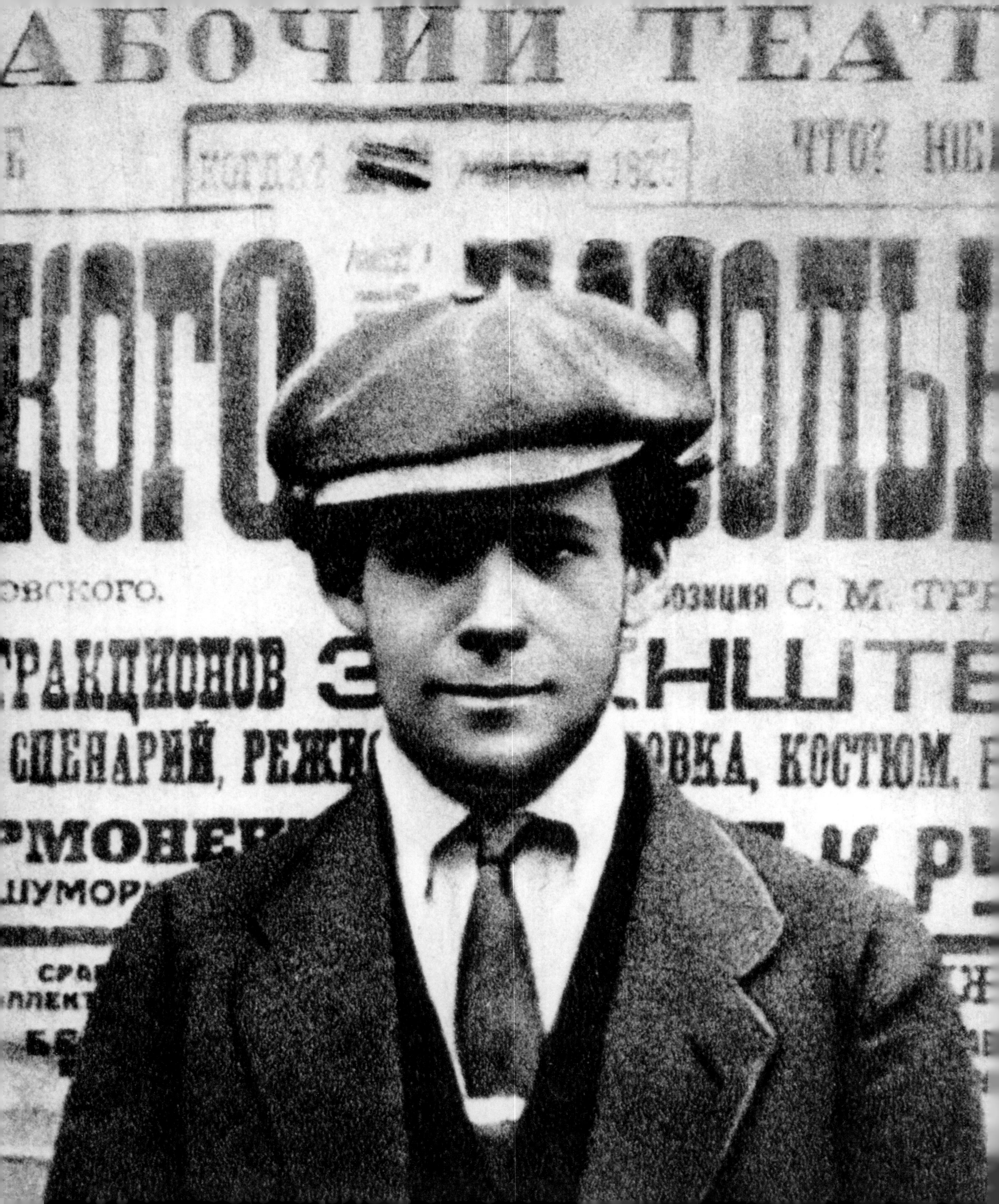
АБОЧИЙ ТЕАТ
ЧТО?
КОГО
ОВСКОГО.
ЗИЦИЯ С. М. ТР
ГРАКЦИОНОВ
СЦЕНАРИЙ, РЕЖИС
ОВКА, КОСТЮМ.
РМОНЕ
ШУМОР

CONTENTS

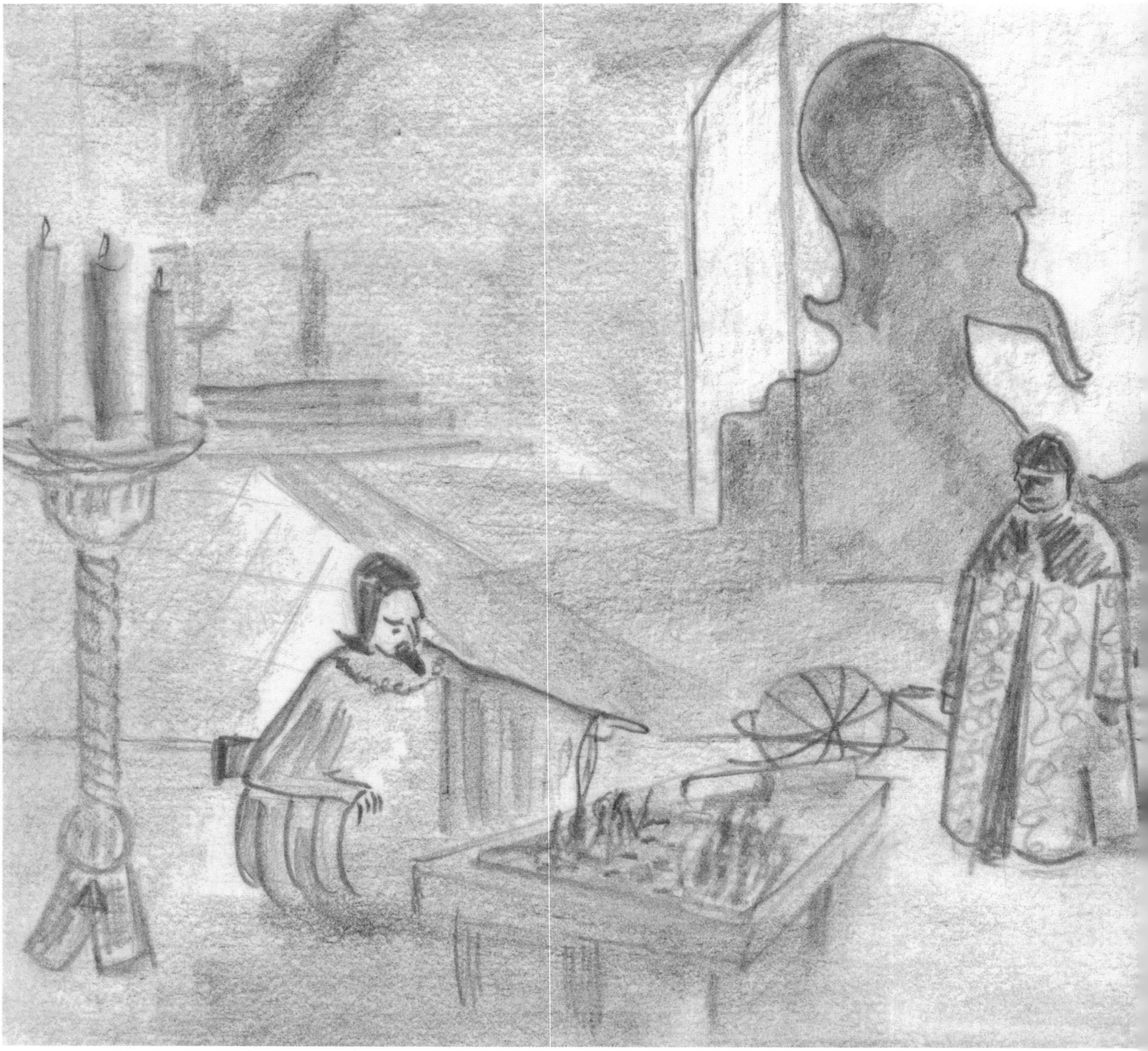

PREVIOUS
Sergei Eisenstein before the premiere of *Enough Stupidity in Every Wise Man*, his first independent production at the Proletkult Theatre (Moscow, 1923)

ABOVE
A sketch inspired by a scene from *Ivan the Terrible Part 2* – featuring Nikolai Cherkasov as Ivan – drawn by the young Martin Scorsese

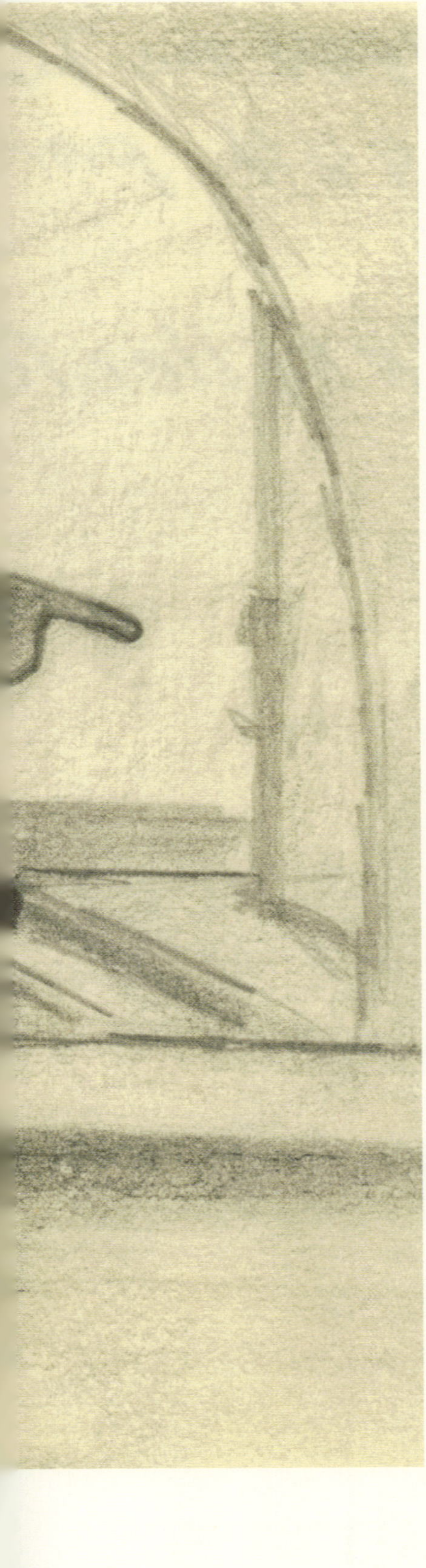

FOREWORD BY

MARTIN SCORSESE

When I was young, Sergei Eisenstein was one of the great canonical names of the cinema. He was one of the only filmmakers (along with Chaplin) revered by the serious intellectuals who decided what was and wasn't great art, and you would see his name mentioned alongside Joyce and Picasso and O'Neill and Stravinsky. *Battleship Potemkin* was generally considered to be one of the greatest films ever made.

The films themselves were something else again. *Potemkin*, no matter how many times you saw it, no matter how often you saw the 'Odessa Steps' sequence broken down frame by frame, had a force that was breathtaking. Rhythm, dynamism, collisions of images and ideas, all of the things that have been analyzed for many years now by so many film scholars. And, a graphic force so powerful that it seemed almost otherworldly. It wasn't just that Eisenstein had a visual gift – it was well beyond that. He visualized in multiple dimensions. It was Dickens, it was Disney (both of whom he famously admired), it was a total mastery of painting and design, and it was a percussive sense of rhythm and counterpoint, all concentrated into every single frame of film.

The first Eisenstein film I ever saw was *Alexander Nevsky*. There was a mention of it in *Cue* magazine, which was a cultural guide for New Yorkers. I took the subway up to the Thalia Theater on 95th Street and Broadway, walked in and sat down in the middle of the picture, right before the 'Battle on the Ice'. I was astonished, by what I was seeing *and* hearing: the ferocious brass in Prokofiev's score made such an impression on me that I went out and bought as many recordings of his music as I could find (I was disappointed by the sound in the restoration of that film: it lacked the raw force of the original).

The picture that really took my breath away was *Ivan the Terrible Part 2*, which was released for the first time in the United States in 1959 (I caught up with Part 1 a few years later). I felt like I'd been dropped into the middle of a secret ancient ceremony, like the Eleusinian Mysteries or the rites of the Roman Vestal Virgins.

As a matter of fact, when I got a little older and I was beginning to take the study of cinema seriously, I drew a frame from the picture, a high angle on Cherkasov standing over a table, the massive shadow of his profile cast against the wall. I might have drawn some other images from the picture. Each and every one of them. I'd never seen anything like it. I still haven't.

In the last few decades, Eisenstein's reputation has not exactly declined, but it has faded a bit. The reasons for this are somewhat mysterious to me. In his introduction, Ian Christie suggests that André Bazin had something to do with it. Maybe. Or maybe it's that the connection with Eisenstein and his world has loosened or been dropped or severed. I suppose the same could be said of Chaplin.

This wonderful book brings the artist and his visual imagination to life in a brand new way. I had seen quite a few of Eisenstein's drawings over the years, but never so many of them all together. The effect is overwhelming. On almost every page, you will find something to astonish you in these reproductions of sketches, line drawings, caricatures and designs for theatre and film. The continual play of volume and form is mesmerizing, the sense of colour (even when there *is* no colour!) and scale and the continual shifting of registers, from satiric to reverent to erotic, always surprising.

As you go through *Eisenstein on Paper* page by page, reading about the all-too-short life, studying the images, you'll marvel, and your understanding of those remarkable films will expand.

PREFACE BY TATIANA GORYAEVA, RGALI

SERGEI EISENSTEIN'S STOREHOUSE

Sergei Mikhailovich Eisenstein (1898–1948), one of the 20th century's greatest cultural figures, is best known as the maker of ground-breaking cinematic classics. His films – of which the most popular are *Battleship Potemkin, Alexander Nevsky* and *Ivan the Terrible* – are still studied today and continue to inspire artists in various fields. His work for the stage has been examined in some detail, notably his involvement with the First Workers' Theatre under the auspices of the Proletkult and his subsequent production of Wagner's opera *Die Walküre* for the Bolshoi Theatre. But it was in the field of drawing that Eisenstein's artistic career began.

We know that he became firmly interested in drawing in 1915. From his childhood, he had looked at the world through the eyes of an artist, dreaming of linking his own destiny with the arts. Even when he was serving as a Red Army engineer in Vologda, in 1918, Eisenstein described his enthusiastic impressions of its architectural monuments and of nature in the Russian north, writing to his mother: 'As I say, you only see landscapes like these in paintings: the perfectly cloudless sky, broad, vast, coloured pale green and orange and pink by the sunset, unbelievably clean, and far away a blue-grey hill and the sharp dark outline of a little village standing out against that amazing sky. Or birch trees with a pine forest behind, in the rays of the setting sun, with blue transparent shadows....' And again, in the same letter: 'The other thing I like here is the village women's dresses. I'm determined to buy one. They're stripy, with thick stripes of bright, bright red, yellow, green, violet, and blue – although it's the red that dominates: the others are only there to add variety.'

We also know that in 1920, after a brief hesitation, it was as a visual artist that Eisenstein began his life in the theatre; and later, he made more than one attempt to acquire a classical artistic education. At the time, he wrote to his mother: 'I am a member of the artists' trade union, my profession is that of an artist, and I specialize in staging and set design!' By 1922, he already had his productions for the Proletkult theatre behind him, as well as those (with Sergei Yutkevich) for Nikolai Foregger, and had taken courses at two drama studios and also at the technical school attached to the Theatre Division of the People's Commissariat for Enlightenment. That year, in another letter to his mother, he noted '... being an artist isn't my vocation at all! God alone knows how I've ended up as an "artist"! But *noblesse oblige*; although I do hope I'll somehow manage to get into directing.' Nonetheless, drawing would always remain a constituent part of Eisenstein's creative activity: it would accompany both his films and his contemplation, and it would be a means of expressing his sense of self.

The heritage of his drawings remained unknown to the public for a long time. His first exhibition, the only one held in his lifetime, took place at John Becker's gallery in New York between 15 October and 7 November 1932. It featured twenty-two drawings taken from 'Salome' and 'The Bullfight', two of the cycles he had drawn in Mexico. It was only after his death that Eisenstein really became known as an artist, however. The first major exhibition of his drawings was held in 1957 at the Central House of Arts Workers in Moscow. It included 200 sketches connected with *Alexander Nevsky, Ivan the Terrible* and the Bolshoi production of *Die Walküre*, as well as drawings from his time in Mexico and theatrical cartoons and caricatures. More than fifty years have passed since then, and in that time Eisenstein's drawings have been exhibited in France, Belgium (Antwerp), Italy, England, Germany, Japan and Canada. In 1998, the organizers of a huge anniversary exhibition of Eisenstein's drawings from the RGALI archive, staged in Moscow's Museum of Private Collections, promised with some fervour that his erotic drawings would be exhibited for the first time. In the end, however, the anticipated drawings were not shown. There was a little eroticism – a naked youth, seen side on – but no more than that. It is believed that the museum management censored the exhibition.

In the past, albums of Eisenstein's drawings and catalogues of his exhibitions have been published in the USSR, Mexico and France. Nonetheless, we can assert with confidence that these volumes do not give even an approximate idea of the place that visual art occupied in Sergei Mikhailovich's oeuvre in comparison to his chief muses: the theatre and the cinema. The largest and most representative collection of Eisenstein's drawings is held at RGALI, the Russian State Archive for Literature and Art. Catalogued as No. 1923 and consisting of 6,081 items dating from the 1870s to 1995 – including Eisenstein's collection of 17th- to 19th-century engravings (fifty-three items in all) – it represents his personal archive. His drawings on particular subjects are grouped into different cycles and series, or else by theme or chronology. Among them are albums of drawings he made as a child and young adult: cartoons, comic strips, illustrations for books he had read and architectural and anthropomorphic fantasias (1900s–1917). There are exercises in expressiveness (1920s) and cycles of drawings on mythological and biblical topics from his Mexican period (1931): 'Piet', 'Golgotha', 'Joseph and Potiphar's Wife', 'Heavenly Dramas', 'Samson and Delilah', 'St Sebastian', 'Prometheus' and 'The Death of King Duncan' (156 drawings on themes from *Macbeth*). The archive also holds drawings on various topics from the early 1940s, when Eisenstein was evacuated to Almaty (known in Russian as Alma-Ata until Kazakhstan became independent in 1991) along with the Mosfilm studio. The series 'At the Doctor's', 'The Military Commissariat', 'The Death of Nero' and 'The Prodigal Son' are included, alongside individual drawings recalling Eisenstein's world travels and his daydreams about unattainable delights. Finally, there are sketches from the post-war years on various themes: the theatre, the circus, the variety stage, Bible stories, reminiscences of the East, the 'Parks' series and drawings on literary subjects.

Eisenstein's sketches for theatrical productions and his films are grouped by title and organized chronologically. The archive includes a substantial collection of sketches for the sets, costumes and makeup to be used in plays for which Eisenstein did the set design or staging. There are a few drawings for his films and film projects – *Chung-kuo, MMM, Frunze, The Great Ferghana Canal* and *¡Que viva México!* – a significant collection of drawings for *Alexander Nevsky* and more than 1,000 sketches of sets, costumes and makeup for *Ivan the Terrible*.

A considerable part of Eisenstein's work is occupied by erotic themes, with their roots in the 'decadent' aesthetic of sexual liberation at the beginning of the 20th century – Russia's first sexual revolution, as it has become customary to call it. This period is characterized by the emergence – alongside imagery typical of Russian Symbolists such as Aleksandr Blok and Konstantin Somov – of the type of the decadent artist (for example Igor Severyanin and Victor Borisov-Musatov) in whom the intimate and sensuous side of love literally took possession of all forms of art.

The overwhelming majority of the material stored in the Eisenstein archive became public property thanks to the efforts of Pera Moiseevna Atasheva, Sergei Eisenstein's wife and friend. She made his acquaintance in the mid-1930s. A short memoir extract:

'... And so – Pera Atasheva! Eisenstein had become famous. Fame came crashing down on him, burying him under its weight, and he was giving way, he wasn't able to cope with it. He carried on living any old how, like a student. And one morning this round ball bounced up to him – cheery, friendly, like Kolobok in the fairy tale [a reference to the Russian fairy tale concerning an animate bread roll named Kolobok, who outwits various animals that want to eat him]. This ball-shaped being kept giggling. And, above all, it was a ball-shaped being of unusual kindliness and initiative. And it took everything onto its round little shoulders. Suddenly there was wonderful coffee, the shopping was dealt with, the papers were in order, a typewriter had been bought and had begun to rattle away against a chorus of perpetual nattering and giggling. I thought a kind sun had peeked into Eisen's room. They'd both chatter, in Russian or in English, and they'd both laugh, and feel cheerful. And in time Pera proved herself to be a loyal, devoted, selfless friend. On one occasion Eisen came down with something like smallpox! He was quarantined at once, and put in a kind of room with glass walls. He sat there as if he were in a cage. They even gave him his meals through a little window, like an orangutan at the zoo. We did visit, but we could only see him through the glass, and converse like deaf mutes. But Pera persuaded them to let her in so she could be with him in that cage, and she looked after him selflessly. I don't think all secretaries would have been capable of that.'

It was chiefly P. M. Atasheva who inspired and organized the transfer of many of Eisenstein's documents and materials to state ownership. Thanks to her, the Eisenstein archive is one of the largest and best-supplied personal collections, a real treasure for people studying this great artist's life, work and theoretical legacy.

The first documents were received from Atasheva in January 1949, and by the end of the year the public archive had received more than 4,000 documents (essays, directing notes for plays and films, screenplays, drawings and letters). The next consignment, of more than 6,000 documents, arrived in May 1957. It included working materials for Eisenstein's films, press articles, texts of lectures and more letters. These documents were acquired by the state, and the archive preserves Maksim Shtraukh's written assessment to the effect that they are of significant value for research into the history of world cinema.

Over the subsequent years, the archive continued to receive articles, drawings and photographs. In 1965, after Atasheva's death, all the remaining materials – drawings, diaries, theoretical notes and biographical documents – were passed to the state for safe-keeping. In total, RGALI received 25,000 documents relating to Eisenstein.

But the history of the formation of the Eisenstein archive did not end there. In 1970, the archive obtained Eisenstein's rough drawings for *Ivan the Terrible*, from costume designer Lidia Naumova. On the backs of two of the drawings were notes naming performers who were missing from the movie's credits, and on the back of one of them Eisenstein has written some instructions during the course of filming.

One of the archive's last acquisitions, in 1985, was a caricature by Eisenstein that dates from 1917–18. Naum Kleiman, the author of this volume, has written of the drawing: 'Eisenstein's cartoon "Life-guard dragoons on parade" is rather unusual: it is executed on a large sheet of card; the unbroken line of the drawing, characteristic of Eisenstein, is replaced here by a solid wash of gouache and by a ragged outline.... During this period Eisenstein was led to reject the sharp graphic style he had already mastered – led by his desire to resemble recognized cartoonists, and by his attraction to depictions of everyday life and to popular political prints. He began to make wide use of colour; his work is characterized by precise character types, the expressive placement of figures and groups on a white field, a mastery of balanced masses in asymmetrical compositions and other features....'

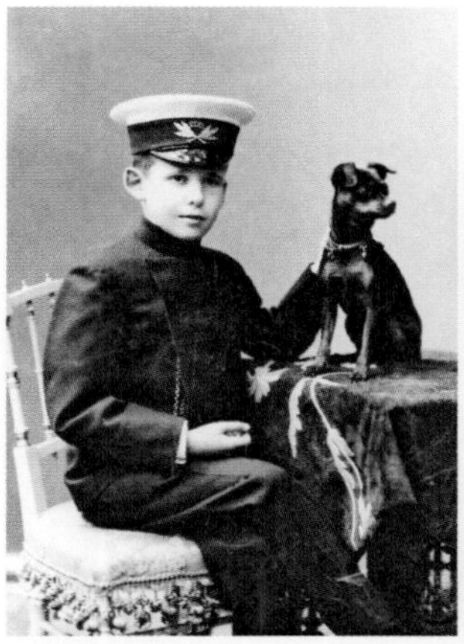

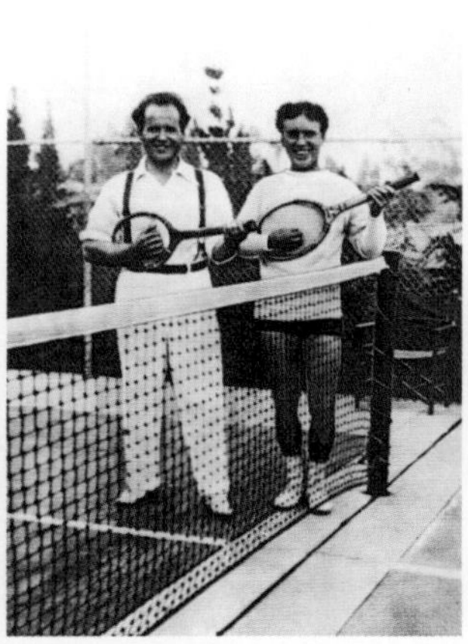

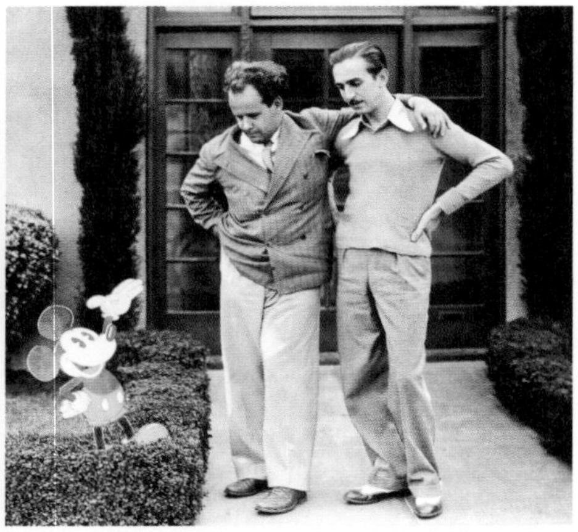

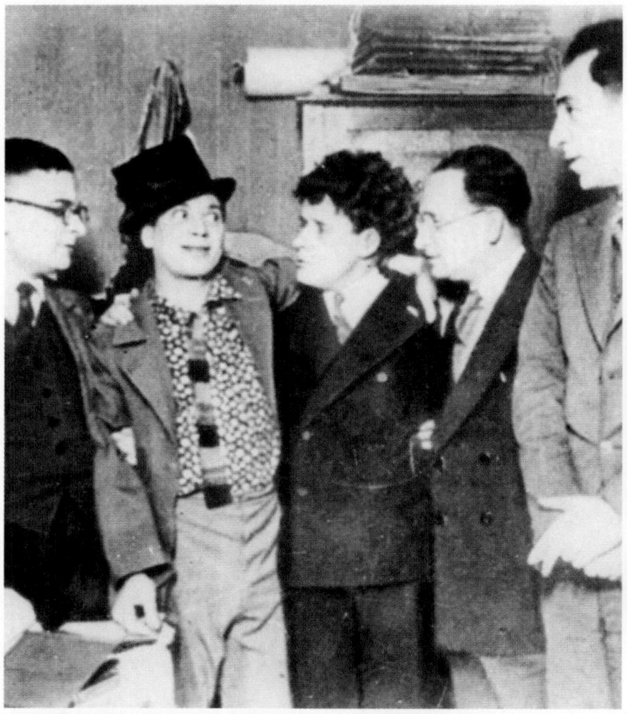

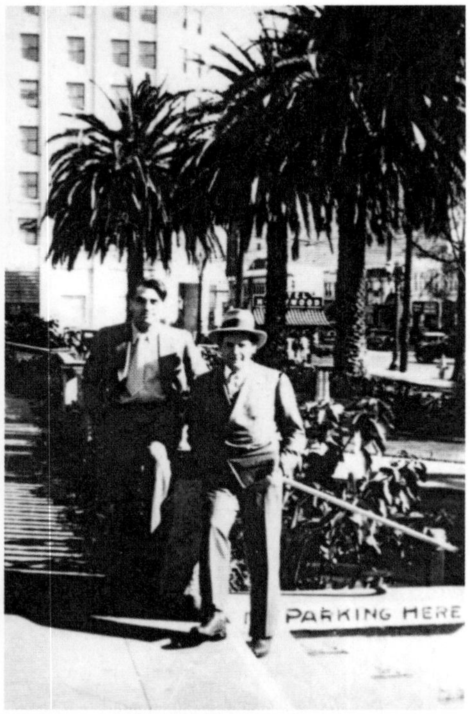

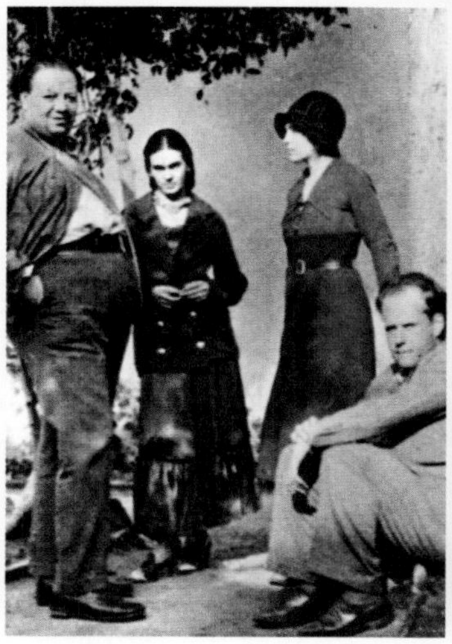

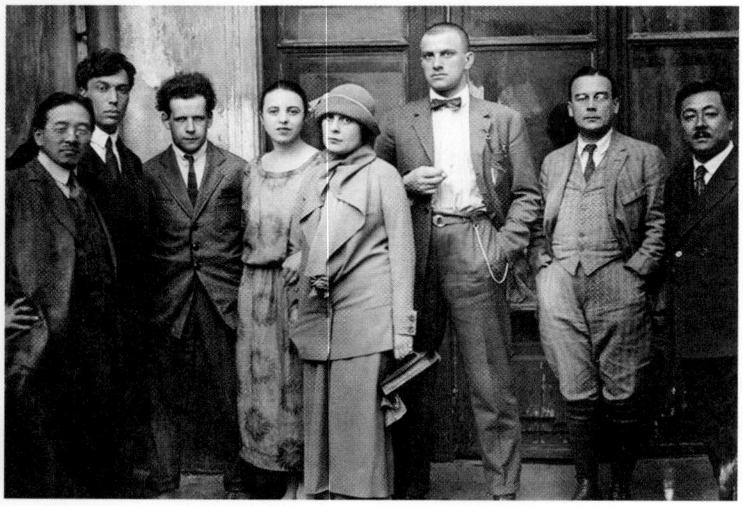

TOP LEFT
Riga secondary school pupil Sergei Eisenstein with his toy terrier

TOP CENTRE
With Charles Chaplin on his tennis court (Hollywood, 1930)

TOP RIGHT
With Mickey Mouse and Walt Disney (Hollywood, 1930)

CENTRE LEFT
With Harpo Marx after his performance in Moscow Music Hall (1933)

CENTRE RIGHT
With Luis Buñuel (Hollywood, 1930)

BOTTOM LEFT
(L–R) Diego Rivera, Frida Kahlo, Frances Flynn Paine and Sergei Eisenstein (Mexico City, 1931)

BOTTOM RIGHT
(L–R) Japanese writer Tamiji Naito, Boris Pasternak, Sergei Eisenstein, Olga Tretiakova, Lilya Brik, Vladimir Mayakovsky, Arseny Voznesensky and an interpreter at VOKS (All-Union Society for Cultural Connections with Foreign Countries) (Moscow, May 1924)

INTRODUCTION BY IAN CHRISTIE

RECONSTRUCTING CINEMA'S RENAISSANCE MAN

When Sergei Eisenstein died, as he had fatalistically foreseen, at the age of fifty in 1948, his reputation was at a low ebb. His last film, the second part of *Ivan the Terrible*, had been banned on Stalin's order and would not be seen for another decade, after both author and sponsor were gone. Indeed, it was the final paradox of Eisenstein's brief yet intense career that it owed so much to the tyrant who made it possible but also held it in check. Stalin received Eisenstein and his leading actor, Nikolai Cherkasov, at a midnight audience in the Kremlin in 1947, and the record of what was said makes for eerie reading.[1] Ostensibly, Stalin and his henchmen, the foreign minister Vyacheslav Molotov and the cultural supremo Andrei Zhdanov, only want to 'help' their leading artist correct his errors and make the film releasable. The parting exchange suggested this was achievable, and Eisenstein was offered anything he needed to 'correct' the film's portrayal of the tsar. Yet Eisenstein must have doubted that his bleak portrayal of Tsar Ivan's last years could ever find favour with the increasingly paranoid Stalin.

Ever since a near-fatal heart attack on the night that he finished editing the second part of *Ivan* in 1946, Eisenstein had been engaged in a journey of reminiscence and introspection. Most of the texts that were later collected as his 'amoral memoirs' date from this period of convalescence and enforced inaction.[2] All around, former colleagues were being hounded and executed in a renewed spasm of terror inspired by Stalin's fear of the post-war world, expressed as a campaign against 'cosmopolitanism'.[3] Eisenstein was forced, we may assume, to denounce foreign film-makers as 'purveyors of spiritual poison' in an essay of 1947.

His resurrection would take another decade to get underway, starting with the release of *Ivan the Terrible Part 2* in 1958 and the belated revival of his first film, *The Strike*, in the same year.[4] In 1958, Jay Leyda assembled a 'study version' of the unedited footage for Eisenstein's never-completed film shot in Mexico;[5] and a palimpsest of the banned film *Bezhin Meadow*, by the veteran film-maker Sergei Yutkevich and the young Naum Kleiman, appeared in 1965. A first selection of his writings, edited by his widow Pera Attasheva, appeared between 1964 and 1971,[6] preceded by a book of his drawings in 1961. Throughout the 1970s and 1980s, more writings appeared in translation, largely through the efforts of Jay Leyda. The first modern biography, superseding Marie Seton's valuable but highly personal 1952 account, was by a Romanian, Yon Barna. Peter Wollen's revisionist essay 'Eisenstein's Aesthetics', first published in 1968, would have a continuing influence on Anglo-American attitudes during the period when 'film studies' began to emerge as an academic field.[7] Wollen later explained his strategic reason for championing Eisenstein: 'I decided to write about Eisenstein rather than Hitchcock, partly because Eisenstein was already accepted as a great artist, even though he had worked with a large budget in an industrial context. He was a kind of wedge that I could use to break open the crust of prejudice and philistinism and hopefully smooth the path for others, like Hitchcock. And then Eisenstein also provided me with a way of linking the cinema to theory and semiotics through his own concerns with the nature of "film language".'[8]

Part of the problem was that the French critic André Bazin, who would exert a major posthumous influence on film studies, had effectively condemned Eisenstein in a widely circulated essay, 'The Evolution of the Language of Cinema', where he declared that 'montage as used by Kuleshov, Eisenstein, or Gance, did not give us the event; it alluded to it'.[9] Bazin was writing in the early 1950s, when Eisenstein's later thinking about montage and 'staging in depth' was still unknown, although it would largely anticipate his own.[10] Nonetheless, this pigeonholing continued, in many widely used textbooks.[11]

There was indeed ample new material available to posit a new and more complex Eisenstein. An Eisenstein who was very much our contemporary in his prodigious variety of expression, even under Stalinist censorship, and in his commitment to theorizing the audiovisual image by all available means. A vital key to this new Eisenstein was the reconstruction of his unfinished essay on Disney.[12] The souvenir pictures of Eisenstein meeting Walt Disney in Hollywood in 1930 and shaking hands with a cut-out Mickey Mouse were well known. But his struggle to identify what gave Disney's 'plasmatic' animation the feeling of life on screen were a major contribution to the theory of animation, drawing on the psychology of art and anthropology. And when Eisenstein speculated whether any of the admirers of his Tsar Ivan had ever realized the kinship between the looming figure of Cherkasov and that of Disney's animated fantasy *Willie the Whale* (1946) – subtitled 'The Whale Who Wanted to Sing at the Met' – he was revealing the same irreverence that had made his *October* and *The Old and the New* so disconcerting to those expecting mere propaganda.

Eisenstein's multifaceted creativity has been compared with that of Leonardo da Vinci, a parallel that intrigued Eisenstein after his precocious reading of Freud's study of Leonardo in 1918.[13] Just as painting was only one aspect of Leonardo's genius, so films were only part of Eisenstein's creative output. And as more of both his exploratory writing and graphic work become available, the challenge – which perhaps bears comparison with new scholarship on Leonardo[14] – becomes how to acknowledge and respond to such an outpouring?

Naum Kleiman here provides a uniquely authoritative commentary on the changing role of drawing across Eisenstein's lifetime. But how would we describe his 'public' career in light of what is now known? Among the many new publications that have taken advantage of post-Soviet access to Russian archives, Oksana Bulgakowa's 1998 biography sheds valuable light on almost every aspect of Eisenstein's public and private lives.[15] Eisenstein himself presented a highly persuasive 'myth of origin' for the Soviet era in Russian cinema which, thanks to his immense prestige, held sway for a long time. According to this: 'We came upon no ready-built city; there were no squares or streets laid out, not even little crooked lanes and blind alleys. We came like Bedouins or goldseekers to a place with unimaginably great possibilities...to a deserted landscape....'[16]

The mass exodus of Russian film personnel in 1917–19 had indeed created a void, which favoured Eisenstein and his contemporaries Lev Kuleshov, Denis Kaufman (soon to become 'Dziga Vertov') and Vsevolod Pudovkin, as they set about creating what amounted to a new industry. However, we now know that a thriving early Russian cinema existed for a decade before the revolutions of 1917 alongside the burgeoning avant-garde theatre that had fascinated the young Eisenstein. After emerging from the Red Army in 1920, amid the cross-currents of Moscow's post-revolutionary society, as full of mystics as of political activists, he was drawn to the febrile world of radical theatre, joining what survived of the Proletkult movement that Lenin had purged. Designing colourful costumes and sets for an adaptation of Jack London's story 'The Mexican', he managed to subvert the director's intended naturalism by siting a boxing match among the audience. Praise for this bold effect inspired him to see theatre as a new profession, although a conflict was already evident between the Proletkult's earnest ideals and the avant-garde elements their designer was injecting.

He took the opportunity to study with his idol, the great theatre director Vsevolod Meyerhold, but rivalry soon distanced them, throwing Eisenstein back into Proletkult, now as a director. In spring 1923, he planned a circus-style 'leftist salon of political crossword-puzzles', travestying a venerable 19th-century play by Ostrovsky – and included among many stunts a short film, purporting to be the diary of one of the characters. Despite no previous experience other than helping re-edit foreign film imports, Proletkult allowed him to make their first feature-length film, the explosive *The Strike*, the following year. With its excellent press reviews, the film provoked envy among many in the cinema community, but immediately marked Eisenstein as a major talent, confirmed by a medal awarded at the 1925 Exposition des Arts Décoratifs et Industriels Modernes in Paris.

However much new information we have about early Soviet culture, there can be no doubt that it was *Battleship Potemkin* that brought its twenty-seven-year-old creator immediate and lasting fame, especially among foreign admirers. Commissioned for the twentieth anniversary of the 'first' Russian revolution of 1905, this focused on the sailors' mutiny and its impact on Odessa, creating indelibly classic scenes and images that continued to fascinate Eisenstein himself, almost as if he had not directed and edited it, from his first polemical essays of the 1920s up to an aesthetic treatise *Non-Indifferent Nature* in the mid-1940s.[17]

Potemkin was not the 'failure' with Russian audience of 1926 that has sometimes been claimed.[18] But its real impact was first felt in Germany, with the benefit of a driving accompaniment commissioned from Edmund Meisel, a composer who had worked for the radical Berlin theatre director Erwin Piscator and with Brecht. Despite censorship and outright bans in many countries, there is ample evidence of the inspirational impact of *Potemkin* throughout the world. *Close Up*, the first journal devoted to film as an avant-garde art form, proclaimed: 'We feel that the future of pure cinema is safe in Soviet hands.'[19] And among the many celebrities on both sides of the Atlantic who paid tribute to *Potemkin* as a radical demonstration of cinema's innate power, there were many young men and women who were inspired by its example. From America, Jay Leyda would succeed in attending the Moscow film school VGIK, where Eisenstein taught during the 1930s, before becoming his main conduit for publishing in English. Later, the young Samuel Beckett, who had acted as secretary to James Joyce and probably knew of the writer's admiration for *Potemkin*, wrote to Eisenstein from Dublin, asking if he might come and study with him.[20]

Even before *Potemkin* reached many foreign audiences, Eisenstein was ordered to set aside his 'village picture', *The General Line*, in favour of another commemorative film, this time for the tenth anniversary of the October Revolution of 1917. The massive production would tax him physically to the point of collapse, and generate much ironic comment about how it had caused more damage to Leningrad (as St Petersburg had now become) and to the Winter Palace than the revolution itself. It also apparently provoked the first direct intervention of Stalin into the course of Soviet cinema. Bulgakowa notes that whereas Stalin's then rivals Trotsky and Bukharin had made literature their priority, cultivating the famous writers of the period, 'the pragmatic politician Stalin chose the new medium of film'.[21] According to Eisenstein's associate Grigory Aleksandrov, Stalin visited the editing room in late 1927, demanding to see any scenes that featured Trotsky – who was naturally included in Eisenstein's account of the events of 1917. These were deleted, as part of Stalin's campaign to eliminate his rival.[22]

When *October* was finally released in March 1928, it did not meet with the same success as *Potemkin*, either at home or abroad. This was largely due to Eisenstein's interspersing the climax of the October Revolution with a series of experiments in 'intellectual montage', notably in sequences set within the Winter Palace, where the vacillating figure of Kerensky, leader of Russia after the February Revolution, triggers a series of ironic comparisons with Napoleon. Or when the tsarist rallying call 'God and Country' is deconstructed in a sequence of increasingly abstract images. Although *October* included spectacular staging of some scenes that had marked the October Revolution, which have since served repeatedly to illustrate that unfilmed event, its formal and aesthetic ambitions mystified many audiences expecting another *Potemkin*.

When Eisenstein was finally able to return to his 'village' film, Stalin's policy on agriculture had changed, and 'the general line' became *The Old and the New*, making its heroine Marfa Lapkina a standard-bearer for the mechanization of Soviet farming – although with a sequence devoted to the mechanical milk separator that manages to combine the erotic and the sacramental, and a balletic vision of massed tractors that has been compared with Busby Berkeley's Hollywood dance routines.

By the time *The Old and the New* was premiered in late 1929, Eisenstein and his colleagues Tisse and Aleksandrov had already left for their supposed fact-finding mission to study sound cinema abroad, which would last over two years. Instructed by Stalin to 'learn from and teach the West', they were reminded how important Soviet films had already been in creating an image of the Revolution abroad. In practice, their progress from Germany to Switzerland, then to Britain and France before setting off for the United States, had the appearance of a triumphal tour, with the young Eisenstein feted on all sides. The range of celebrities he met, as the most admired film-maker of the era, underlines the impact that *Potemkin* had made. From Luigi Pirandello, George Bernard Shaw and James Joyce to Albert Einstein and the physicist Pyotr Kapitsa, many sensed that Eisenstein was much more than a maker of incendiary film propaganda. His views on a wide range of subjects were sought, his lectures were packed, and he in turn took every opportunity to experience what he had only read about.

Money had been a constant problem since leaving Russia. But just when returning to Moscow seemed inevitable, an invitation from Jesse Lasky and Paramount took the Russians to their goal – Hollywood – and guaranteed them a salary. Eisenstein's Atlantic crossing and progress from New York and Boston to Los Angeles seemed like a dream come true, offering a further round of meetings with celebrities who ranged from the philosopher John Dewey to Charlie Chaplin. However, the discussions about possible film projects never reached fruition, with *The Glass House*, *Sutter's Gold* and *An American Tragedy* were all rejected by Paramount. By the end of 1930, Eisenstein had only one backer: the radical novelist Upton Sinclair and his wife were willing to finance a film that would present a fresco of Mexican history and landscape.

The ensuing fourteen months that Eisenstein spent in Mexico would include some of the happiest periods of his life, and would release a torrent of creative self-expression through the hundreds of drawings that he made. Their uninhibited and often blasphemous sexual imagery, however, would also lead to accusations of 'perversion' by his backers. And the broken promise that the 200,000 feet of film he had shot would follow him back to the USSR became a defining tragedy in his life. The climate of the Soviet Union under Stalin's increasingly dictatorial regime provided Eisenstein with a series of unwelcome surprises. His first projects, about Moscow through the ages (echoing his historical treatment of Mexico) and a comedy about a 'little man', were rejected as unsuited to the new spirit of heroic 'socialist realism'.

A 1935 conference organized to set the approved direction of Soviet cinema saw many of Eisenstein's former colleagues taking turns to berate him for not putting his talents to constructive use.[23] He continued to teach at VGIK, and the energy and range of his classes was captured in students' notes, and to plan a systematic exposition of his aesthetics. But the most vivid insight into his state of mind comes from drawings made in the mid-1930s, some of which express profound despair, especially as it became clear that the Mexican footage would never reach Moscow. The question of what Eisenstein's next film would be was finally answered in 1935 by a script from Aleksandr Rzheshevsky which seemed to combine approved contemporary themes with his growing anthropological interests. *Bezhin Meadow* took its title from a classic story by Ivan Turgenev, yet was based on a recent incident that had been heavily promoted as a model for young communists to follow. Pavlik Morozov was a boy who had denounced his father, chairman of the village Soviet, to the GPU for anti-Soviet activities, and been killed by his own family in revenge, thus becoming an official Soviet martyr.

In Eisenstein's and Rzheshevsky's version, young Stepok tries to protect the crop of his collective farm from political 'sabotage' by his father, and his death at the hands of the reactionaries leads to a peasant demonstration in support of his bravery. But even this exemplary fable did not win approval, in part due to the unwelcome religiosity of a sequence about ransacking a church. Despite the wide international interest it aroused, *Bezhin Meadow* was subject to heavy demands for revision and never released. Eisenstein's career was only saved by his acceptance of another commission, to celebrate the medieval prince and later saint, Alexander Nevsky, revered for his defence of Kievan Rus against the Tatars, and eventually the Teutonic knights, in a battle on the frozen Lake Peipus in 1242.

Recreating medieval Russia allowed Eisenstein to pursue his scholarly and art historical interests, while also staying far from the treacherous field of contemporary political issues – until Stalin and Hitler's non-aggression pact of August 1939, which led to the film being temporarily suppressed. But the Nazi invasion of 1940 gave it a new topicality, and *Alexander Nevsky* became not only Eisenstein's first sound film to be released, with a stirring score by Sergei Prokofiev, but also his most popular. For some admirers of his earlier work, it seemed like a capitulation to the demands of Stalin's nationalistic 'romanticism', even a film that Hollywood would have been proud to produce. But while it rehabilitated Eisenstein as the USSR's most internationally renowned artist, it also allowed him to experiment practically with audiovisual montage, as he would explain in an essay that appeared in his first book on film aesthetics.[24] And it would have other unexpected consequences, such as helping to inspire *Henry V*, starring and directed by Lawrence Olivier in 1944.[25]

While *Nevsky* restored Eisenstein to the forefront of Soviet cinema, much as *Potemkin* had first placed him there a decade earlier, it also made him even more beholden to Stalin's ambitions. Eisenstein may have dreamt of making a film about Pushkin's emotional life, but Stalin had other plans for his leading film-maker. Another celebration of an illustrious forerunner was decreed, and so Eisenstein set to work on a chronicle about the reign of the 16th-century Tsar Ivan, nicknamed 'the Terrible' on account of his bloody despatch of opponents, including his own son. Now he could write his own script and supervise every aspect of the film's production, which was evacuated to Alma-Ata (now Almaty) in Kazakhstan, as German forces drove into western Russia. Far from Moscow, Eisenstein was able to immerse himself completely in creating the world of Ivan's court, acting as the film's designer in addition to his other roles.

As the conception expanded to a planned three parts, tracing Ivan's trajectory from a youthful puppet of the aristocratic boyars, through early manhood and losing his consort Anastasia as a victim of court intrigue, to becoming the saturnine figure of his maturity, so Eisenstein invested more of his own inner life in this intimate portrait of a lonely autocrat. The young Ivan's insecurity and traumatic witnessing of his mother's murder was a scene that clearly meant much to Eisenstein, and was moved from its original place in *Part 1* to become a flashback in *Part 2*. Sequences such as a people's pilgrimage to beseech Ivan's return from his self-imposed retreat, and his attempt to woo his youthful friend Kolychev, now an archbishop, seem imbued with Eisenstein's own sense of isolation.

In the event, the first part of his *Ivan* was greeted with rapturous praise in 1944, only for the second to be banned in 1945, soon after Eisenstein had suffered a heart attack. The memoirs that he started compiling during his convalescence were written as if posthumously.[26] Eisenstein's portrait of the ageing tyrant, trapped in a labyrinthine world of his own making, had clearly disturbed its Kremlin patron, yet who seemingly still wanted to 'correct' it as late as 1947. Considering the near-paralysis of Soviet film-making in these post-war years, the fact that Stalin wanted to discuss Ivan with its star and director seems remarkable, and a clear sign of the film's tremendous symbolic and psychological significance. The very fact that Eisenstein had wanted to extend what was already a risky scenario as far as Ivan's final despair suggests that either he was oblivious to the film's immediate referent, or that he did not care about his own fate amid the continued arrests.

When Eisenstein died during the night of 10 February 1948, he had been hard at work on an essay about the new world of colour film. Writing, and a limited amount of drawing, such as the cycle 'Les dons', had become his way of surviving the maelstrom of Stalin's last years. In one text from this period, he wrote rapturously about an American wartime film, *A Guy Named Joe* (Victor Fleming, 1943), in which Spencer Tracy played a pilot who is killed but returns as a guardian angel to protect a younger flyer who was his rival in love.[27] Eisenstein discerned in this romantic fantasy a message close to his heart:

'The idea that the hands of each trainee would be guided by the thousands that perished before him attains the height of pathos....

The death of one is the guarantee for others of being able to fly.

Victims are not without value.[28]

The chain of transmission of experience is uninterrupted

And each flight is the creative performance of all....

The story of *A Guy Named Joe* is magnificent...precisely because of this idea of creative heritage which is transmitted through generations in whatever domain.

And especially in our domain of creation.'

If this sounds fanciful, even heretical in a Soviet context, it makes sense as a restatement of the earlier tradition of Russian Symbolism as a collective transgenerational enterprise, and even of the late-19th-century mystic Nikolai Fedorov and his 'philosophy of the common task'.

The Eisenstein that we can now reconstruct from the growing body of his writings being published and translated, and especially from the drawings, his least public form of expression, is much more

1898
Born on 23 January to Mikhail Osipovich and Yulia Ivanovna Eisenstein in Riga, Latvia.

1909
His parents divorce and his mother moves back to St Petersburg. Eisenstein remains with his father.

1915
Enrols at the Institute of Civil Engineering in what becomes Petrograd and develops a love of theatre.

1918
Is drafted into the Red Army as an engineer and starts to work as an actor and designer in army clubs.

1920
Works with various theatre groups, designing *Macbeth*, *The Mexican*, *Heartbreak House* and other productions.

1923
First film experience is an insert made for his penultimate Proletkult production, *The Wise Man*.

1924
Works with Esfir Shub on re-editing imported films and writes his first feature, *The Strike*.

1925
Films *Battleship Potemkin* in Odessa, commissioned to mark the 20th anniversary of the failed 1905 revolution.

1926
Travels to Berlin before the triumphant release of *Potemkin*, and returns to start *The General Line*.

1927–8
Commissioned to commemorate the Bolshevik revolution of 1917, *October* is subject to political censorship.

1929
When work resumes on *The General Line*, the title is changed to *The Old and the New*.

1929–30
Travels to Western Europe and the USA, spending six months in Hollywood on projects that are rejected by Paramount.

complex than either his reputation as a solemn theorist of intellectual montage, or his image as a loyal servant of the Soviet state. It was not that 'the little boy from Riga', as Eisenstein always felt himself to be, was in obvious revolt against the Stalinist state. Indeed, his later writings continue to profess a belief in the eventual triumph of Communism that we may find difficult to credit as sincere:

'Time and time again our understanding of immortality was emphatically defined as immortality in the struggle for the revolutionary idea of freedom.

The bookish platitude for many, for our generation – I say again – was the emergence of a new awareness of life and reality.'[29]

Eisenstein also confessed in his memoirs to a taste for self-abasement, a willingness to accept cruelty and the exercise of tyranny, which had made the subject of Russia's notorious 'Ivan the Terrible' a congenial one. Eisenstein's Ivan might not have been terrible enough for Stalin – 'you can show him as a cruel man, but you have to show why he had to be cruel', according to the midnight discussion.[30] But the pathos of his isolation, surrounded by a romanticized homoerotic portrayal of the band of ruthless oprichniki sworn to absolute loyalty, certainly appealed to Eisenstein's own complex psyche.

We are now free to reassess the films, released from the need that their contemporaries felt to judge Eisenstein in relation to the USSR's policies and, ultimately, Stalin. Every Soviet citizen had to reach their own accommodation with this terrifying regime; Eisenstein had less reason to be apologetic than most, considering his acts of personal defiance and bravery, such as concealing Meyerhold's archive after his murder. But how to read them from a post-Soviet perspective?

Here, the graphic legacy provides a vital insight. After the fascination of the precocious drawings from childhood and early youth, two categories represent the most public of aspects of Eisenstein as draughtsman: his theatre designs of the early twenties, and those more or less directly linked to the later films, where he largely served as his own production designer. What remains, and forms by far the largest category, is Eisenstein's self-exploration through drawing, across a period when writing and even talking among supposed friends was dangerous. I have elsewhere described Eisenstein's drawings as a 'third text' in his creative output, which is to claim even more importance for them than, say, the rich marginalia of such major writers as Victor Hugo or Pushkin.[31] This first published selection to appear since the dissolution of the Soviet Union offers a chance to test such a claim. Among all the series and groups, attention will inevitably focus on those that seem to offer insight into Eisenstein's most personal and necessarily secret impulses. The 'Murder of Duncan' group, produced in an outpouring during his year in Mexico, belong to the period of Eisenstein's most uninhibited exploration of psychosexual themes, when the often farcically erotic and blasphemous 'secret' drawings accelerated his departure from the Americas in 1932.[32] But separate drawings from the 1930s and 1940s also clearly relate to crises in their author's life ('That's how I do feel' is a caption to one), as well as his most grandiose intellectual ambitions ('The Building to be Built').

Often, Eisenstein seems to be reaching out towards an intellectual and emotional synthesis that recalls the cultural world of his youth. The accusations of Symbolism and 'formalism' that pursued his films from *October* onwards are perhaps evidence that his contemporaries perceived this undercurrent, which we are free to explore without prejudice. And it may be significant that Eisenstein was keen to collaborate with the Symbolist writer Andrei Bely, also a prolific graphic self-analyst, before the latter's death in the early 1930s.[33]

As we contemplate the tragic disparity between Eisenstein's boundless ambition and the mere seven films he was able to complete, the drawings provide a uniquely valuable record of his unquenchable appetite for 'life creation'.[34] However scandalous and even infantile some of these may seem (often making their reproduction problematic) Eisenstein's almost continuous practice of drawing cannot be considered merely symptomatic or reflex. Because he 'never learned to draw' – any more than he 'learned' how to make films – drawing would serve many functions at different stages in a life that required the adoption of multiple personae. It was the fate of some of the most talented among the first generation of the Soviet intelligentsia to combine aspects of Symbolism and Modernism with an idealistic Communism, creating a distinctive aesthetic utopia that both fed, and was frequently annihilated by, Stalinism. Prominent among those celebrants and victims was 'the little boy from Riga', who was also Soviet Russia's greatest artist in the very public medium of cinema.

1931 • **Receives private funding from the USA and shoots *¡Que Viva México!*. He never gets to edit the footage.**

1932 • **Returns to USSR and to teaching at the film school GTK. His projects *MMM* and *Moscow* are rejected.**

1935 • **Criticized for inactivity by many former colleagues at a major conference on Soviet cinema.**

1936–7 • **Is forced to revise a major film, *Bezhin Meadow*. It is not released and is destroyed by an order from above.**

1938 • **Biopic *Alexander Nevsky* – Eisenstein's first sound film – is well received and restores him to favour.**

1940 • **Production of Wagner's *Die Walküre* is staged at the Bolshoi Theatre during Nazi-Soviet pact.**

1941–4 • **During the wartime evacuation of Mosfilm, *Ivan the Terrible* is filmed in Almaty, Kazakhstan.**

1945 • **Premiere of *Ivan the Terrible Part 1*. Works on *Part 2* and writes the book *Non-Indifferent Nature*.**

1946 • **Wins the Stalin Prize for *Ivan Part 1*; *Ivan Part 2* is banned and not released until 1958.**

1947 • **Becomes director of the cinema section in the Institute of Art History. Meets Stalin to discuss modifying *Ivan Part 2*.**

1948 • **Dies of heart failure on 11 February in Moscow. The funeral is held on 13 February.**

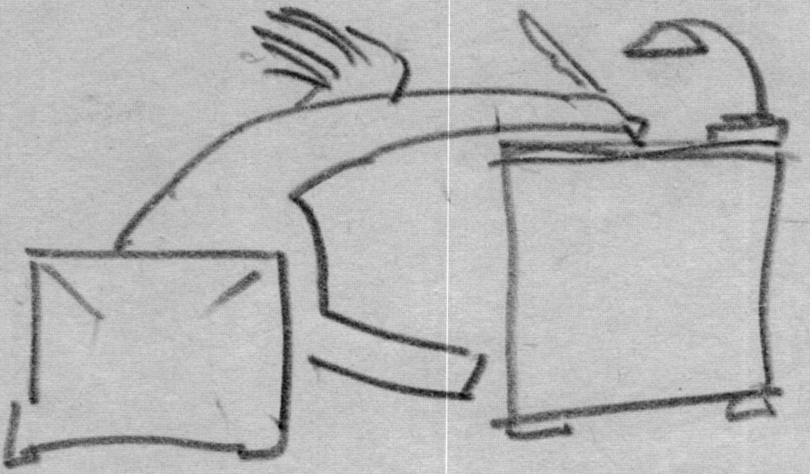

Моя посадка за столом.
И даже не слишком очно́.

30 Мч

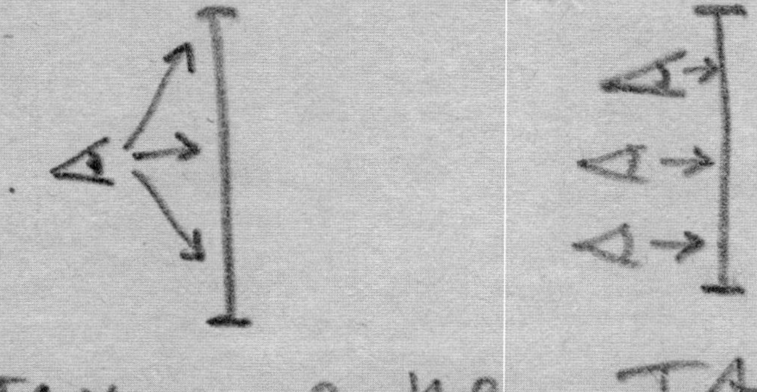

ТАК, а не ТАК.

PREFACE TO THE DRAWINGS

RULES OF THE GAME

'What's important isn't what an artist does, it's what he represents.' — Pablo Picasso

'Man only plays when he is indeed a human being, in the full sense of that word, and he is only completely a human being when he is playing.' — Friedrich Schiller

Eisenstein's fame as a draughtsman took much longer to establish than his fame as a director and his authority as a cinema theorist. Those usual scapegoats, the audience and the critics, are not to blame this time. During Sergei Mikhailovich's lifetime, they had no idea his drawings even existed.

Not that Eisen (as his colleagues called him, familiarly but also with respect) made a secret of the fact that he drew. When he lectured at the Cinematographic Institute in Moscow, the students watched his chalk fly across the blackboard as he used drawings to illustrate the laws of the directing game, both on the stage and on the screen.

Mostly, he drew sketches of a *mise-en-scène* (a scheme of movements on a horizontal surface) or of what he called *mise-en-cadres* (how to film the action of an episode as a series of shots from different points and angles, to produce a montage). But there would also be quick outline drawings of characters, showing how they looked or how they moved, how they interacted in space or how they changed in time. The drawings, in white chalk on the blackboard, would appear rapidly, like lines of light on a film negative – and just as instantaneously they would vanish as a damp rag swept over them. Some students tried to copy these seemingly simple pictures in their exercise books, but the expressiveness would somehow disappear, the lines would wrinkle up like a leaky balloon. The copyists' pencils would be unable to keep up with Eisenstein's chalk, and in the end they would give up. Nobody ever recorded these improvisations on photographic film, and not only because Leicas were a rarity in Moscow at that time and film itself in short supply. In the end, his drawings were no more than supplementary visual explanations – ephemeral butterflies in the flowering meadow of his lectures.

At the Mosfilm studio, Eisenstein's collaborators on *Alexander Nevsky* (1938) and *Ivan the Terrible* (1944/45) received his *croquis* (rough sketches). These were usually done in plain, graphite pencil on ordinary paper, sometimes on the backs of old typescripts, on scraps of paper with roughly torn edges, or on the envelopes of letters he had just received. Clean paper was then in short supply in the USSR, too.

We cannot say that these little drawings were not valued: on the contrary, people hoped for them, even demanded them. The designers used them in creating their detailed, full-colour drawings of the sets and costumes to be made. Cinematographers obtained from them a visual impression of the themes or the composition of the scenes that were to be shot. Makeup artists understood from them how the director wanted the actors to look when transformed into characters. Before the composer Sergei Prokofiev wrote the music for one of the director's films, he insisted on seeing if not the material that had been already been shot, then at least Eisen's drawings. Nikolai Cherkasov, who played Ivan the Terrible, complained half-jokingly that Eisenstein was 'contorting him to make him fit the picture': the director used drawings to explain the tsar's character, or how the actor was to play him in the shot. The drawings did not only lay down an interpretation of the role, they also provided a standard against which the expressiveness of the acting could be measured – a standard that creatures of flesh and blood did not always find easy to meet.

But there were also times when an actor or cinematographer or makeup artist would receive their latest *croqui* and burst into laughter. The drawings presented Eisenstein's ideas in the form of acute caricatures or graphic jokes, sometimes very salty ones. Here again, the director had to engage in a kind of playing. Precisely because the desired result was difficult to achieve, it must – according to Eisenstein's rule – be done joyfully.

Sergei Mikhailovich's drawings went around the film crews; some of them would be returned to him, others would be quietly kept as souvenirs. Some vanished without trace once they had been transformed into a prop, a set or a shot. Assistant film editor Esfir Tobak once admitted: 'I was gluing together coils of film, and all the time Eisen was drawing. On anything that came to hand: scraps of wrapping paper, labels that were waiting to be attached to film canisters....By the time I'd finished work, there were piles of his drawings all over the cutting room. I got angry, and I threw the whole lot in the bin.' And, with a sigh of regret: 'If I'd only known how people would come to value them....'

At home, Eisenstein liked to play a game with his guests: he would open one of his numerous folders, which would turn out to contain not sketches for a film but drawings of the most unexpected things. He would then watch, with probing irony, to see how the astonished guests reacted. Years later, some of those who first saw these papers in Eisenstein's flat in the Potylikha neighbourhood, or at his *dacha* in Kratovo, admitted their surprise that the drawings resembled neither the familiar Eisenstein of the film screen nor conventional, fine-art draughtsmanship. They were something like caricatures, something like anthropomorphic sketches, something like outlines – which, academic convention would dictate, should be filled in with form and colour. But, for whatever reason, these outlines touched a nerve. Better-educated guests would launch into analogies ('Almost like Matisse', 'No worse than Cocteau'). Plainer ones would ask, in all honesty, how they were to understand the strange themes or the non-realistic style. The writer Boris Agapov didn't say a word: he just gestured, reproducing the kinked line of the pencil – and saw Eisen's eyes shining with approval.

Did Eisenstein want his drawings to be seen by a wider audience than that of his pupils, colleagues and friends? We know he tried several times to make his drawings public. As an adolescent (when he was known to his family as 'Rorik'), Eisenstein wrote from Riga to his mother in St Petersburg, telling her that his father had recommended that his drawings be published in 'Golden Journal' – a proposed avant-garde periodical that was planned to be the Baltic analogue of *Apollo*, an important arts magazine in St Petersburg. Alas, this project was interrupted by the outbreak of war.

In 1917, Eisenstein – by then an architecture student – sent a number of political cartoons to the St Petersburg papers. One or two were even printed. The well-known humorist Arkady Averchenko took notice of them, but the general public forgot them. In the early 1920s, when he was starting work as a director and scenographer, Eisenstein sent several of his sketches to magazines. They were published as illustrations to articles and notices about the productions to which they were related. They went along with other revolutionary innovations in the theatre, they were quite fit to stand alongside the work of avant-garde artists...and they dissolved in the period colour of the time.

Eisenstein returned to drawing in Mexico in 1931, after an eight-year gap. He agreed to have a few sketches published in the American magazine *Creative Art*, and even wrote a crib about them for Anita Brenner, who was to write an article about his drawings. But for some reason, neither the article nor the artwork made it into print.[1]

Three years later, he intended to include a few sequences of drawings on a theme taken from *Macbeth* – 'The Murder of King Duncan' – in *Directing* (a textbook on the creative process), in order to show the subconscious paths by which an idea takes form. They were improvised drawings that he had made in Mexico and he himself had been surprised at what appeared beneath his pen. But the drawings, along with all the other manuscript material for the book, remained unpublished in his archive.[2]

Ten years later, during wartime, it was suggested to him that he publish the screenplay of *Ivan the Terrible*. Along with the text, Eisenstein thought it would be necessary to publish a historical commentary and (of course) his sketches. To explain them, he wrote an essay under the title 'A Few Words about my Drawings'.[3] But in the end, the text was published on its own – and abridged, at that.

Only once in Eisenstein's lifetime did his drawings find their way into a public exhibition (although without his knowledge or consent). It was staged in 1934, in the foyer of a New York movie theatre, and was arranged by the gallery owner John Becker, who had bought (almost by chance) some of Eisenstein's Mexican drawings. In 1946, 'strolling through his past' with the aid of his diaries after his heart attack, Sergei Mikhailovich remembered with some pride – as well as his customary irony – a tiny but approving notice of the exhibition that had appeared in *The New York Sun*: 'That was the first and last time I've earned press recognition for my talents as a draughtsman.'[4]

But he did nothing to solicit greater recognition for these works. Perhaps his fame as a film-maker was enough for him – fame that served him well both in his years of triumph and during the time when fate was less kind to him. Or did he feel that the game he played with his gift, his public and his fame had different rules when it came to drawing?

The first real exhibition of Sergei Mikhailovich's drawings took place in 1957, at the Arts Workers' Central House in Moscow. This was a trial panorama consisting of some 300 sheets, including a little of everything: a few childhood drawings, the most realistic of the theatrical sketches, rough drawings of characters and scenes for his late films, impressions from his life, fantasias on the theme of art, and friendly caricatures and cartoons. Visitors were unanimous: it was the name of the famous director that had brought them to the exhibition, but they left feeling surprised at the encounter with an unknown Eisenstein.

It was a case of being famous but unknown. The newspapers saw him as one of the classic Soviet artists, but the cinemas only ever showed *Battleship Potemkin* (during revolutionary holidays) and *Alexander Nevsky* (during patriotic holidays). It was not until the year after the exhibition that the ban on Part 2 of *Ivan the Terrible* was lifted. And it was ten years before *October* could be shown – albeit deformed by cuts, re-orderings and new intertitles, and smothered by the music.

It was this 1957 exhibition, together with the publication a year earlier of the first book of Eisenstein's essays to appear in Russian, that marked the beginning of his renaissance. In 1961, the first album of his drawings was published. They were very cautiously selected, but confirmed that Eisenstein's sketching had been something more than a hobby.

The drawings were accompanied by two texts, written by Eisenstein as keys to the work. The first consisted of fragments from his memoirs, under the title 'How I Learned to Draw' and bearing the subtitle 'A Chapter about Dancing Lessons'. The second was the essay 'A Few Words about my Drawings', which had been cut (like the sketches) from the 1944 publication of the *Ivan the Terrible* screenplay.

The first text provided critics with an admission by the author that his drawings were 'as if danced out', that their light and 'mathematical' lines resembled the trace of a dance. The phrase 'visual shorthand', employed in the second text, would be extracted and quoted many times in exhibition reviews and in biographical articles. But art critics have not explored his metaphor of drawing as dance. Eisenstein's biographers have never asked just what sights it was that he was taking down in this 'shorthand'; and professional artists praise him as a 'director who drew'.

Yury Pimenov, famous in the USSR as a painter, visited the 1957 exhibition and was delighted at how expressive Eisenstein's uncanonical drawing was. The art publishing house Iskusstvo invited Pimenov to write a foreword for *Drawings* (the first album of Eisenstein's graphic art, published in 1961), partly to establish an authoritative opinion in the face of any attacks on the work from dogmatists. Emphatically supportive in its tone, Pimenov's foreword made a serious attempt to explain the peculiarities of Eisenstein's drawings and to define their position:

> ***These little drawings and sketches are full of something that is always very lively and passionate: Eisenstein says what he wants to say, and he says it exceptionally convincingly.***
>
> ***They are very theatrical, in the very highest sense of the term. And they also contain the acute, eccentric spirit of the circus: he probably needed theatricality and circus to raise the depiction of reality to the maximum of expressiveness.***
>
> ***In this relationship to the theatre and the circus, Eisenstein's drawings resemble – not as a result, but in their soul and inner essence – the world of Lautrec's drawings. But here we are at once faced with a difference both of approach and of intention: Lautrec, as an artist, finds the measure of exaggeration and the degree of expressiveness that permit him to present his idea in a drawing in the most concise and complete form possible; Eisenstein, on the other hand, thinks and draws above all like a director. His are a director's drawings: he does not check the degree of their expressiveness, he allows the character and form of his drawings to vary; for him they are not distinct works of his art, they are a meditation, or a run-up, or an experiment for his future directorial work. He sees beyond what he depicts.***[5]

In this flattering comparison with Henri de Toulouse-Lautrec, do we not hear a subtext? Not, perhaps, an accusation of dilettantism, but a somewhat patronizing attitude towards these drawings as something intermediate, as 'applied' art, something created to serve a purpose outside itself?

And, hand on heart, do we really disagree that a drawing by Toulouse-Lautrec and a drawing by Eisenstein cannot, in the final analysis, be compared? Is it not obvious that Eisenstein's drawings belong to some different category, so that some different parallel must be sought?

If we were to begin an imaginary conversation with Eisenstein, we might begin with: Why are you ashamed of being a dilettante?

An entry in his 'Mexican' notebook, dated 8 July 1931, could furnish the reply:

> ***Don't forget the enormous role of the dilettante (according to the*** **Film Spectator**, ***von Sternberg somewhere called me a dilettante – thanks, "von" – meaning someone who [is] outside the rhythm of generally accepted doctrine when it comes to progress and new discoveries in the arts and sciences.***[6]

If we tried to find our 'different parallels', he might admit – quoting another diary entry (made at the Hacienda Tetlapayac and dated 16 December 1931):

> ***I don't like (and I don't respect) analogies, but it seems I always fall into making them [myself].... Analogies form the extreme of brevity in the possible coordination of static comparison with the dynamics of principles' dialectical unity (becoming).***[7]

Pushkin recommended judging an artist against 'those laws that he himself accepted as binding him'. If we asked Eisenstein about the laws that bound his drawing, he might reply using the words he wrote in his diary on 25 December 1931, at a moment of extreme exhaustion, which makes them rather chaotic (an effect emphasized by their polyglot character – the original is written in a mixture of Russian, English, French and Spanish):

> ***Apologia for my drawings:***
> ***I draw for myself: since it is impossible to collect and get into the right order all the drawings that form a theme. And they take a long time, and myself I condense a month into half an hour. Like a fruit fly, that reproduces 12 times a year (?): you can learn the laws of inheritance quicker from a fly, who happens to develop just like a cow does....***

I attach no greater absolute importance to my drawings [compared] to those of real draughtsmen than to a fruit fly compared to a Piedras Negras bull.

Sincerity and completeness replaces quality (high quality).

The main thing I've discovered (above all from the Pietà at Tehuantepec) is the conflict of the impulsive, sensuous, instinctive – the WHAT – with the conscious, intellectual – the HOW (form).

Noticed in accordance with the principle of amplifying now one, now the other, and registering (as far as possible) motifs and documenting how they change.

Only one thing [established] so far about Macbeth *(the Death of Duncan):*

Lady Macbeth, unsuccessful on sheet x, is 'punished' on sheet x+1: she is suddenly teeny-tiny and in an unimportant place.

All Macbeth *– more than 200 of them!*

And, again, a drawing is the easiest thing to reproduce in order to explain things: just try to describe a conflict of attitudes, in motion or over the course of an argument! [...]

Sometimes – when I'm worn out, and that happens terribly often – and there's somewhere to write, but you can't [resist], you sit down and you feel an impulse to draw – not on any particular subject. You ask yourself what to draw. You don't feel like drawing anything in particular. And you start sketching heads, or more often the same one over and over again, and new fragments. In corpore *this is the lowest form of expression given to a formula that hasn't yet been formulated. (Lowering by way of exhaustion.)*[8]

The paradoxes in this self-critical apologia are obvious, but that is exactly where to look for the author's hints to the viewer.

Thus, according to the artist himself, it is in the traditional *content* (theme, subject, motif) that he is revealed as sensuous and instinctive, while what he termed the *form* of his 'transparent', 'quickly danced-over' pages is the field of the intellect. It would seem that Eisenstein could not manage to get his impulsively running line under the control of his reason. It is the subjects of the drawings that actually seem maximally intellectual: all these Madonnas balancing between kitsch and high baroque, these *corridas* where the bull and the toreador run each other through at once, the 'Murder of King Duncan' with its echoes now of Zola's *Thérèse Raquin*, now of the fantasies of the Marquis de Sade, now of a solemn rite of *hara-kiri*.

But let us look at them through Eisenstein's eyes. He admitted more than once that he would examine the results of his spontaneous drawing with curiosity. And it was the form, the flow of the lines, the rhythm, the relations between the figures, on which he would base *a diagnosis of the state of his own soul*. Of course, the form of a drawing would also reflect his mental attitude to the intimate emotional material that took on the form of one or another subject. The HOW really did belong to the sphere of the intellect – reflection, analysis and conclusion.

Eisenstein wrote of a conflict between the WHAT and the HOW. His fleeting lines are not only visual shorthand, noting down striking observations and temperamental fantasies that wanted to be recorded on paper. They are also:

• *encephalograms* of secretive thought processes going beyond reason and consciousness. And at the same time, they are:

• *cardiograms* of that no less mysterious and powerful sphere of feeling that lies at the foundation of all our many-storeyed intellect.

In other words, drawing played just the same role in his artistic activity as the experimental use of *automatic writing* did for the Surrealists. Do not Eisenstein's invectives against Surrealism in his speeches, articles and books seem exaggerated? One can understand his distaste for the paintings of the 'mystificator' Salvador Dalí (who did, however, receive his constant attention). It is harder to explain his irritation with the theory and practice of Surrealism as such, however. He enjoyed good relations with many of the masters of Surrealism, including Luis Buñuel, Paul Éluard, Max Ernst and Hans Richter. For all the difference between the ultimate aims of the Soviet director and the European Surrealists, they had much in common, in terms of their shared curiosity about the subcortex of consciousness and even their artistic toolkit. We know that Eisenstein, influenced by André Breton's ideas, made attempts at the automatic transcription of his thoughts for psychoanalytic purposes. On one occasion he (a teetotaller!) even consumed a large portion of alcohol in order *to liberate his subconscious*.

He was not content with his experiment in automatic writing. Perhaps the failure was caused not by the arrangement, but by the method used to realize it. Eisenstein himself admits in his 'Apologia' that he would start drawing, without consciously willing it, when he was too tired to be able to write.

When the eminent psychologist Aleksandr Luria undertook a post-mortem analysis of his friend Eisenstein's brain, he discovered an asymmetry between the two hemispheres. The visual and musical right hemisphere was markedly larger, and had clearly been dominant. So it was not a stream of words, as with Breton, that was Eisenstein's chosen method of self-analysis but rather the flow of the line. Drawing, not literature, allowed the right-brained Eisenstein to express himself in the most organic way.

This is precisely why it is appropriate to compare his drawings less with other artists' drawings than with literature. And not just the Surrealists' spontaneous automatic writing, but also the bold experiments of his beloved James Joyce, who contrived to interweave records of everyday life with mythological reminiscences and the reconstruction of interior monologue. There is even a comparison with the poetry of Aleksandr Pushkin – outwardly light and unforced, but actually compressed to the transparency of a diamond – in whose manuscripts the process of composing verse is mysteriously connected with drawing.

Examining these spontaneously born drawings, Eisenstein understood that they allowed him an insight into his mental state at that moment. They were also a means of working out innate or acquired psychological traumas and complexes. And, perhaps, they provided a way *to decipher the genetic code of the creative process itself.* It was only in drawing that this process was contracted to the lifespan of a fruit fly.

In these drawings, the form (the HOW) and the content (the WHAT) keep changing places before our eyes, keep passing into one another. They are inextricable in their contradictory unity. But we would be equally justified in concluding that, for Eisenstein, his drawings were *a genuine confession* – or, if we emphasize its therapeutic function and use Freudian terminology, *a sublimation*. If the viewer is interested in Eisenstein's spiritual, rather than outward, biography, then his drawings taken together form *a visual diary of his inner life*.

We can find another important hint in the 'Apologia'. Eisenstein denies any independent value in an individual drawing. For him, *the unit of his drawing is the series*. This may be a cycle of drawings more or less linked by their plot (for example, a kind of adolescent comic he created about visiting Trouville, or the *Fall of Adam and Eve* sketched in Mexico, or the *Story of the Prodigal Son* that he drew in Almaty). It may be variations on a single theme (the many pages of the *Murder of King Duncan*, the St Sebastians that repeat themselves down the years, or the late *Parques*). Or it may be the development of a theme (the early juxtapositions of people and animals, the Mexican bullfight-crucifixions, the tragic cycles of 1937, the *Les dons* drawn towards the end of his life).

What all these types of series have in common is their *development in time*. Even within each page of Eisenstein's drawings, 'the line speaks of motion'. That is how he remembered the words of Wang Bi, a Chinese philosopher of the 3rd century: 'What is the line? The line speaks of changeability.'[9]

But the trace of time on one sheet of paper was not enough for Eisenstein. After finishing the outline of a figure or completing the composition of a given sheet, he needed to continue the movement (the lines? The themes? The ideas?) on the next sheet, and then the next and the next.

The artist Jean Charlot suggests that Eisenstein 'thought of [his drawings] like shots on a ciné reel'. But he was drawing in series even in his Riga notebooks of 1912–13, long before Rorik became a film director. And it is quite logical to suggest that that was why he became a film director. By nature, and by the specific cast of his talent, he had been unable – from childhood on – to think of space without time, to see a picture outside its development and its juxtaposition with others that are similar or opposite.

Eisenstein made a note of these words from Wang Bi's treatise 'The basic principles of the *Book of Changes*': 'Only he who has understood [the essence of] the line can evoke joy in everyone, can penetrate into everyone's cares, can recognize in opposites their similarity and in distinct things their unity.' Eisenstein undoubtedly felt joy, underlining this postulate in the Chinese philosopher's book. Not just the joy of understanding this law, a law that he knew from his own creative work, but the joy of recognizing it.

There is a third and final significant hint in the 'Apologia'. It turns out that for Eisenstein, automatic drawing (whether of unconnected heads or of whole compositions) is a lower form, which anticipates *a formula*. What did he understand by the term 'formula'? What kind of 'formula' did he have in mind? Graphic? Literary? Scientific?

In his draft note of 15 September 1945 entitled 'The Line', Eisenstein uses this word again – and again in connection with his employment of the 'mathematically pure line' in his drawing:

> ***The line as trace, as process. The line as sensory image, as formula, as concept of the same thing. Every profile can be described by a formula. 'Regiments of the infinitesimal...' 'Quantities that seek the limit...' The poet Sokhotsky. Who dynamized, animated.***
>
> ***I love Disney, because he actually does make the line run: he sets Sleeping Beauty free (not just the partner of the seven dwarfs, but the sleeping beauty of the Line).***
>
> ***Chinese painting: the cult of the stroke (I get to know the visual quality of the hieroglyphs [...] during the civil war).***
>
> ***A 'typage' as a trace, as a process by which the history of a whole life comes into being. And the faces where you find this: those are the type's characteristic faces....***[10]

This note interweaves terms from Eisenstein's directing ('typages' are characters from his silent films) with theoretical themes that he develops in his books *Method* and *Non-Indifferent Nature* and in his essay 'Disney'. The name of Yulian Vasilievich Sokhotsky, a professor

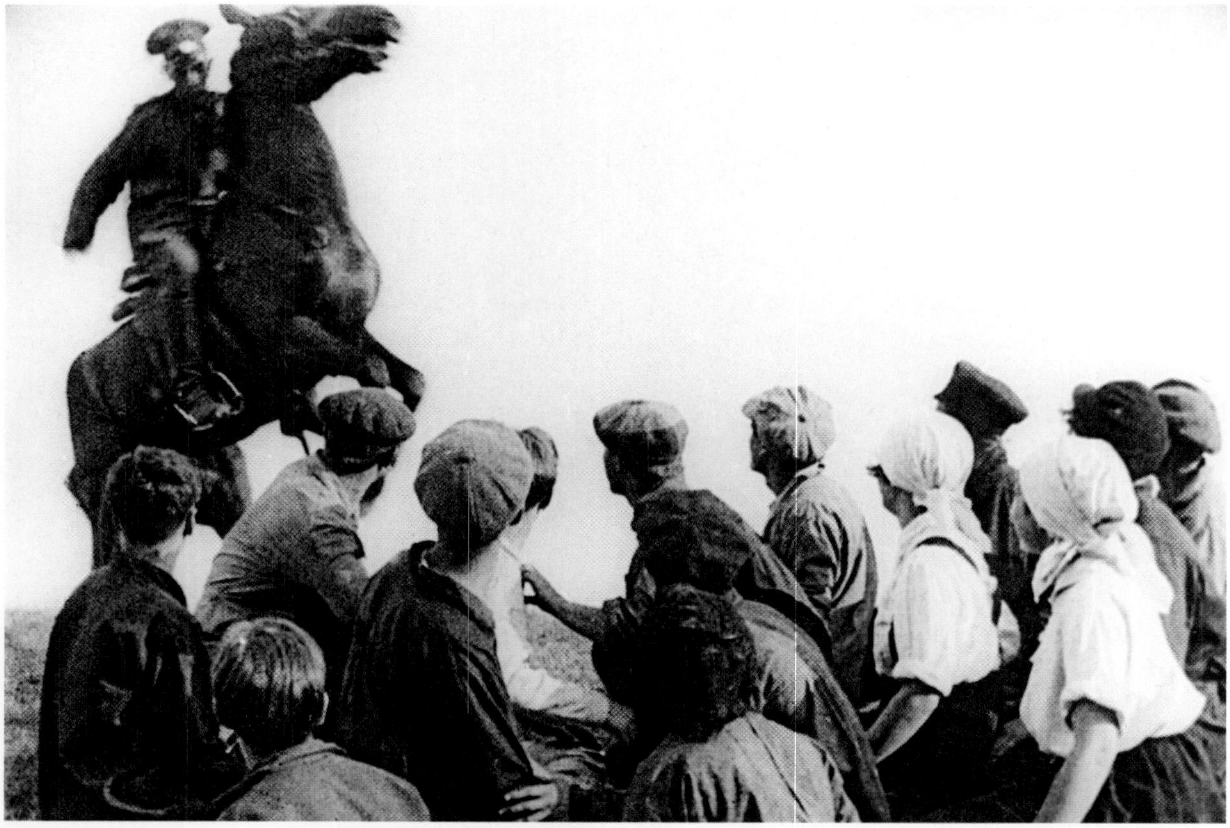

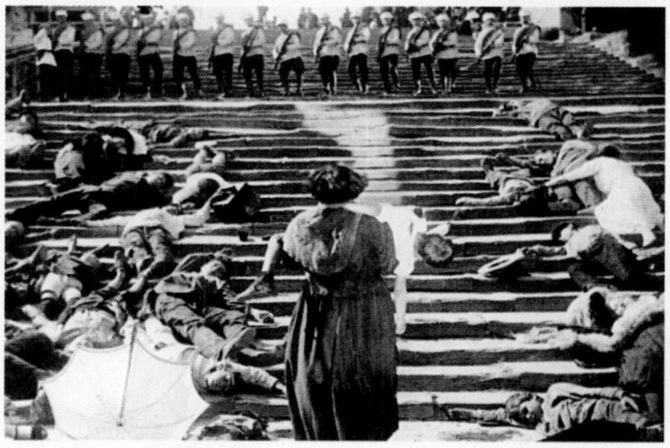

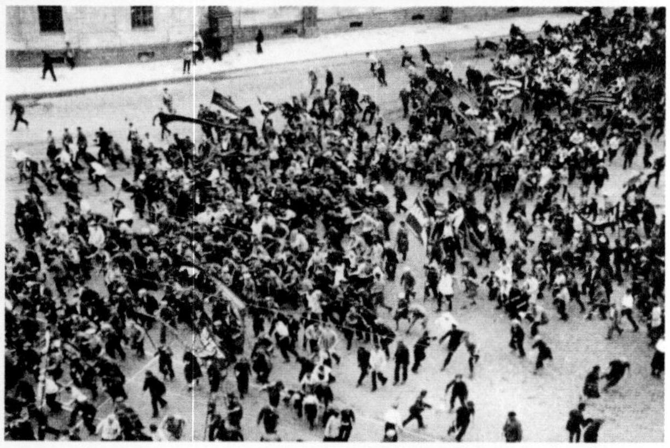

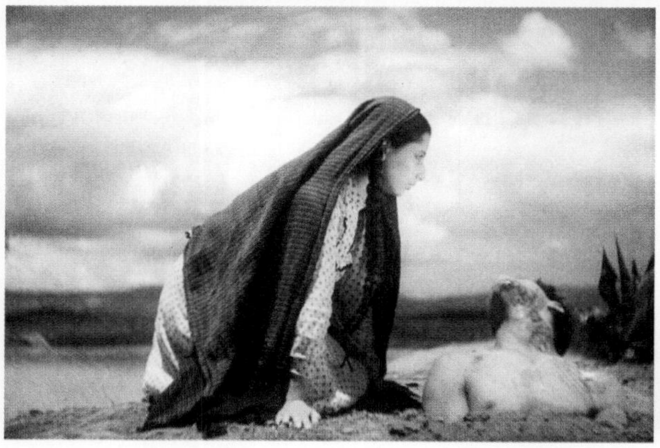

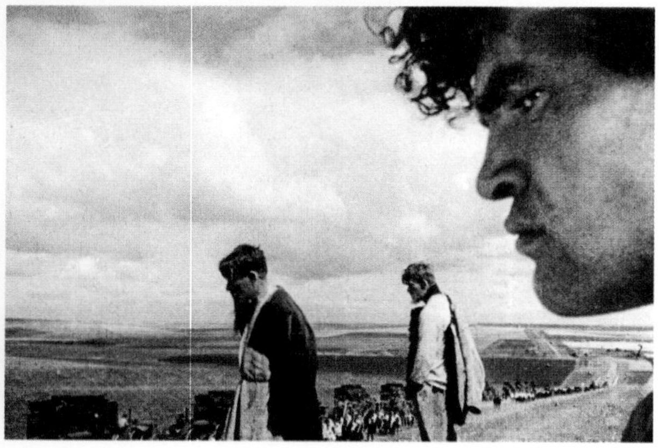

—PAGE 16

Text: My position at the table. And even not too outré. So, but not so. (Almaty, 1942)

—THIS PAGE

Shots from Eisenstein's films:

TOP

Cossacks against the workers, from *Strike* (1924)

CENTRE LEFT

Massacre at Odessa staircase, from *Battleship Potemkin* (1925)

CENTRE RIGHT

Scene from the demonstration of 3 July 1917, from *October* (1928)

BOTTOM LEFT

Lamentation of the executed rebel, from *¡Que viva México!* (1931–32, unfinished)

BOTTOM RIGHT

Arrested peasants, opposers of the collective farms, from *Bezhin Meadow* (1935–37, unreleased) of mathematics whose lectures he had heard in his youth at the Petrograd Institute of Civil Engineers, floats to the surface. In his essay 'Perspectives' (1929), Eisenstein describes Sokhotsky's method of introducing students to higher mathematics:

> ***An auditorium. A lecturer. Of course, not an emasculated bureaucrat of education: but one of those flaming old fanatics (of whom there are fewer and fewer), like the late Professor Sokhotsky, who could talk for hours about integrals or the analysis of infinitesimals with the same fire as Camille Desmoulins, Danton, Gambetta, Volodarsky, thundering against the enemies of the people and the revolution.***
>
> ***The lecturer's temperament grabs you completely. And all around you the auditorium is electrified, held in the steely grip of suddenly rhythmic breathing.***
>
> ***The auditorium has suddenly become...a circus, a hippodrome, a rally, the arena of a united collective aspiration and a pulsating united interest.***
>
> ***Suddenly, the mathematical abstraction becomes flesh and blood.***[11]

After such an ecstatic description, it no longer seems surprising that the note cited above should mention in the same line, separated only by a comma, the following as stages of the same phenomenon's coming into being: 'the sensory image -> the formula -> the concept'.

Is the formula a halfway stage on the way from the spontaneous image to the abstract concept? Perhaps the formula is a dynamic synthesis of both: it generalizes from particular sense data and at the same time it makes the intellectual abstraction concrete? In rather the same way, the 'typage' is 'a person's story, turned outwards'.

The crib we mentioned earlier, 'Notes for Anita Brenner's Article on my Drawings for *Creative Art*', also puts drawing in an intermediate position – but in rather a different way. In this text, striking in its openness albeit written in the third person, Eisenstein divides his activity into three kinds:

> ***First, and generally known: his 'objective' cinematographic [...] and public activity.***
>
> ***Second: activity of an 'intimate' nature. Subjective/personal. <...> The main activity by which he realizes this is drawing. [...]***
>
> ***The third kind of activity unites, as it were, the two previous kinds: it is his deep-theoretical work on the conception of art in general, where art is derived from ecstasy, just as Nietzsche has tragedy being born from the spirit of music [...].***

Thus, if we do need to compare Eisenstein the draughtsman with anyone, it is above all with himself: Eisenstein the director and Eisenstein the theorist. His drawing stands revealed as a necessary link joining his directing with his theory. He himself seems almost to think that these three kinds of activity form an equilateral triangle.

One could remain satisfied with this ideal geometrical figure as the graphic formula of Eisenstein's work. One face of it, the public and political face – the face addressed to the masses – consists of *film as poetry or as symphonic music*. The second face, subjective/personal and intimate, consists of *drawing as lyric poetry or as chamber music*. And the third is the impersonal and abstract face: *theory as objective science*.

But here's the problem: a 'formula' like that is too static to be acceptable to Eisenstein.

In dividing his activity into three kinds for Anita Brenner's benefit, Eisenstein actually admitted that such a division was essentially only for convenience. His films were not meant only to meet objective needs, but also for 'scientific vivisection' – and 'Bacchic' ecstasy is present in them no less than in his drawings. As the years went by, his learnt books, articles and lectures took on more and more of the character of a free, subjective train of thought, just as capricious and unacademic as the lines of his drawings.

Everything is entangled with everything else, or changes directly from one thing into another.

It was only the materials and the conditions that varied. Never the rules of the game.

The static 'triangle' logically leads to a dynamic circle, in which it is sometimes all but impossible to say where one kind of activity ends and another begins.

From the recognition of these transformations there flows, logically, a hypothesis that we have already come close to stating a few times in the course of our reflections. It is connected with the puzzle of the eight-year break in Eisenstein's drawing.

Eisenstein practically stopped drawing altogether in 1923, when he was working on a theatrical production entitled *Enough Stupidity in Every Wise Man*. In 1931, in Mexico, his magical line awoke again (like Sleeping Beauty being kissed by the prince). From then on, it did not leave the artist for the rest of his days. Perhaps this mysterious 'taboo' on pen and pencil only signified that *drawing had metamorphosed into directing*?

Yury Pimenov suggests: 'In the first instance Eisenstein thinks and draws like a director, and his drawings are a director's drawings.'

But perhaps the opposite conclusion would be equally justified: Eisenstein thinks and directs like a draughtsman, and his films are a draughtsman's films? Perhaps the clear lines of his *mise-en-scènes* or the graphically precise composition of his montages was his drawing, in another guise?

It was not his sketches for sets and costumes that were the extreme expression of his theatrical draughtsmanship. It was the imaginary lines of the staging, drawn scenically with living actors. In *Enough Stupidity in Every Wise Man*, it was the diagonal line of rope, from the arena to the balcony, that Grigory Aleksandrov (playing the adventurer Golutvin) used to 'cross the border'; or it was the vertical line of the 'priapic' pole that Vera Yanukova ran up against (in the role of the super-sexual Madame Mamaeva).

The cinema once again gave the draughtsman-director a frame, the screen, and replaced flesh-and-blood actors with their images, whose metamorphoses and ways of moving could be controlled and recorded. What is more, the series of edited film sequences and episodes allowed him to realize his inclination (which he had had since adolescence) to develop his drawings in time.

In that case, the line *through theatre to film* in Eisenstein's biography, a line Eisenstein himself (in the book *Film Form*) has persuaded us to trace, actually has a longer and more complex trajectory: *from drawing, via the theatre, to the cinema.*[12]

This hypothesis radically increases the scope of Eisenstein's graphic art. Besides the several thousand surviving paper pages covered with drawings in ink, pencil, or (during his theatrical period) gouache, it would now include his *cinematographic* art: tens of thousands of images created with light and lenses on a prepared surface of perforated photosensitive ciné film.

Animator Juri Norstein believes that *Ivan the Terrible* is a 'super-animation' – and not just because 'Eisen drew the whole film before it was shot'. Incidentally, *Ivan* – uniquely among Eisenstein's films – permits us to see how, and by what rules, the drawings were transformed into acting and filming. For, despite the legend that the director drew every shot in advance and then filmed the scene in accordance with what he had drawn, the film came into being as a *metamorphosis of graphic art.*

The relationship between drawings and film was different in *¡Que viva México!* even in *Alexander Nevsky*, although the drawings were of vital importance here too in forming the idea and its embodiment.

The absence of sketches for *Battleship Potemkin*, *October* (1927) and *The General Line* (1929) only confirms our hypothesis: the shots in these films were themselves the form of drawing that Eisenstein was using in the second half of the 1920s. And if we compare *Strike* (1925) with the young Rorik's drawings in Riga, then the film takes on a new dimension. It suddenly becomes obvious that Eisenstein's film-making began (although he himself did not suspect it) with the drawings in his notebooks of 1912–13.

Rorik's drawings also include the depiction of people as 'typages', and a mastery of the art of showing the crowd as at once differentiated and united, and the desire to reveal reality through metaphor, and a premonition of the tragic nature of life (hidden, for the time being, by humour).

But right there, in their flawlessly flying strokes, in their tense yet translucent compositions, in their instantaneous and unforced projection straight from the imagination onto the paper, we see a harbinger of Eisenstein's emancipation from all intermediaries on stage or on screen.

Eisenstein called his abandonment of drawing and subsequent return to it 'a paradise lost and then regained anew'. It was in Mexico that his *pure graphic art* awoke to independent life. He assures us (or himself?) that this happened under the influence of the 'linear' Mexican landscape, of the designs of the serapes worn by the peons and the painful ropes that bound their naked bodies, of his encounter with the works of the great muralists. He probably wasn't being disingenuous. But this is clearly not the whole truth.

In Mexico, Eisen felt that a line on paper was the only way he could freely express things he could neither say in words, nor write with his pen, nor shoot on film. And how well this served him back home, where you could neither speak, nor write, nor film frankly!

Drawing became the most sovereign and sincere form of his creative art: it became his vitally important game. And it is for this very reason that Eisenstein's drawings can do without any obligatory comparisons – even the comparison with his own principles as a film-maker or conceptions as a theorist.

It is a quite autonomous phenomenon, and addresses us in its own language – if we choose to look, listen and understand.

Shots from Eisenstein's films and a Wagner opera:

TOP LEFT
Single combat between Prince Alexander and Von Balk, Master of the Teutonic Order, from *Alexander Nevsky* (1938)

TOP RIGHT
The combat between Hunding and Siegmund, from *Die Walküre* (The Valkyrie) by Richard Wagner (Bolshoi Theatre, 1940)

CENTRE LEFT
Ivan and Nepea, the Russian ambassador to England, from *Ivan the Terrible Part 1* (1945)

CENTRE RIGHT
Metropolitan Filipp and Archbishop Pimen with the tsar's victims, from *Ivan the Terrible Part 2* (1946)

BOTTOM
Ivan's confessor accuses the tsar of repression, from *Ivan the Terrible Part 3* (1943–46, unfinished)
Photo by Victor Dombrovsky

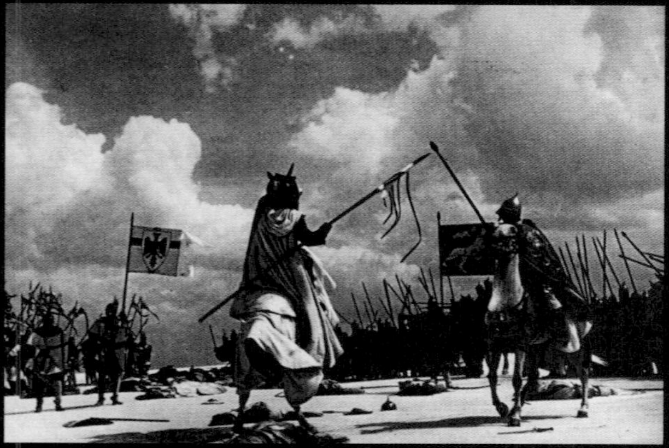

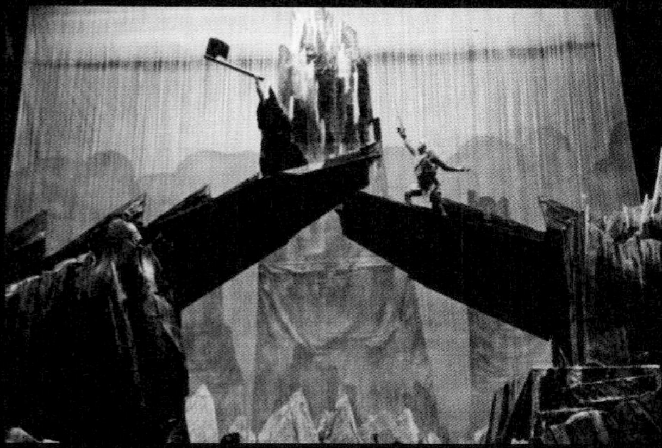

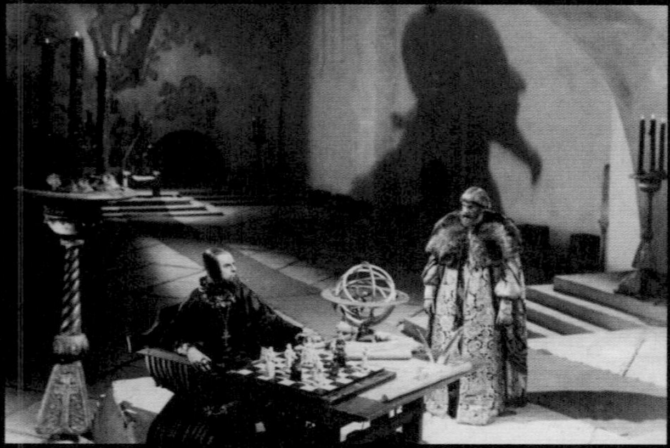

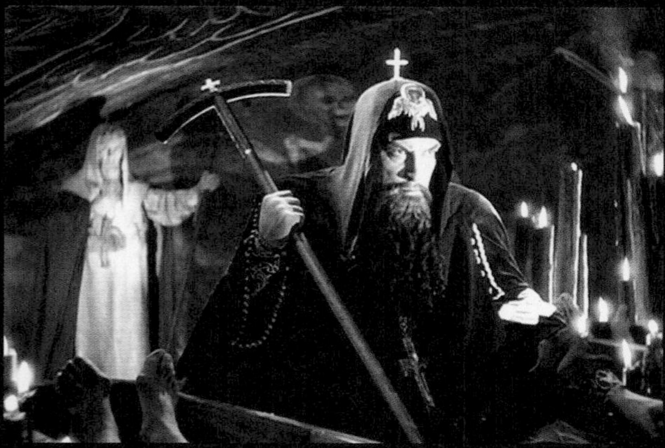

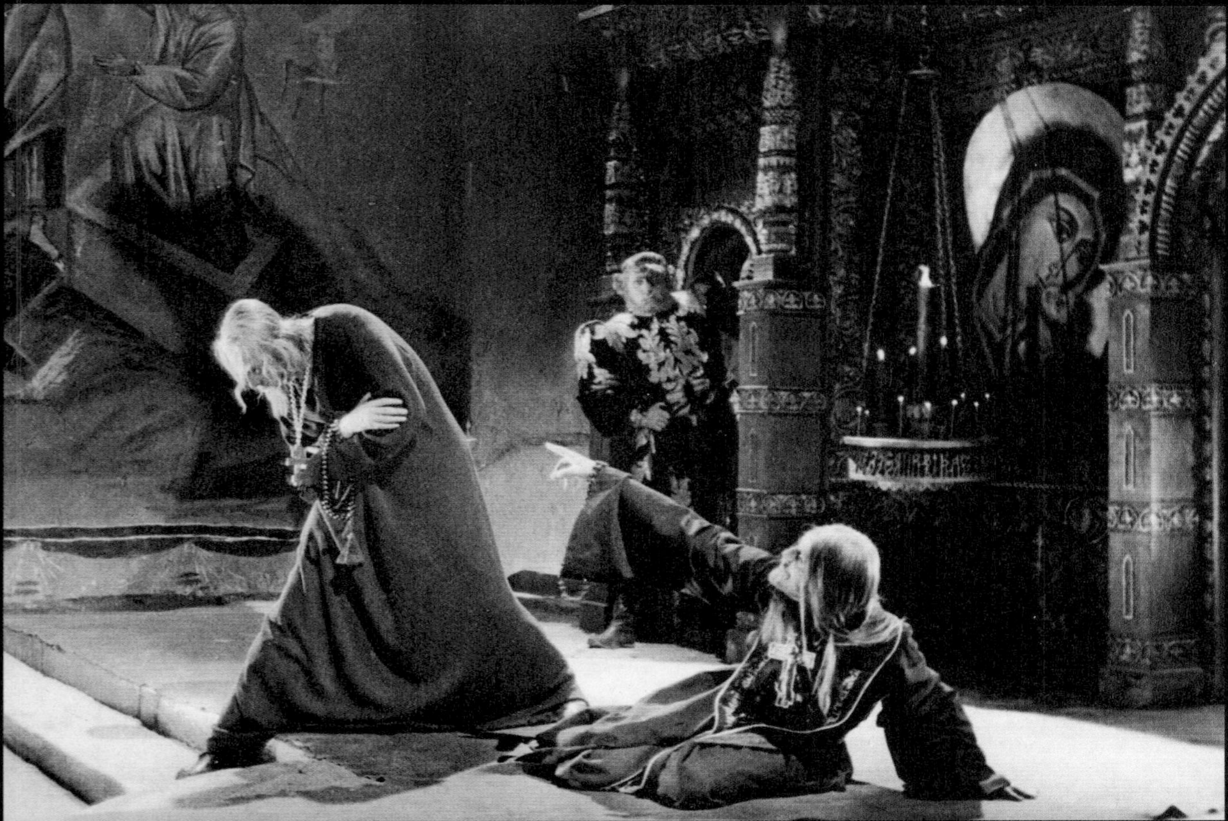

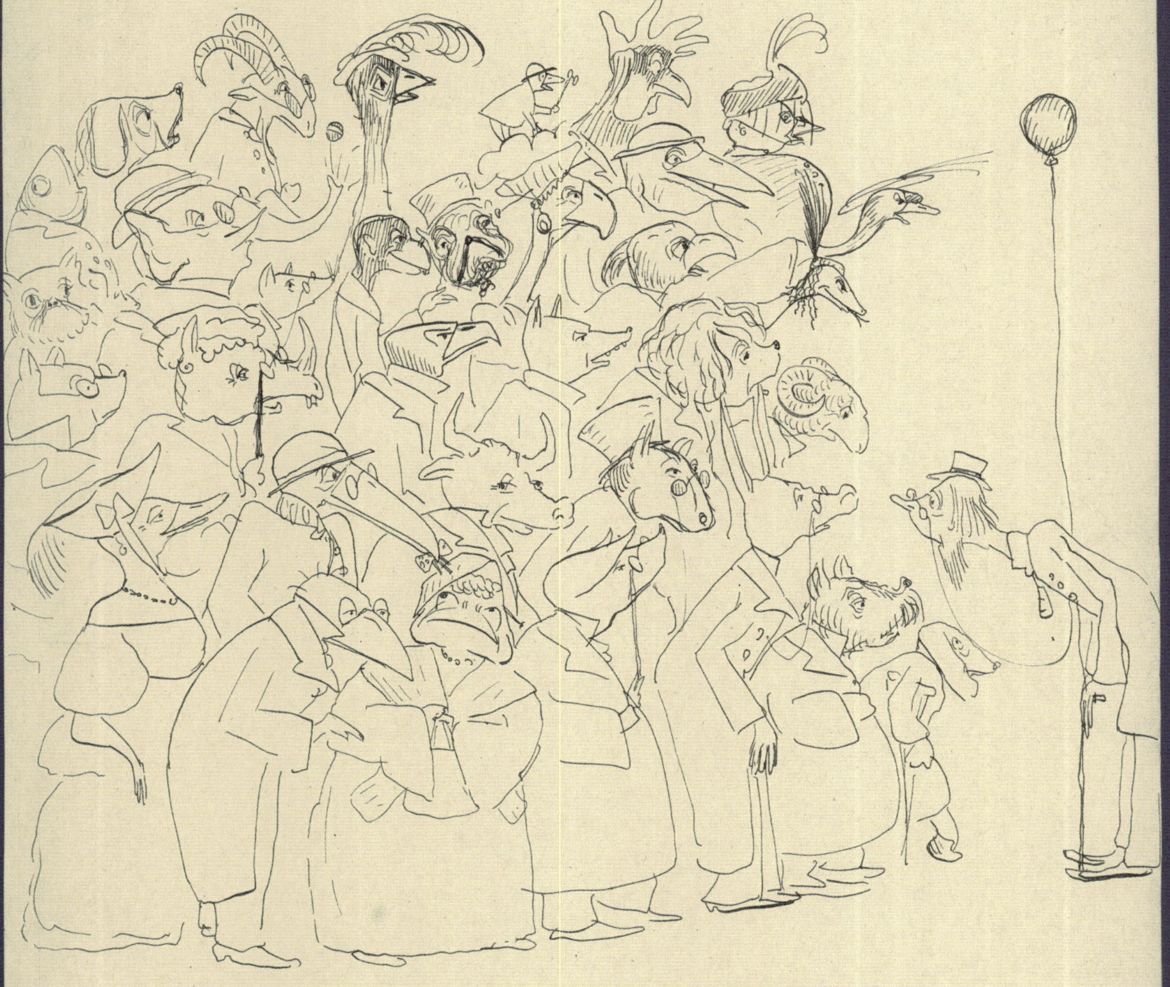

„И этого типа называютъ царемъ Вселенной?!"

РИГА-ПЕТРОГРАД 1912—1917

THE KING OF THE UNIVERSE?

RIGA–PETROGRAD

1

'And they call this fellow the king of the universe?'...ask the crowd of animals, as they gaze in surprise at a little human being, frozen in fear, and ready to hide once again in the place he's peeped out from so timidly – beyond the edge of the notebook page, in non-existence.

...exclaims the fifteen-year-old Riga High School student Sergei 'Rorik' Eisenstein, whose light and confident pen created this cartoon – or fable? Or visual treatise? – in 1913.

Even if it were revealed that the teenager had not thought of the idea for himself but had borrowed the theme, or even copied the whole composition (he had already seen and remembered a great deal for his age), this drawing would still not seem like an idea taken from another person, an imitation of an alien approach to drawing and thinking.

The 'Riga' period in Eisenstein's life lasted from 1898, when he was born, until 1915, but his drawings fall naturally into two stages. Firstly, a childhood phase, of which all that survives is a few sheets and letters with naive pencil and watercolour figures that depict relatives or fairy-tale characters. Secondly, an adolescent phase, which began in 1912 and is represented by drawings in thick school exercise books, or on paper torn or cut from them. The multitude of surviving drawings from this second phase demonstrates that the theme, the style and the very way of thinking expressed here, on the first page of the first notebook we have, belonged wholly to the young Rorik.

In this drawing, and on many other pages of the exercise book, two worlds confront one another. One might call them the Animal World and the Human World, if not for the fact that the borderline between them is an extremely notional one. The two worlds interfere, like waves from two stones that a boy has flung into the water at once.

Even in the few purely 'animal' drawings, the animals behave either like happy, mischievous children or respectable, incurably serious adults. But it is particularly clear in the 'narrative' drawings that the animal world is actually the human world that surrounded the adolescent Eisenstein. The only difficulty is in deciding whether it is the animals that are given human traits, or the human beings who reveal animal traits.

In some of the rough sketches, the process of transference is clear. People sprout fur and feathers; horns and beaks appear on their faces. Elsewhere, thoroughly human attributes and expressions appear on the animals' faces – pride and stupidity, irony and spite, naivety and obedience. These conjunctions of human and beast already reveal the metaphorical overtones that are so characteristic of Eisenstein's mature work and thought.

The animal imagery he had loved from childhood would play an active part in the multi-layered metaphors of his films. Early on, it is declared openly in comparison cuts that express 'assessments'. Thus, in *Strike*, the police spies are animals and the shooting is a slaughter. In *October*, images of Aleksandr Kerensky, the chief of the Provisional Government, are intercut with those of a peacock.

In later films, zoomorphism infiltrates scenarios, shots, and the appearance and behaviour of the characters. In *Alexander Nevsky*, the conquering knights wear helmets adorned with symbols of beasts and birds of prey and the Teutonic bishop turns into a wolf. In *Ivan the Terrible*, the executioner Malyuta is given the look and the mannerisms of an angry bear, and the knight-errant Staden resembles a plucked eagle. Eisenstein liked to use animal images in explaining a character's personality to the actors, too. He once told the actor playing Kurbsky (the emperor's former friend, then his adversary and finally his enemy): 'The prince is like a powerful, passionate, impatient steed, who has scented his favourite mare over the horizon in the steppe and is racing towards her; that's just the way Kurbsky hungers for power and glory.'

Eisenstein's writing – his memoirs, his articles and even his theoretical work – is full of animal imagery. 'It is Done!', he writes, in an essay from May 1945. 'In the age-old struggle of man and beast, man has again been victorious. The beast has been brought low: the beast of fascism. And we want to believe that this time it is forever.'[1]

It was present in his day-to-day life, too. In numberless Eisenstein witticisms or aphorisms that have entered the folklore, this childhood enjoyment reappears. He once won a competition to find Moscow's finest wit. The theme of the contest was 'who was like which animal'. Eisenstein's winning remark was: 'He's like a bear, he's like a goose, but N. B. is like...a boa.' He had a lot of experience for a competition such as this, going back to the animal-human sketches he had drawn as a child.

In Rorik's exercise books we see the young man mastering the skills and habits needed for art: the suite of mental operations and the necessary tools. The drawings he was producing by the age of fifteen show us that he could distinguish, remember and reproduce human facial expressions and the mannerisms of animals. He could denote the nuances of gait characteristic of an old man or a drunkard, a giraffe or a monkey; shapes of noses, tails, bustles, chignons; ways of balancing, or of holding a head or a cane; the peculiarities of the courtly bow and the servile bow; the hunched posture of a peasant woman and the stoop of a clerk.

To assemble this 'mental Scotland Yard card index', as Eisenstein later jokingly referred to it, called for the gift of dissociating the characteristic features that make up a visible whole. Such a gift was made possible by three personality traits in particular: an analytical mind, a sharp eye and a receptive memory.

But Rorik the draughtsman and future director also revealed an opposing trait in his thinking: the gift of association, the ability to link disparate phenomena on the basis of the smallest hint that they had

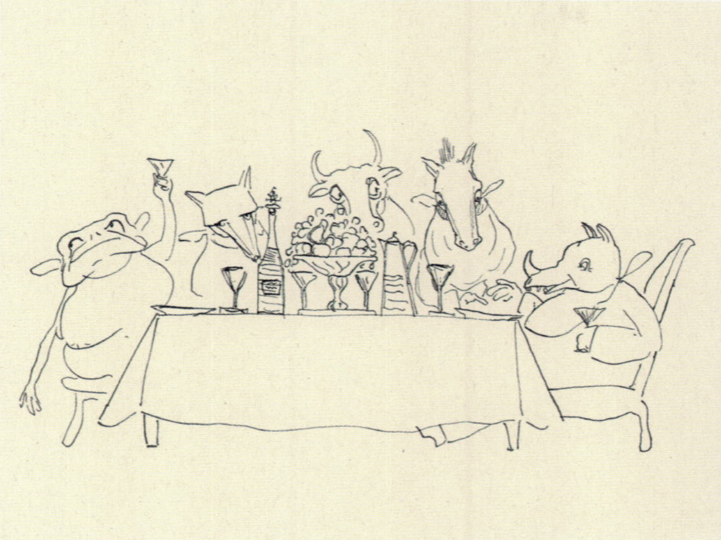

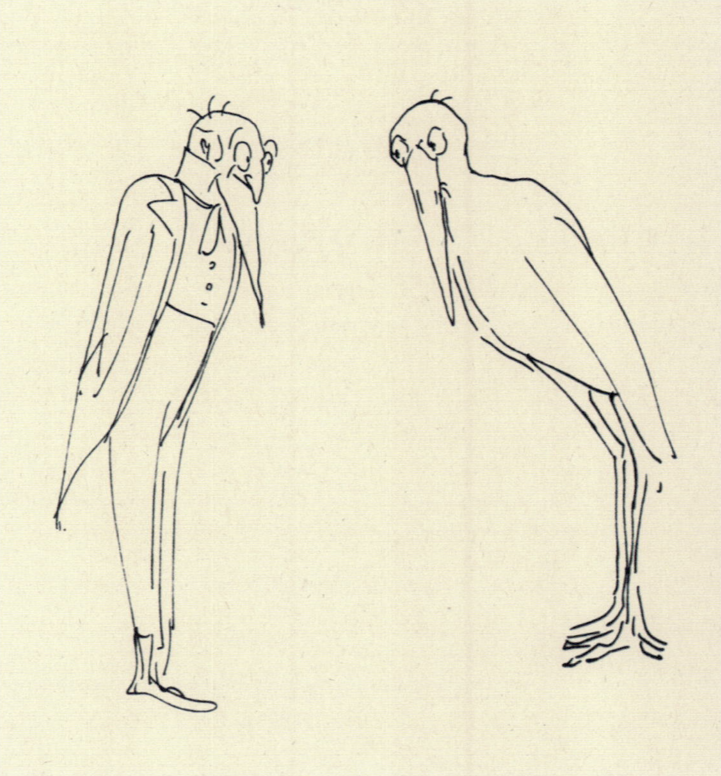

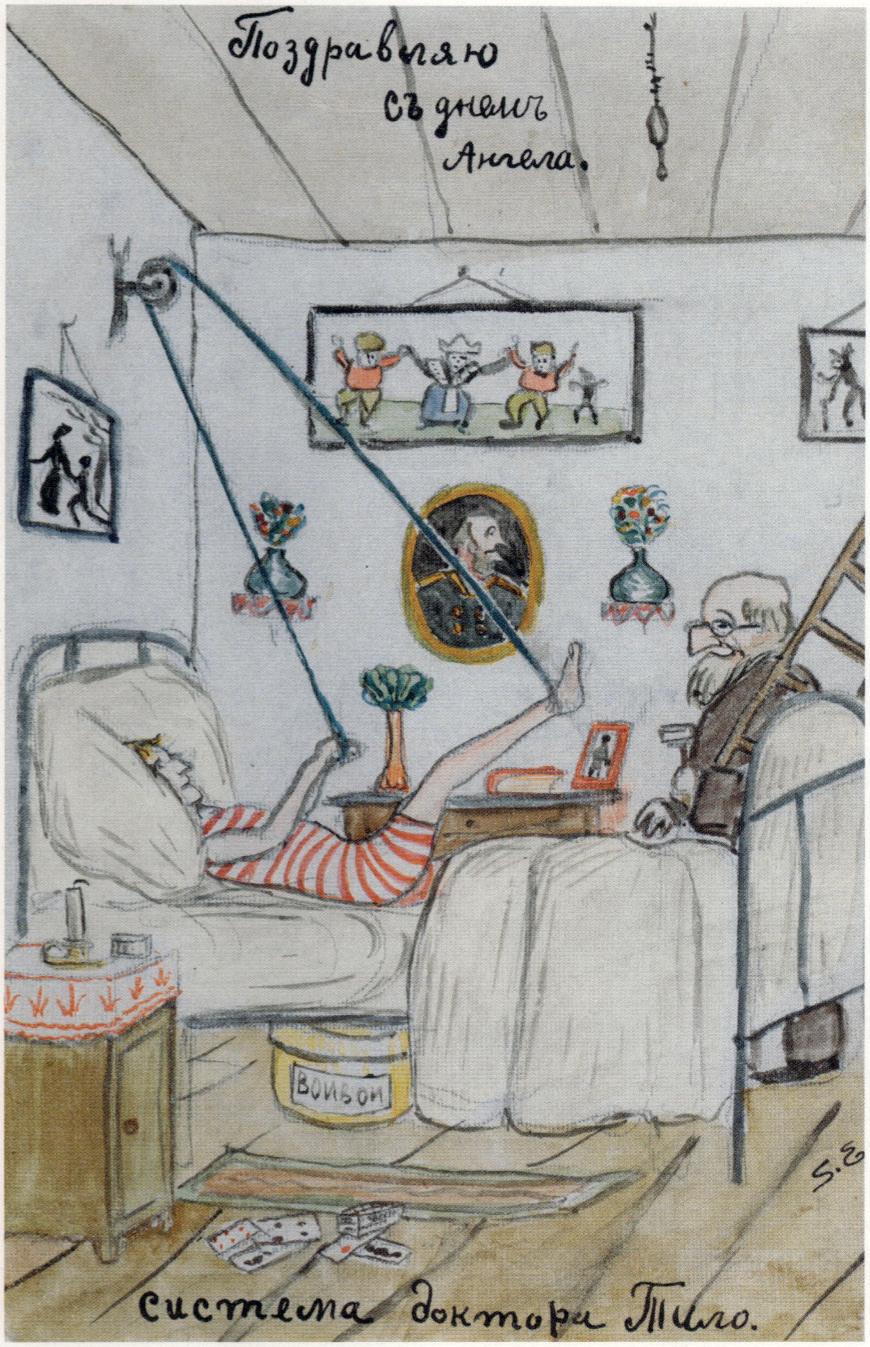

—PREVIOUS
And They Call This Fellow the King of the Universe? (1913)

—THIS PAGE

TOP LEFT
'Dinner in honour of the dignitary' (1913)

BOTTOM LEFT
'Who looks like who?' (1913)

RIGHT
Postcard sent to Katya Bertels (1911)
Text: Congratulations on your Angel Day (Name Day). The Dr Tylo method.

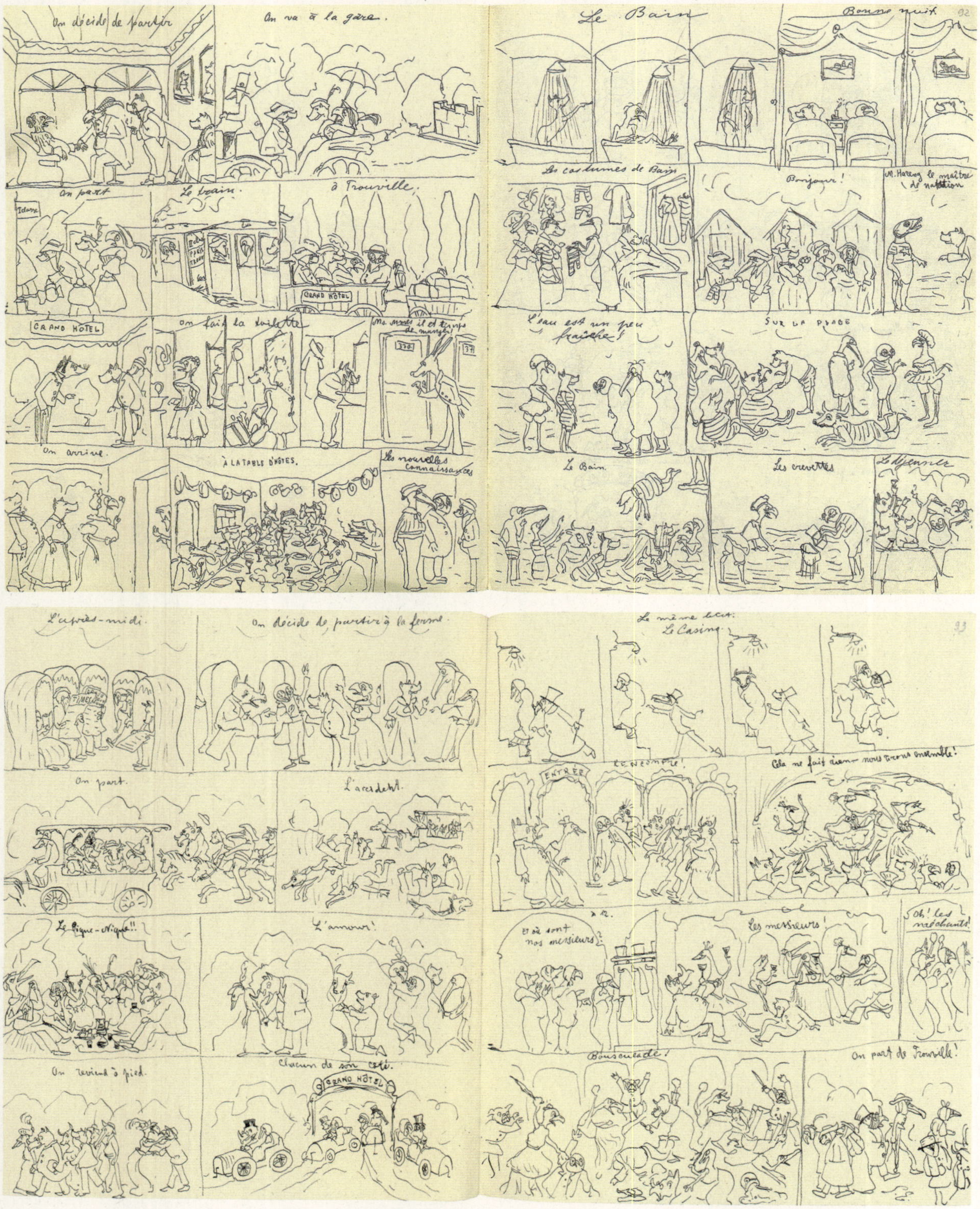

From 'Travel to Trouville' (1914)

TOP LEFT

Text: *On décide de partir – On va à la gare – On part – Le train – À Trouville – Grand Hôtel – On fait la toilette – Ms, Mmes, il est temps de manger! – On arrive – À la table d'hôtel – Les nouvelles connaissances*

(We decide to leave – We go to the station – We leave – The train – To Trouville – Grand Hotel – We wash – Gentlemen, ladies, it is time to eat! – We arrive – At the guests' table – New acquaintances)

TOP RIGHT

Text: *Le Bain – Bonne nuit – Les costumes de Bain – Bonjour! – M. Hareng, le maître de natation – L'eau est un peu fraîche! – Sur la plage – Le Bain – Les crevettes – Le déjeuner*

(The bath – Goodnight – The bathing costumes – Hello! – M. Hareng, the swimming teacher – The water is a little fresh! – On the beach – The bath – Shrimps – Lunch)

BOTTOM LEFT

Text: *L'après-midi – On décide de partir à la ferme – On part – L'accident – Le Pique-Nique!! – L'amour! – On reviend à pied – Chacun de son côté*

(The afternoon – We decide to go to the farm – We leave – The accident – The picnic!! – Love! – We return on foot – Each their own way)

BOTTOM RIGHT

Text: *Le même bût: le casino – Rencontre! – Cela ne fait rien – Nous rirons ensemble! Et où sont nos messieurs? – Les messieurs! – Oh! Les méchants! – Bousculade! – On part de Trouville!*

(To the same destination: the casino – The encounter! – It doesn't matter – we laugh together! And where are our gentlemen? – The gentlemen! – Oh! The villains! – Crush! – We leave Trouville!)

something in common. In fact, the word 'like' or 'similar' seems too anaemic to fit the conjunctions he made. A more suitable term might be something like 'visual rhyme' or, if you prefer, 'optical harmony'.

For what happens in the drawings is not simply that a nose is replaced by a similar-looking beak, or a pair of wings by the tails of a coat. One thing has to be visible through the other, to respond to the other, so that zoomorphism and anthropomorphism turn into one another – not statically, as a comparative exercise, but dynamically, as one examines the drawing. The sketches capture the transformation of a human being into an animal, or the resemblance between animals and people, but in Rorik's pictorial compositions the metamorphosis that takes place is more complicated. The 'King of the Universe' has a chicken's weak neck, a duck's bluntish nose, a goat's feeble beard, a monkey's degenerate skull – and deeply human office-worker's shoulders.

There is no doubt that this timid clerk is the characteristic petty Russian urban official of the early 20th century. Rorik would hardly have been conscious that in this drawing he was dealing with one of the central motifs of Russian literature: the 'little man' as the innocent victim of circumstances or of the authorities. But it seems he had already realized the gulf between this typical character of modern times and the Renaissance ideal of man (as 'the beauty of the world').

It was not until 1924 that Eisenstein introduced the term 'type' to the lexicon of the cinema. Ten years after that, he defined 'typehood', in his textbook *Directing*, as 'a social and personal biography turned outwards, to become an appearance'. A type – whether a real person or an actor – must possess the psychological, social and temporal characteristics needed for the film, and these must be clearly expressed in his or her appearance. The type is at once a 'he' or a 'she' and an 'it' (a social and historical phenomenon).

Thus, in *Battleship Potemkin* the Odessans who gladly greet the rebel ship and who die tragically under the gunfire of the tsarist forces are types: the Schoolmistress, the Worker, the Intellectual, the Flower Girl, the Student. Neither the plot nor the intertitles explain their identities, but the audience clearly understands who is who: they understand the types instantly. The menagerie gazing at the 'King of the Universe' includes a snapshot of Russian society in 1913. The Toad, of course, is the petty Home-owner. The Raven is probably the Banker. The Vulture is the Aristocrat. The Elephant is the Teacher, the Dog the School Janitor, the Rhinoceros the Inspector – or even the Head of the Department of Education.

The sketchbooks of the boy from Riga form a visual encyclopaedia of tsarist Russian types. Both the animal and the human worlds depict every class in society, mock the 'beau monde', wax ironically over 'revenue house' residents and over his father's guests, over monarchs and schoolteachers.

In 1915, influenced by a visit to a military hospital, Rorik classified the types of Sisters of Mercy. But it seems that he felt it was not enough simply to grasp individual people's weaknesses and characters. He tries to portray the vices of humanity, as one sees them in medieval cathedrals, in the form of bestial chimeras.

At the end of 1915 and the beginning of 1916, he created two panoramas showing the hungry queues in the second year of the war: 150 Petersburg types, 150 characters and fates, reflecting different strata of residents in the imperial capital. Eisenstein would certainly remember these drawings of queues eleven years later, when he was shooting *October*. A mass of characters – a small group, or a genuine mass scene – fills the page, sometimes to overflowing, but it does not lead to any sense of pointless crowding or tautology.

In 1926, the German press would hail the director of *Potemkin* as the 'master of the mass film' (Meister des Massenfilms). After the grandiose crowd scenes of D. W. Griffith's *Intolerance* (1916), Abel Gance's *Napoléon* (1927) and Fritz Lang's *Metropolis* (1927), Eisenstein's films were more modest in number of participants – but were felt to be incontestably more 'mass'. Even in his adolescent drawings, Eisenstein had understood one of the secrets of achieving a mass effect that he would later use as a director: what matters is not how many people are on the screen, but how diverse they are. The collective life of the people is to be depicted as an interaction among distinct types, so that the grey crowd becomes differentiated.

From childhood, Rorik had felt that any monotony, any unified sameness, was clumsy or dangerous. A crowd of stock exchange traders in identical beards (with the biggest difference being their head gear: either a top hat or a bowler) strikes him above all as amusing. But a procession of uniformed civil servants (with variations in only two or three kinds of faces) oppresses the young man no less than the gorilla-like Clerk. As early as 1914, identical tunics – the uniform worn by disembodied souls in the afterlife – were linked in his imagination with the idea of death. The boy used irony to overcome a frightening facelessness, whether in a crowd or in an individual: he laughs at the paranoid fear of modern rulers, given material shape in an iron mask and armour.

Years later, the theme of the helmet or mask substituting for a living face would recur in *Alexander Nevsky* in the appearance of the Teutonic Knights, those ancestors of the Nazis' tank columns. In *Potemkin*, the file of soldiers present identical backs, boots and rifles to the viewer, and their faces are always out of shot. In *Ivan the Terrible*, the grim, deep-hooded costumes turn the tsar's guard – the oprichniks – into a ruthless, repressive force.

Diversity, in depictions of the mass, is a synonym for Life. Rorik felt that intuitively, rather than understanding it, when he drew the mass scenes of the cheerful 'Beach', the bustling 'House', the ancient

'Monastery' and the futuristic 'Airport'. Eisenstein the director would consciously contrast the facelessness of a repressive force with the faces of people showing a very broad palette of lively reactions. This principle would be maintained in his films even in the context of grief, which one might expect to erase all differences.

In *Non-Indifferent Nature*, Eisenstein wrote about one episode from *Potemkin* – the mourning for Vakulinchuk, a sailor killed in the uprising:

> ***...the theme of grief is developed through differentiated actions on the part of individual people from the crowd, from the mass. The polyphony of collective sorrow includes parts played by the blind singers, and the weeping women, and groups of two, three, four, and five people – sad, angry, or indifferent (so as to draw out all the shades of grief among the others), young and old, women and men, children and adults.***[2]

The key word here is 'polyphony'.

Even at fifteen, Rorik was intuitively mastering a visual 'polyphony'. In the 'King of the Universe', the general amazement of the crowd of animals is woven from the sincere bafflement of the Lion, the arrogant indignation of the Eagle, the astonishment of the Sheep, the slyness of the Raven, the scandalized surprise of the Peahen, the mockery of the Monkey, the despair of the Hare, and the self-satisfaction of the Toad.

Looking at the animals' reactions, the viewer's eye involuntarily focuses, like a camera, on individual characters, pairs, or groups, discovering within the whole (the 'mass') the part as another whole (the 'type'). The combination of these reactions leads naturally to montage, in one of its most important functions: developing and varying the material. In the 'King of the Universe', our eye falls from time to time on the object of everyone's amazement – the Man: his figure (so clumsy next to the animals); his scared face (recalling that of the Hare); his skinny legs (forming such a vivid contrast with the might of the Elephant). The cutting and arrangement of 'zooms', to which Eisenstein would later devote so much attention in his cinematic theory and practice, here has a dramatic function. It makes manifest the conflict between opposing characters, forces and worlds.

The majority of Rorik's mass-scene drawings can be easily broken down into a series of depictions. Sometimes, the young Eisenstein even draws a whole narrative in pictures – a precursor of the comic strip, or a premonition of the film storyboard. It might be the tedium of his classes – a schoolboy's diary. Or the trial of a bird, probably an echo of the regular police-and-crime reports in the papers. Or the adventures of a well-to-do family at a French resort – recalling the Eisenstein family's trip to Normandy in 1906. In fact, even within the bounds of one situation Rorik succeeds in maintaining the development of the action. He does so, for example, in presenting all the royal affairs troubling a Sultan: harem matters, medical issues, financial business, judicial proceedings, astrological aspects and military affairs. In drawings such as this, the action again unfolds on a single piece of paper. Even at a young age, Eisenstein knew how to play with time, contracting it and extending it as he needed, or combining several 'times' into a single moment. One should not be fooled by the reportage-like character of his Riga sketches – or, indeed, the films he went on to make. Into the bustle of a modern city he can introduce a group of astonished Old Russian boyars and *streltsy* (guardsmen), or ironic medieval minstrels. In the same way, Eisenstein's aborted film *¡Que viva México!* (begun 1930, released 1979) shows how several historical systems and social formations become visible at once through his 'chronicle' of modern times. And his draft for the comedy *MMM* (1932–33) directly brings 16th-century boyars and headsmen into the reality of Soviet Russia.

Thanks to the presence of the fourth dimension, time, it is not real space that dominates in the two-dimensional flat drawings so much as thought space, where all combinations and metamorphoses are possible. They happen on that borderline between documentary reality and pure imagination, where one changes into the other, or one can be seen through the other.

The bear that wanders into town and flees back into the forest is by no means a living beast: it is an inappropriately decorated lamppost from a building entrance. The sly Son has sent his architect Daddy's latest brainwave 'home'! In just the same way, Rorik sends back to Egypt the sphinx that was to recline, according to Daddy's whim, at the doorway to a revenue house in the Albertstrasse in Riga.

It is only at first glance that the encounter between the Office Worker and the host of animals seems fantastical: not for nothing did the playful draughtsman supply his urbanite with a stick with a balloon attached to it when he took him out for a stroll amid unspoilt nature. Where else, after all, is the 'King of the Universe' going to encounter his subjects?

The humour and the impact of these caricatures rest on the way they slide from the realm of everyday into that of the fairy tale and back again. One simple example of visual wit is the Lady taking a stroll not with her pet dog, but with her pet fish.

Leaning over his exercise book, holding the pen in his strange way (pinching it with all five digits), Eisenstein would extract his drawings from his imagination and translate them onto the blank white page. All he needed to do this was a simple line of black ink, flowing freely across the page. The unbroken line made it possible to put onto the paper, at one and the same time, an expressive outline, an indication of size, a characteristic look and a motion in space.

He did not master this ascetic line immediately. In the very earliest of his surviving drawings (from 1908 to 1910), the still-unsure pencil

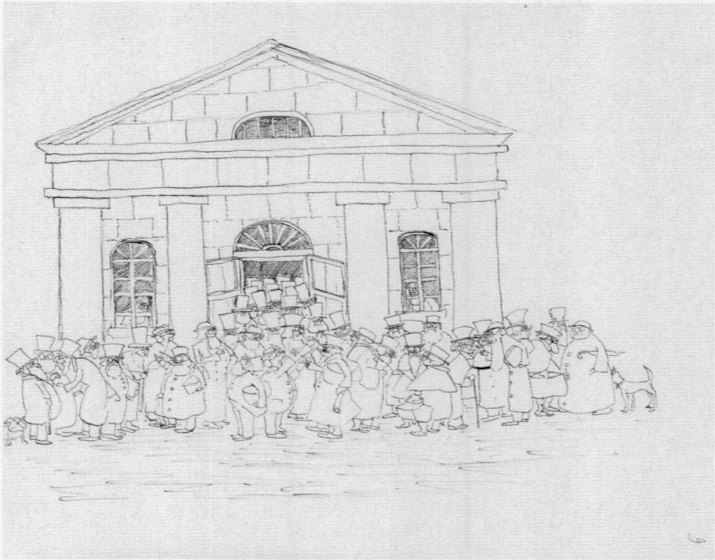

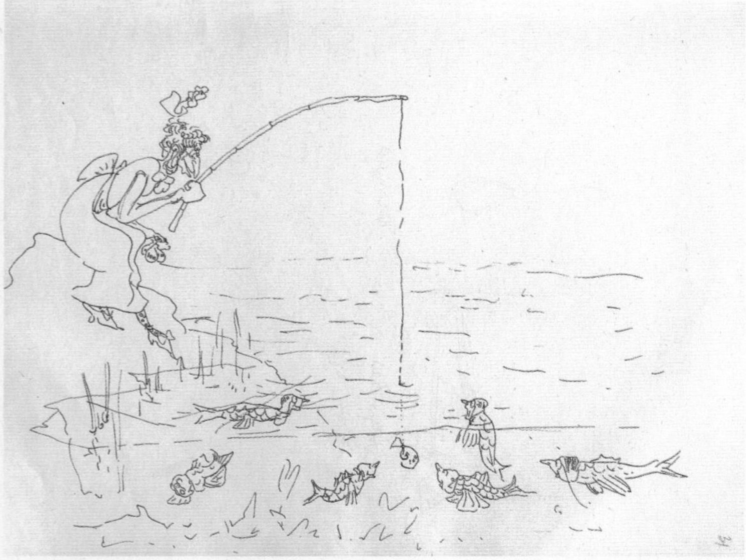

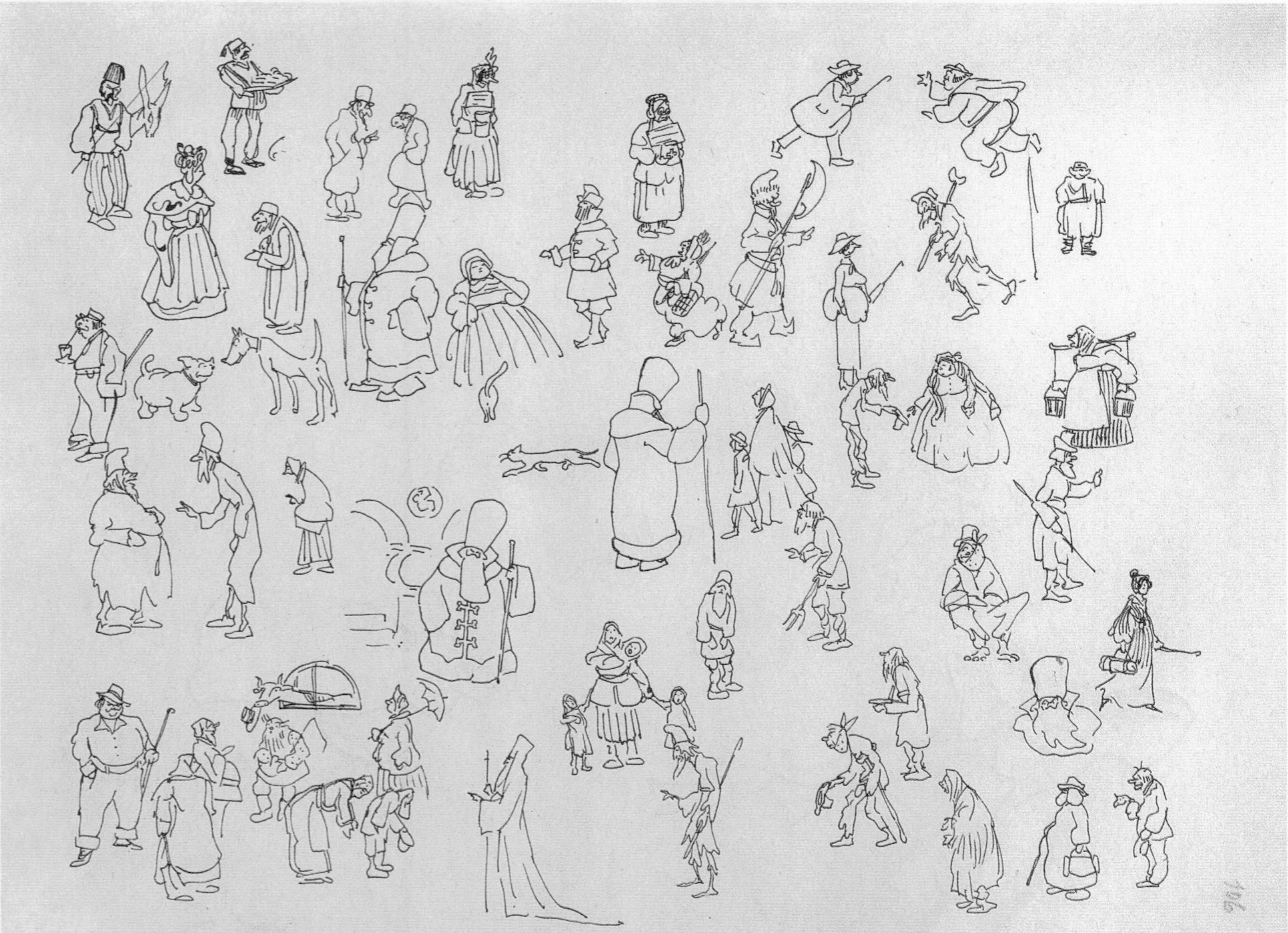

TOP LEFT
'Stock Exchange' (1914)

BOTTOM
'The boyars in modern Russia' (1914)

TOP RIGHT
'Rich bride' (1914)

outlines are artlessly filled in with watercolours – as in his get-well card for Katya Bertels, his schoolfriend Alyosha's sister, who had had the bad luck to break her leg on the eve of her name day. Rorik clearly tried hard to follow the rules of correct drawing here: the room is depicted according to the laws of perspective, the whole area of the paper is filled up, forms keep their proper sizes and everything is anatomically accurate. Between a year and eighteen months later, however, the outline was gradually freeing itself from elegant but irrelevant colour and the uncertain pencil work was giving way to a thin, firm, monochrome line. The rubber had been discarded altogether and the hand was flawlessly accomplishing rapid turns and pirouettes – as though it were tracing some other drawing, clear to the young artist, but invisible to anyone else. Of course, the foundation of this kind of drawing is an insuperable natural gift for plastic thinking, to which Eisenstein himself admitted in his memoirs:

> ***When I read about something, or it just comes into my head, I see it before me unusually clearly.***
>
> ***This is probably a combination of a large store of visual impressions with a lot of training in 'daydreaming', when you make the thing you're remembering or thinking about run before your eyes in images, like a ciné film.***
>
> ***Even now, when I draw, it is almost as if I am 'tracing' with my hand the outlines, as it were, of drawings taken from the unending sequence of visual images and events that pass in front of me.***
>
> ***These impressions, acutely visual above all, beg with a painful intensity to be reproduced....***[3]

Here is a revealing piece of evidence from his childhood – a slip of the pen in a letter from Riga to his mother in St Petersburg, dated 4 December 1908:

> ***Dear Mama, I forgot to tell you one other thing, which is that Daddy is very kind to me really and has never banned me from writing to you, only you know yourself that I don't much like [drawi: CROSSED OUT] writing....***[4]

What did this slip let pass from the unconscious into the text? Was it the fact that, for this boy, drawing did mean writing – that the drawing and the word were, for him, interchangeable?

Here is another example, from this earliest phase: a letter about a new servant, in which letters take on the shape of a figure, with Russian characters added above it for the sake of the likeness.

Perhaps Rorik did not like the fact that he drew, and the slip was a characteristic repression of his dissatisfaction with himself. All the same, it does seem that visual depiction was for him more basic than words. From the moment when his mother left for St Petersburg, Rorik sent her letters and drawings. Beginning from 1912, however, the style of these illustrated letters changes drastically: the boy masters the clear, flexible line and learns to tell a story in pictures without verbal explanations.

In the same chapter of his memoirs, Eisenstein recounts one of the most shattering events of his early childhood. During a big family party (before his parents' scandalous divorce), an engineer by the name of Afrosimov drew him some animals on the card table in chalk...using a flowing line. Did the boy try then and there to imitate this way of drawing, and this subject matter? It is very probable. Did he succeed? Not immediately, of course – judging by his later drawings from 1908. No examples from the very earliest period have survived. Perhaps Rorik destroyed them himself, when he was a bit older. Or perhaps they perished in 1918, when Engineer Eisenstein's flat was plundered under the slogans of 'the struggle against autocracy' and 'equality among citizens of free Russia'.

Perhaps it was under Afrosimov's influence that there awoke in the boy that irrepressible striving that Eisenstein referred to as 'Me too' in English, or 'Yo también' in Spanish. It's possible that this chance meeting helped to conjure up that mighty impulse, without which Eisenstein's natural talent would have been no more than potential.

But let us not forget that his architect father did not just sketch the plans of future buildings every day at home. He also drew the ornamentation for their façades on sheets of Whatman paper – gigantic plaster figures and mask-like faces, miniature capitals, enlarged emblems and ornaments. There is no doubt that this gave his son training towards his destined profession.

Eisenstein's father was also generous in buying books and albums and subscribing both to Russian and foreign magazines. Over time, Rorik's eye began to distinguish between the drawing masters he might choose. Among the cartoons published in the German humour magazine *Simplicissimus*, he unerringly picked out the drawings of Olaf Gulbransson, and among his illustrated children's publications the graphic poems of Wilhelm Busch. His first independent purchase in a bookshop was an album of drawings by Honoré Daumier, but his great passion was J. J. Grandville's *Un autre monde* (1844). It was probably in the pages of the latter that Rorik learnt to use the World of Animals to laugh at the World of People.

Unfortunately, Eisenstein's formal artistic education offered little in the way of help or inspiration. His schoolteacher, Herr Nieländer, insisted that he had to draw as instructed, following the conventions by which accepted artists learnt. For instance, he would be required to reproduce a still life with an eagle's perch and the corner of a cupboard in the background, with all its wealth of bodies and tints. Alas, the young Eisenstein received no better than average marks in his drawing classes. And so this well-brought-up boy from Riga learnt that there were three kinds of drawing: the kind that was accepted at school; the kind that was needed for a career; and the kind that you wanted to do yourself.

A threefold division also reigned in society in Riga, which was the provincial capital of the Lifland Governorate of the Russian Empire. The most influential group among the ethnically diverse population were the Baltic Germans, descended from the region's former colonizers. Hostile to them were the 'aborigines': the taciturn Latvians, closed off in a powerless nationalism. Rorik belonged to the third layer, that of Russian officialdom, but among the children of his community his only friends were fair-haired Alyosha Bertels and (in the summers, when they came for the seaside) Max von Strauch, the son of a Moscow doctor.

Of course, his parents' divorce had something to do with this. The question of whether children from 'good homes' should be allowed to see the son of 'those people' outside school was debated long and heatedly in local society. But, over and above this scandal, the residents of these three worlds were suspicious of the name Eisenstein for other reasons. In vain did his father, Mikhail Osipovich, introduce himself with the words, 'Eisenstein. I'm Orthodox.' In vain did his mother, Yulia Ivanovna, display a portrait photograph of Grandpa, Ivan Konetsky, who had come from the neighbourhood of ancient Novgorod. He had become a millionaire, a merchant of the first guild, an honorary citizen of St Petersburg, and the owner of a home not far from the resting place of Prince Alexander Nevsky. A saint to the state and the family alike. And in vain did the parents hang over their son's cot an image (not an icon, it is true, but a typographical reproduction) of his patron saint, St Sergius of Radonezh.

Educated members of Riga society would not let themselves be fooled by such measures. 'Mikhail', or 'Michael', is, of course, a name that would cause no alarm among these Christian folk. But it does come from the Old Testament; and 'Osip' is just a Russianization of 'Joseph'. And anyway, who was the unknown other grandfather?

'Sergei' comes from the Greek word for 'respected'. But, as soon as Sergei learnt to say his name, when he was out strolling in the noble Kronvald Park with his governess, Filya, anyone who heard it would likely become suspicious. For this was tsarist Russia, and the sound of his name might well prompt the response: 'God forbid, you aren't one of those Jews, are you?'

Eisenstein would sign his letters to his mother 'Cat' or 'Kitten', and that was also how he signed his drawings – until he had mastered the line, which was when he thought up his first pseudonym: $\sqrt{2}$. This sign, a simple mathematical symbol standing for the square root of the number two, appears on drawings in the correct (in his opinion) 'linear manner' from the school year 1912/13 onwards.

What lies behind this playful signature? A desire to escape verbal self-identification in any language? A striving to 'take the root' of what seems simple? A premonition of the irrationality hiding within the 'natural series'? A bit of naughtiness from a boy who had solved the mystery of how he had come into the world? Or all of these at once?

Whatever the answer, this radical signature became a symbol of the best period of Eisenstein's early drawings, which lasted until 1915. This was the year in which his life in Riga life ended and his life in Petrograd (St Petersburg's name from 1914 to 1924, when it became Leningrad) began. As his father had intended, the high-school pupil became a student at His Imperial Majesty Nicholas I's Institute of Civil Engineers. He moved to live with his mother, in Nicholas II's capital. And, in the same year, he thought up a new pseudonym for his drawings: Sir Gay, a Russo-English pun on his first name that, at the time, meant simply 'Sir Happy'.

The seventeen-year-old Eisenstein bade farewell forever to his childhood nickname of Rorik, and began to get used to his adult name and patronymic: Sergei Mikhailovich. And his drawing took on new features. The student drew for himself less and less: much of his time was now taken up with sketching acanthus leaves, technical drawings and homework. True, from time to time there would appear from his pen little linear graphic jokes, sometimes on architectural themes.

Increasingly, he drew images on themes concerning the life and tastes of the average person in the street: a disaster on the way to a picnic; someone being tight-fisted at Easter; or a typical scandal among the petit bourgeois. His drawings of his fellow students and teachers, shaded in pencil, are perfectly good likenesses of their subjects. But in striving to show forms bodily and to be an accurate depiction of its subject, the picture loses something of the wit and lightness given to an image by the flying line.

In his Petrograd drawings of 1915–16, there is evidence that he was attempting to draw 'properly' – just as the student S. M. Eisenstein's appearance and behaviour at the time reveal ever more of his father's desire to become 'Monsieur du Comme-il-faut'. For his father, a typical son of the 19th century, the ideal figure was, of course, Napoleon. Eisenstein admits in his memoirs that in 1915 he invented and wrote down his first maxim: 'Napoleon didn't do all the things he did because he was talented and a genius. He made himself talented so as to do all the things he did.'[5]

Had the young man perhaps decided that his own initials should stand for 'Self-made Man'? The change of pseudonym, from the root to the play on his own first name, reveals a crisis of self-consciousness that brought on a crisis in his drawing too.

It was in Petrograd that the possibilities for his future biography began to become clear. If he were fortunate, the likelihood was that S. M. Eisenstein would become a fashionable architect with a lot of commissions, and, therefore, a man of means. In his rare moments of free time he might collect books and drawings (only first editions and originals). If he was extremely lucky, he would become the patron of a magazine, which he would graciously permit to publish his architectural drawings (signed with his full name) and – who knows? – funny sketches (signed with a transparent pseudonym). He would ride, like an aristocrat, and would visit the circus (as his father did) to see the horses – although, in truth he had a plebeian enjoyment of the clowns. And perhaps this Eisenstein would forget that it was not him who had made the choice between the Clown and Monsieur du Comme-il-faut – both of whom had once met in one of his Riga exercise books.

If he was not so lucky, he might get a respectable civil-service job as his father had. He would dress in an official uniform, collect reproductions (only of the best quality), and – who knows? – occasionally he might entertain children at a party by drawing funny animals. In the very worst case, he would drift down into being an office worker, like 'that fellow', and would stop thinking about his childhood games with paper and India ink. But, God willing, his mother's money and his father's connections meant things would not come to the very worst.

One or other of those three scenarios would most probably have come to pass if it had not been for politics, and all that happened in Russia in connection with it. In the capital of the empire, Eisenstein was closer to current politics than he had been in the capital of the Lifland Governorate. In Riga, this sphere of life had taken two forms for him. On the one hand, it was part of the world of adults, and reached him in important but little-understood remarks after a good dinner. When he drew commentaries on the latest 'happenings in the Balkans' in letters to his mother (fairy-tale Sultans playing the fool with their neighbours), it was more a hint that her Kitten was becoming a grown-up Cat than it was a sign of real interest in the area known as the 'Balkan cockpit'. And his anti-German cartoons of the Devil Kaiser and his associates, which appeared at the outbreak of World War I, were less because he was seriously influenced by Russia's chauvinist press and more because he wanted to settle accounts with the Riga Germans who had treated his father and himself as upstarts from who-knows-where.

On the other hand, Rorik learnt to see and understand what real political art meant. He was attracted by a visual form – angry and irresistibly funny – that Daumier had found for the sins of society. He was fascinated by the hidden intrigues and tragic conflicts of the real history inside the romantic fictions by Victor Hugo and Alexandre Dumas. He discovered an impersonal force, similar to the ancient Greek goddess Moira, or Fate, to which the immortal gods and the purportedly all-powerful rulers of states, who already seemed to the young man to be no more than history's puppets, were equally subject.

In Petrograd, politics came to seem much less mysterious to the young Eisenstein. Initially, Sir Gay's drawings continued with the caricatures of the monarchs who were at war with the Allies, just as in Riga. Then, political figures from the Russian Empire began to appear in his drawings too. They were nothing like the immortal gods: they were his neighbours from the Tauride Palace, beside which he and his mother lived. Even the tsar himself, and his associates from the Winter Palace, did not resemble chosen ones: they were parodies of characters from literature, drama and mythology. Prime Minister Goremykin was such a reactionary that he was attacked by newspapers of all shades of opinion – even conservative ones. Eisenstein drew him as St Sebastian. Next to the imperial family's all-powerful favourite, Rasputin (who could end a political career with a word), any Salome seemed a pitiful beginner. And Kaiser Wilhelm was no longer a devil: he was an epigone of the bloody Lady Macbeth.

Contemporary issues would evidently have remained, in Sir Gay's drawings, a play of two mutually illuminating worlds – newspaper politics and bookish history – if it had not been for the revolution of February 1917, when the Russian autocracy crumbled like a wretched piece of decor. And the image of the tsar of all the Russias with the double-headed caged bird turned out strangely similar to the feeble 'King of the Universe', who had discovered four years earlier that –

Exactly ten years later, Sergei Eisenstein the director would shoot the symbolic prologue to his film *October*. The crowd is flinging nooses at the statue of the autocrat, and the ropes suddenly make the secret threads of history visible: they reveal that the Idol, gigantic, empty, fallen under its own weight, is a puppet.

Amusingly, the first echoes of the revolution to appear in the architecture student's drawings did so through the filter of ready-made images from books, music and the theatre. Moreover, many of his political cartoons resemble his very first attempts to draw, or the caricatures that he had recently created at the Institute. Eisenstein subsequently admitted that they were 'drawn first in pencil. Then I traced them in India ink. Broken outlines, no dynamism, no expression of the spontaneous flow of thoughts and feelings. Rubbish!' Sir Gay really was starting to draw again from scratch. A fourth possibility for his future life now became apparent: he might become a newspaper cartoonist, working on themes from politics and life.

His first attempt to publish a political drawing ended in disaster. The famous humourist Arkady Averchenko, the publisher of *Satirikon* magazine, brusquely rejected his submission. But the *Peterburgskaya Gazeta* did print one of his cartoons about the 'civil militia', whose 'C. M.' armband Eisenstein himself had worn in the first days of the

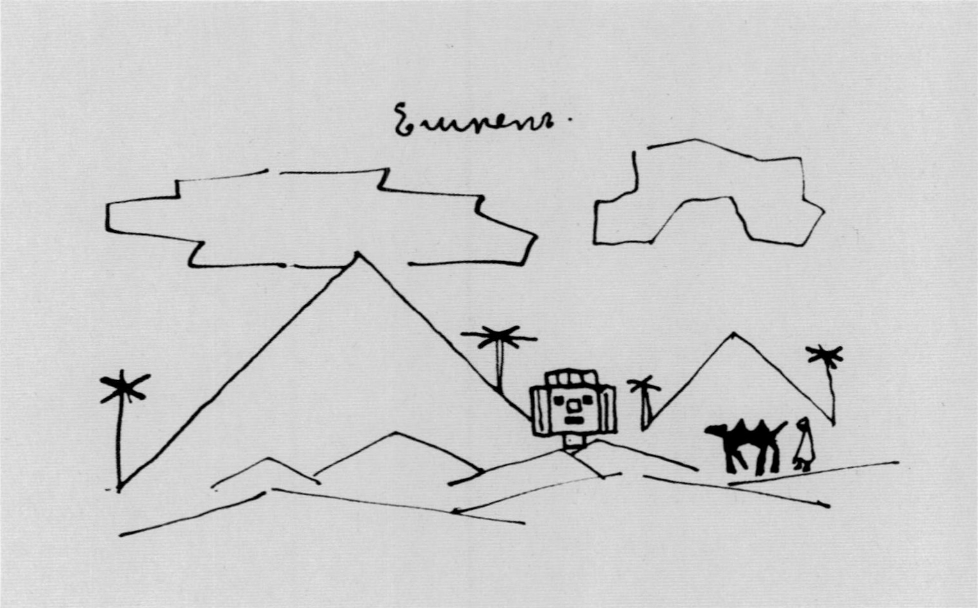

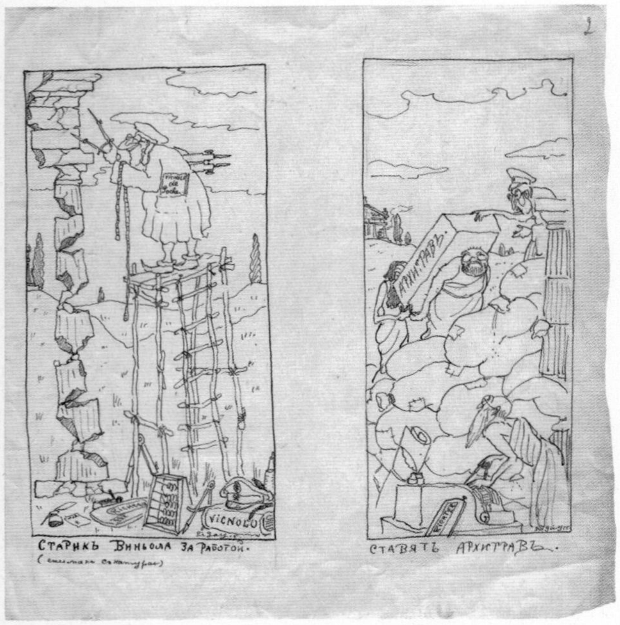

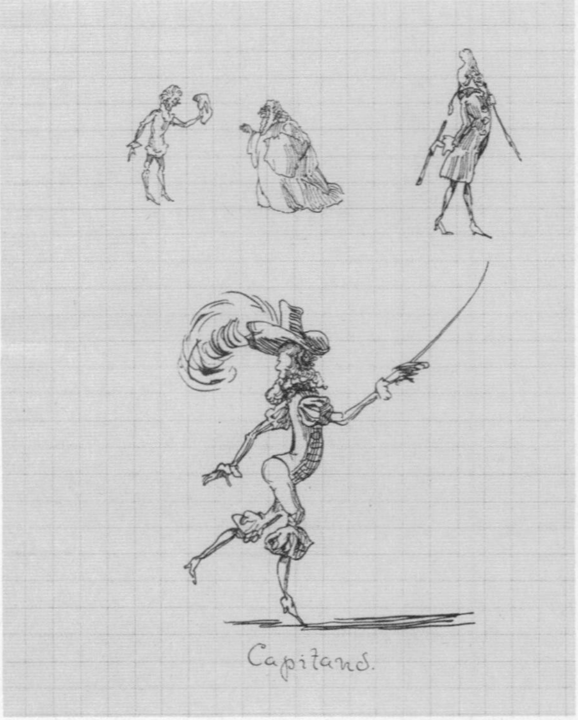

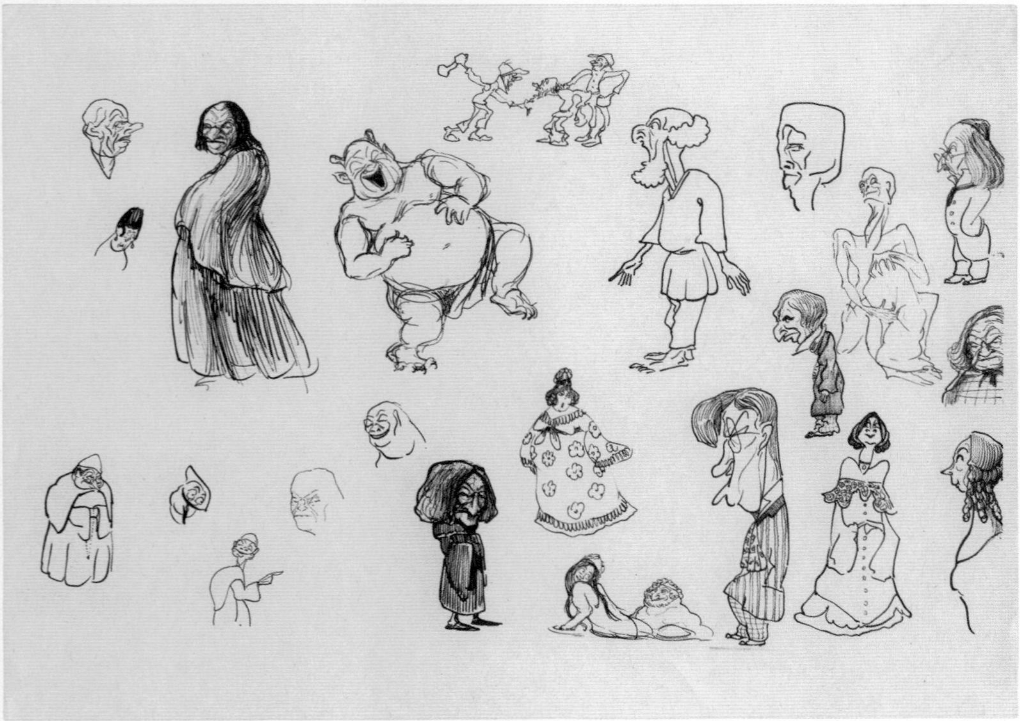

—THIS PAGE

TOP LEFT
Egypt (1915)

TOP RIGHT
Old Man Vignola at Work (1915)

BOTTOM LEFT
Captain, from 'Masks of *commedia dell'arte*' (1917)

BOTTOM RIGHT
'Expression of feelings' (1917)

—OVERLEAF

TOP LEFT
'Monarchs as the puppets of history' (1915)

TOP RIGHT
'Cinema at the front' (1915)

BOTTOM
'The beginning of the Trojan War' (1918)
Text: Banking House Menelaus, Agamemnon & Co. – Recording volunteers – Openwork stitching, pleated – War to victory! – Ultimatum – For Faith, Tsar and Elena!!!
– Hector

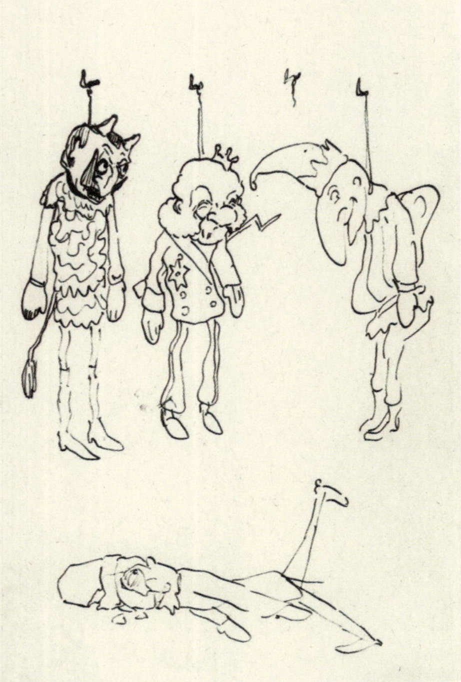

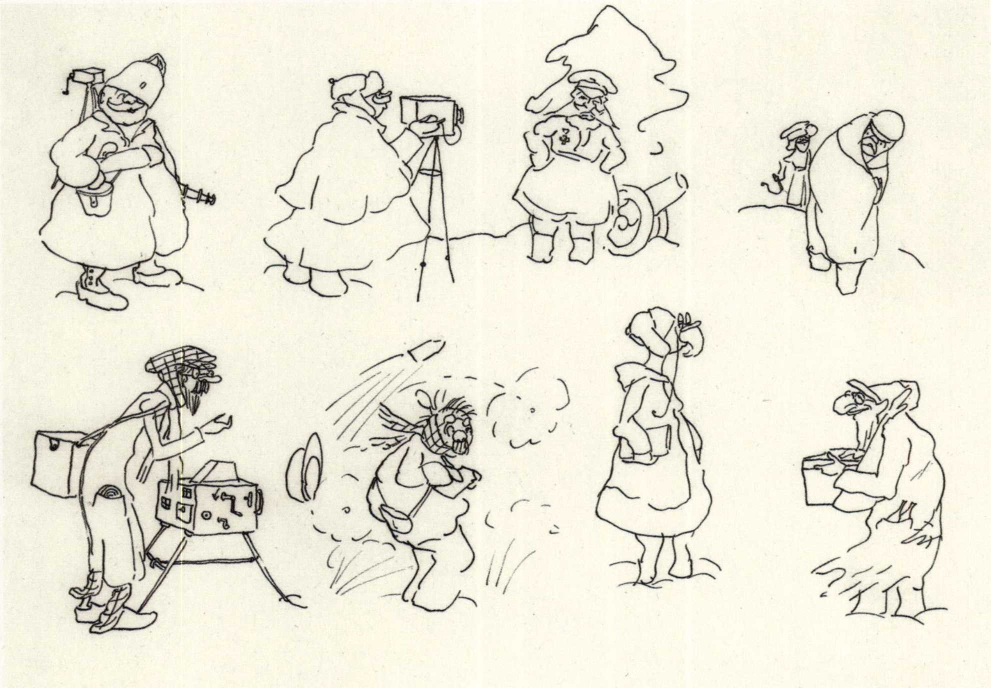

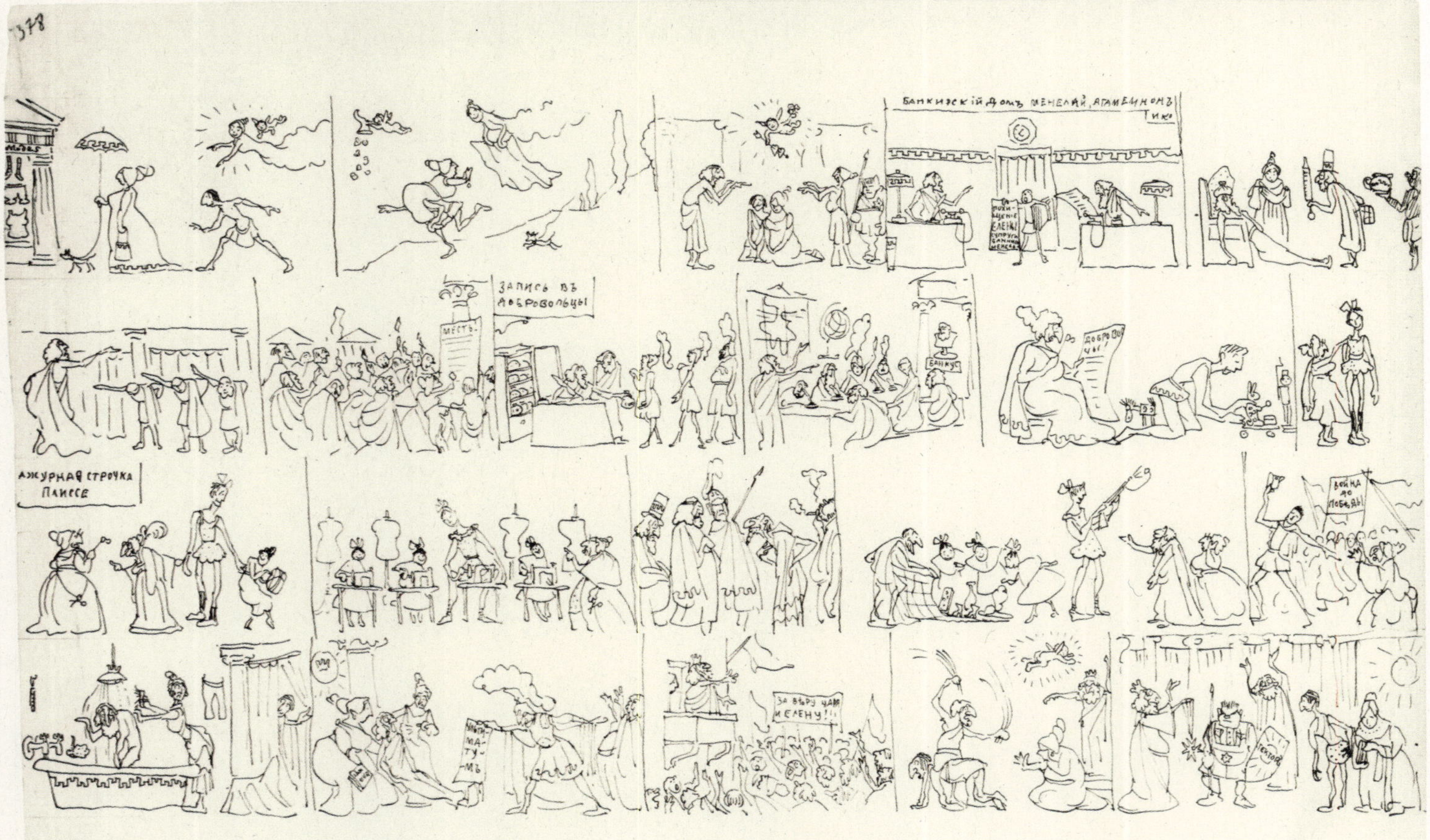

БАНКИРСКІЙ ДОМЪ МЕНЕЛАЙ, АГАМЕМНОНЪ И Ко
ЗАПИСЬ ВЪ ДОБРОВОЛЬЦЫ
МЕСТЬ
БАНКУС
ДОБРОВОЛЬЧЫ!
АЖУРНАЯ СТРОЧКА ПЛИССЕ
ВОЙНА ДО ПОБЕДЫ
ЗА ВѢРУ ЦАРЯ И ЕЛЕНУ!!!

February revolution. The militia's job was to prevent a putsch by the tsarist army. Eisenstein's impressions of the 'first days of freedom' not only gave him new subjects, but also freed up his line, which became once more flawlessly fine and light.

Even a family tragedy that happened in 1917 – the death of his mother's relative General Butovsky from an attack of apoplexy after his bank bonds were annulled – struck Sir Gay as a story about Monsieur du Comme-il-faut, frightened by history. He drew it with a fluent line of India ink in his best style, and then did something that was perhaps a surprise even for him: he swapped his pen for a brush, soaked it in crimson watercolour, as he had done in early childhood, and with a single sweep he coloured in the flag flying from Petrograd's Peter and Paul Fortress. Eight years later, he did the same thing in a black-and-white film, when he boldly coloured in crimson the flag on the mutinous battleship *Potemkin*.

In the context of 1917, Bonaparte no longer seemed the image of an ideal self-made man, but rather the symbol of a usurper and dictator. Wisely, Eisenstein remained silent about his 'maxim' of two years previously – although he had not forgotten it.

Was he satisfied with his new possible biography: not Architecture, but 'Politics and Drawing'? He thought about it, no doubt, when his cartoons appeared on the pages of a newspaper. But another alternative to the destiny his father had mapped out also appeared, in the same year. More and more often, very strange visions had been appearing before the eyes of the boy from Riga. Not caricatures. Not graphic reportage. Not political or everyday-life cartoons. But sketches for sets, costumes and theatrical characters. One of the first such visions was, of course, *Hamlet*. The young Eisenstein had loved the theatre when he was still in Riga: his letters and his school sketchbooks reflect his regular visits to see German opera and Russian drama.

In Petrograd, he tried not to miss the most talked-about productions: *Boris Godunov* with Feodor Chaliapin at the Mariinsky Opera; Vsevolod Meyerhold's shows at the Alexandrinsky Theatre and in 'decadent' studio theatres; Nikolai Evreinov's sketches at the Curved Mirror. From his nineteenth birthday onwards, however, the student from the Institute of Civil Engineers felt drawn to the theatre not merely as a spectator, but as a potential participant in the mysteries of stagecraft. Would he have enough energy and determination to ensure that his theatrical visions became more than spectres on sheets of paper? Would the Theatre not cast him out, like poor Pierrot from the pantomime *Les Millions de Pierrot* – a project that he had undertaken to compose in the spirit of Molière and of the *commedia dell'arte*?

Who can say what would have happened if it had not been for the second revolution, in the Russian October (European November) of 1917? Eisenstein was being quite honest and sincere when he observed that:

The revolution gave me the most precious thing in my life – it made me an artist.

Without the revolution, I'd never have 'broken' the tragedy: I'd have been an engineer, like father, like son.

I had the ideas, the desires, but it was only the wind of revolution that gave me the main thing: freedom of self-determination.[6]

He wrote that in his autobiography of 1939. At that time, during the Great Terror, the done thing would have been to write something along the lines of: 'Sergei Eisenstein, architecture student, just turned twenty, son of a monarchist, grandson of a merchant and honorary citizen of Petrograd, rejected his inherited millions and joined up with the Red Army to construct bunkers and trenches.'

In fact, events had turned out rather differently. In February 1918, his mother Yulia Ivanovna had found an escape from all the predicted possibilities into an unpredicted reality. Faced with the total mobilization of young men into the Bolshevik army, rich families who were unable to leave the country decided to hide their children in the 'jaws of the lion'. An engineer, Sergei Peich, crafty as Harlequin, organized the military construction of defensive fortifications on the very quietest section of the front in the Civil War, where there was allegedly a danger that British intervention forces would attack on their way from Archangelsk to Petrograd. Besides his folders of paper, his pens and his ink, Eisenstein also took with him to the North his paints and brushes for sketching imaginary theatrical productions.

The line from Rorik to Kitten to $\sqrt{2}$ to Sir Gay had made a sharp turn: away from the 'King of the Universe' and towards 'S. M. Eisenstein'.

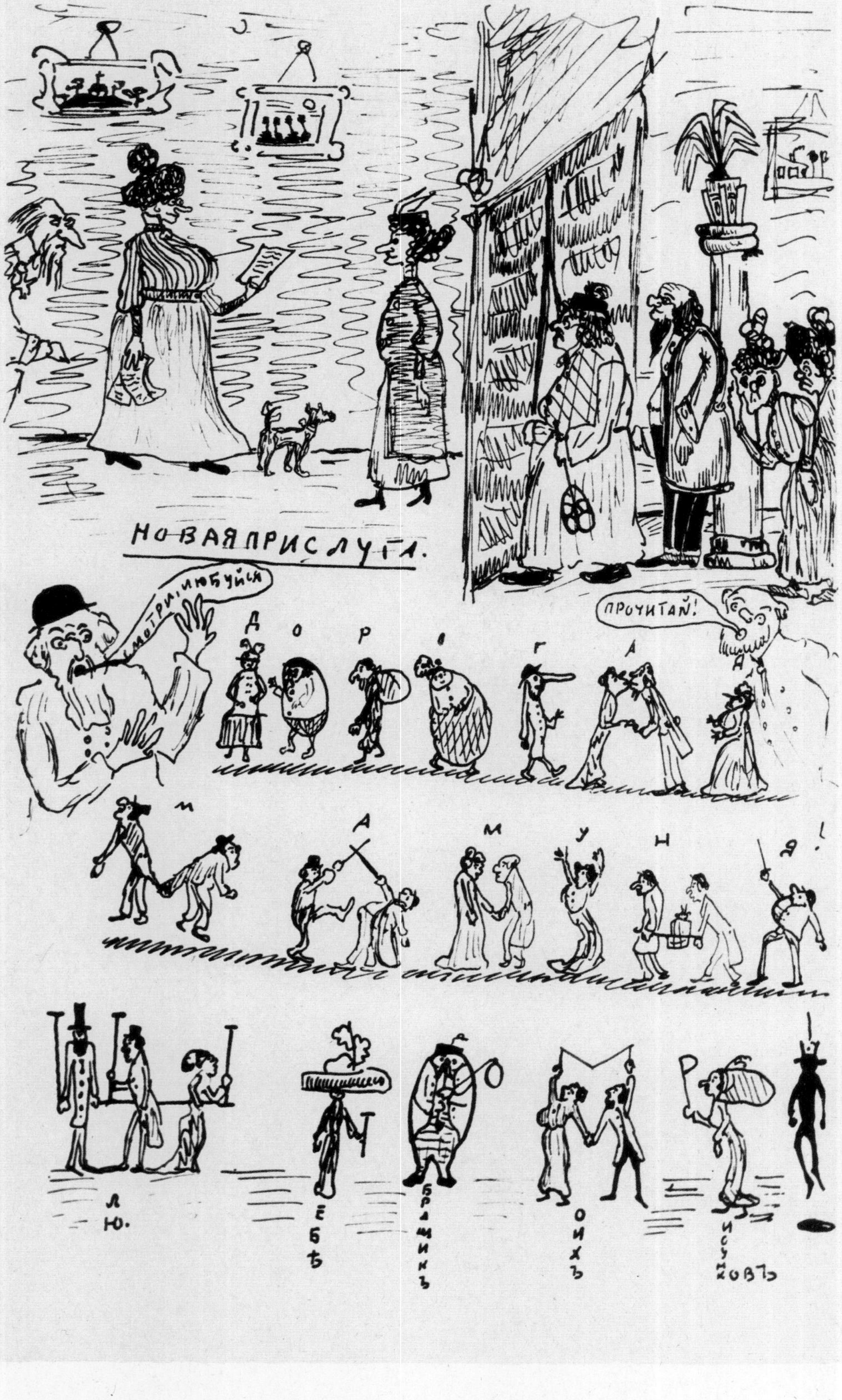
НОВАЯ ПРИСЛУГА.
Смотри и любуйся
ПРОЧИТАЙ!
Д О Р Ѣ Г А
И А М У Н Я !
Л Ю.
ЕБЪ
БРАШИКЪ
ОИХЪ
ИСУМКОВЪ

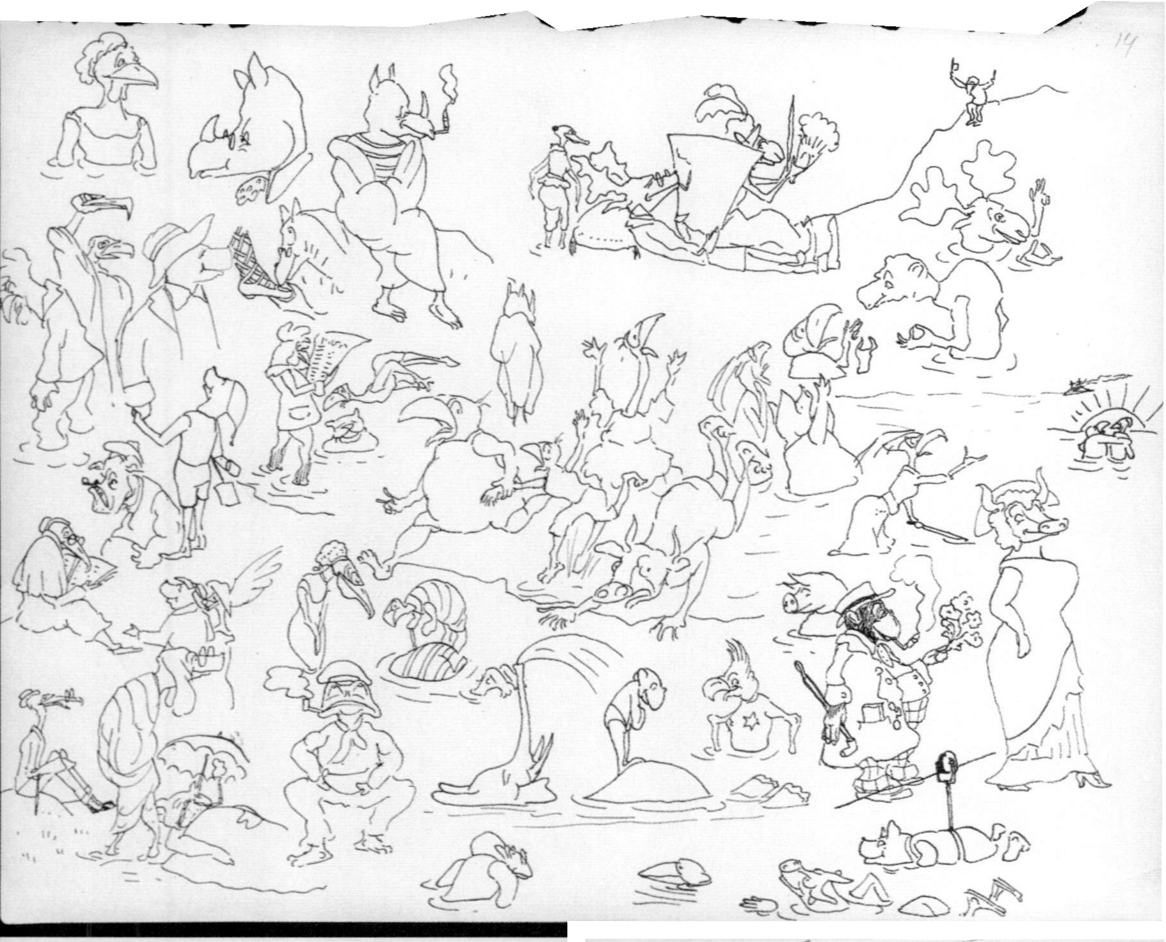

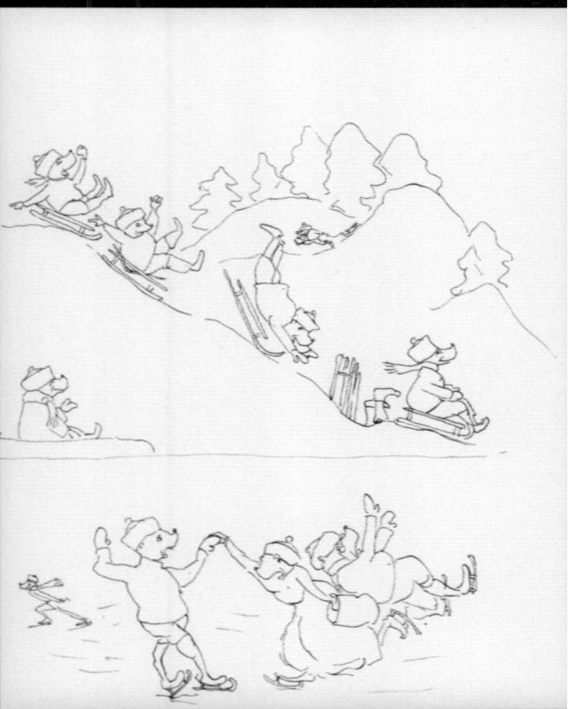

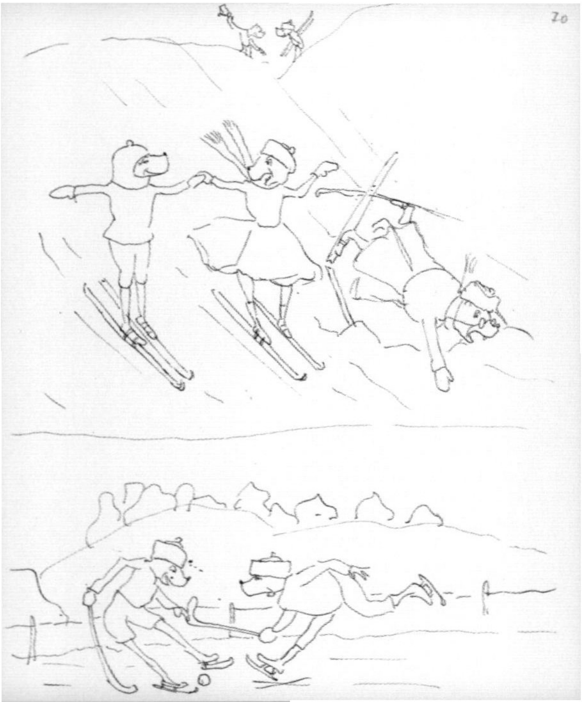

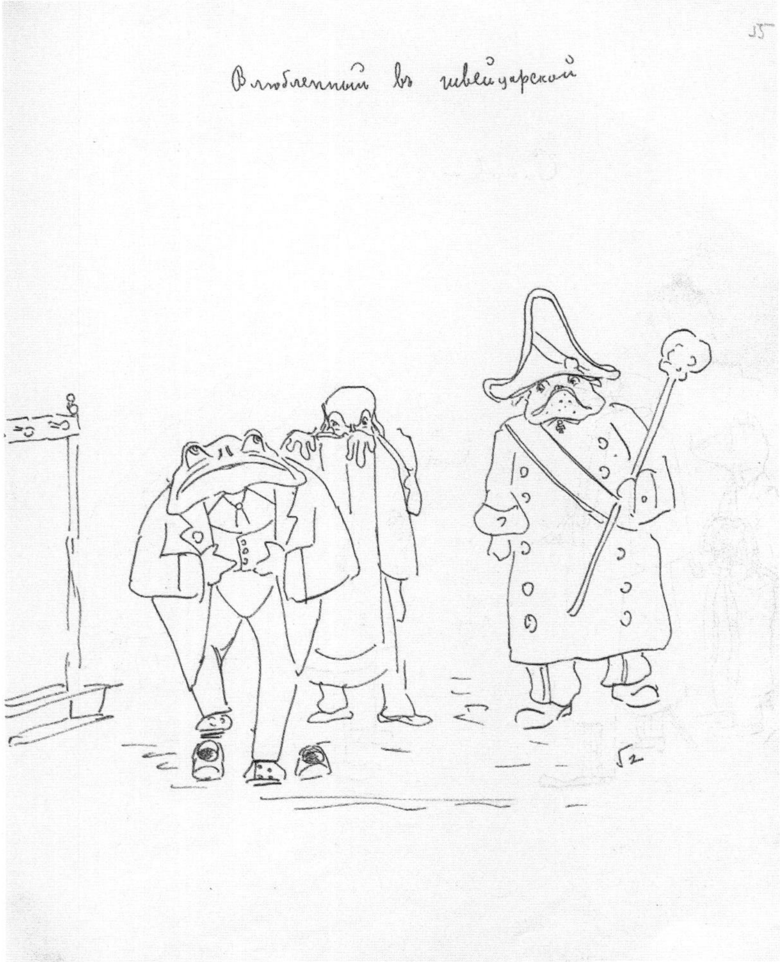
Влюбленный въ швейцарской
√2

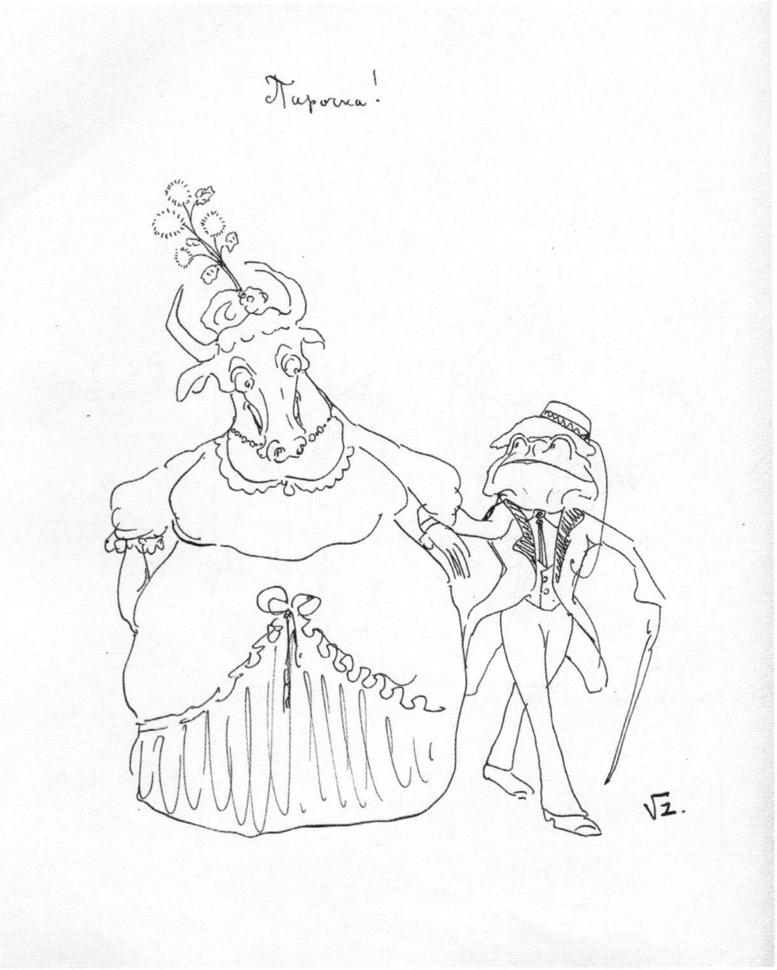
Парочка!
√2.

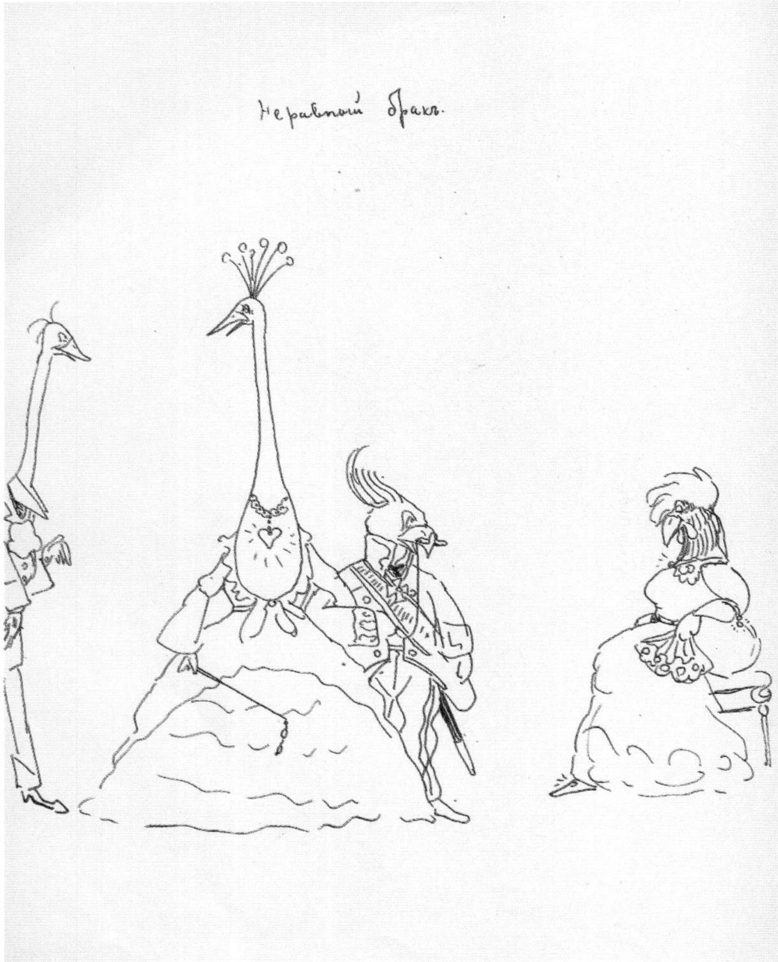
Неравный бракъ.

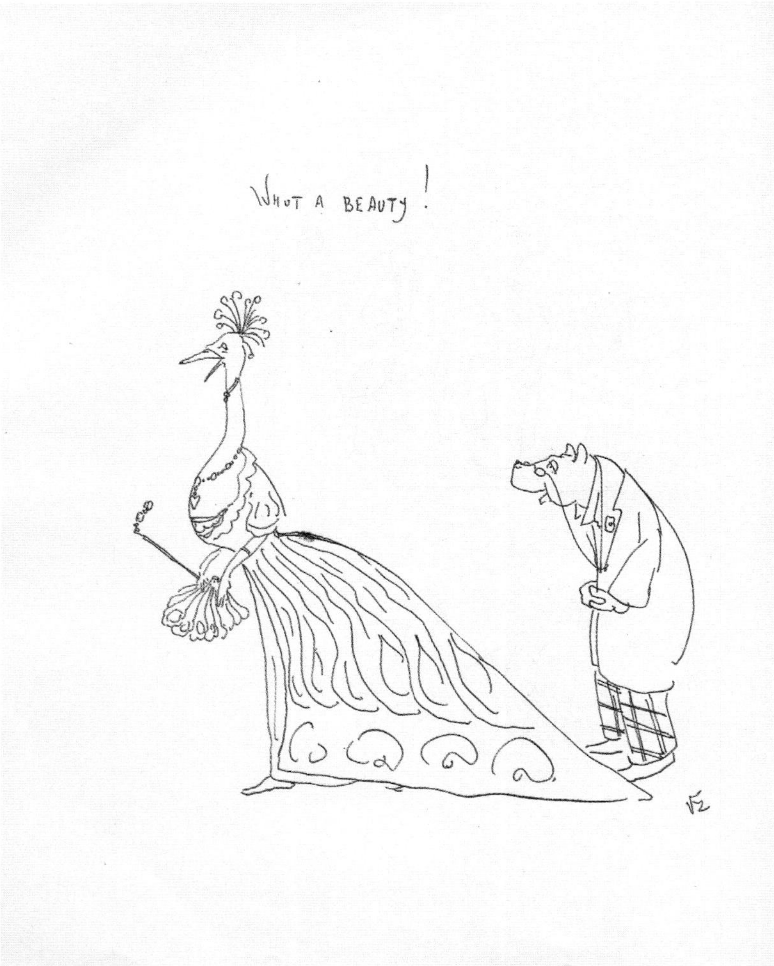
WHOT A BEAUTY!
√2

—PREVIOUS

LEFT PAGE
A letter to mother, *The New Maid* (1911)
Text:
(On the left): Look, admire!
(On the right): Read!
(Written by figures forming letters): Dear mother! I send you a sample of my drawings!

RIGHT PAGE TOP
'Summer' (1914)

RIGHT PAGE BOTTOM (LEFT AND RIGHT)
'Winter' (1913)

—OPPOSITE

TOP LEFT
The Lover in the Antechamber (1914)

TOP RIGHT
The Couple! (1914)

BOTTOM LEFT
Misalliance (1914)

BOTTOM RIGHT
What a Beauty! (1914)

—THIS PAGE
Estates (1914)

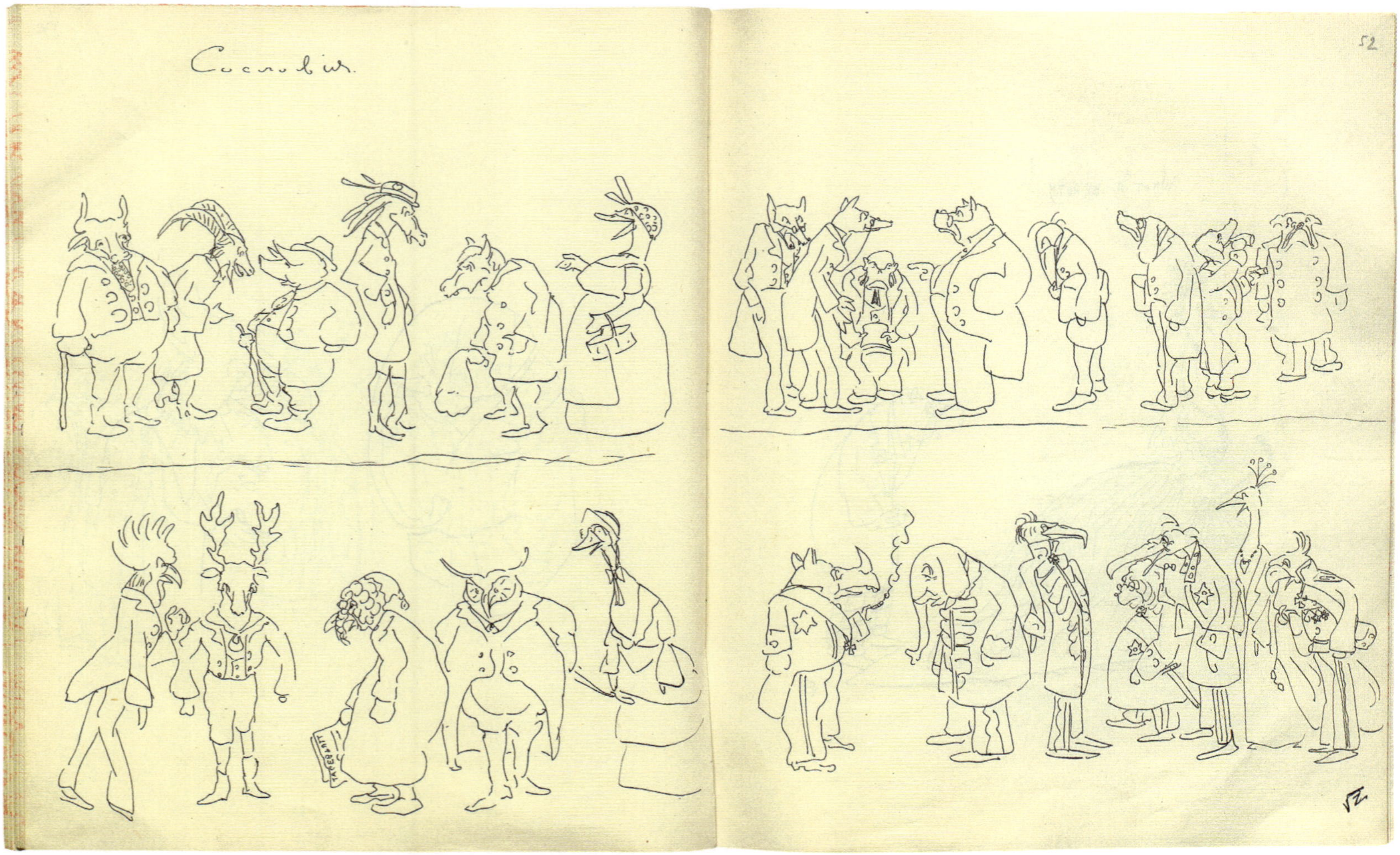

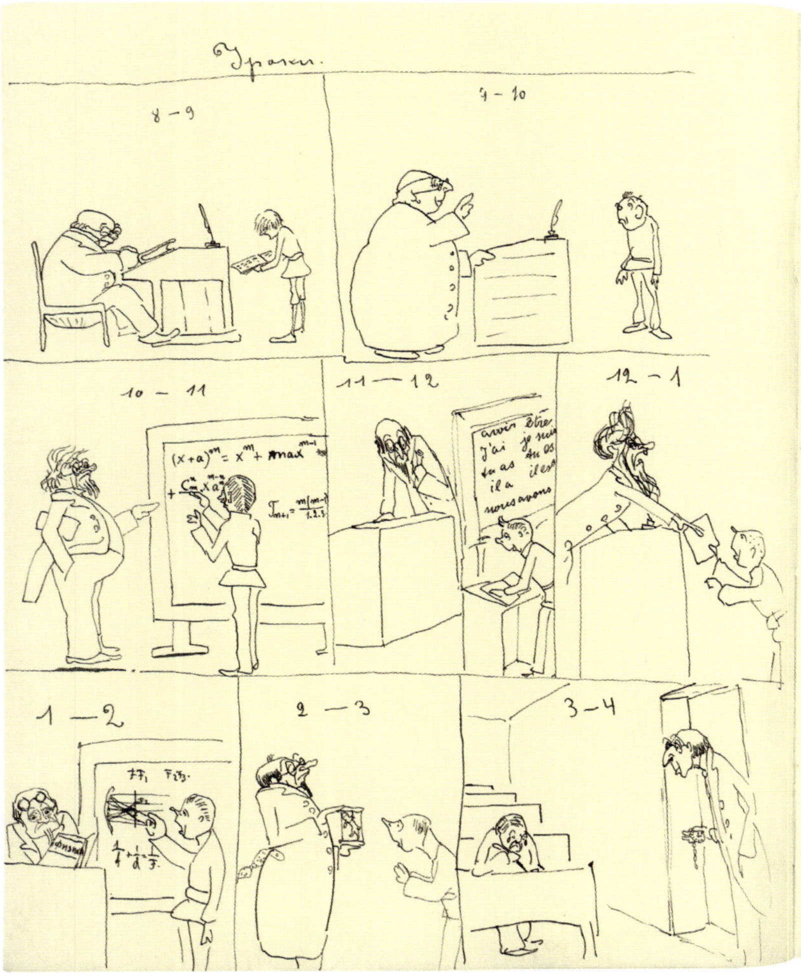

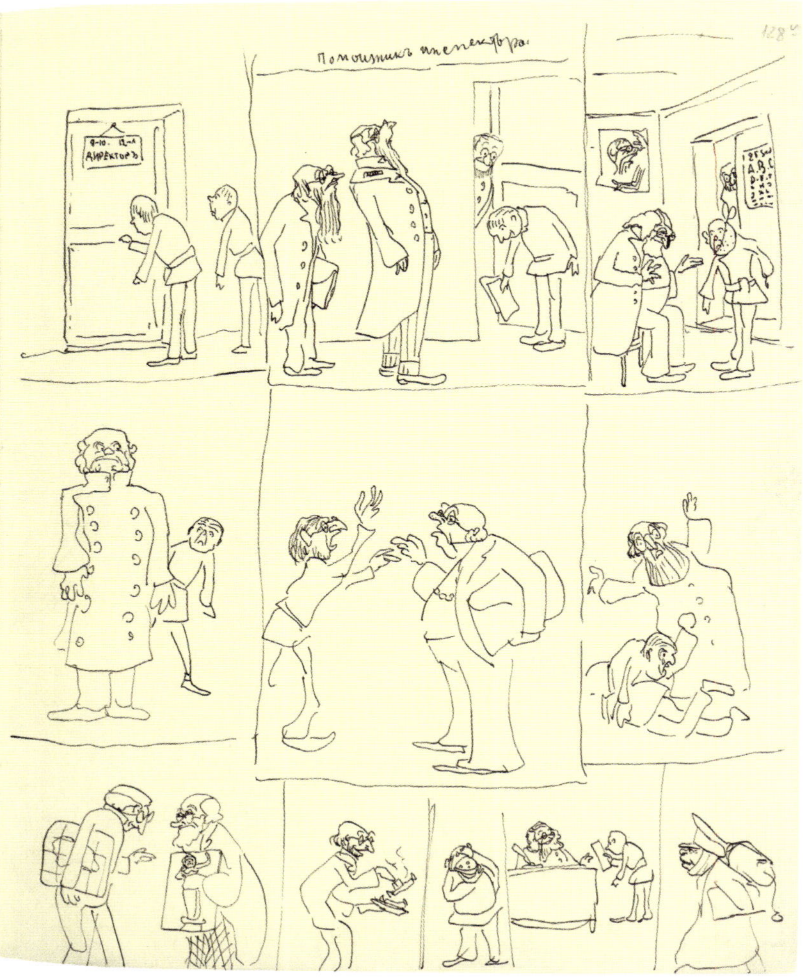

—THIS PAGE

ABOVE LEFT
Lessons (1914)

ABOVE RIGHT
Assistant Inspector (1914)

—OPPOSITE
An Error!! !! !! (1914)

—OVERLEAF LEFT

TOP LEFT
'Civil servants' (1914)

TOP RIGHT
'Clerk' (1914)

BOTTOM LEFT
'Clown' (1914)

BOTTOM RIGHT
'Monsieur du Comme-il-faut' (Gentleman) (1914)

—OVERLEAF RIGHT
'The house' (1914)

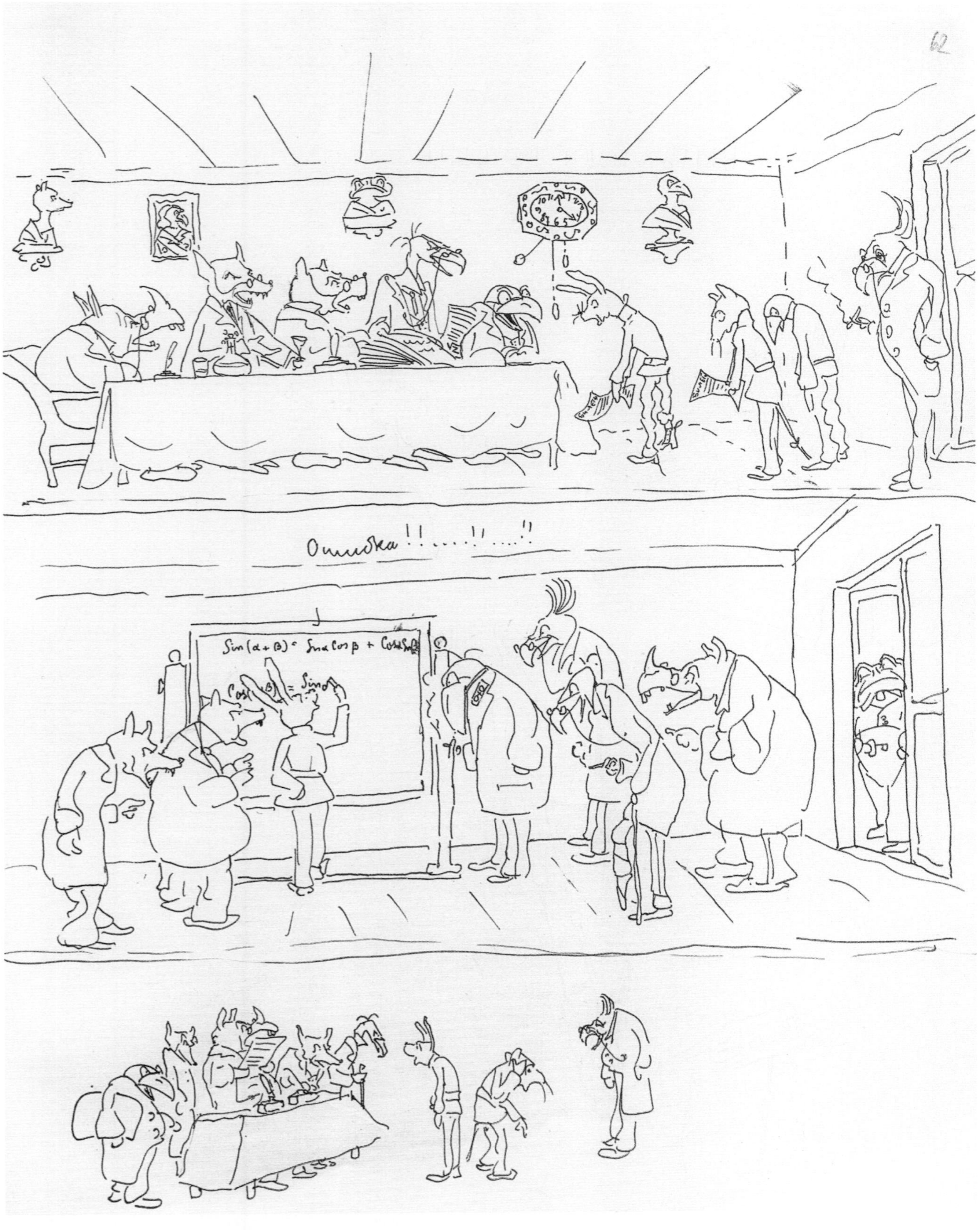
62
Ошибка!!....!!....!!
Sin(α+β) = Sinα Cosβ + CosαSinβ

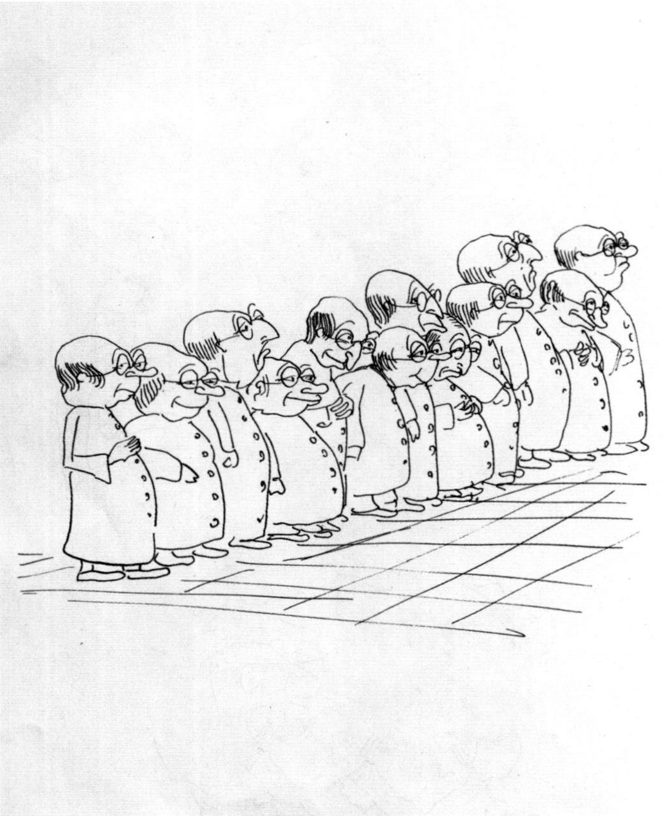

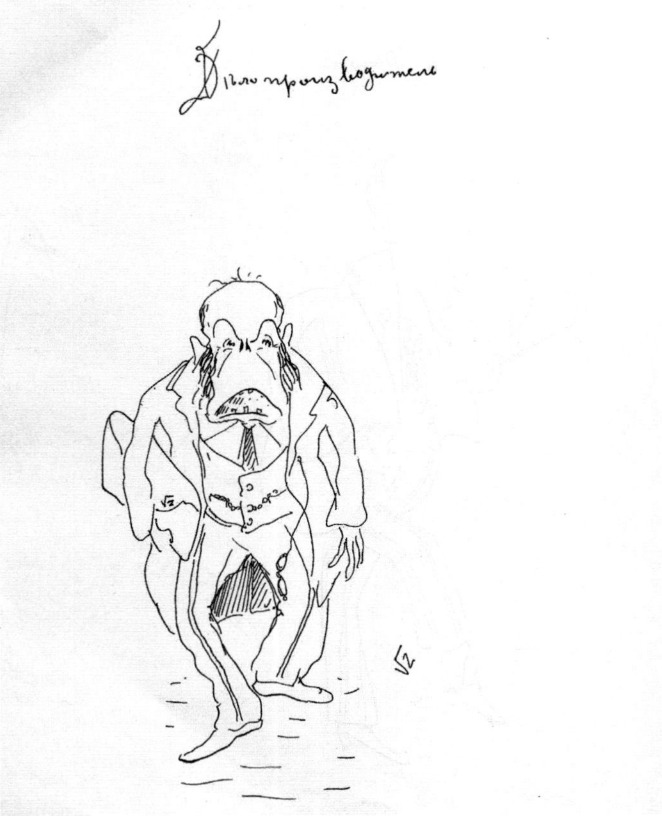
Дѣло производитель

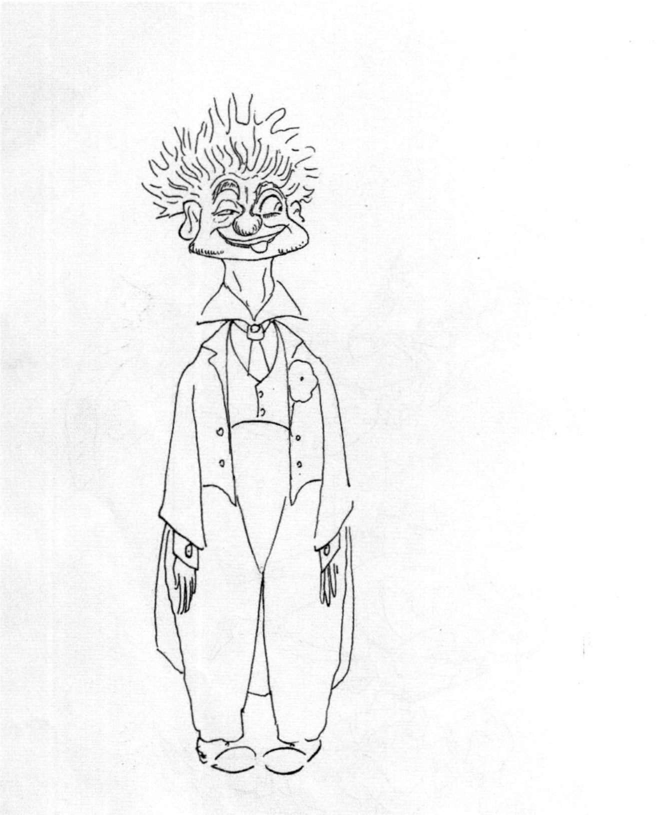

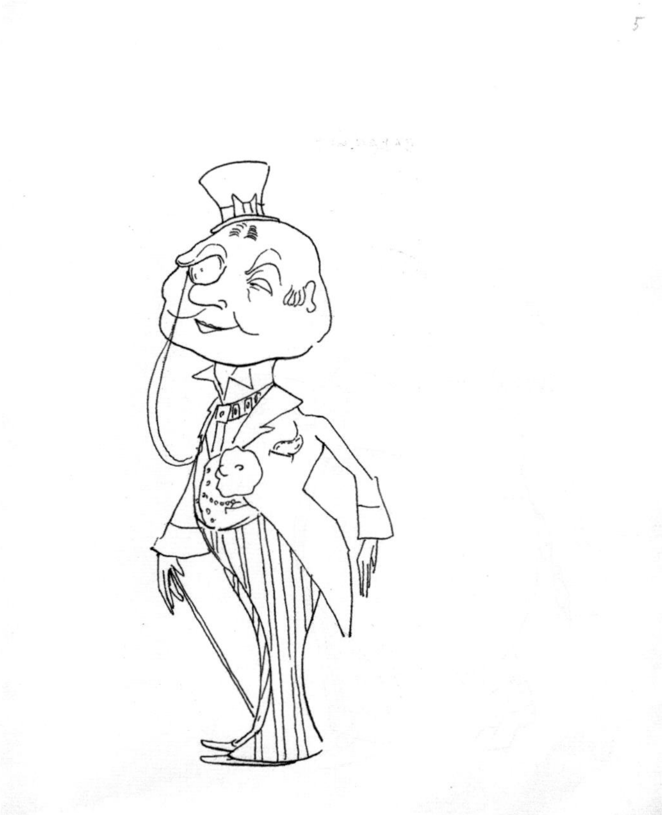

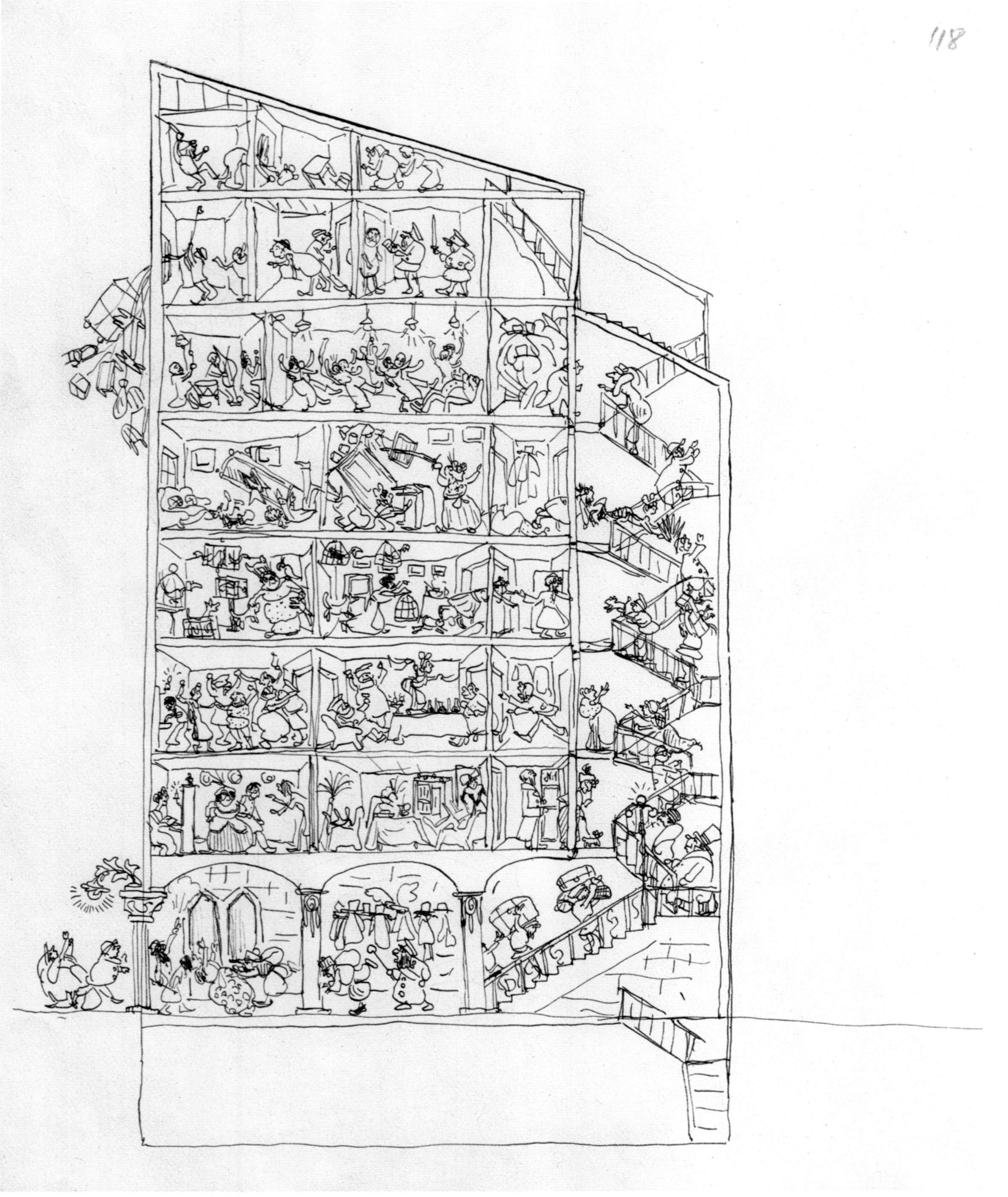

Пріюхали.

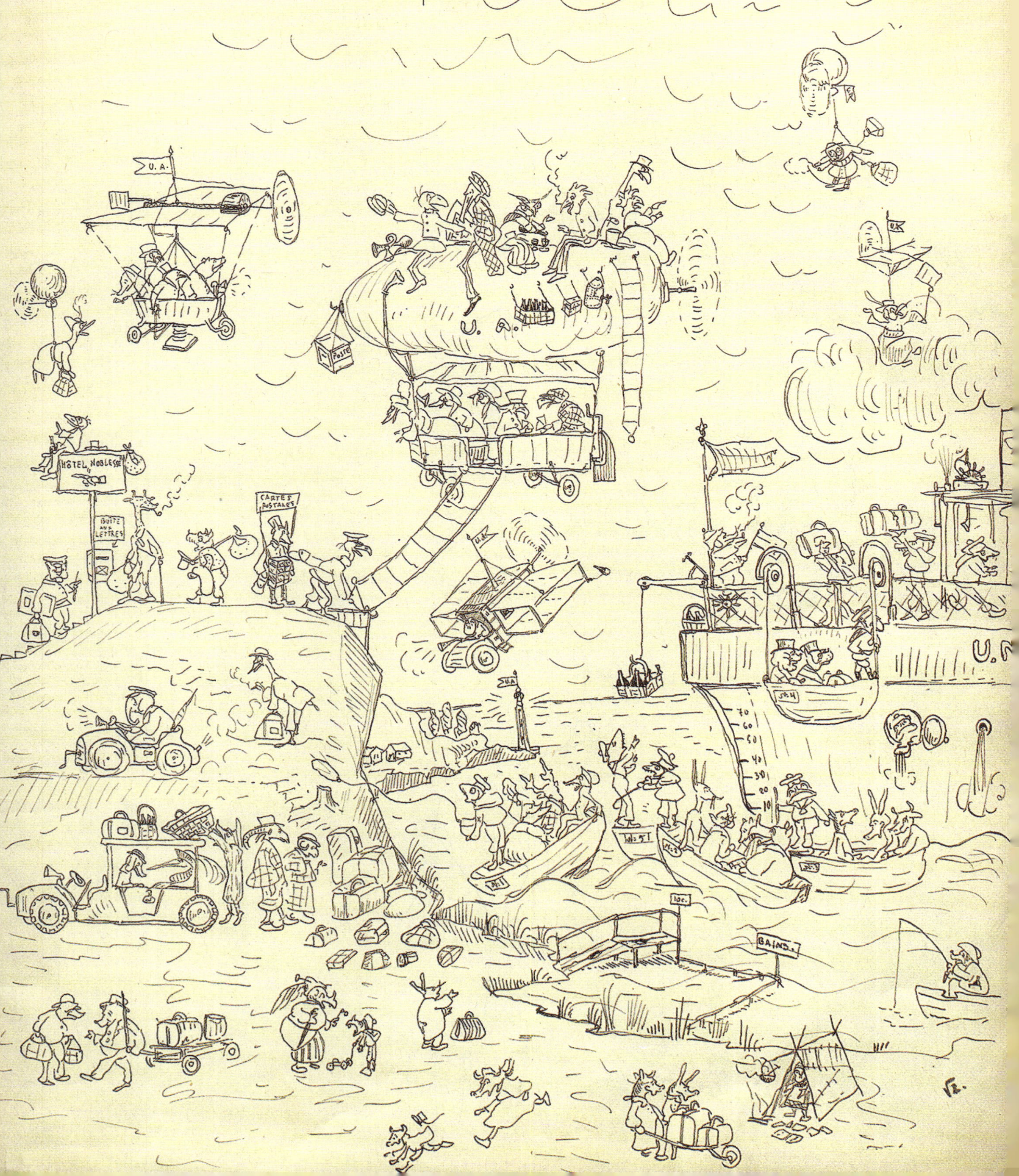
U. A.
U. A.
POSTE
HÔTEL NOBLESSE
BOITE AUX LETTRES
CARTES POSTALES
U. A.
BAINS.
√2.

OPPOSITE
Arrived (1914)

THIS PAGE
Monastery (1914)

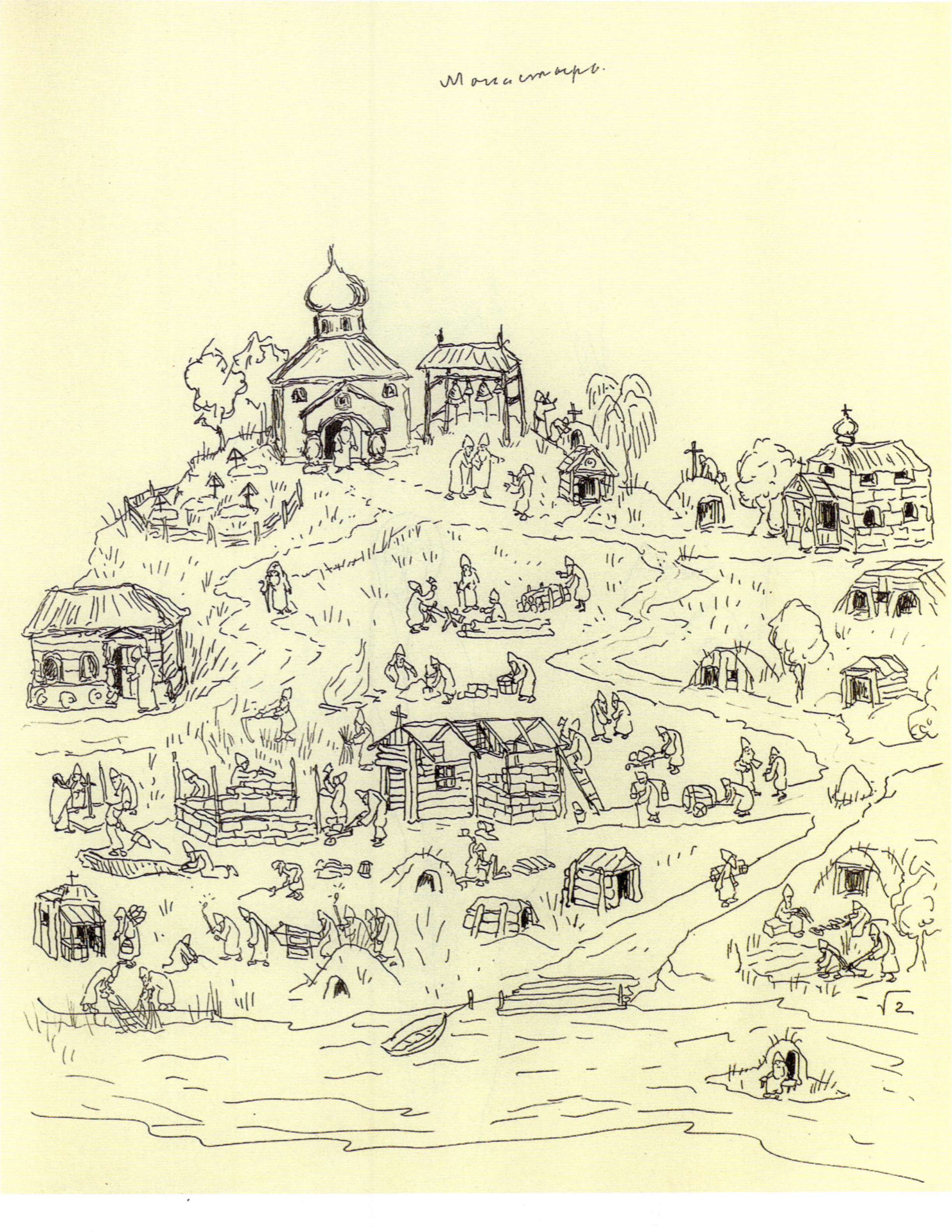

—THIS PAGE

BELOW LEFT
Destiny (1914)

BELOW RIGHT
'The gods and the citizens of ancient Athens' (1914)

—OPPOSITE

TOP (LEFT AND RIGHT)
'Orpheus in the Underworld' (1914)

BOTTOM
Where? (1914)

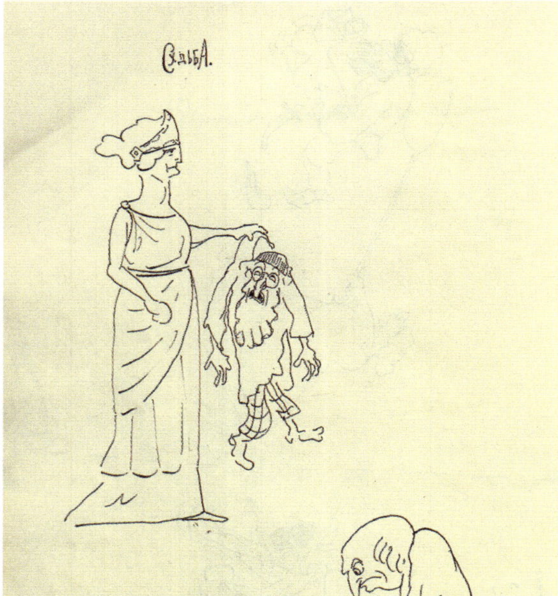

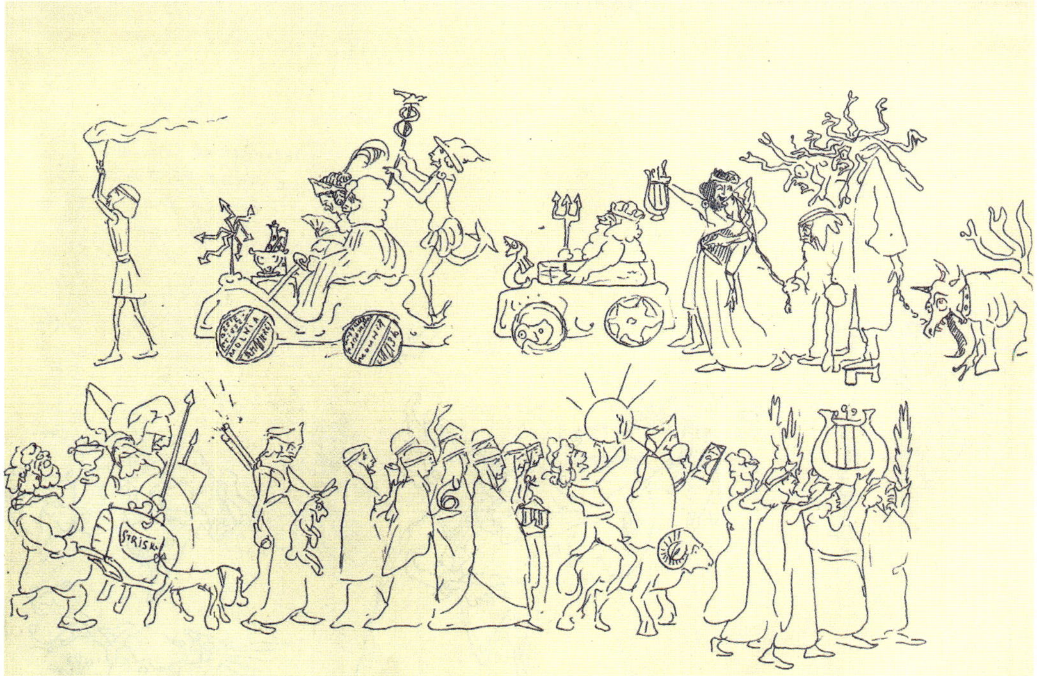

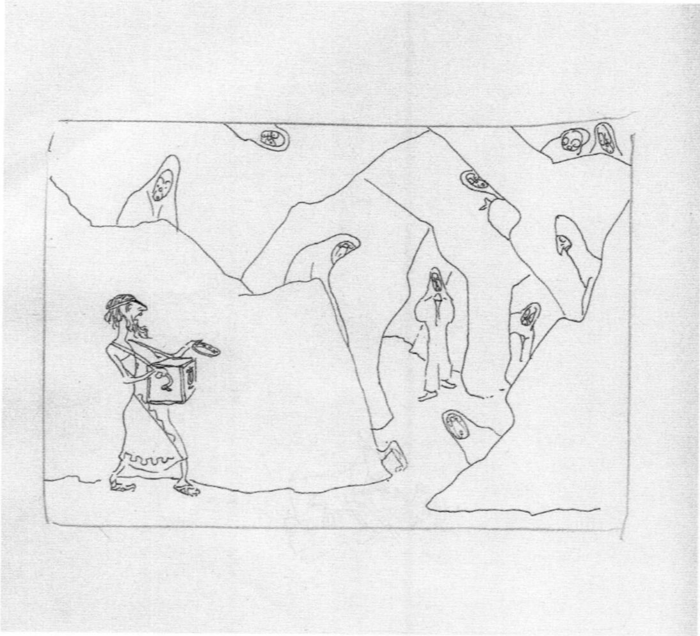

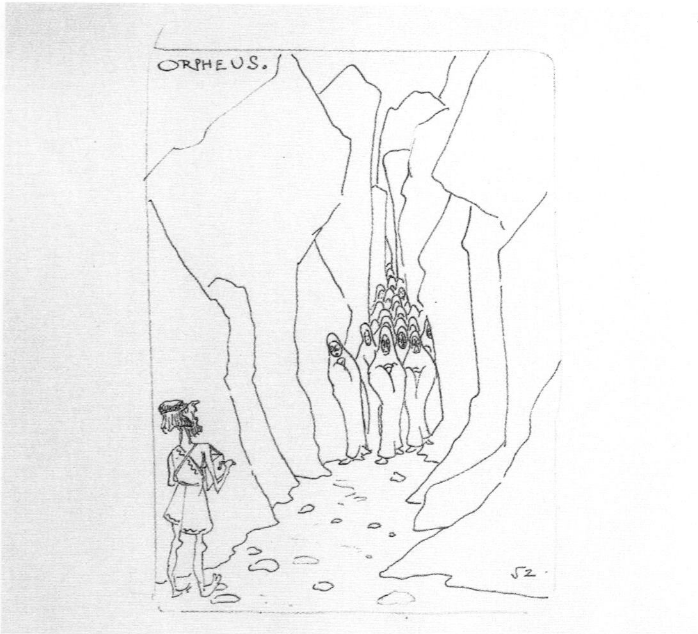
ORPHEUS.

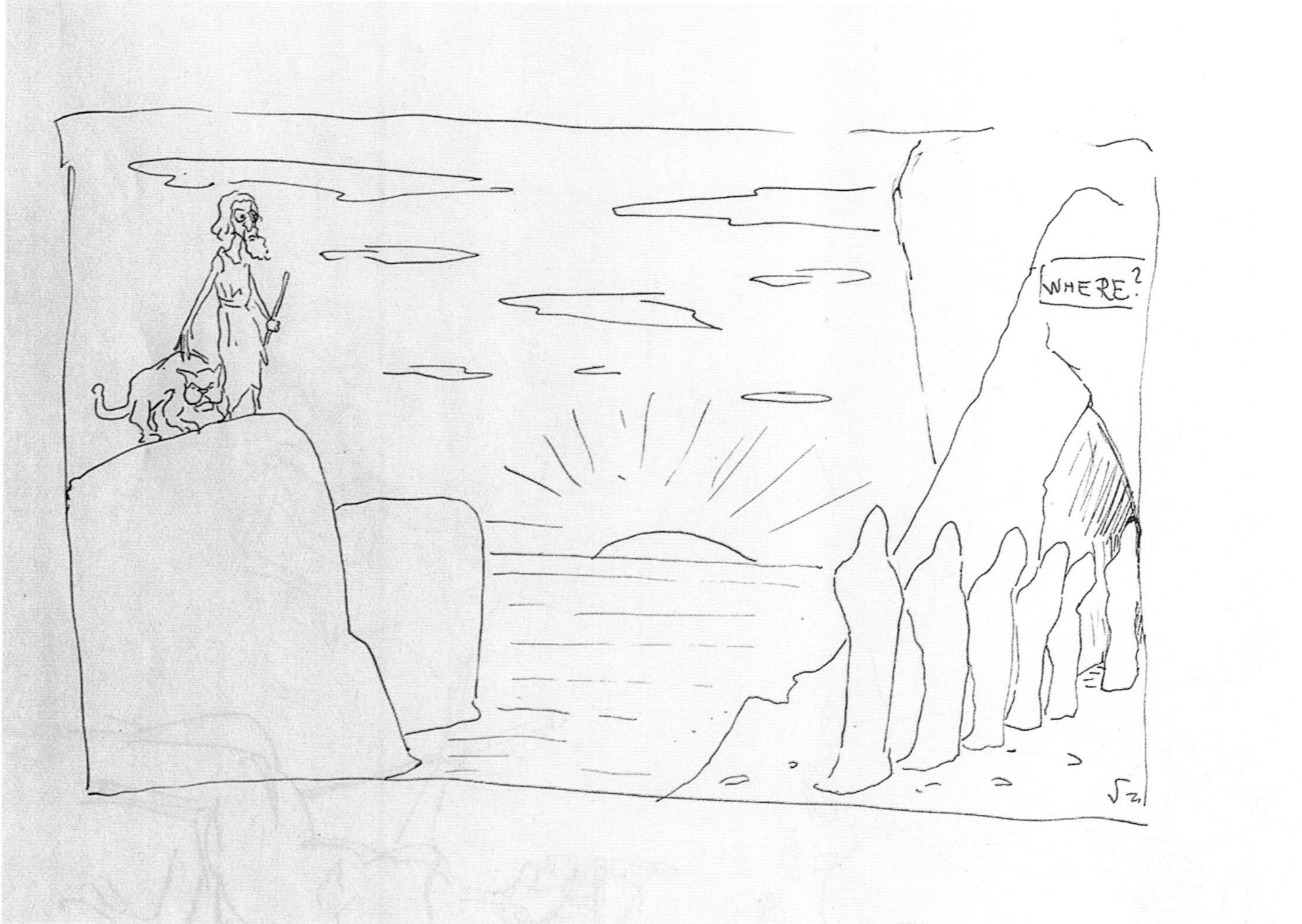
WHERE?

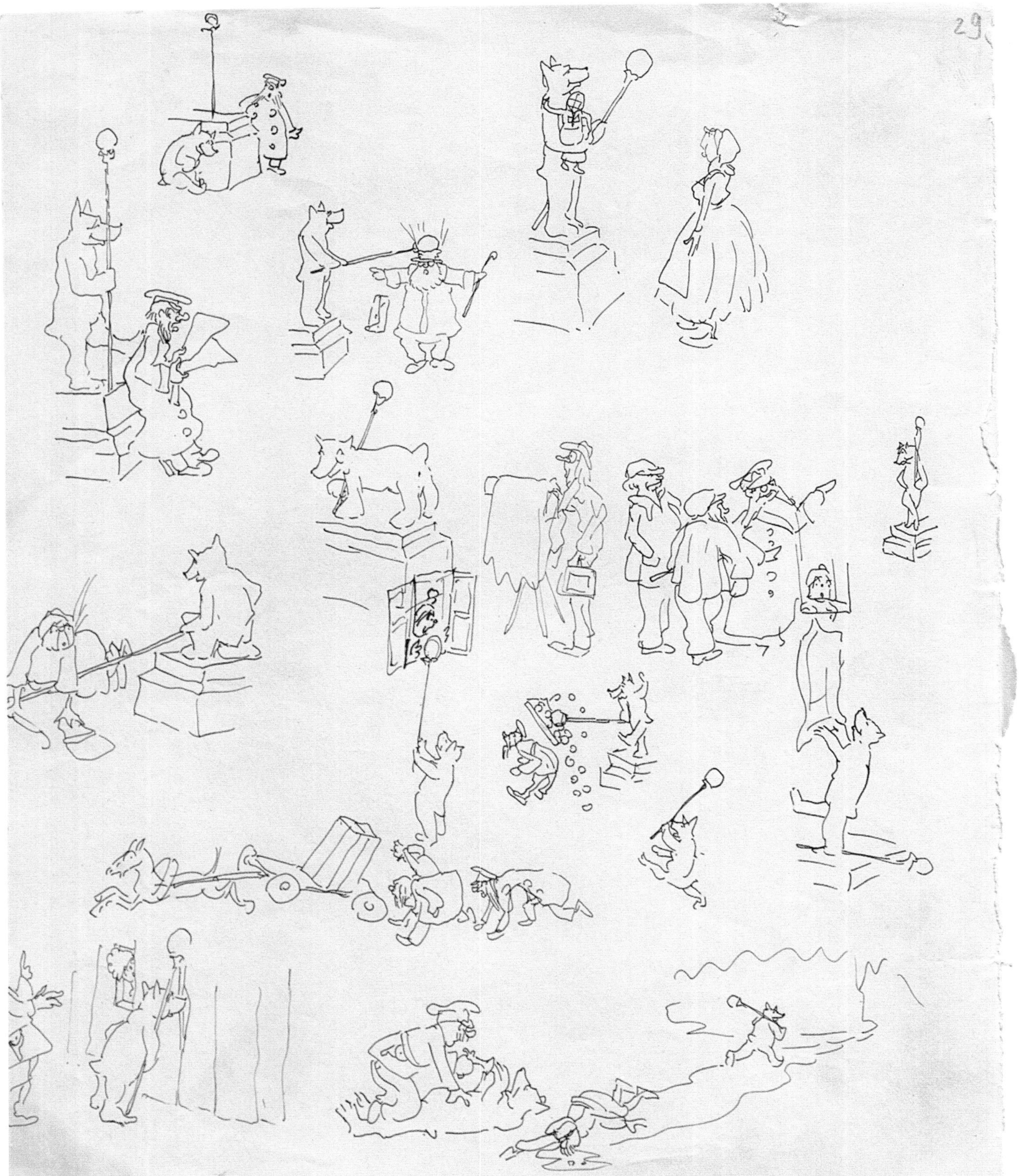

29

—OPPOSITE

'The mischievous acts of a bear with a lamp' (1914)

—THIS PAGE

TOP

'The sphinx's adventures in Riga' (1914)

BOTTOM

Cinema 64 – 'Shooting the Tsar Cannon at the circus' (1914)

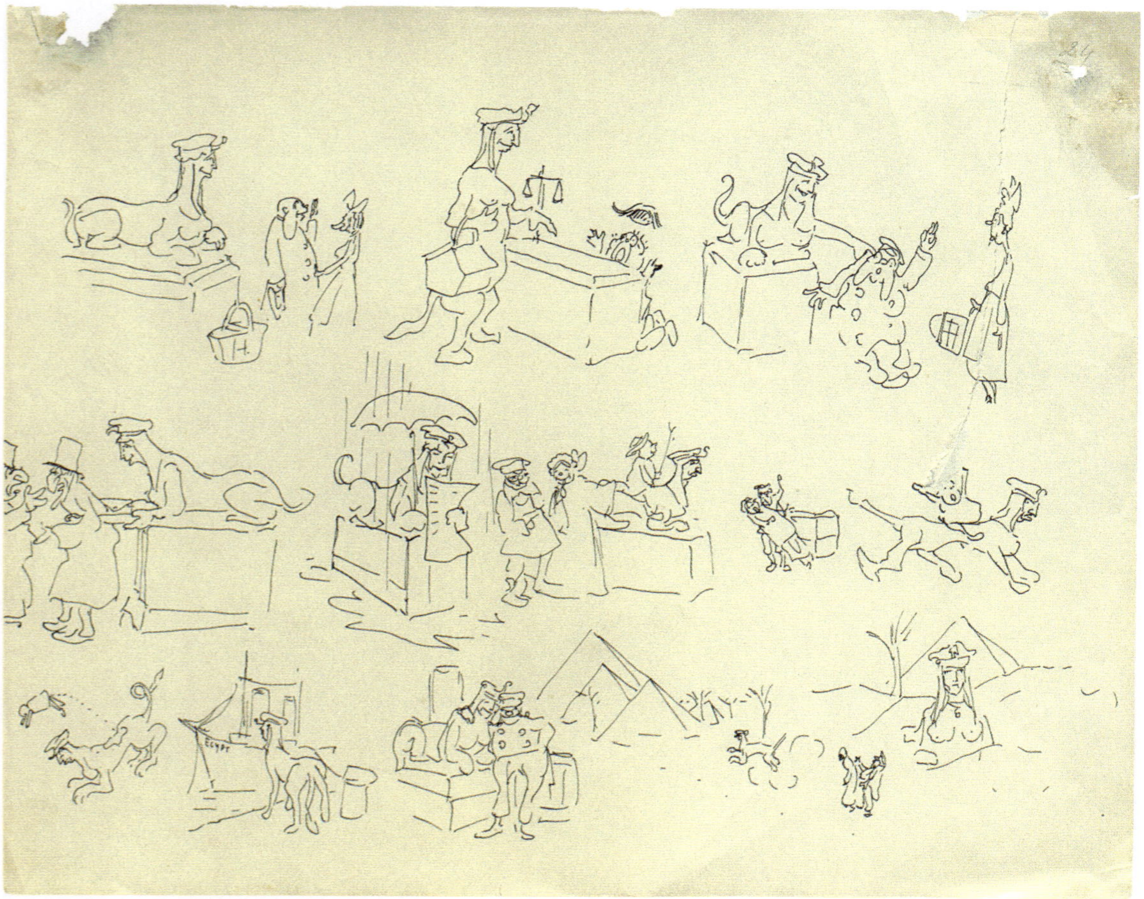

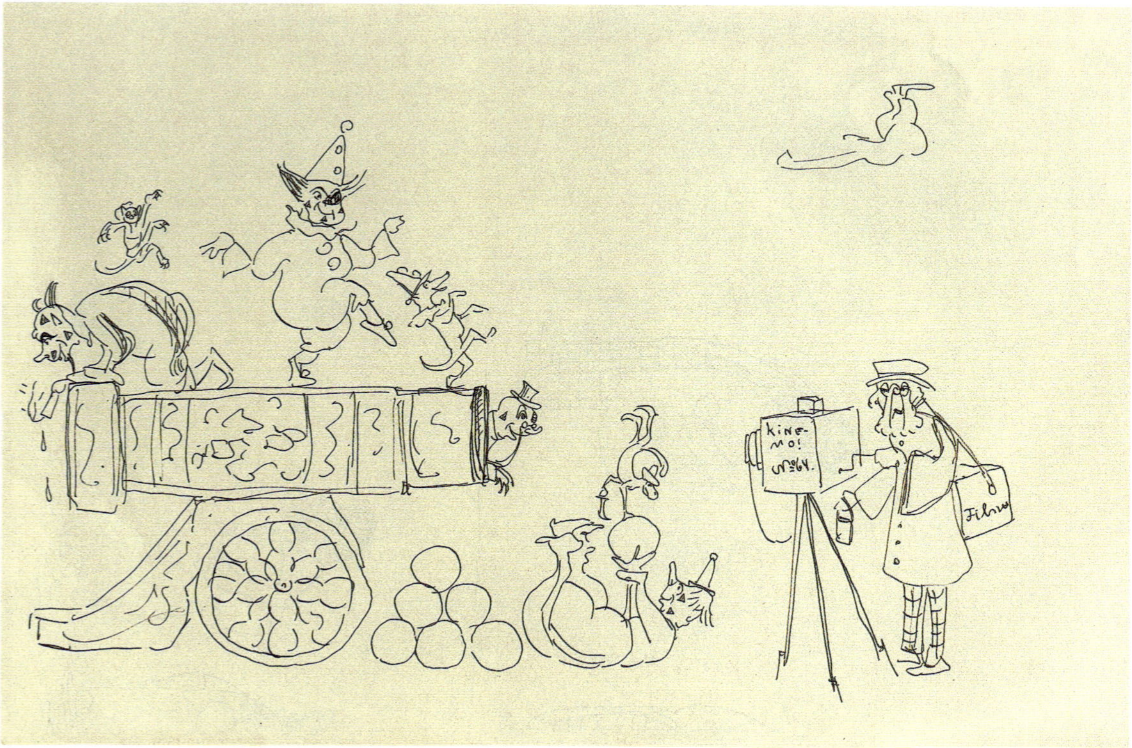

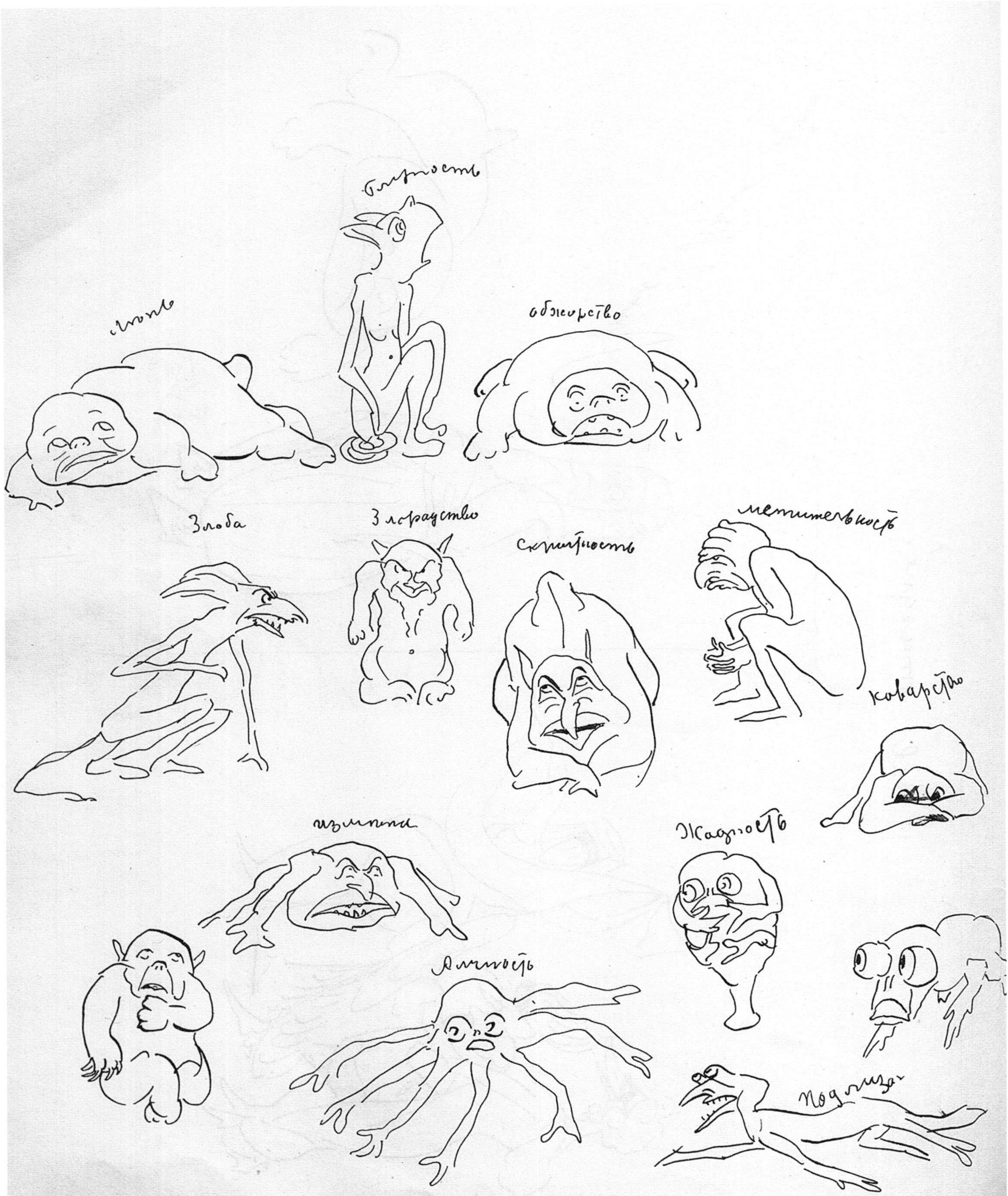
Глупость
Лень
обжорство
Злоба
Злорадство
Скрытность
мстительность
коварство
измена
Жадность
Алчность
Подлиза

Сестры.

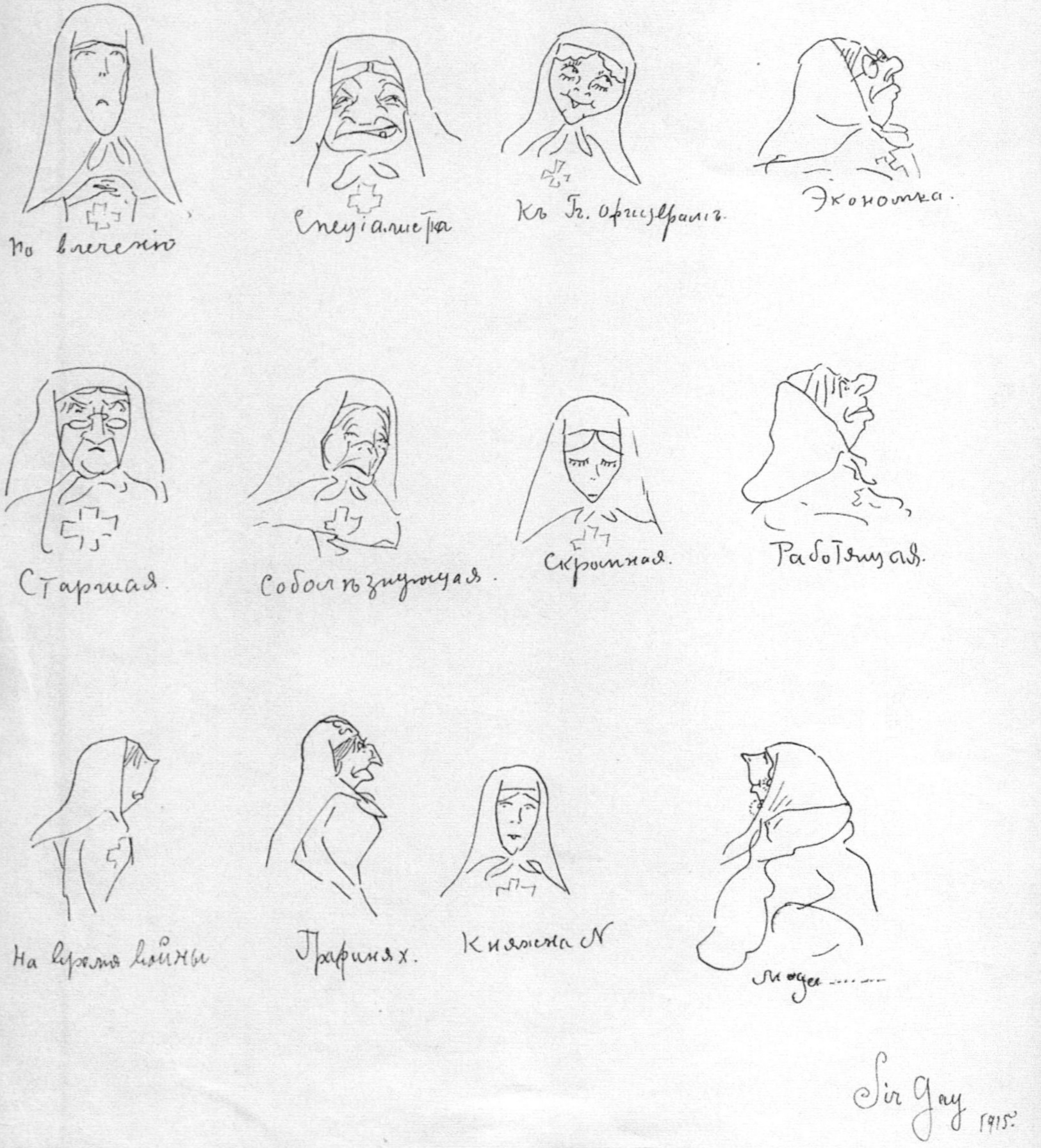
По влечению
Специалистка
Къ Г. Офицерамъ.
Экономка.
Старшая.
Соболезнующая.
Скромная.
Работящая.
На время войны
Графиня X.
Княжна N
Мода......
Sir Gay 1915.

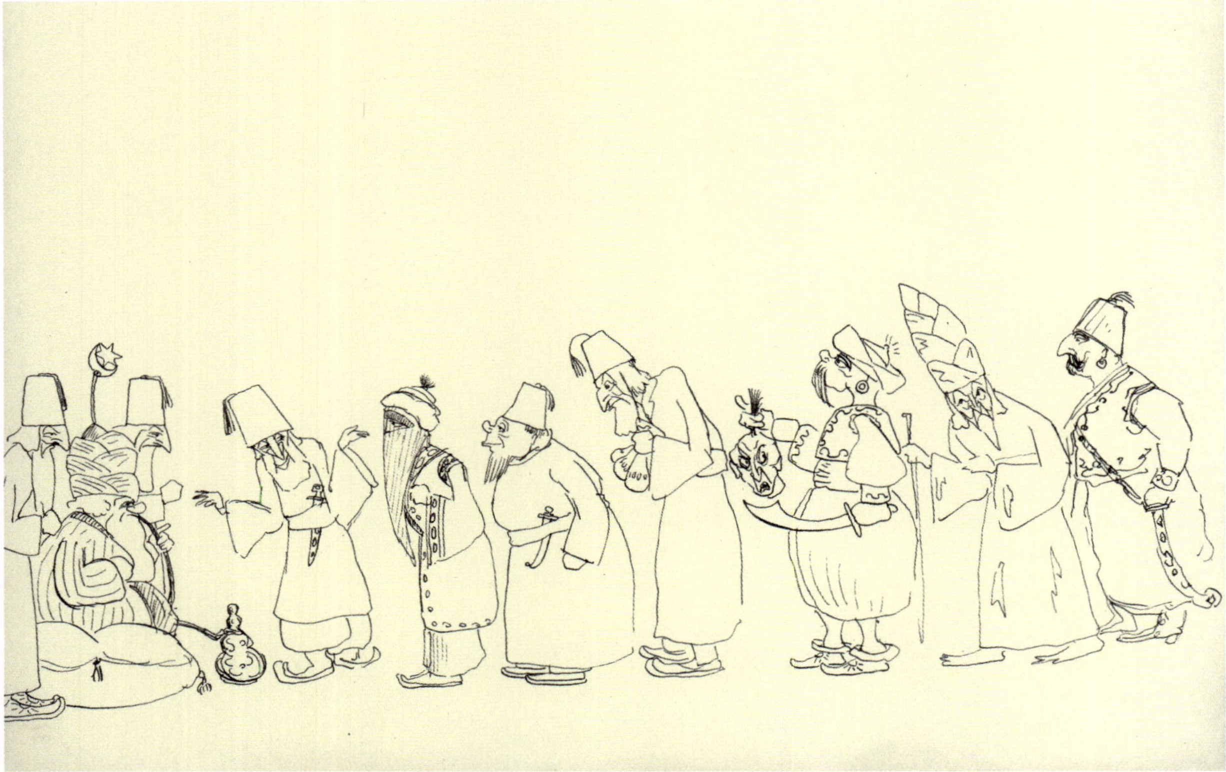

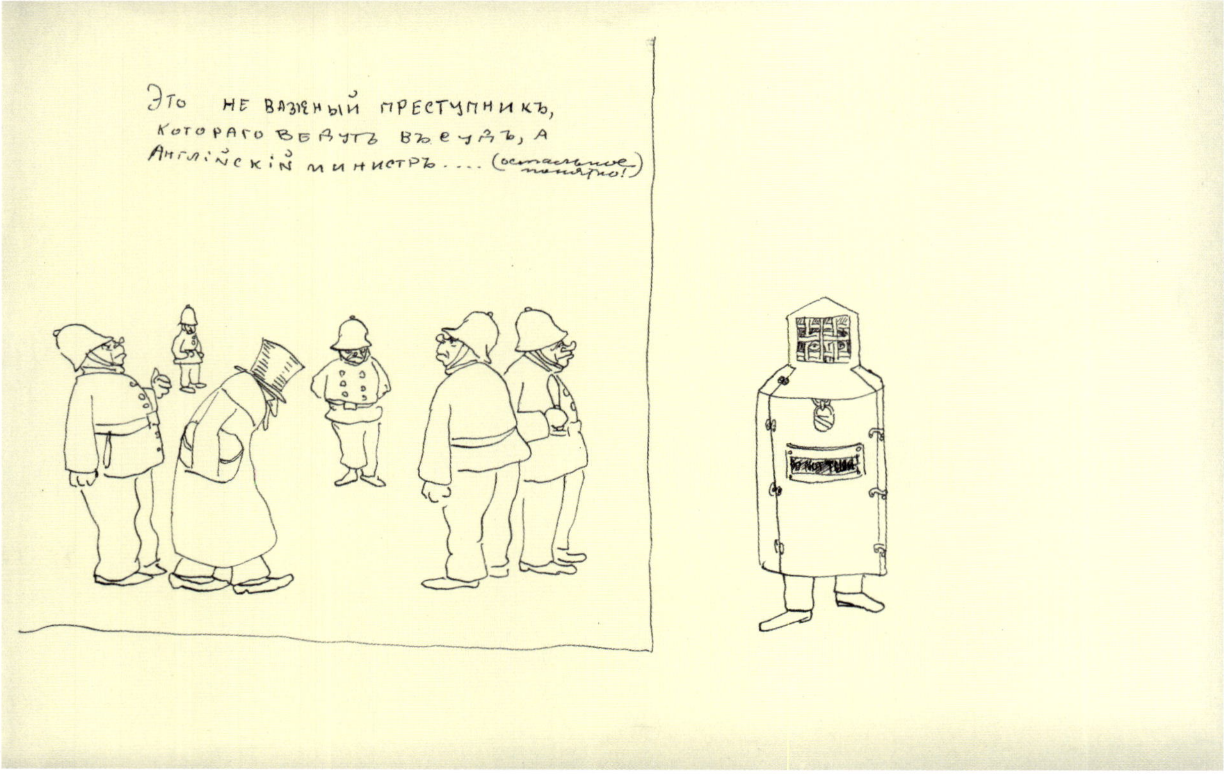

—THIS PAGE

TOP
'Sultan's affairs' (1914)

BOTTOM
Text: It is not an notable criminal who is being led to the court, but an English minister… (the rest is understandable!)

—OPPOSITE
People of the XXI Century (1913)

—OVERLEAF
The Queue (1916)
Text: Tea. Coffee. Sugar – 150 people

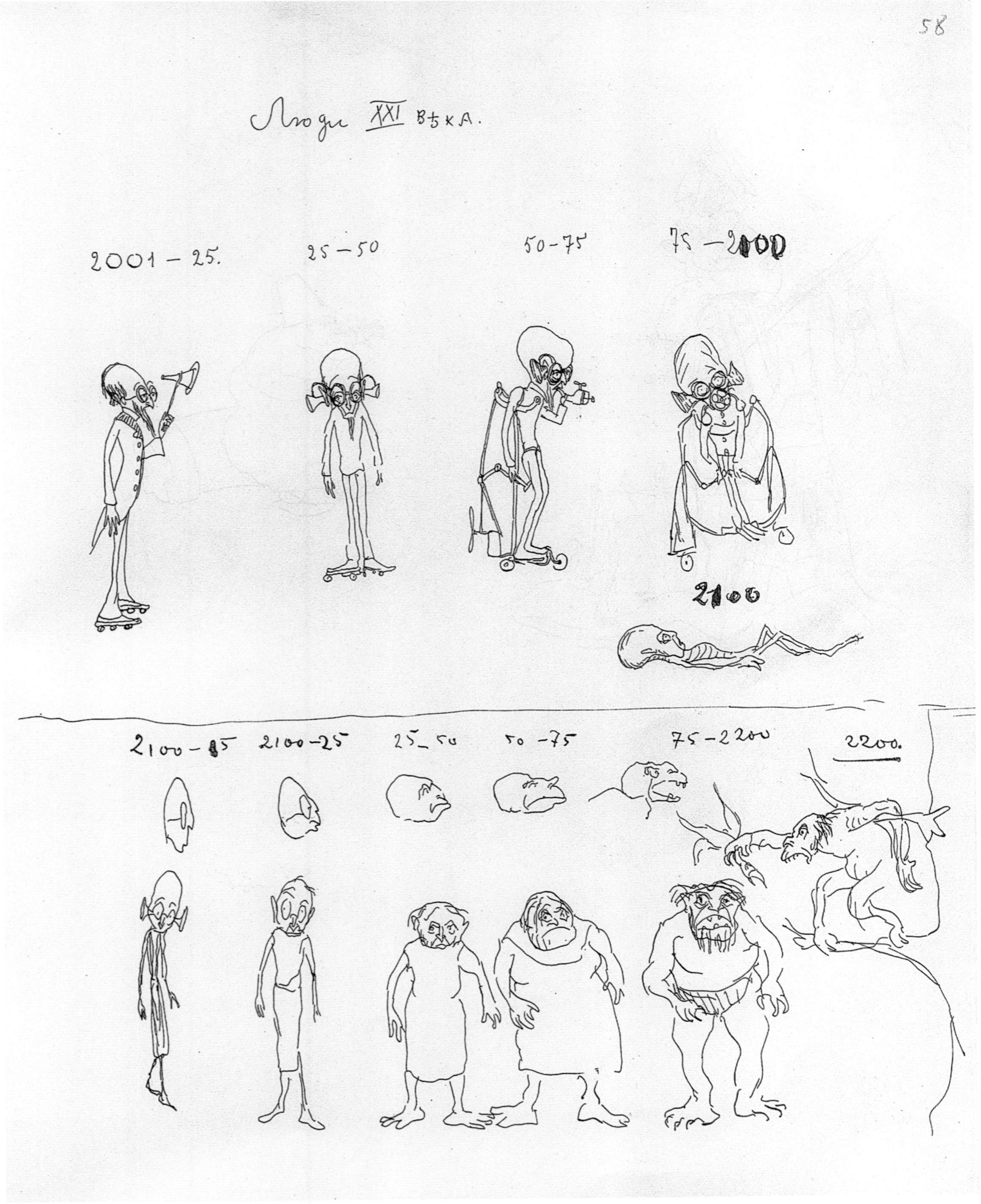
58
Люди XXI вѣка.
2001 – 25.
25 – 50
50 – 75
75 – 2100
2100
2100 – 25
25 – 50
50 – 75
75 – 2200
2200.

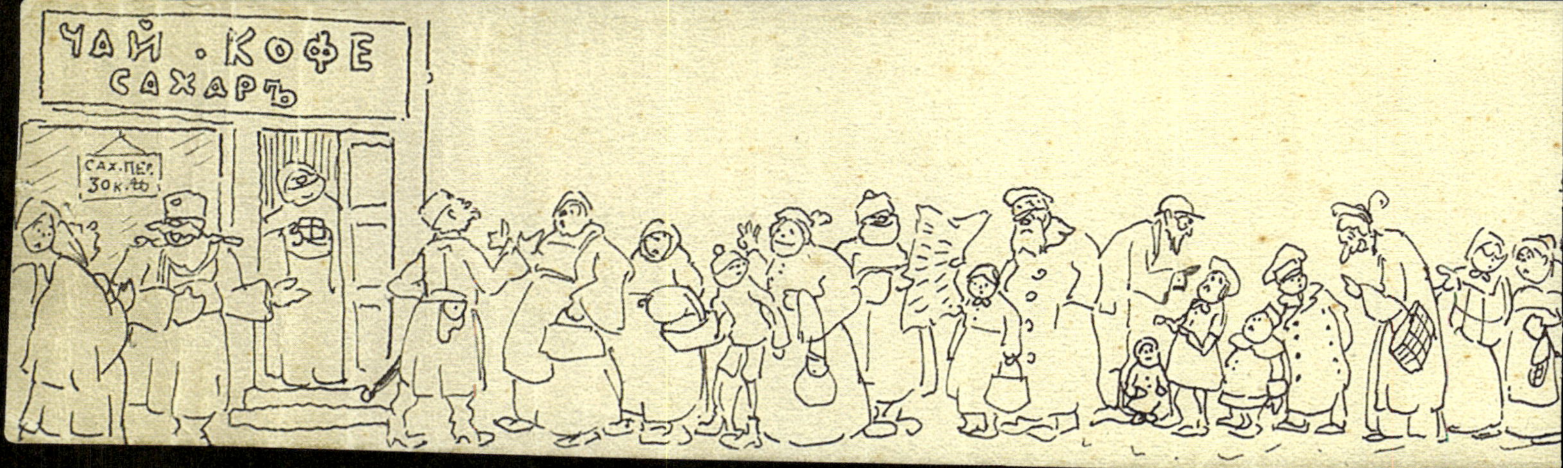
ЧАЙ · КОФЕ
САХАРЪ
САХ.ПЕР.
30 К.

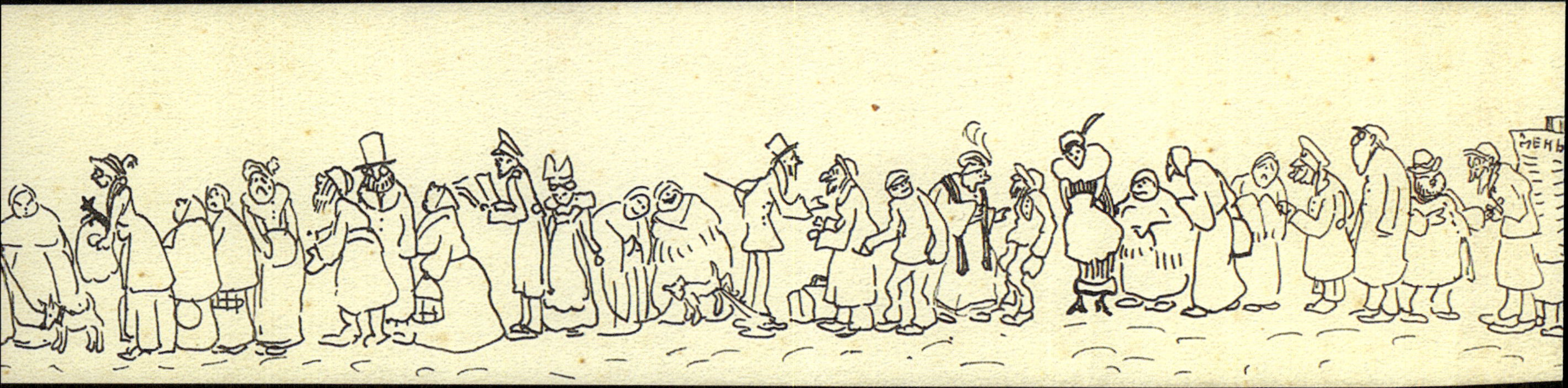

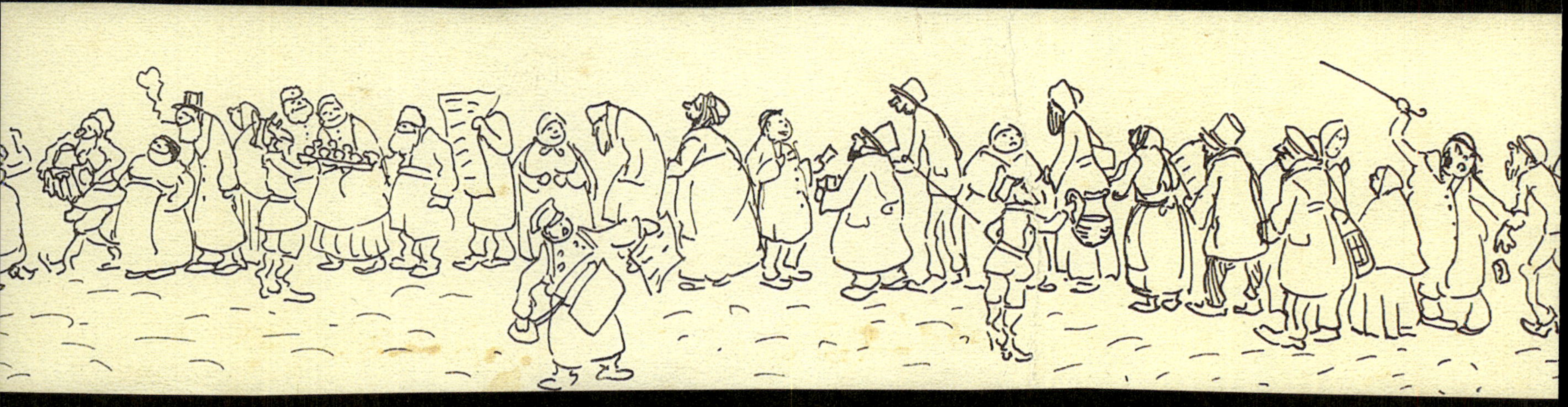

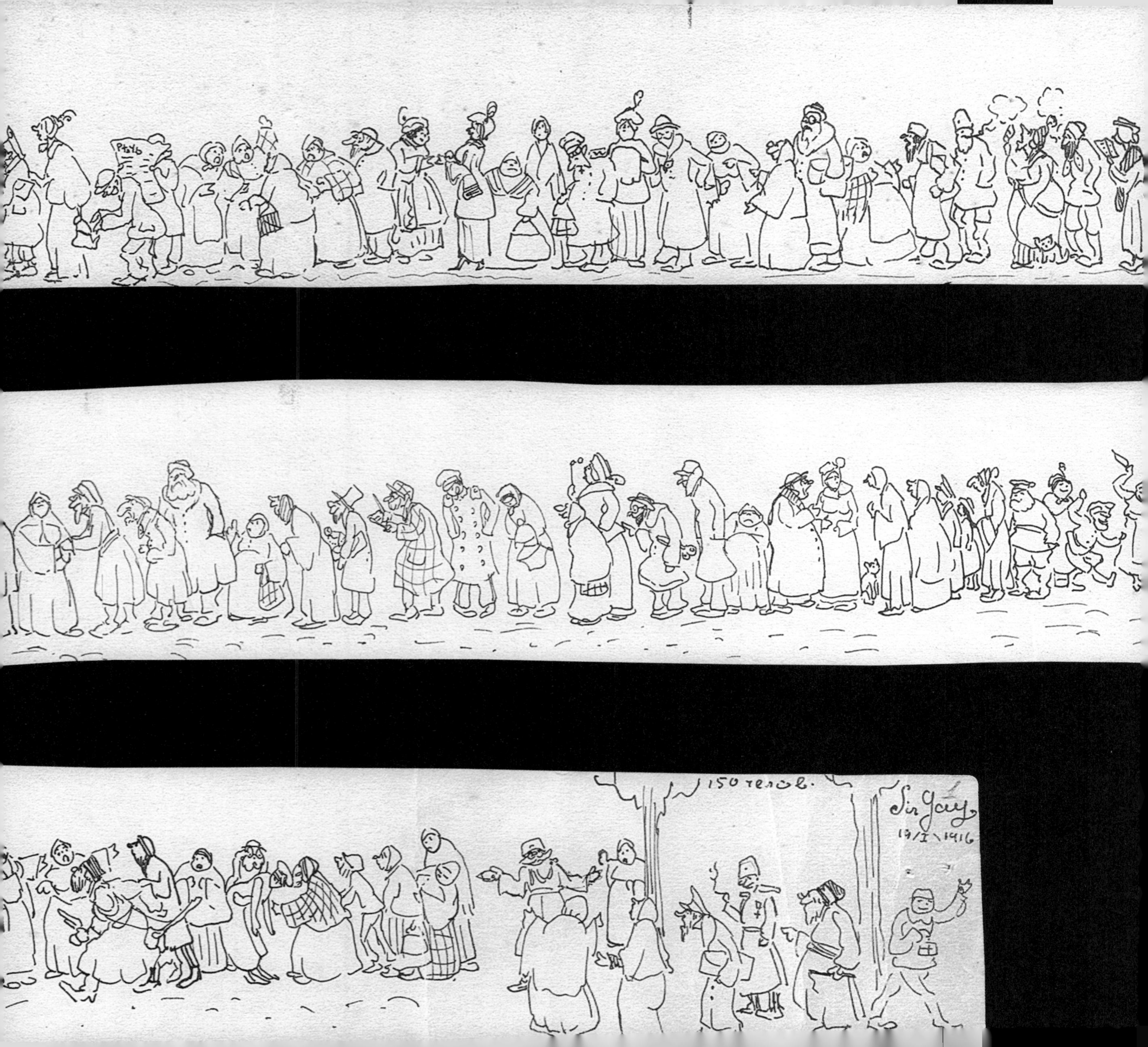
150 челов.
Sir Gay
19/I\1916

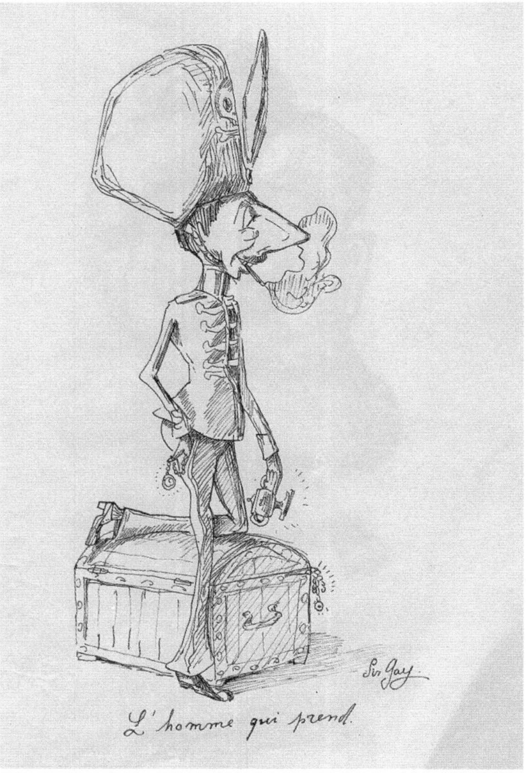
Sir Gay
L'homme qui prend.

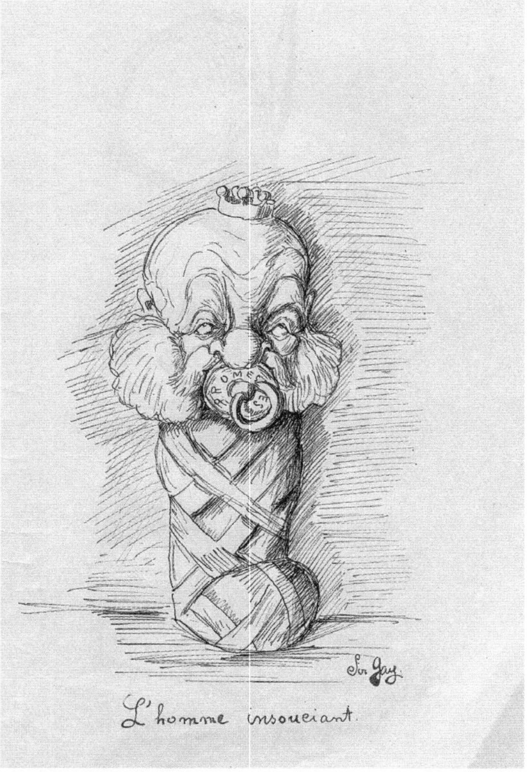
Sir Gay
L'homme insouciant.

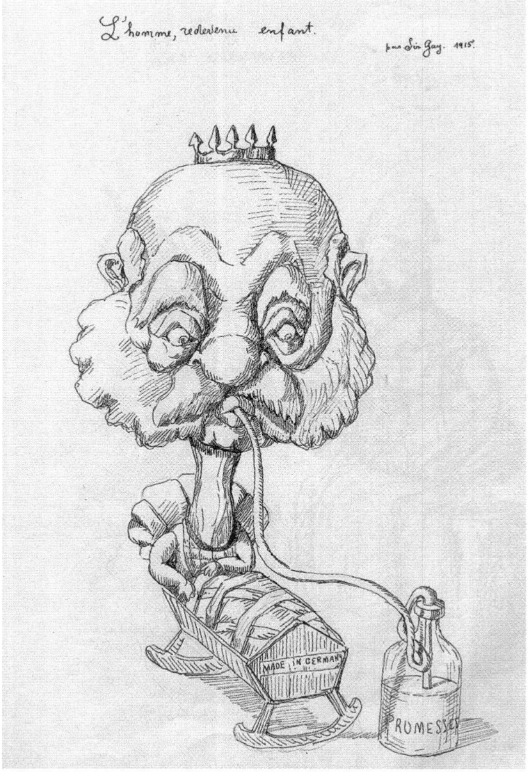
L'homme, redevenu enfant.
par Sir Gay. 1915.
MADE IN GERMANY
PROMESSES

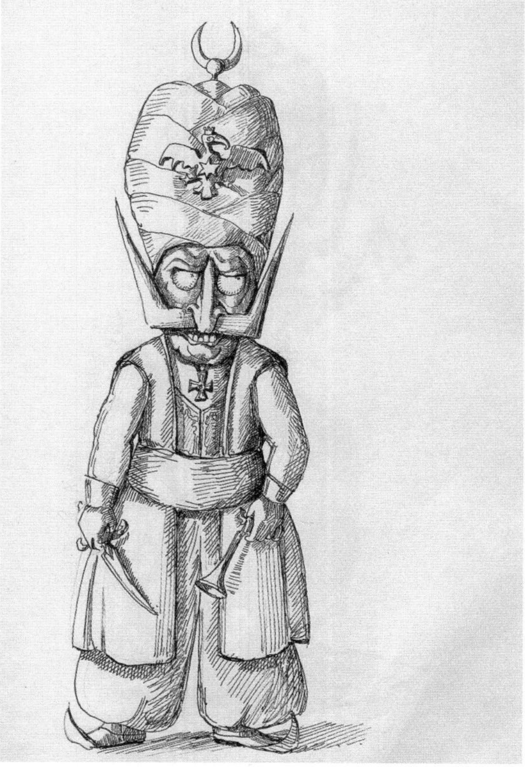

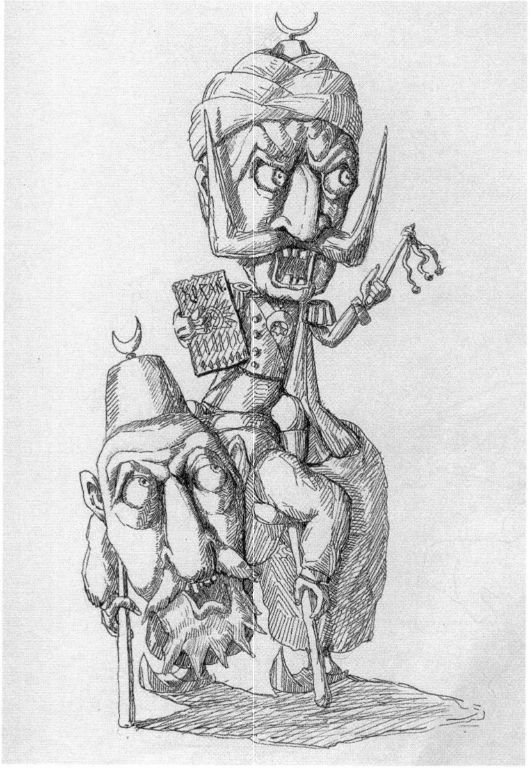

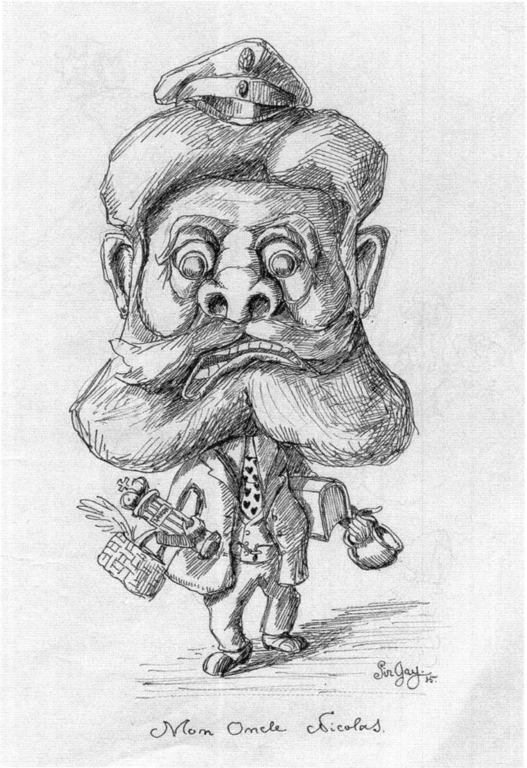
Sir Gay 15.
Mon Oncle Nicolas.

—OPPOSITE

Monarchs of Belligerent Countries (1915)

TOP ROW L–R

Albert I, King of Belgium

Text: *L'homme qui prend*

(The man who takes)

Franz-Josef II, Emperor of Austria-Hungary

Text: *L'homme insouciant*

(The carefree man)

Franz-Josef II, Emperor of Austria-Hungary

Text: *L'homme, redevenu enfant*

(The man becomes a child again)

BOTTOM ROW L–R

Wilhelm II, German Kaiser

Wilhelm II with Sultan Mehmed V

Mon Oncle Nikolas (Russian Emperor Nicholas II)

—THIS PAGE

TOP

Le Martyre (Goremykin, Russian prime minister) (1915)

BOTTOM (LEFT AND RIGHT)

I've Surpassed You, Mlle Salomé! (Rasputin) (1916)

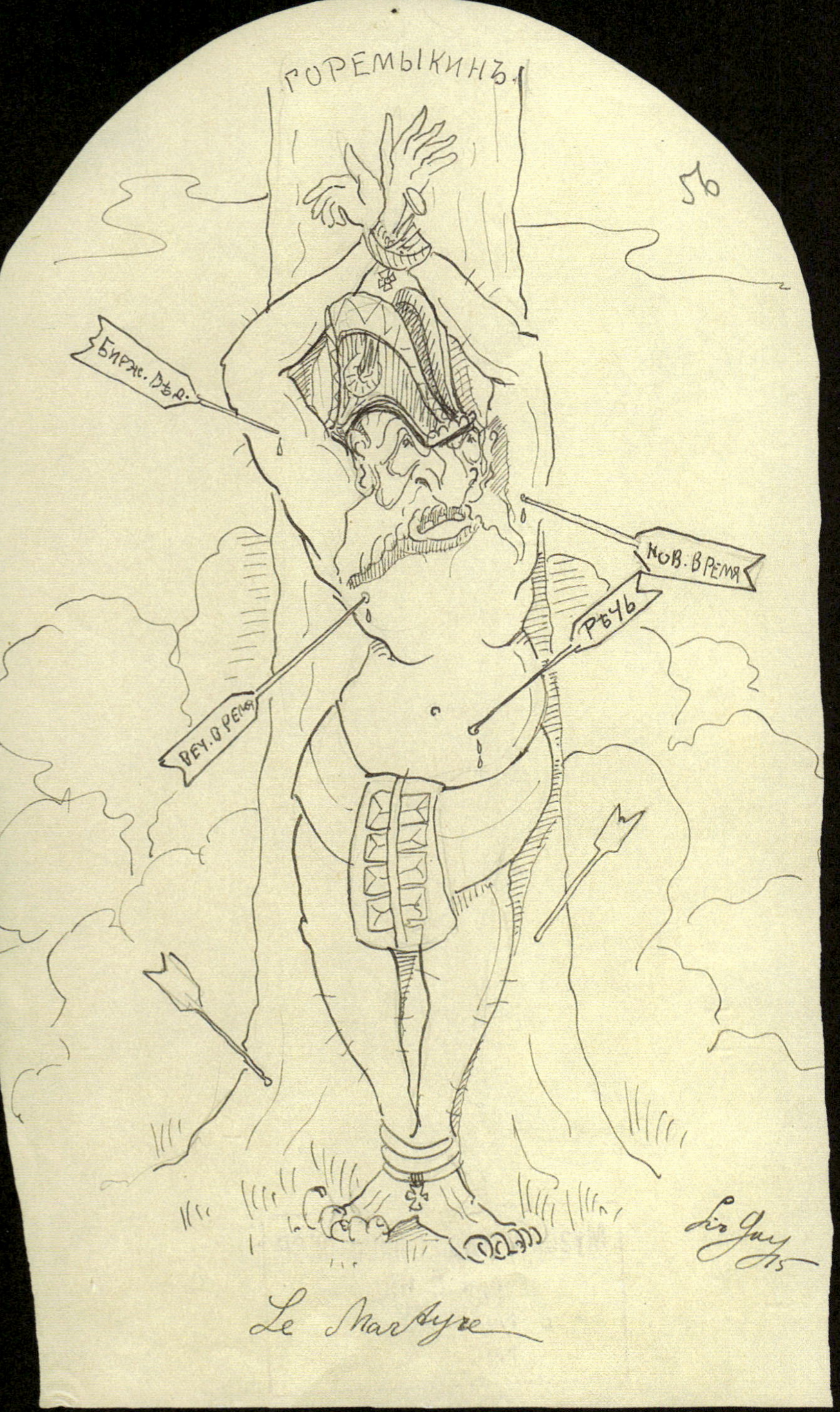

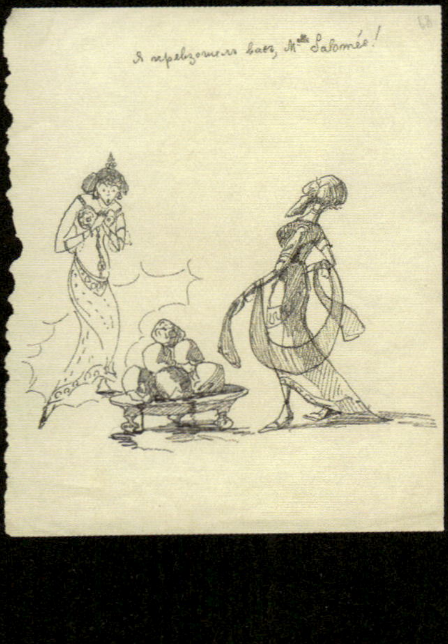

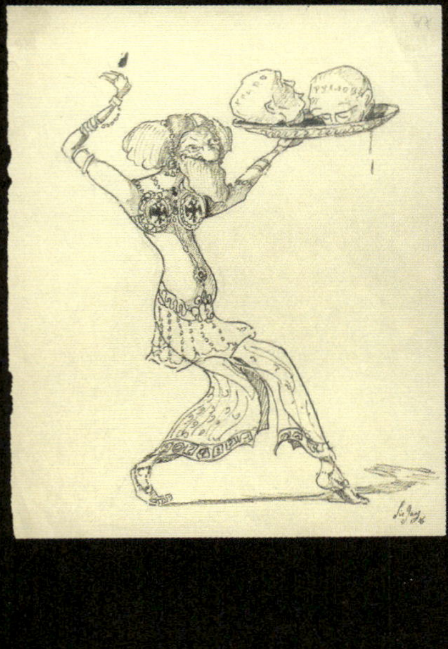

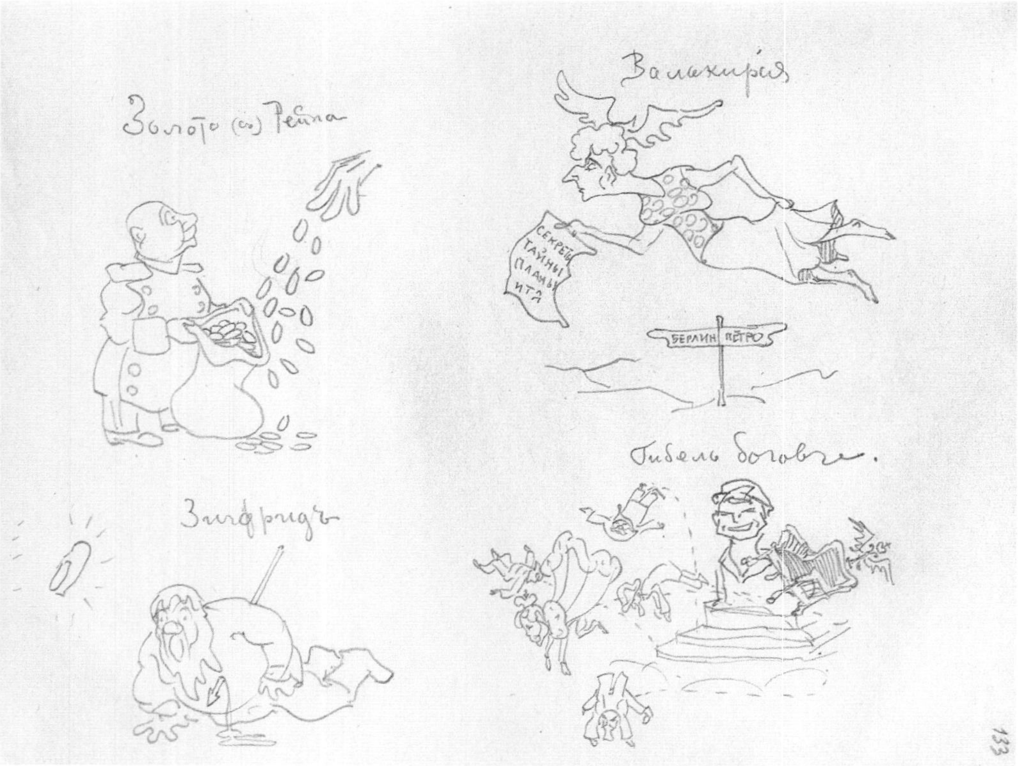

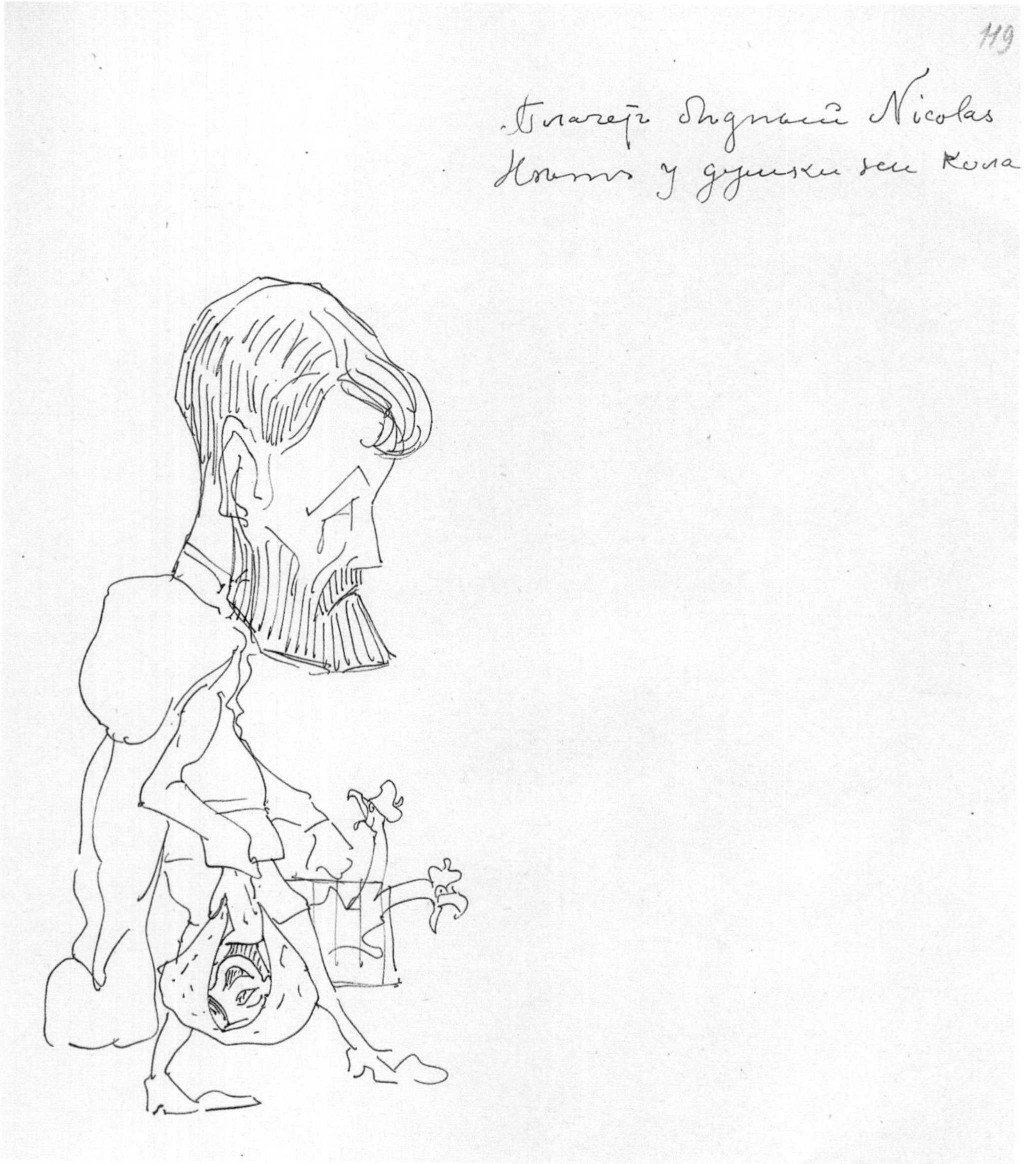

—THIS PAGE

TOP

'Tetralogy of revolution' (1917)

Text: Gold (from) the Rhine, Valkyrie, Siegfried, Death of Gods

BOTTOM

Poor Crying Nicolas, He Has Neither House Nor Home (1917)

—OPPOSITE

'Revolution in Petrograd' (1917)

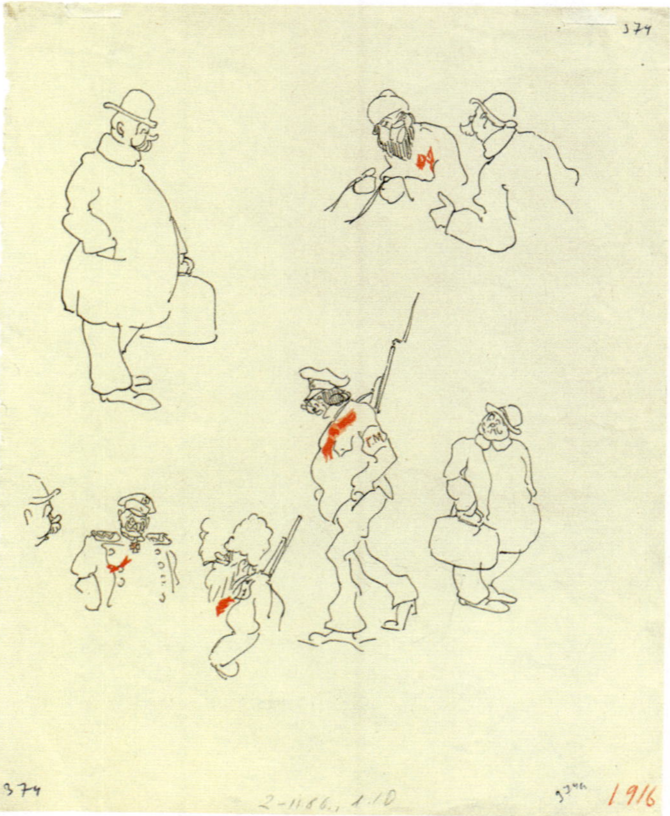
1916

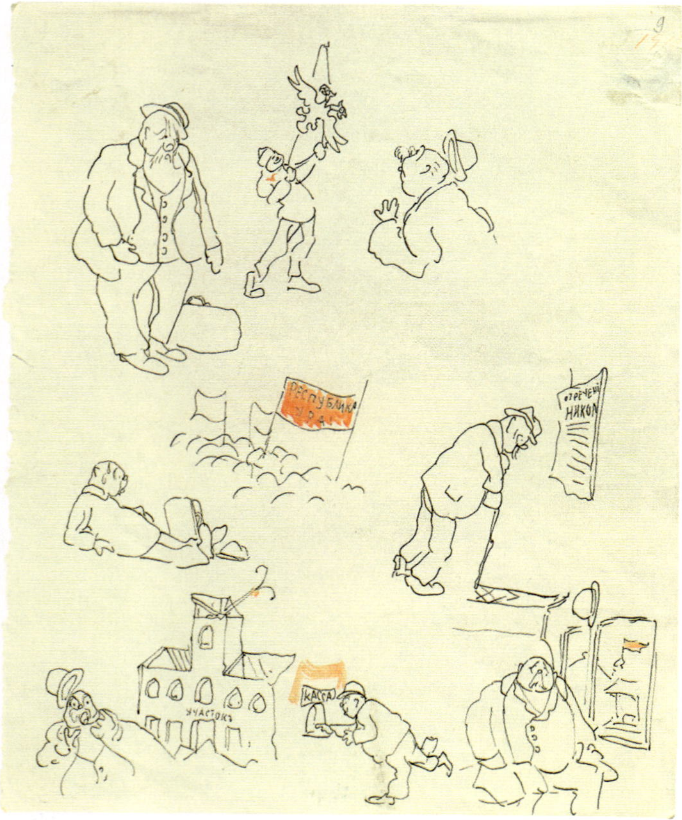
УЧАСТОКЪ
КАССА

1916

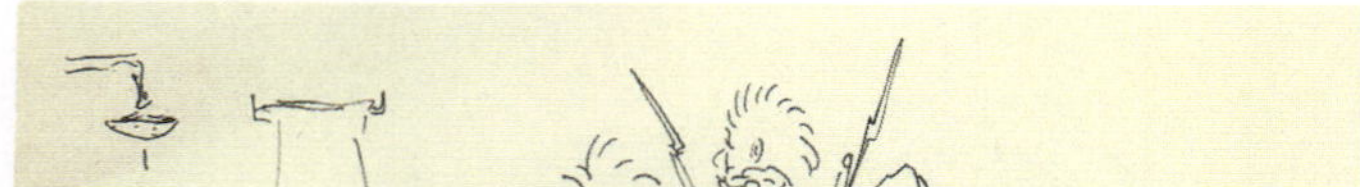
ГМ

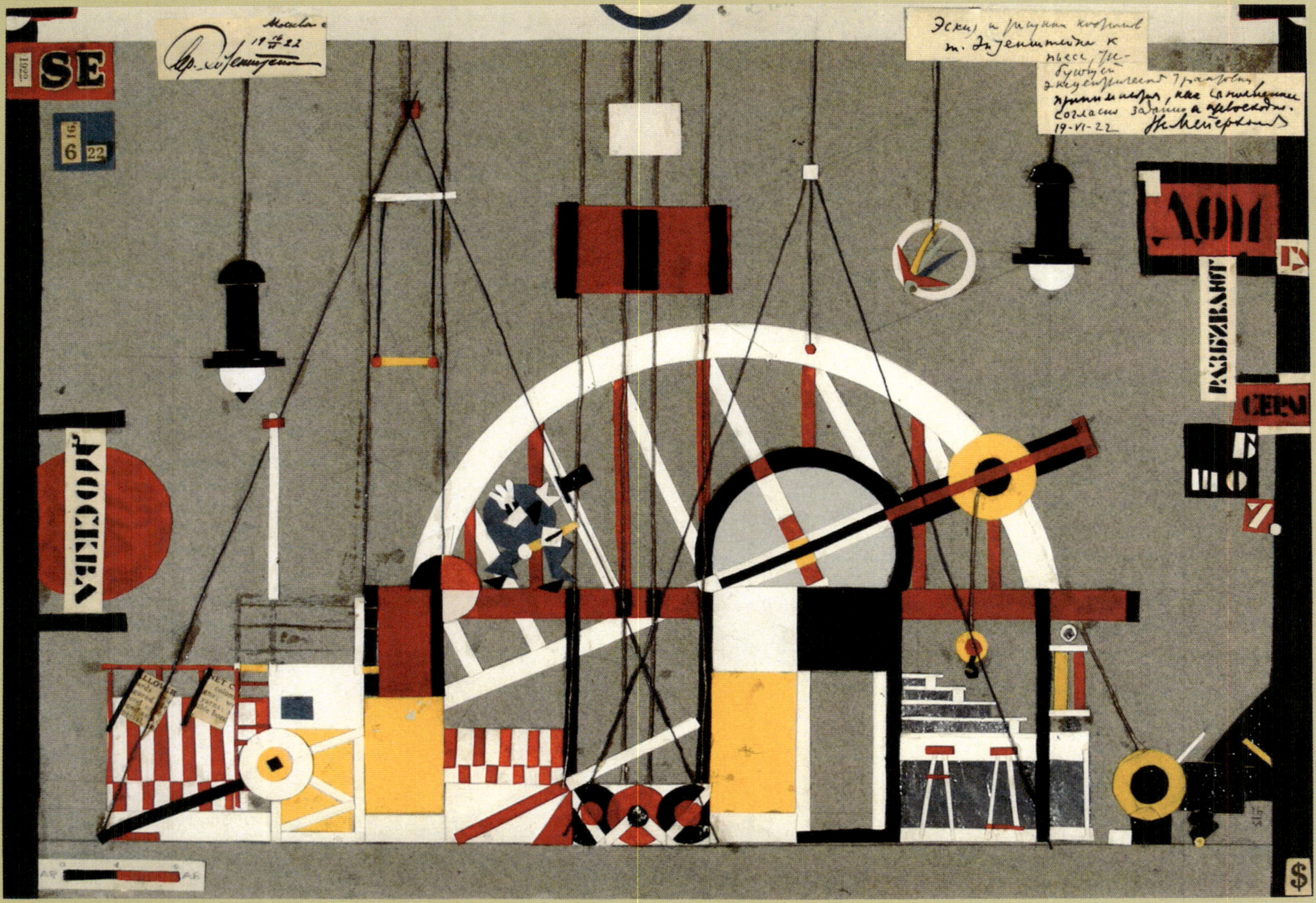
SE
ДОМ
$

ПЕТРОГРАД–МОСКВА 1917—1923

HEARTBREAK HOUSE

PETROGRAD–MOSCOW

2

I

It is June 1922. Moscow. The last exercise at Vsevolod Meyerhold's school – the State Higher Directing Workshop, or GVYRM.

The last bit of stage work by Eisenstein that would not be for his own shows. And, as it later turned out, a crucial point on the journey from the theatre to the cinema.

Of course, Eisenstein, the student, could know nothing of that when he submits his latest piece of homework: a design for Bernard Shaw's 1919 play *Heartbreak House*, where hearts do not break, they are broken, as translated by Ivan Aksenov – an essayist, expert on Elizabethan drama, and teacher at GVYRM (Aksenov could not then have known it, but he would also become his former student Eisenstein's first biographer).

Eisenstein's sketches of sets and costumes for Shaw's play were, in fact, the third version of his designs. And this time they were not sketches, but collages and technical drawings; not sets, but a *machine for acting*; not costumes, but *prozodezhda* (work clothes).

The terminology is the teacher's, not the pupil's. It is the fourth month of what Meyerhold has proclaimed as the era of 'October in Theatre'. The fourth month of thunderous slogans promoting the latest revolution in the art of the stage:

> ***DOWN WITH PICTURESQUE COSTUMES AND SETS! (Irrespective of whether they are realistic, as in Stanislavsky's Arts Theatre, or archaeo-cubo-futurist, as with Aleksandr Tairov's Chamber Theatre. Meyerhold is now convinced that picturesqueness on the stage only obscures the work of the director and the actors.)***
>
> ***LONG LIVE NON-REPRESENTATIONAL CONSTRUCTION ON THE STAGE! (It lets the director create*** **mises-en-scène** ***that will be clearly comprehensible from the stalls.)***
>
> ***LET 'WORK CLOTHES' TRIUMPH! (They help the actors to demonstrate absolute mastery of their bodies: the 'biomechanics' of acting, as Meyerhold called it.)***
>
> ***TOWARDS AN ART THAT IS CHEERFUL, JOYOUS, AND HEALTHY, AND THAT MAKES THE AUDIENCE ACTIVE! (Only an art like that is worthy of the new social epoch – the time of the hope for a healthy society.) And so on, and so forth.***

It is the fourth month in which the appeals of the revolutionary Meyerhold have been underpinned by the merriest and naughtiest show in Moscow – *Le Cocu magnifique*, a farce by the Belgian playwright Fernand Crommelynck: 'On the stage, in front of the bare brick of the back wall, stands a wooden construction of gangways, staircases, and wheels (the artist, Lyubov Popova, has nonetheless managed to hint gently at a windmill, where the action is set). All the actors are dressed in identical blue canvas overalls.'

The Beginning of the New Era (i.e. the premiere of Crommelynck's play) took place on 25 April 1922. And it was on 19 June that Meyerhold, the Master, received the third set of drafts by Eisenstein, the Pupil, for *Heartbreak House*.

The first version of his designs had been submitted in January, before the premiere of *Le Cocu*. Instead of a conventional set for the character Captain Shotover's house, included in the 'box' of the stage behind the footlights, the Pupil proposed to build an extra-proscenium construction (which was independent of the proscenium and could move out into the hall), with a gentle hint suggesting Captain Shotover's house. The characters' costumes, however, as befits characters belonging to British high society in the early 20th century, were designed in a noble Belle Epoque style.

The second version came in March, on the eve of Meyerhold's 'October in the Theatre'. The Pupil perfected his set design both functionally and visually. The 'house' was now more reminiscent of a sinking packet boat, while a sofa in the middle became (in the absence of wings) a place where actors could rest when they were not involved in the action. And the characters' costumes were transformed into luxuriant Cubist fantasias that could put the actors' outfits at Tairov's Chamber Theatre in the shade. That said, it was not very clear how the actors, whose costumes sported extravagant trains, would be able to move around the decks and ladders of the extra-proscenium house.

Both versions were handed in by the Student but not accepted by the Teacher. They were not exactly rejected, but neither were they taken forward.

The third draft differs radically from its predecessors, both in design and in essence. It is no longer a matter of elegant line drawings or of exuberant costumes in baroque-Cubist gouache, or of sketches for scenographic spaces, it is a draft for a material design. Attached to the sheets of grey card (sometimes with glue, sometimes with wire) we now find little fragments of the future stage set, and two-dimensional puppets representing the performer of each part. All the fragments and figures can be turned around, changing and restructuring the model. And the collage part of the draft comes with an accompanying text.

Here are some excerpts from it, divided into paragraphs and with some interpolations (in square brackets) to clarify what is outwardly a businesslike commentary on the sketches but is in fact a bold manifesto. The author is using his official engineer's style to hide the extreme radicalism of his new scenographic ideas.

EXPLANATORY NOTES ON THE DRAFT MATERIAL DESIGN FOR HEARTBREAK HOUSE[1]

...Assignment: to design sets and costumes for a play that demands eccentric treatment; the former to hint at a ship (the action takes place in the home of a half-crazy sea-captain); a cupboard and a sofa.
Solution: <...> To construct, based on the particular way this play is put together, a special mechanism or machine suitable for this play only that will determine and define the way the performers act. As far as possible, [one must] avoid representational machinery or machinery that is associated with factory settings.

Data concerning the play:
The play is conversational. As in the majority of Bernard Shaw's plays, all the value and wit – except for a few comic moments (the Zeppelin scene, the hypnotism, catching the thief) – is in the dialogues. Result: wishing to maintain the play's conversational character, which excludes active dynamics on the part of the actors, [it has become necessary] to construct the mechanism taking account of the actor's passive kinetics, i.e. to construct a mechanism that moves and relocates the actor independently [of the dialogue], i.e. rather in a specific comic coordination with the verbal material.

(For instance: a love dialogue on the two platforms of the lift, which move up and down separately from one another.

One partner in a similar dialogue falling, with no change of tone, through the collapsing ladder of the red walkway onto the sofa below.

One [partner] leaping up to a springboard and thereby flinging the partner standing at the other end onto a trapeze, etc.)

(signatures on the drawings) Rapid ascent – Seesaw descends, and the other side launches upwards with a turn in the air – [Nurse] Guinness offers tea.

The conclusion from this [is] to find corresponding apparatuses with the greatest possible diversity of trajectories for relocating the actor's body in space (in the plane of the proscenium or in depth).

In this respect the richest ground-level apparatus is undoubtedly the springboard, which for a given grouping of the figure to be thrown provides a whole series of distinct relocations of that figure in space (forward and backward salto (1) away from the springboard, (2) across it, vertically, (3) to the side, etc.)

The Teacher must have shuddered at this suggestion. These relocations would have meant the actors risking breaking their own necks, or their partners', or – God forbid – those of members of the audience. Would the show end up being known as 'Spinebreak House'?

And there is an equally risky *entrechat* with the mechanisms to come:

[The springboard permits] both parabolic and linear (vertical) relocations.

The other [apparatuses] are non-ground-level: two curving trapezes operating in perpendicular planes, the collapsing parts of the red walkway, bascules *<seesaws (French)> set up on supports, inclined – the inclined running walkway (shock task: the comic effect of chasing the burglar in Act 2, approaching his movement from the opposite direction, running on the spot), etc.*

The same arrangements are also designed to facilitate active movement by the actors: the top is covered with a series of beams, making it possible to move around the external radius (for instance, in developing the chase scene); a vertical pillar on the bridge (N) – for Nurse Guinness to climb (in the scene where they extinguish the lights when the Zeppelin is approaching) in order to 'blow out' the Lux hanging above it – which her blowing sends soaring into the fly-loft....

The Teacher could not but reflect on the fire risk that this 'invention' might pose in the theatre. And the Pupil's constructions for the actors to wear were no less radical. Here, for instance, is how he envisages Nurse Guinness's costume:

Travesti. *A short – above the knees – crinoline like an umbrella, beneath which there hang unseen the whole collection of the most varied odds and ends that [will] be used at various points during the action: a coffee pot, a tea service, a brush, candlesticks, keys, a lifebelt, etc. The wig is a bald cap like a boat with three red balls swinging from a frame. A clown-style bonnet to the side; clown-style feet with swinging ball-shaped toes and double tap sole....*[2]

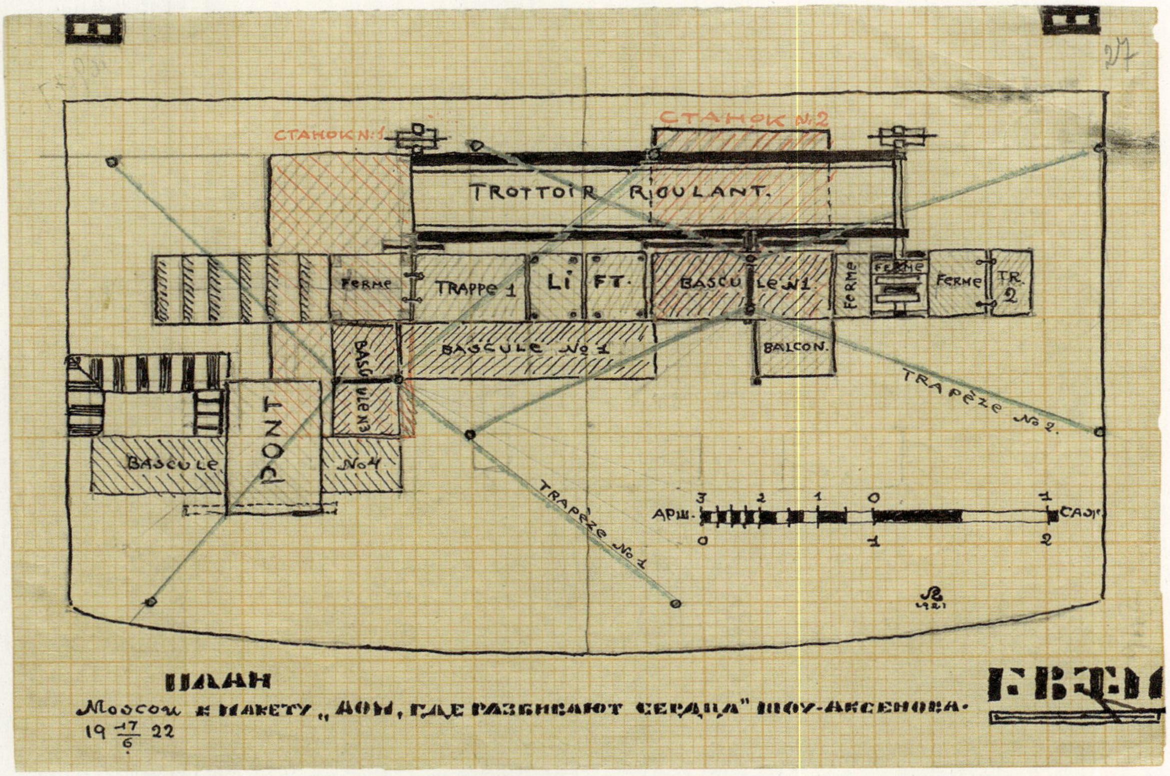

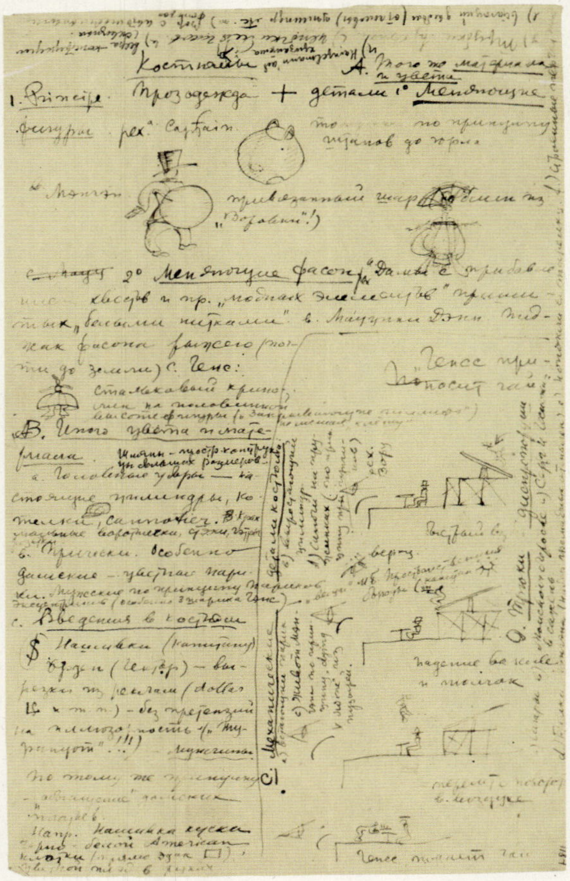

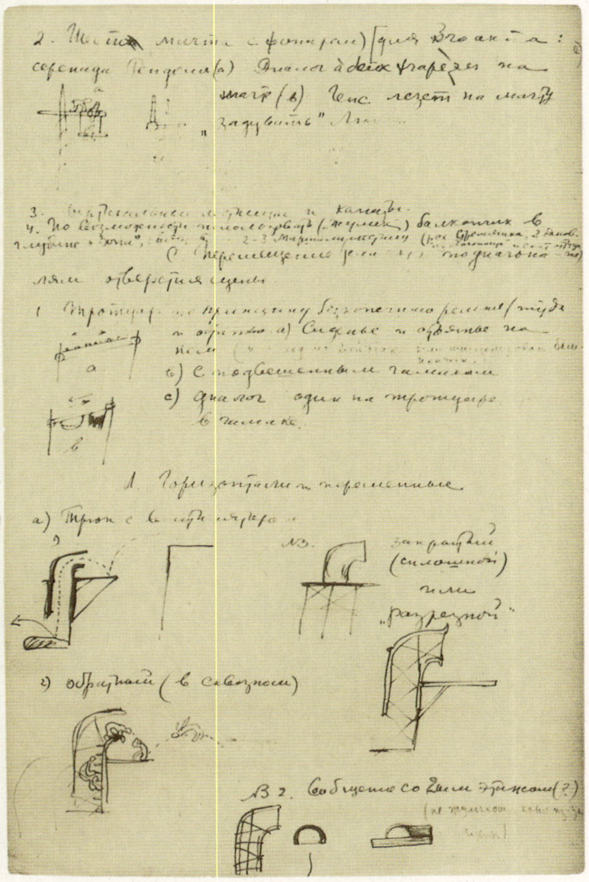

—PAGE 64
Stage construction project (3rd version) for *Heartbreak House* by Bernard Shaw (1922)

—THIS PAGE

TOP
Plan of the mechanisms used in the stage construction (3rd version) for *Heartbreak House* by Bernard Shaw (1922)

BOTTOM (LEFT AND RIGHT)
Two pages of explanatory notes for the draft designs for *Heartbreak House,* with illustrations of the seesaw ('Nurse Guinness brings tea') and the mast with a lantern ('Randall playing the clarinet')

How was the Master to react to this 'circusification' of Shaw? On the one hand, all the initial ideas were Meyerhold's: the 'machine' on a bare stage instead of sets, *the biomechanical play* instead of *flabby 'inner emotions'*, characters moving actively in space instead of sitting tediously at table or on the garden benches of gentlefolk.

On the other hand, though, all these ideas were taken to extremes – and beyond. The stage construction was no longer a platform on the stage, it was a cunningly assembled combination of new electrical gadgets (a lift, a moving walkway) with old circus devices (ropes, trapezes, seesaws). *Prozodezhda* took the form of clown coats, the product of centuries of tradition, but also crinolines and bonnets. Biomechanics had turned into acrobatics, juggling, a balancing act. Isn't all this a parody of the theatrical Constructivism that the Master has proclaimed – of the style of 'October in the Theatre', and its very principles? It is not difficult to imagine the mistrustful Meyerhold's inward reaction to Eisenstein's draft.

The Pupil is courtesy itself (a 'lad from a good family', as they would say in old Russia), and the embodiment of erudition in theatre history. He is ready, of course, to demonstrate the total propriety of his solution for the play. Impish laughter appears in the depths of his grey eyes at any opportunity – surely, though, he wouldn't be laughing at the task that the Teacher has set him?

But what if this student has picked up on the trend before Meyerhold – the leader of the 'Left' theatre?

And the Master attaches his written decision to the 'stage machine' collage – a decision that repeats verbatim the general formulation from the 'Explanatory Notes':

'Comrade Eisenstein's sketch and drawings, for a play that demands eccentric treatment, are accepted as having fulfilled the task that was set – and fulfilled it excellently. 19/VI 1922.'

Which play, Meyerhold does not specify. The remark 'fulfilled the task that was set' preserves his priority, and the comment 'excellent' preserves his status as a progressive-thinking, well-intentioned Teacher, encouraging his Pupil to develop the Master's line.

Did the Pupil guess that no production of Shaw's play with such a hyper-eccentric treatment would go ahead? He probably suspected as much even in March, when he was completing the second version of his design. And he was probably almost sure of it when he was thinking up the third. But he could not stop: his movement towards this version of the project was so natural.

The 'machine for acting', with all its consequences for theatre shows, only seems to be something that has appeared unexpectedly, like the *deus ex machina* of the ancients – although, actually, the Greek μηχανῆς (*mēchanēs*) is actually its direct ancestor.

The Master himself had long been fond of Shaw's prophetic comedy in the Russian (Chekhovian) style, and dreamt of putting it on the stage. In early 1922, the opportunity (almost an obligation, in fact) to announce it as part of the planned repertory arose: by the will of the authorities, Meyerhold's company was amalgamated with the troupe of the former Nezlobin Theatre (founded by Konstantin Nezlobin), Once upon a time, the Nezlobin had been thought one of the most cultivated and even advanced theatre companies in Russia. But by 1922 this theatre had lost much and had fallen hopelessly behind in the turbulent movement of theatrical innovations. Even so, the Nezlobin demanded that the 'leftist' Meyerhold give them their accustomed acting material. Agreement was reached on Shaw's *House*. Meyerhold called this new centaur-like company the Actor's Theatre, and entrusted the design for the play to his most radical student: Sergei Eisenstein.

In fact, Eisenstein is just paying back some of his debts.

The Teacher could scarcely have known that his surprising decision was prompted by the finger of fate! Precisely ten years earlier, in 1912, none other than the Konstantin Nezlobin Theatre had presented Fedor Komissarzhevsky's production of *Princess Turandot* (1762), by Carlo Gozzi, on tour in Riga. And it was at this very play that fourteen-year-old Rorik's passionate interest in stagecraft had begun. What had struck the teenager back then was not the contrast between this vivid spectacle and the well-ordered routine of Riga, the dim respectability of local plays. Instead, he was shaken by the perpetual violation of what he had regarded as taboo since he was little, when his father had started taking him to the theatre: the sacred line of the footlights as a barrier between the magical world of the play and the reality that included the audience. Now it had been broken through!

Many years later, on 1 January 1947, Eisenstein would recall his youthful excitement in his note 'Division':

> ***I first saw action drawn 'outside the plane' of the theatre in Komissarzhevsky's* Turandot *(1912–1913?): Italian masks coming into the stalls, sitting on the prompter's box, etc. The masks were 'half-on, half-off' the face. (Pirandello later [used this], but less so.) This aspect of the theatre of convention captivated, of course, by way of a principle (besides the immediate effect): the principle of division.***
>
> ***The acuteness of the bifurcation between illusion and fact (the 'image' of the mask and the 'wearer' of the mask), and their reunification: Harlequin has only just climbed across the footlights, but here he is again, 'within' the action, and participating in the illusory events 'behind the footlights' just as much as the imaginary reality of the whole action and all the characters 'there'....***[3]

The young man found out about the *commedia dell'arte*, with its *lazzi* (buffoon's tricks), *aparte* (witty asides), and standing characters or 'masks' with their instantaneous improvisations. And he sensed, even if he did not understand, the basic question of the theatre: the face-to-face meeting of two kingdoms, even two worlds: Art and Reality. He felt how blatantly they are opposed, how mysteriously they turn into one another, and how paradoxically they are one. This was no less attractive – perhaps more so – than his drawings' metamorphosis of the Human World into the Animal World and back again.

And one more opposition – that between the theatre and the circus – lost its absolute character. It turned out that the things that so excited Rorik in the vulgar circus were also possible in the real, *comme il faut* theatre. The clowns' wilful behaviour and witty jokes, which shattered the hierarchical rigidity of society. The way the characters seemed to be able to speak directly to him, the well-brought-up Riga boy sitting in the stalls next to Daddy. The very possibility (the sweet danger!) of being dragged into the Red Clown's act or soaked in the White Clown's fountain of tears.

The shock he had felt as a child was repeated and strengthened five years later, in 1917 when Eisenstein, by now an architecture student, saw Meyerhold's adaptation of *Masquerade* (1835), by Mikhail Lermontov. He tried to attend the long-awaited premiere at the Aleksandrinsky Theatre (the work had been in preparation for many years) but could not get in because that was the very night when the February Revolution broke out. Soon afterwards, however, Sir Gay did make it to the show, staged at what had until recently been the Imperial Theatre.

The columns and mirrors and the lights still burning in the chandeliers united the stage with the stalls. A whole system of curtains and strictly honed *mises-en-scène* now fixed the action to a proscenium that projected far out towards the audience, and now drew the characters (and with them the audience's heart and eye) deep into the stage. What took place above the footlights was less a 19th-century costumed ball in Petrograd (the city nicknamed the 'northern Palmyra') than a luxury carnival that would have been the envy even of Venice in the days of Gozzi, Carlo Goldoni and Casanova. The actors were transformed by a system of different masks: carnival masks, mime masks, society masks. And, by some miracle, the tragedy of the demonic hero Arbenin's jealousy became a requiem for – and a condemnation of – the collapsing regime of Nicholas II. In the luxurious hall that passed almost imperceptibly into the luxurious stage, the spellbound Eisenstein became a witness (or a co-participant?) in a baleful spell: tragic art and the tragedies of life turning one into the other.

Meyerhold and the Revolution were linked not only in life and in the history of the Russian theatre, but also in Eisenstein's destiny. The stunning show, with its Venetian masks at a Petersburg ball, awoke in the young man an attraction that had been created by Gozzi and Komissarzhevsky's *Princess Turandot*: the *commedia dell'arte*. *Masquerade* helped the student to decide to bid farewell to the career in architecture that Daddy had planned for him, to the career as a cartoonist that had seemed possible after February, to any career at all except the theatre!

Sir Gay did not immediately give up drawing political caricatures: after all, there was inspiration aplenty in the elemental forces of the Revolution that were raging all around. But in 1917, academic projects and characters from the political stage were increasingly driven out of his head, and off his sketching paper, by mischievous Harlequins, sad Pierrots, playful Colombinas, sinister Smeraldinas, miserly old Pantalones and others.

The Italian street theatre, with its system of standing characters or masks and its dramaturgy that was ceaselessly renewed by way of improvisations on current themes, made its initial appearance in Russia as early as the first third of the 18th century – the era of Russian society's Europeanization. It was driven out of the country at the end of the century by Paul I, the eccentric son of Catherine the Great. But the images of the *commedia dell'arte* returned to Russia in the early 20th century, first in the poetry of the symbolist Aleksandr Blok, and then on the stage too: at the very end of December 1906, a young Meyerhold put on *The Fairground Booth*, by Blok, himself taking the part of Pierrot. The production was a *succès de scandale*: the actors in it are presented as the puppets of Fate, Harlequin dies in the finale ('Help, I am bleeding cranberry juice!'), and the *commedia dell'arte* concluded as a tragedy, full of dark symbols and forebodings.

Meyerhold used the pseudonym 'Doctor Dapertutto' (borrowed from the German Romantic writer E. T. A. Hoffmann, also an admirer of the *commedia dell'arte*) to publish a magazine, *The Love for Three Oranges*, whose title came from Carlo Gozzi. It was under the direct influence of Meyerhold and his magazine, among other factors, that the young Sergei Prokofiev composed his comic opera of the same title in 1919.

Doctor Dapertutto also played his part in inspiring Sergei Eisenstein to create sketches for theatrical productions – imaginary ones, for the time being.

The architecture student imagined them endlessly: first in Petrograd in 1917, and then, for almost three years during the Civil War, in small towns in north-western Russia, where the 18th Engineers were hastily building fortifications against an imaginary offensive by British forces.

Of course, the seeds of this tempestuous attraction fell on fertile soil, made ready by Eisenstein's early drawing. The masks of the *commedia dell'arte* drew into a cohesive system the numberless multitude of types (in human or animal guise) from Rorik's Riga notebooks, and the shifting relationships and magical adventures of all these Tartaglias and Brighellas chimed with the Riga characters' metamorphoses and their mischievous doings. And Sir Gay's early graphic habits proved perfectly suited to sketching imaginary productions: his ability to capture what was sharply characteristic in a face, his way of varying his motifs, his gift for seeing an inner similarity underlying the most divergent forms. His Harlequin is recognizable in the air-headed young carnival dancer of Casanova's time, and in the comically sinister Turkish pasha from the playlet *Fun on the Water and in the Field*, and in the Devil's cunning servant in the satire on red tape, *The Man Who Fell in Love With a Doll, or, The French Knight*.

The neophyte found plots in anonymous 18th-century libretti (published in a separate collection, as it happens, in 1917). He went back to the tales of Carlo Gozzi. He made up his own, mentally transporting himself from legendary Venice to the fantastical East and from the fairy-tale past to recent reality. In 1919, working on the French Second Empire satire *Les 12 heures de Colombine*, Sergei recognized the foppish idealist as Pierrot and the gouty swindler – reminiscent of his beloved Honoré Daumier's Robert Macaire – as the crafty Harlequin.

From his very first theatrical sketches, Sir Gay discovered a striving to be not a costume designer, but a director. What he drew was not the actors' clothes but the characters themselves, as though snatched out of the action on stage. And what he imagined was not just moments of the acting, but the acting space itself.

In his idea for *Hamlet* – still fully academic in style – he initially thought of historically accurate sets, which would easily change from Elsinore castle to the castle hall and back again with the aid of curtains and props. At once, though, he also created a second version: an abstract, metaphysical space defined by a semicircle of columns, in the spirit of Leonid Andreev's Symbolist drama *The Life of Man* (1906) as produced by the very same Proteus-Meyerhold.

But influential as Doctor Dapertutto was, neither he nor the *commedia dell'arte* were the only landmarks for Russian theatre – nor, indeed, for the trainee architect Eisenstein, who had developed such a serious interest in it.

Before the Revolution, a rebirth of theatre had been proclaimed. Its advocates included not just the vehement modernist Meyerhold, but also another erudite and imaginative playwright, director and theorist – Nikolai Evreinov, the originator of the concept of 'ancient theatre'. According to Evreinov's proposal, antique and medieval dramas must be shown in ancient ways – in amphitheatres, on city squares, in front of cathedrals. At the same time, Evreinov invented 'theatre for oneself' – life as a theatre, where each person is an actor and a spectator. Both were supported (although they quarrelled among themselves) by Symbolists enchanted with the Middle Ages and by Futurists dreaming of what was to come. And the student Sir Gay watched and listened to all of them.

Under the influence of this polyphony, but especially under that of Evreinov's ideas, the neophyte grew increasingly convinced that the 'box', divided by the footlights into the stage and the stalls, was unnatural for the theatre. It had not existed for the Elizabethans – and theirs was the great theatrical culture of Christopher Marlowe, Shakespeare and Ben Jonson. It had not existed in the Middle Ages: then, the stage had been placed in cathedral porches or inside the church. For the mystery plays, multi-storey constructions had been erected, with levels for Earth, Hell below it and Heaven above. For morality plays, 'mansions' (small houses on platforms) were built, open to the audience on all sides; for farces, a simple platform amid the crowd sufficed. Nor had the *scēnē* of Aeschylus and Aristophanes been a 'box': their *orchēstra* was almost surrounded by the amphitheatre.

Before leaving Petrograd, Sir Gay drew 'A general view of the theatre'. More precisely, this is a theatre within the theatre: on the stage of the modern 'box' theatre is constructed a set resembling a cathedral square from an old European city, and in the porch there is erected a platform where it seems that the play (a morality?) will be acted. The old townsfolk, the audience for the show, are to walk around it. Who are they? Intermediaries, through whose eyes the modern audience is to look? Or types from 1496 played by actors, as an alter ego for the 1917 audience – a chance for modern people to participate actively in the antique spectacle? Or is this project something like the 'mousetrap' set up by Hamlet himself: a demonstration of how the scene played out by the actors directly affects real life? Here, the young Eisenstein is unwittingly encountering a problem that is both practical and theoretical – one that he would spend his whole artistic life trying to resolve.

Sir Gay tried using a stage on a stage for the *commedia dell'arte* too, in a production of Carlo Gozzi's *La Donna-Serpente* (The serpent woman). He would have brought the proscenium for the intermezzos and *aparte* as close as possible to the public, even closer than Meyerhold had in *Masquerade*. And he would have moved the small stage (for magical transformations) way back – even beyond the limit of the firewall, the rear wall of the stage 'box'.[4]

The concept of the 'limit' had entered his consciousness back in the Civil Engineering Institute, at Professor Yulian Sokhotsky's lectures. The so-called 'poet of mathematics' had explained the principles of differentiation and integration by way of metaphors, drawing captivating pictures of how 'regiments and hordes of infinitely small quantities approach their limit', as Eisenstein wrote in his *Memoirs*.

In the student Eisenstein's imagination, the mathematical abstraction went beyond the framework of mathematics to become an image with two meanings: limit as the absolute boundary of a given phenomenon, and limit as the extreme degree of definiteness, 'the state of being completely expressed'. This last quote is from 'Notes on the Theatre' (17 April 1921), where Eisenstein writes 'a definition of the beautiful: the state of being completely expressed – Richard III is just as beautiful as Ophelia, who is no less beautiful than Falstaff'.[5]

Throughout his subsequent life, Eisenstein would strive to reduce any task – whether practical or theoretical – to its limiting resolution. And he would never be able to resist the temptation to peek beyond the limit.

What if the limit represented by the footlights is cut through? The imaginary action will end up in the audience's real space – as in Komissarzhevsky's *Princess Turandot*, or in the circus. The boundary between stage and stalls, between spectacle and audience, between art and reality, will be destroyed. Which side will subordinate the other? Which is the stronger? The young Eisenstein is convinced (as are, indeed, a significant part of the Russian intelligentsia) that theatre (art) can transform society (reality) in accordance with the laws of aesthetic (i.e. universal?) perfection.

But what if we now cut through the limit represented by the back wall? Will the theatrical action go out into a transcendent world, as with Maurice Maeterlinck? Or will the theatre break out, beyond the limit of the firewall, into the real city square, which is in fact where the folk comedy of the masks once originated? After the two revolutions of 1917, things that would previously have seemed nonsensical, or an aesthetic pose, or mere grandstanding, took on a new meaning. The street was breaking in on the theatre, and the theatre too was breaking out of its enclosed box into the street outside. The famous 'fourth wall' of Stanislavsky's theatre, imagined by the director and the actors in place of the 'stage mirror', now seemed anachronistic: it was obvious, whatever version one accepted, that it needed to be broken through.

Eisenstein the fortification-builder was an active participant in the garrison club's amateur theatre, acquiring a mastery of scenography and of the history of the theatre. He drew ('staged') the most all-embracing repertoire – on plans of trenches, on accounting statements, on the backs of military maps and secret reports.

He seems to have been testing to the limit not just the stage 'box', but whole theatrical systems. He discovered the history of strolling troupes of fairground barkers, with dancers, jugglers, *trouvères* (epic poets), jesters and exotic animals who were concurrent with the *commedia dell'arte*. Still further back in the past was the comedy of Terence and Plautus, mocking the morals of Rome. Before that, the masks of Aristophanes, embodying the right of the free citizen in the *polis* to laugh, to argue and to debate. And even further back, the ancient Saturnalias, where there was as yet no distinction between those who participated in the action and those who watched it.

On the other side of the Harlequinade – the side facing the 20th century – Sergei followed its transformation into Molière's high comedy, and Count Gozzi's attempts to preserve 'the folk comedy of the masks'. Outside the limits of strict classicism he discovered the fantastical grotesqueries and dark irony of the Romantics Ludwig Tieck and E. T. A. Hoffmann, and the realist (i.e. social and psychological) comedy of Aleksandr Ostrovsky and Émile Zola. And the neophyte observes: if we scratch (scrape?) each of these theatrical systems, we will discover not merely the eternal masks, under the cover of various characters, but also, behind the various principles by which stage action is constructed, the same continual attempts to break through the boundaries of the footlights, the wings, the 'box'. It was this very tendency that most attracted the young military engineer who longed to work in the theatre.

As early as 1918, his attention had turned to the 'mansions', dating from the Middle Ages, from which the theatre had originated. At first, mansions were built inside churches for performances of early mysteries and morality plays. Then they broke out into the porch, and then the square, where the residents of the town surrounded them on all sides. And in 1919, Sergei saw such a mansion in a reproduction of one of Giotto's frescoes from Padua – a mansion that could have been used for *The Miracle of St Nicholas*.

The old French miniatures give an indication of how one of *The Miracles of Notre Dame* might have looked to a contemporary audience.

In Eisenstein's sketches for Gogol's *Marriage* (1842), which he was thinking about staging in 1920, the proscenium has become a circle and the whole stage turns into an arena on which there stands an almost medieval mansion with almost ancient *periaktoi* (wooden prisms rotating about their axes), which could change the set from 'the groom's house' to 'the bride's house' in an instant. In the finale, Podkolesin flees from his bride not 'out of the window' (as in Gogol's play), but 'in across the footlights into the audience and thence into the foyer, where he calls his coachman'.[6] Gogol's hero breaks the taboo of the footlights even more decisively than Harlequin had in Fedor Komissarzhevsky's production of *Princess Turandot*.

Eisenstein was convinced that this decision was anything but a sign of eclecticism. It was a single principle, hidden in various eras and styles, in the transformations of the theatre down the centuries. He joined them into an unbroken line: 'playing with the audience'.

This is also confirmed by the activity of the innovators, which had occupied Sir Gay's attention in Petrograd. The tireless Proteus-Meyerhold, in the first years after the revolution, staged Vladimir Mayakovsky's bizarre hybrid *Mysteria-Bouffe* (1918/1921), in which

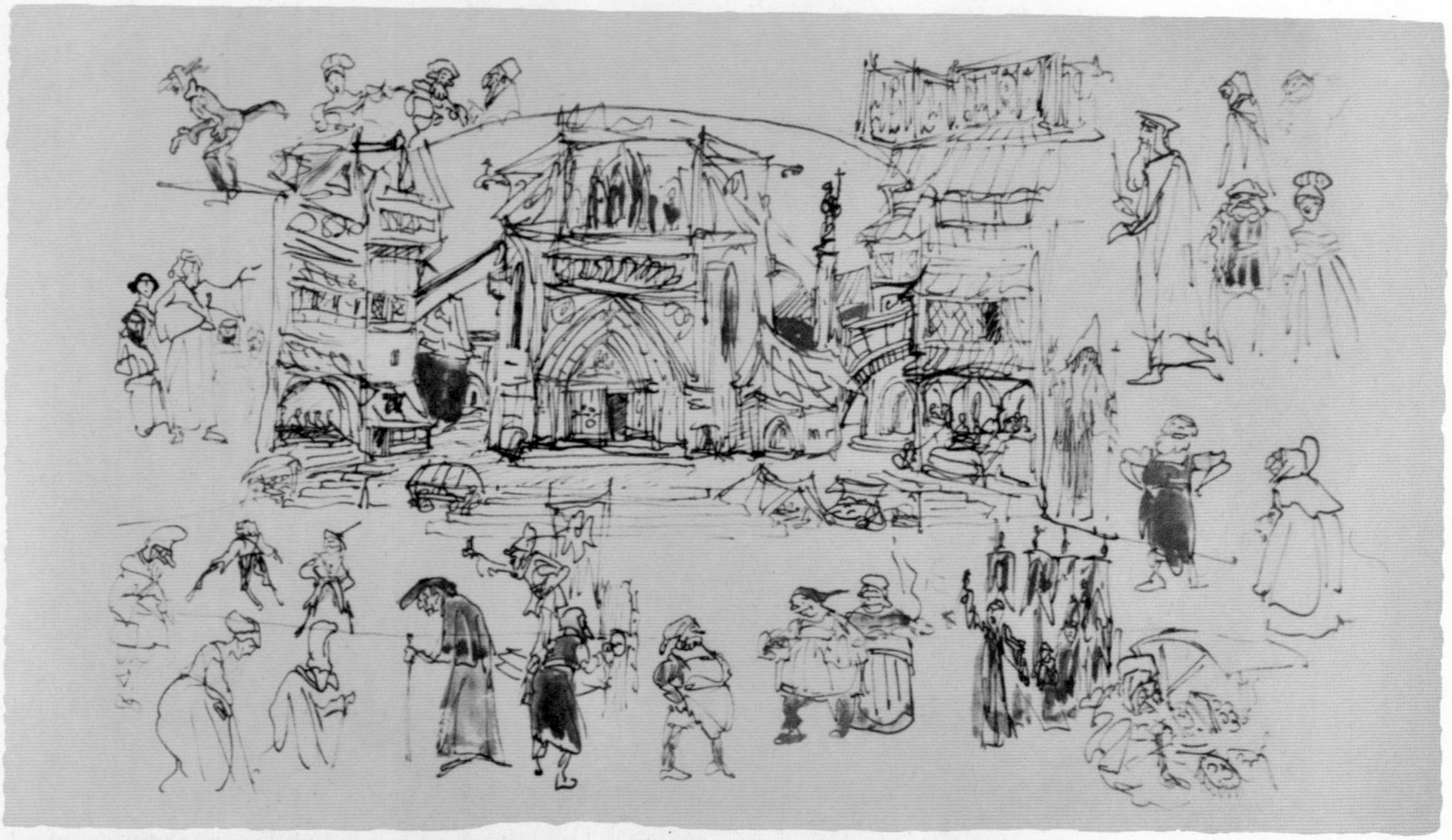

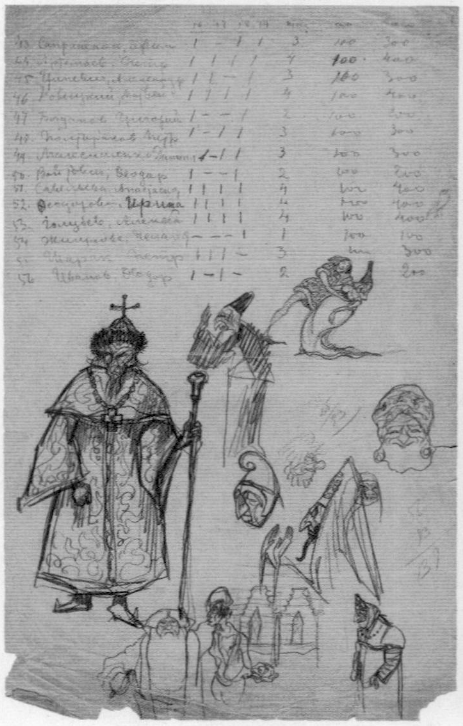

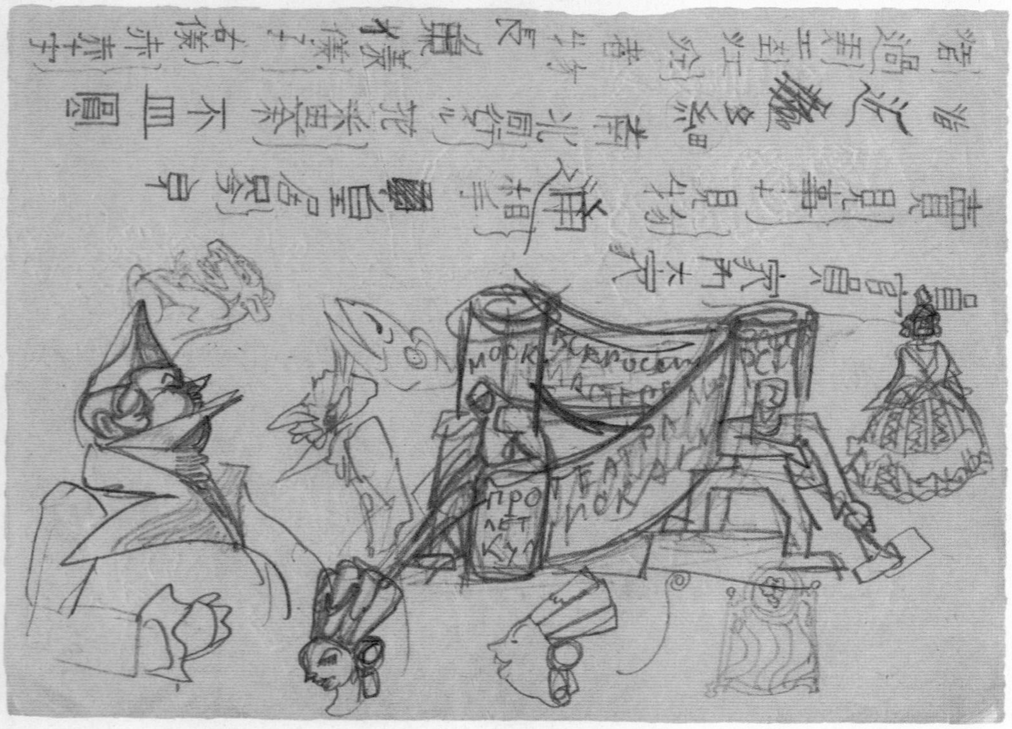

TOP
Sketch for a performance at the Ancient Theatre: Town Square, with the platform in front of the porch of the cathedral surrounded by 'ancient spectators' (Petrograd, 1917)

BOTTOM LEFT
A list of workers engaged in digging trenches, and a sketch of Ivan the Terrible for the historical drama *Vasilisa Melentyeva* (1867) by Aleksandr Ostrovsky (Polotsk, June 1920)

BOTTOM RIGHT
Sketches of theatrical figures in a notebook that Eisenstein used for his Japanese studies at the General Staff Academy (Moscow, 1920)

—THIS PAGE

TOP LEFT
Builder of Cologne Cathedral
Construction of the mansion for the mystery play (Smolensk, 1920)

BOTTOM LEFT
Stage design for the comedy *Marriage* by Nikolai Gogol (Moscow, November, 1920)

TOP CENTRE
Builder of Cologne Cathedral
Personages in the mystery play (Minsk, 1920)

BOTTOM CENTRE
Avocat Patelin by David Augustin de Brueys, based on a medieval farce Personages in the comedy (1920)

TOP RIGHT AND BOTTOM RIGHT
Personages in a satirical play: Zagrebalo (Mr Capture) and Podbiralo (Mr Pick) (Velikiye Luki, 1920)

—OVERLEAF

TOP
Geometrization of the Periwig
(Moscow, 1920)
Text: *Le XVIII-ième siècle géometrisé*
(The 18th century geometrized)

BOTTOM
Geometrization of the Periwig
(Moscow, 1920)
Text: NB. Hairstyles (smooth hair) – sparse soft cap, on which hang the curls. Suede cut wig and favori (a lock of loose hair at the temple) are worn together. Hair sticks to the cheek.

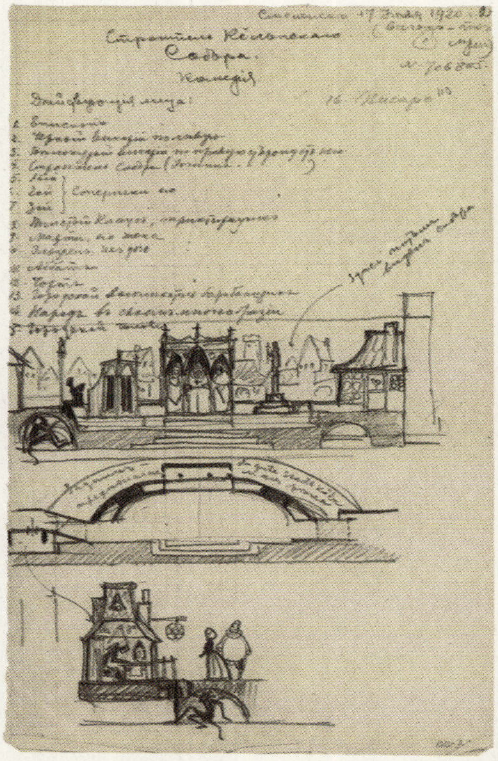

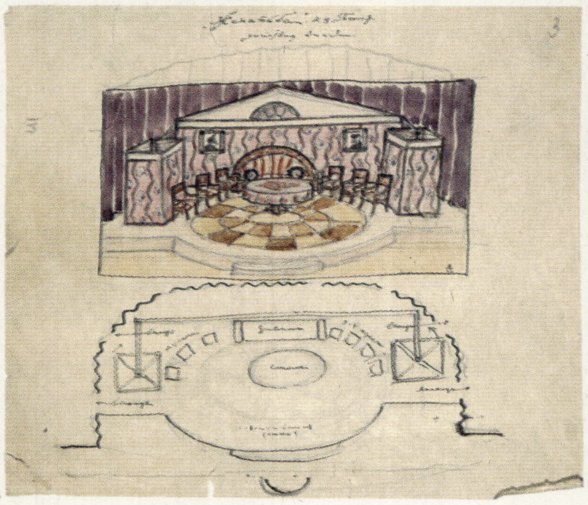

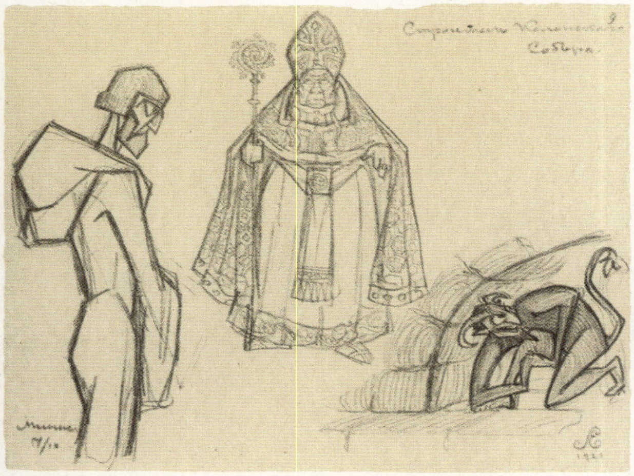

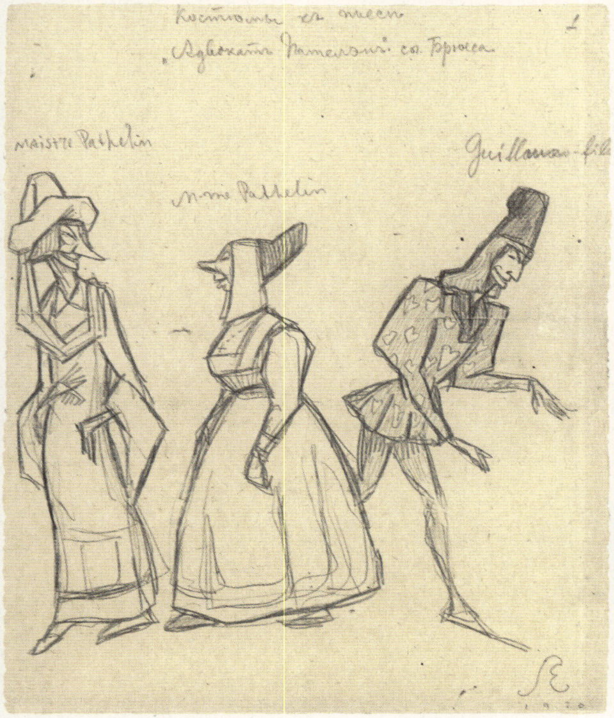

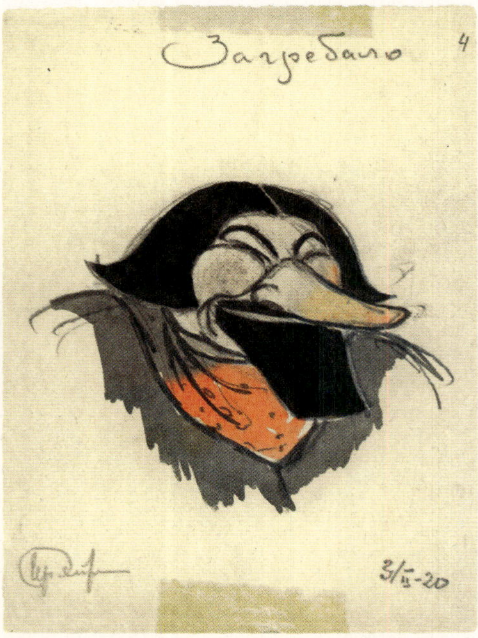

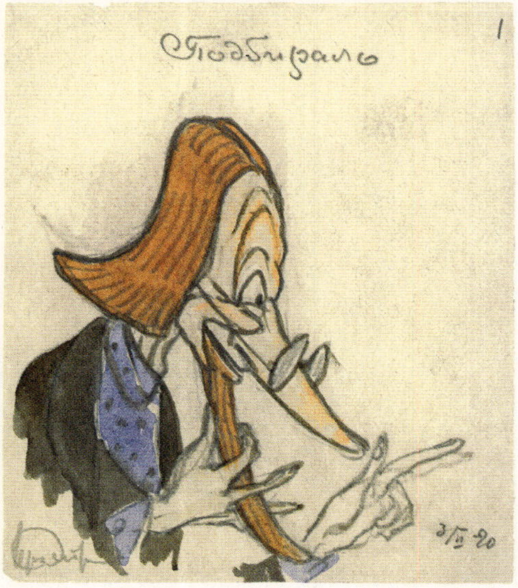

the action unfolded on several planes at once. And in 1920, Evreinov, the advocate of so-called 'ancient theatre', organized a mass action – essentially an agitprop morality play – entitled *The Taking of the Winter Palace*, in the very Petrograd square where the real events had taken place three years earlier. The times themselves demanded a rebirth of mass holidays with marches and carnivals, with historic actions in historic places: grand games played with the 'plane of the fact' and the 'plane of illusion'. Were these actions not the harbinger of a new fusion between the thespian and the public?

At the same time: the free citizen also had to become a free viewer – to acquire an unhampered choice of viewpoint on the show. That meant being able to walk around the spectacle. It called for the complete independence of the stage space from the 'box', and for 'democratic equal rights' for the various points from which it could be viewed – and which the director had to take into account.

While the flames of civil war were raging across Russia, technician Sergei Eisenstein, in the calm of the 18th Engineers, was doing more than simply studying the books, plays and albums about the theatre that were sent to him from Petrograd. He was also acquiring practical experience, on the garrison's amateur stage as a set designer, costume designer, director and even actor (although not too successfully in this last capacity). In June 1920, he was transferred from peaceful Polotsk and attached to the theatre section of the Western Front's political department, based first in Smolensk and then in Minsk. It was there that Rorik, now grown up, took his first independent decision – perhaps the most important one of his life: he would return neither to Petrograd, where Mummy was waiting for him, nor to the Civil Engineering Institute, as Daddy wanted. Instead, he would get himself demobbed (the war was coming to an end) and head for Moscow. In essence, he would be demobilized from architecture and join the theatre.

Formally, he – together with two other theatre enthusiasts with whom he had served – would become attached to the Oriental Department of the General Staff Academy, to study Japanese. There was a long-range calculation behind this metamorphosis: becoming an interpreter was the only way for Eisenstein to get to Japan and see the astonishing Kabuki theatre he had read about in *Love for Three Oranges*.

As his notebooks from his brief period at the Academy bear clear witness, the trainee Japonist's interests were divided in two. Alongside neatly written *kanji*, we see theatre characters. And not just that: rough sketches of advertisements for the Proletkult [Proletarian Culture] Theatre, an experimental Soviet artistic body.

Sergei Eisenstein was lucky: that same October of 1920, he was accepted as head of the Proletkult's set design department. And at once he was entrusted with the task of creating the set (alongside Leonid Nikitin, his old comrade-in-arms from the garrison amateur theatre), the costumes and the makeup for a stage version of Jack London's short story *The Mexican* (1911). The director, Valentin Smyshlyaev, was an employee of the Stanislavsky theatre. He was impressed with the speed and quality of Eisenstein's work, with the laconic way in which his sketches depicted the appearance of the main characters and the various second-string ones, and with the expressive precision of their characterization in terms of age, ethnicity and psychology.

The authority of this newcomer to the Proletkult theatre, who was not yet twenty-three years old, was expressed in the nickname of 'the Old Man'. He was already being addressed by his first name and patronymic, as Sergei Mikhailovich (or S. M.), and he was trusted to teach the art of the theatre at the Proletkult's workshop on directing. But within three months, the artist had started to change the thoroughly realistic costumes and makeup laid down by the director – to make them more 'geometrical'. Then he went over entirely to combining two generalized geometrical shapes – in the costumes, in the props, even in the makeup. He explained this decision by reference to the plot: a Mexican, who needs to box to earn money for the revolution, fighting an American, for whom boxing is purely a matter of money and fame. The supporters of one and of the other are like two different worlds – one ball-shaped, the other cuboid. It appears that S. M. was not joking when he said this.

At the time, Cubism was proclaimed to be the most modern style, almost the worldview of the industrial, electrical, scientific age, and for nearly two years it was uppermost in Eisenstein's thinking. Or perhaps it was the other way around: Sergei Mikhailovich was getting on top of the possibilities Cubism offered for the stage; and he was testing this too to its limits.

His first encounter with the new style came right at the beginning of his time in Moscow, at performances by Aleksandr Tairov's Chamber Theatre – and at once he was bewitched by it. Molière's comedy *George Dandin* (1668) was going round in Eisenstein's imagination at the time, and he tried to 'Cubize' (or modernize) the wigs of the 18th century – almost in the style of Aleksandr Vesnin, who turned the ancient helmets in Racine's *Phèdre* (1677) into Cubist constructions.

During the Civil War, Eisenstein had started preparing a production of Offenbach's *The Tales of Hoffmann* (1881): he had made a series of sketches combining the Biedermeier style with Romantic irony. In September 1921, this project came back to him in a Cubist guise. In January and February of the same year, Eisenstein had modified not only the costumes and makeup but also the sets for *The Mexican*.

In the Prologue, the mountains (where the junta of Mexican revolutionaries gather for their underground meeting) is represented by a composition of simple cubes and parallelepipeds, on which is sketched (just as in the German Expressionist film, *The Cabinet of*

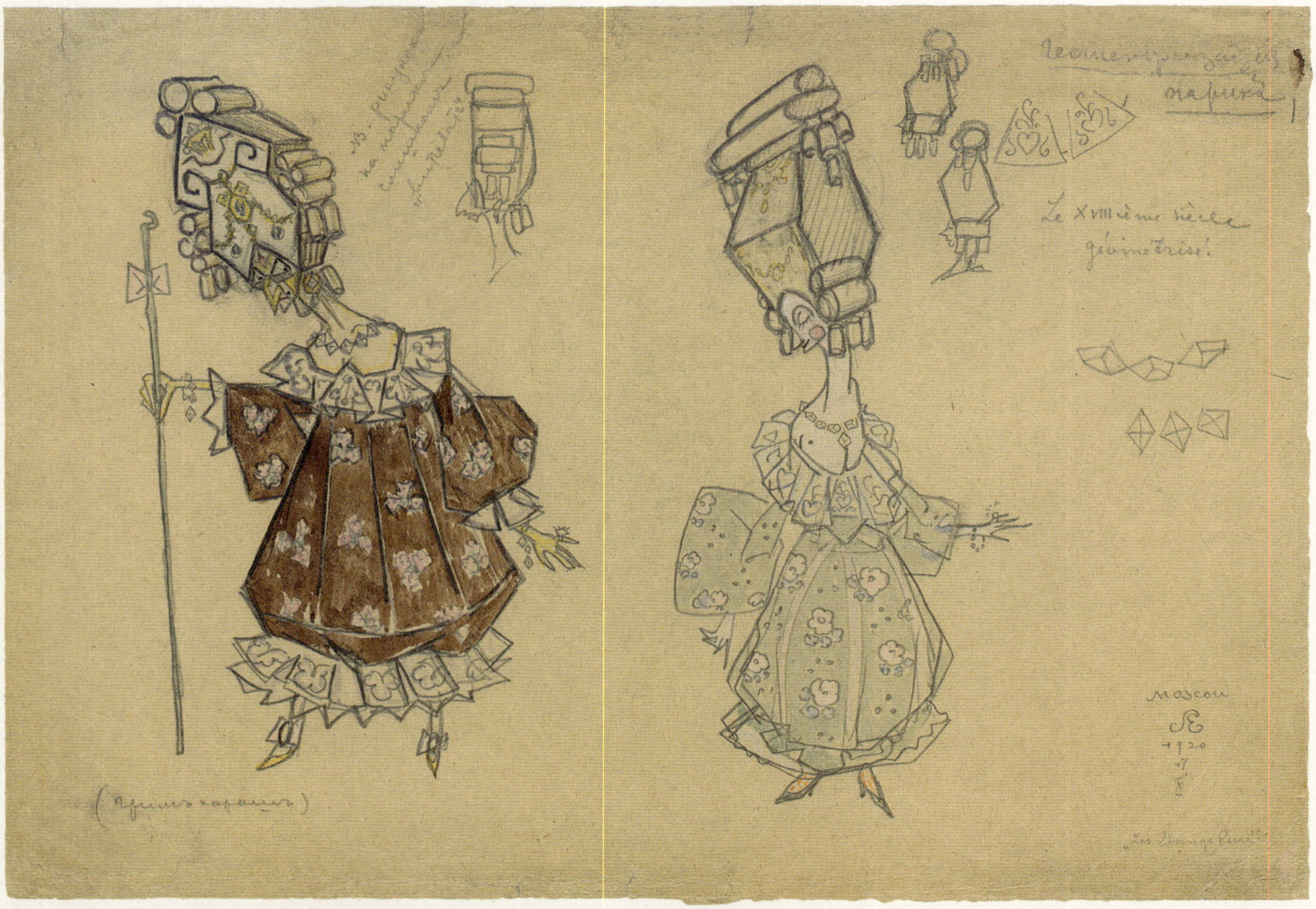
Le XVIIIème siècle géométrisé
Moscou
1920

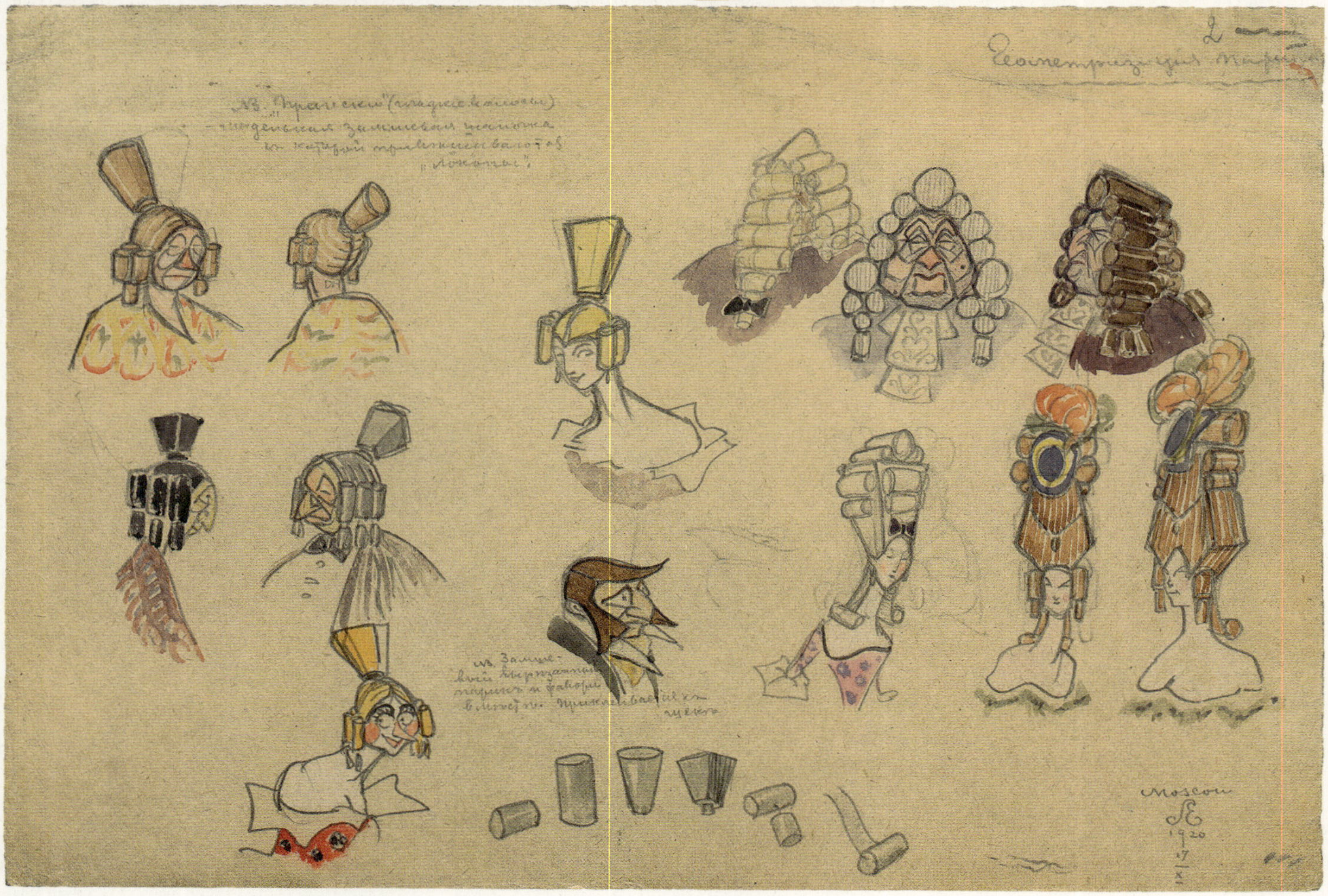
Moscou
1920

Dr Caligari, released the previous year) a light that shines into the ravine or into the cavern.

What is more, he had designed intermezzos featuring clowns: they were to use *aparte* to comment on what was happening and to make the audience respond more actively. And then came the chief innovation (a blatant encroachment on the role of the director!): a direct, rather than a merely verbal, crossing of the footlights. Eisenstein proposed to set up the boxing ring not on the stage, but in the centre of the stalls – amid the real audience. He wanted to teach the actors the rules of boxing, and to prepare two endings depending on the outcome of a real boxing match (i.e. whether the Mexican won or lost): the triumph of the revolutionaries would either happen at once, or else it would be delayed. In both versions, he wanted to finish the spectacle with a joint procession of the actors and the audience from the theatre out into the street.

The Proletkult would not agree to a boxing ring in the middle of the stalls, but it did name Eisenstein as Smyshlyaev's co-director. The 'Old Man' disagreed with the leadership's decision, and went his own way. The sacral space of the actors had to break into the sovereign region of the audience – if not in *The Mexican* then in the Tonplassos (tonal and plastic numbers): group gymnastic mimes to music, cultivated by the Proletkult, which claimed to give a symbolic embodiment of revolutionary themes such as 'The Emancipation of Labour', 'Victory over Capital' and 'The Solidarity of the Workers of All Countries'. For these agitprop exercises, Eisenstein suggested a movable Cubist 'platform', which could be easily installed in a factory workshop, a city square or the outskirts of a village.

Alas: Cubism, as a theatrical style, soon revealed an inclination towards stylization. Its pioneer in Russia, Aleksandra Ekster, supported Adolf Appia's sensible idea of 'three-dimensional sets for three-dimensional actors' and the bold experiments of Pablo Picasso and Jean Cocteau (in Erik Satie's ballet *Parade* [1917]) aiming at 'the integration of the actor and the set' on stage. Soon, however, Ekster had started running into mannerism in Tairov's productions – from Wilde's *Salomé* (1891) to Shakespeare's *Romeo and Juliet*. The turbulent expansion of 'volume painting' on the stage led to stylized painterly poses for the actors, and to *mises-en-scène* that were completely integrated with the set – drawing criticism from Meyerhold and his supporters.

In 1921, when he became a student at Meyerhold's GVYRM, Eisenstein was fated to clash with the stylizer Tairov. Along with his fellow student Sergei Yutkevich, he did the design for Nikolai Foregger's production (on the small stage at Print House) of Vladimir Mass's parodic sketch *PhèTre, or, A Phenomenal Tragedy*. Instead of buskins, the performers wore children's highchairs with a hole in the middle, tied to their feet. But this was just 'petty hooliganism'. The real quarrel with pseudo-Cubist stylization came within the style: in the Central Educational Theatre's *Macbeth*, where the two Sergeis designed sketches for the sets and costumes. The most indicative example came with the costume of the main character, the criminal Usurper of Power.

Even during the Civil War, Eisenstein had drawn various old helmets from books, and he remembered them. Some were topped with regal emblems: the heads of lions or eagles, predatory beaks and teeth, taloned paws. These motifs could be used, with changes to a few lines, to give the whole helmet the look of an eagle in rapid flight. But it was possible to go further: to turn the helmet into a gigantic comb, with a broad cloak like King Herod's in *Salomé*, but not the way Ekster had done it – rather, as a spreading plumage of scarlet, black and gold. And suddenly, the costume is no longer a Cubist stylization of historic dress, it is a metaphor: Macbeth, the usurper of the throne, is not an Eagle at all – he is a spiteful, lascivious, bloodied Cockerel.

By the same token, the 'horns' of his crown and the 'hooves' of his buskins transform the lawful king Duncan (whose only function in Shakespeare's tragedy is to be murdered) into a sacrificial animal.

And Lady Macbeth, sealed into a stiff costume with a heavy headdress, is less a lady than an inhuman siege tower!

Metaphor – the transference of meanings and significance – becomes a means of interpreting the play even here, in a show for which Eisenstein is merely the designer, not the director. And this metaphor materializes into an image through a process of analyzing and then synthesizing anew the fundamental elements. Surely, this is the way and the goal of genuine Cubism!

The Tonplassos stage, escaping the theatre building, comes to be known as 'portal-free construction'.

Eisenstein would bring this idea to Meyerhold and GVYRM, and, in a slightly more radically 'Cubized' form, would propose it as the basis of the sets for *The Merchant of Venice*. The Teacher accepted this study – not a classroom assignment – favourably, but then unexpectedly asked the Pupil to work out a design for a completely different project – a production of his beloved *Puss in Boots*, by the German Romantic playwright Ludwig Tieck.

Written in 1797, this biting satire is a play within a play. Charles Perrault's fairy-tale story about a talking cat who brings his owners good luck unfolds on the boards and becomes the trigger for a series of scandals: the Actors do not play what the Author wrote, the philistine audience eagerly discuss the action and interfere in it, the Theatre Owner clashes with the Author, the Prompter and the Stagehand add to the chaos. Tieck's merciless irony engulfs everyone and everything: the state of affairs in the decaying German principalities and the tastes of the man in the street, the ultra-rationalism of philosophy and the conservatism of the theatre, the illusions of life and the illusions of the stage. In neighbouring France, the revolution was in full flood.

A translation of Tieck's play appeared in 1916 in Meyerhold's *The Love for Three Oranges* magazine. A production of this old comedy that had not lost its innovative spark would be a good way of ridiculing the enemies of his 'theatre of convention'. While he was in search of a stage for it, revolution broke out in Russia, and the idea seemed to become less acute. Five years later, the project was becoming relevant again. With the help of his GVYRM students, the Teacher hoped to stage *Puss in Boots* and use it to mock his new enemies and critics. He entrusted the design for *Puss in Boots* to his most learnt and most imaginative student: Sergei Eisenstein.

On 27 December 1921, in the GVYRM library, the Master gave the Student a sheet from a notebook with a drawing and an explanatory note, dating from 22 December: 'Secret. My plan for the production: facing us – the audience, the conductor, the prompter; underneath the stage – the author, the stagehand, workers'. Below, in Meyerhold's jealous and suspicious way, was written: 'Return immediately after reading'.[7]

The Master's idea had the simplicity and wit of genius: turning the stage into a kind of mirror image of the real theatre. At the back of the stage would be the stalls and circle for the 'audience'; at the front, between the real audience and the actors playing the audience, there would need to be a platform on which the fairy-tale action would take place. Things would thus be turned back to front: the plot would be played out by actors with their backs to the audience, who would hear the lines first from the prompter and only then – in tones of exaggeratedly theatrical declamation – from the actors, and it would see all the machinery of theatrical marvels; at the same time, the conflict among the 'creators of the show' would take place also at the front of the stage, underneath this platform. Above the show and the conflict, noisy heckles from the 'philistine audience' would float down from the back of the stage. Let the real, 'new' audience, no less conservative than the old, catch sight of itself in the mirror of the stage!

What about the Master, the Innovator? Is he not repeating – albeit in a new variant – the principle of a mirror uniting stage and stalls that he had used in his four-year-old production of *Masquerade*?

Overnight, from 28 December to 29 December, Eisenstein made his plan of the set for *Puss*, following Meyerhold's idea and his assignment to the letter.

But then something happened that the Master had not foreseen. The very next day, 30 December, the Student sketched a new draft in which he violated one very fundamental condition of the assignment: the set did not remain on one side of the footlights. The stage construction was brought out beyond the limits of the proscenium. What is more, the stage opening no longer had any frame (the 'mirror of the stage') separating the audience from the space of the action. The double spectacle was to be surrounded by audience: part of the audience (played by actors) would be located on the stage platform while the others sat in the real theatre stalls – to provoke, as it were, the remaining (real) audience.

In the sketch from 30 December, there is still a curtain separating the stage from the orchestra pit and the audience. Four days later, on 3 January 1922, Eisenstein produced a yet more radical draft, in which everything is laid bare and fused into one: the stage and the wings, the orchestra (turned back to front) and the noisy audience.

We do not know what the Teacher said in response to this wilfulness from the Pupil. Perhaps he asked how, in this version, the real audience was to act: should they play along with the actors, and heckle in reality? Or did he perhaps think the Pupil had found a means of making the audience active?

It seems that the Master resolved to seize the initiative back, and at the same time to put everything in its place. Ivan Aksenov, not just a witness to events but a participant, asserts in his essay 'Sergei Eisenstein. Portrait of an Artist' (1934):

> ***Meyerhold was a little troubled by the turn that matters had taken, but then he seemed to get his bearings and he hurried to take up a position on the extreme left wing of this innovative step and to defend his challenged right to extreme radicalism. Eisenstein played the role of a tireless inciter, finding technical justifications for the most fantastical suggestions from Popova and Bebutov – ideas that they themselves had thought were only possible as aspirations....The kinetic sets Bebutov had dreamt about when they started working on the show were quite forgotten. Sets were only mentioned at all in order to ridicule the term. Its place was now taken by the concepts of stage space, stage arrangement, and construction for acting. It was in this fantastical and seemingly irresponsible work on crazy projects that would never see the light of day that all the elements that would come together in the production of*** **Le Cocu magnifique** ***were created.***[8]

Aksenov's statement cannot be valued too highly: it provides a direct indication that the artist Lyubov Popova's famous 'workspace for acting', in *Le Cocu*, was closely related to the 'non-portal construction' that Eisenstein invented for *Puss in Boots*. But the Teacher made one fundamental correction to the Pupil's project 'that would never see the light of day': he put the construction back on the stage, i.e. he re-drew the boundary between the spectacle and the audience!

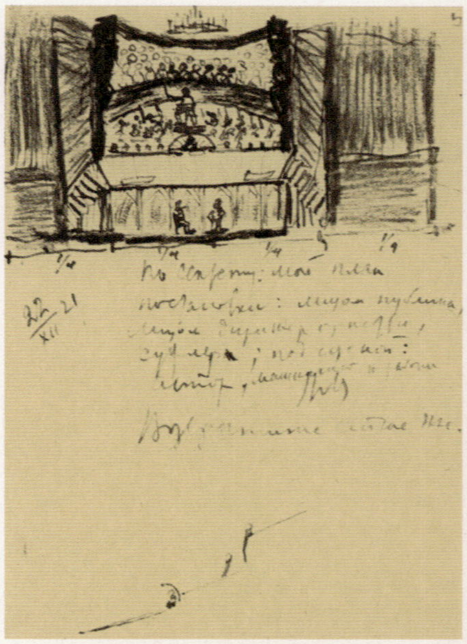

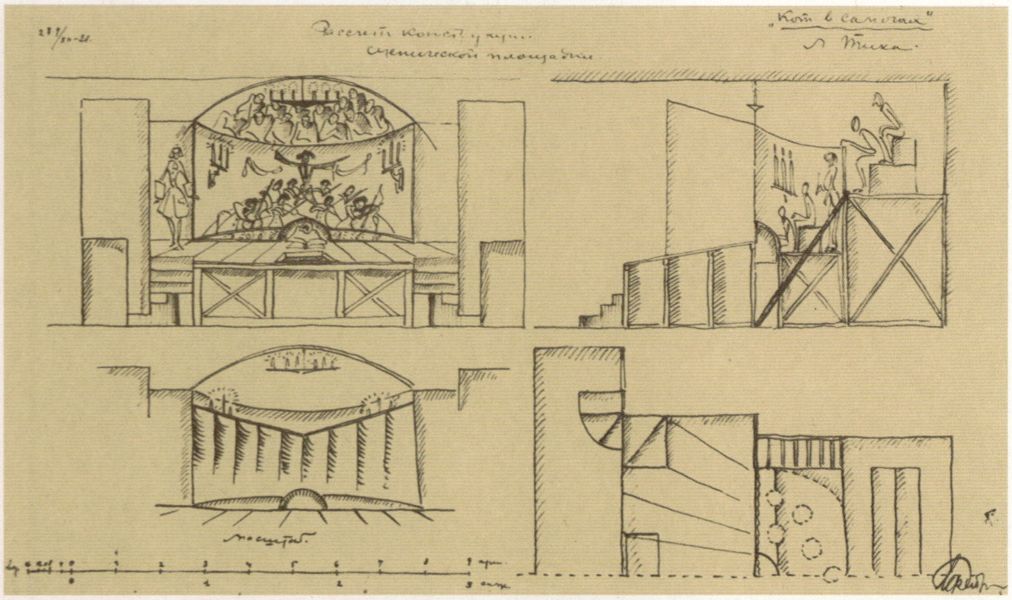
„Кот в сапогах"
Л. Тика

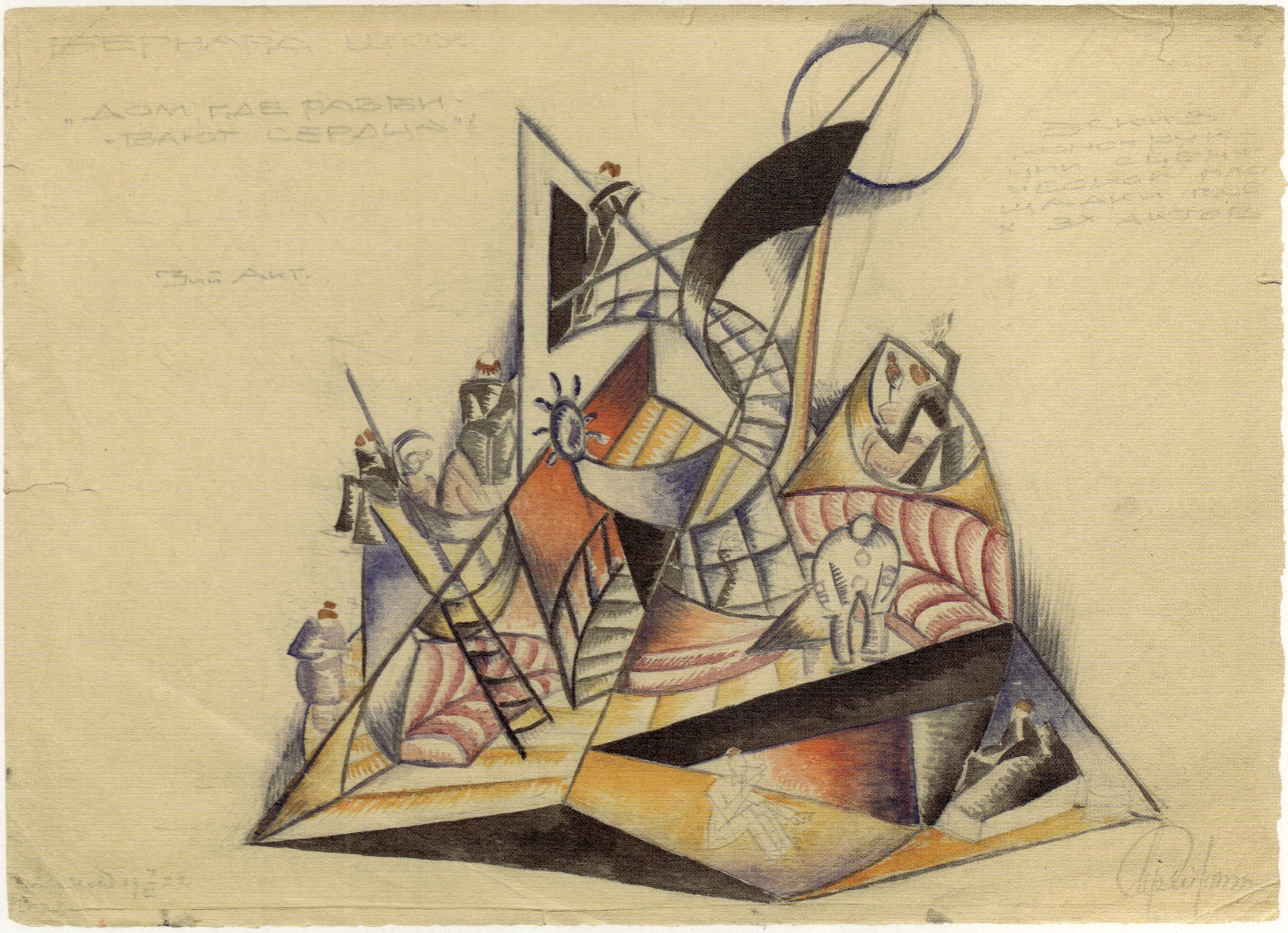
БЕРНАРД ШОУ
„ДОМ, ГДЕ РАЗБИ-
-ВАЮТ СЕРДЦА"
3ий АКТ.

Now it was the Pupil's turn to take care. What did the Master know (or feel) that made him advocate a conciliatory, opportunistic compromise even while he was unwilling to relinquish his position as leader of the radical 'theatre front'?

For the time being, however, in January 1922, it was Eisenstein who received the commission to do the design for *Heartbreak House*. And, of course, his starting point was 'portal-free stage construction'.

The first version, in March, was still very reminiscent of his construction for *Puss in Boots*. But the design (to say 'decoration' was forbidden!) of this construction was slightly different, with its suggestion of ship-like motifs in the half-mad Captain Shotover's villa.

This version was rejected: Eisenstein was accused not of imitation, but of insufficient radicalism. 'Backwardness' here found expression in his being obviously influenced by a style that was thought to have been transcended. 'Solutions in terms of volume and space' had been a distinguishing feature of the Chamber Theatre's Cubism.

The second version of the stage construction for *Heartbreak House* was also put together in March 1922 (a month before the premiere of *Le Cocu!*), and it was the result of a compromise. 'The top was three-dimensional and graphical, but the bottom was still in terms of volume and space. The artist sought to justify this by saying that he had to take account of what was realistically possible for actors of the old school.'[9]

This version, unlike the first, abolished the separation of distinct spaces within the house: everything was laid bare, and the interior was combined with the exterior. The inclined mast, the ropes, ladders, hammocks and rings in the shape of lifebelts make the half-mad captain's house look like a sinking packet boat: the metaphor was accomplished using techniques that are 'Constructivist' in style. And the merging of the three spaces – stage, wings and audience – was carried out even more consistently than in the second version of *Puss in Boots*. But how could the audience, sitting motionless in their seats, feel the benefit of this fusion?

The premiere of *Le Cocu magnifique*, with its clear, constructional arrangement on the stage (not in the stalls!), its ascetic *prozodezhda* (neither picturesque nor metaphorical) and its actors demonstrating real actions, i.e. biomechanical mastery, marked a way out of the contradictions and obscurities of the school hypothesis. The Master did not bring the spectacle to the limit proposed by the Pupil. But the result was still a revolutionary one for the theatre. The Master raised the 'construction for acting' onto the stage, and thereby made clear that the line of the footlights and the mirror of the stage did have to remain as a boundary between the spectacle and the audience.

Did the Pupil agree with this practical lesson? Without looking back, he goes forward.

A week after the *Le Cocu...* premiere, on 1 May 1922, he began working on how to direct Arthur Schnitzler's *Colombina's Veil* (1910), with musical score by Ernö Dohnányi. This would hardly have been a GVYRM assignment. Rather, it was the Pupil's response in his hidden polemic with the Master. And with Tairov too. Both the 'antipodes' of the new Russian theatre had staged Schnitzler's pantomime before. Meyerhold had produced it twice, under the title of *Colombina's Scarf*: once in October 1910 and once in April 1916. Tairov 'monumentalized' the same pantomime, giving it the title of *Pierrette's Veil*, in November 1913.

The traditional plot of the Italian masked comedy – Colombina cheating on Pierrot with Harlequin – acquires a tragic coloration. Pierrot drinks poison and dies, and Colombina runs in horror from the body to the wedding ball, where she dances with Harlequin before returning to Pierrot and draining a glass of poison in her turn.

Eisenstein took his impressions of *Le Cocu...* and of the Shaw and Schnitzler texts, and also his sketches for them, back to Petrograd with him when he went to stay with his mother during the holidays. In the former capital (Moscow became the new capital in 1918), he encountered friend Sergei Yutkevich. The two Sergeis fell to a heated discussion of the latest rival 'isms'. Eisenstein proposed to use good old pantomime for a parody of everyone and everything: Cubism, Suprematism, Expressionism, Constructivism, Stanislavsky's 'fourth wall', Meyerhold's idea of 'bas-relief' theatre (fixed to the footlights), Tairov's sugared aestheticism and the acerbic eroticism of Foregger's 'dances of the machines'. At the same time they would parody Hollywood cop movies with their society adventurers and brutal criminals, French series with their Vampires and Fantômases, and German mystical films with their Golems and Sleepwalkers. The new version of the pantomime would be entitled *The Columbia Girl's Garter*, in English, and the two Sergeis would stage it under the clown-style pseudonyms of Pip & Fax.

The stage literally had to be lifted up on its hind legs, so that the set could cover the whole 'mirror of the stage'. The action would play out on this 'bas-relief fourth wall' (as if on a cinema screen). 'Pierrot's boudoir', in the first act, was to look like this:

> ***The space is constructed vertically, in the shape of a semicircular window (whose size is that of the portal of the stage). The casement would give the actors somewhere to act and to move around. The upper frame of the window would form a bow-shaped bridge (making it possible to pass from one side to the other). A sofa would hang from the top (house) right of the window, with an 'intimate' light above it. Below that, an electricity meter and a fusebox.***

Below and to the left an armchair, with its back to the audience. Further left, a telegraph machine and an X-ray screen. Above, on the window frame, an oval mirror (the silvered side to the audience). Behind the window and to the left, a lift.

The back of the stage is darkened, with a structure of narrow beams of light....

And here are the main characters of the updated pantomime:

PIERROT: a viscount and an aesthete. Soft in the head at 34. Wig. False teeth. Morphine user...
HARLEQUIN: factory owner... The bastard son of Irma Vep and Buffalo Bill....In act 2: black turtleneck, à la Fantômas...
COLOMBINA: 'The Columbia Girl'. Soon to be made an honest woman by her marriage to Sir Archibald Harlequin, Straps and Garter Manufacturer, of 60 High Street, Boston, USA.
Her MA and PA: high-society émigrés, 'Russia No. 2'. A former baroness with a German surname, Fräulein to Her Former Imperial Majesty. Kammerjunker, Knight of the Order of the Garter....[20]

In the finale, Colombina dies in the arms of the dead Pierrot, whom Sir Harlequin has garrotted with a steel garter, mummified and then electrified. This point could be made particularly amusing: the electrified lover would perform the celebrated biomechanical exercise of 'jumping up to the chest and stabbing'. On the title page, the pupils wrote a respectful dedication: 'For V. E. Meyerhold. *Au patriarche de l'Echarpe – les novices de la Jarretière* [To the patriarch of the Scarf from the novices of the Garter]'.

The fundamental question about the theatre for Eisenstein is now not about how the characters and their environment, the actors and the space could be fused into a unity on stage, and even not the problem of the boundary between the stage and the audience. He had solved assignments of that kind easily, and in the most varied styles.

No, the question was of making the stage commensurate with the stalls, the spectacle with the audience, and – in the final analysis – art with life. A common unit of measurement needed to be found.

In other words, he needed to find the elementary particle of art: something like the recently discovered electron, proton and neutron. For the atom, which had been thought to be the minimal particle of matter, had now turned out – as Lord Rutherford had said – to be something like a 'little Universe'.

Once Sergei Yutkevich comes to see him, unusually excited: he had been in Luna Park funfair, riding the railroad-themed 'American mountains' (which in America are called 'Russian'). Now, this was the tempo of the 20th century, this was an attraction! It makes Eisenstein start. Had the thing been found? After all, the word 'attraction' did not refer only to a ride in a park or a trick in the circus. Its Latin root (meaning to 'drag', 'pull' or 'draw') also contained the goal and the key idea of any art – impact. Was this not the main thing in the theatre? Was it not for the sake of impact that all of the playwrights, directors, artists and actors concentrated their gifts, their knowledge and their talents in the hall? Did the audience not attend the theatre in order to feel an impact, to be drawn out of the 'plane of the everyday' into the 'plane of creation'? Art was an 'impact machine', an 'impact mechanism':

So, what is valuable in art [is] only the element of the 'attraction'. The 'blow to the nerves'.... And the task of studying an artform can be reduced to studying the conditions of under which a work exerts 'maximum attraction', on the basis of the techniques available to that form....

The impact of the theatre takes two forms: [constructions] acting on the imagination (spiritualistic), and acting on the feelings (sensory), [in other words] mental (i.e. apprehended by the mind, weighed up, and 'evaluated': 'oh, how horrible', etc.) and emotional (a drumbeat, a boxer's punch). It is evident that the latter are attractions.

The former can be attractions only if the viewer 'identifies' with the actor (in the representational theatre), by ducking into the illusion...., disconnecting oneself from reality, 'concentrating'.

The second [type of theatre] does not require this: its impact is founded, in contrast, on connecting all the viewer's faculties. [This is assisted by] a bright light that makes demands on the eye, a drumbeat that mobilizes the ear, and a restless rhythm that forces the knees to shake.

Leaving the theatre in a dream, with Fiers's words sounding in one's mind [in the first type] and...wanting to turn cartwheels [in the second].'[11]

The last sentence of this note, which was written *pro domo sua* (not for publication), is a protest against Stanislavsky's elegiac and nostalgic treatment of Chekhov's *The Cherry Orchard*, in the finale of which old Fiers (a servant whom the owners of the now-sold estate have abandoned like a thing) speaks the famous words: 'They've forgotten a man'. Is he not laughable, this willing slave, freed by his masters, who would not leave them and who paid the price for it? Chekhov himself was not very happy with the way the play was treated in the Arts Theatre, and kept repeating: 'It's a comedy! A comedy!' In Eisenstein's opinion, Fiers should be played by none other than Charlie Chaplin!

Shaw had written his satire on a dishonest and hypocritical society under the influence of Chekhov's plays, and he said as much in a preface as a warning to people who would stage it. Meyerhold and Eisenstein's show was to finish like this: after the bombing of Captain Shotover's house, a secondary character by the name of Randall would soar to the top of the mast, and the painful melody of his clarinet would become a tragic parody of Fiers's famous line. But would such a finale leave the audience wanting to 'turn cartwheels'?

Eisenstein knew that Stanislavsky – his Teacher's Teacher – was busy on some kind of mysterious 'system'. His actors spent years sitting at their desks in search for the kernel of a part (which was why they were nearly always sitting down on stage, during the actual play). In the staging of *Heartbreak House* by himself and Meyerhold, there would not be one static second. The actors must only speak their lines in motion! Perhaps Stanislavsky's actors really did experience their parts, but what mattered in the theatre was what the audience experienced. In their *Heartbreak House*, the audience would experience joy in the art itself – and not just the craft of the actors. Eisenstein did not agree with the sophistical remark made by Vladimir Nemirovich-Danchenko (Stanislavsky's 'companion-in-arms') that 'The director must die in the actor!' Why must he die? He must turn into the actors, and into the performance as a whole!

He, S. M. Eisenstein, would create a stage construction that would lay the secret wellsprings of the show bare before the audience, that would materialize the invisible lines of the *mises-en-scène* that his Teacher would devise with such brilliance (let the audience be shaken by the craft of the director!). This construction would precisely define the actors' movements, counteracting their perpetual itch to improvise for themselves and disrupt the strict delineation of their parts. He would turn the lines of their movements into ropes, narrow bridges and walkways. The will of the director would be embodied in springboards that would fling the actors from one place to another. The actors would have to devote themselves to the study of acrobatics and biomechanics, if they did not want to break their own necks or those of the audience!

The tyranny of the word in the theatre had to be overthrown! The democratic equal rights of all means of achieving impact – all attractions – had to be established! But 'unit' attractions were not to be confused with trick attractions (the latter being only a special case of the former). What needed saying was involuntarily said by Ilya Ehrenburg, that 'Russian Frenchman'. He had just dispatched to Petrograd the latest edition of *Veshch* ['Thing'], the magazine he published in Berlin, devoted to *the assemblage of machines, skyscrapers, things, films* – to a *universal montage*.

And what about *shows*? asks Eisenstein. For what, in fact, is the coupling of personality and image in each character and in the ensemble of them – the elements of stage design, music and noises into the unitary composition (the 'machine') of the show – if it is not a montage of all these impact devices and materials? He had found the word he had been missing in his reflections on the new, third version of the Shaw-Aksenov *Heartbreak House* – and on theatre as such.

The directing machine that Eisenstein would construct for *Heartbreak House* would have to give material form to the idea of the 'subject-free theatre'. For the truly subject-free theatre was not Kazimir Malevich's prehistoric (1913!) experiments in the sets for the opera *Victory Over the Sun*, but rather constructions that did not depend on the play's verbal content, perhaps not even on its plot. In fact, he makes an important correction to the idea of being subject-free by introducing that associativity of apprehension that the spectacle needs:

> ***The preliminary schema of movement is abstract and formal, after the selection of people moving up into the air for reasons outside themselves as the main attraction. The objective is not at all to fill the proscenium with drawings of flying figures: it is to create a sensory impact on the audience, by means of human figures in flight…but once that is present in the background…the background imposes obligations. That is how the process of construction goes. And here comes the point of combining this construction [of the action] with the construction associated with the 'ship' [the stage set], what was not quite obligatory. However, it was Meyerhold's assignment.***
>
> ***In fact, the aspiration to create a theatre that would be subject-free 'at all costs' is pure snobbery, although of course it has colossal 'purificatory' value, making it possible to judge that element without which the theatre would be unthinkable,– to judge it from without, and from a distance. Because, as it seems to me, associativity par excellence is the characteristic that distinguishes the theatre from other genres: the circus, gymnastics, etc.***[12]

It seems that Eisenstein was catching himself in the act of snobbery, and of holding to his own contradictory idea of 'subject-free construction of the show'.

Of course, his directing machine was not at all subject-free. It strove to act on the audience by means of the human body in flight. Did the proposed 'sensory impact' not contain a certain measure of 'associativity'? The motif of 'people moving...for reasons outside themselves' could, after all, be understood in more than one way!

And did all his musings about attractions not have as their subject that mysterious space, the field of associations that the audience would perceive? The audience's 'imagined' field within the 'real' space of the theatre is initially included in the performance, alongside the acting space of the stage. And that is where the *'machine' of the director's conception* must work, a machine that is also imaginary, constructed from all the materials and means of impact available to the theatre. In Petrograd, he had found a name for this machine: *the montage of attractions*. Its first material embodiment would be this very stage machine or construction designed for *Heartbreak House*.

Eisenstein was convinced that the production of Shaw's play would be a step forward from *Le Cocu magnifique* – a new revolution in the theatre. The restrained decision that the Teacher had affixed to his draft collage project in June had been the first cold shower that the Pupil's imagination had had to endure.

The second shower was chillier: the former Nezlobin players quit Meyerhold's theatre. It is possible that the rumours about the forthcoming 'eccentric treatment' of Shaw had played their part in this decision. At the end of the day, they were not puppets, and they were not 'weightless'. They would not allow themselves to be 'blown' into the air, breaking their bodies, not their hearts.

The temperature dropped fast. The Master suddenly wrote a letter to the Pupil, in official tones:

> ***Comrade Eisenstein,***
> ***Please hand over the staging work on the Shaw play to Comrade Z. N. Raikh, who has been given a permanent post at the Actor's Theatre assisting me with mounting.***
> ***V. Meyerhold.'***[13]

The exclusion from mounting was a warning. What came next was exile.

The blow was struck by Zinaida Nikolaevna Raikh, Meyerhold's wife. At a GVYRM lecture, Aksenov had seen her tear a strip off a poster that was lying on the table and write a note on it in pencil:

> ***Seryozha,***
> ***I love you. I admire your talent and your vivid personality. I think you need to leave M-d, just as M-d once left Stanislavsky. You have reached maturity. I advise you to bring your studies here to an end of your own accord. It would be the noble and sensible thing to do. In principle I myself am an enemy of yours, although personally I have warm and tender feelings for you.***
> ***Z. Raikh.***[14]

This piece of advice would have been impossible unless it had been suggested by the Teacher.

Aksenov reports in his essay that:

> ***After the lecture he went up to his teacher and they spent a long time discussing various questions that had been touched on in the lecture without being developed. Meyerhold promised he would finish his exposition the very next day, and insisted that Eisenstein not miss that lecture. For the first time in the whole season he was gentle and friendly. The two of them parted with professions of love, and agreed to see one another at the following day's lecture. But the following day never came. Eisenstein vanished from his teacher's circle for many years.***[15]

The first biography was not very accurate: after this exile Eisenstein still worked as 'laboratory assistant' on Meyerhold's production of *Tarelkin's Death*, by Aleksandr Sukhovo-Kobylin, in the Theatre GITIS. The director's conception, as well as Varvara Stepanova's set design, included some ideas from the *Heartbreak House* project. But Shaw's comedy remained unrealized.

It is easy to imagine what the break cost him. Who knows whether a crack did not appear in the Pupil's heart muscle in the autumn of 1922, during his flawlessly noble and sensible departure from the Teacher's school? How prophetic was the title of his final assignment: *Heartbreak House*. Eisenstein was suspicious too: but, unlike Meyerhold, his suspicions were directed not at other people but at himself. Perhaps the phrase 'you have matured' was only there to sugar the pill, and in fact Eisenstein was not a director at all. In that case, what was he?

He had thought up all those masts and ladders, attaining to precision and clarity in line and movement. More than anything else, in art he disliked scruffiness – in anything apart from a clown's messy wig (which so resembled his own disobedient locks). The Master was not fond of untidiness either. As early as 31 December 1920, Eisenstein had copied out a passage from *The Love for Three Oranges* magazine that struck him as important:

'The actor is an artist, and his business is to live in the form of a drawing. The actor may be his own draughtsman, or he may reproduce a drawing by another master, just as a pianist plays notes that he did not compose.'

What if 'filling the proscenium with drawings of flying figures' was not directing but merely graphic art, drawing lines in real space (albeit scenographically organized) using real actors (who were not at all 'weightless')? What if his whole idea of the 'directing machine' had just been an intervention by his old interests, or (to permit oneself to be immodest) his innate gifts: an eruption of his 'repressed' (as Freud would say) but ineradicable instinct to draw?

And then Eisenstein might have thought back to the pantomime he had created during the Civil War:

> ***...the story of an unfortunate young man, wandering among fellow creatures who are forced to move and run through orbits that have been laid down forever.***
>
> ***Some go in zigzags, some in figure-eights, some sweep into the stage space out of the unknown, following the track of a parabola, only to vanish back into the unknown after a brief interaction with the hero. An especially pathetic episode is that of the hero's girlfriend, who at the very moment when she is nearest to him has to leave, because that is 'prescribed' by the curve she must follow.***
>
> ***Most terrible was the moment when the hero, so proud of his ability to go in a straight line, cutting across the twisting sinusoids and lemniscates of his fellows, that his trajectory is not the result of a free choice either, and his straight line is just part of a curve – true, about a distant centre, but just as determined as the other characters'.***[16]

Was the 'acting machine' not the very materialization of his youthful Schopenhauerian pantomime, whose scenes played out 'the world as will and representation'? And had he, who had imagined he was a director, a demiurge of the theatre world, proved to be no more than his own character, with a predetermined trajectory? Still worse, had he become the slave of someone else's representation? Should he not, then, return to drawing, where he could be his own master?

Eisenstein did the opposite. He remained a director – and ceased to be a set designer. After his sketches for the Shaw comedy he did not create another colour sketch, even for his own three shows at the First Workers' Theatre of the Proletkult: he limited himself to hasty cartoons in graphite pencil for the first of them, with a bitterly ironic, proverbial title: *Enough Stupidity for Each Wise Man*.

Eisenstein had been working on this Aleksandr Ostrovsky comedy since 1922, and the style of his production of it had changed radically. The first steps in the work were taken under the sign of the *commedia dell'arte*. But the futurist poet Sergei Tretyakov, a comrade of Vladimir Mayakovsky's and a fellow countryman of Eisenstein's, reworked the classic text to incorporate a series of up-to-the-minute sketches about swindlers, political adventurers and time-servers. Eisenstein said his work on *Wise Man* used devices from the arsenals of the music hall, street satire and the circus. It also (although hardly anyone knew it) used a lot of devices that he had invented for Aksenov's translation of the Shaw play.

No, he would not use a 'stage machine', with lifts and moving walkways. Instead, he would apply the new 'mechanism' he had invented – the montage of attractions. He would put the means of achieving impact that he had prepared for *Heartbreak House* (sensory, associative, rhythmical) to new use. Even some 'individual cases' of circus attractions: the gymnastic ring above the stage (for the clown's reprises); the wire (stretched over the audience's heads), which would carry the Adventurer in the black mask 'abroad'; the pole that the hyper-sensory Madame Mamaeva would climb up, eventually slipping easily out of her cloak-like dress and being exposed in flesh-coloured knitwear (an ideal *prozodezhda*, with the restriction on movement reduced to the limit!).

There was no stage mirror at all. The stage space was demarcated by the complete circle of an 'arena': the carpet on the floor was on the same level as the first row of the amphitheatre where the audience sat, as in the circus. In the arena there was a small stand with a curtain: a *scēnē*, as in ancient Greece. And there was also a low box: a stage on the stage. Nothing had been forgotten from his experience of four years' early fantasies about the theatre, and one year's study with Meyerhold. But everything had been transformed.

Not all his ideas found a use, of course, and it seems that he rejected some of them himself – including, for instance, the main idea he had so long fought for: the idea of abolishing the demarcated boundary between the stage and the stalls.

In *Wise Man*, a broad bright frame surrounded the carpet-arena, emphasizing the line where the footlights would have been. It seems that Eisenstein had accepted that his Teacher had been right: what attracts the audience, what creates impact, is precisely crossing the line that divides the actors' space from the audience's space. Eisenstein invented a multitude of such crossings: clowns and jugglers 'throwing' various objects into the stalls; the erotic Mamaeva playfully jumping onto the knees of somebody sitting in the front row; bold couplets and *aparte* addressed to the audience by clowns in *travesti*; and more. The line of the footlights in the theatre seemed to be an important component in the invisible mechanism, the mechanism that was one and the same both for the composition of a spectacle and for the laws of its apprehension. The mechanism that Eisenstein called the montage of attractions.

—PAGE 79

TOP LEFT
Meyerhold's note, with a sketch of the stage design for *Puss in Boots* by Ludwig Tieck (Moscow, 1921)

TOP RIGHT
Sketch for *Puss in Boots*, based on the Teacher's idea of the stage as a 'mirror of the auditorium' (1921)

BOTTOM
Stage construction for all three acts of Bernard Shaw's *Heartbreak House* (1st version, 1922)

—THIS PAGE TOP
Sketches for *Enough Stupidity in Every Wise Man* by Aleksandr Ostrovsky/ Sergei Tretyakov, staged by the First Workers Theatre of the Proletkult (Moscow, 1923):

LEFT
Glumov's Costume for Prologue, Interludes and Epilogue (1st variant, 1921)

RIGHT
Mamaeva (2nd variant, 1922)

—THIS PAGE BOTTOM
Photographs of scenes from the performance (April 1923):

LEFT
'Adventurer Golutvin (Grigory Aleksandrov) goes abroad'

RIGHT
'Rendezvous Mamaeva (Vera Yanukova) and General Krutitsky (Aleksandr Antonov)'

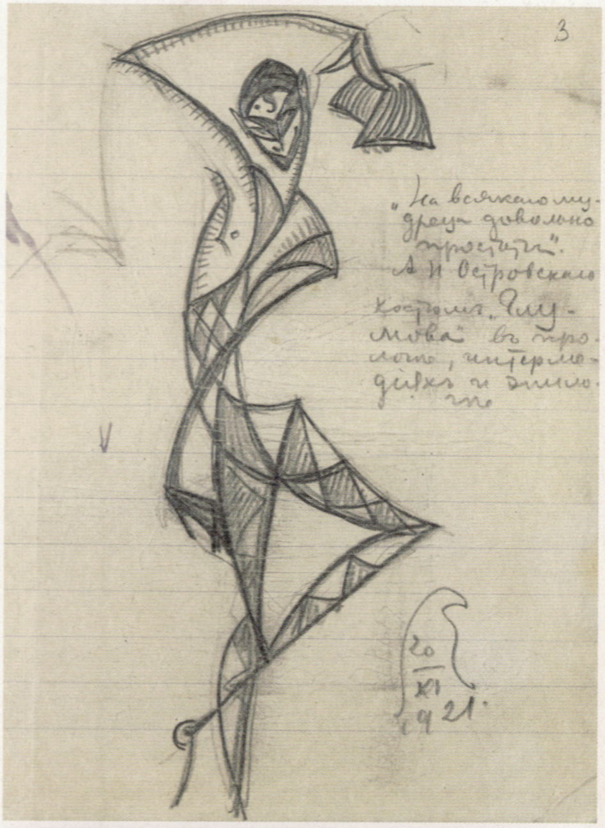

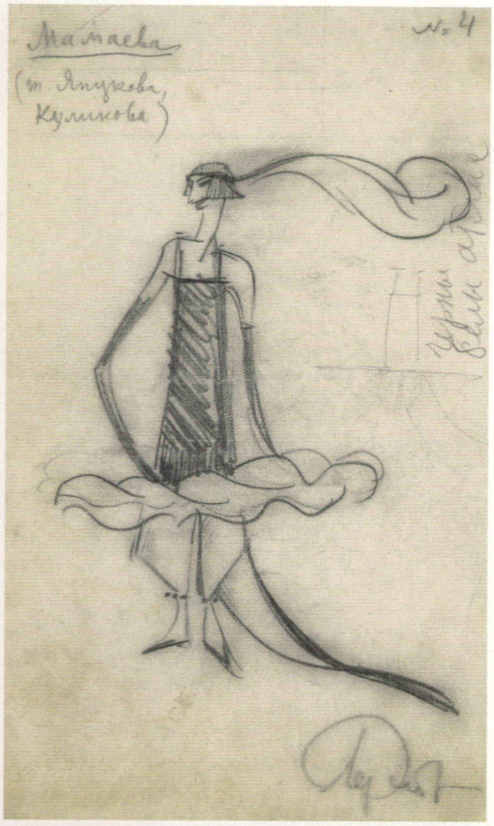

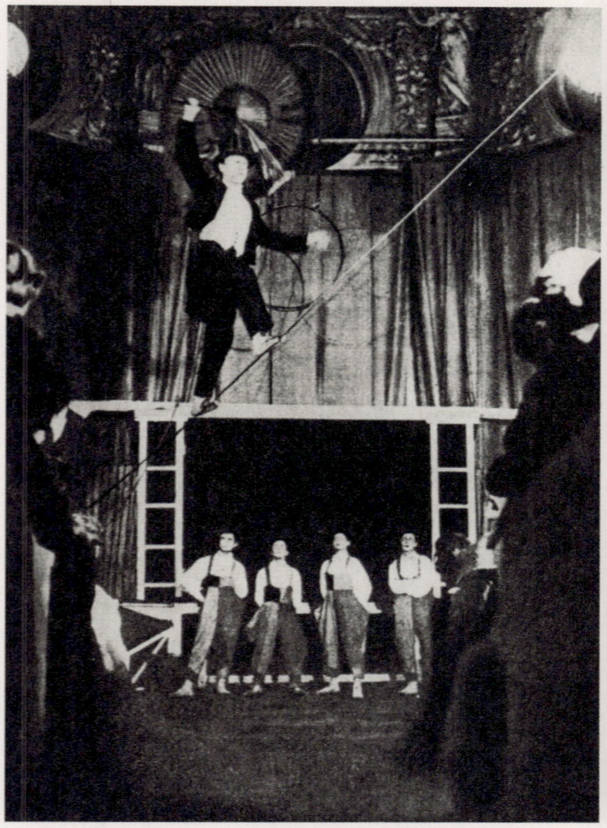

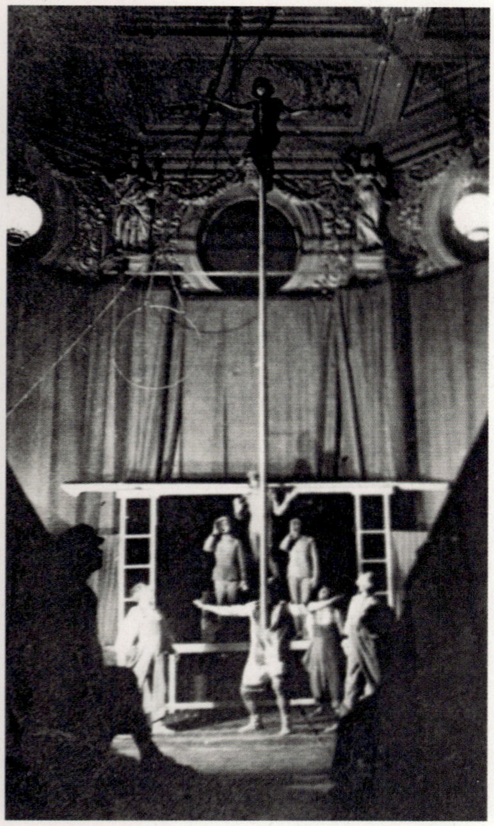

On 2 April 1923, a concert was held to mark the 25th anniversary of Meyerhold's work at the Bolshoi Theatre. On the most academic stage in the country, Eisenstein presented the riskiest scene and the biggest attraction from *Wise Man*: the meeting between Mamaeva and General Krutitsky. The hero's amorous 'auntie' climbs up the priapic column that protrudes shamelessly from the General's wide trousers.

Perhaps the Teacher realized how eccentrically the Pupil had transformed the finale of their ill-fated *Heartbreak House*. There, it had been Randall who was to climb the mast after the bombing, to produce on his flute an elegiac melody about the cosy domestic hearth.

When the audience burst into applause, Eisenstein was overcome, and forgot to give the order 'Curtain!' In fact, his show was not supposed to feature a curtain at all.

The premiere of *Wise Man* was to take place in three weeks. Soon, Meyerhold would bring his workshop students to see it, indirectly praising it. He would still express his opinion of his Pupil's ideas in deeds, not in words.

On 19 January 1924, the Meyerhold Theatre put on its first performance of *The Forest* – a production of another comedy by Ostrovsky – first published in 1871. The 'declaration of love' scene was executed as follows. Two long ropes with loops at the ends ('giants' footsteps'), were attached to the top of a tall pole. The actor and actress each put one leg through a loop, exchanged some lines of seemingly insignificant dialogue, but at the same time kept circling round the pole – chasing, chasing, but never catching one another. In the other lyrical scene, meanwhile, the partners held their dialogue seated on the ends of a plank balanced across a beam (like a seesaw) and, 'inappropriately for the words', they kept bouncing one another up and down, which lent the whole scene a rather frivolous and very amusing character.

Eisenstein was excited. He could not but see these quasi-circus attractions in *The Forest* as the Teacher's response to his own *Wise Man*. And he would certainly have recognized in them the ropes, masts and springboards that would have featured in *Heartbreak House*: the great Master had slightly altered them, and given them legitimacy on the stage (a step back from the limit!), but he had not forgotten them.

In fact, by this time Eisenstein himself had taken a decisive step forward, and crossed the limit by undergoing the most important transformation of his life.

As early as March 1923, he had decided to include a special attraction in *Wise Man*: a 'cinematic sketch' in which Golutvin's scheme – the theft of a diary from the main character, Glumov – would be shown on the screen. This would be a parody of Méliès's *féeries* (fairy-tale films), which he had loved since childhood; of the Pathé company's news sensations; of the serial dealing with the criminal Fantômas; of the crime drama *Secrets of New York*; of Vertov's *Cinema Eye*.

Eisenstein approached Dziga Vertov for help. Vertov dispatched a cameraman, Boris Frantsisson, with a camera and some film. Eisenstein brought the actors to the courtyard of the General Staff Academy, which he had left for the theatre some two-and-a-half years previously. The actor Aleksandr Levshin, who had appeared in *Wise Man*, recounts:

> ***For a long time, during the shooting, he did not come up to the camera: he was shy, or scared, perhaps, and he trusted entirely to the magic art of the cameraman, B. Frantsisson. In the end, it was the cameraman himself who insisted that Eisenstein take a look through the lens himself. For the first time in his life, Sergei Mikhailovich came into direct contact with a ciné camera.***
>
> ***I cannot recall those moments, which were truly historic for the art of the cinema, without feeling profound excitement: Eisenstein's first approach to an instrument he would wield, like a magician, to bewitch audiences the world over....***
>
> ***The camera was mounted high on a tripod, and inclined at some fantastic angle. Eisenstein was a great artist, but he wasn't a tall man. We were worried for him, so we put a film box on top of the camera's case. Eisenstein clambered carefully atop this unsteady structure, and leant over the camera tripod....***
>
> ***We regarded this first approach of Eisenstein's to the film camera, at the cameraman's bidding, as a funny spectacle: he was 'poking his nose into somebody else's business'. And we were waiting to see what 'trick' he would use to get down. We watched it like an entertaining show, with mockery: would he fall down, or would he not?***
>
> ***But he literally hung from the tripod and looked [through] the eyepiece. Who could have foreseen that in that moment he was assisting at the mystery of a great change in cinematic art!***
>
> ***It's hard to say what Eisenstein saw through the lens that day....***[17]

Knowing what Eisenstein would do and write over the next twenty-five years of his artistic career, we can propose, with a high degree of likelihood, what might have taken place in his imagination during his long look through the viewfinder before shooting his first frame.

Before him was a *mechanism*, or something we might call *an acting machine*: a ciné camera. It had been invented quite recently, only twenty-eight years earlier, just three years before he himself was born, as a way of giving movement to the static art of photography. In those twenty-eight years, the Lumières' camera had conquered the whole world and had even forced its way onto Mount Parnassus, becoming the attribute of the Tenth Muse.

Instantly, and with a precision that was carried to the limit, the ciné camera recorded a moment that was seen, making it possible to fix either an instant one had noticed or else selected types in whole series – the way Rorik had once loved to draw, back in Riga. And every cell, every frame of the film that stretched into the bowels of the camera, was none other than a drawing made using light, or, if you prefer, an engraving on a light-sensory surface. The 'impression' did not at all have to be of chance material in chaotic form: in various countries, expressive *ciné graphic art* was taking shape.

At the same time, the cinema gave a new meaning to ideas that had attracted Sir Gay in turbulent, revolutionary Petrograd and in the small, quiet towns during the Civil War. Just as in the theatre of antiquity and the Middle Ages, acting here took place in the squares and the streets, the temples and the fields: it transformed the whole world into a stage. But did the lens of the ciné camera, moving from point to point around the action or driving into the middle of it, not become the eye of a free spectator of a mystery or a street farce, more than one inside a 'box' theatre – whether fixed to a seat or not?

Suddenly, Eisenstein's boldest fantasies from his Proletkult theatre days were becoming realistic. A real boxing match, not an imitation of one; bringing the action to the audience member at work, at home, at rest. And Cubism, too, was no longer a matter of stylized costumes, makeup and sets. It regained its original meaning. The cinema made it possible to see a thing or a process the way Picasso or Braque, Delaunay and Gris wanted to – from various points of view. It gave one the chance of analyzing its properties, introducing time into space and turning space into time, synthesizing a new unity in time and space, and mounting it, without losing the natural form of objects.

Even the radical third draft for *Heartbreak House*, wherein Eisenstein had carried Meyerhold's Constructivism to the limit, was given a new twist. In the cinema, the machinery was not subjected to the will of the actors so much as the other way around. What the actors did, and the spectacle itself, was determined by a highly complex mechanism that combined the achievements of stagecraft and technology.

What about the question of the footlights, the sacred boundary between spectacle and audience? Here there was a real paradox: the screen onto which the action was projected was like a materialization of Stanislavsky's fourth wall along the line of the footlights, and indeed of the whole 'mirror' of the stage, the imaginary wall that had not existed through the whole history of theatrical art and which had been subjected to criticism by the leftist theatre after the revolution. But the cinema was not the theatre, and the spectacle that the cinema-goer saw on that fabric stage was only real in part. In fact, there was no movement there, only a sequence of motionless light-engravings that flashed past in quick succession, so that they fused in the mysterious space of the viewer's imagination – and there, as Eisenstein had once dreamt, 'attract the field of associative elements of perception'. Or 'plough up the consciousness', as he would write after his first film, *Strike* (1924).

Of course, when he first touched a ciné camera he was not thinking about all these ideas, all this potential, all these paradoxes. He would reflect on them, and write about them, once he had gained experience as a cinema director. So far, all Eisenstein saw through the lens was an agglomeration of people and objects in real space, confined within a rectangular frame. And they needed to be composed into a composition, the lines of their movement defined, so that they turned into a ciné frame.

Perhaps it was at this very moment, thanks to God knows what effort of will and power of imagination, that Eisenstein reforged his instinct for drawing into clear lines of movement on the screen.

In early 1924, after his break with the Proletkult and with theatre in general, he would join the cinema – and effectively stop drawing.

In the next seven years, he would make four films, and shoot several thousand images for them. Each of them can be seen as another form of Eisenstein's graphic art.

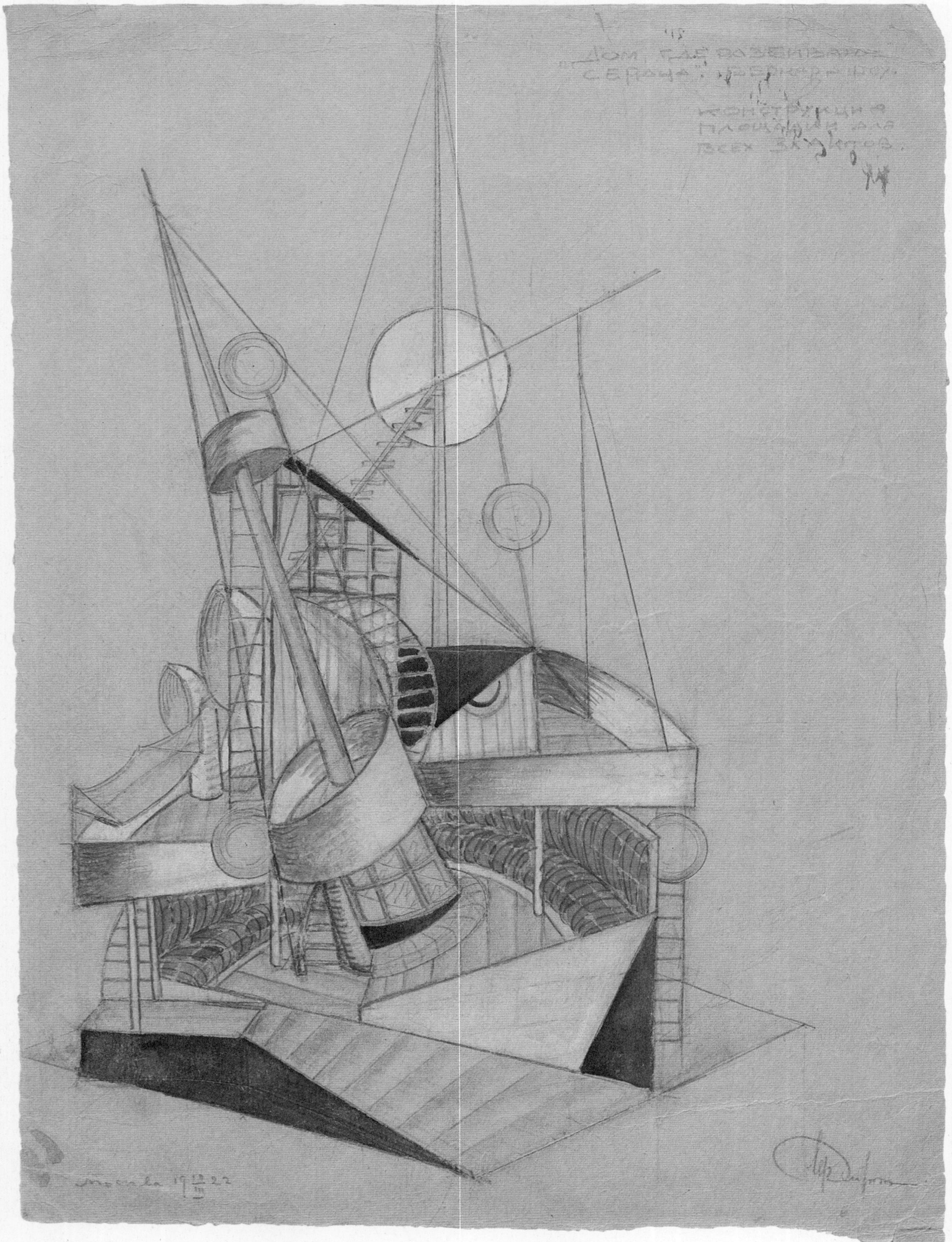

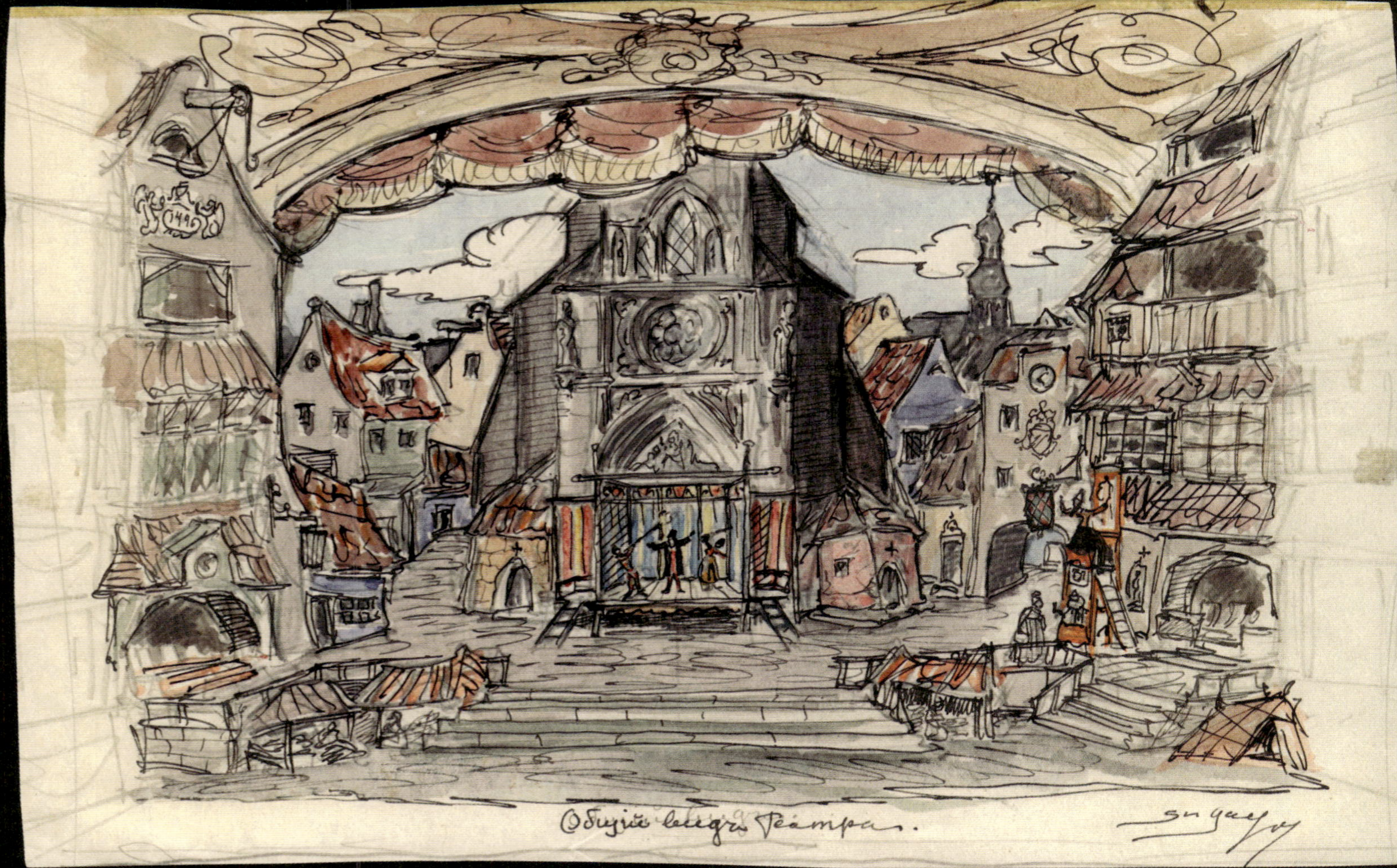
Общій видъ театра.

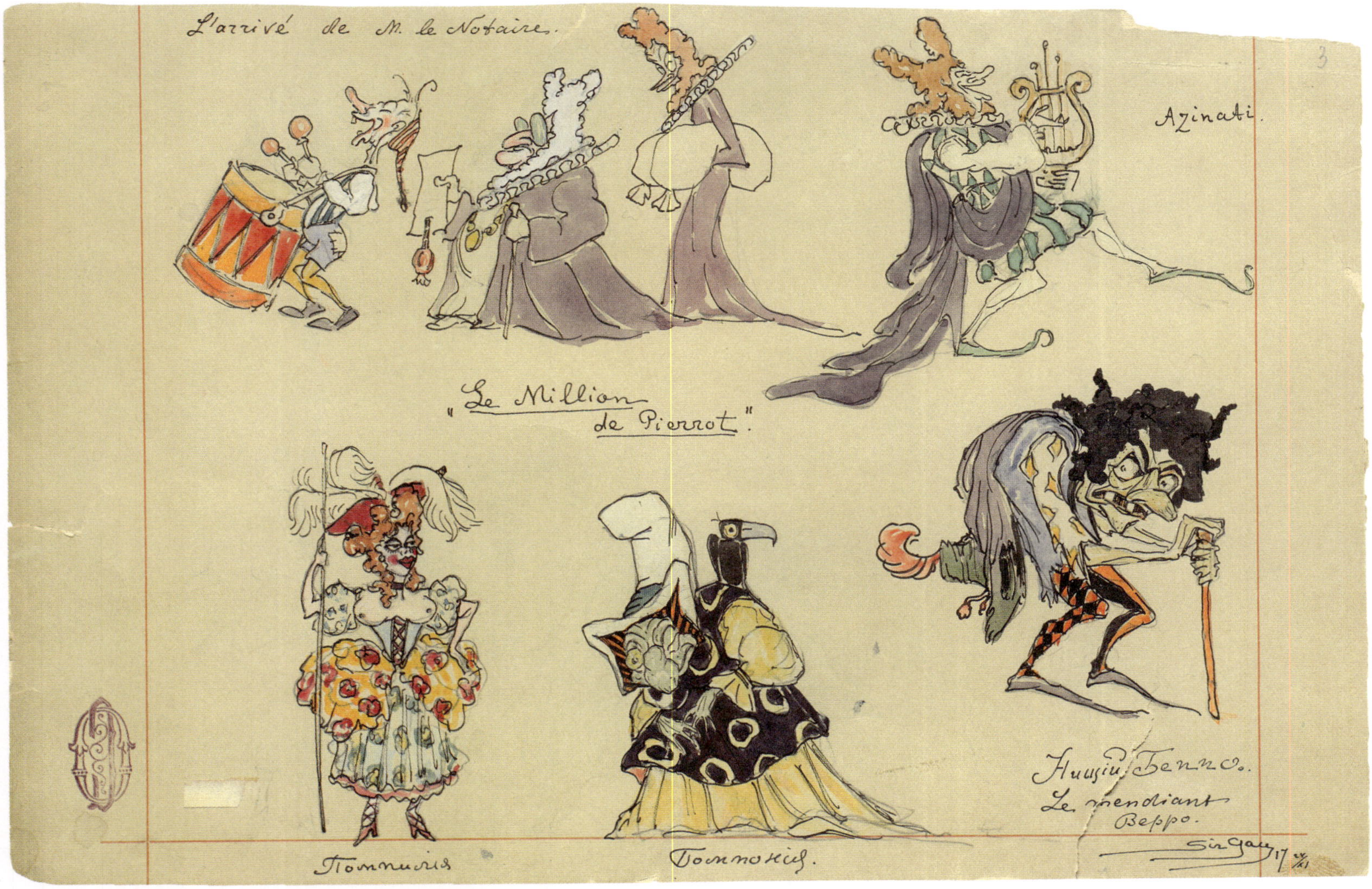
L'arrivé de M. le Notaire.
Azinati.
„Le Million de Pierrot".
Нищiй Беппо.
Le mendiant Beppo.
Помпилія
Бомбокія.
Sir Gay 17

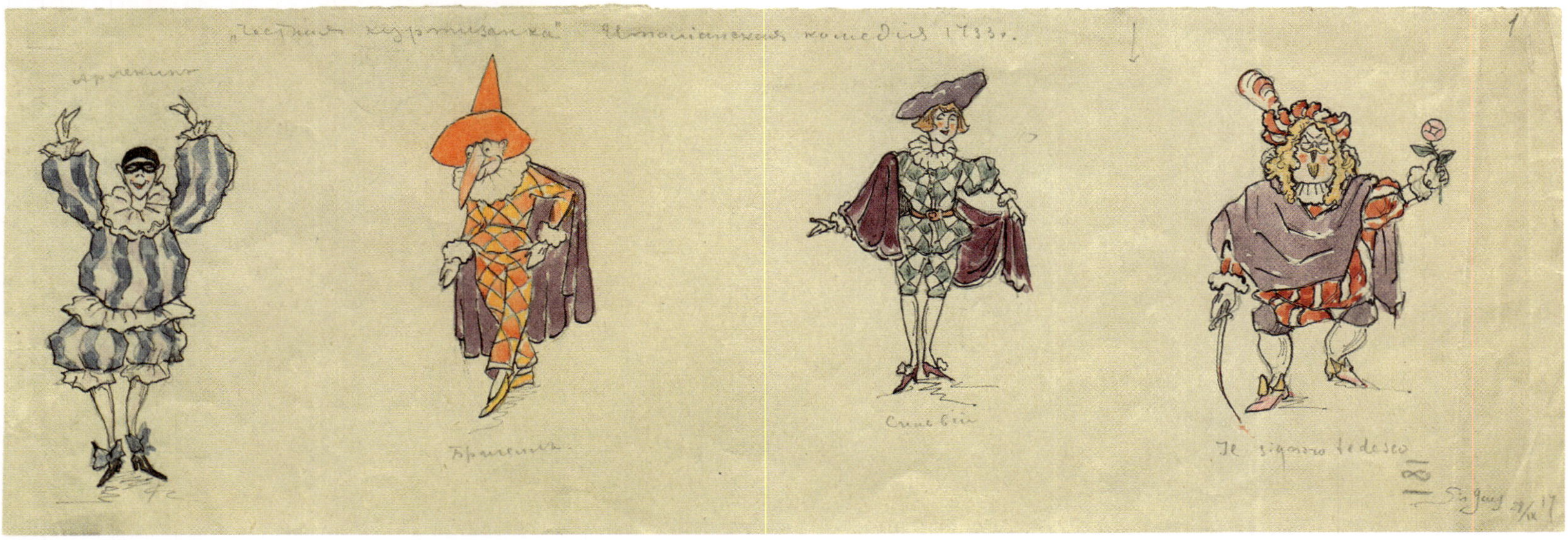
„Честная куртизанка" Италiанская комедiя 1733 г.
Il signore tedesco

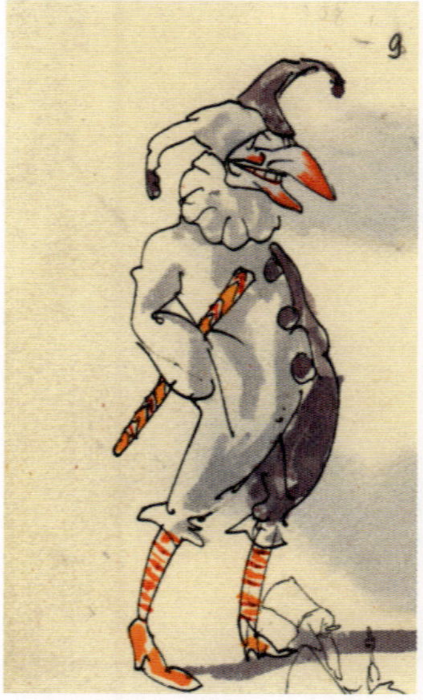

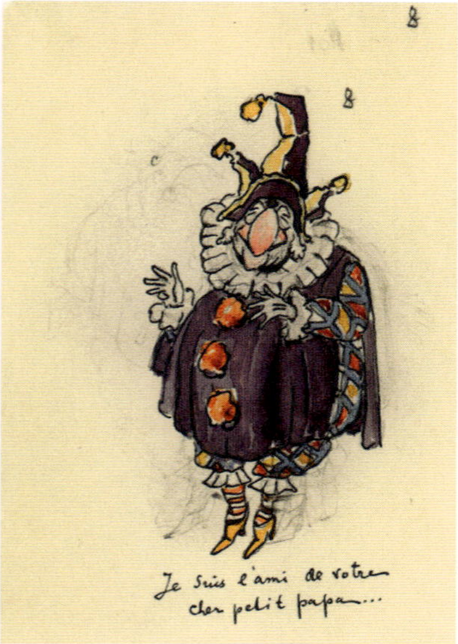

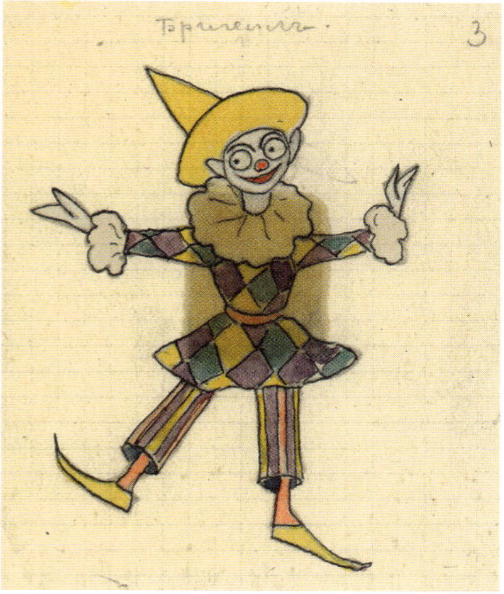

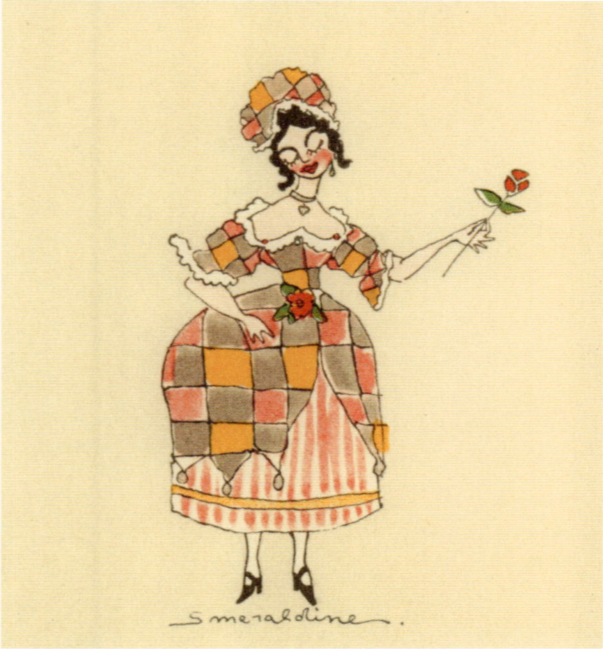

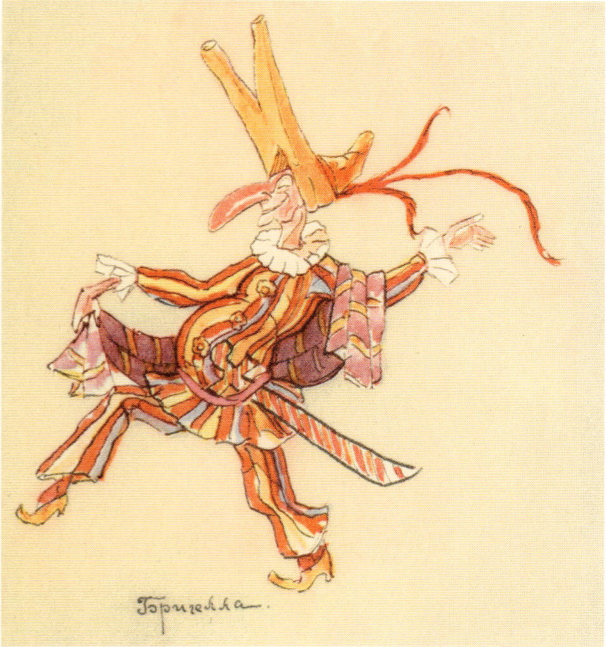

—PREVIOUS LEFT PAGE
The stage construction for all three acts of *Heartbreak House* by Bernard Shaw (2nd version, Moscow, 1922)

—PREVIOUS RIGHT PAGE
General view of the [Ancient] Theatre (Petrograd, 1917)

—OPPOSITE

TOP
Character drawings, *Le Million de Pierrot* (Pierrot's Millions) (Petrograd, 1917)
Text: *L'arrivé* [sic] *de M. le Notaire* (The arrival of the notary) – Azinati – Pompilia – Pomponia – *Le mendiant Beppo* (The Beggar Beppo)

BOTTOM
Commedia dell'arte masks for *La putta onorata* (The honorable maiden) (1733) (Petrograd, 1917)
Text: Harlequin – Brighella – Silvius – *Il signoro tedesco* (The German gentleman)

—THIS PAGE
Commedia dell'arte masks (Petrograd, 1917):

TOP LEFT
Pantalone

TOP CENTRE
Old Harlequin
Text: *Je suis l'ami de votre cher petit papa...* (I am your dear little papa's friend)

TOP RIGHT
Young Brighella

BOTTOM LEFT
Smeraldina

BOTTOM RIGHT
Old Brighella

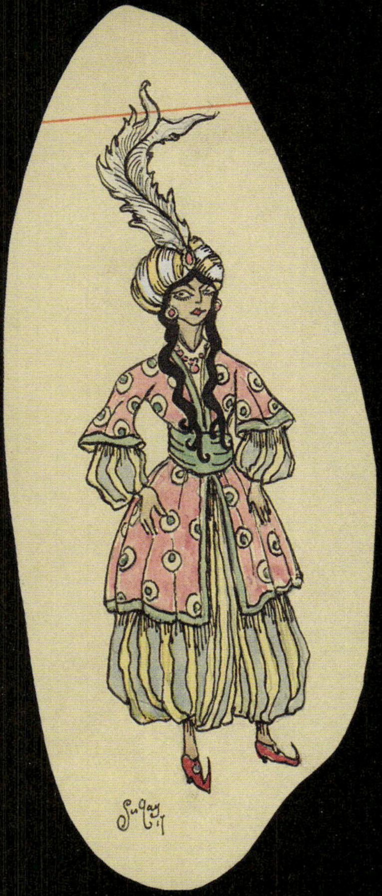

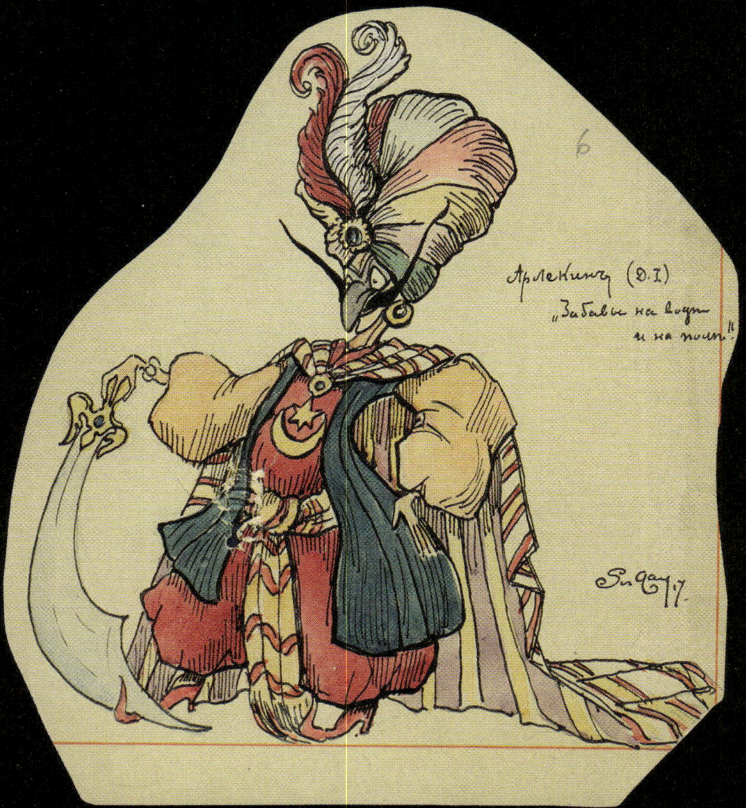
Арлекинъ (Д.I)
„Забавы на воде
и на поле!“

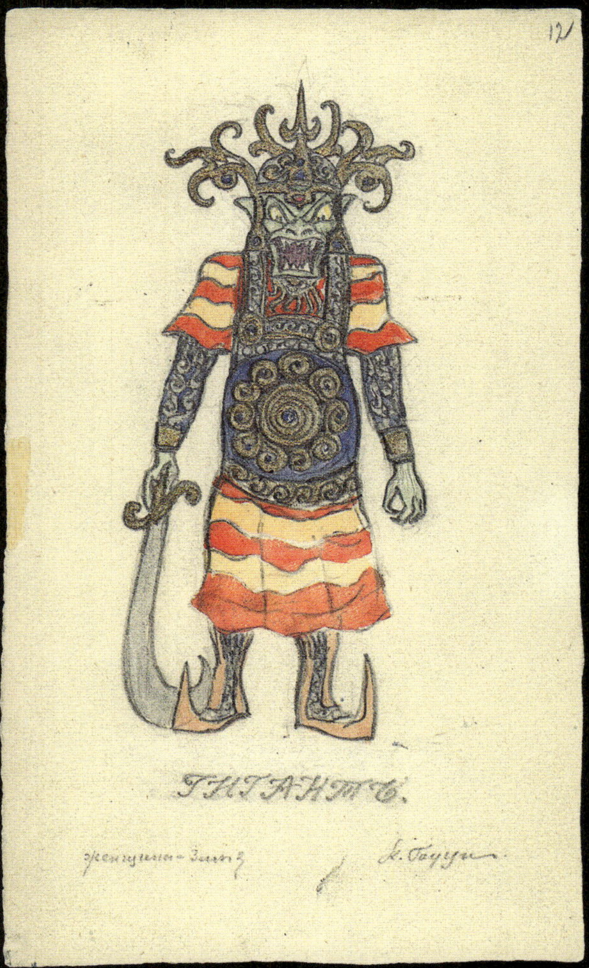
Гигантъ.
Женщина-Змея
К. Гоцци

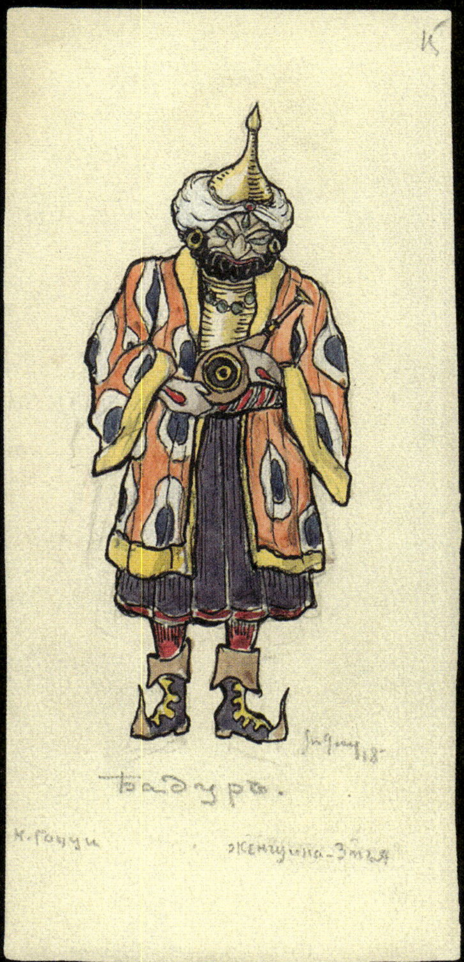
Бадуръ.
К. Гоцци
Женщина-Змея

—OPPOSITE

TOP LEFT
Smeraldina, from the comedy *Fun on the Water and on the Field* (anon, 1734) (Petrograd, 1917)

TOP RIGHT
Harlequin, from *Fun on the Water and on the Field* (1734) (Petrograd, 1917)

BOTTOM LEFT
Giant, from the extravaganza *La Donna-Serpente* (The serpent woman) by Carlo Gozzi (Petrograd, 1918)

BOTTOM RIGHT
Badur, from the extravaganza *La Donna-Serpente* by Carlo Gozzi (Petrograd, 1918)

—THIS PAGE
General view of the proscenium for *La Donna-Serpente*, the curtain arrangement (for the small stage on the stage) and a costume sketch for a servant (Petrograd, 1918)

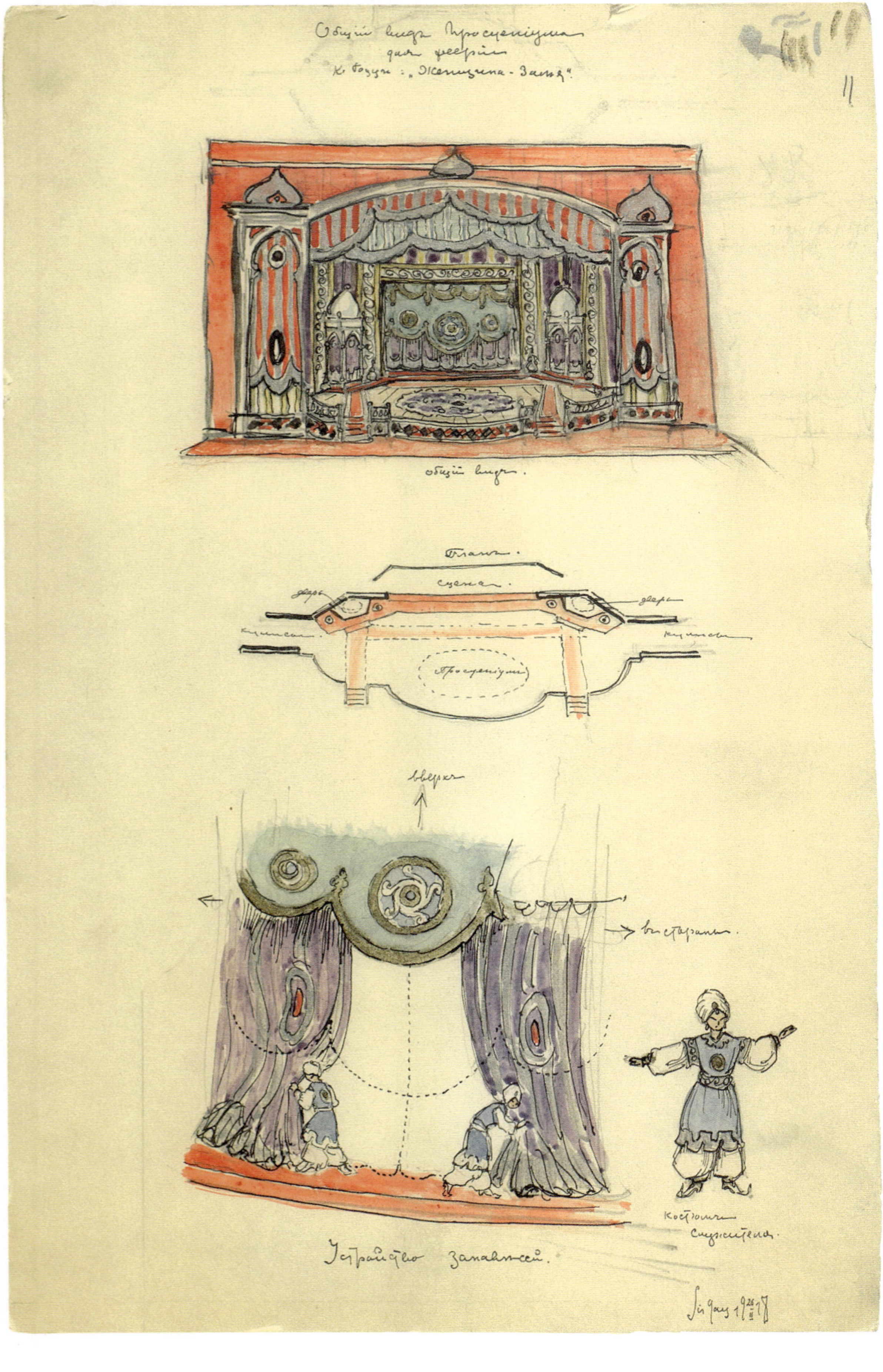

RIGHT
'Comedy of power' (Queen Isabella)
The Government of the Rebellious Citizens (Kholm, 1919)

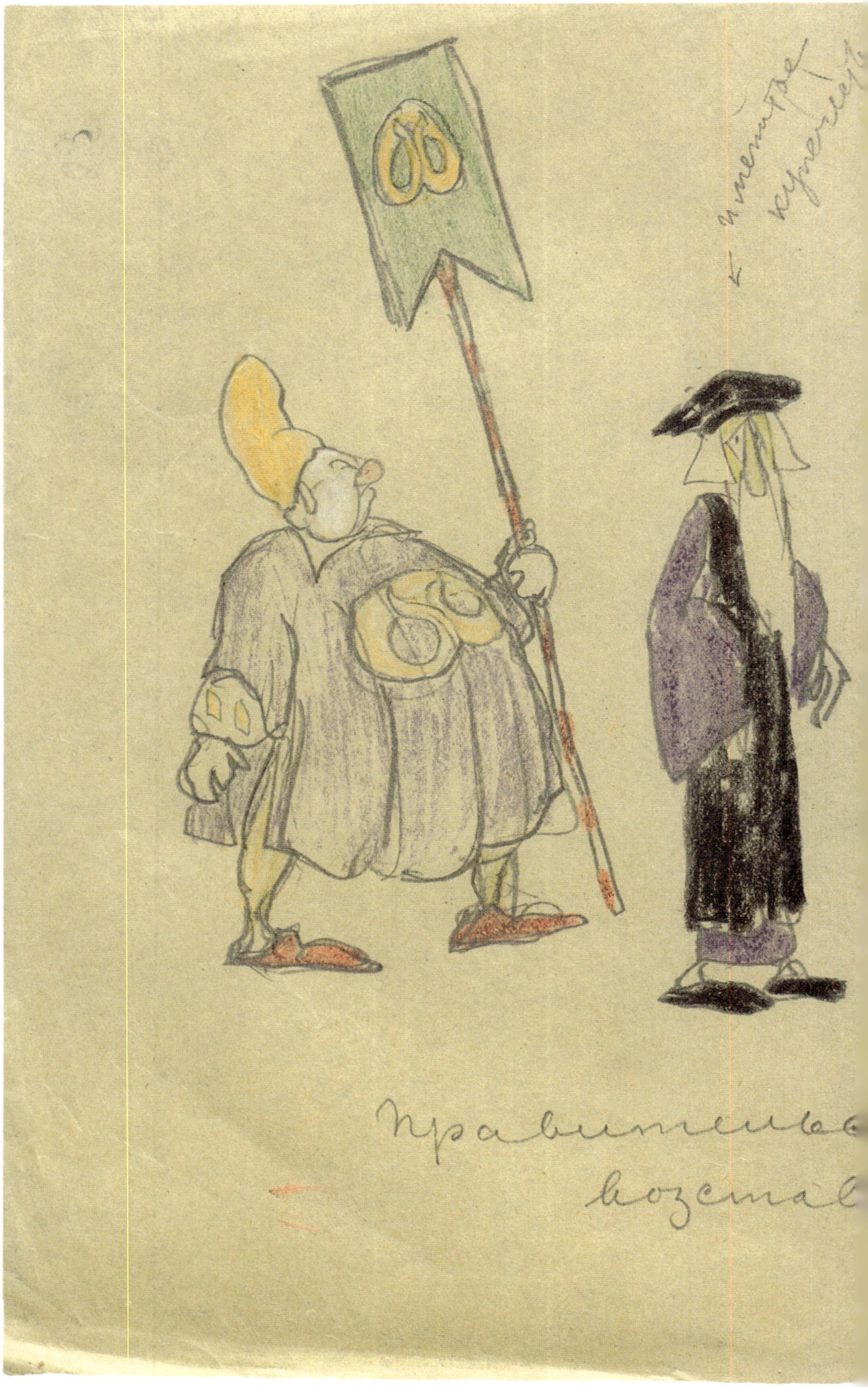

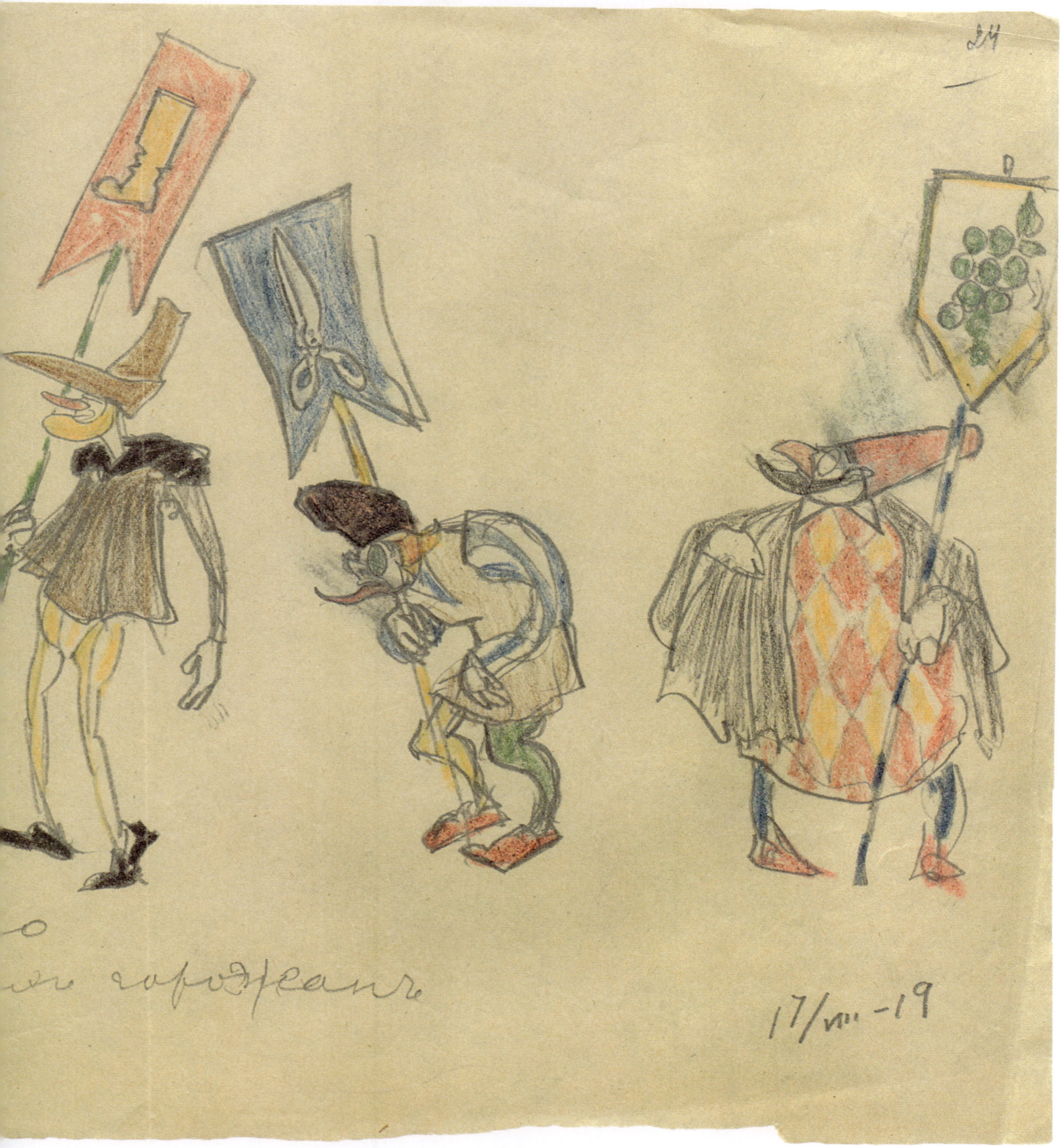

—THIS PAGE

Characters from the miracle play *Queen Theodora* (Dvinsk, 1919):

TOP LEFT

La Reine Theodora

TOP RIGHT

Knight

BOTTOM LEFT

Youth

BOTTOM RIGHT

Le Mari de la Reine Theodora (Queen Theodora's husband)

—OPPOSITE

TOP

Scenery and costume sketch for *Moralité de L'Empereur Qui Tua Son Neveu* (XIVth Siècle) (Moral story of the emperor who killed his nephew) (1920)

BOTTOM

L'Abesse Grosse, mansion for 'The Miracles of Notre Dame' (1919)

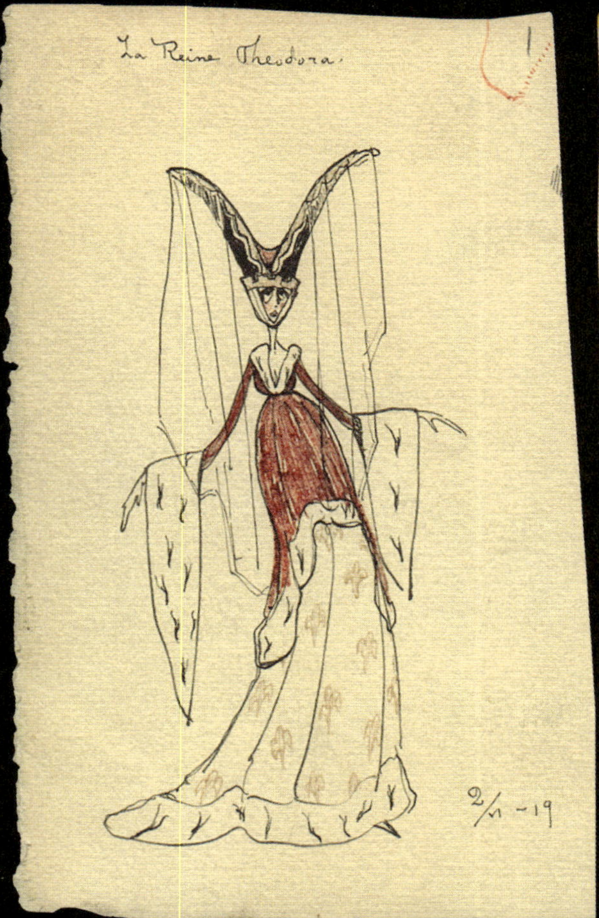

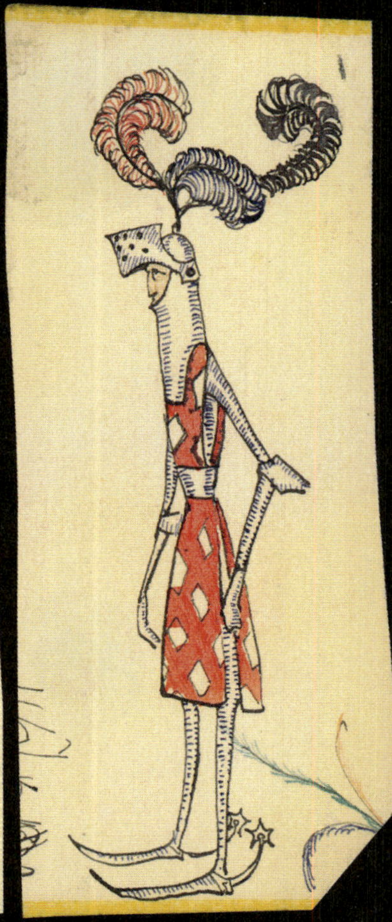

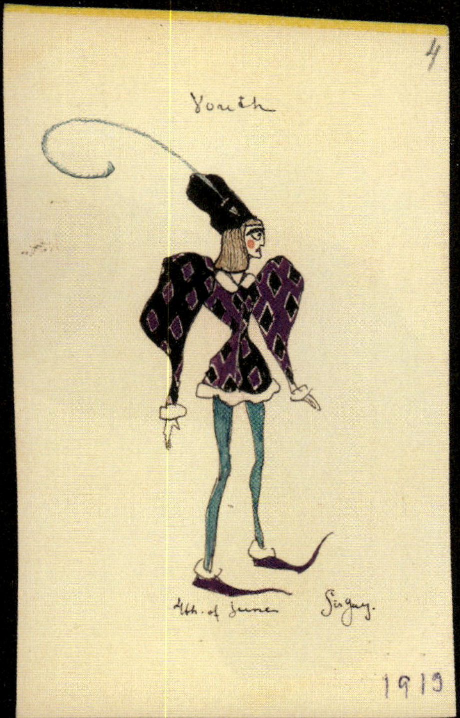

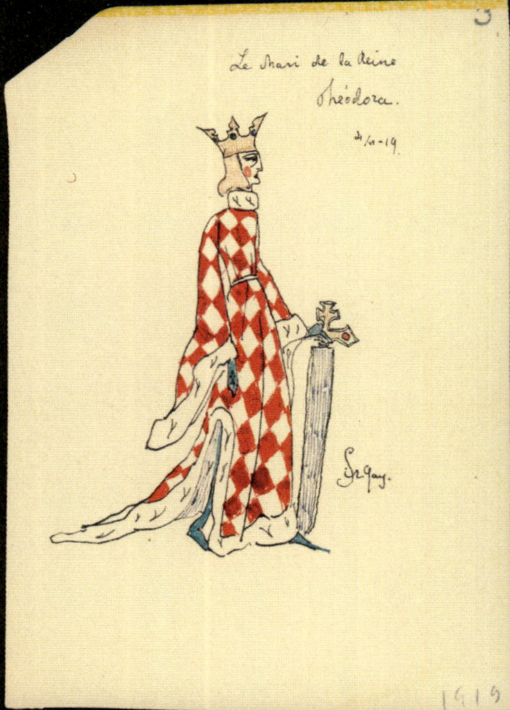

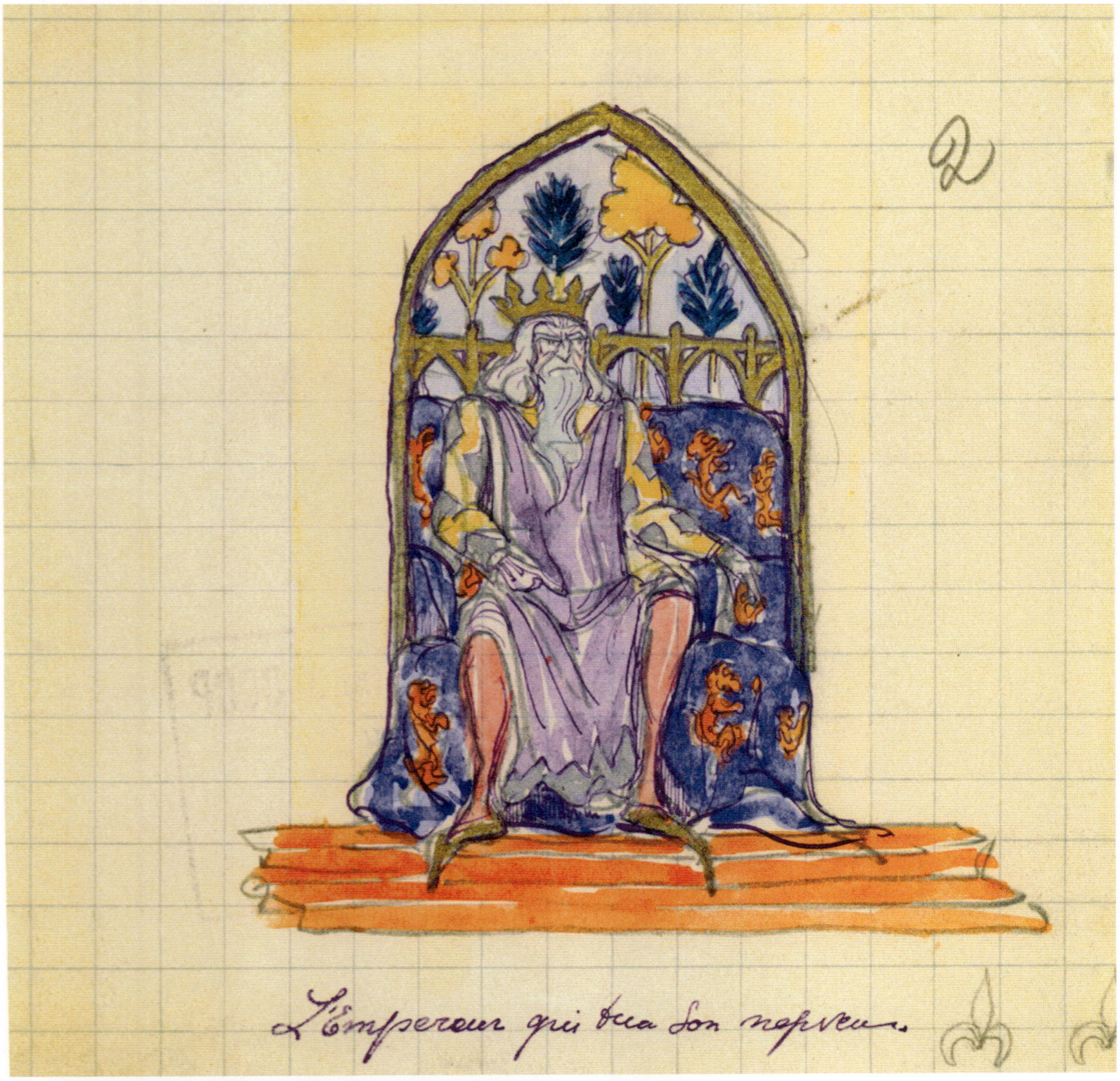
2
L'Empereur qui tua son neveu.

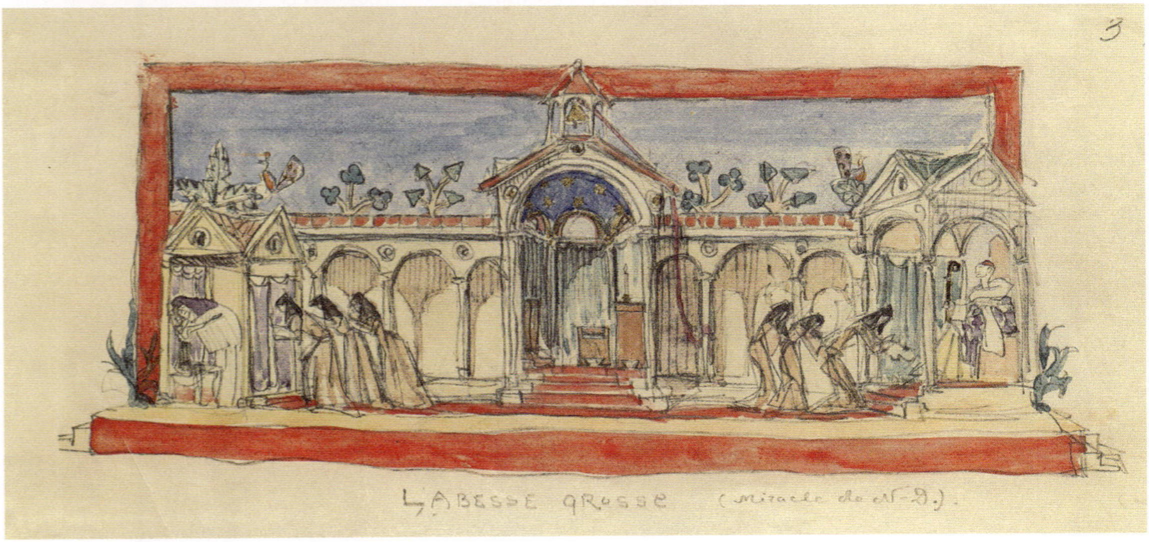
3
L'ABESSE GROSSE

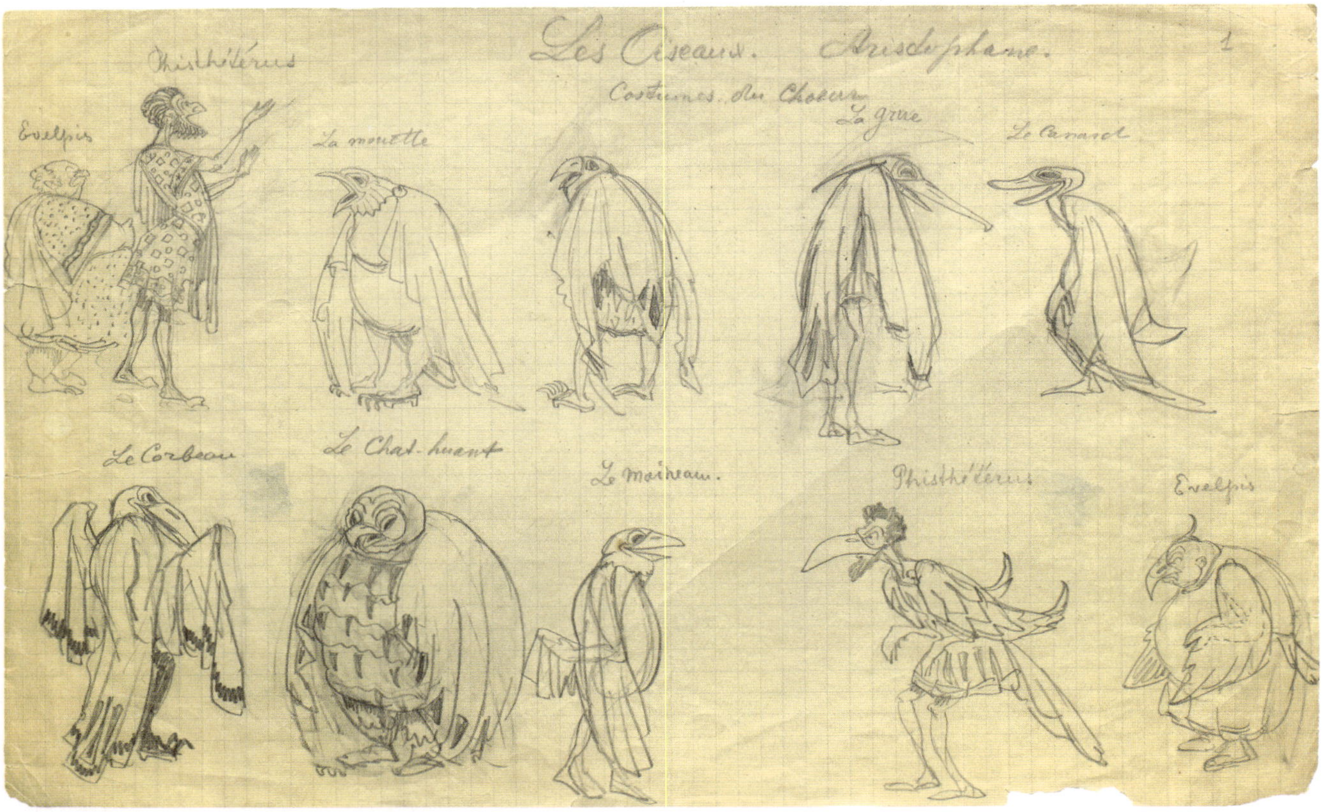

Les Oiseaux. Aristophane.
1
Costumes du Choeur
Evelpis
Pisthétérus
La mouette
La grue
Le Canard
Le Corbeau
Le Chat-huant
Le moineau
Pisthétérus
Evelpis

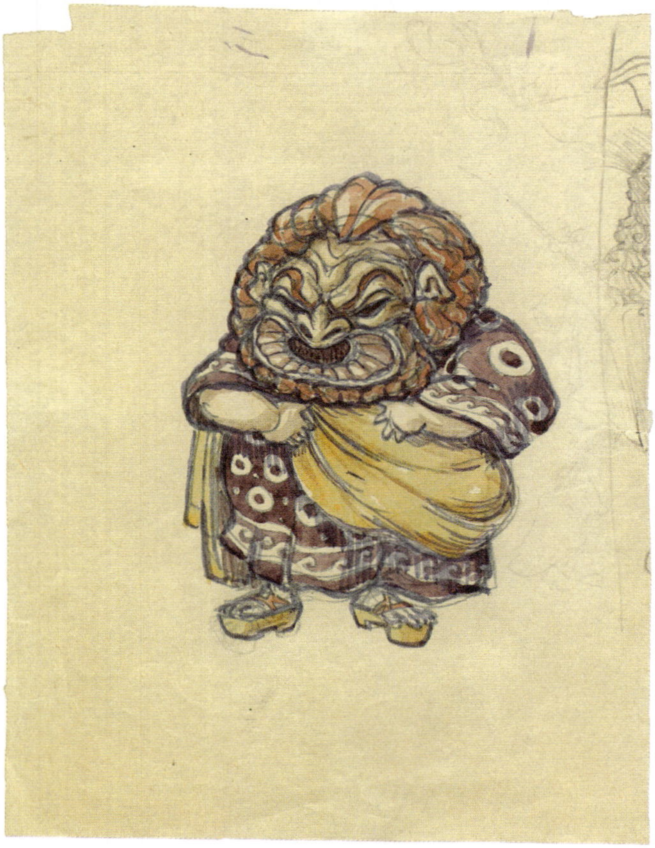

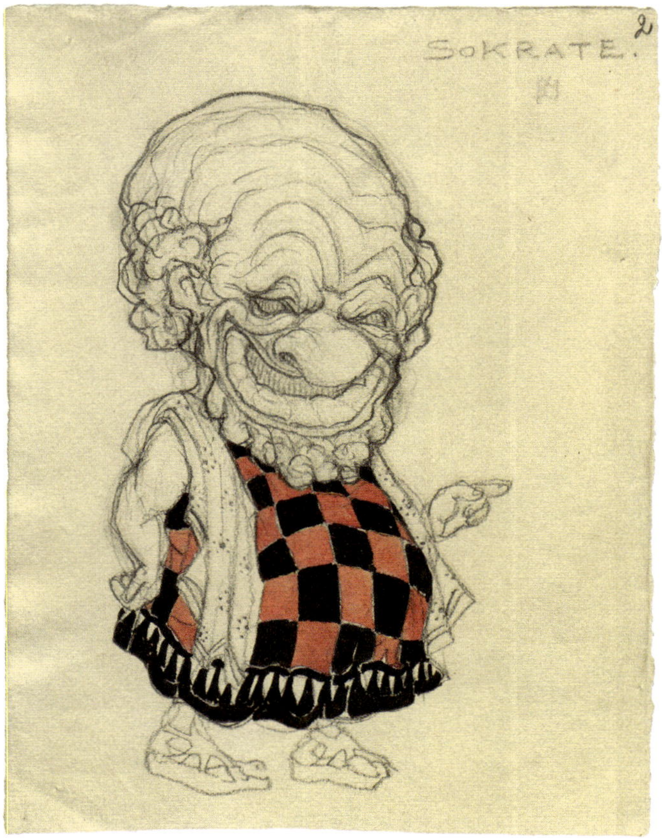

SOKRATE.
2

5

STREPSIADE.

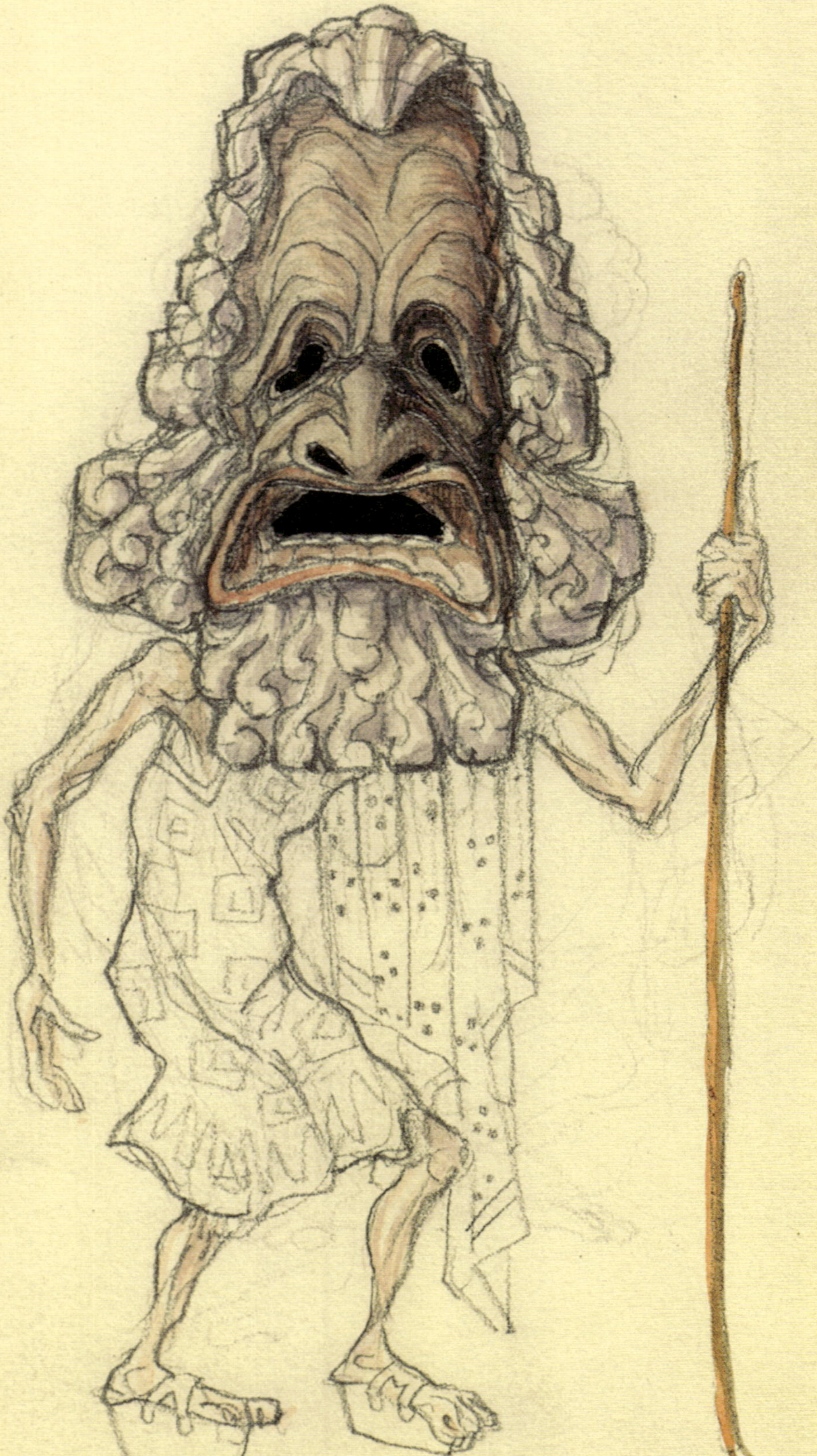

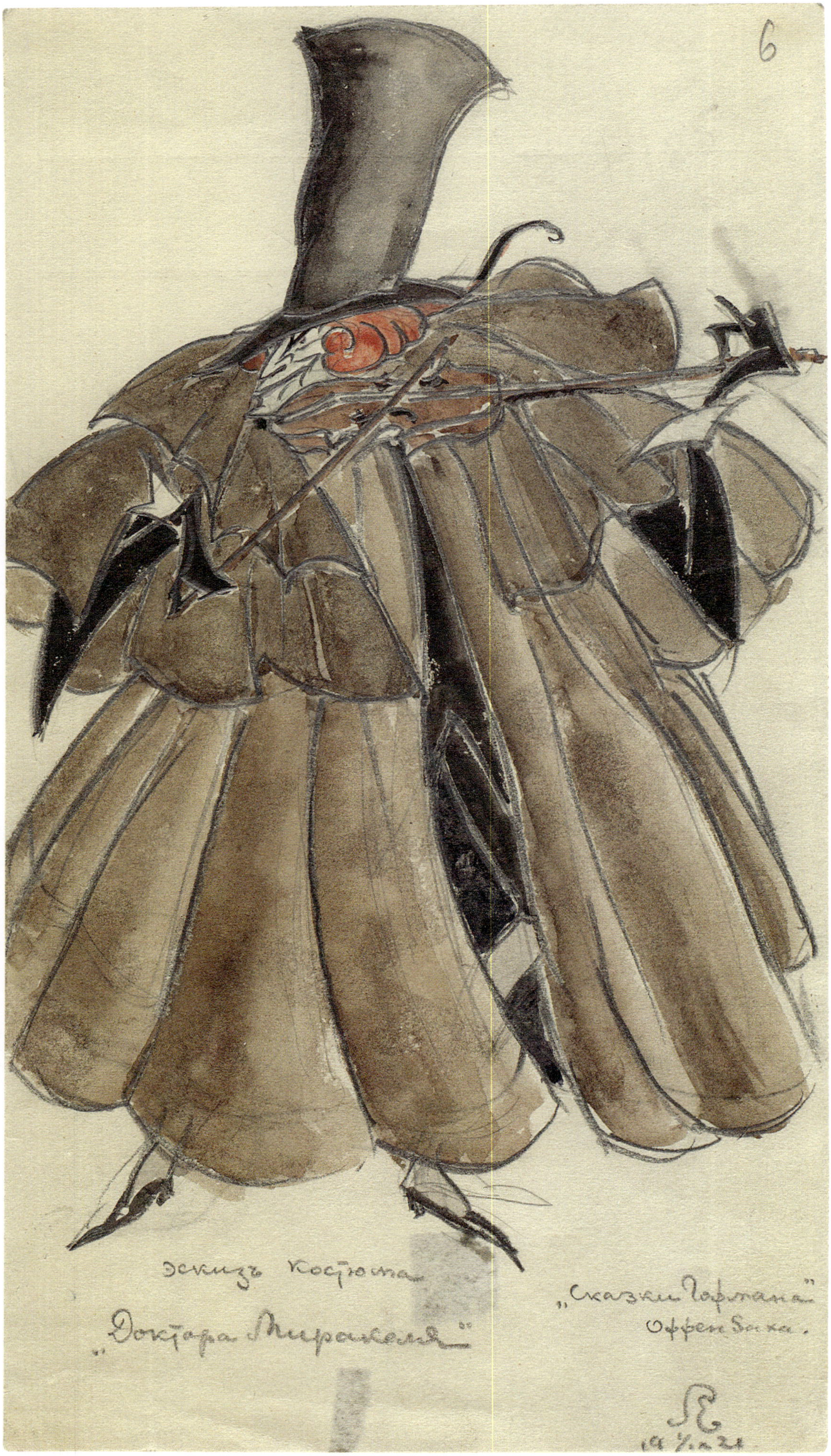
6
Эскизъ костюма
„Доктора Миракеля"
„Сказки Гофмана"
Offenbaха.

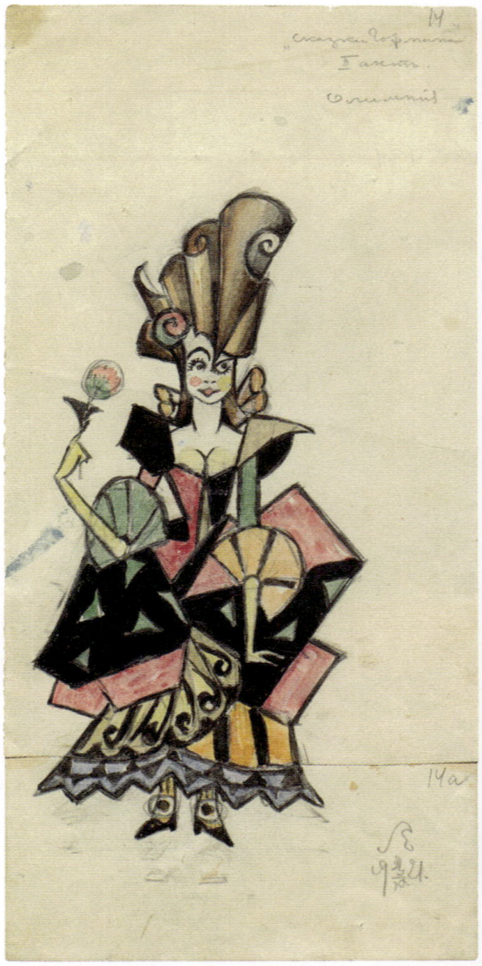

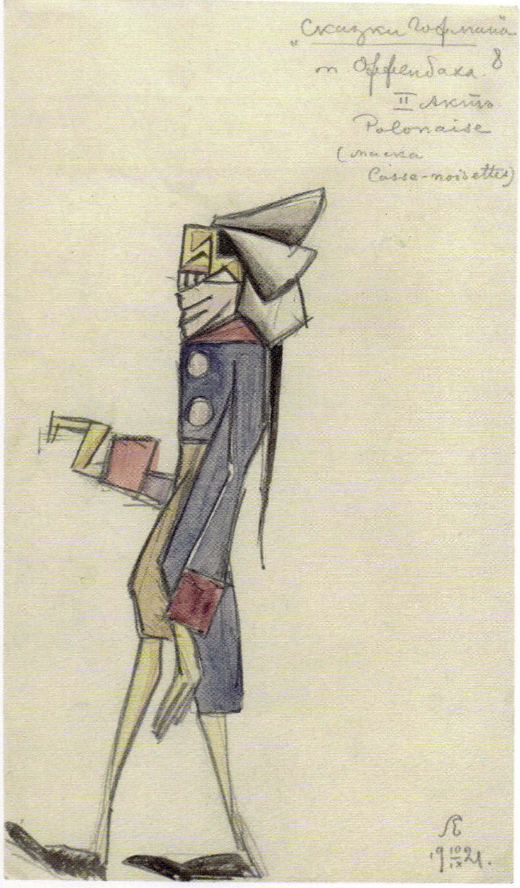

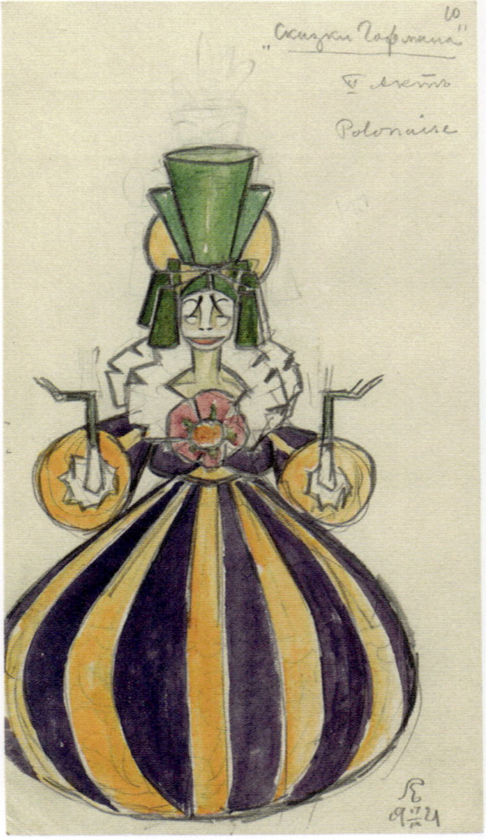

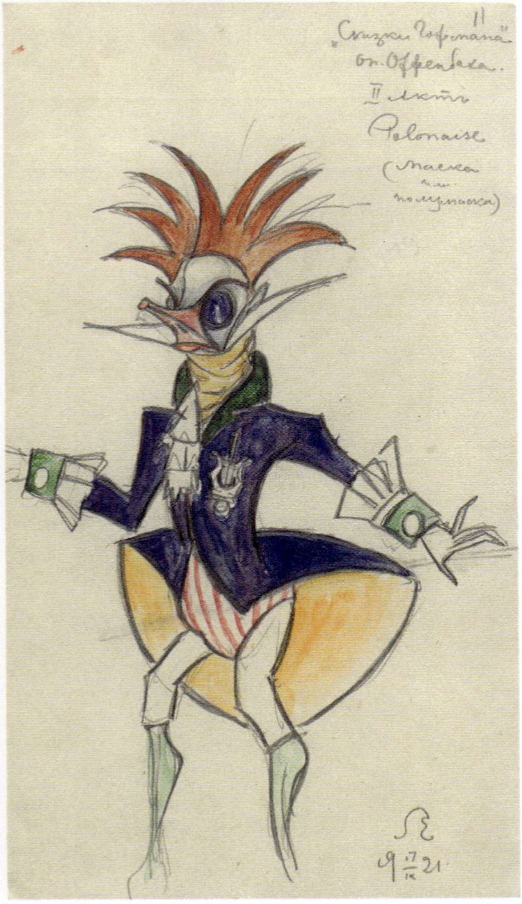

—PREVIOUS LEFT PAGE

TOP
Costumes for the comedy *The Birds* by Aristophanes (Dvinsk, June 1918)

BOTTOM LEFT
'Antique comedy mask'

BOTTOM RIGHT
The mask of Socrates for the comedy *The Clouds* by Aristophanes (1919)

—PREVIOUS RIGHT PAGE
The mask of Strepsiades for *The Clouds* by Aristophanes (1919)

—OPPOSITE
Costume for Doctor Miracle (Dr Dapertutto) for *The Tales of Hoffmann* by Jacques Offenbach (Moscow, 1921)

—THIS PAGE
Characters from *The Tales of Hoffmann* by Jacques Offenbach:

TOP LEFT
Olympia (1921)

TOP RIGHT
Nutcracker (1921)

BOTTOM LEFT
Polonaise, Act V (1921)

BOTTOM RIGHT
Polonaise, Act II, Mask or Half-Mask (1921)

—THIS PAGE
Characters from *Dawn of the Proletkult* by V. Ignatov (Moscow, 1921):

TOP LEFT
A Peasant

TOP RIGHT
Head of the Punitive Squad

BOTTOM LEFT
Masks for the Second Act, Pope

BOTTOM RIGHT
Masks for the Second Act, Pedagog

—OPPOSITE
Costume and mask for Capital from *Dawn of the Proletkult* by V. Ignatov (Moscow, 1921)

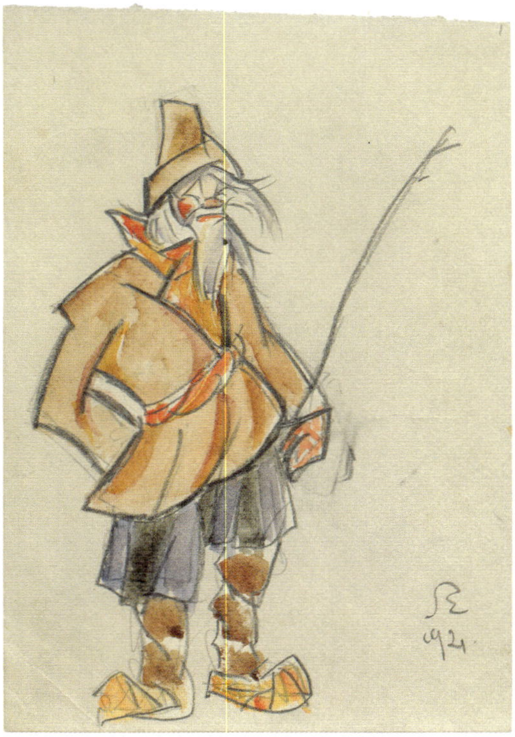

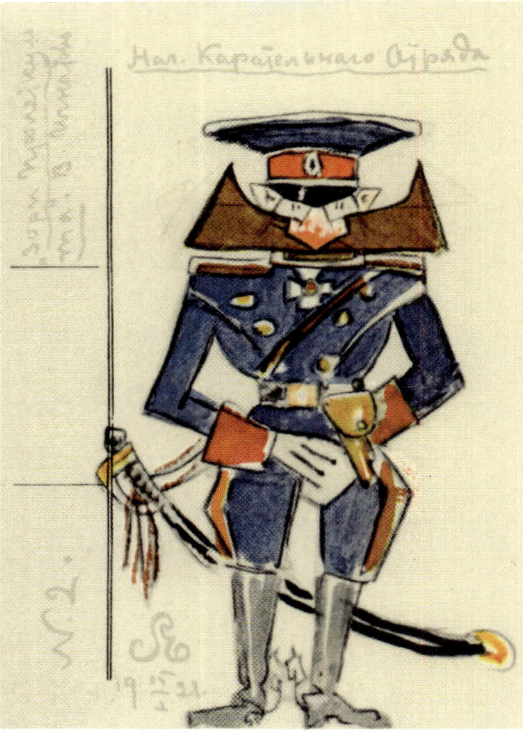

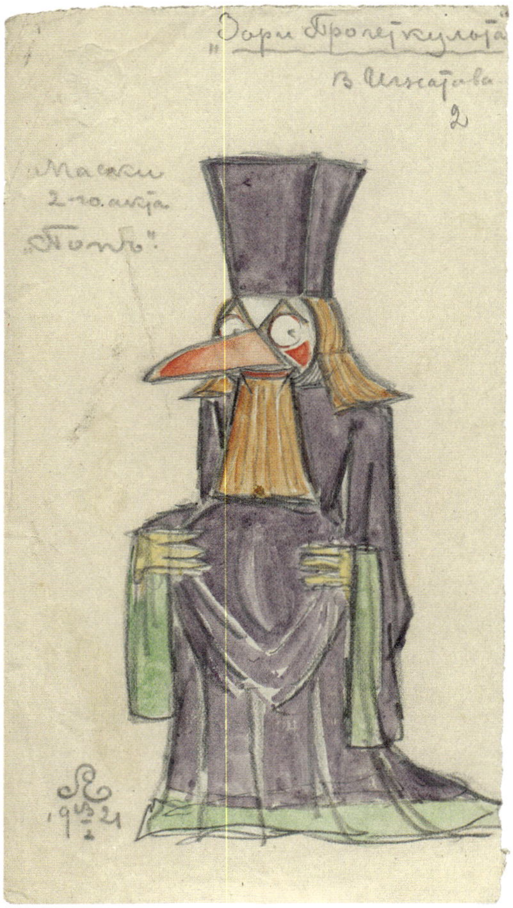

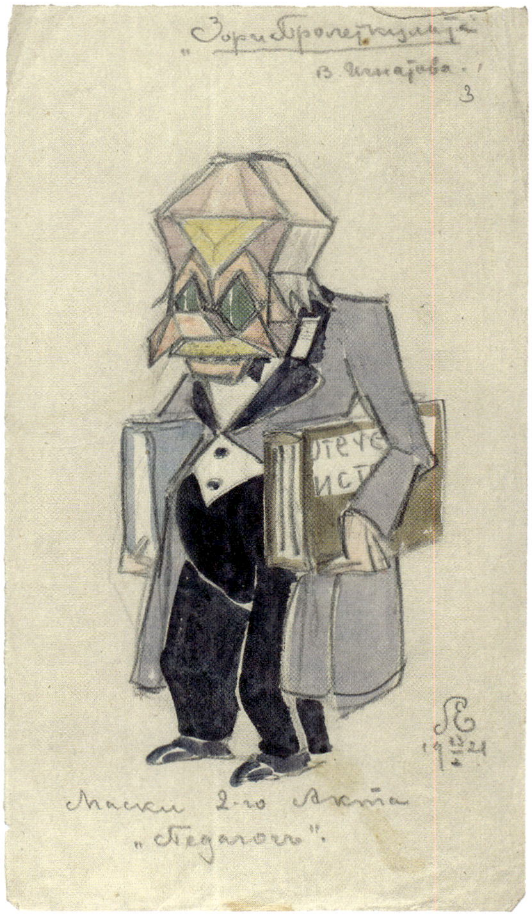

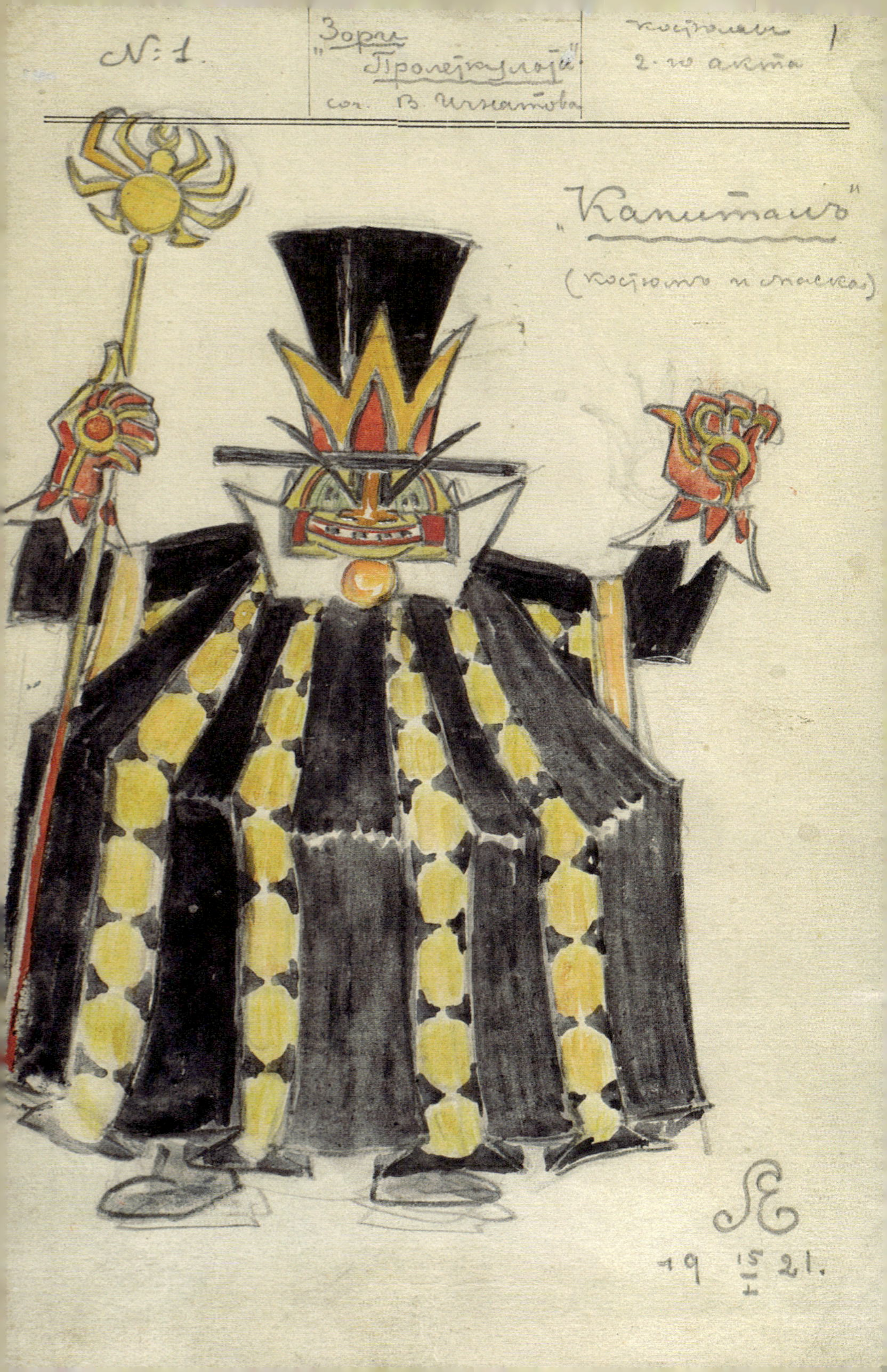

№ 1.
Зори
"Пролеткульта"
соч. В. Игнатова
костюмы 2-го акта
1
"Капиталъ"
(костюмъ и маска)
19 15/I 21.

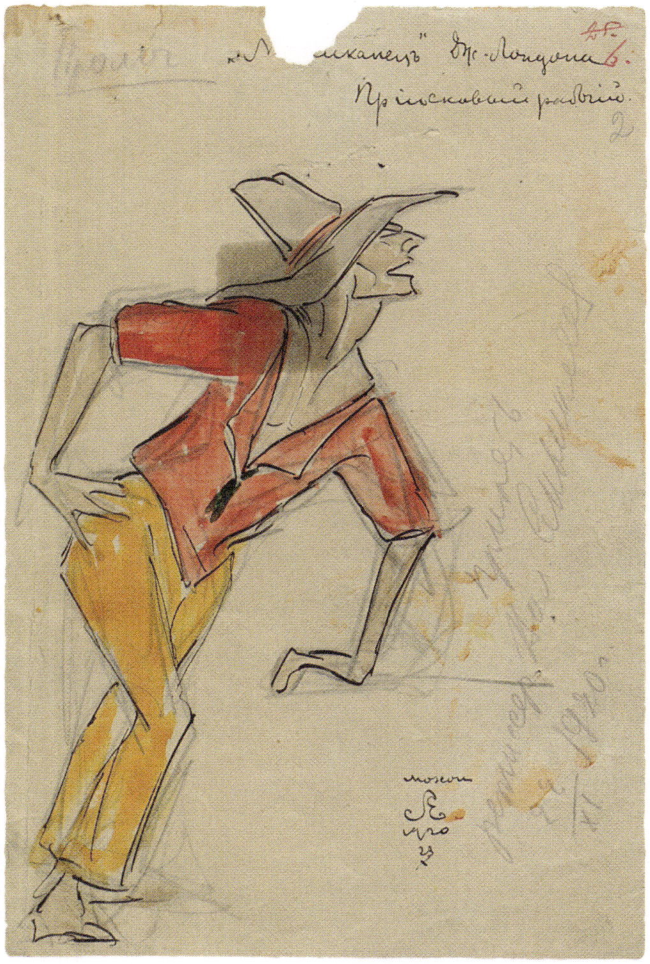
„Мексиканецъ" Дж. Лондона

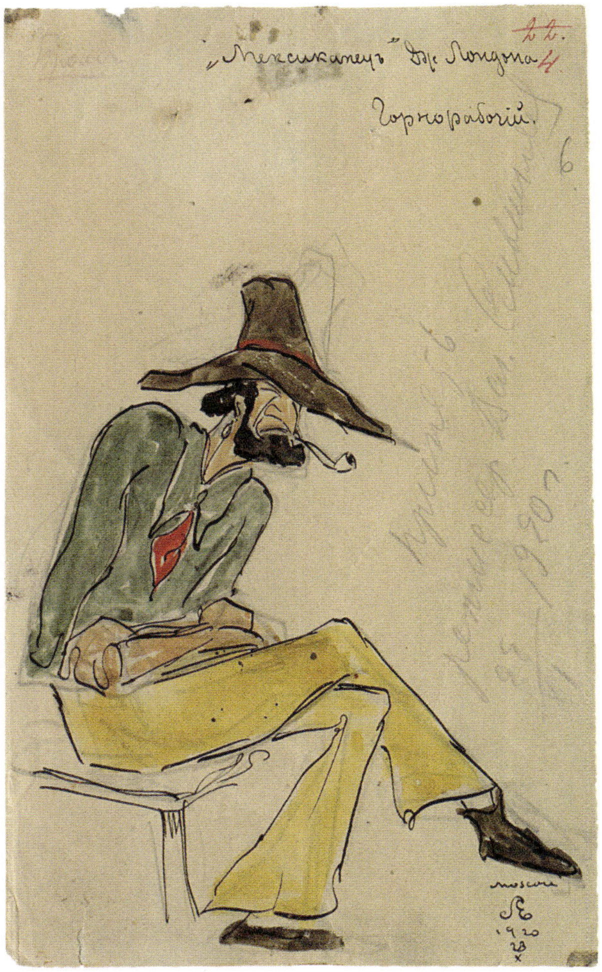
„Мексиканецъ" Дж. Лондона
Горнорабочій

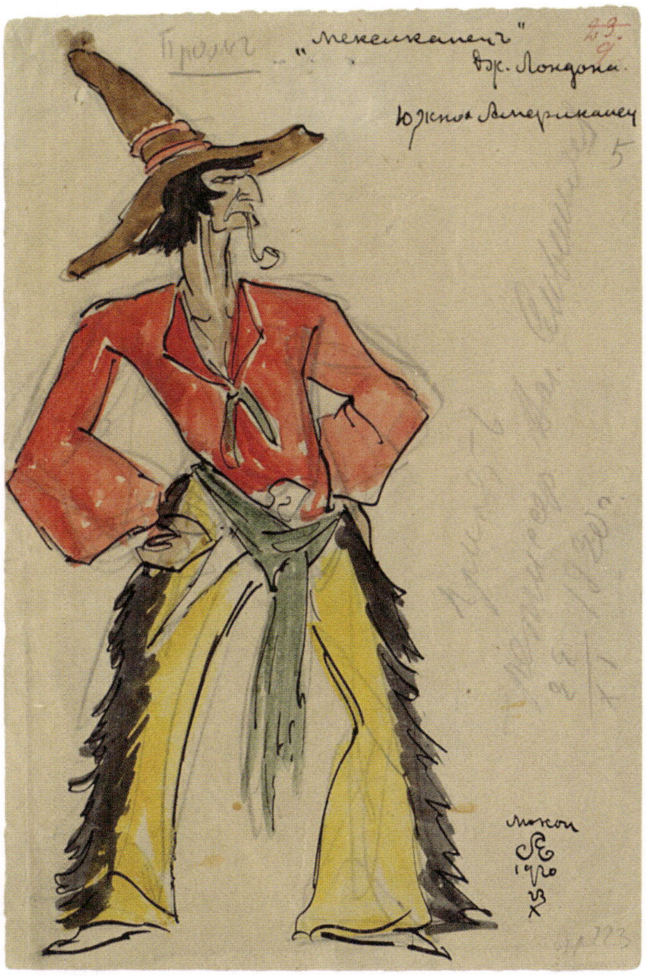
„Мексиканецъ"
Дж. Лондона

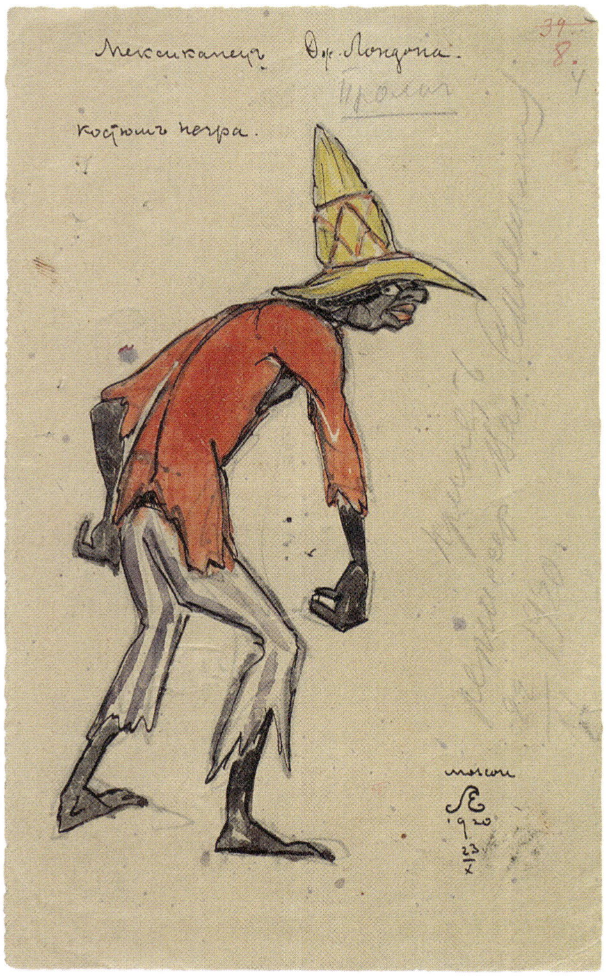
Мексиканецъ Дж. Лондона
костюмъ негра

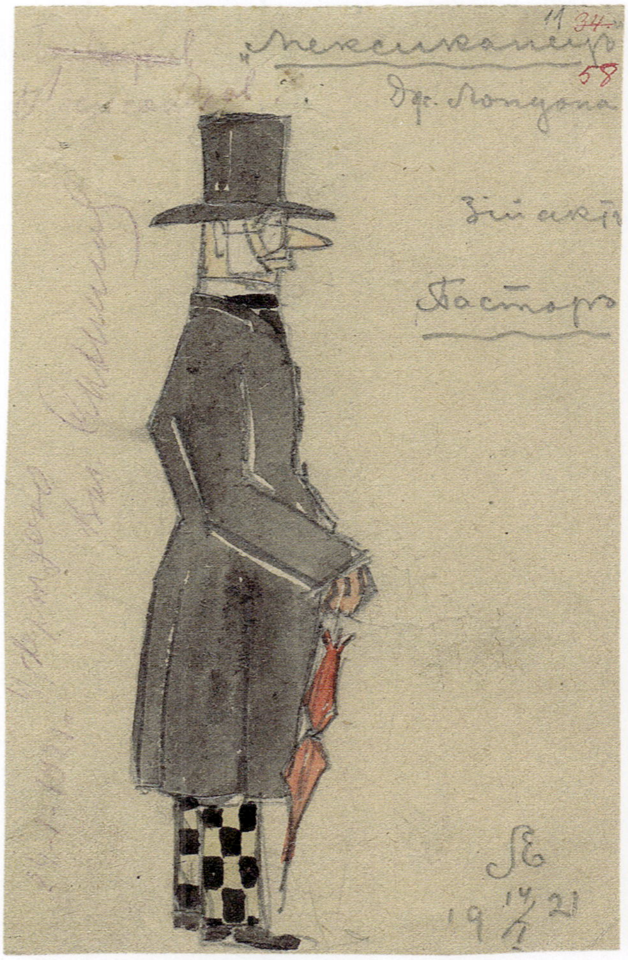

"Мексиканецъ"
Дж. Лондона
3й актъ
Пасторъ

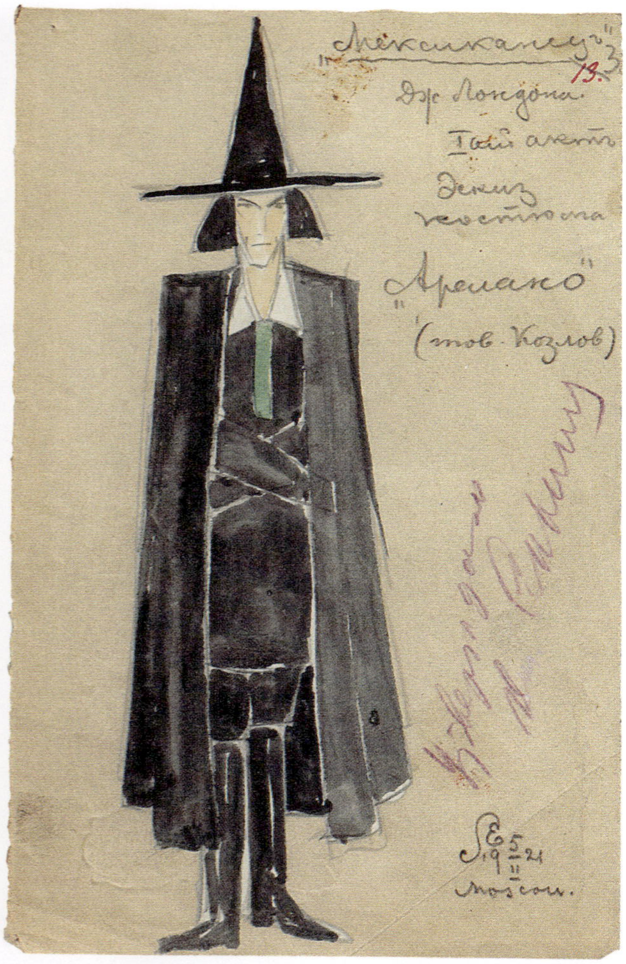

"Мексиканецъ"
Дж. Лондона
I-ый актъ
Эскиз костюма
"Арелано"
(тов. Козлов)
Moscou.

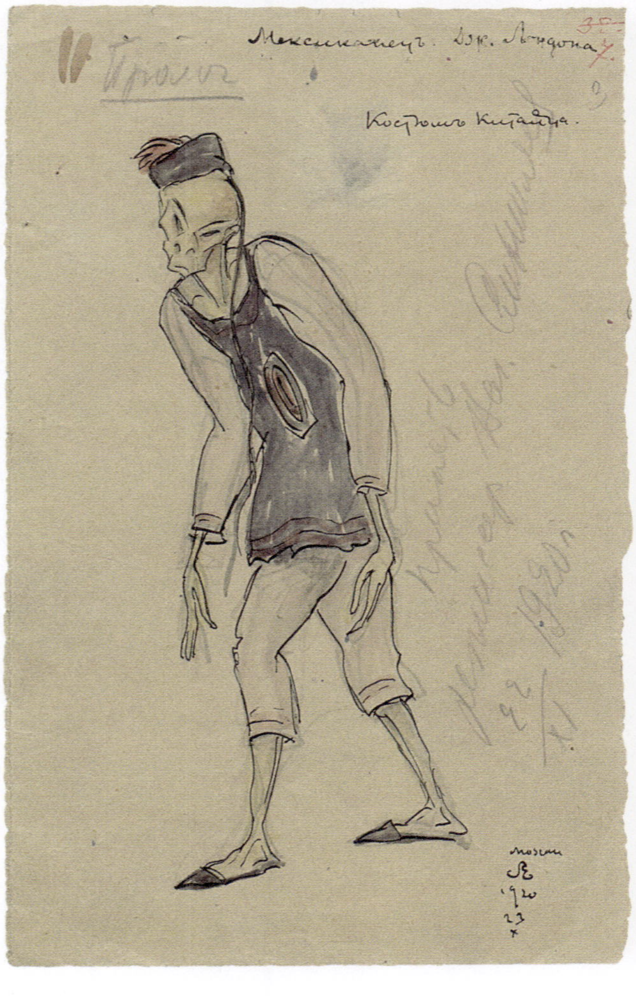

Мексиканецъ. Дж. Лондона
Прологъ
Костюмъ Китайца.

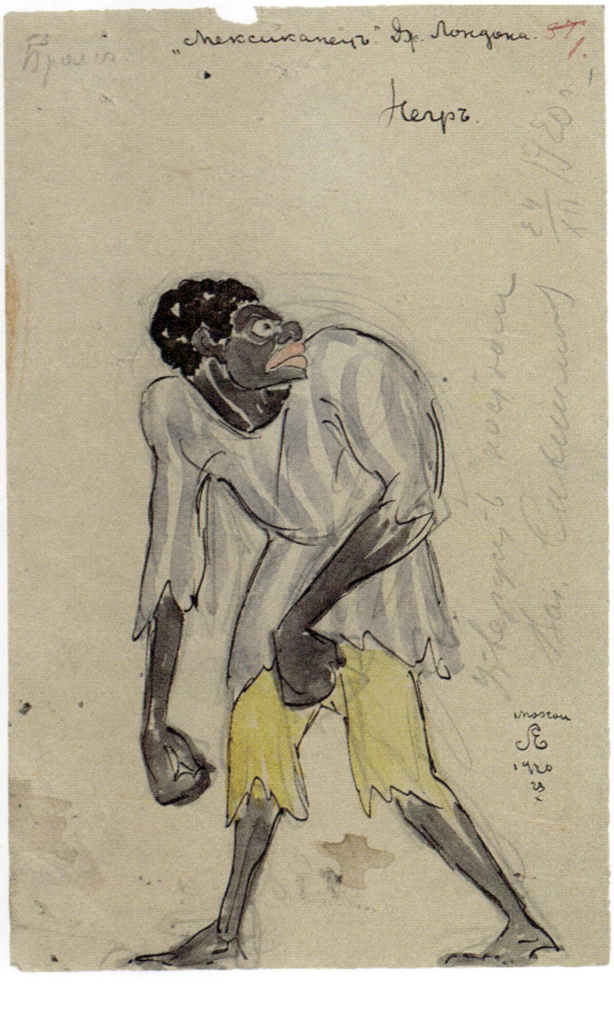

"Мексиканецъ" Дж. Лондона
Прологъ
Негръ.

—PREVIOUS LEFT PAGE

Typages in the crowd from *The Mexican* (after a story by Jack London) (Central Arena of Proletkult, Moscow, 1920–21):

TOP LEFT
The Gold Digger (1920)

TOP RIGHT
The Miner (1920)

BOTTOM LEFT
The South American (1920)

BOTTOM RIGHT
Negro (Prologue) (1920)

—PREVIOUS RIGHT PAGE

Typages in the crowd from *The Mexican* (after a story by Jack London) (Central Arena of Proletkult, Moscow, 1920–21):

TOP LEFT
Pastor (1921)

TOP RIGHT
Arelano (1921)

BOTTOM LEFT
Chinaman (1920)

BOTTOM RIGHT
Negro (1920)

—THIS PAGE

Set design for the first act of *The Mexican* (sketch of the definitive variant): *The Meeting of the Revolutionary 'Junta'* (1921)

—OPPOSITE

Greasepaint of characters in *The Mexican*:

LEFT
Maïkail (1921)

RIGHT
The Souteneur (Pimp) (1921)

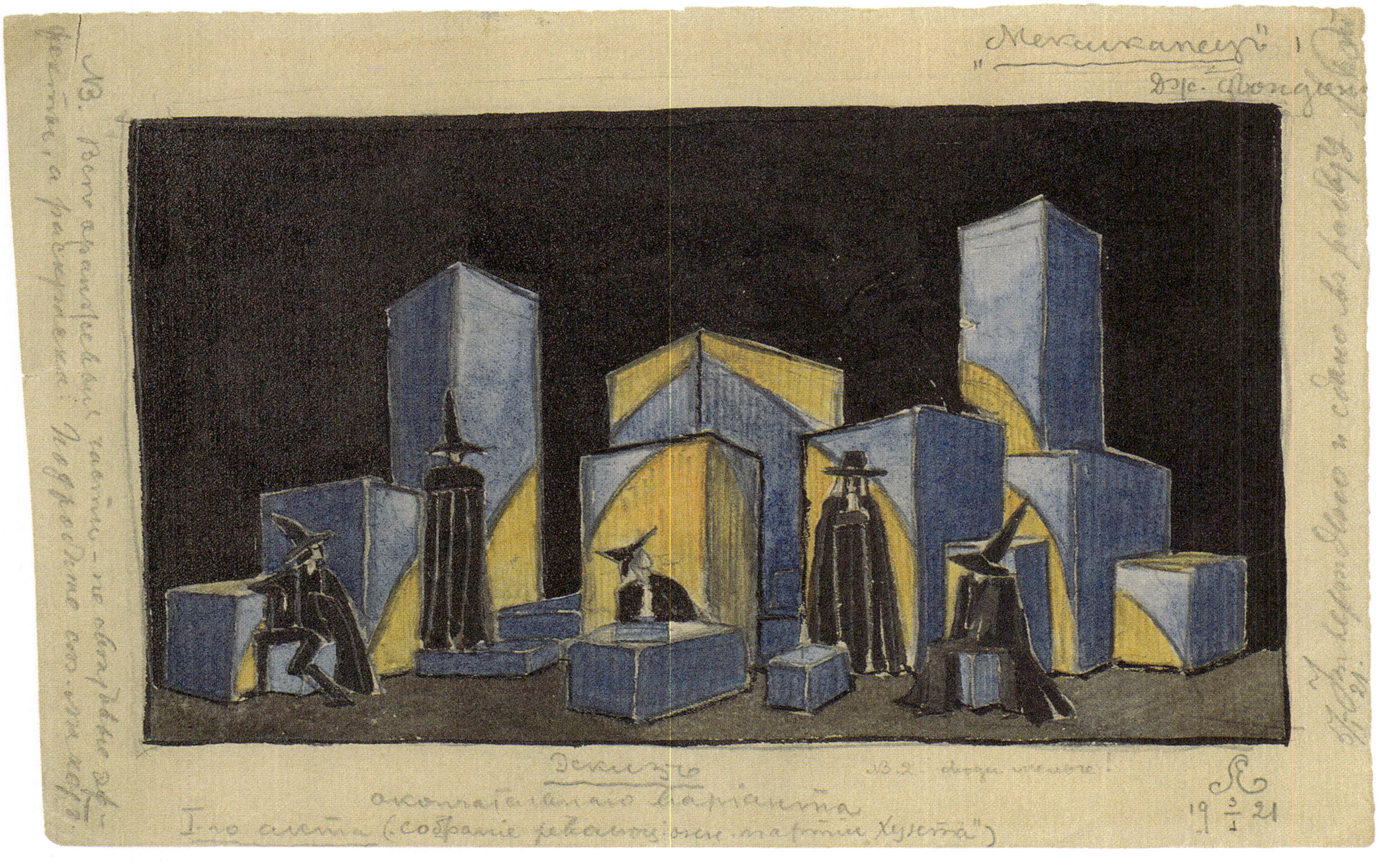

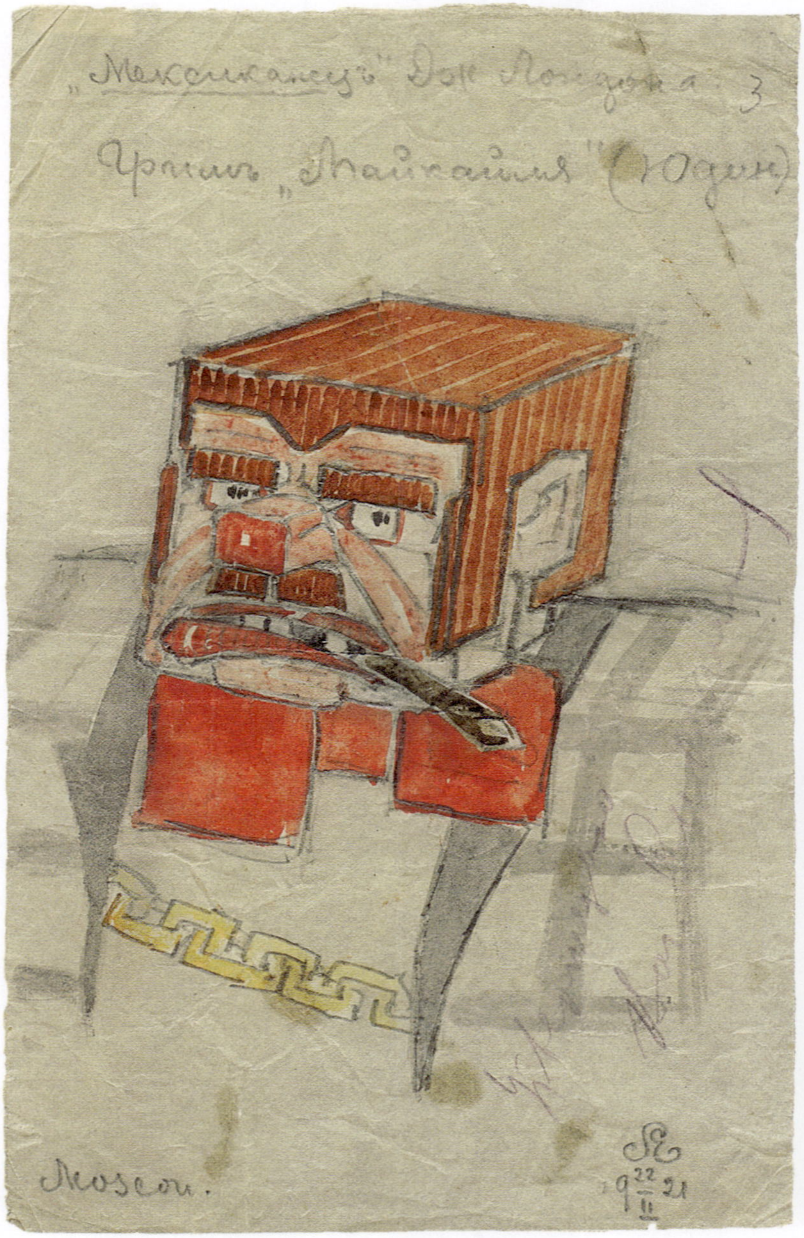
„Мексиканецъ" Дж. Лондона
Moscou.

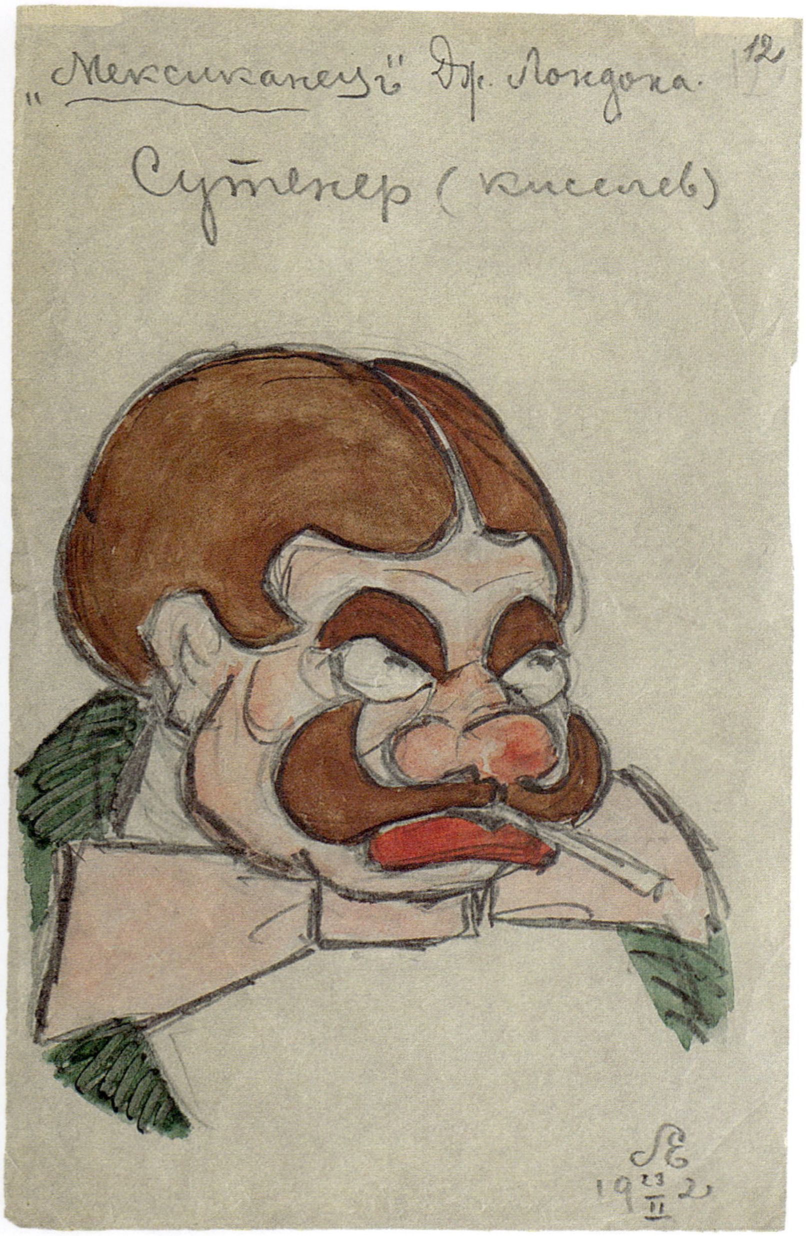
„Мексиканецъ" Дж. Лондона
Сутенер (Киселев)

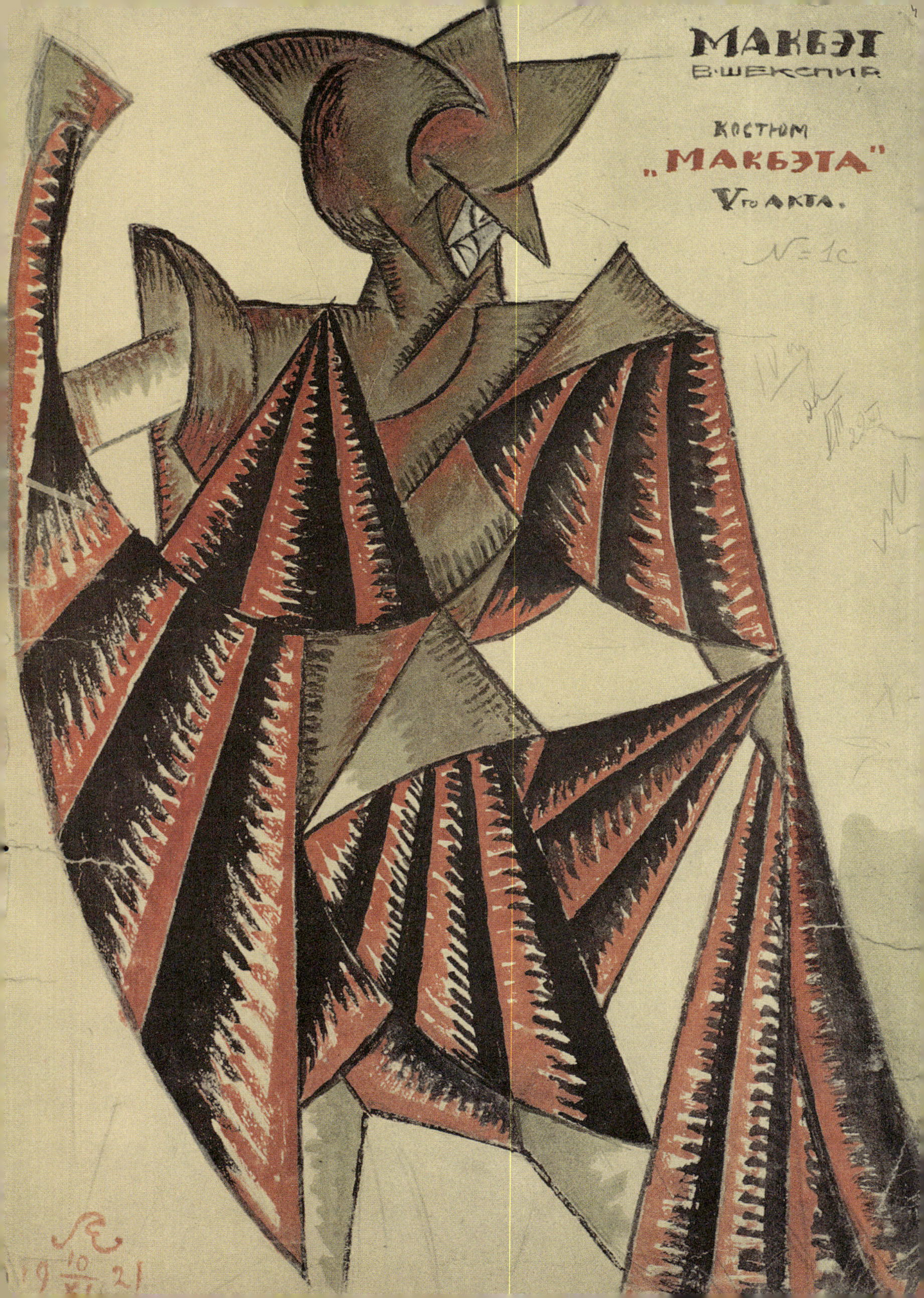
МАКБЭТ
В·ШЕКСПИРА
КОСТЮМ
„МАКБЭТА"
V-го АКТА.
№=1с

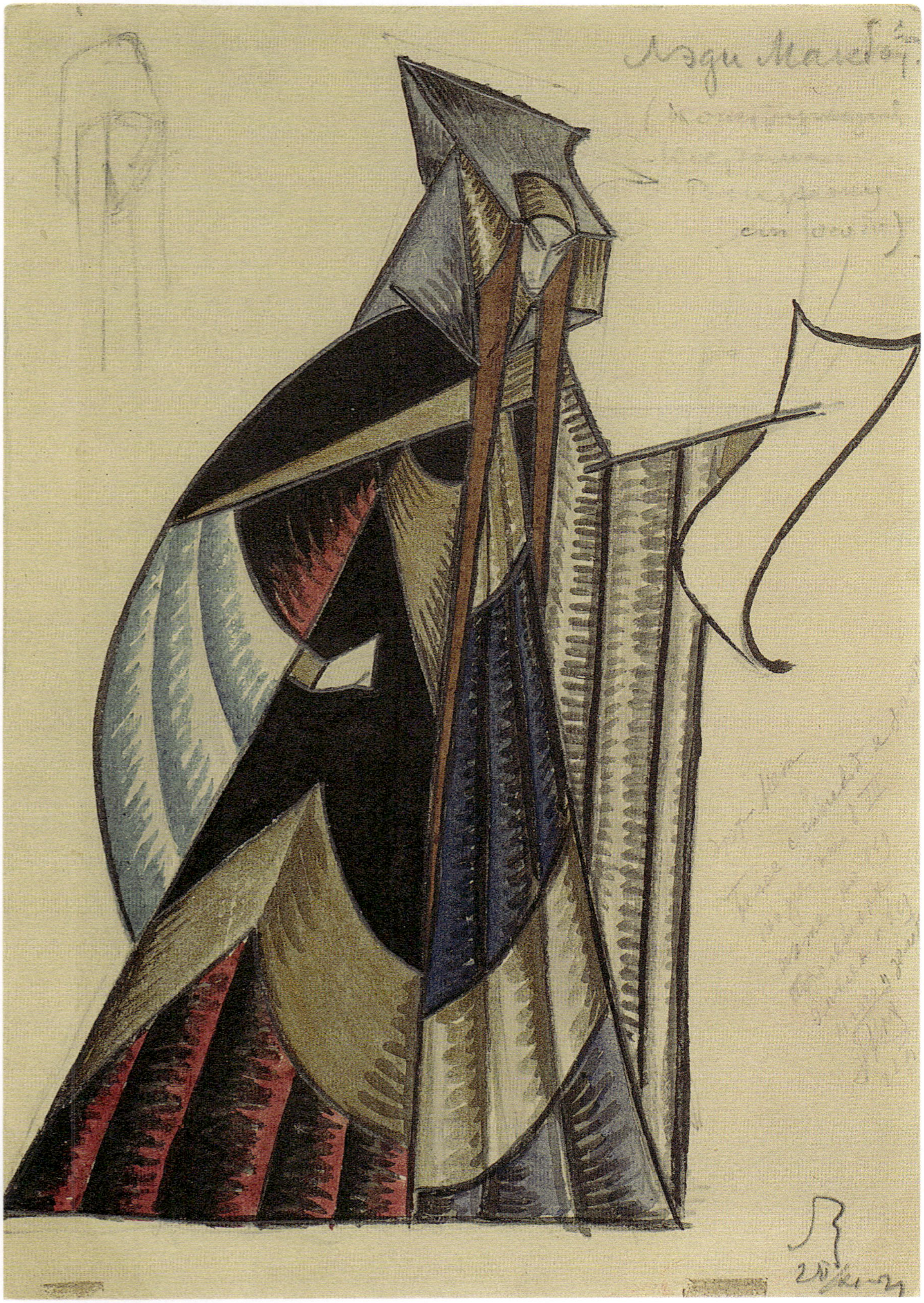
Лэди Макбет

—PREVIOUS

LEFT PAGE
Macbeth by William Shakespeare
Costume for Macbeth in Act V
(Central Educational Theatre
[director V. Tikhonovich],
Moscow, 1921)

RIGHT PAGE
Costume construction for Lady
Macbeth (Central Educational
Theatre [director V. Tikhonovich],
Moscow, 1921)

—THIS PAGE
Costumes for the First and Second
Killers in *Macbeth* (Central Educational
Theatre [director V. Tikhonovich],
Moscow, 1921)

—OPPOSITE
Motif for the costume of Duncan
in *Macbeth* (Central Educational
Theatre [director V. Tikhonovich],
Moscow, 1921)

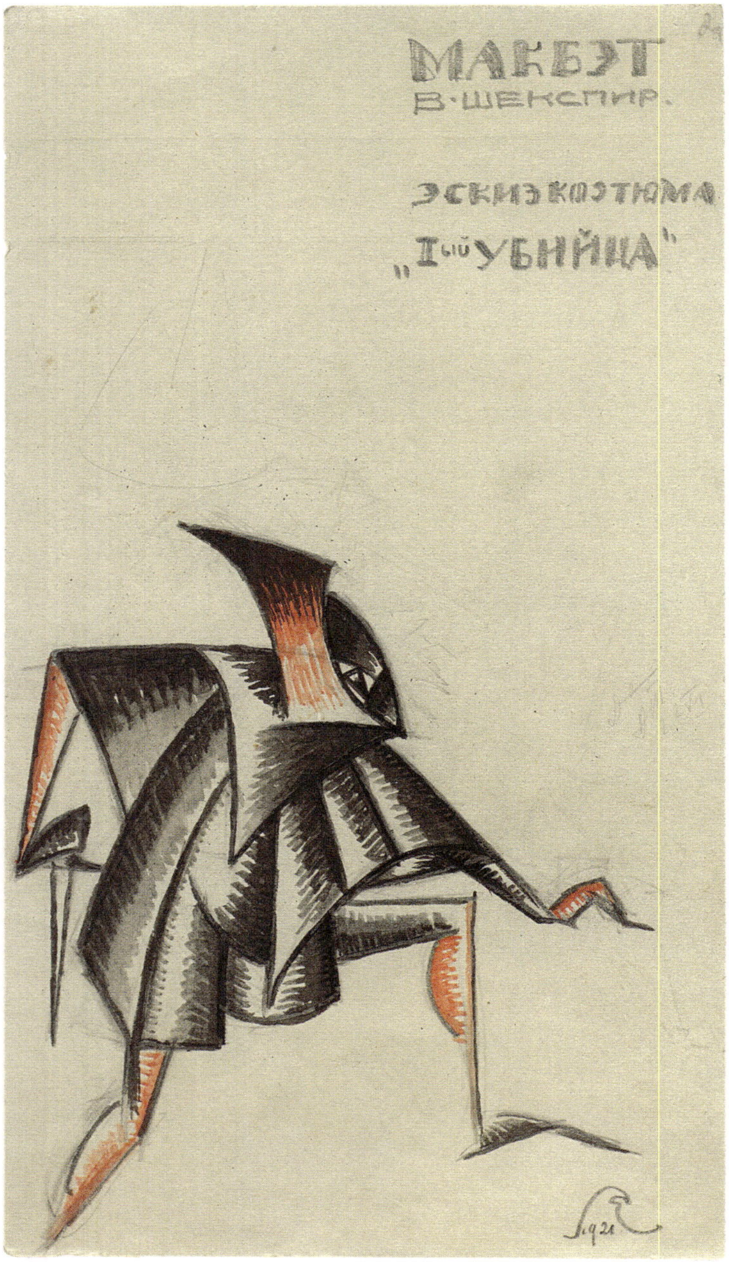

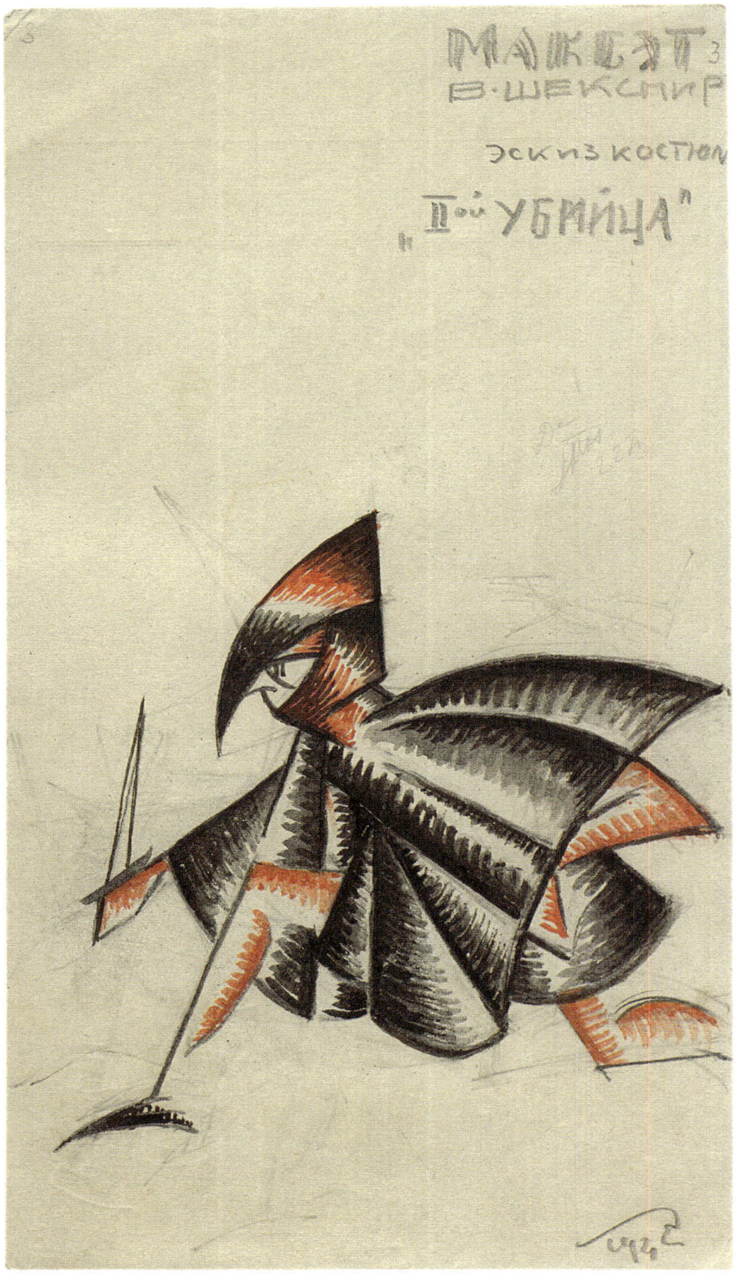

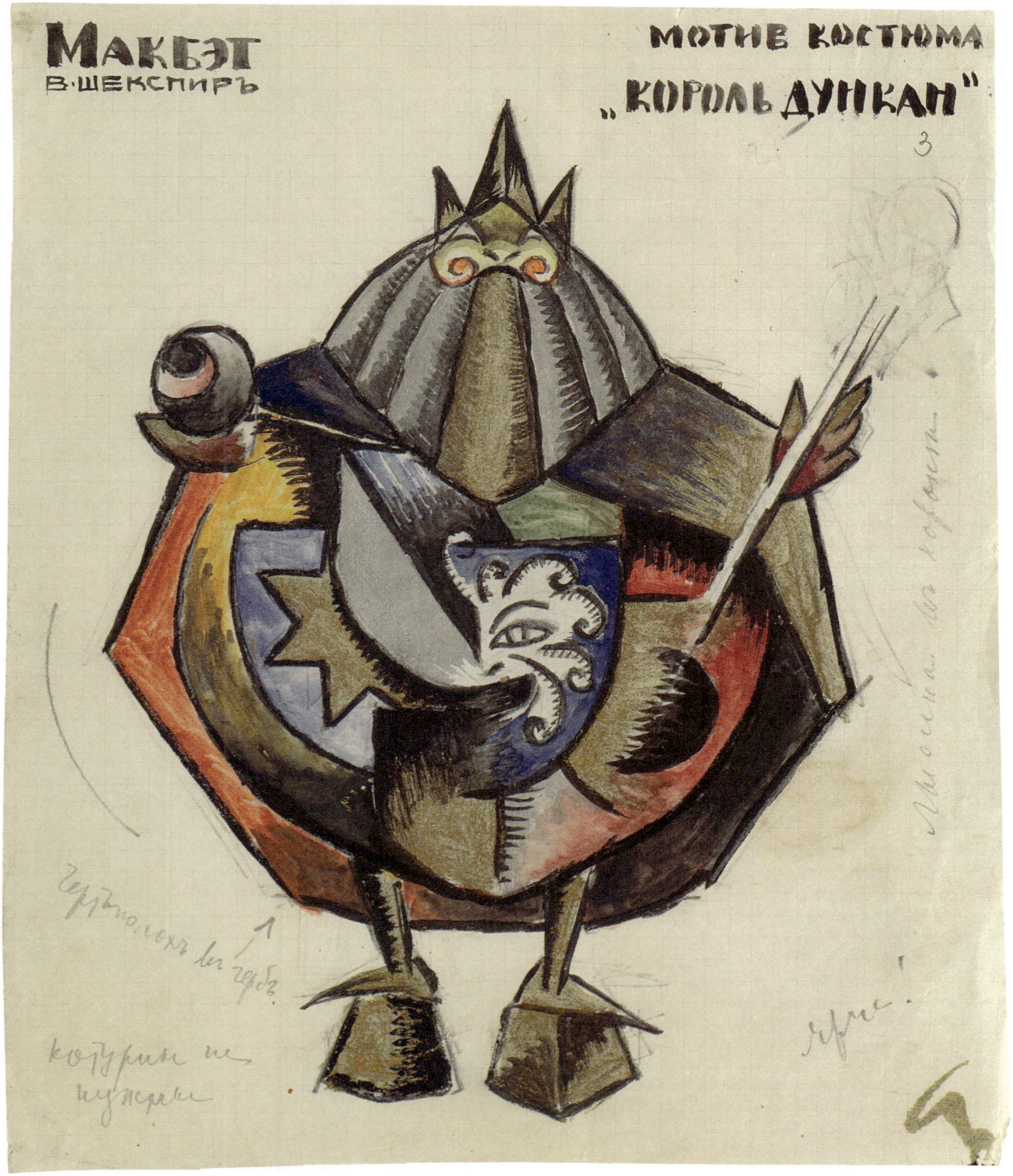
МАКБЭТ
В·ШЕКСПИРЪ
МОТИВ КОСТЮМА
„КОРОЛЬ ДУНКАН"

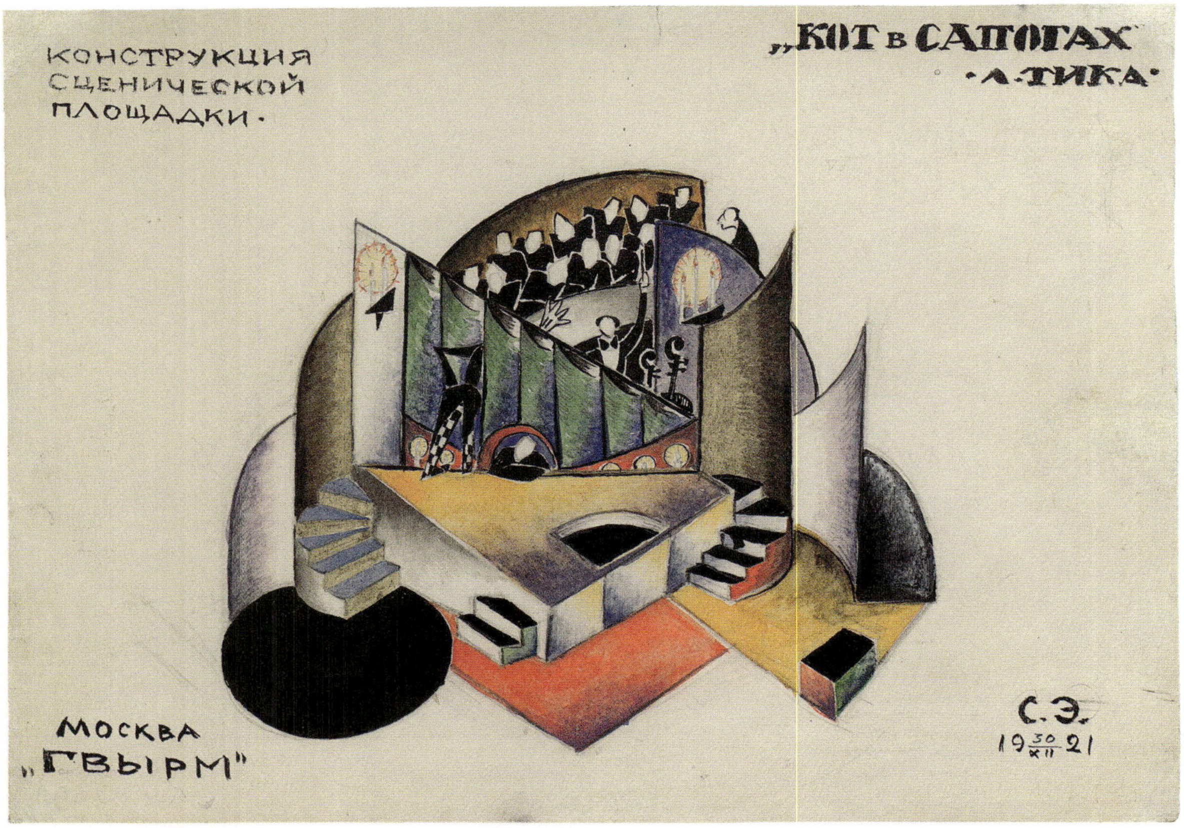

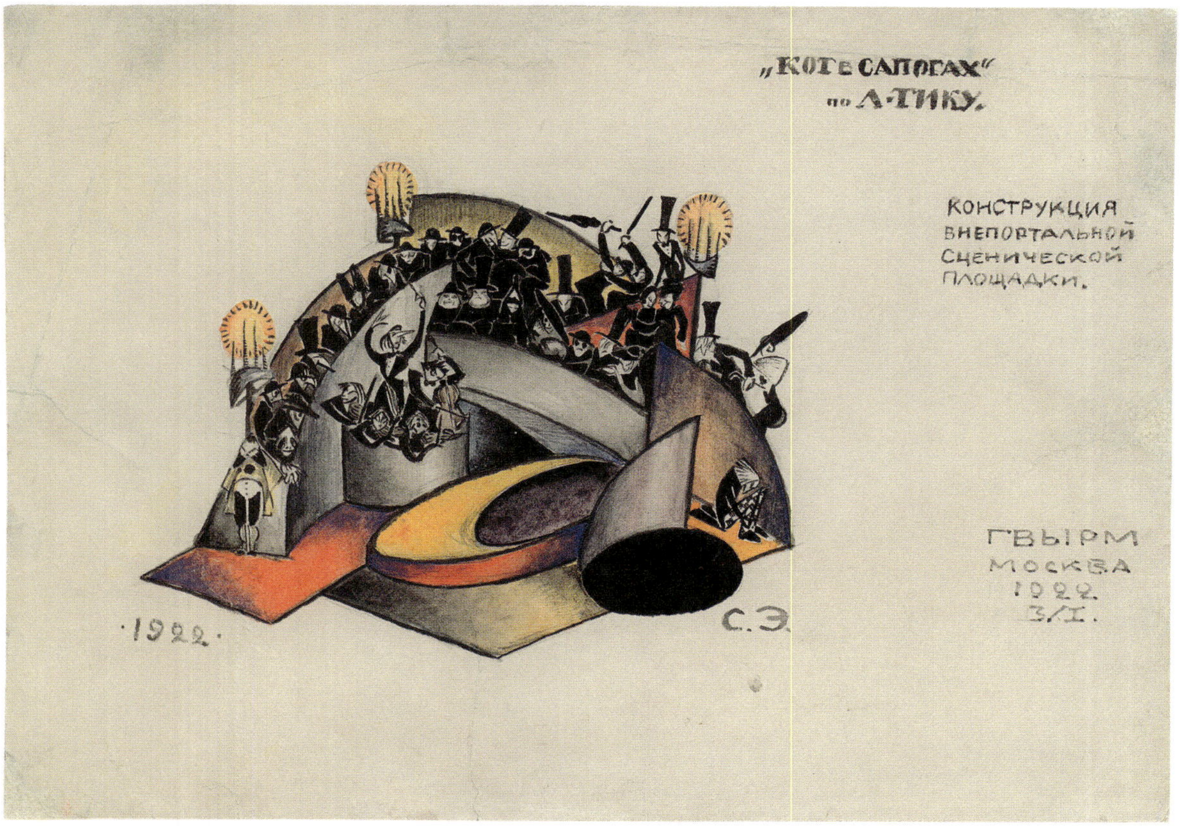

—THIS PAGE

TOP
Stage construction [outside of the portal] for *Puss in Boots* by Ludwig Tieck (1st variant, Moscow, GVYRM, 1921)

BOTTOM
Stage construction outside of the portal for *Puss in Boots* by Ludwig Tieck (2nd variant, Moscow, GVYRM, 1922)

—OPPOSITE
'A good attitude towards horses' by Vladimir Mayakovsky, English singer of couplets (MastFor [Foregger's Workshop], Press House, Moscow, 1921)

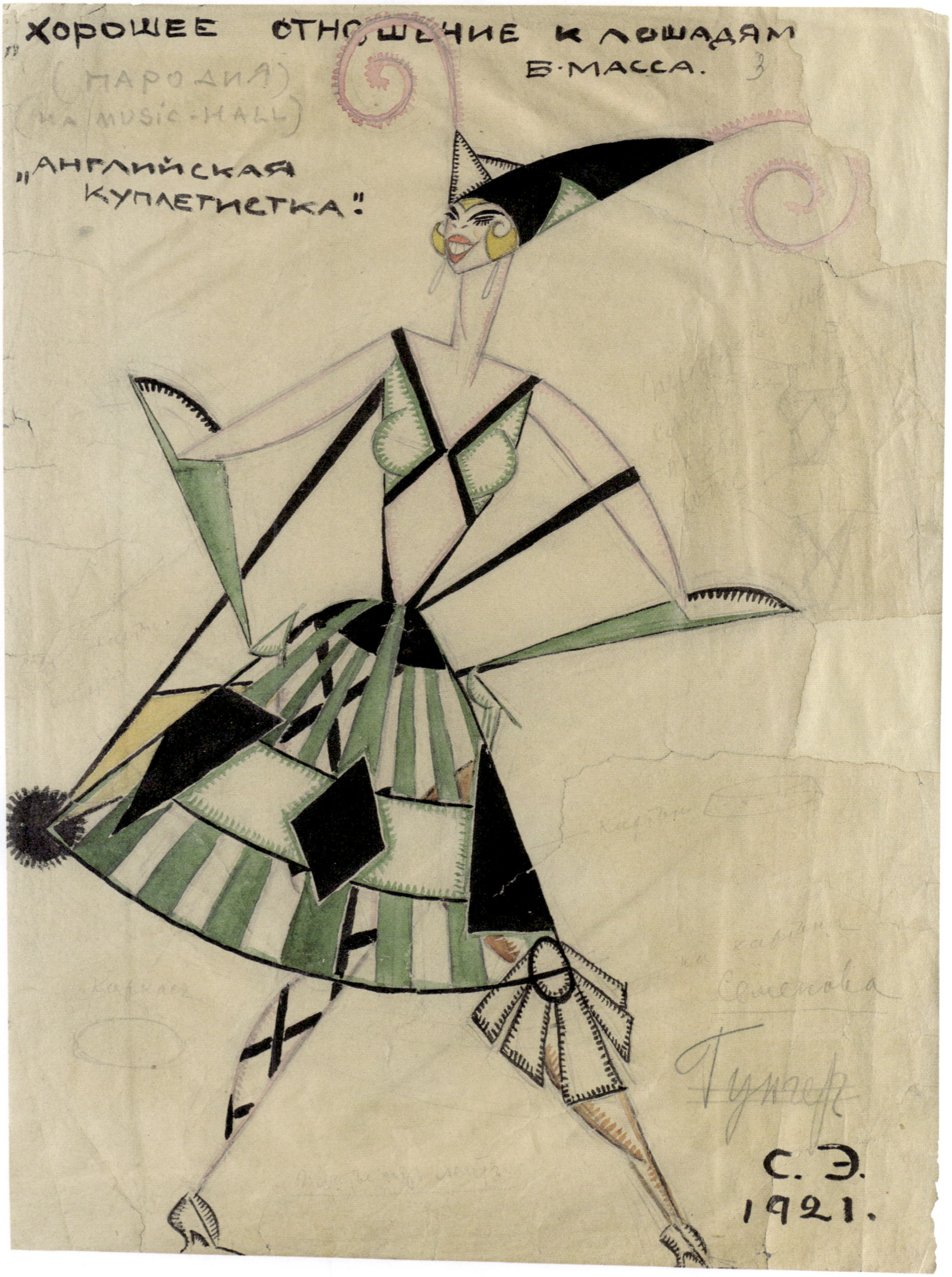
ХОРОШЕЕ ОТНОШЕНИЕ К ЛОШАДЯМ
Б·МАССА.
(ПАРОДИЯ)
(НА MUSIC-HALL)
„АНГЛИЙСКАЯ КУПЛЕТИСТКА!"
С. Э.
1921.

RIGHT
Set design for *Masques* by Claude Debussy (MastFor, Moscow, 1922)

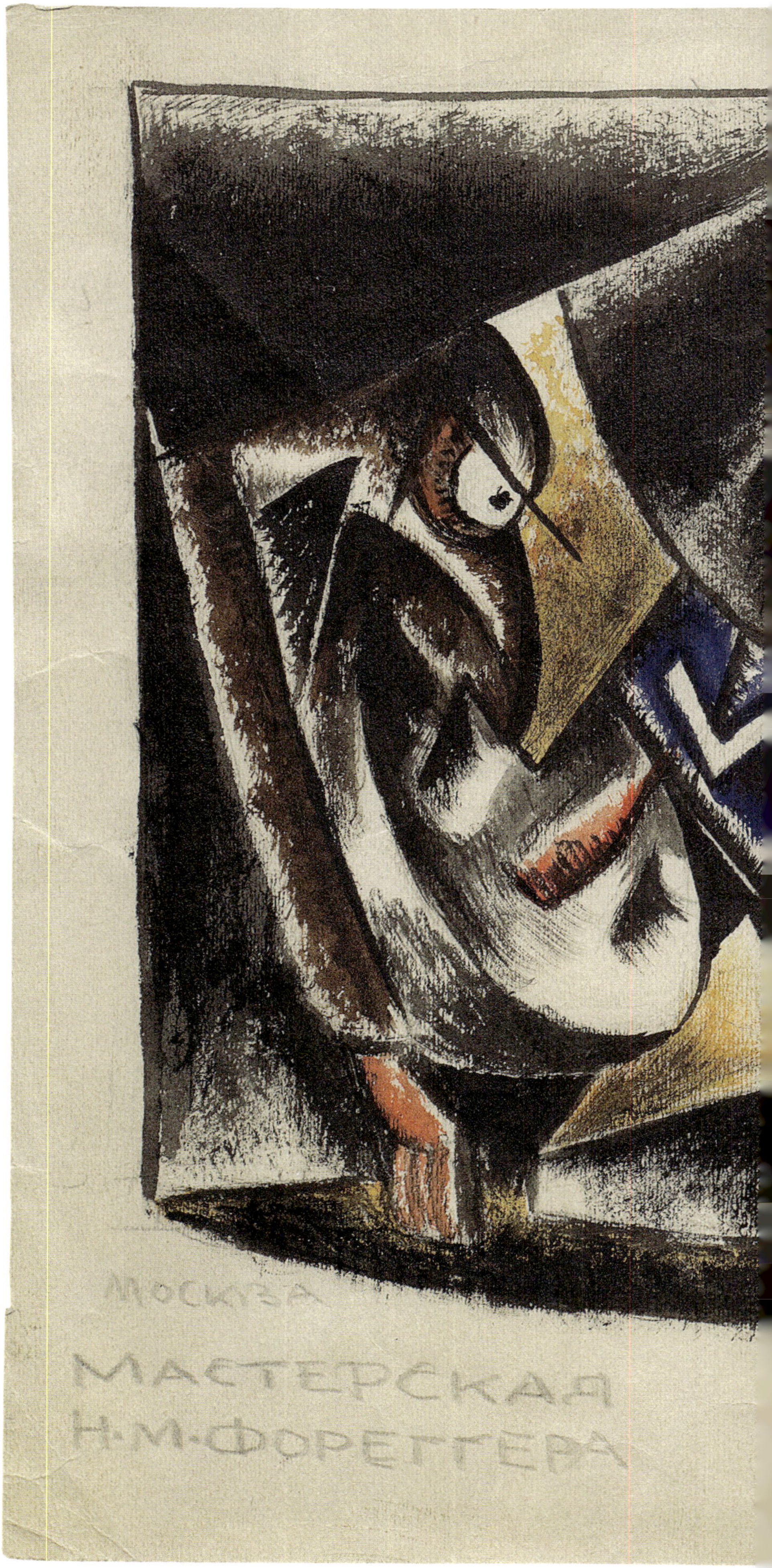

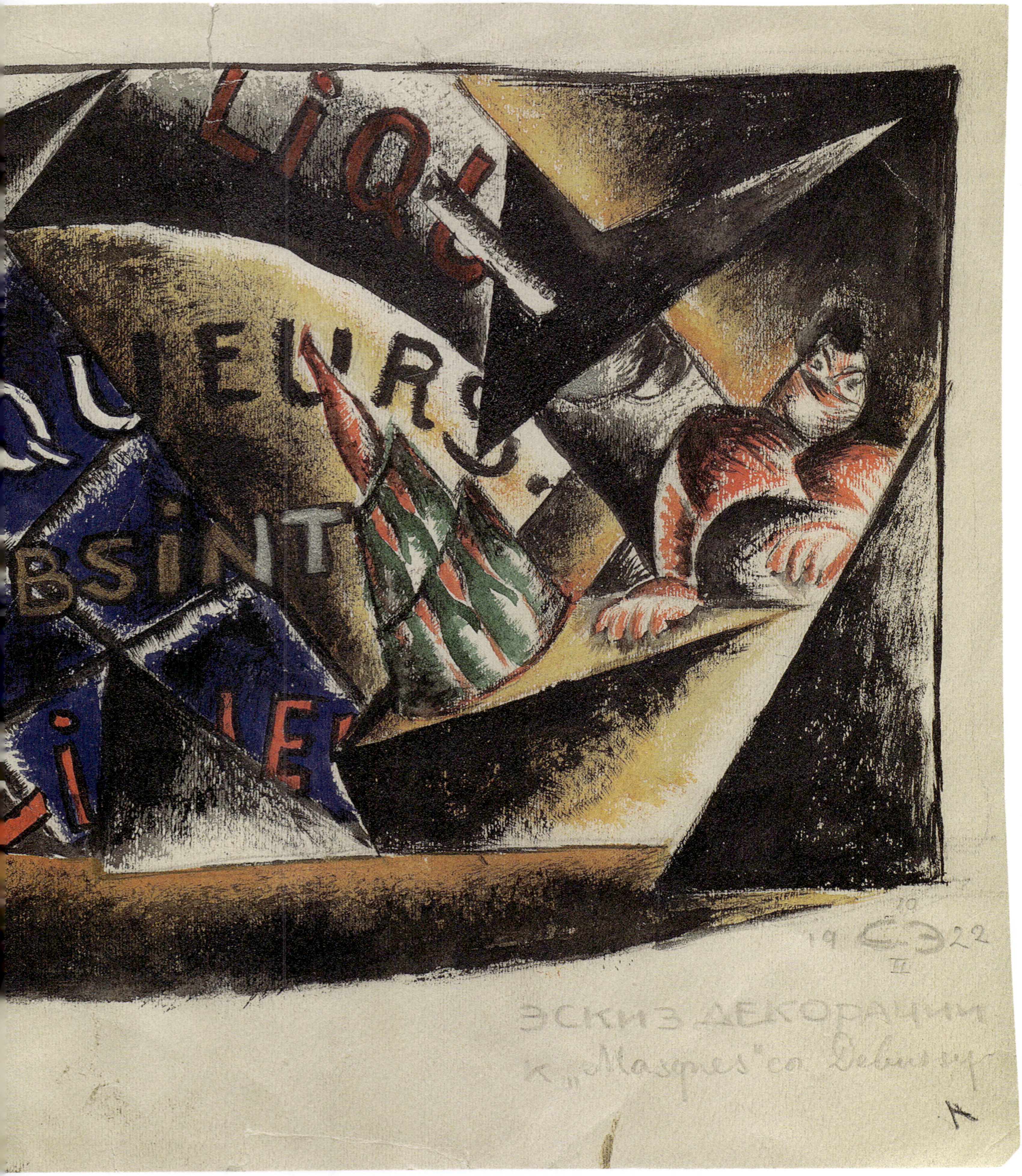

LiQ
IEURS
BSINT
ЭСКИЗ ДЕКОРАЦИИ

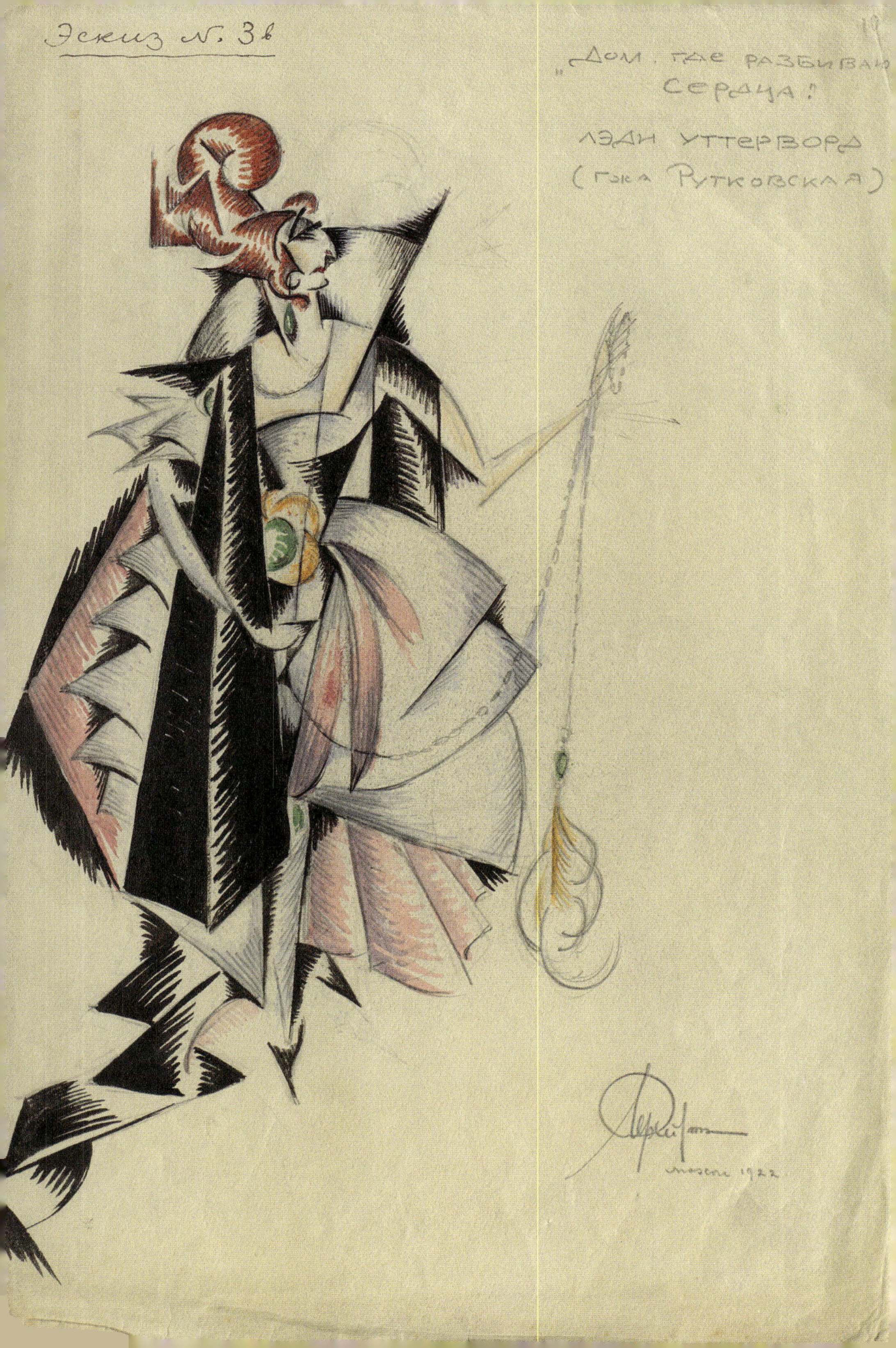
Эскиз N. 3в
„Дом, где разбиваю
сердца!"
Лэди Уттерворд
(г-жа Рутковская)
Москва 1922

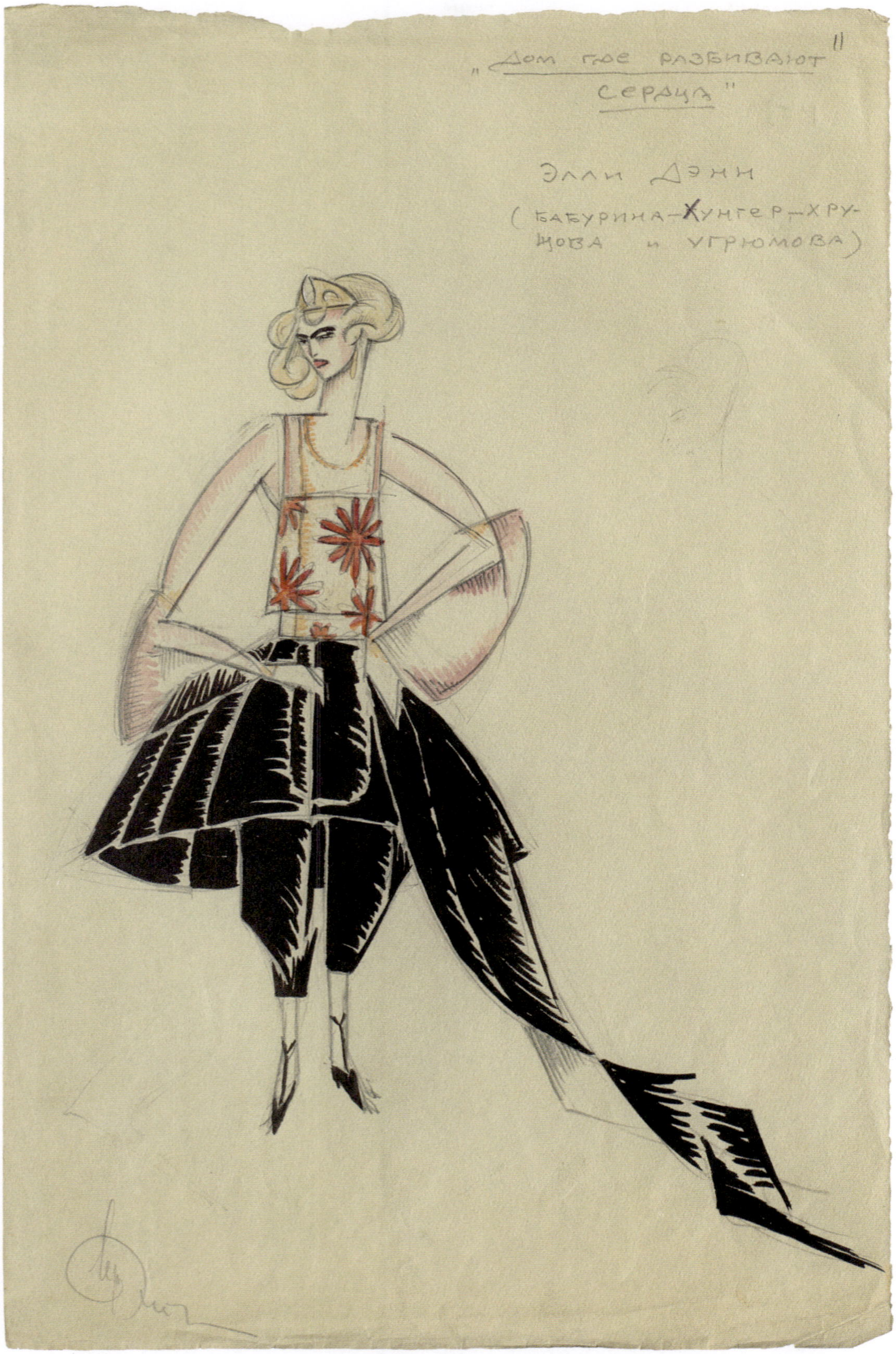

—OPPOSITE
Lady Utterword, from *Heartbreak House* by Bernard Shaw/Ivan Aksenov (GVYRM, Moscow, 1922)

—THIS PAGE
Ellie Dunn, from *Heartbreak House* by Bernard Shaw/Ivan Aksenov (GVYRM, Moscow, 1922)

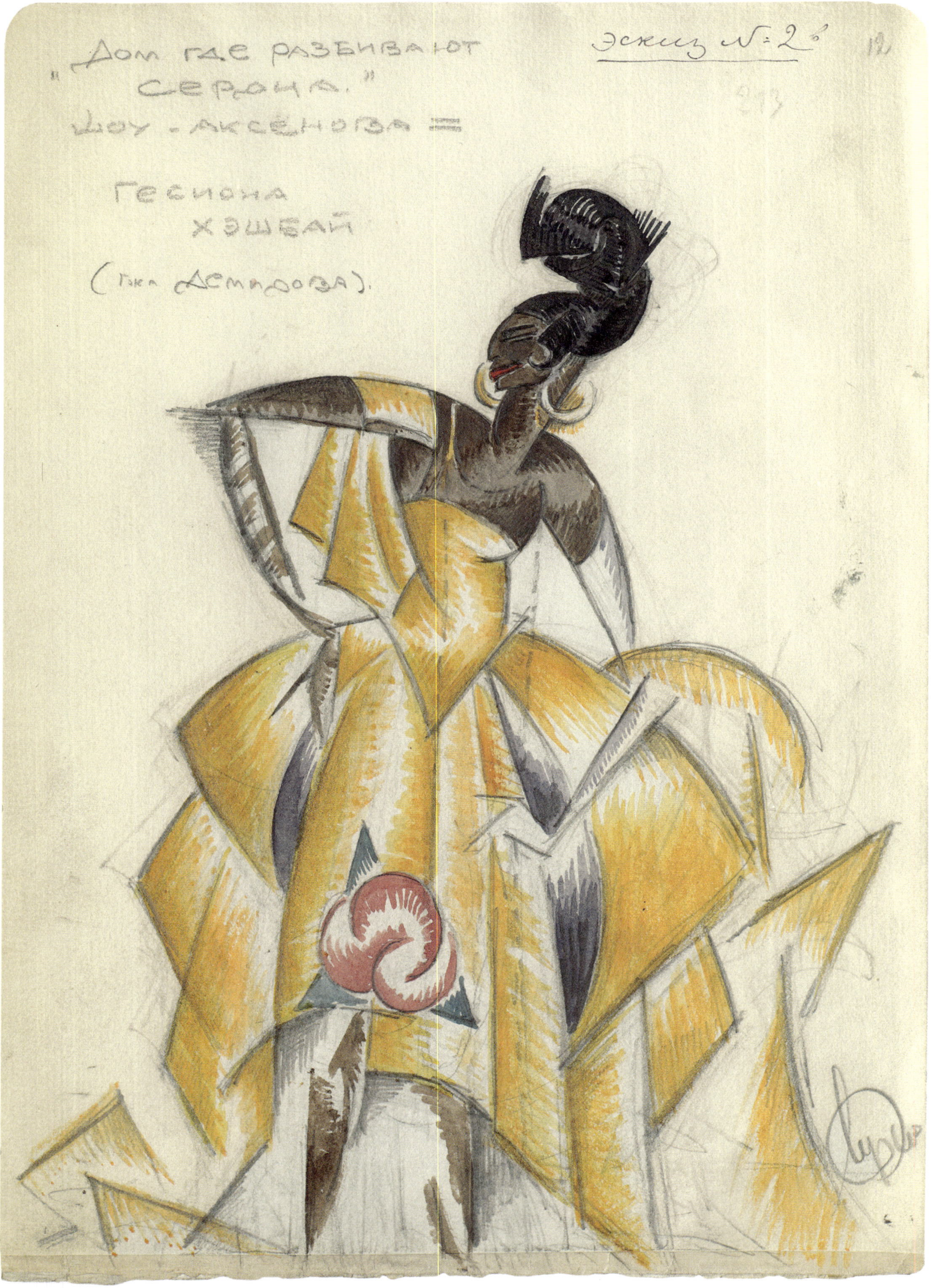
"Дом где разбиваюТ
сердца."
Шоу - Аксёнова =
Гесиона
Хэшбай
(г-жа Демидова).
Эскиз № 2

—OPPOSITE
Hesione Hushabye, from *Heartbreak House* by Bernard Shaw/Ivan Aksenov (GVYRM, Moscow, 1922)

—THIS PAGE
(Alfred) Mangan, from *Heartbreak House* by Bernard Shaw/Ivan Aksenov (GVYRM, Moscow, 1922)

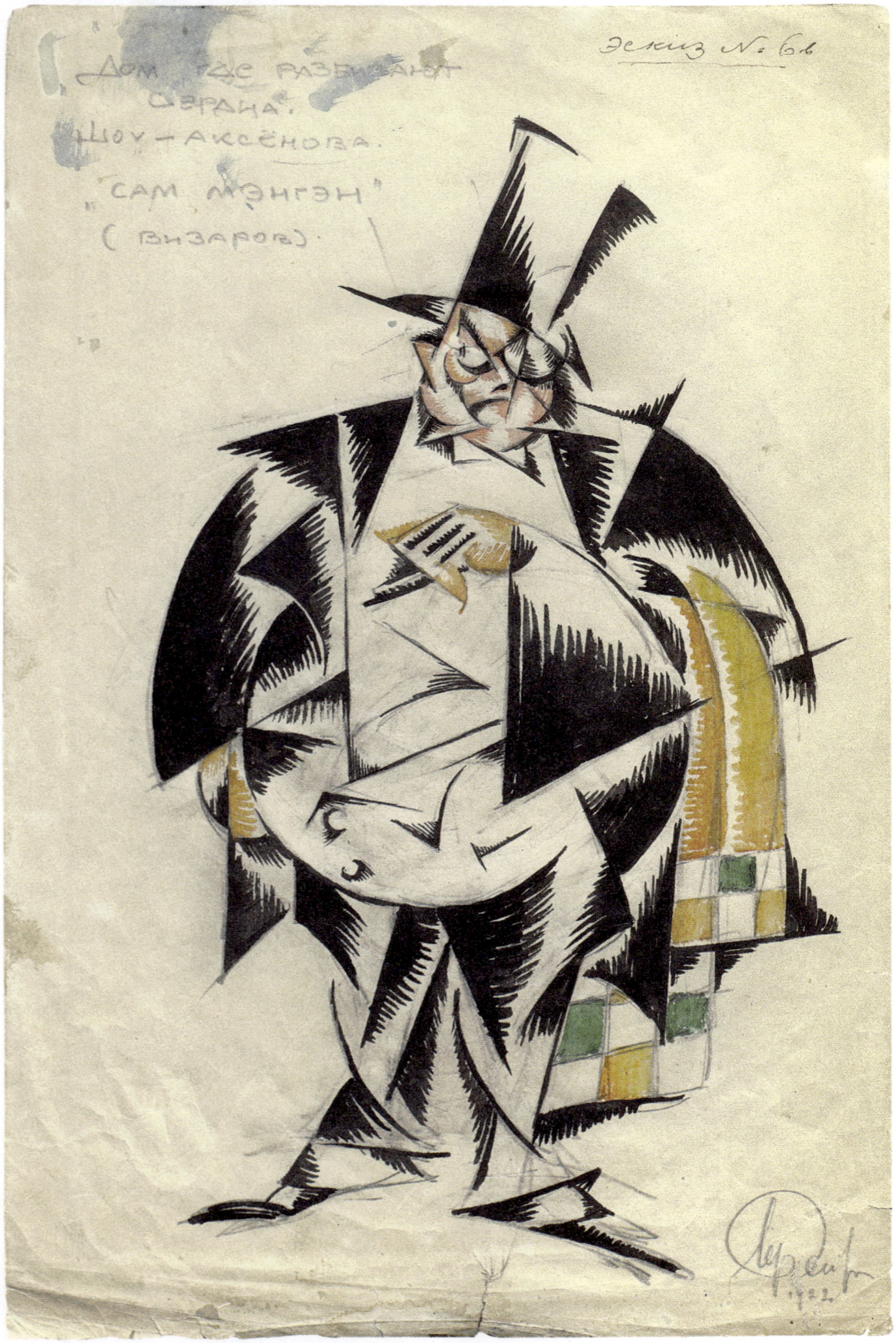

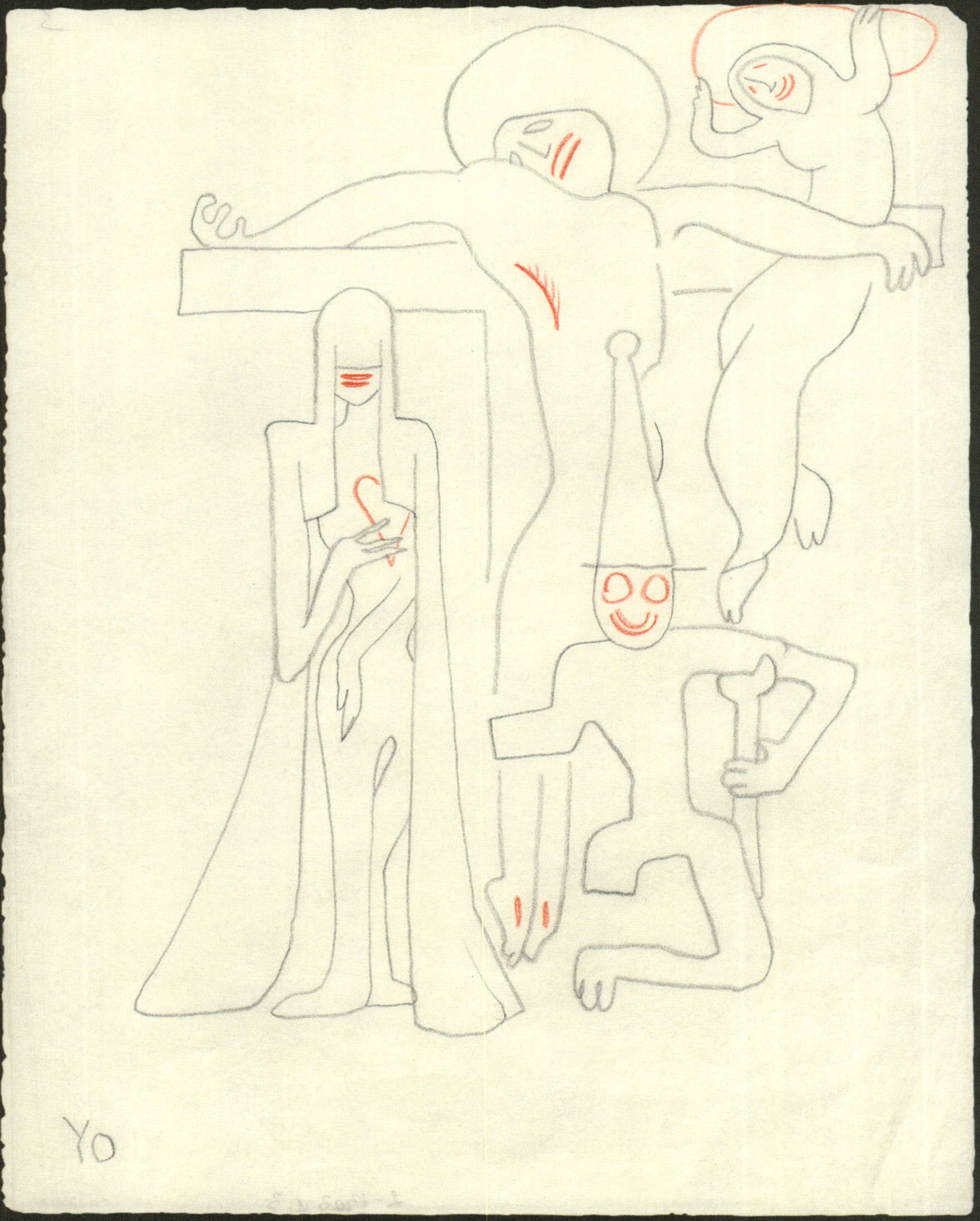
YO

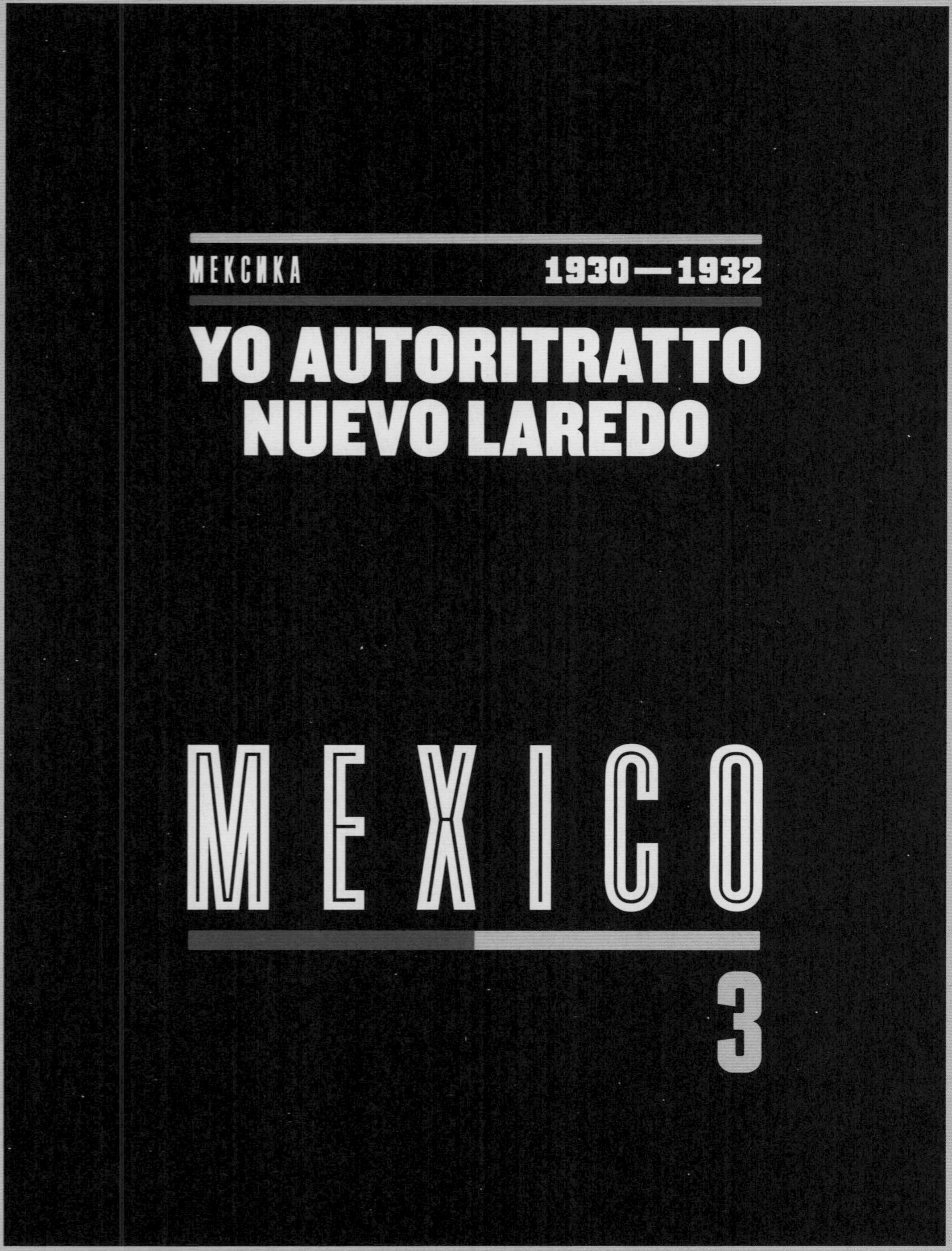
МЕКСИКА 1930—1932

YO AUTORITRATTO
NUEVO LAREDO

MEXICO

3

That mixture of Spanish and Italian, which means 'Me – Self-portrait – Nuevo Laredo', was the title Eisenstein gave to a strange composition of five figures that he drew on 25 February 1932. And then he immediately reduced the number of characters to four, giving each of them a somewhat changed metaphorical meaning in the process. The second version was titled simply *YO*. But the sense of the drawing's time and place of birth was even more clearly expressed.

A second week had passed since Sergei Eisenstein, Grigory Aleksandrov and Eduard Tisse had arrived in the northern Mexican border town of Nuevo Laredo. They had already visited the other side of the Rio Grande twice, but this time the 1930 visas that they had used to enter New York were not accepted by the border guards at Laredo, Texas, and these suspicious Russians with their Soviet passwords were not admitted to the United States (Mexico had broken off diplomatic relations with the USSR two years earlier, and the United States had never had them).

The three's indefinite status was on top of all their other troubles. Moscow had refused to extend the trip and was demanding their immediate return to the Soviet Union. There were suspicions that Eisenstein had become a 'non-returner' – that he had defected. Pera Atasheva's letters hint at it, linking rumours he had decided to remain in the West with his mother's tearful plea to come home at once, as otherwise she (the daughter of a millionaire merchant) might be exiled to Siberia as an 'alien class element'. Eisenstein seems not to have known yet about the wire Stalin himself had sent to Upton Sinclair, where he ominously wrote that 'Eisenstein has lost the confidence of his comrades'. At the same time, the Mexican Film Trust – an independent company Sinclair had organized to support the Soviet film-making team – had withdrawn its financial backing and demanded that the filming, which had overrun, should be brought to a halt. Hunter Kimbrough, Sinclair's brother-in-law who claimed to be the producer, was clashing with the director, and also suspected Eisenstein of having a secret business plan: to shoot not one but four or five films using the Trust's money (why else try to jam more than one plot into just the one movie?), give the Trust one of them and smuggle the rest back to the USSR! Sinclair did not have enough of a sense of humour to enable him simply to laugh at this nonsense.

Eisenstein would spent the best part of a month writing to his influential American friends and colleagues asking for their help. And privately he would keep blessing his unexpected confinement in Nuevo Laredo, which gave him time to read the books he had bought in Mexico City and ordered from Paris and London, time to think, to compare, to write... He even thought of Friedrich Nietzsche, who, according to Stefan Zweig, received his 'greatest revelations holed up in a disgusting hotel'.[1] Eisenstein devoted particular attention to *Des grâces d'oraison* (On the Grace of Prayer), by the Jesuit priest Father Auguste Poulain. The spiritual exercises of St Ignatius Loyola and the ecstatic revelations of other saints, published by Poulain, confirmed the common psychological 'mechanisms' of ecstasy, which grant human beings – depending on their attitude – either a religious experience of the Godhead, or erotic pleasure in love, or creative inspiration and the joy of embodying it in art. Eisenstein had looked into the book when he was still in the capital, but now, in the middle of nowhere and with his status so indeterminate, he could not stop: he wrote out into the margins, copied whole pages as quotations into his notebook and hurried to record his observations and associations alongside them.

It was also at this time that he remembered he had promised to write a 'crib' on his drawing for Anita Brenner, the delightful American researcher whose *Idols Behind Altars* had offered precious help when he was trying to grasp the culture and the very spirit of Mexico. Anita, who had published articles in *Creative Art* about Mexican artistic life and the artists behind it, had expressed a desire to present the Russian director's drawings there. She did not hide the fact that she found them striking and even a little frightening, but her intention was less to 'judge' them than to explain them from the standpoint of the artist himself.

In two sittings, on 23 and 25 February, Eisenstein wrote these Notes,[2] full of his thoughts on the nature of ecstasy – creative, erotic, and religious. Here is this text:

Notes for Anita Brenner's article about my drawings for* Creative Art*, Nuevo Laredo [Mexico], 23–25 February 1932

1. One aspect of E.'s theoretical work at the present moment is the unification of the two conceptual poles, idealism and dialectical materialism.

By means of identifying in them a gradated distinction in the phenomenon of perception of the basic driving principles.

Working from a comparative study of their apogees: for idealism, the state of ecstasy (which is erroneously dubbed mystical insight), and for materialism of the highest quality, dialectical perception.

The conclusion from the detailed study (from all angles) of both these phenomena is the proposition, to formulate it briefly, that one and the same actually existing law of being has been observed from the Vedas down to Engels: [the law of] coming into being, development.

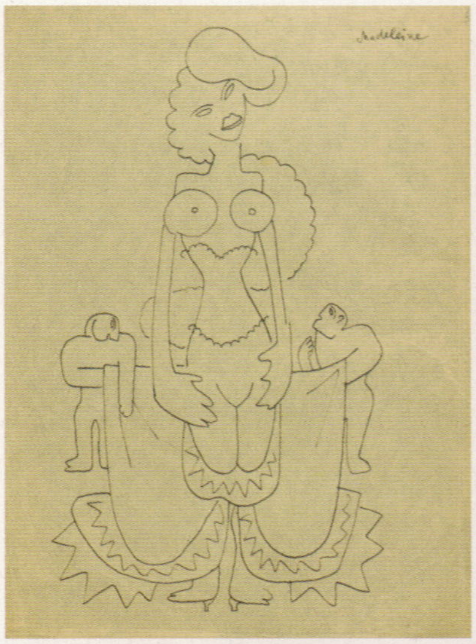

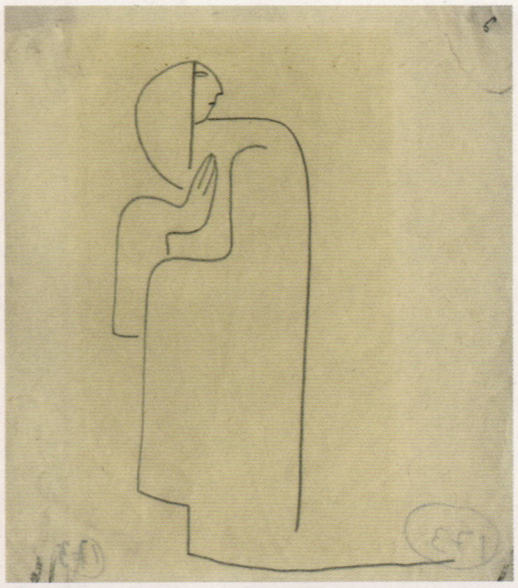

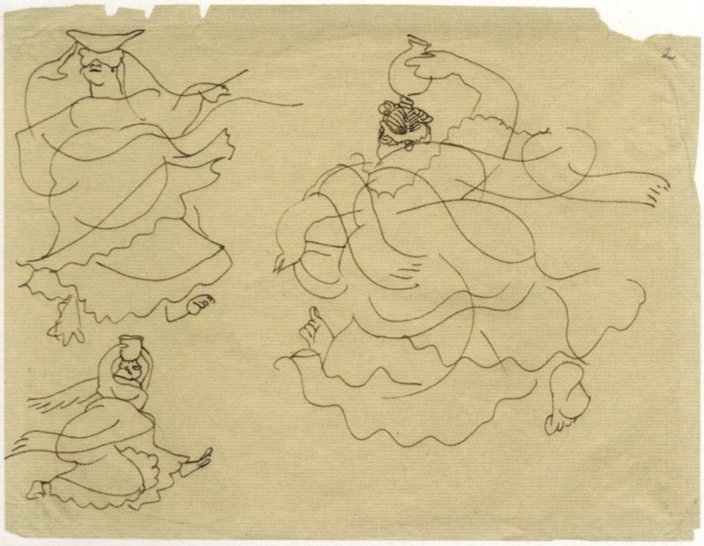

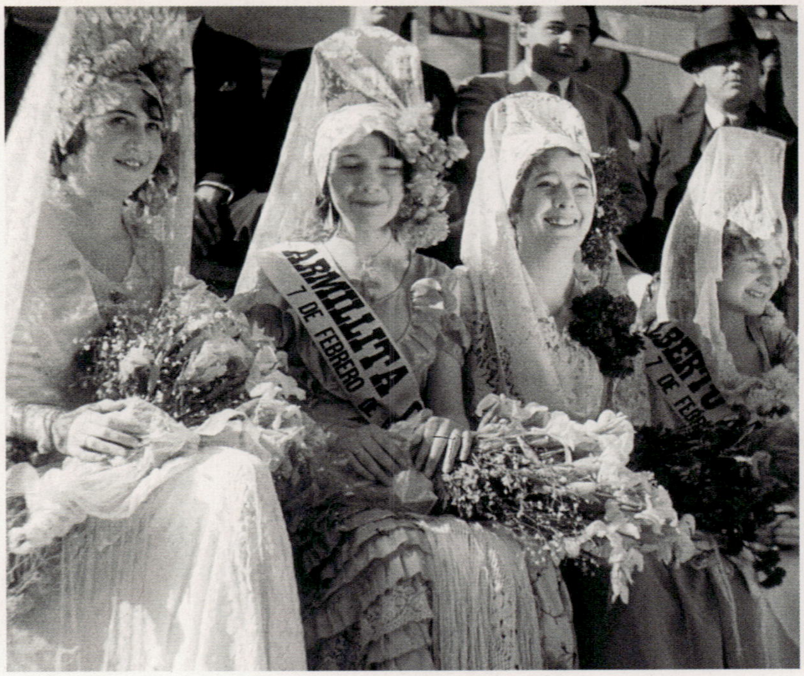

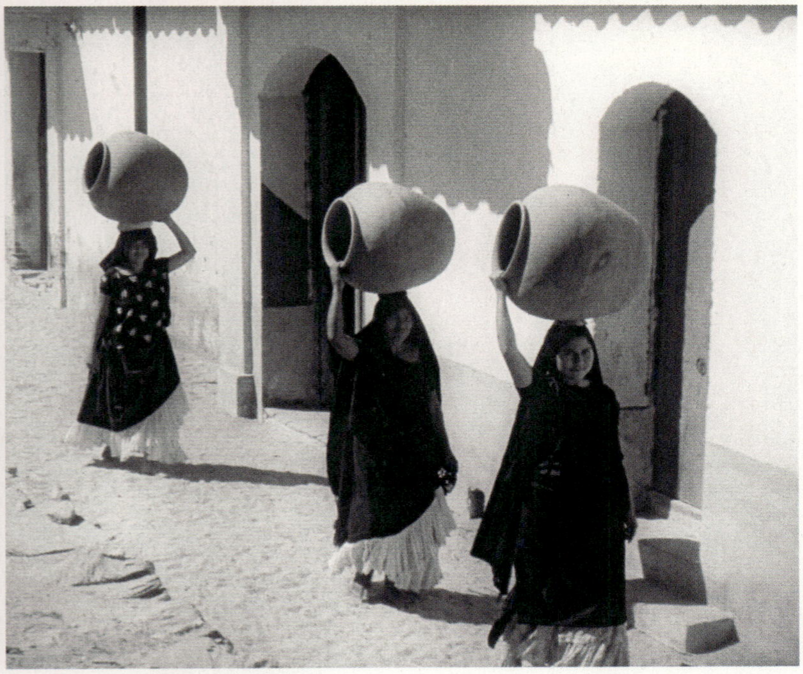

—PREVIOUS
YO (Nuevo Laredo, Mexico, 1932)

—THIS PAGE
Motifs for the film *¡Que viva México!* (1930–32):

TOP LEFT
Madeleine

TOP CENTRE
'Isabel Villaseñor as Maria'

TOP RIGHT
'Women of Tehuantepec'

Shots from the film *¡Que viva México!*:

BOTTOM LEFT
Queens of the *corrida* ('Fiesta' episode)

BOTTOM RIGHT
Women of Tehuantepec ('Sandunga' episode)

—OVERLEAF
Motifs for the film *¡Que viva México!* (1930–32):

TOP LEFT
'Peon Sebastian caught with a lasso'

TOP RIGHT
'The death of a revolting peon under the hoof'

—OVERLEAF
Shots from the film *¡Que viva México!* ('Maguey' episode):

BOTTOM LEFT
Peon Sebastian caught with a lasso

BOTTOM RIGHT
Execution of the peons who revolted

But in the lower stages of intellectual development the recognition of these propositions/laws could not take objective form in an independently-existing group of concepts United into a group of propositions that could be formulated abstractly (abstracted from the experience of them).

In these lower levels the perception of dialectical order in the course of events remained at the subjective stage – that is, it could not be separated from the subject of cognition by way of a formulation: [there exists] 'cognition' only at the level of experiencing a proposition through the most intimate communion with the course of this Universe via fusion with it – an identificational and unitary [cognition] by artificially returning oneself to spheres that came closest to the stage of minimal differentiation from this Universe.

Experiencing a dialectical phenomenon, rather than grasping it and cognizing it: this is how E. characterizes the ecstatic state and its urge towards the basic secret of existence, which can be approached through ecstasy (the Vedas, Catholicism, the Eleusinian mysteries – all these ecstasies lead to the same place, and all turn out to be identical in their goals and methods, with no more than local variations).

Dialectical insight remains at the stage of subjective experience until there is sufficient social differentiation to permit the objective discoverability [of the phenomenon] in the social organism (which corresponds to the emergence of the proletariat as a sharply distinct class).

Until then, the chief object of observation of the dialectical phenomenon was merely introspection, with a corresponding inability to abstract (just the same happens historically in the case of, for instance, psychology, where intuitive individual-subjective 'psychology' gives way to objective-experimental reflexology).

This, by the way, is the reason for the sexual colouration given to ecstasy and the study of ecstasy in recent periods.

The bisexual conflict, the most salient within the subject, becomes the main factor of observation and the main mechanism by which the phenomenon is realized.

Therefore, the dialectics of the subjective period (stage) is closely linked to religion (having not yet become a scientific discipline, it appears as a discipline of behaviour: religion is a collection of disciplines), [to] the orgasm of acute sexuality in general and to the bisexual character in particular.

The main distinction between the periods is that in the first case the 'knower' is passively subjected to the dialectical order and course of things, while in the second he actively masters the course of developments, knowing the l[aw]s of their emergence.

2. The enunciator[3] of this thought, E. himself is the best illustration of the truth of his hypothesis, for he strangely possesses within himself both successive stages at the same time. He differs sharply from the biographies of Rimbaud and Huysmans, which he himself adduces [as examples], where he traces phylogenetically, over the course of their personal biographies, the development that takes place ontogenetically through the course of the centuries during which humanity has been approaching objective dialectical cognition.[4]

In fact, E.'s activity is divided into three kinds.

The first is his well-known 'objective' activity as filmmaker, film polemicist, and theorist, profoundly linked [with his time and manifesting itself] as social and public activity. Maximally close approach (at least in his intentions) to objective dialectical principles. E. as he is known on the screens and by the political police of foreign powers. Progressive.

The second is activity of an 'intimate' nature. Subjective and personal. Known only to a comparatively small number of his close friends. Here everything is very closely linked to the past. To the infantile and personal. The subjective past. Or the cultural and historical past. His main activity to realize this is his drawing. And this is his very earliest kind of expressive activity (he's been drawing since he was in the cradle), in his career too (he started out as a costume-designer and set designer in the theatre). And it is here that we see the full flowering of indicators of dialectical perception at the stage of undifferentiated subjectivism. Like Japanese wooden flowers: formless coloured fragments, when they are curled up, which only unfurl into a completely concrete sketch of a plant when they are brought into objective contact with water…

This E. is like a mediaeval erotomaniac monk and mystic.[5] An ecstatic and a cynic. A singer of orgasms

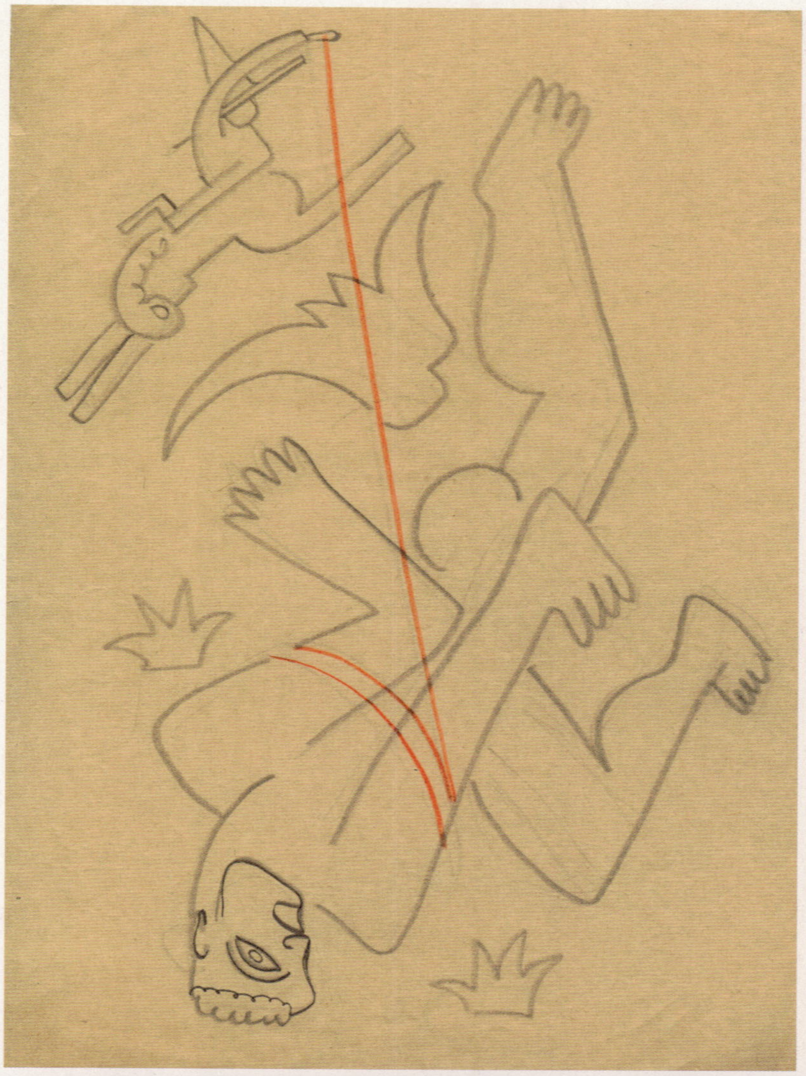
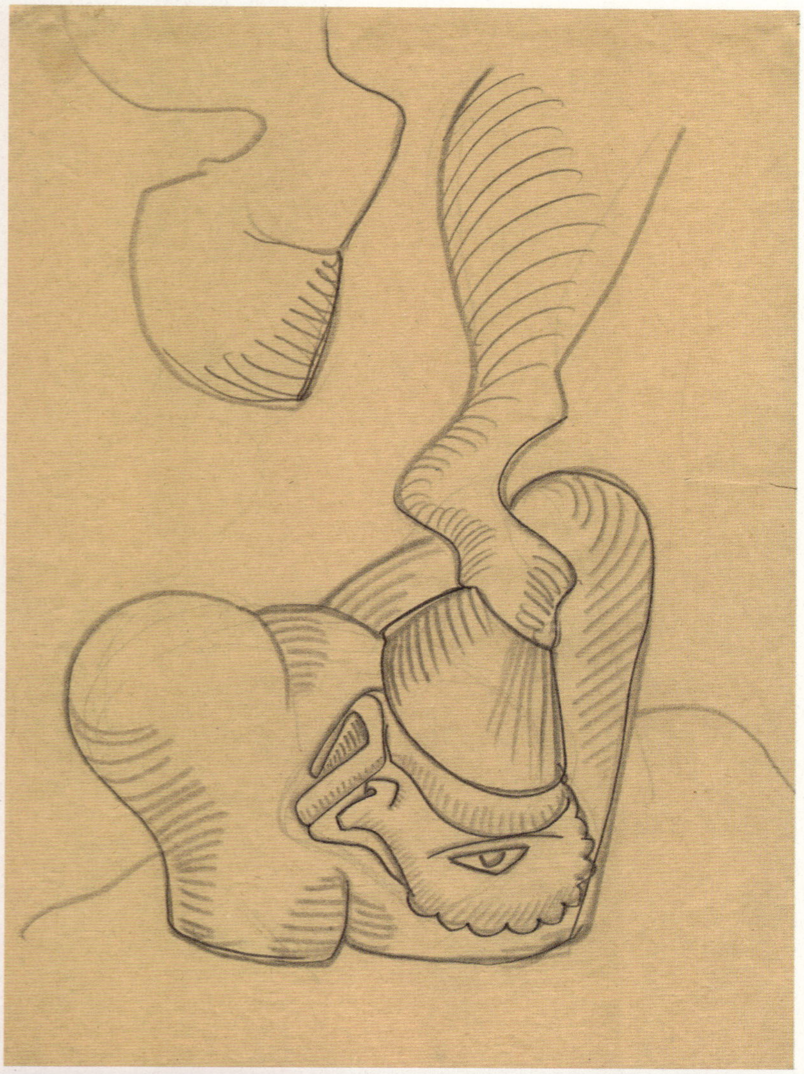
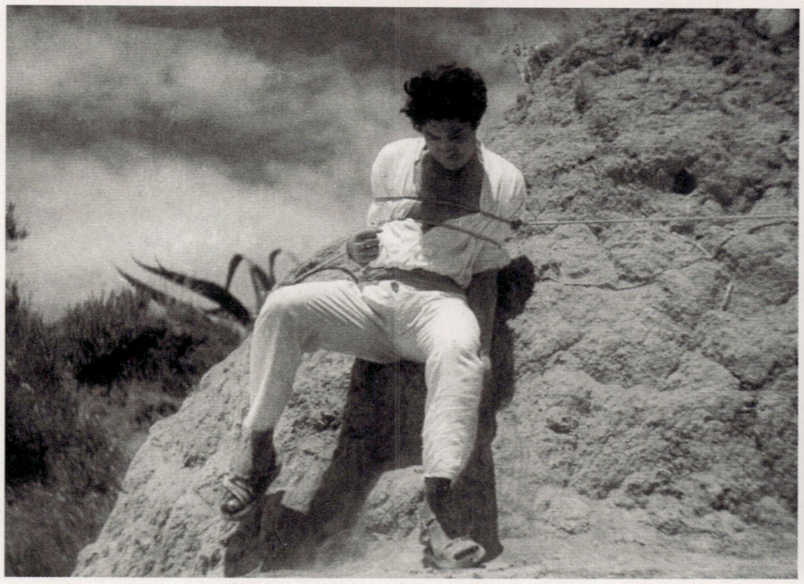
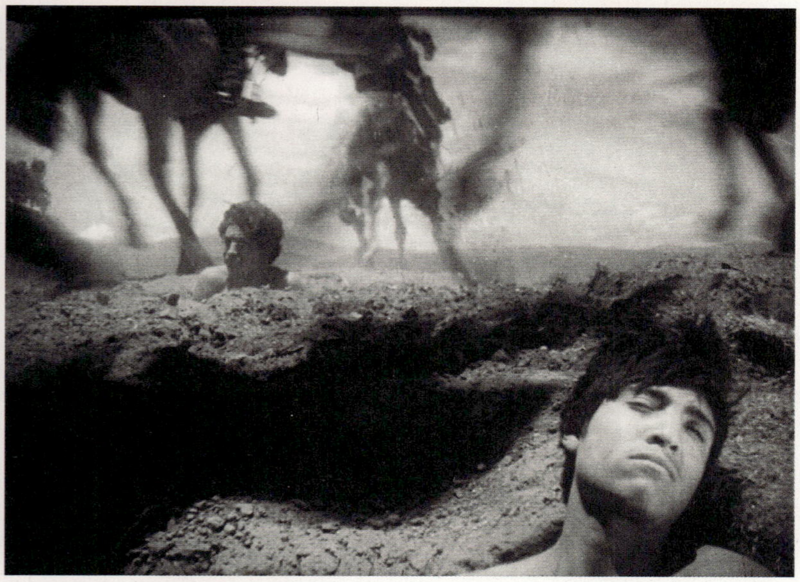

Drawings from the cycles dedicated to the *corrida* (Mexico, 1931):

TOP LEFT
Synthèse: Eve-Europe-Jésus-Torero
(Hacienda Tetlapayac, 1931)

TOP CENTRE
The Mutual Cross
(Hacienda Tetlapayac, 1931)

TOP RIGHT
'Bullfight as crucifixion'
(Mexico City, 1931)

Shots from the film *¡Que viva México!* ('Fiesta' episode):

BOTTOM LEFT
Matador with a muleta and the bull

BOTTOM RIGHT
David Liceaga, the best Mexican *torero* of the year (1931)

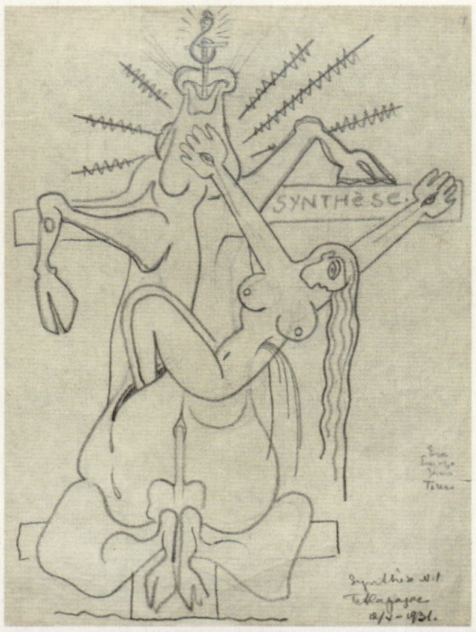

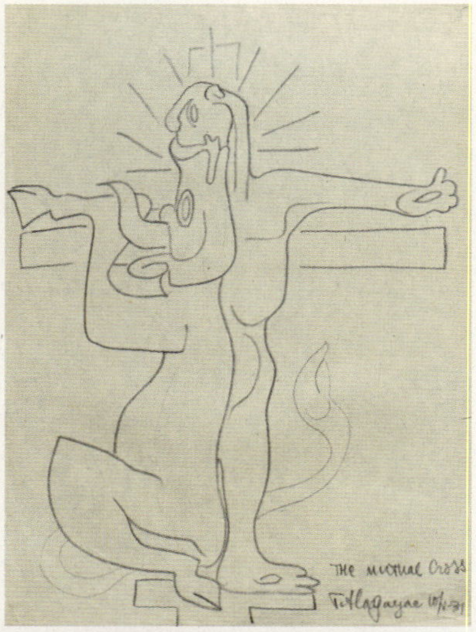

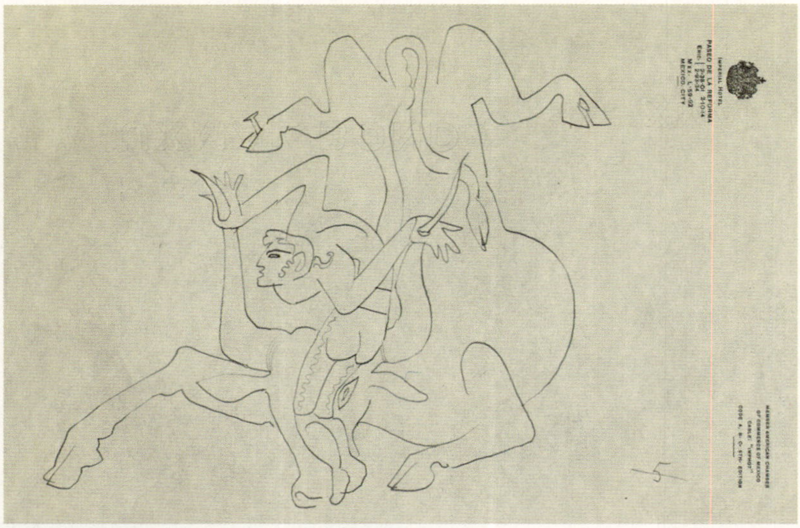

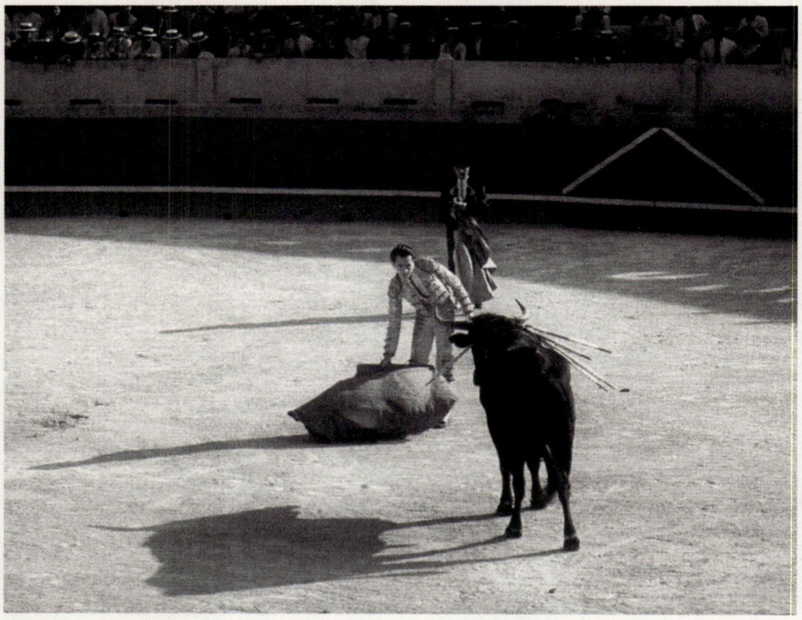

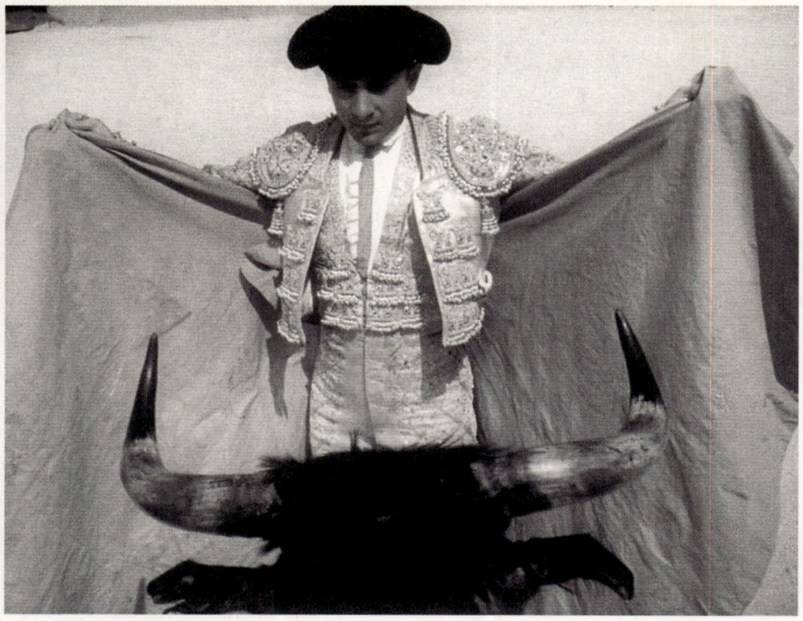

of all known and unknown varieties. An ecstatic who blasphemes in the religious aspect just as intensely as he expresses passion for the social ideal in his objective output.

This atavistic field of E.'s activity is shot through with religiosity in its 'head-over-heels' aspect, déchaînement érotique, *and a sharp expression of the bisexual line, from its crudest animal interpretation to elegant formal and stylistic twists.*

Combining in the monstrous double crucifixion of the fused matadors and bulls in their bloody death-marriage. [Embodied in] the forbidden love triangle among the crosses of Golgotha. The cohabitation of St Teresa with the shadow of the cross. Or the cross as the source of hot and cold water in the bathroom at a Catholic club. Or the cross as a wine dispenser in a bar. A money box. Or, finally, a pen, in the Mrs Crane-Gartz production. (Everything, basically.)[6]

The third kind of activity embraces the two previous ones, as it were: it is his profoundly theoretical work on the concept of art in general, where art is derived from ecstasy just as with Nietzsche tragedy is born from the spirit of music. The medically exhaustive scalpel of materialism, directed into what seem the most esoteric areas of human experience and 'spirit'.

It is not only the fact of this activity, but also its theme (its basic theme, for all the endless variations of nuance and level) that allows this third kind to be a synthesis of the other two, turning the objectivized tool of dialectics back towards the mystic womb that bore it, to illuminate the hidden corners of this mysterious and ancient phenomenon. E. sometimes accumulates research material – drawings – blindly and automatically, and at other times he makes dynamic incisions into the formation of these materials with the microscopic objectivity of a surprised outside observer. (It is just the same within the objective wing of his activity, where his films seem to have been made solely in order to be pinned down on the operating table of theoretical analysis. Dr Jekyll and Mr Hyde, within his own work.)

One must suppose that this supplies a certain additional load of possible insights, for the unity that inevitably connects both principles makes possible a certain orientation during the dark and vague period of the work's birth and a certain intuitive linking at moments of abstract analytical consideration, which preserve a connection to the pulse of the dissociated process.

In the most successful flights of resolution within his films ([in his] activity en grand) there also pulses this primitive, Bacchic image, connected very closely to the intellectual abstraction of the materialized thesis. For instance, in part 2 of The General Line,[7] *where the animal ecstasy of orgiastic symbolism and power is also the most refined bearer of the thesis.*

But sometimes, at times when the weaknesses of the wicked monk of the Middle Ages (the comparison with a bad monk belongs to Anita Brenner, after looking at my drawings) crash against the steel of the intellectual constructions, there suddenly appears an atavism of 'perversion' and of pathologically personal neurotic symptoms... The ecstatically personal liturgies of October, or the pantheistic rites of The General Line. *The Mexico film seems in its conception to be the most complete and flexible with regard to the elements of its realization, embodying this interior skein in all its aspects, fertilized by the highest stage of ecstatic dialectical insight: irony, from crude farce to witty formula or from the example image to the most abstract proposition.*

In Mexico, had Eisenstein not been struck by the combination of different eras, different religious conceptions, different social forms? Travelling from one state to the next was like travelling in time, rather than in space: from modern Mexico City to the matriarchy of Tehuantepec in the South, by way of Yucatán with its pre-Columbian customs and then to the agrarian life of Hidalgo state, recalling feudalism. It was as though historical eras did not replace one another, or drive one another out, but were instead layered one on top of the other, building up a soil out of which the future would emerge, growing from all times at once.

Eisenstein had discovered a similar contemporaneous existence of different periods in the Soviet Union in 1926, when he was preparing to shoot *The General Line* – a film about the destiny of rural Russia. Even Lenin, obsessed with the country's socialist transformation, was forced to admit that 20th-century Russia presented five different socio-economic orders at the same time: primitive communism, semi-feudalism, weak capitalism, imperialism and early socialism. The existence of the crude log house (with no chimney) alongside buildings made from concrete and glass, the wooden plough along-side the tractor, the wise woman alongside the genetics laboratory:

these are only the outward signs of Russia's profound diversity of social formations. Eisenstein also noticed the conjunction of the most varied and blatantly contradictory ideas and norms in people's thinking; but he prioritized a social interpretation of them. Mexico palpably confirmed that historical development was non-linear, and refuted the abstract notion of consistent progress.

But what particularly struck Eisenstein about Mexico was another paradox – one he discovered in himself and described rather openly, fifteen years later, in his memoirs:

> ***I think that what's swum into my mind and my feelings isn't the blood and sand of the bloodthirsty spectacle of the* corrida*, the spiced sensuousness of the tropics, the asceticism and self-mortification of the monks, the scarlet and gold of* Catholicism*, the cosmic timelessness of the Aztec pyramids: no, what's happened is that the whole complex of my own emotions and characteristics has grown out of me here and expanded infinitely, becoming an entire vast country with its mountains, its forests, its cathedrals, its people and its fruit, its beasts and its breakers, its herds and its armies, its painted saints and the majolica of its blue domes, with the necklaces of gold coins that the girls of Tehuantepec wear, and the play of reflections in the canals of Xochimilco....***
>
> ***...when I encountered Mexico, it seemed to me that in all the multiplicity of its contradictions it was something like an outward projection of all the separate lines and characteristics that I had been carrying around inside me like a complex, a tangle, and that I still do.***[8]

A whole country – as a portrait of one man! And Eisenstein goes on to list cultural, natural and ethnic characteristics that one would think were unique to Mexico, but which he felt analogous to his own seemingly Russian and European personality:

> ***Monumental simplicity and baroque abandon – in both its aspects, the Spanish and the Aztec....The duality of these sympathies is repeated anew in my simultaneous attraction to the severe white of the peon's dress – an outfit whose colour and whose linear silhouette make it seem the first step, the* tabula rasa*, of clothing in general – and to the gold and silver bas-reliefs, overloaded with a fabric of gold sculpture, flaming above the blue, green, orange, and cherry-red satin and the black caps of the heroes of the* corrida*...***
>
> ***I loved both, and I felt that both were close to me.***
>
> ***I harmonized with both.***
>
> ***And both seemed to harmonize with me.***
>
> ***And I sank my teeth into both, greedily, using the lenses of Eduard Tisse's incomparable ciné camera.***[9]

Eisenstein recollected another resonance that Mexico had aroused in him: the 'string of cruelty', which had been touched in his heart since childhood. His very first films had seen him accused of sadism, despite the fact that his imagination created horrific scenes simply in order to teach both himself, the director, and the audience to overcome their fear of cruelty and death. That was why, even before he travelled to the New World, he had been attracted by the Mexicans' (superficially) paradoxical sense of humour: their laughter at death, their life-affirming *danse macabre* every 2 November on the national Day of the Dead. And that was why the first thing he drew in Mexico, in December 1930, was the comic cycle 'Duncan mort', as if the tragedy of Macbeth and his wife were staged by clowns and acrobats in the circus. Over a period of six months, Eisenstein would draw more than two hundred variations on this theme: these highly refined depictions of murder, decadence and torture contained an antidote to Mexico's brutal humour and to his own personal irony.

Eisenstein also acknowledged something that he could not discuss openly in Russia, but which comes through strongly in his 'visuastenography' of 1931. He was attracted by the Mexicans' almost androgynous unity of the masculine and feminine principles:

> ***This 'race' is dear to me, concealing muscles of steel under flowing coverings, free of spite, but at the same time as capricious as a child: this combination of features in the Mexican* indio *make him or her –* muchacho *or* muchacha *– a kind of perpetual unity of monsieur, madame et bébé. Even adults, people who have become men and women, seem like a race of adolescents compared to other races, a race of youth, where the young men have not yet lost their primordial girlishness, the young women are still boyishly mischievous, and both still have the charm of childhood.***
>
> ***Of course, I am thinking of an ideal, collective, average type, and of the best examples of women and men, youths and girls, who passed before my camera and before myself in the long months when I was***

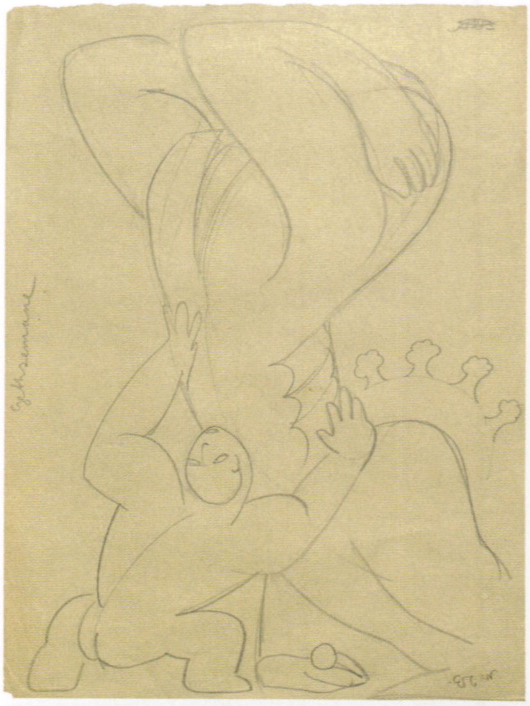

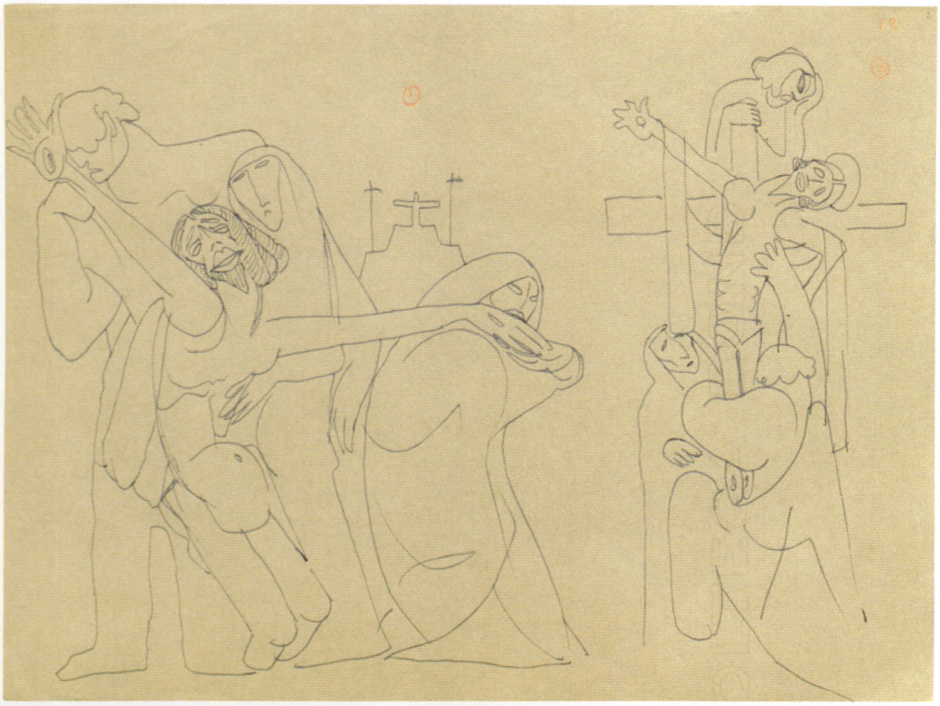

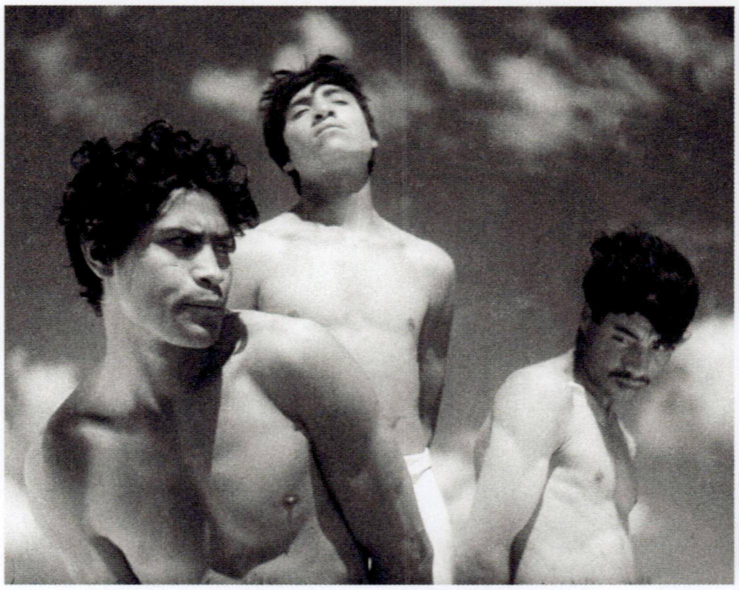

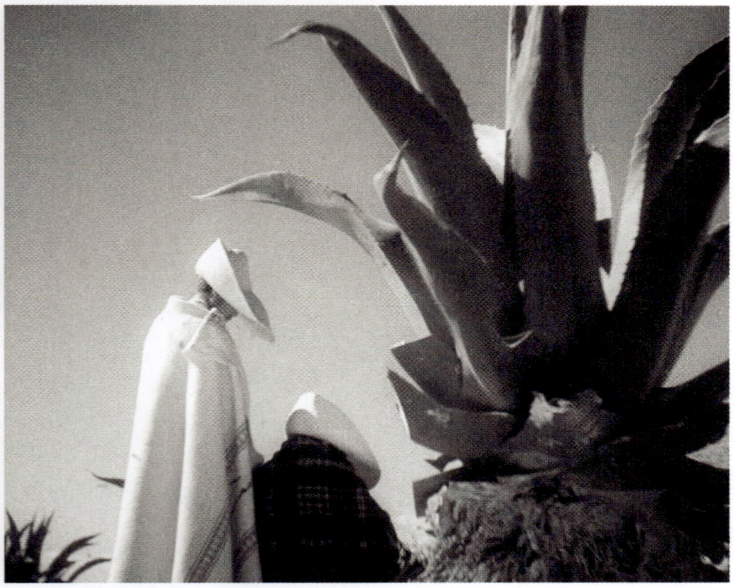

Drawings from cycles with religious motifs (1931):

TOP LEFT
'Gethsemane', drawing no. 23 from the cycle 'Crucifixion'

TOP RIGHT
Pietà

Shots from the film *¡Que viva México!* ('Maguey' episode):

BOTTOM LEFT
Golgotha of the rebels

BOTTOM RIGHT
Sorrow of the peons

—THIS PAGE

BELOW LEFT
'Swaddling Christ', drawing no. 26 from the cycle 'Crucifixion'

BELOW RIGHT (TOP AND BOTTOM)
Shots from the film *¡Que viva México!* ('Maguey' episode): Preparation for the execution

—OVERLEAF

TOP (LEFT AND RIGHT)
Drawings from the cycle 'La Fuite en Egypte' (Flight into Egypt) (1931)

BOTTOM
Shot from the film *¡Que viva México!* ('Maguey' episode): Sebastian brings Maria to the hacienda

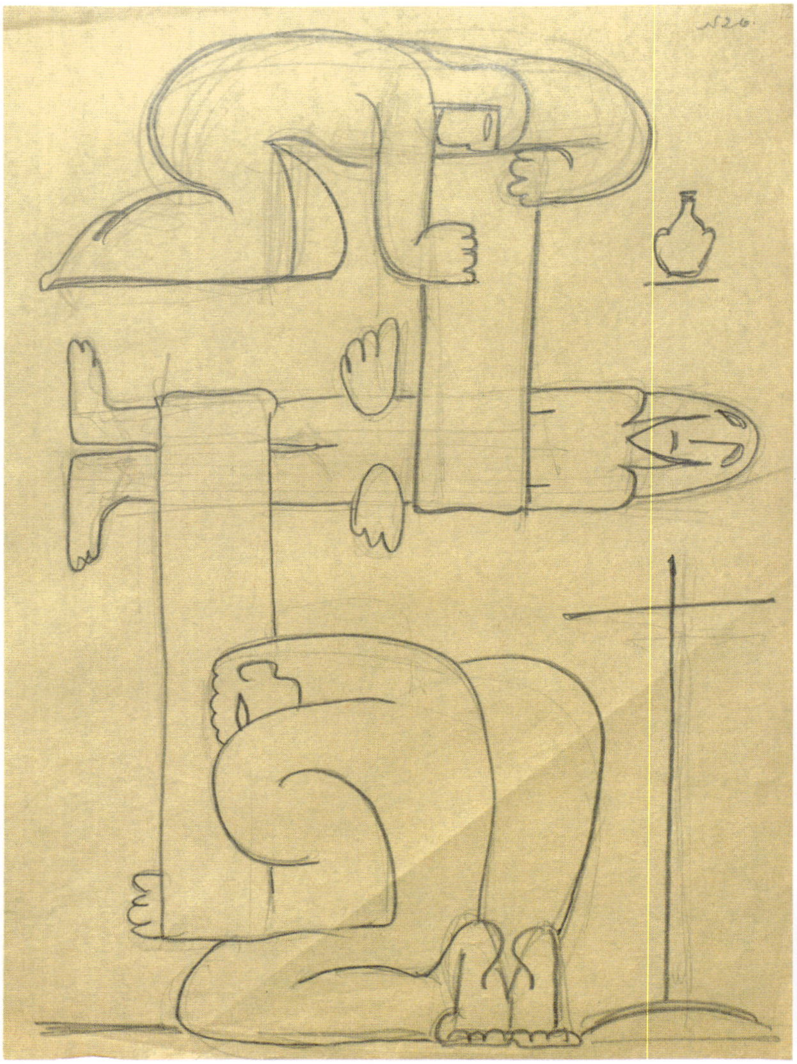

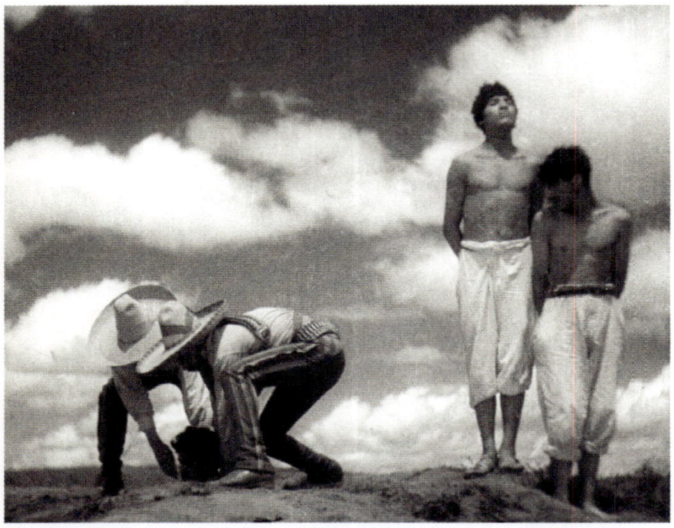

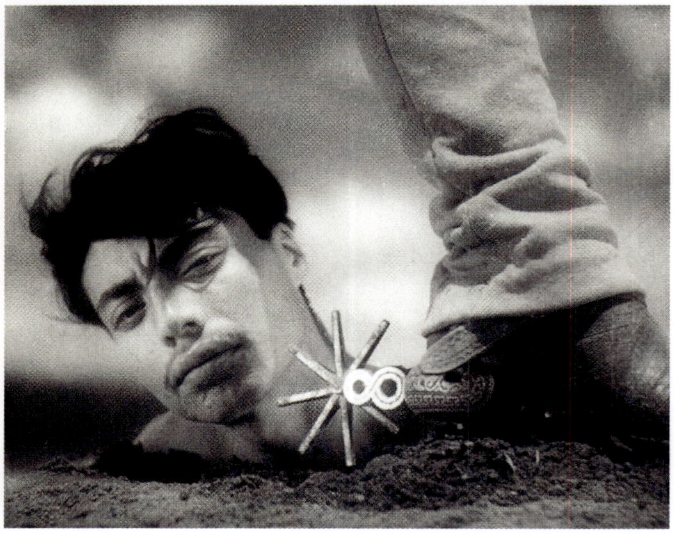

travelling through this strange and peculiar, cruel and tender, and childishly delightful Mexico.[10]

Eisenstein even drew a 'formula' for this unity. Not exactly a pair of lovers, nor exactly one combined being that has survived from antiquity (see Aristophanes' myth in Plato's *Symposium*).

He experienced the return to drawing as a return to himself:

And it happened in that very Mexico, where drawing is undergoing a stage of inner purification in its quest for the mathematical, abstract, pure line.

The effect is particularly acute when this abstracted ('intellectualized') line becomes the means for drawing deeply emotional combinations of human figures, usually in some kind of especially weird and abstruse situations! [Maurice] Bardèche and [Robert] Brasillach consider my basic characteristic as an artist to be a very strongly expressed sensualism combined with a capacity for the most extreme abstraction. That is a great compliment to me, and I am thoroughly happy with it....[11]

And this is where Eisenstein made his fundamental discoveries. His drawings, spontaneous in origin, carried images up from the depths of his unconscious: images that were often surprising, sometimes even frightening, and which invariably attracted his own investigative attention. He formulated in German this property of his graphics: '...meine Zeichnungen sind emotionelle Hieroglyphen der Vor-Erkenntniss...' 'my drawings are emotional hieroglyphs of pre-cognition'.[12]

This 'atavistic sphere of E.'s activities', expressed in graphic art and made into an object of contemplation, led Eisenstein to the conclusion that the human consciousness was also multi-layered. It included not only different forms of thinking, but also forms belonging to different (historical) times, based not on rational logical categories but on proto-logical images. Above all, these forms were based on methods and 'mechanisms' that had taken shape in profound antiquity and that continued to operate in the unconscious perception and interpretation of reality – and especially actively when reality was creatively transformed into art.

Why are these 'bizarre double crucifixions where the matador and the bull fuse in a bloody marriage of death' (as Eisenstein, writing in his private journal, described the depictions of the *corrida* in his drawings) so disturbing? And why do they seem inexplicable? Is it not because these plastic metaphors have a kind of resonance, on the level of feelings? That they awaken impulses in layers and forms of the ancient mythological consciousness where it still seems quite natural that man and beast, wedding and death, should be inseparable?

The *corrida* struck Eisenstein as more than just an intensely passionate and picturesque spectacle, more than a genuine fight to the death between man and beast. Neither was its appeal limited to the selflessness and choreographic precision of the *toreros*' movements. No: in a bullfight, Eisenstein discovered a conjunction of historically diverse religious beliefs, opposing ethical norms and multiple ethnic customs and ways of life. He would later comment:

The 'bullfighting suite', where the theme of the bullfight is interwoven in the most various ways with the St Sebastian theme. And sometimes the martyr is the matador, sometimes...the bull.

There is even a drawing of a bull crucified, transfixed with arrows, like St Sebastian.

None of this is my fault.

It is Mexico that combines the blood of Christ at morning mass in the cathedral, and gouts of bulls' blood at the **corrida** ***in the city arena after lunch, into a single atmosphere of Sunday festivities; and tickets for the bullfight are adorned with an image of Our Lady of Guadalupe, whose four hundredth anniversary is marked not only with pilgrimages of many thousands, with dozens of South American cardinals in crimson-red robes, but also by particularly splendid*** **corridas** ***'to the glory of the Mother of God'*** **(de la Madre de Dios).**[13]

Eisenstein was struck by this public slaying of the beast, at the risk of the slayer's own life, in the name of the Virgin Mary, or to the glory of a saint – after humble prayers in church!

The ancient pagan ritual of killing the sacred bull – the most ancient of gods, to whom man was once offered as a sacrifice! A ritual inherited from the Iberians, or established in the Pyrenean peninsula at some point in the past (by the ancient Greeks? Or the Arabs?), to be taken from there by the Spanish and instilled along with Christianity into Mexican culture. And did the archaic European Minotauromachy not answer also to the human sacrifices practised in the ancient religion of the Aztecs and Incas? The Latin American phenomenon, that interweaving of the Old and New Worlds, found expression not only in the nature of the ethnic groups – for which Eisenstein found an amusing graphic 'formula' combining faces and 'masks' – but also deep in the Latin American perception of the world.

David Liceaga – in 1931, the finest *torero* in Mexico – was filmed by Eisenstein for the 'Fiesta' episode in *¡Que viva México!*. He told

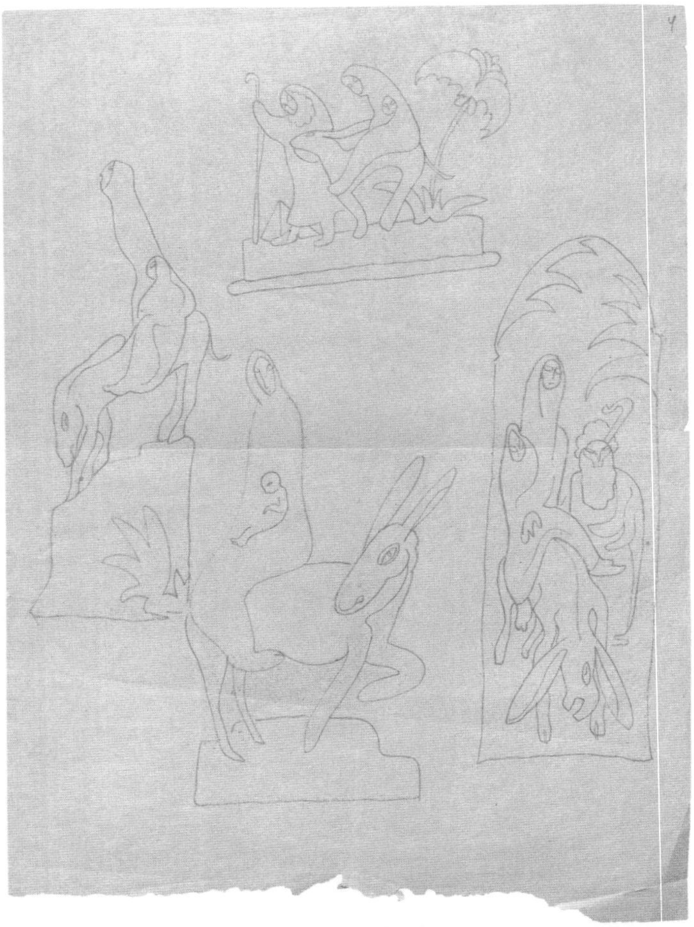

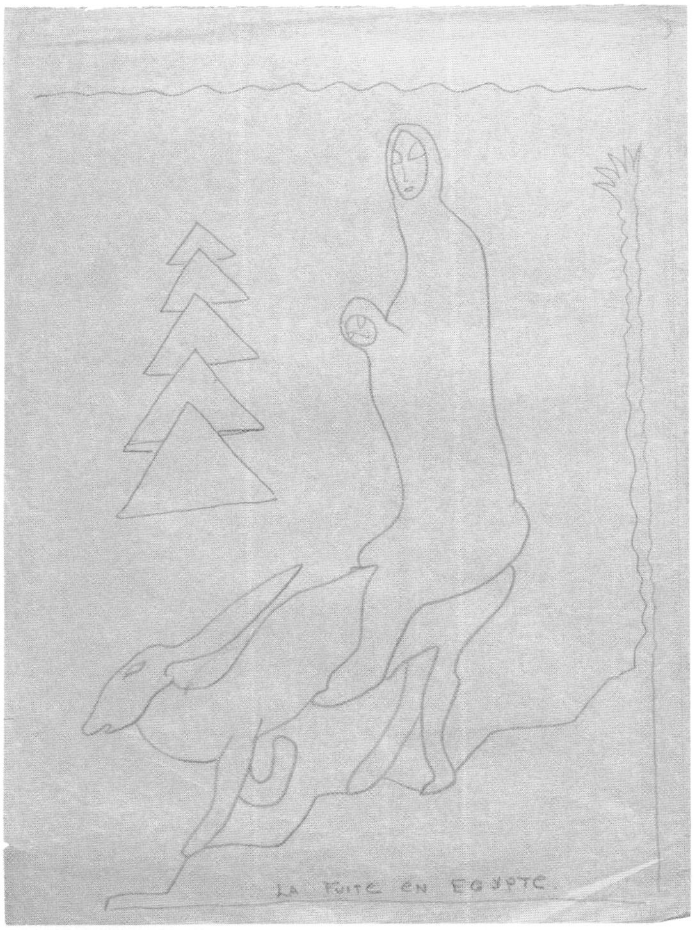
LA FUITE EN EGYPTE.

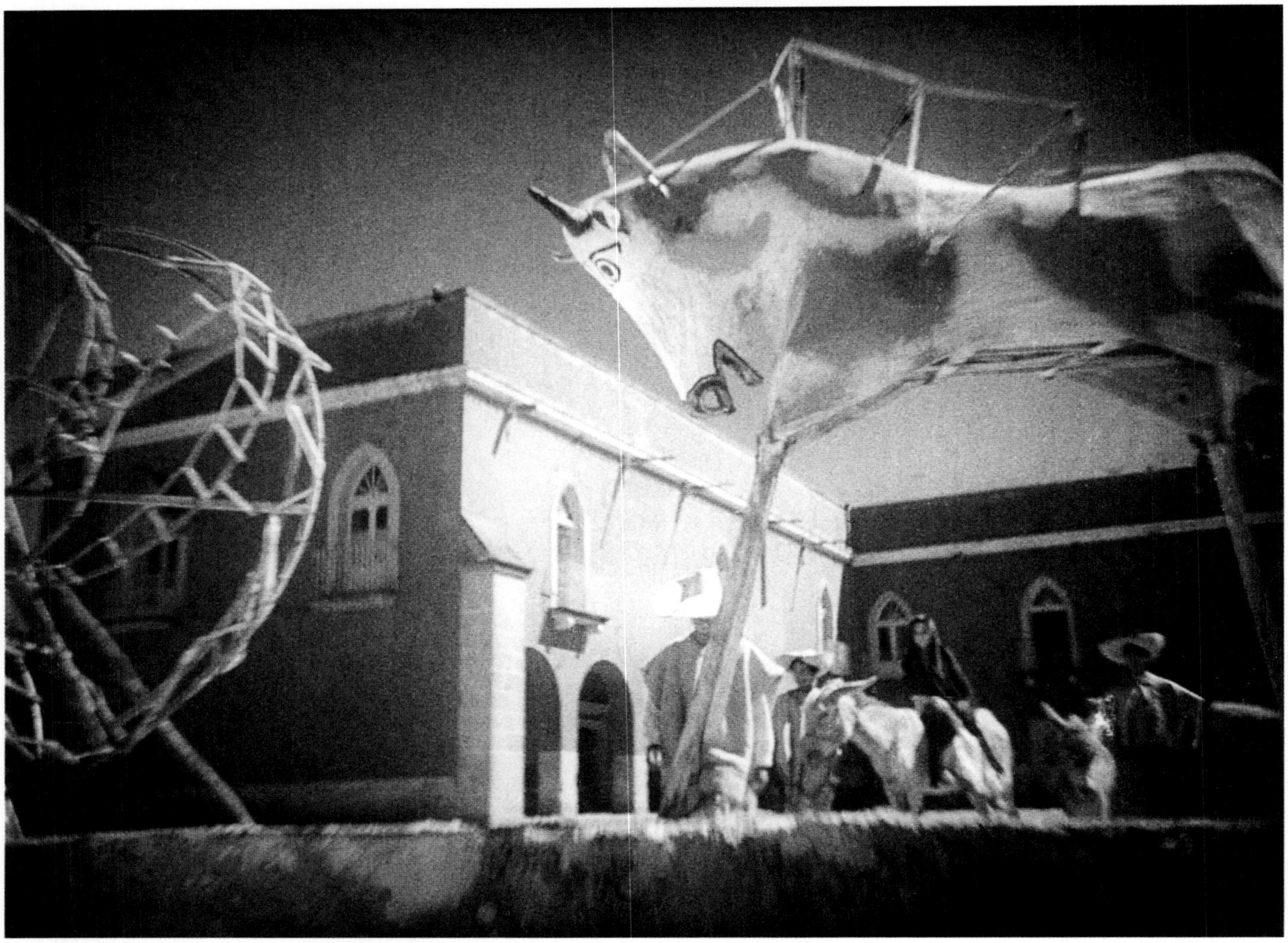

the Russian director how, when he was fatally close to the horns, he would almost stroke the bull's face with his *muleta* (the toreador's cape, which hangs from a hollow staff) – a motion known as a 'Veronica', because it recalled the gesture of St Veronica in wiping the sweat from Christ's face as he carried the cross to Golgotha. Blasphemy? Or, on the contrary, a sign of a profound religious sensibility? Or an insight belonging to a wise popular intuition, which had detected in the compassion of St Veronica a trace of ancient rites in which the divine victim was tenderly adorned – before being killed? The toreador also admitted that when he ran the bull through with his sword, he felt genuine love for it: an almost erotic oneness with the Beast that was his victim and his own potential killer.

Is it any wonder that the images that welled up in Eisenstein's imagination – and were then immediately transferred onto paper by his pencil or his pen – fused the bull, the *torero*, Christ and Sebastian? On one occasion, he added to this 'synthesis' the myth of the rape of Europa by Zeus as a bull – and also the theme of the serpent deceiving Eve.

It was no coincidence that the name Sebastian was given to one of the heroes of *¡Que viva México!* in 1931. In the episode titled 'Maguey', the indigenous peon Sebastian asks the hacienda owner for permission to marry. His bride, María, falls victim to the *droit du seigneur*, and the proud descendant of the Aztecs, who bears the name of the Christian saint, is killed in the course of a rebellion against this survival of feudal customs. He is not killed by the arrows of the pagans, but under the horses of the heirs to the Spanish colonizers. In a sketch for this episode, Eisenstein hints at the character's mythological prototype: the *charros'* rifle barrels are pointed, like arrows, at Sebastian, who has been caught in the agave fields and dragged back to the hacienda. And we can see in the sketch to the scene of the cruel execution, that the face of dying Sebastian becomes alike to the head of a slain bull.

It would be naive to see nothing more in these echoes and interweavings of disparate themes than a merely irresponsible and wilful play of associations – cynical and godless. The *corrida* arena was not transformed into Golgotha, the swords and *banderillas* (the metal-tipped spiked that the toreador drives into the bull's neck) into arrows, as a result of the learning of the scholar, so much as by the intense emotions that shook the artist, the bold insights that occurred to the attentive observer.

Eisenstein's drawings, first in Mexico and then in Moscow, brought the profound impulses of his imagination to the surface. And they clearly influenced his reassessment of some ideas and concepts from the school of Sigmund Freud. Thus, for instance, he arrived at a different interpretation of the so-called unconscious, where sinful urges are exiled (or 'repressed'), as if to a prison cellar, and where at the same time suppressed erotic desires continue to dwell:

> ***It takes a whole series of years to realize [that] the stock of primordial impulses is wider than the narrowly sexual, as Freud sees it, i.e. is wider than the boundaries of the personal biological adventures of the human individual.***
>
> ***The sphere of sex is no more than a knotted concentrate, which recreates through numberless spiral repetitions the laws of a much more extensive radius.***
>
> ***This is why I like D. H. Lawrence's conceptions, which have forced him beyond the boundaries of sex into cosmic forms of integral fusion (which are inaccessible [...]).***
>
> ***this is why I am drawn to my own conception of the proto-logical belt: that subconscious that includes [sensuality], but is not enslaved by sex.***
>
> ***And this is also why the subconscious itself is depicted above all as a reflection of earlier and less differentiated stages of social being – above all.***[14]

Is it a coincidence that Eisenstein should have used the word 'depicted' in characterizing the subconscious? Hardly. Drawing was – by way of his own subconscious – the very means he used to try to glimpse the depths of thinking, so as to understand the ontogenetic and phylogenetic sources of creative processes. The process of his renewed drawing, and subsequent analysis of what he had drawn, was a substantial influence on what Eisenstein called the 'Grundproblem', the basic difficulty on the road to an understanding of the artistic method in general.

But this road in the creative art did not lead only through an immersion in the depths of the subconscious. Eisenstein, in a passage quoted above, also writes of a movement in quite the opposite direction – out into the cosmic forms of integral fusion through the ecstasy. Elsewhere, he directly names ecstasy as the experience that Mexico had given him – or rather, restored to him – an experience that was also connected to drawing and one that he had known since his youth.

Later, in Moscow, in his lectures at the Institute of Cinematography and in his theoretical works on pathetic composition, Eisenstein would offer a derivation of the word 'ecstasy' from the Latin *ex-stasis*: exit from stasis, transition from one state to another. Such etymology was incorrect, in fact, but it would damp down suspicions about the word's mystical meanings, which were dangerous under Soviet dialectical materialism. And it was only at the end of his life, in a chapter of his memoirs, that Eisenstein admitted that he himself had participated in ecstatic religion in his youth: in St Petersburg in 1916, before he did so for the last time before the Revolution, he had seen his spiritual father experience a true ecstasy during prayer.[15]

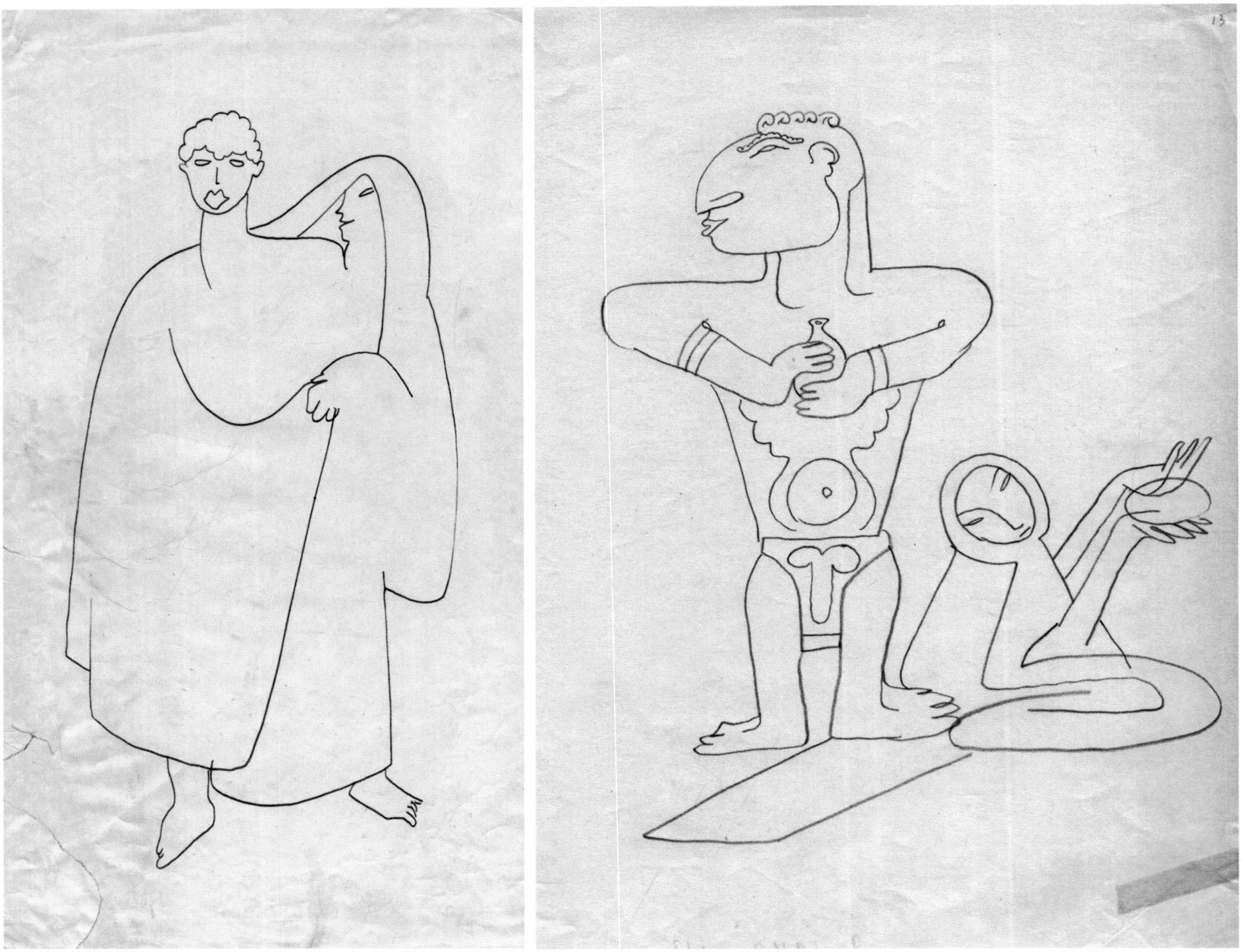

—THIS PAGE
Drawings with the 'Male-Female' motif
(Mexico, 1931)

—OVERLEAF

LEFT PAGE
Yo Autoritratto Nuevo Laredo
(1st version, 1932)

RIGHT PAGE
Arrested Sebastian at the Hacienda
Motif for the film *¡Que viva México!*
('Maguey' episode) (1931)

In Mexico, he saw the *indios* dancing at the festival for the 400th anniversary of Our Lady of Guadalupe – and for Eisenstein, the religious ecstasy was no less important an experience than the bullfight. Busy as he was with shooting his film, he bought up books on the great ecstatics of the Catholic world – Ignatius Loyola, St Teresa, St John of the Cross. He sought accounts of manifestations of ecstasy in other religions. And in Chapter 11 of Théophile Gautier's *Constantinople*, he found a description of whirling dervishes. It was not just that they were strikingly similar to the dansantes: their motions gave Eisenstein the explanation for his own drawings from the 'Corrida-Crucifixion' cycle.

They waltz, arms extended in a cross shape, their heads leaning on their shoulders, their eyes half-closed, their mouths half-open, like confident swimmers who let the river of ecstasy transport them... Sometimes their heads would go back and we would see the whites of their eyes, and the light foam on their lips...

The point is the cross shape... The cross-like position of the arms is a direct centrifugal result of the 'waltzing', circling motion, since the cross is the attitude of maximum expansion and DISSOLUTION: i.e. it is a furthest point that self-dissolution can reach. (NB. the two legs are at the same time drawn together, forming a trunk!)

This is why the practice of ecstasy knows of two positions, which are polar opposites: fetal contraction (which is also one of the attitudes adopted in fakirism) and maximal expansion [....]

The cross is also a hypertrophied maximum, '180°' embrace....[16]

The descriptions of Ignatius Loyola's exercises and of the prayerful ecstasy of the saints that Eisenstein found in Father Augustin Poulain's book *Des grâces d'oraison* convinced him that erotic and religious 'tension' were related. It was this profound inner relationship that came to the surface in the 'maximally ecstatic embrace' in the form of cross, uniting his cycles on the *corrida*, on Golgotha and on the stigmata of St Francis. Here is another fragment of the same journal entry from 28 February 1932:

NB. It's as though even if my drawings do not reveal much, or much new, in the field of the expressive attitudes of the draughtsman (and I 'play' my drawings, the way Disney 'plays' Mickey before he starts to draw – Walt himself told me that), they will still illustrate a whole series of propositions – and the whole 'basic proposition' as such – about the sensory pre-complex of philosophical speculation.

Eisenstein the draughtsman did not, of course, deny the existence of erotic ecstasy. He could depict it very openly – sometimes in 'graphic sublimations', sometimes in ironic 'provocations for friends' that he rarely titled or dated (a sure sign that he did not count these drawings among the body of his serious graphic work).

Eisenstein found a serious 'cosmic formula' for erotic ecstasy in his cycle 'Ex-stasis', born in the same Nuevo Laredo. Here, the image of Monsieur and Madame 'beside themselves', their unity, their self-denial and their immortality, is embodied in Bébé. The image of the interrelation between death, birth and eternal life is expressed through bodiless mask faces that soar in weightlessness and through maximally (diagonally) extended arms, which form a square and are sometimes again enclosed in a circle.

We can now return to the strange self-portrait that Eisenstein drew on the very day when he finished his Notes for Anita Brenner. Which came first? It is conceivable that the drawings did not arise as an illustration to the text at all: Eisenstein could easily have first 'sharply seen' his various hypostases and put them down on paper in the form of different people, even people of different genders, and only then formulated the qualities of these symbolic images (images of his activity? Or of his personality?) in words. The first version of the drawing was still just a ranging shot aimed at the target he saw glimmering in his imagination. The androgynous, self-absorbed being in the rear contrasts with the crucified male figure and the playful, coquettish female. Who are they? The suffering spirit and the amorous soul? The mortified flesh and the compassionate heart? And is the stern woman in monastic habit, lying face down (on the ground? Like the warrior in Diego Rivera's fresco!), the dead muse?

But Eisenstein, clearly unhappy with the drawing's imprecision or with its obviously allegorical character, found himself other visual metaphors. We can interpret them like this. Along with the physically strong, but already wounded Youth (the Artist? The Flesh?), his ecstatically illuminated Faith (Thought? Soul?) is also nailed to the cross, wearing a radiant halo.... The Beautiful Woman with the bare heart, ready to love, hides her eyes behind a stern monastic veil (out of modesty? Or embarrassment? Or because she has been ordered to?)

And in front of them all we have the crippled Invalid Clown, Rorik's childhood symbol for Art itself.

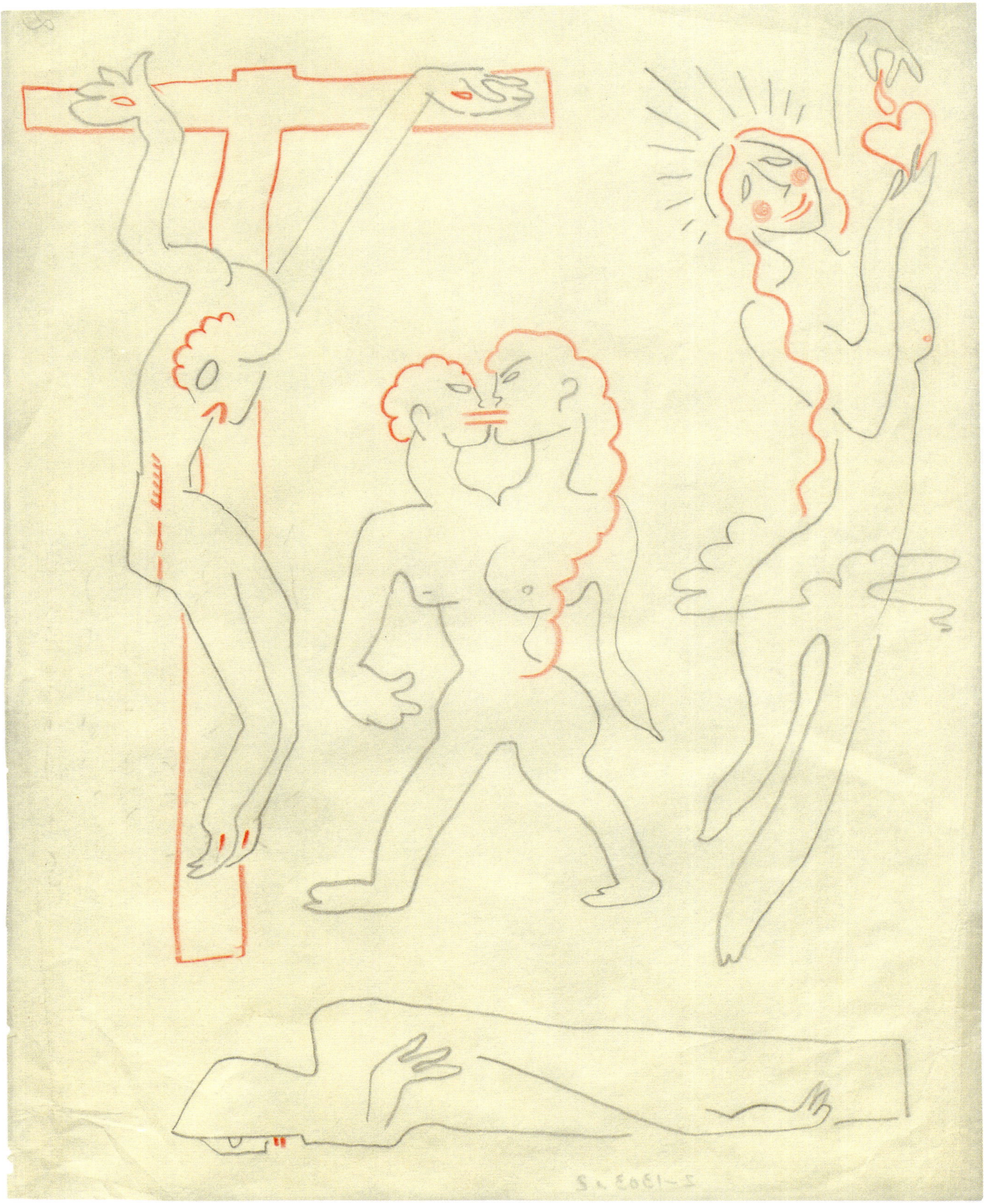

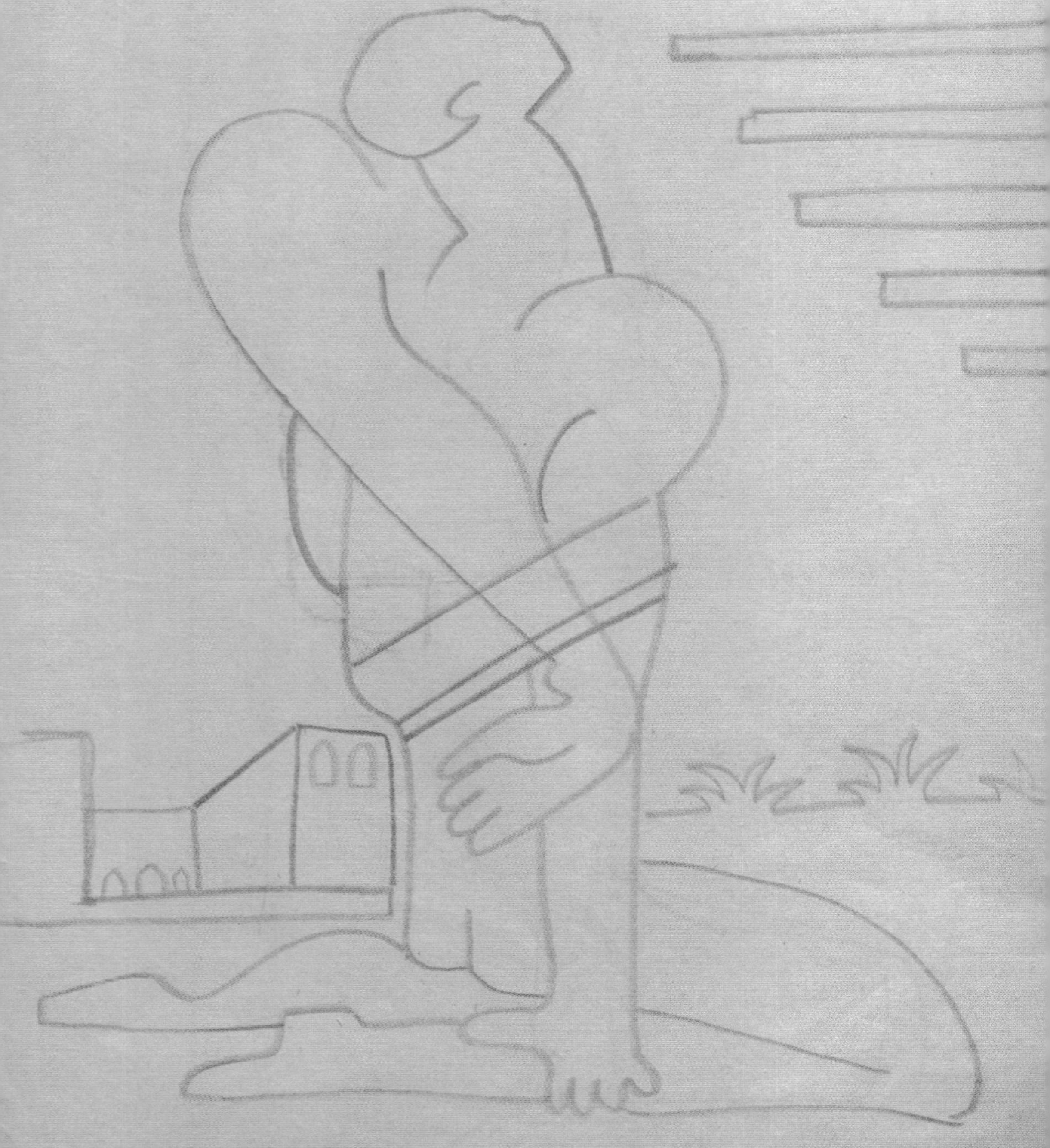

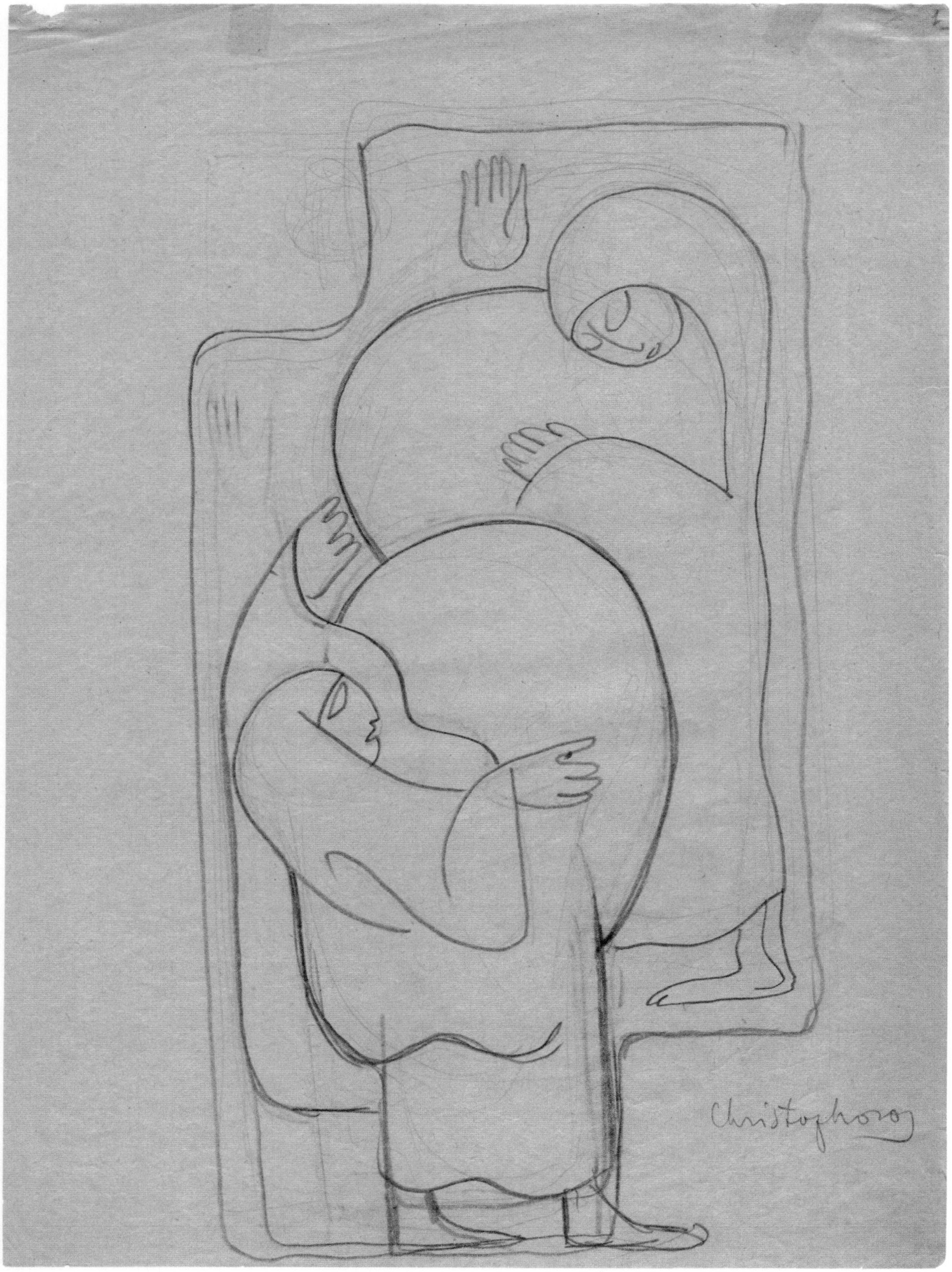

—THIS PAGE
Christophoros (1931)

—OPPOSITE
Motifs for the film *¡Que viva México!* (1931)

TOP LEFT
'Mexican Madonna' (1931)

TOP RIGHT
'Peon in sorrow' (Hacienda Tetlapayac, 1931)

BOTTOM (LEFT AND RIGHT)
'Peons at Hacienda Tetlapayac' (1931)

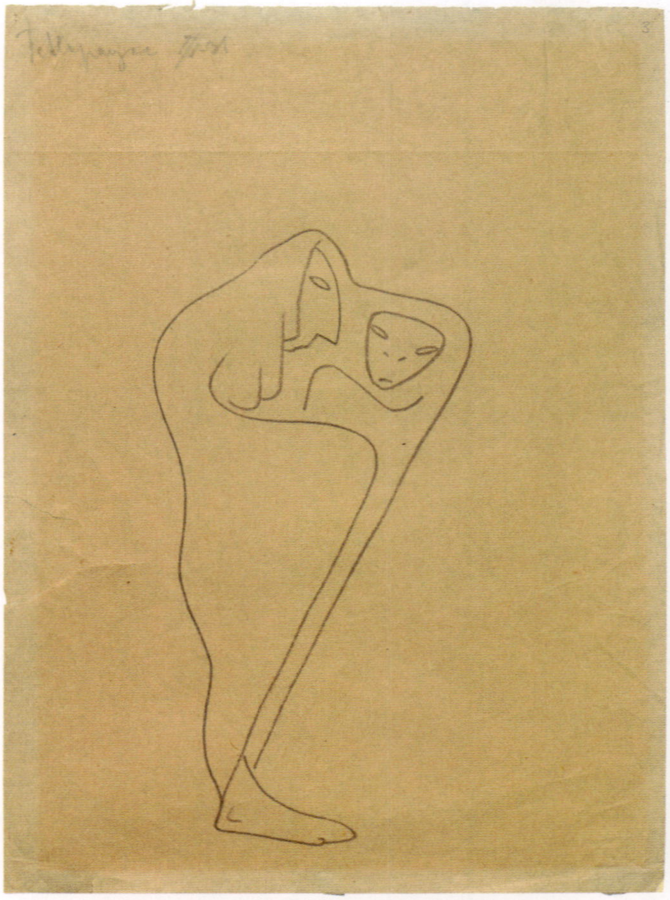

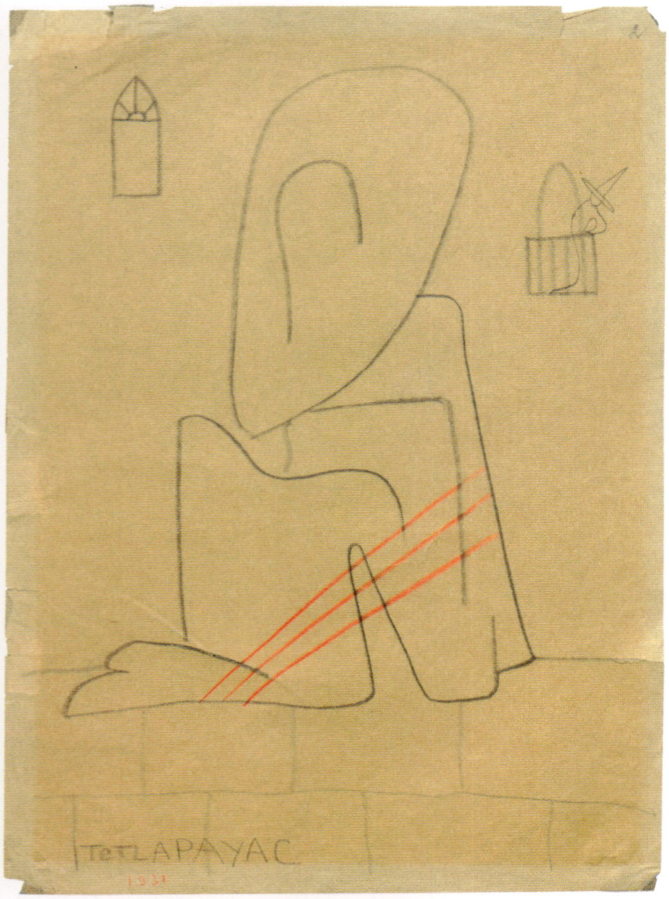
TETLAPAYAC
1931

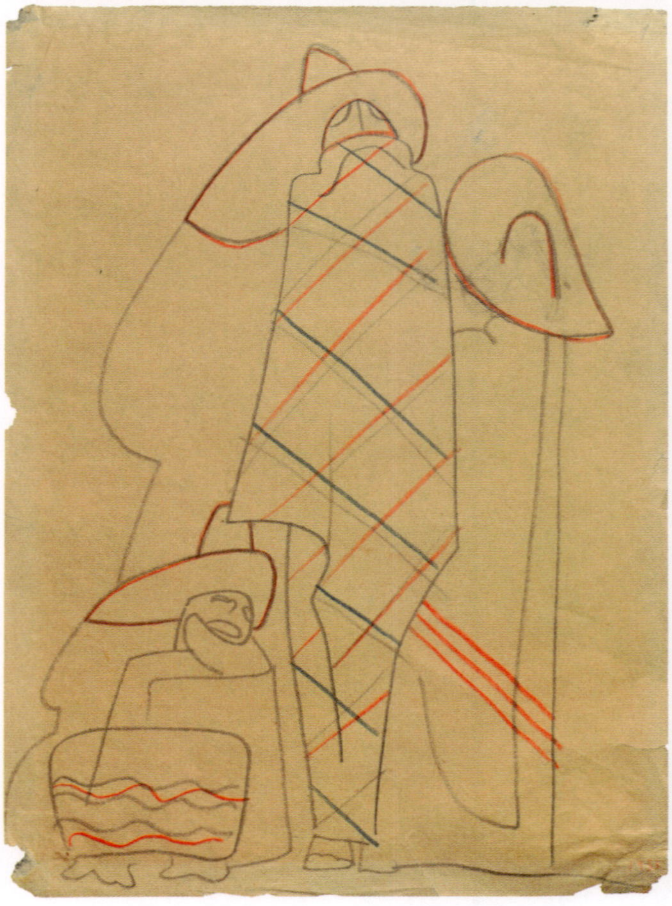

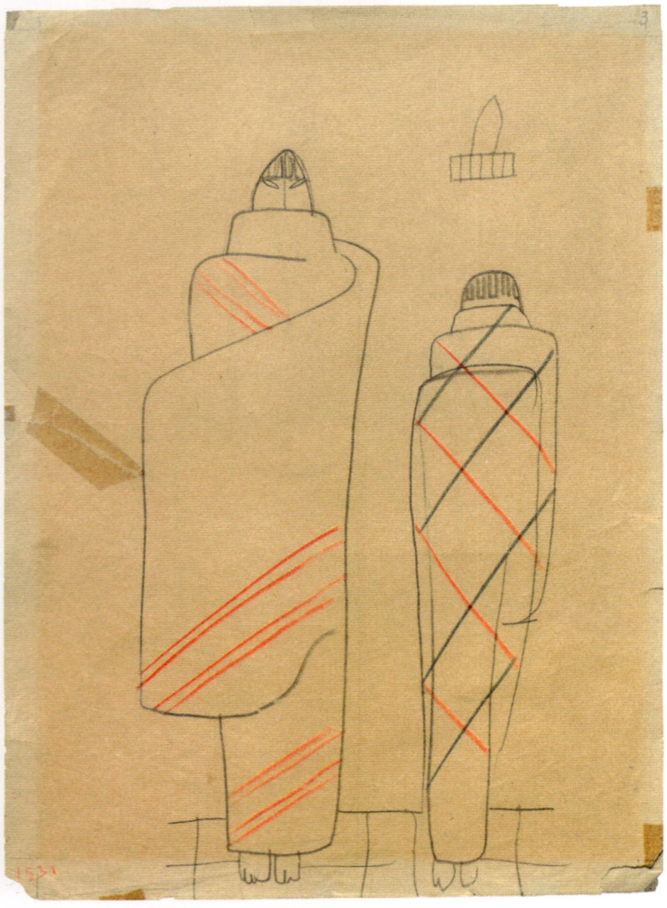

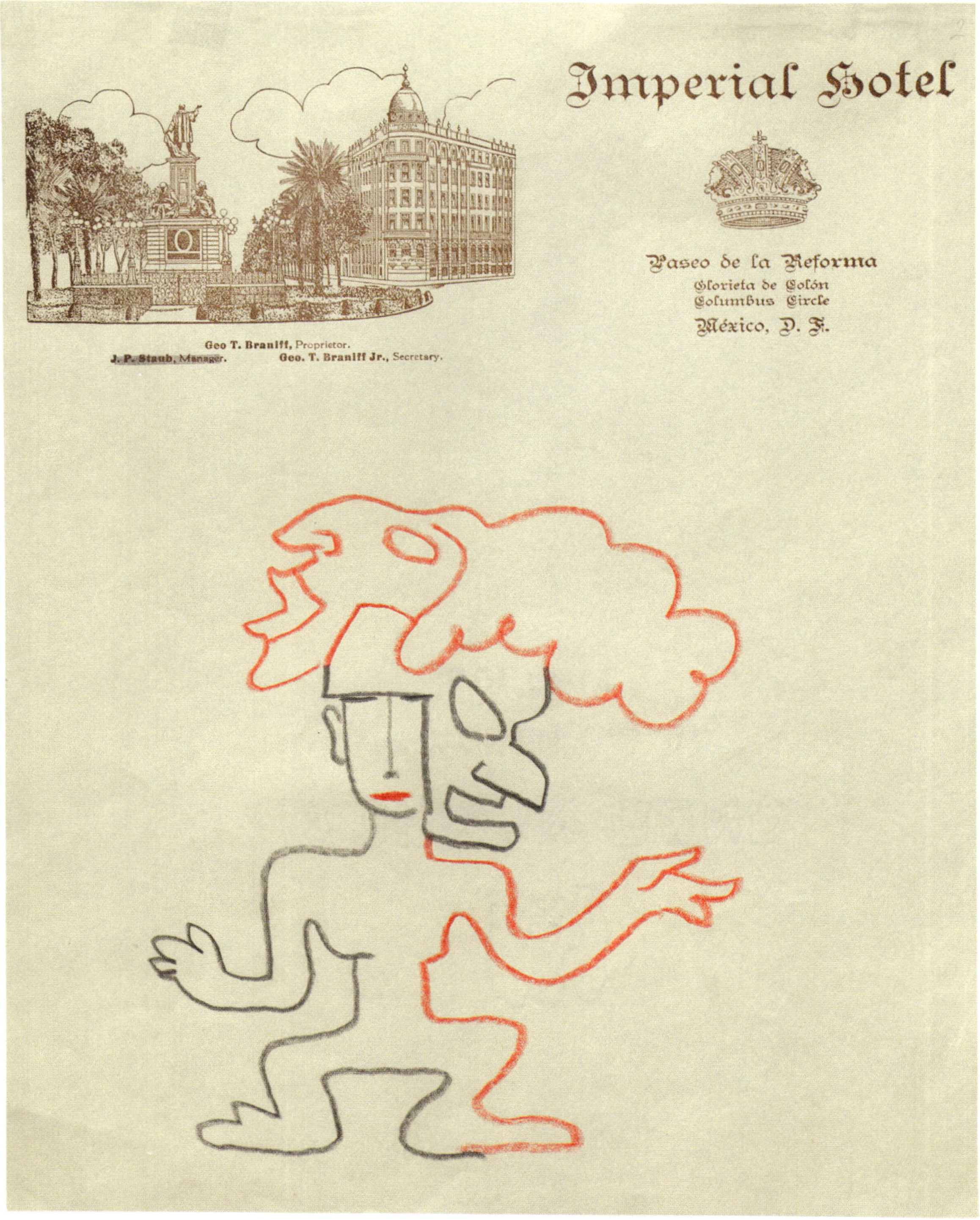

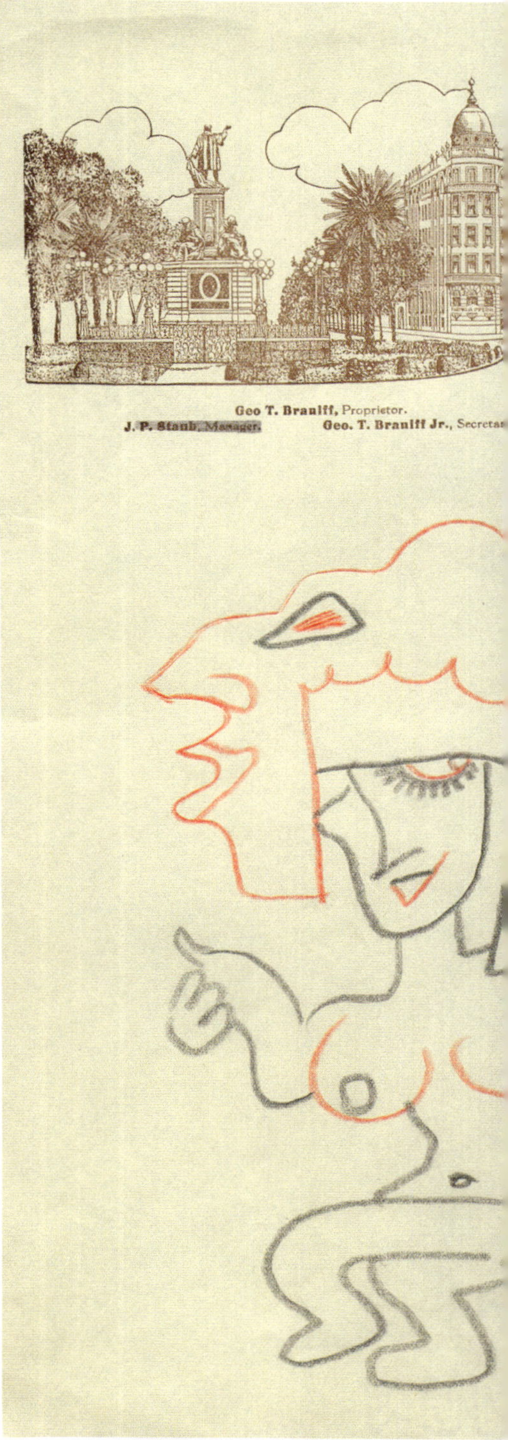

ABOVE
From the cycle 'Three faces of Mexico'
(Mexico City, 1931)

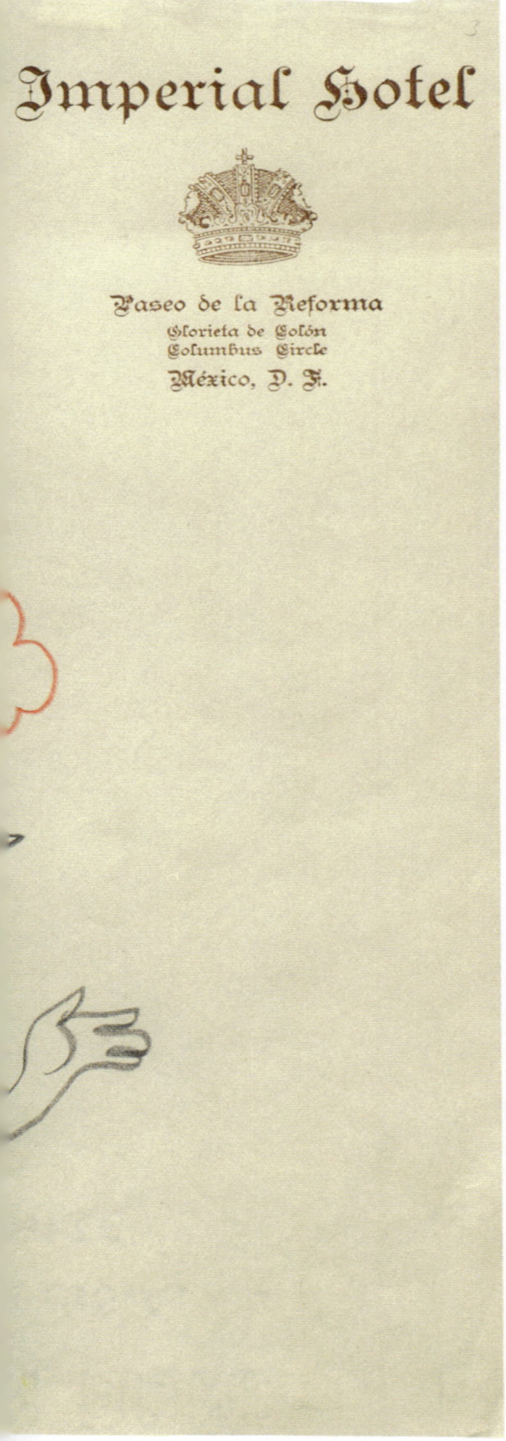
Imperial Hotel
Paseo de la Reforma
Glorieta de Colón
Columbus Circle
México, D. F.

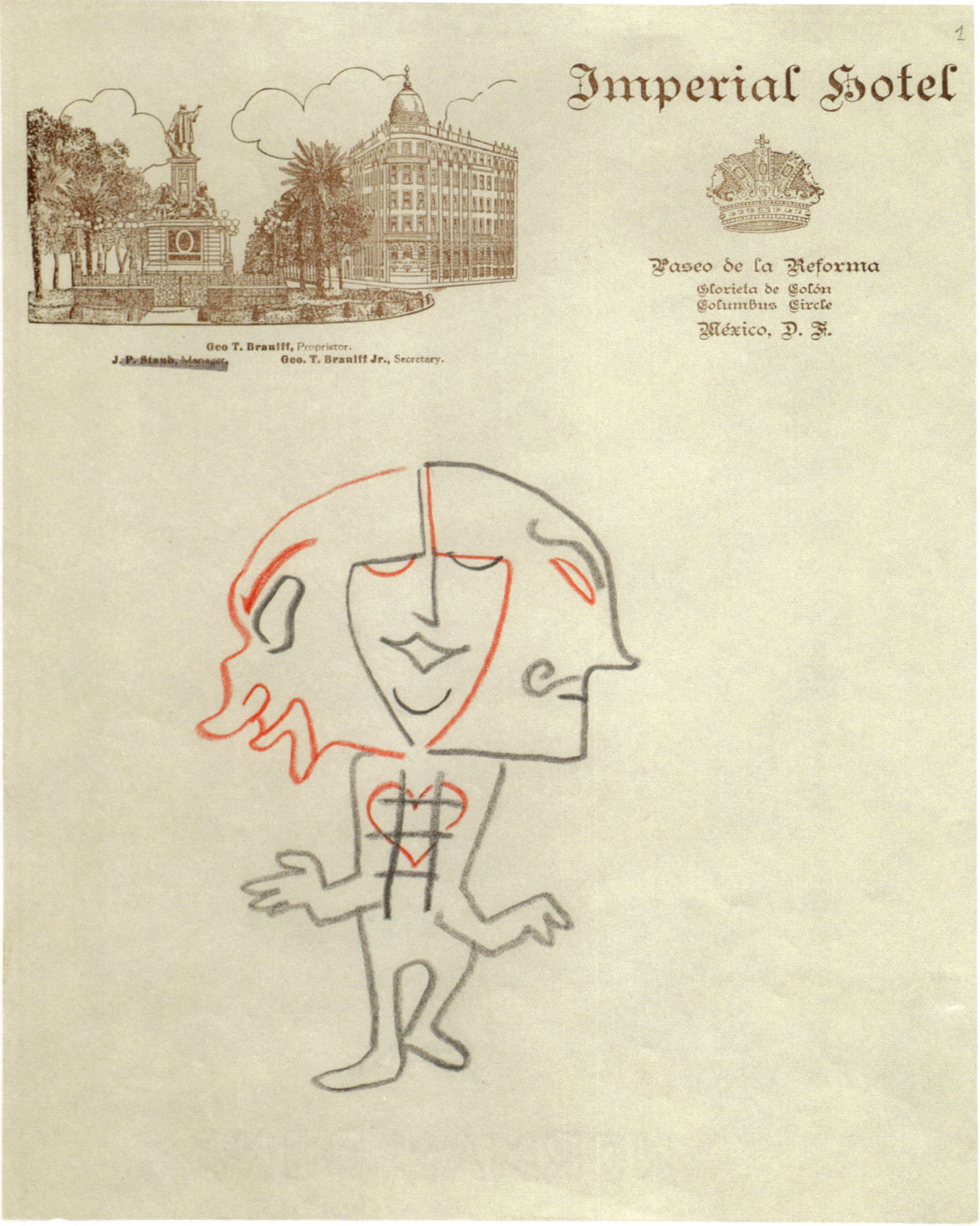
Imperial Hotel
Paseo de la Reforma
Glorieta de Colón
Columbus Circle
México, D. F.
Geo T. Braniff, Proprietor.
J. P. Staub, Manager.
Geo. T. Braniff Jr., Secretary.

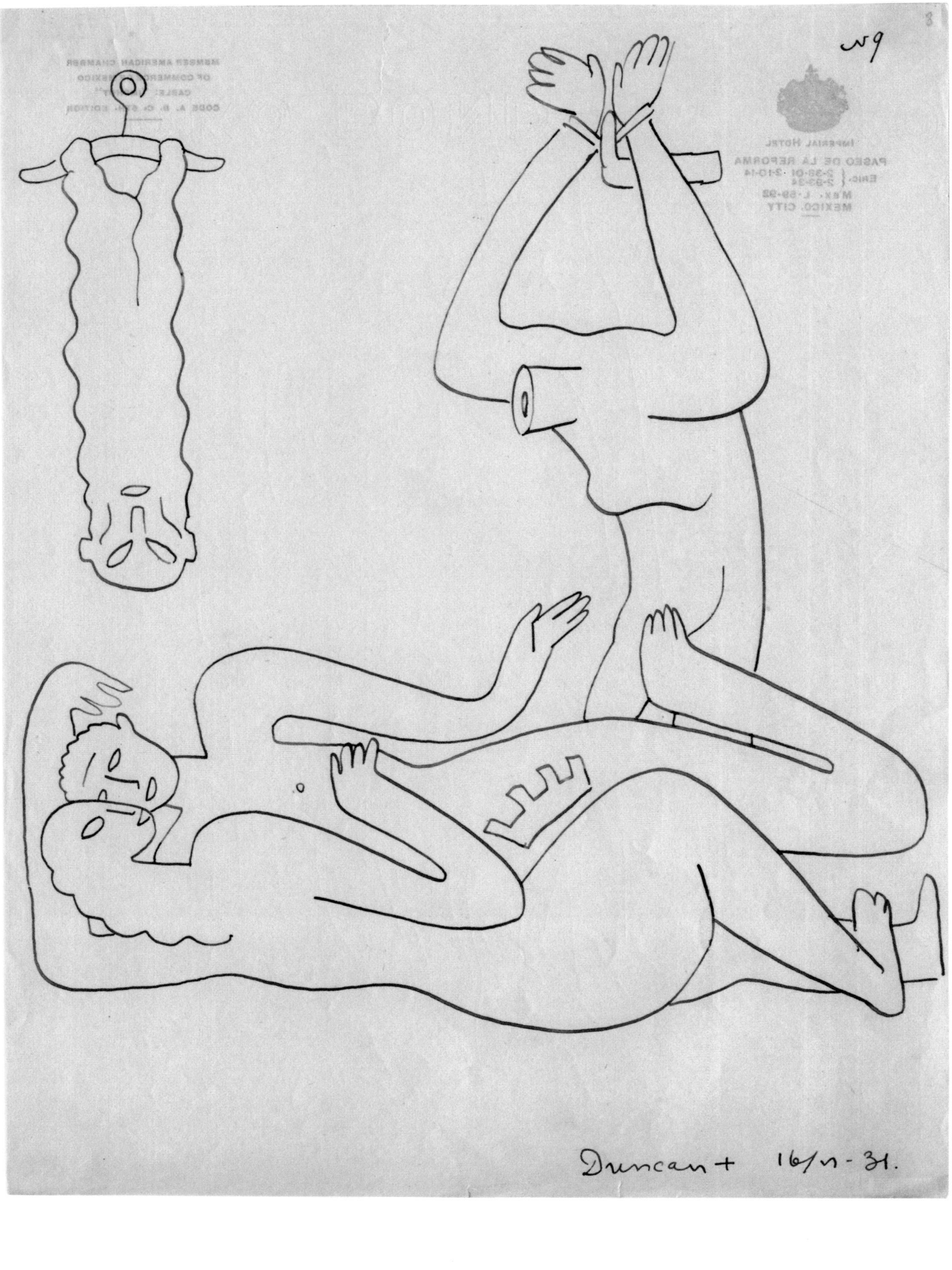
№9
Duncan + 16/11-31.

—OPPOSITE
Drawing no. 9 from the cycle
'Murder of King Duncan' (1931)

—THIS PAGE (LEFT AND RIGHT)
Drawings nos. 1 and 4 from the cycle
'Murder of King Duncan' (1931)

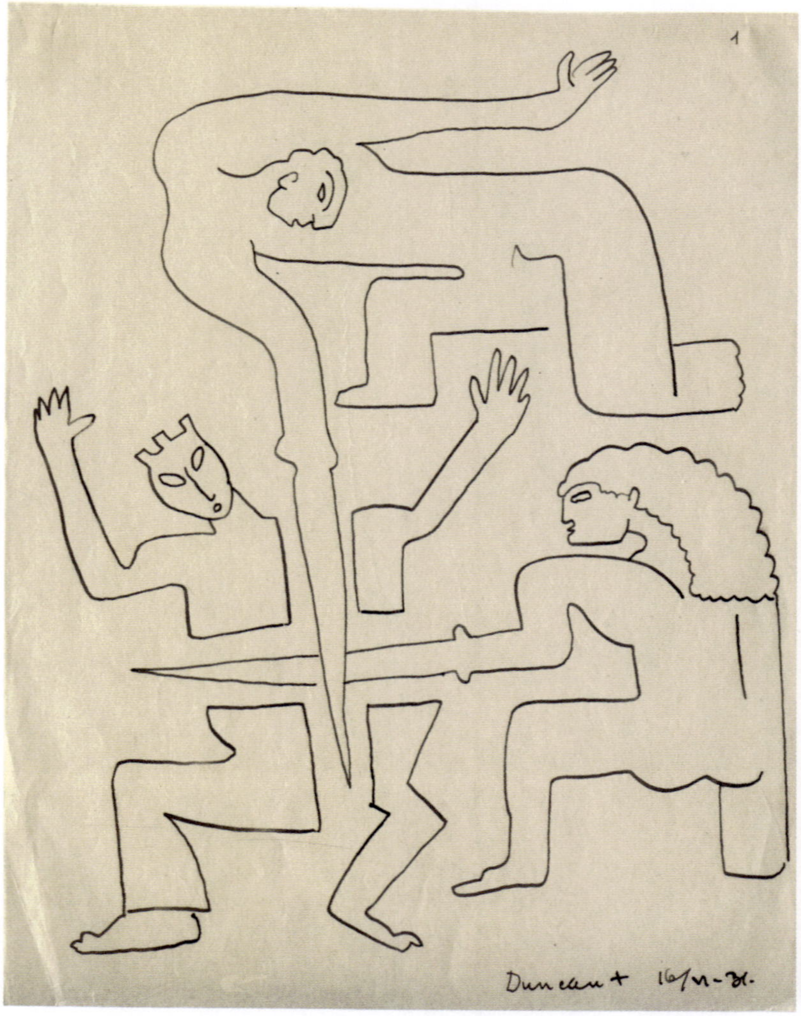

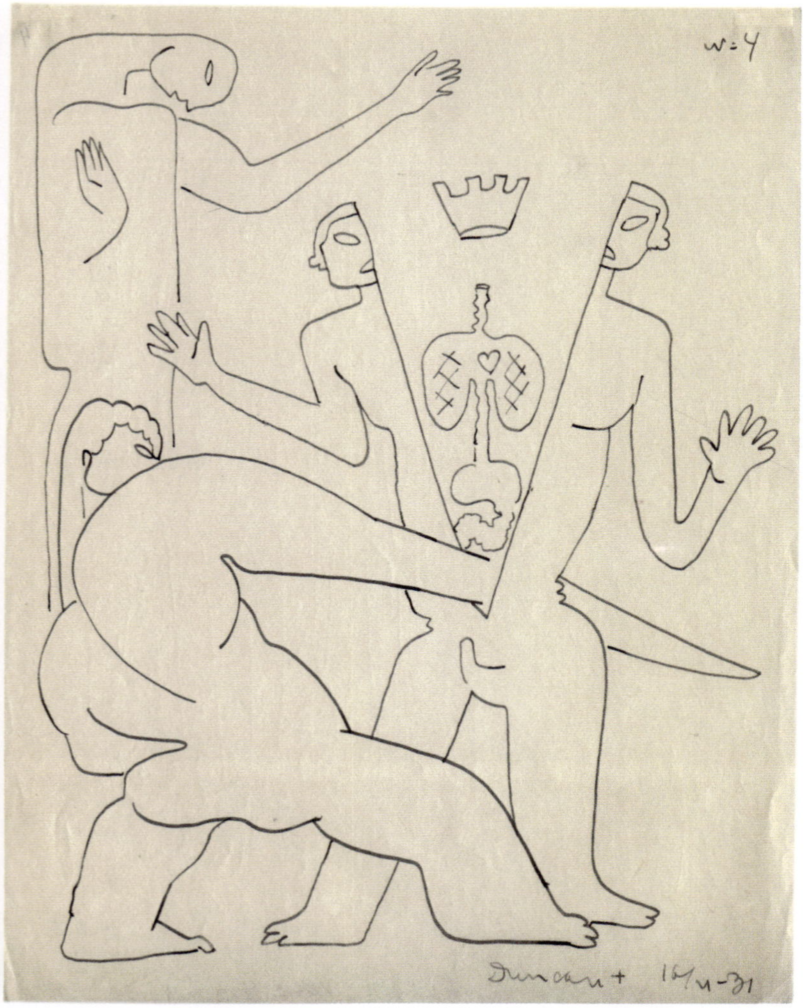

RIGHT
'St Genevieve of Paris'
(Mexico City, 1931)

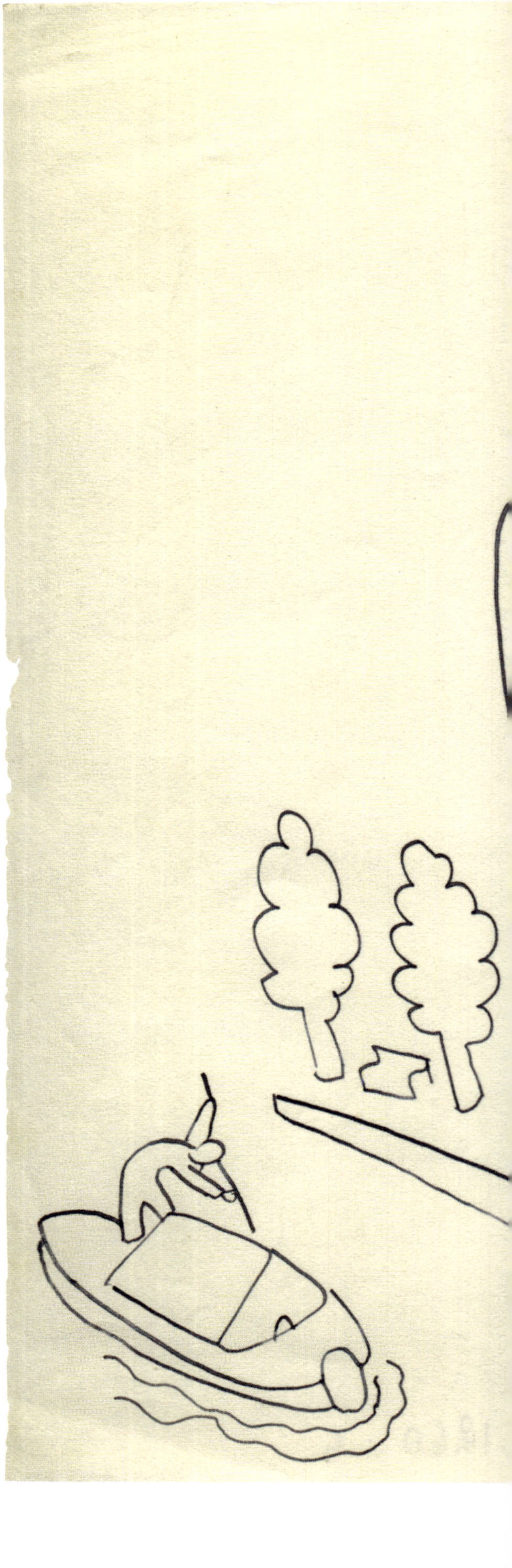

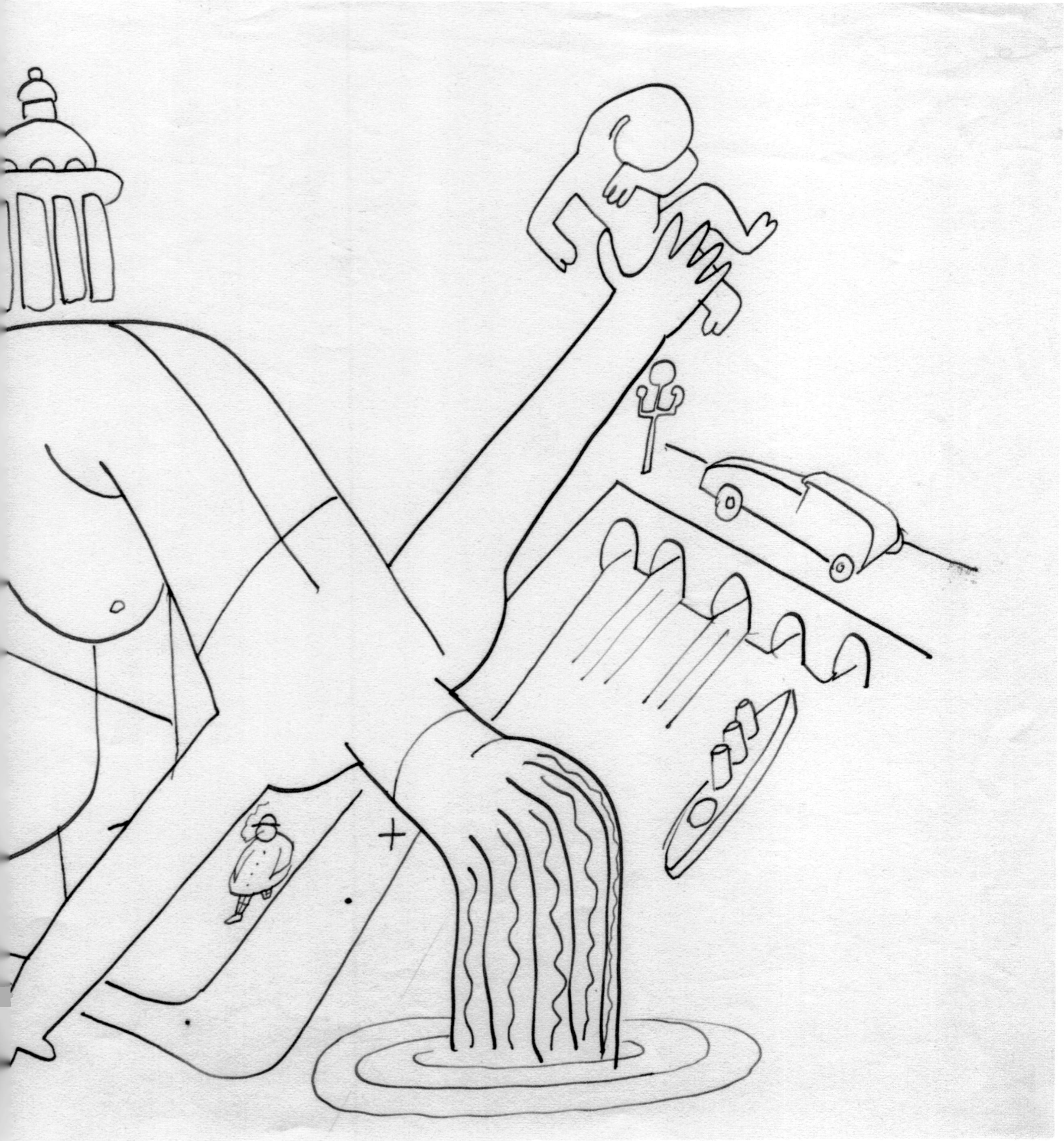

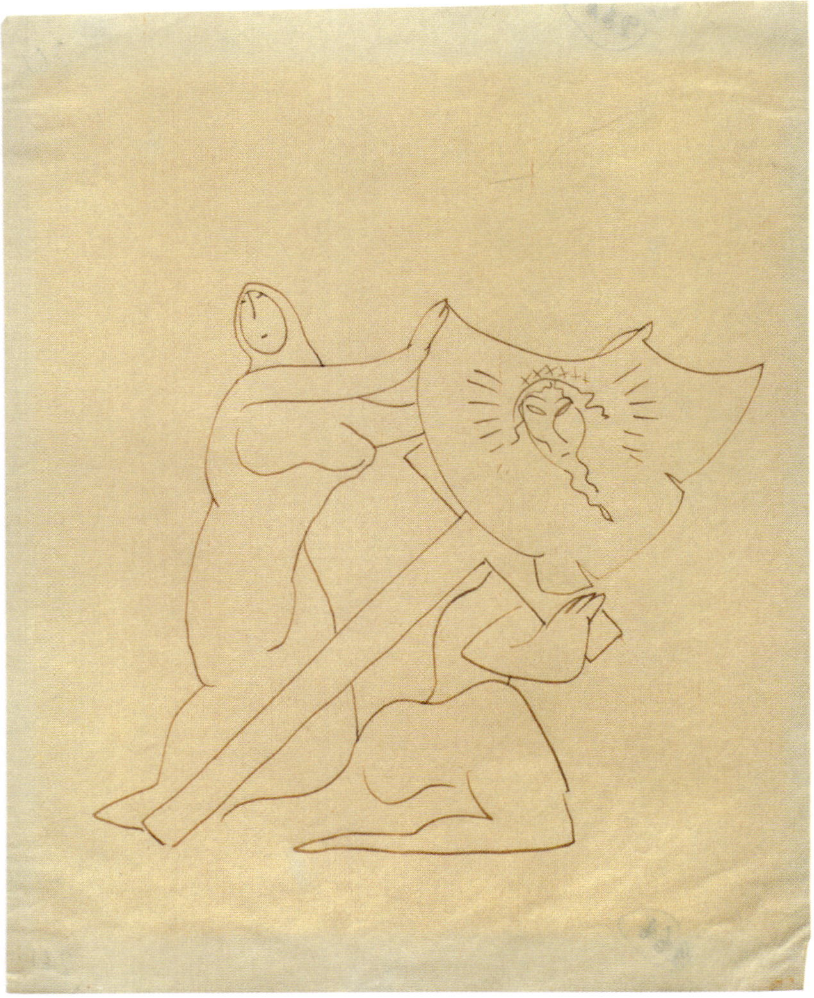

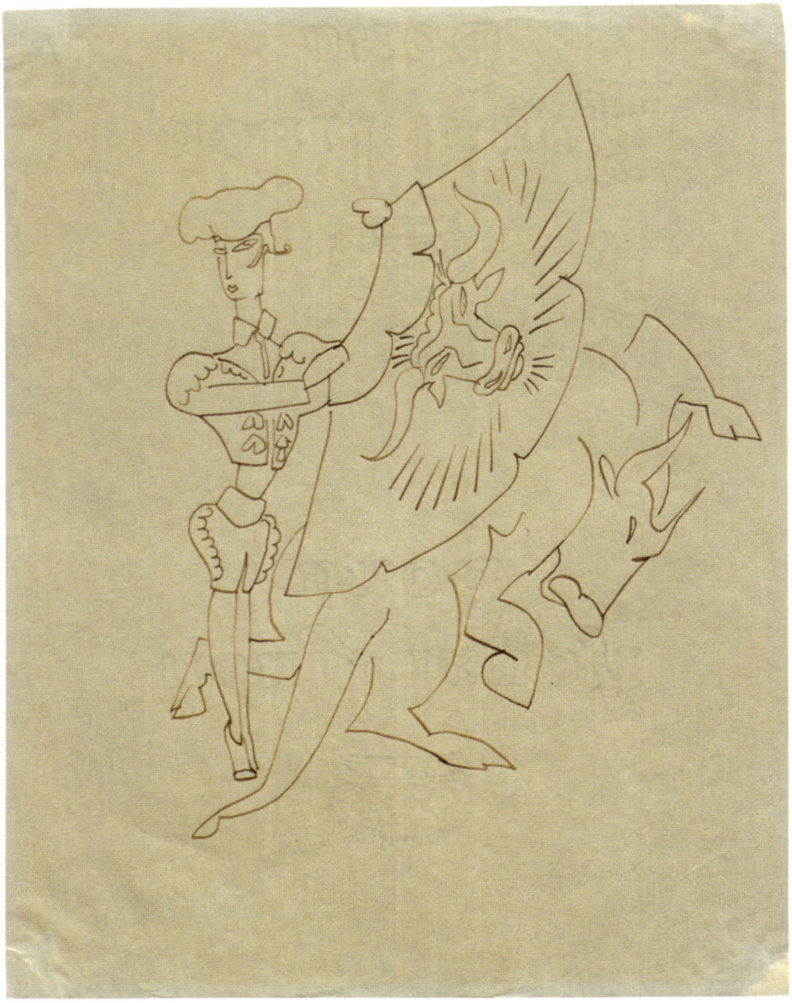

—THIS PAGE

TOP LEFT
'St Veronica' (May 1931)

TOP RIGHT
'Veronica', a matador posing with his muleta in a bullfight (May 1931)

—OPPOSITE
From the cycle 'St Veronica' (March 1931)

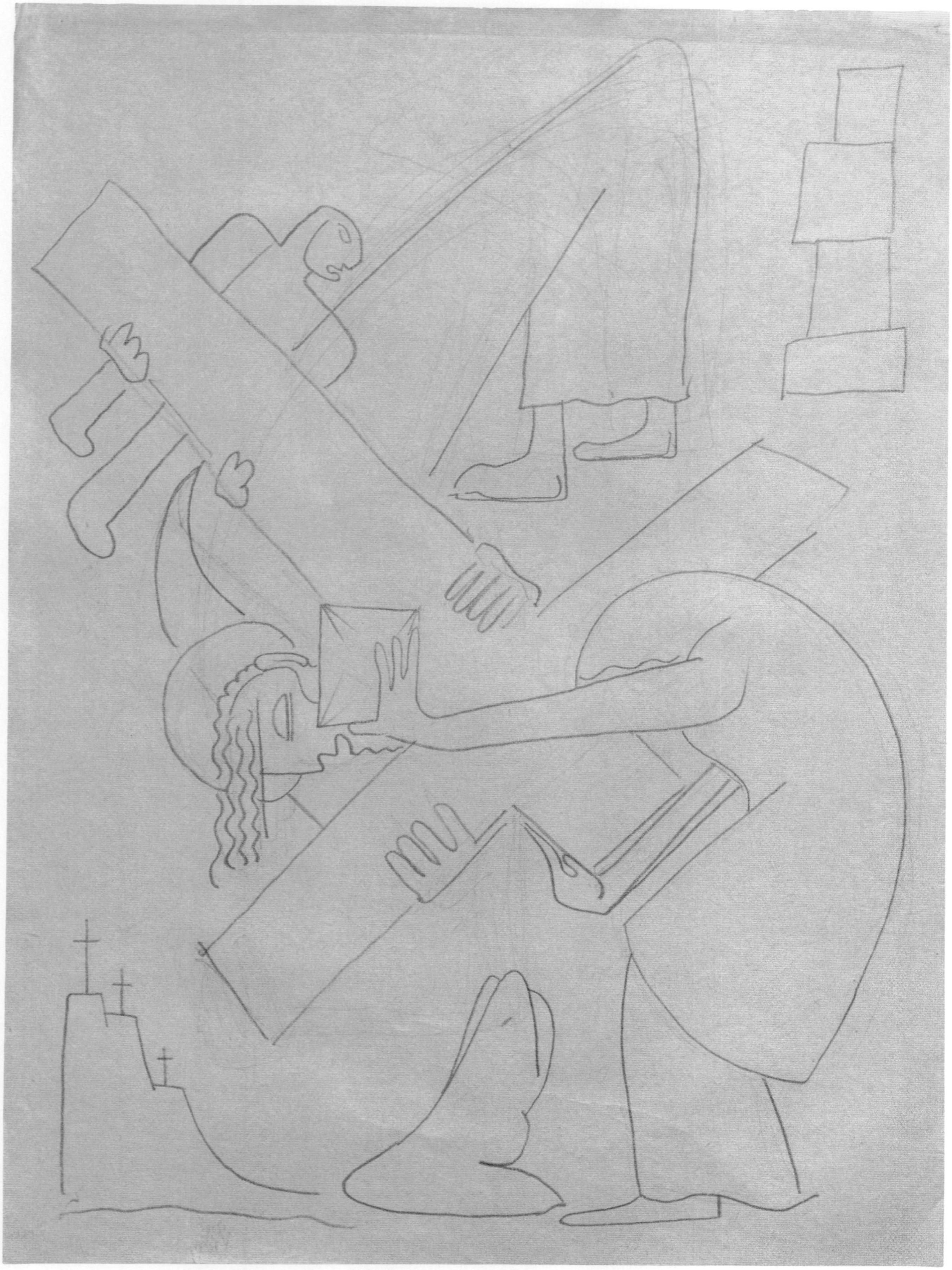

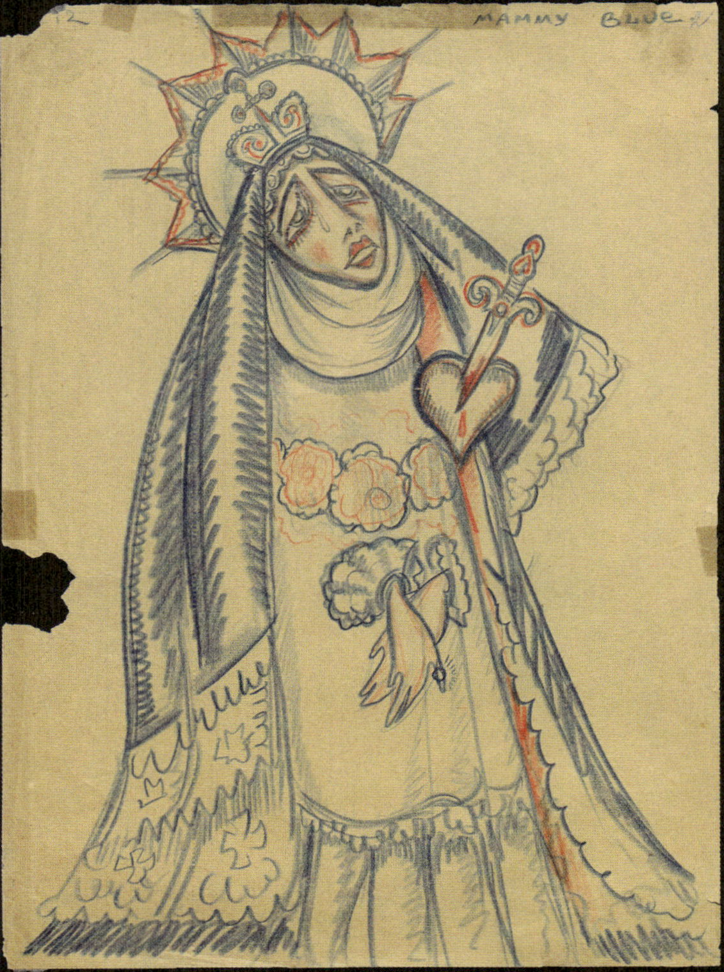
12
MAMMY BLUE

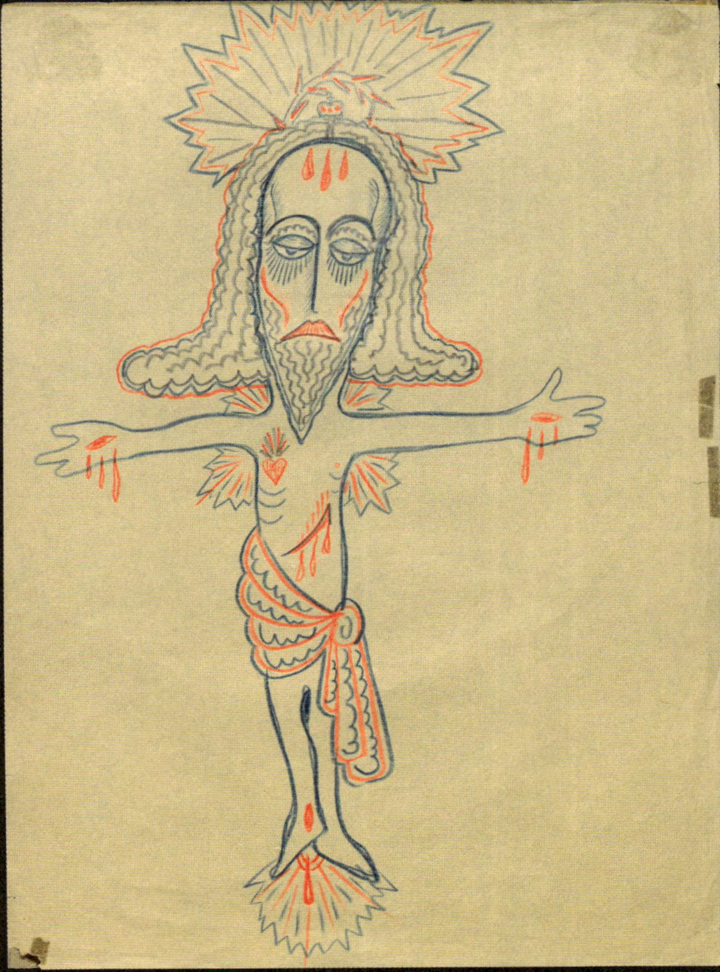

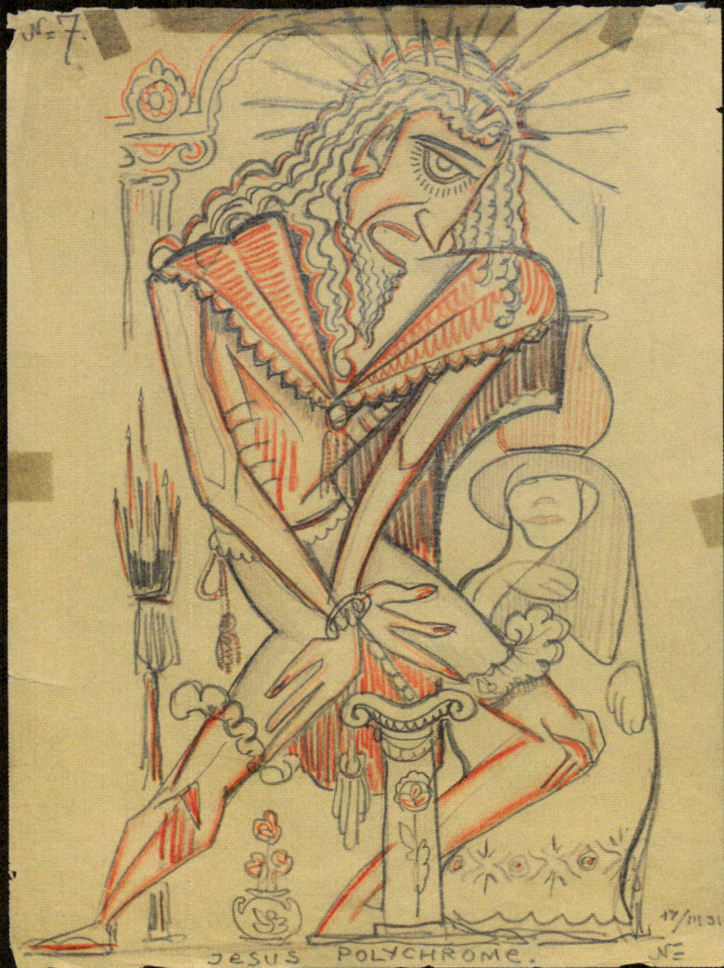
N°7.
17/III 31
JESUS POLYCHROME.

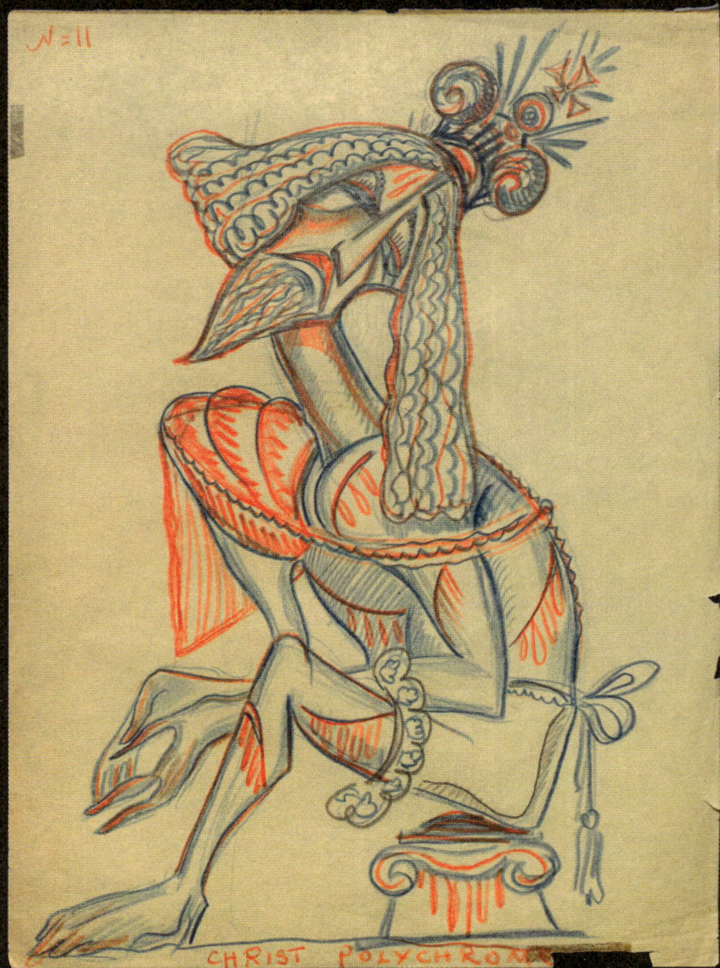
N°11
CHRIST POLYCHROME

—OPPOSITE
From the cycle 'Mexican baroque' (March 1931):

TOP LEFT
Mammy Blue

TOP RIGHT
'Crucifixion'

BOTTOM LEFT
Jesus Polychrome # 7

BOTTOM RIGHT
Christ Polychrome # 11

—THIS PAGE
Judas Kiss # 13

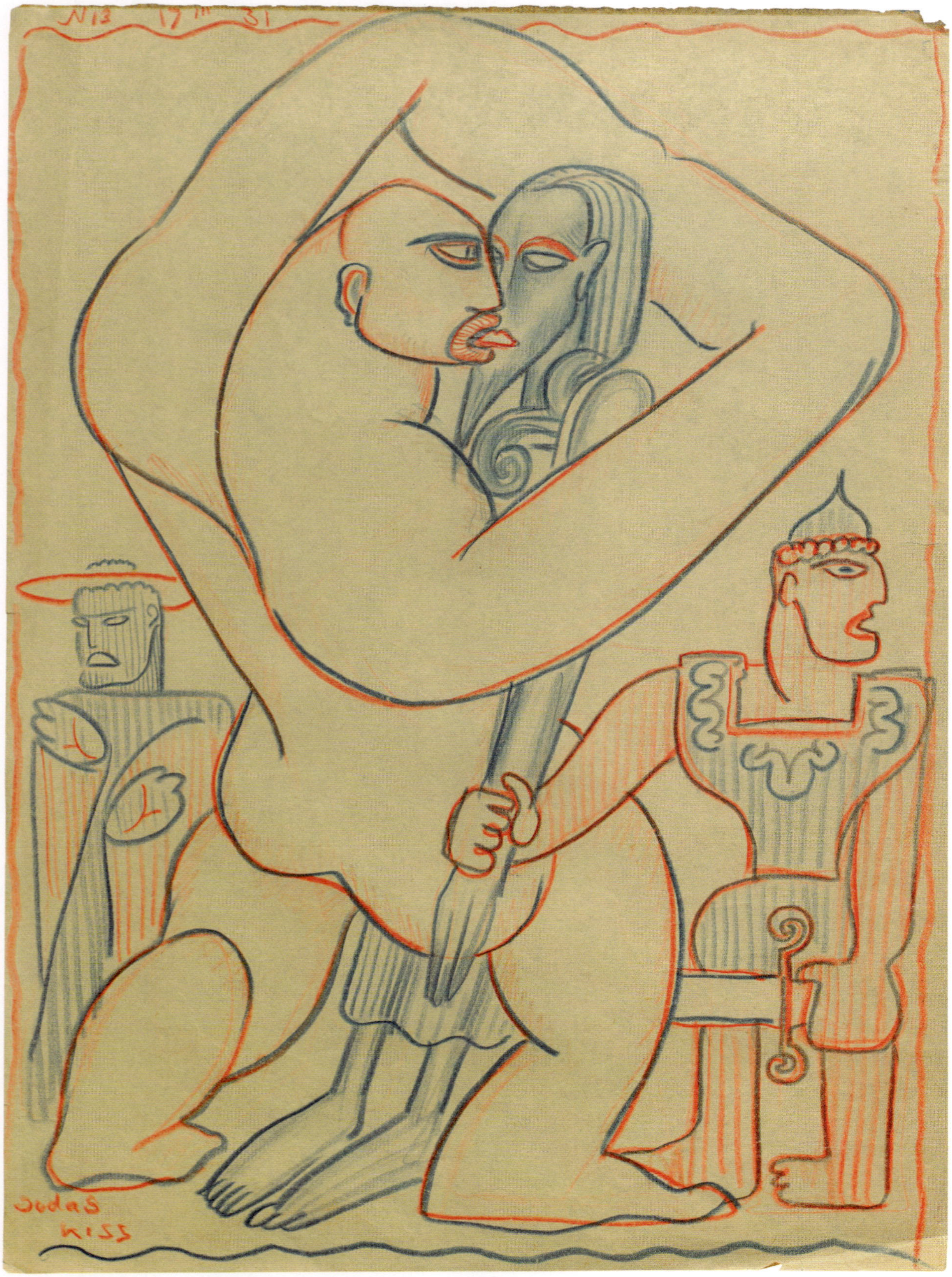

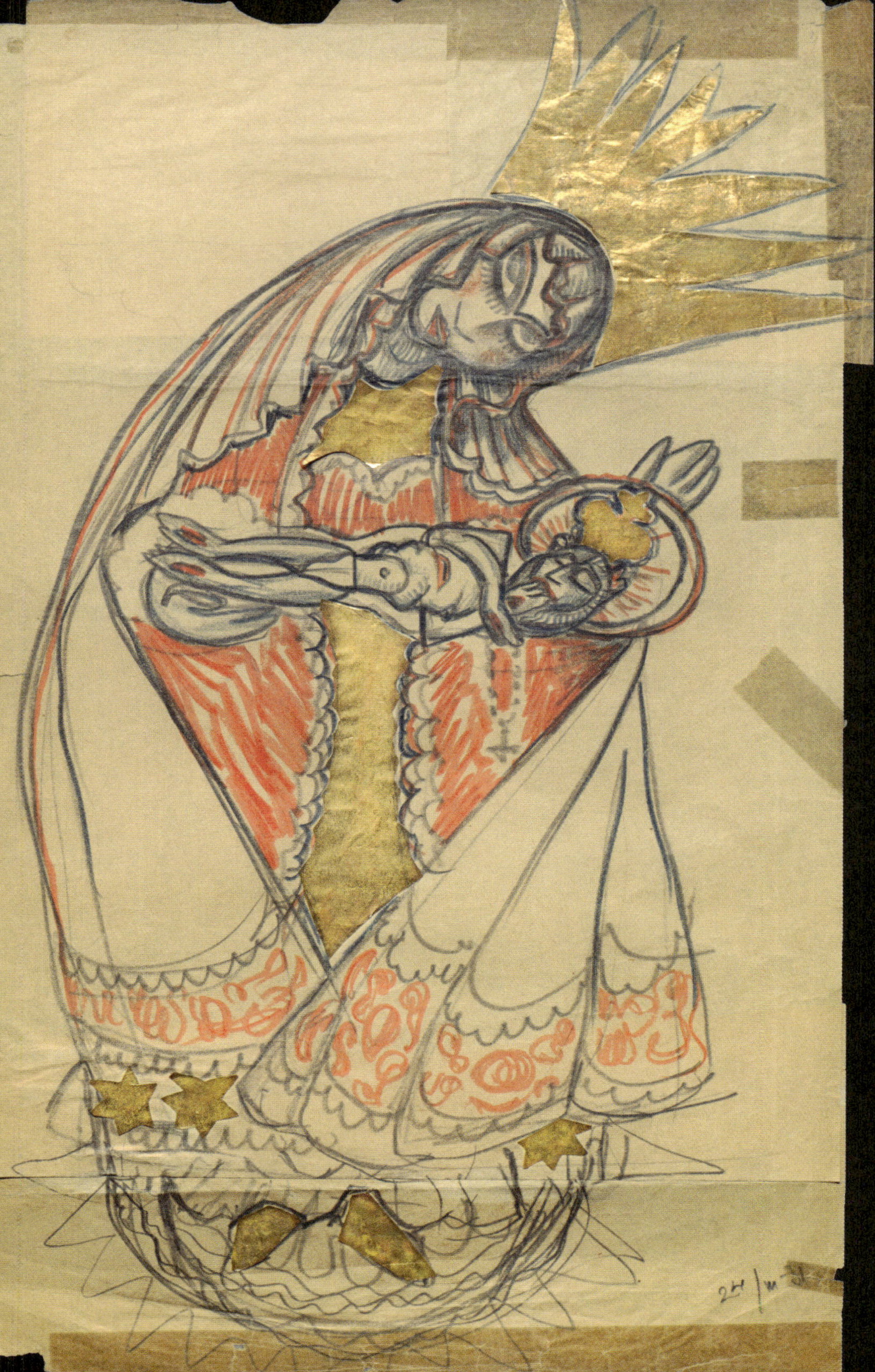

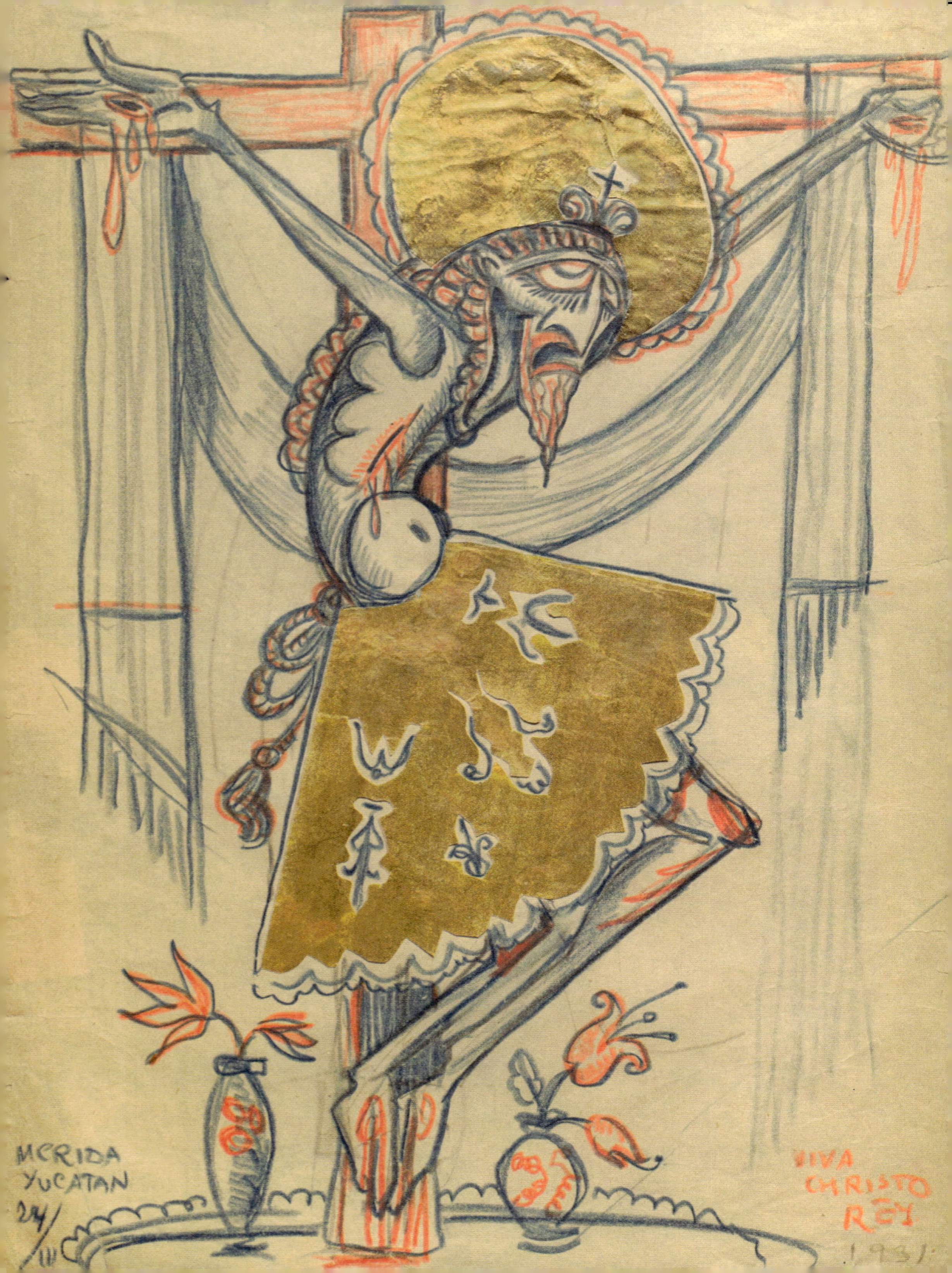
MERIDA
YUCATAN
24/III
VIVA
CHRISTO
REY
1931

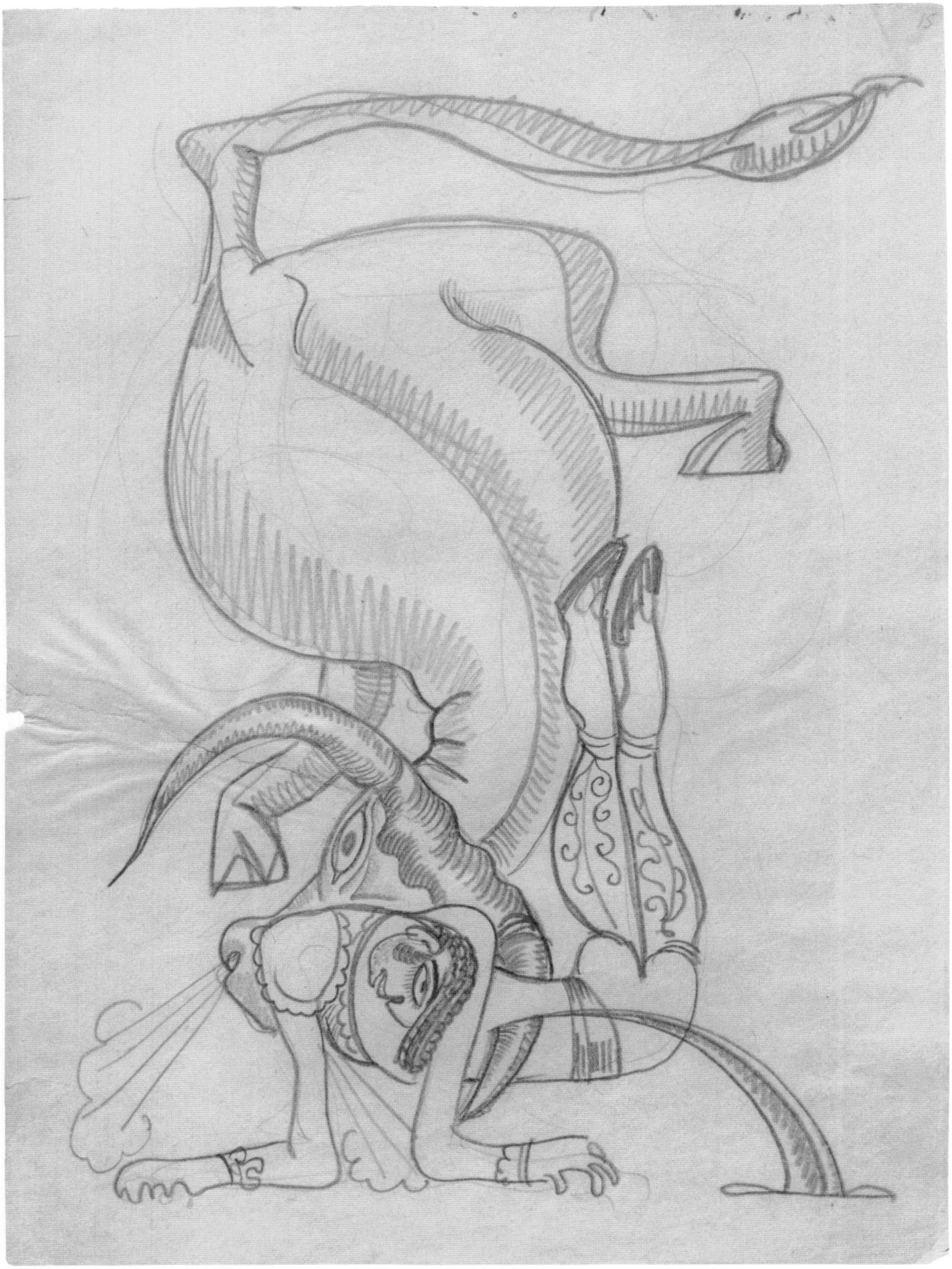

—PREVIOUS

LEFT PAGE
'Madonna with Jesus' (1931)

RIGHT PAGE
Viva Christo Rey (Merida, Yucatán, 1931)

—THIS PAGE
Corrida (1931)

—OPPOSITE
From the cycle 'Los todos toros' (All the bulls) (Tetlapayac, 1931):

TOP (LEFT AND RIGHT)
'Crucifixion of the bull'

BOTTOM LEFT
Les Martyrs

BOTTOM RIGHT
The Fusion

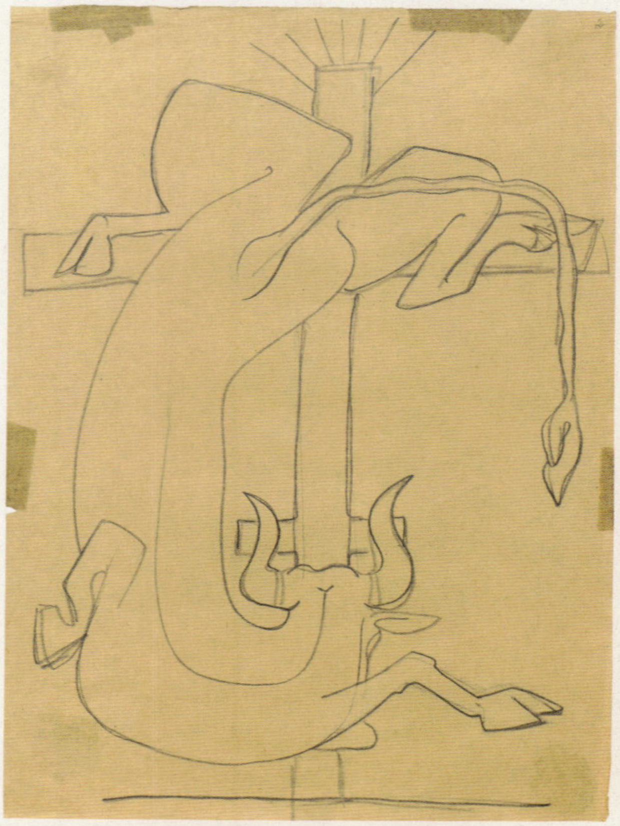

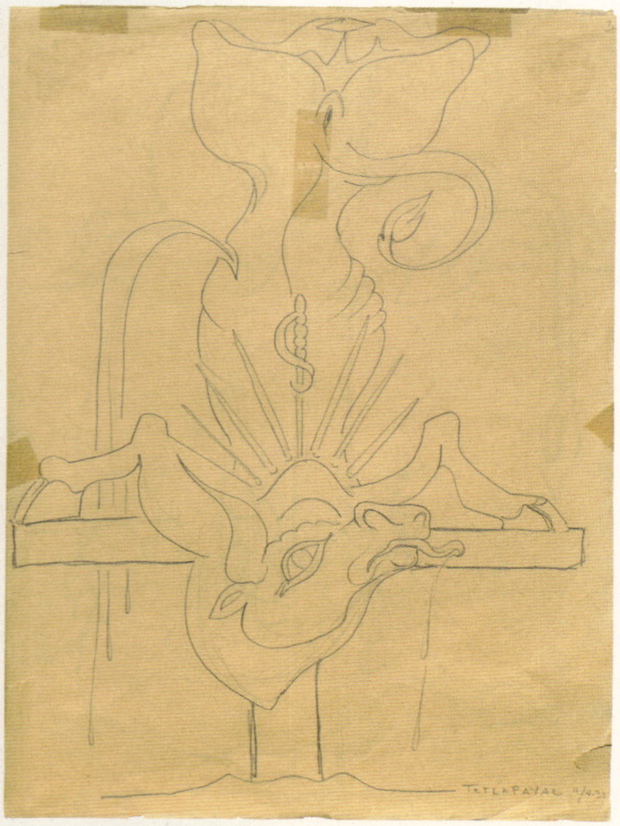
TETLAPAYAC

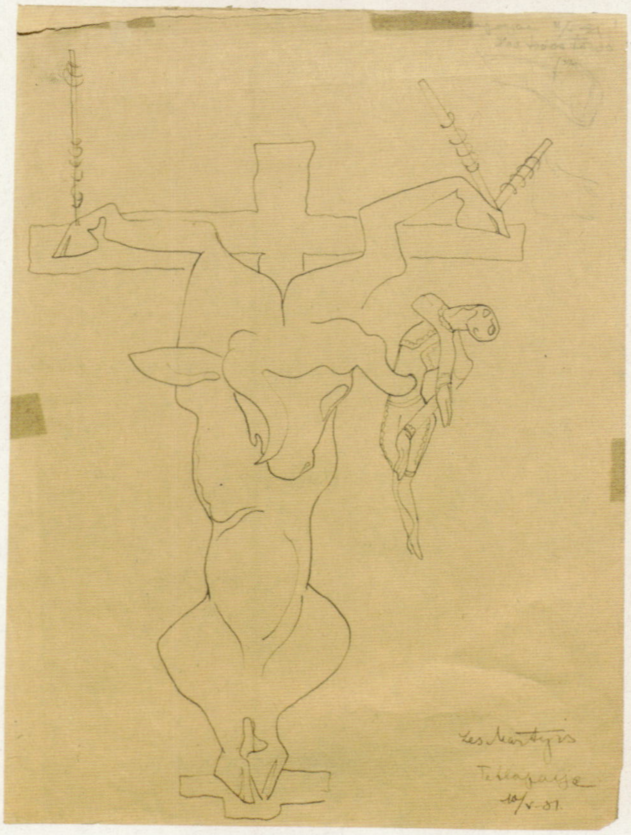

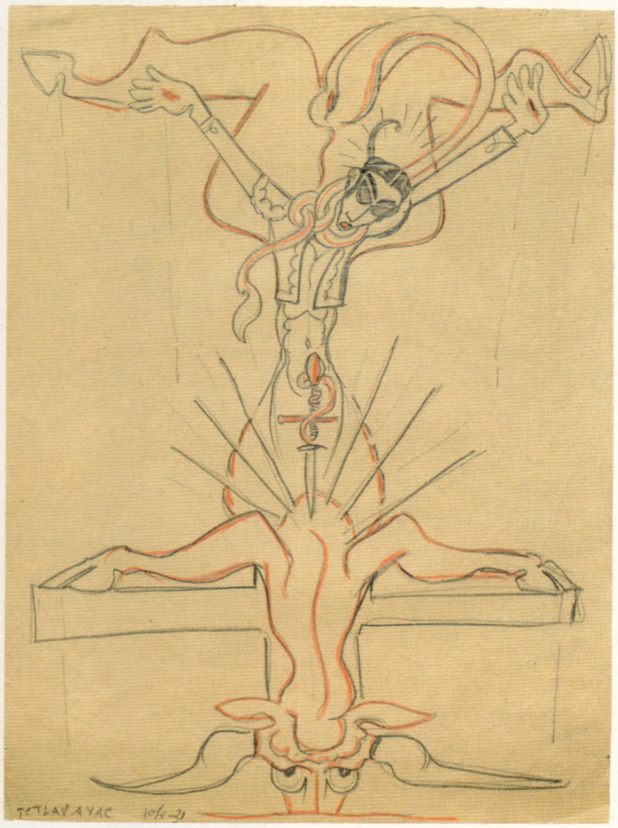
TETLAPAYAC

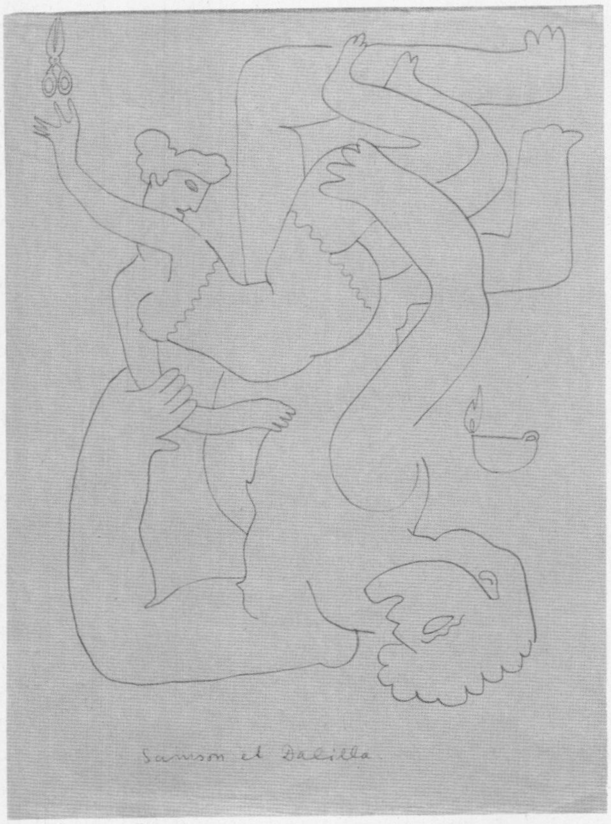

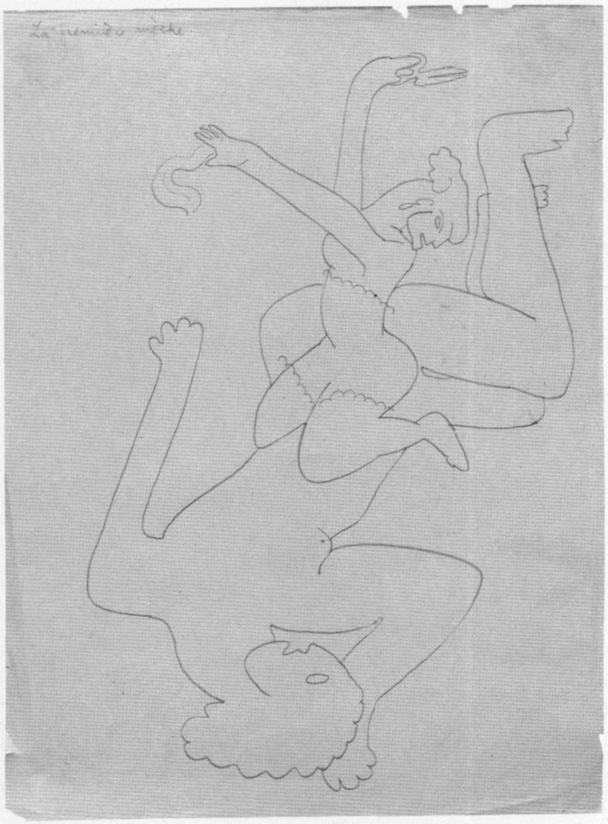

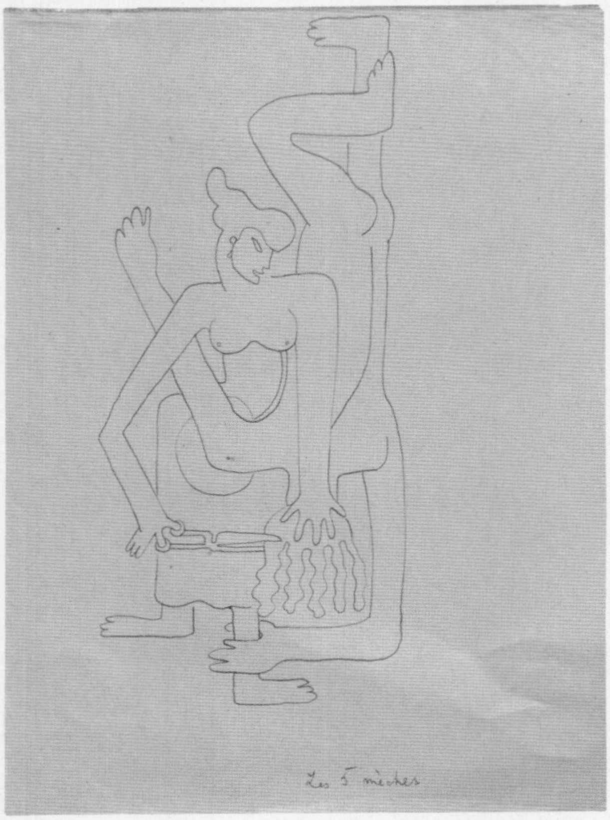

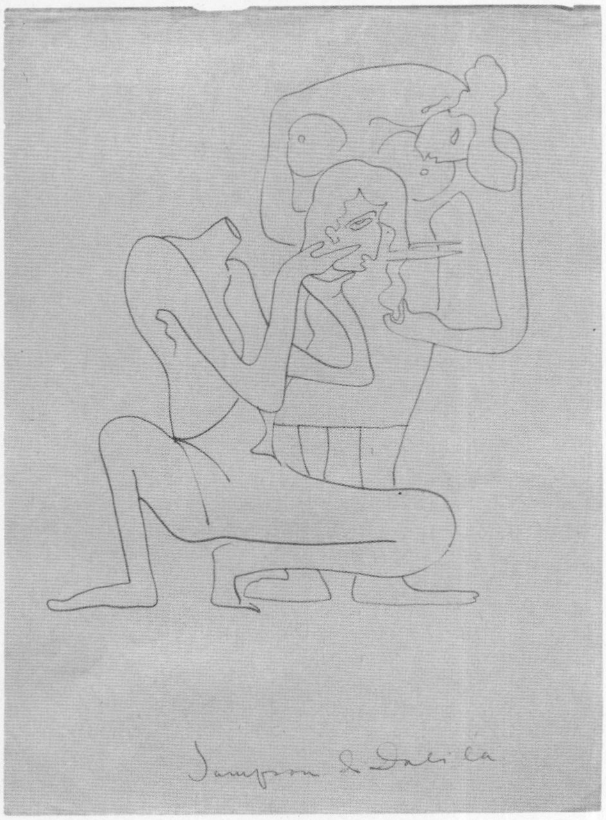

—THIS PAGE

From the cycle 'Samson et Dalila' (1931)

—OPPOSITE

TOP LEFT

Le Crime de M. Cain
(The crime of Mr Cain) (1931)

TOP RIGHT

From the cycle 'David and Goliath' (1931)

BOTTOM (LEFT AND RIGHT)

From the cycle 'David and Goliath' (1931)

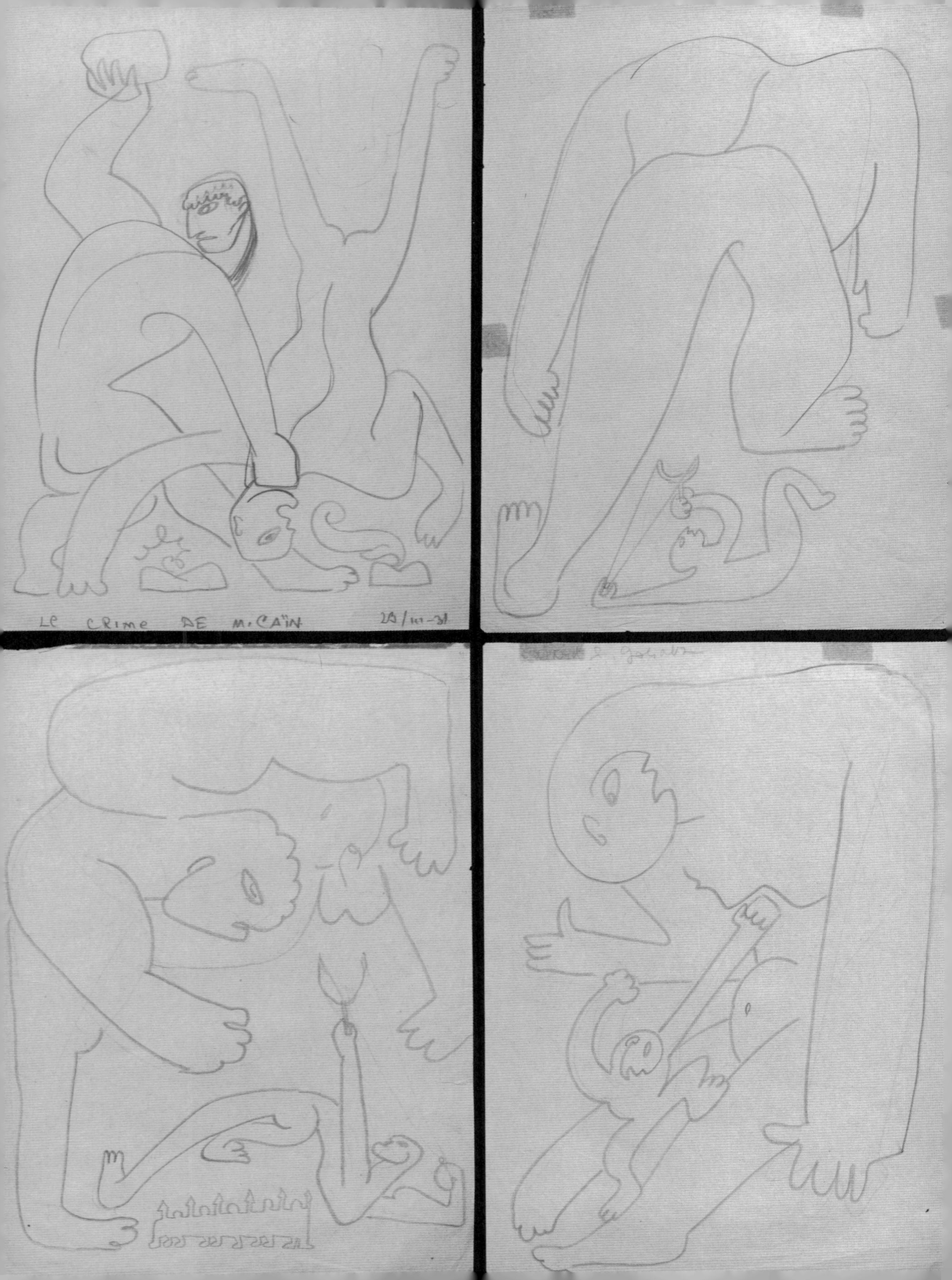

LE CRIME DE M. CAÏN

—THIS PAGE

BELOW LEFT
Question de Pomme (The question of the apple) (1931)

BELOW RIGHT
From the cycle 'The Fall of Adam and Eve' (Yucatán, 1931)

—OPPOSITE
From the cycle 'Stigmatization' (Nuevo Laredo, March 1932)

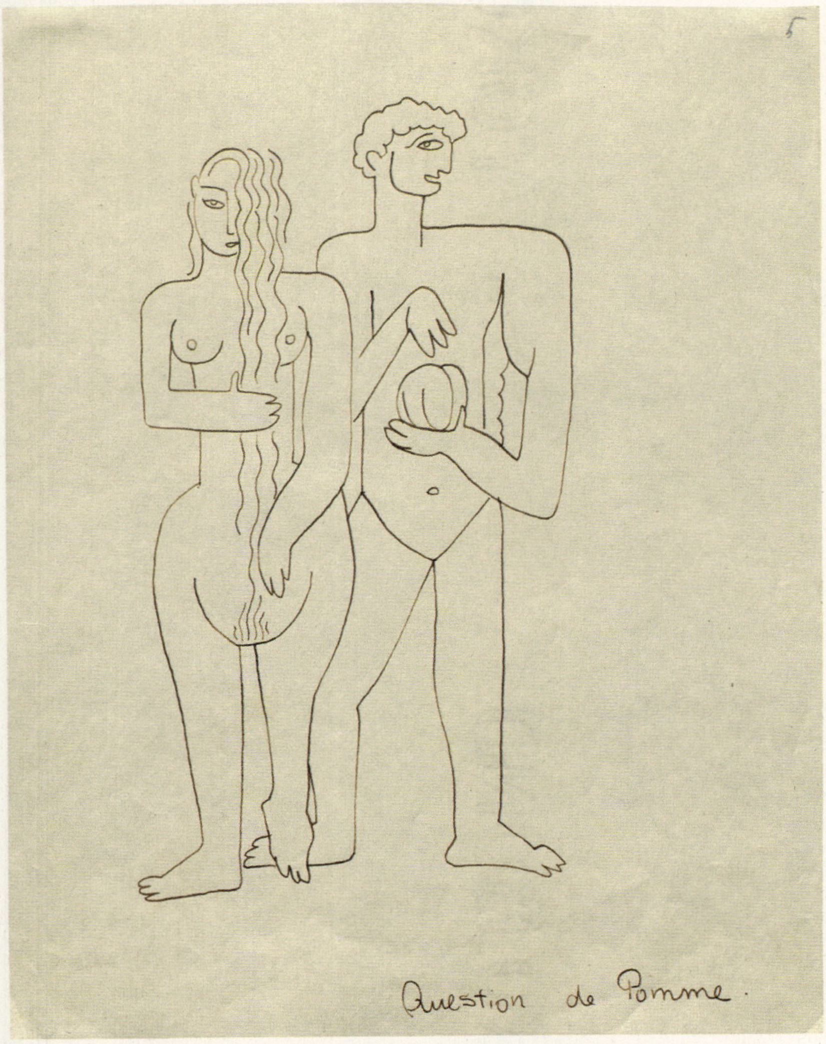

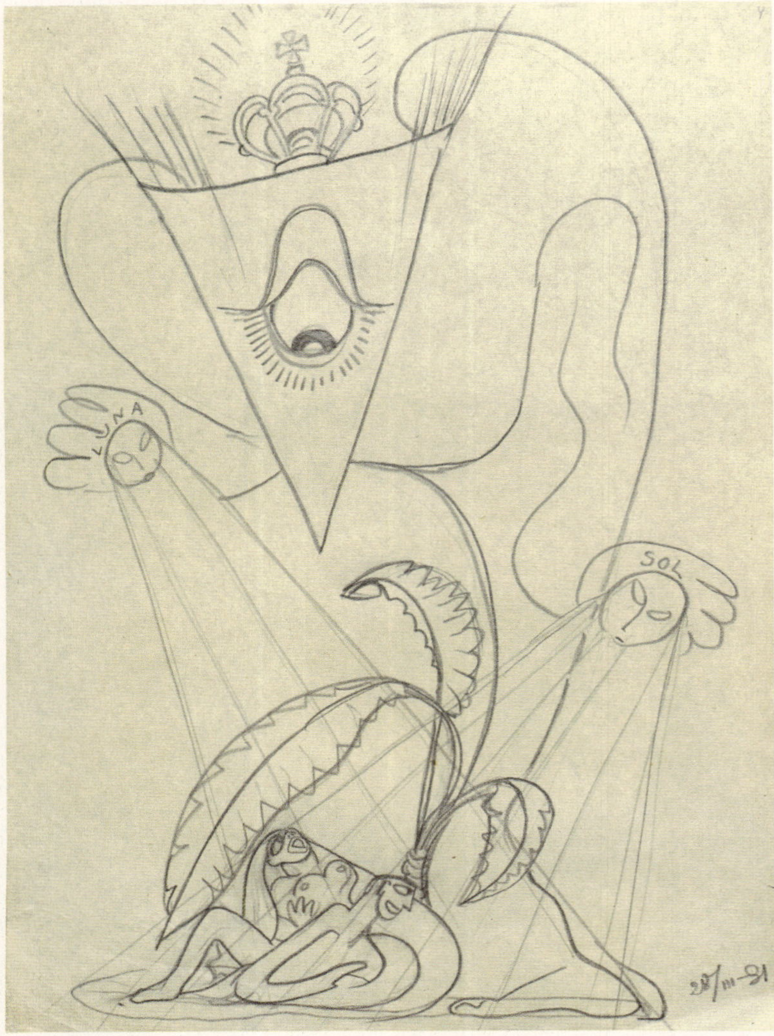

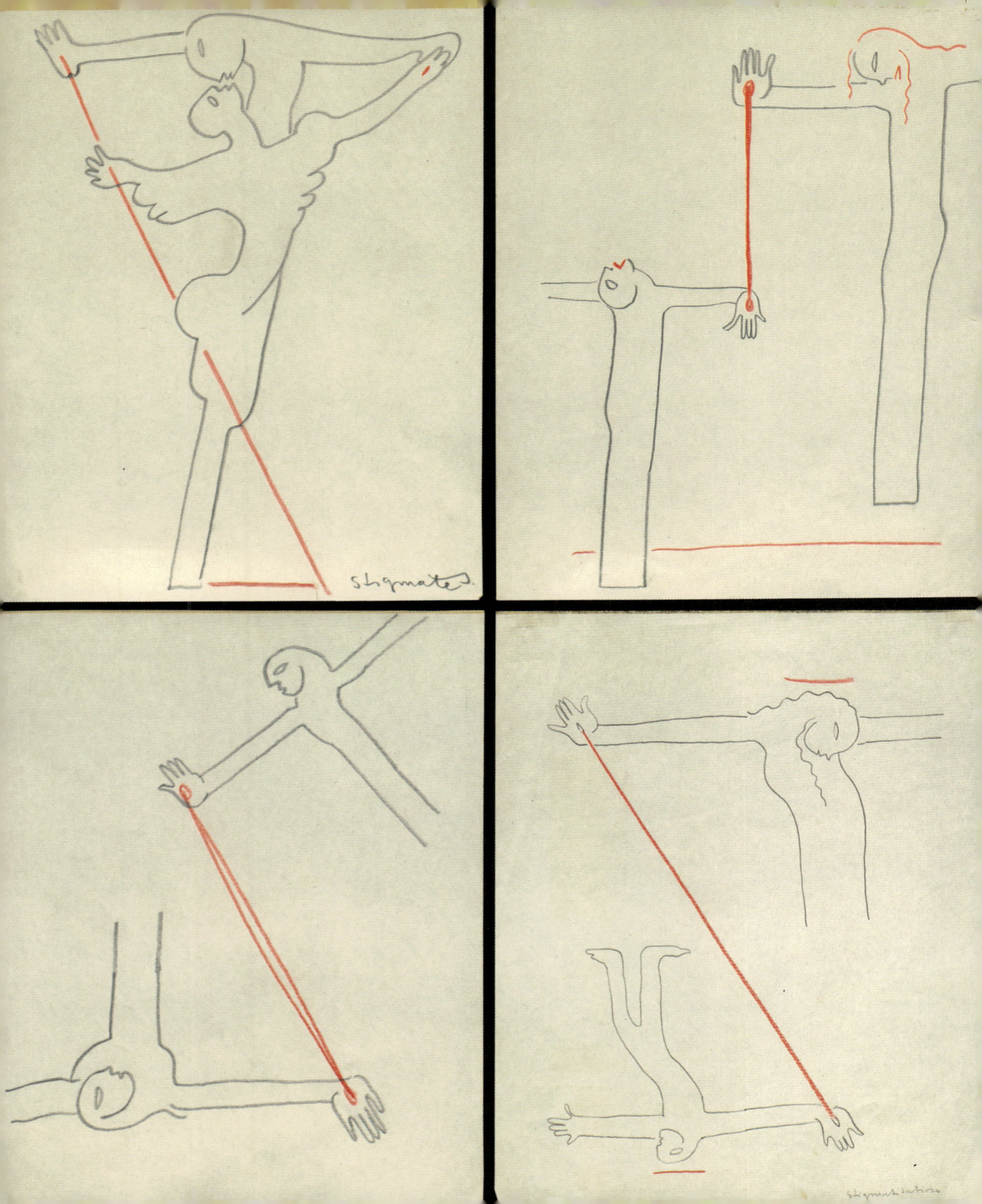
Stigmates.
Stigmatisation

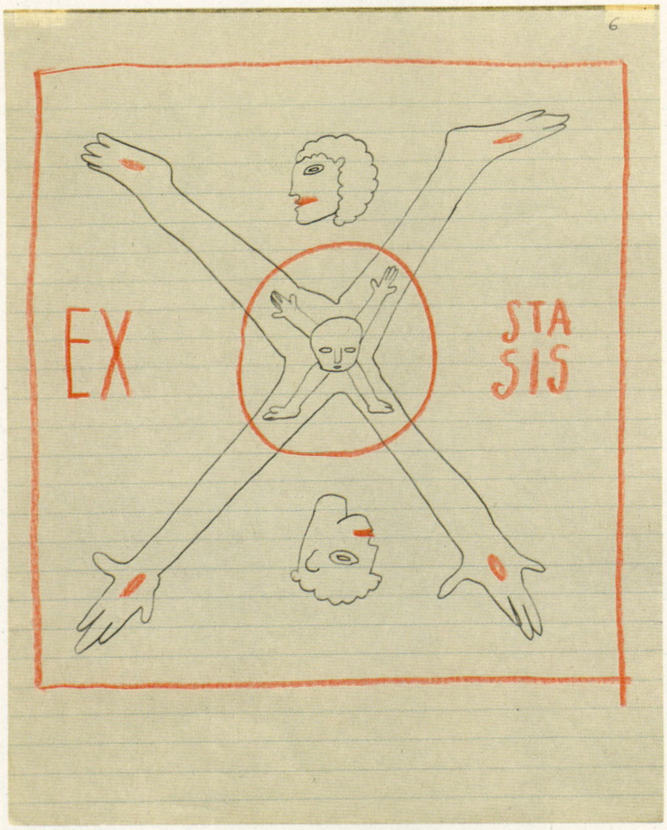
6
EX
STA
SIS

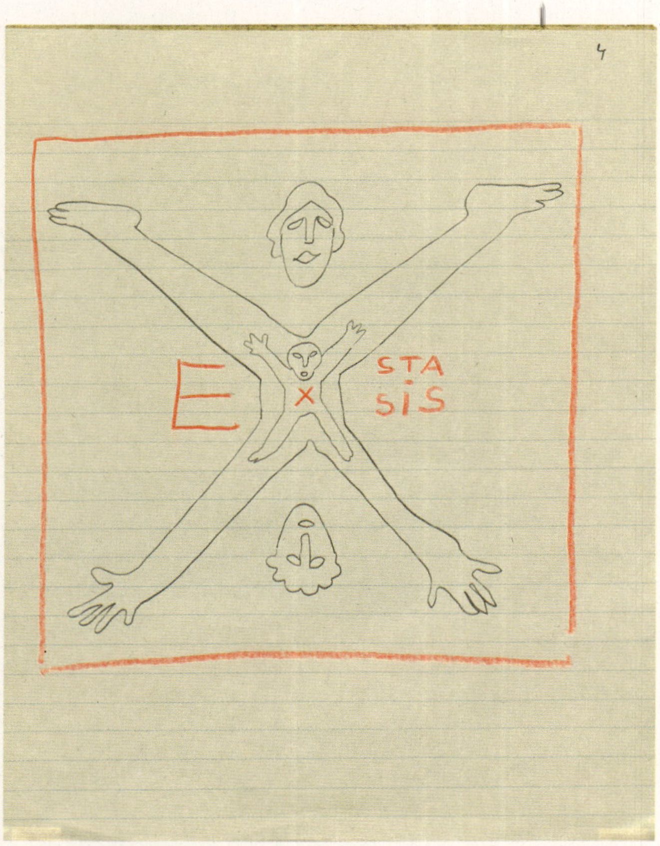
4
E
X
STA
SIS

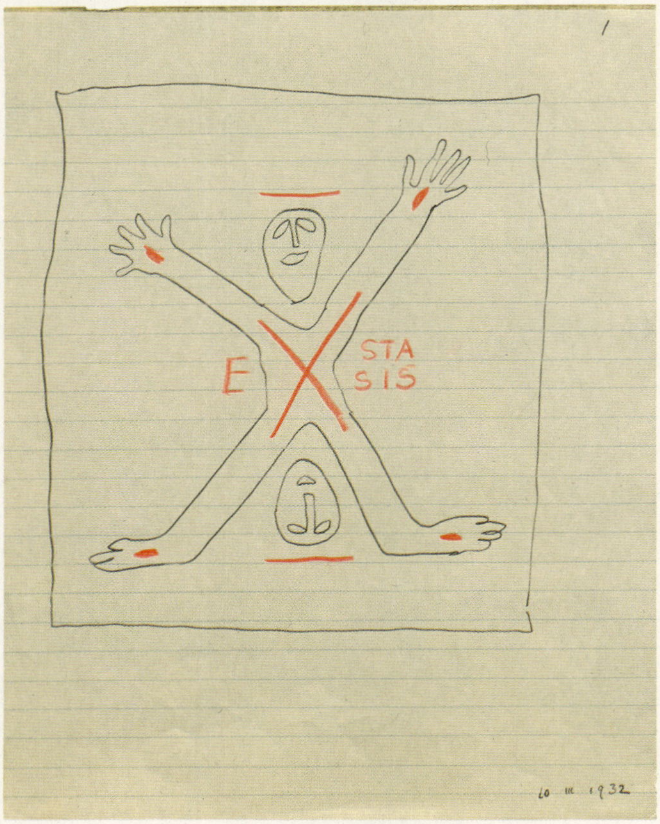
1
E
STA
SIS
10 III 1932

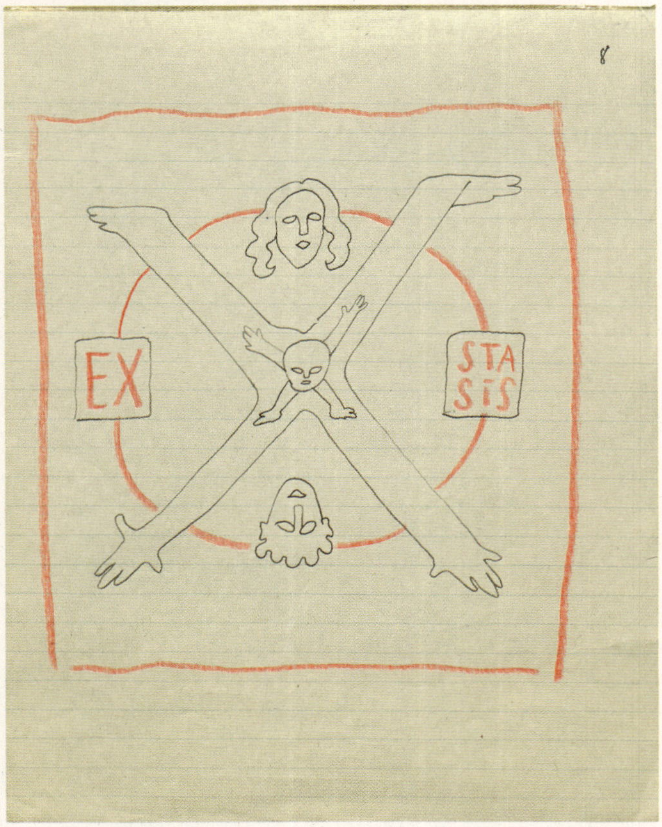
8
EX
STA
SIS

OPPOSITE
From the cycle 'Ex-stasis'
(Nuevo Laredo, 1932)

THIS PAGE
Leonard (Leonardo da Vinci)
(Mexico, 1931)

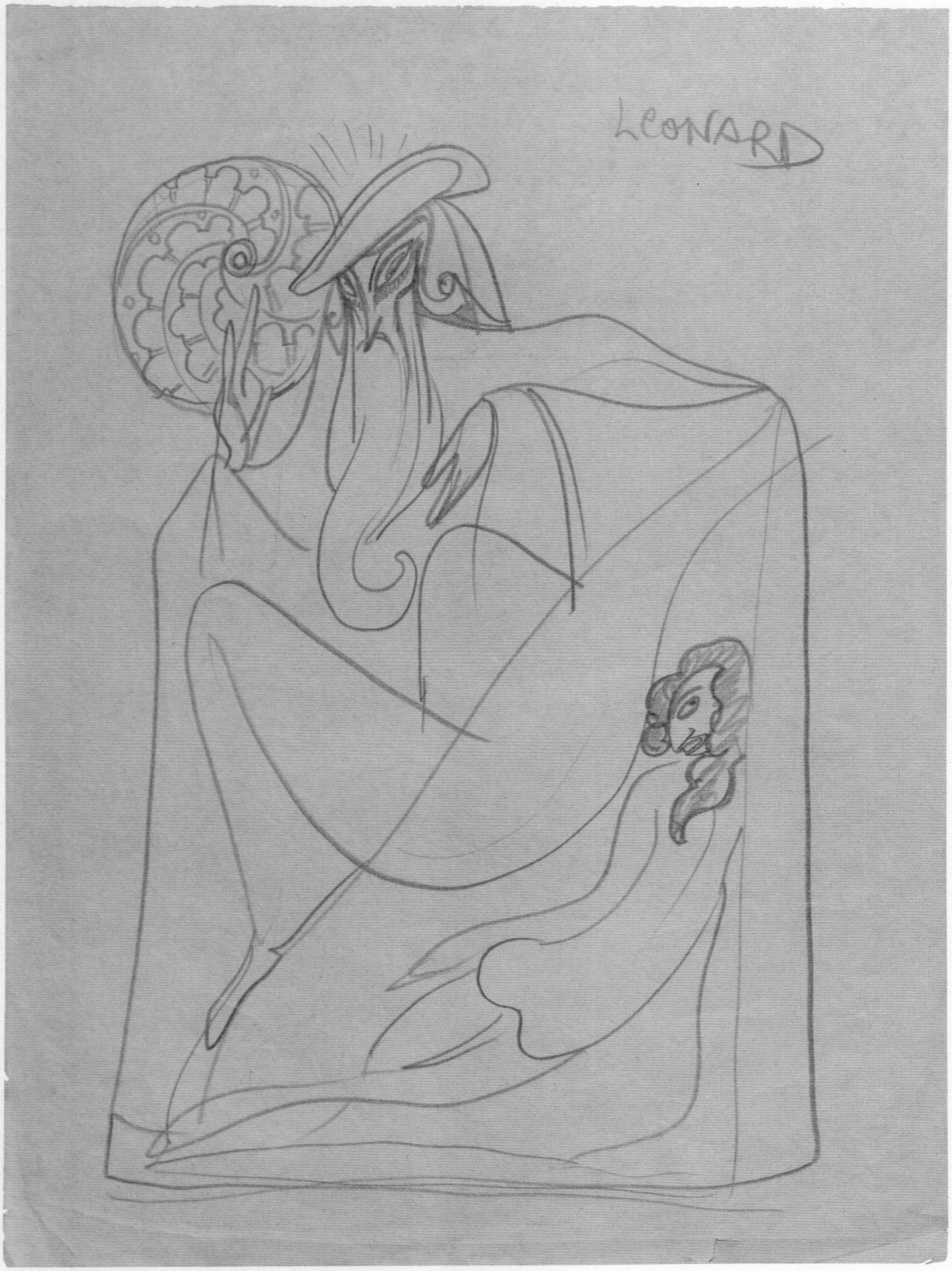

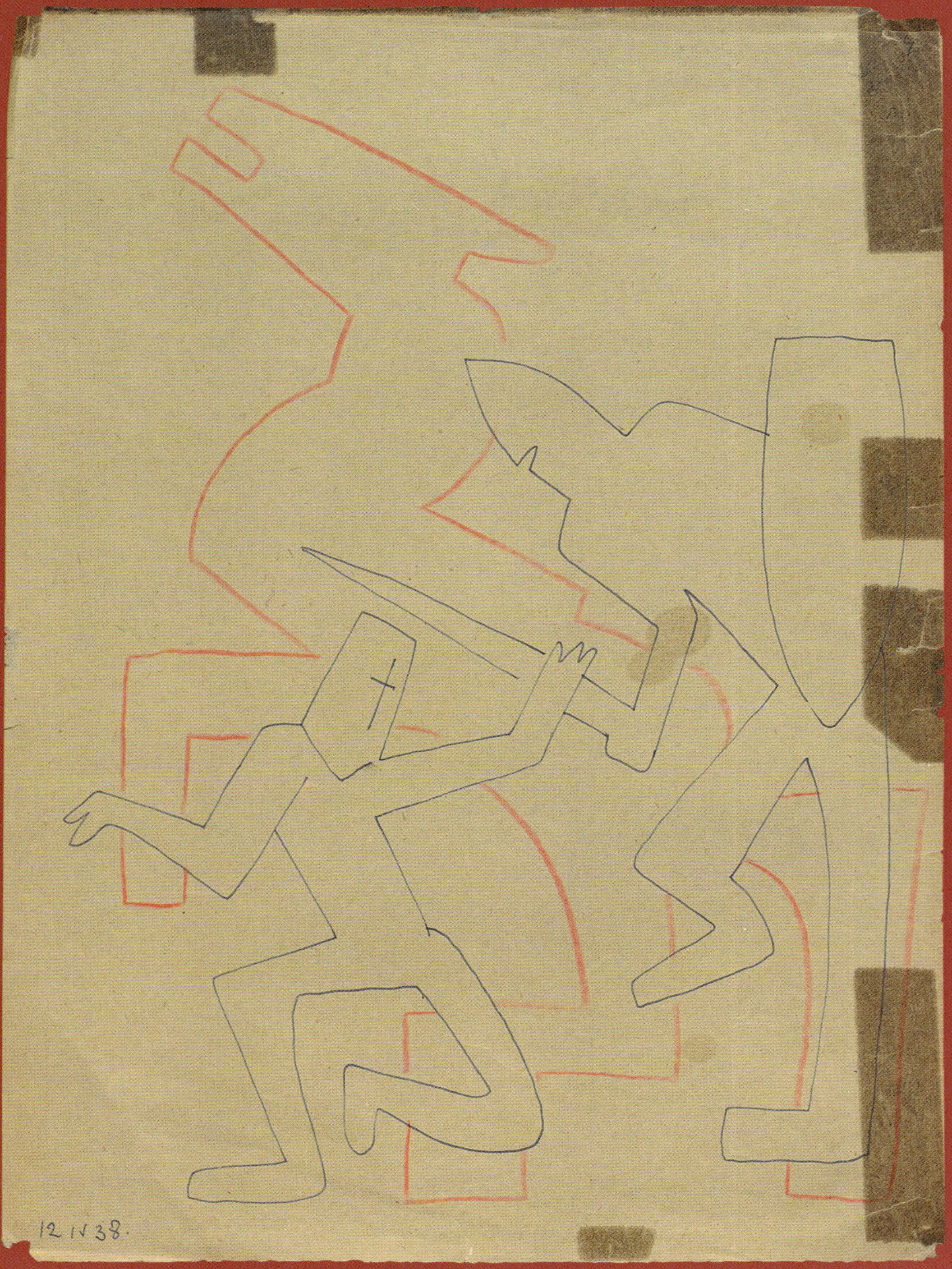
12 IV 38.

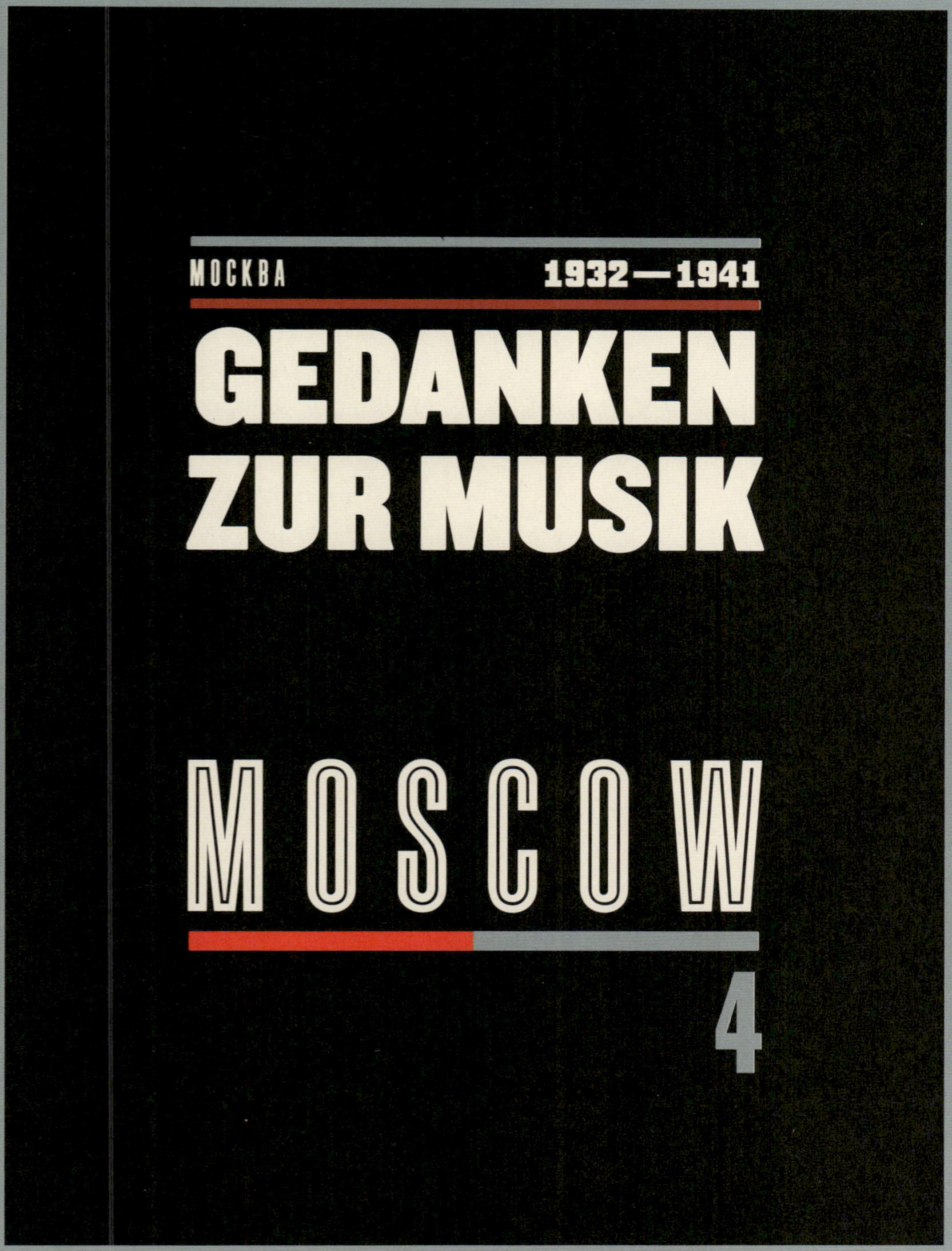
МОСКВА
1932—1941
GEDANKEN
ZUR MUSIK
MOSCOW
4

On Tuesday, 12 April 1938, Eisenstein was using an ordinary graphite pencil to prepare for the shooting of *Alexander Nevsky.*

He had again been cleared to work at the film studio. The sword of Damocles that had long been suspended above him, and which had almost fallen on him in the spring of 1937, was still there but it had moved a little further from his head. The order to arrest the director of *Battleship Potemkin* as an 'enemy of the people and of socialism' – drawn up after the near-complete film *Bezhin Meadow* (1937) had been banned and destroyed – had already been signed by several members of the Politburo. But at the last minute, Stalin cancelled it: he had decided to give the disgraced film-maker a final chance of proving his loyalty. *Alexander Nevsky* – a film about the victory of Prince Alexander's Russian armies over the knights of the Teutonic Order in the 13th century – would stir up the Soviet people's patriotism ahead of the war that was coming, inevitably and soon (so everyone felt), with Nazi Germany. Eisenstein understood that for him, just as for his hero, this was a battle he needed to win. It was not a question of artistic success, but of life and death. There could be no delay! The legendary battle on the frozen Lake Chudskoe would be filmed in summer, in the studio's courtyard, using a mixture of chalk and naphthalene to simulate the snow.

Eisenstein devised and sketched the sets and models that would transform Zvenigorod, outside Moscow, into ancient Novgorod. Then he turned to the tragic moment in the Battle on the Ice: the Germans, who have failed to overcome the Russian fighters' resistance to the attacks of their mounted knights, form an unbreakable square with their shields and pikes. The Russians, lightly armed with hammers and clubs, try to get through the Teutons' armour, and blond young Savka from Prince Alexander's close entourage falls victim to the German pikes.

Eisenstein was aware, of course, that in Savka's death scene the imagination pictured him as a somewhat transformed, but clearly recognizable icon of St Sebastian. And, that very day, alongside his sketches for the film, there appeared a cycle of nine illustrated variations on the death of the early Christian saint, who is honoured in a highly reserved way among Orthodox worshippers but is ardently loved by Catholics. Eisenstein was no Catholic, but he did not conceal the fact that this saint, meek but indomitable in his faith, was a permanent presence in his creative imagination: 'My automatic drawings very often take the form of St Sebastian.'

What a striking difference there is between the figure of the protomartyr – calm, though pierced with arrows – and the agonizingly tense body of Savka upon the pikes! And the contrast is still greater between this young man, who seems as fragile as the tree shoots beside him, and the tragic Sebastian whom Eisenstein had drawn five months earlier, at the height of the Great Terror.

Then, on 13 November 1937, one of the red arrows had put out one of the strong and cypress-slim saint's eyes, and the other eye, ringed in blood, wore an expression of the most extreme horror – just as Michelangelo, in the Sistine Chapel, had painted one of the mortals covering his left eye with his hand and holding his right eye open wide, unable either to look on the Last Judgment or to turn away from it. That Sebastian was the culmination of 1937's series of crazed cycles of drawings: 'Vision de délire', 'Wir klagen in Kreisen', 'Despair', 'La Garotta' and 'Nichts'. The fear and desperation that were enthroned in Eisenstein's heart, as they were in the whole country, were transformed from the mass repression of innocent people – something absolutely outside the logic of any normal mind – into plastic metaphors. If they had been seen by those people to whom they could never under any circumstances be shown, it would have been possible to try explaining them away: 'No, no, these are symbolic depictions of what is happening in Germany, in Spain, abroad!' But this image of the Christian martyr, refusing to abandon his convictions, came dangerously near to the limit of what was permissible.

The geometric nature of the non-figurative forms that sometimes appear in the Mexico drawings, although they are especially frequent in Eisenstein's work from the 1930s in Moscow, would seem to contradict the free flexibility of the 'organic' line with which he played out his figurative characters. How are we to reconcile this with the fact that it was the geometric nature of the Constructivist project for *Heartbreak House* that represented the barrier after which he stopped drawing – turning graphic art into staging and actors' gestures in the theatre, and then into the composition of shots and scenes in the cinema?

Eisenstein had always been interested in the relationship between strict geometrical forms and 'plasmatic' freedom (of lines, movements, compositions), between natural observation and intellectual generalization. He wrote on 14 September 1932 in his diary:

> ***Why are my drawings, despite a complete lack of anatomicalness, humanly physio-logically emotional for viewers? It should seem that 'not anatomical' means 'not imitative'. The point is that these drawings are protoplasmic, avant tout. And elemental because they capture the process between the primal protoplasm and formed man.***
>
> ***In my drawings, the truly appealing theme is the coming into being of the human form from plasma [...].***
>
> ***Mickey Mouse – the first factual dynamic drawing – has this plasmation*** **par excellence** ***[...]***
>
> ***This is the plasmatizing of solid objects: the stretching of necks, legs, the rhythmical swaying of trees, of solid figures, etc.***[1]

One week later, he made a small drawing with a commentary:

> *In drawings of the accompanying type (NB.: very similar to the* Macbeth *series) there is yet another 'plasmatic' factor: the figures 'hover' in space; that is, the atavism in them belongs to the period before being set upon solid ground, to the amoebic-plasmatic stage of movement in liquid.*
>
> *This is the graphic equivalent to the sensation of 'flight' among ecstatics: an identical uterine sensation of gyroscopicness and the identical phylogenetic pre-stage – the floating of the amoebic-proto-plasmatic state in a liquid environment.*[2]

Through his graphic art Eisenstein explored several problems that troubled him since his work in Mexico: the spontaneity of creation and discipline of form, sensual perception and logic of thinking, ecstatically enlightened spirit and sinking into the dark depths of the sub-consciousness – almost into the state of an embryo in the mother's womb. While conceiving the book *Method* Eisenstein started from the idea that art itself would clarify these issues by the process of creativity and by the patterns of composition.

On 3 January 1944 in Kazakhstan, during his work on *Ivan the Terrible* and on *Method*, he was thinking about the difference between representation and generalization in art:

> *I'm slightly troubled by one apparent controversy in my conception of the principle of composition.*
>
> *Namely: the principle consists of the fact that a compositional formula is the content of what is represented, taken to the limits of generalization – the three or four strokes dividing the canvas and indicating the direction of the leading sections.*
>
> *The unity of the representation and the thus-understood principle of composition also constructs that which we (I) call – an image, imagery. [...]*
>
> *Each taken separately is incomplete and lacking imagery.*
>
> *Representation alone is naturalism and 'itinerancy'.*
>
> *Composition alone is constructivism.*
>
> Nun aber kommt die Frage *[Now, however, arises the question]: how does this fit into the general formula of the concept of art as a unity of the logical and the prelogical, the sensuous?*
>
> *In other words: the 'logical' side – this, of course, is 'subject', 'anecdote', theme, content – that is, a narrowly understood representation (a horse, a bouquet, a flogging, a bankruptcy);*
>
> *the prelogical and sensuous component must comprise composition – and this* par excellence, *for it is the limit of maximal emphasis on form (even the conception of form).*
>
> *It turns out, however, that composition is the (even highest!) degree of generalization; that is, something which would seem to be the furthest removed from the sensuous and prelogical – rather the abstract and super-logical?!*
>
> *The controversy is seeming, and results from a superficial understanding of the nature of ... generalization, or rather from a lack of indoctrination in the problem of the nature of generalization, resulting from the purely colloquial use of this word.*
>
> *Generalization is truly super-logical, but at the same time, unavoidably dialectical. And as such, it is also simultaneously (Lenin's as if!) sub-logical.*[3]

This conclusion, made in the 1940s, was a natural result of Eisenstein's evolution from his radical experiments of constructivism in 1920s through the experiences and reflections on geometry in 1930s.

On 28 March 1939, considering some additions to his nearly complete but unpublished book *Directing: The Art of the Mise-en-scène*, he wrote in his diary that:

> *Geometry is the commodity that comes als Anhang [as an addition].*
>
> *The dual tendency in composition: depiction and generalization.*
>
> *The limit of the first is naturalism.*
>
> *The limit of the other is geometry.*
>
> *If a work includes the unity of both, then it is evident that the process of its creation must have involved a rhythmic alternation of both tendencies: in other words, if we have a series of sketches for a picture, we shall see that the two tendencies alternate in successive sketches.*
>
> *The example of 'The Murder of [King] Duncan' (as an experiment).*[4]

The experiment to which reference is here made was the Mexican graphic cycle on a theme from Shakespeare's *Macbeth*. Eisenstein wrote an analytical study of it in 1934, in which he revealed the course and result of his experimental drawing with striking clarity:

In 1931, in Mexico, I became very attached to drawing. Drawing, and the process of drawing. In the long days of the rainy season, when I had no outlet for my creative energy, I devoted more than a little time to it. I had no illusions of becoming a draughtsman (because of my age), and I was more interested in accumulating material for possible future research [....] To observe step by step, phase by phase, the genesis and movement of the idea I was embodying: that is what interested me. [...]

I drew completely freely. My own task was to establish where the compositional possibilities and varieties of one and the same situation would be exhausted. What I produced was: [for] two or three days, unnumbered sheets. Then I made myself number the drawings, and after a few days I had the following:

8 June 1931 – 16 motifs; 9 June 1931 – 20; 12 June 1931 – 32; 15 June 1931 – 19; 16 June 1931 – 20.

IN TOTAL – 127 motifs on the same theme.

I took as my theme the murder of King Duncan by Macbeth and Lady Macbeth. The attributes were reduced to a minimum. The characters were naked (a reminiscence of Zola's La Bête humaine, *where they strip after the murder in order to wash themselves and remark the fact that the murderer strips completely naked so as to make sure that not a trace of the blood and the crime stays on him). [...]*

I worked with great intensity, almost in a trance; by the 52nd drawing I was exhausted! And a post-analysis of what I had done immediately drew my attention to the first thing I noticed: the alternation between acutely stylized drawings and everyday, naturalistic ones.

Almost every motif started out strictly representational and everyday. Then it was 'shaped' into a composition. Then it would freeze as a conventional sign. Finally, a new concept of the situation would arise to reject the old, a concept that would entirely replace the former and start the cycle afresh. The schematism would begin to be infused with blood, and would come to life. But it was the fact of the phased alternation between generalized (almost ornamental) and everyday (almost cartoonishly naturalistic) composition, between the 'general' and the 'particular', that I could not help but notice." [5]

In Eisenstein's Moscow drawings from the 1930s, the two tendencies alternated over the course of the various cycles. The series of cartoons on themes from everyday life – whether modern ('Soviet holidaymakers', 'La Vie quotidienne') or historical and mock-mythological ('Olympians and Athenians') – gravitated towards the freer 'naturalist' manner. The tragic cycles – mythological ('Prometheus', 'Golgotha', 'Oedipus') and contemporary ('Bombs. Spain', 'Vision de délire', 'La Garrotta') – were drawn with a tenser, 'generalizing' line.

On one occasion, in February 1934, Eisenstein had an idea for a strange kind of stained-glass window. In blue ink, he depicted ancient, oriental and 'eternal' love motifs. Then, in red pencil, he added geometrical figures to define 'zones of glass' from mural 'outline frescoes'. But here the geometry was more ornamental than conceptual, and belongs rather to the art of framing, separating the part from the whole, than to the interpretation of the design.

At around the same time, he copied out an extract from Will Durant's *The Story of Philosophy*:

> ***...Plutarch tells us that according to Plato 'God always geometrizes'; or, as Spinoza puts the same thought, God and the universal laws of structure and operation are one and the same reality. To Plato, as to Bertrand Russell, mathematics is therefore the indispensable prelude to philosophy, and its highest form; over the doors of his Academy Plato placed, Dantesquely, these words, 'Let no man ignorant of geometry enter here'*** [6]

It was not for nothing that Kazimir Malevich traced the genealogy of his Suprematism back to the transcendent geometry of Byzantine icon painting. He could also have referred to Platonic cosmogony!

But Eisenstein's dialectical mind refused, as always, to accord phenomena an unequivocal and immanent meaning – whether they were lines or colours, gestures or scenes. On several occasions, he observed in his own drawings that a geometrical general composition, or a geometrical outline of a figure, or a geometrical abstract line could turn out to be a manifestation not of the life-giving (divine) principle, but of the fatal 'earthly order' – the order of the state, of society, dogma and formal rationalism.

He spent the late summer of 1937 in Kratovo, outside Moscow, at the dacha built under his mother's supervision (it took a year) in parallel with all his cinematographic troubles. After *Bezhin Meadow* was banned, he worked feverishly on his book *Montage*, driving away the thought that he was likely to be arrested. This book detailed the film-maker's noble ancestry: among many forebears, Eisenstein recalled ancient Greek culture – from the myth of the god Dionysus, who was torn to pieces and rose from the dead, to the architecture of the Athenian Acropolis.

—PAGE 160
From the cycle 'Gedanken zur Musik' Drawing of the motif for 'The Battle on the Ice' from the film *Alexander Nevsky* (1938)

—THIS PAGE

TOP LEFT
'Antique motifs' (Kratovo, 1937)

TOP RIGHT
St Sebastian Surcharge (Moscow, 1938)

BOTTOM
Idée sur la Musique (Musical idea) (Moscow, 1946)

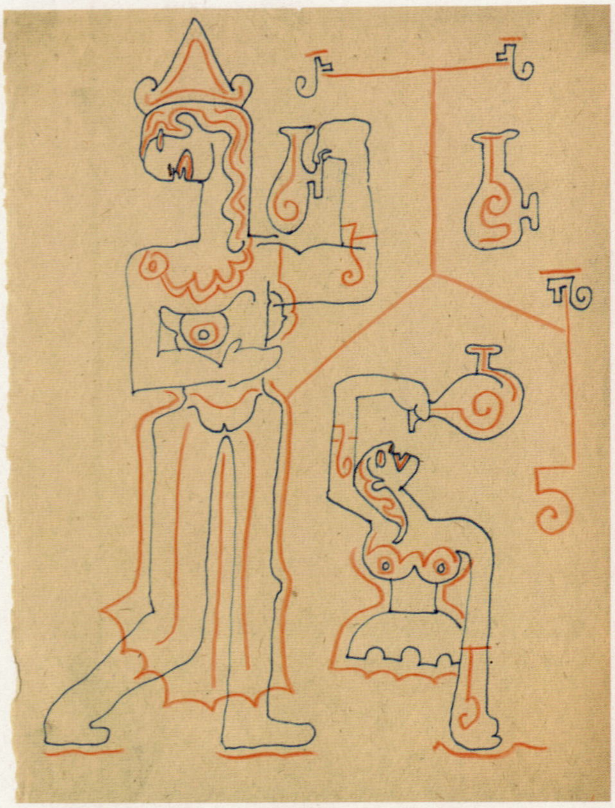

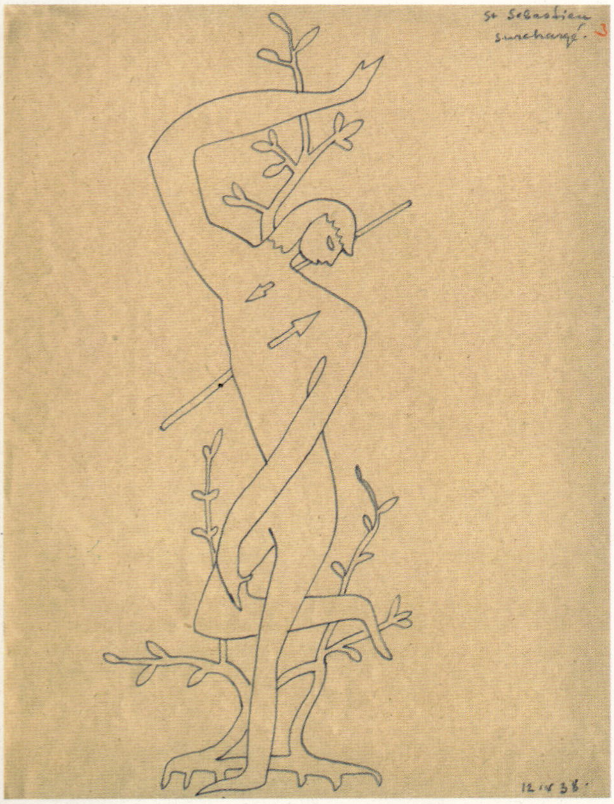

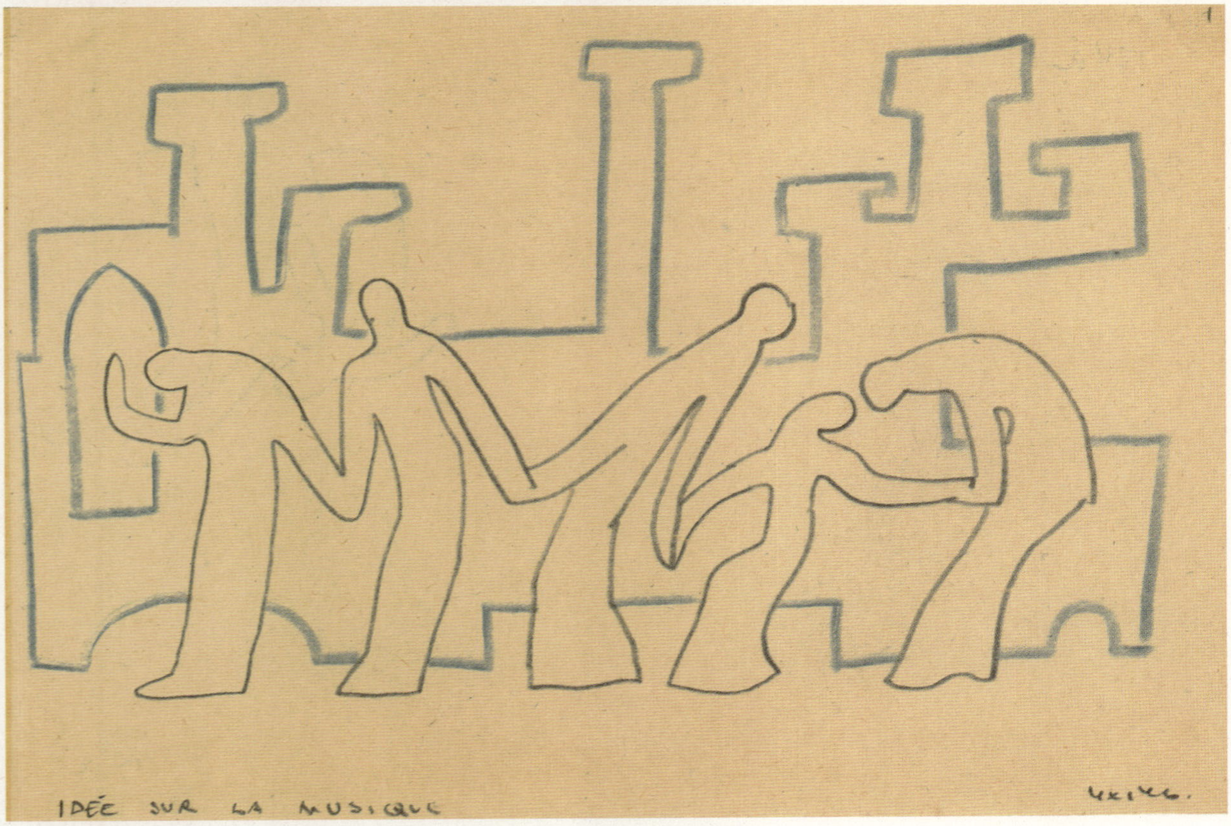

On Tuesday, 24 August, he took a break from the manuscript. In the same ink he was using to write the book, he drew some semi-parodic Greek female figures with amphorae. Then, to the blue lines he added water, hair, tunics and simple ornamentation, all in red pencil. And suddenly, on the next sheet of paper, what appeared under his pen and pencil was an overseer holding a whip, more Roman than Hellenic, with geometrical figures in the background.

The same day saw the birth of a cycle of drawings that falls, as it were, into two halves. In one half, we see stories from antiquity: the punishment of a slave, the transportation of a mummy and an idol, the worship of a bust of the sovereign. And in the other half there are typical scenes from Soviet dacha life: digging up tree stumps, planting trees and strawberry bushes, clearing paths. It was the final drawing of the cycle, the fourteenth, that seems to have given Eisenstein a title for the whole series: 'Histoire des petits chemins'. It is noteworthy that the flower beds and vegetable patches are enclosed in 'correct' geometrical figures, while all the little paths end in dead ends in the form of porticos, busts and urns – echoes of the 'monumental' world of geometrized idol-worshippers and mummies. The 'August' cycle was no less rebellious, in its metaphorical meaning, than the dangerously open, 'despairing' drawings of 1937.

On 12 April 1938, after the sketches for *Alexander Nevsky* and the series of St Sebastians, Eisenstein appears to have remembered the experience of the 'Histoire des petits chemins' – and then turned it inside out, creating his third graphic cycle of the day. The first title he gave it in his diary was in German, 'Gedanken zur Musik' (Thoughts on music); but he later changed it to a slightly different Russian name, translating as 'Musical ideas'.

In blue ink, Eisenstein drew the Battle on the Ice: moments from the fight between the Teutonic Knights and the warriors of Alexander Nevsky. In red pencil, he added abstract geometrical figures, which, however, sometimes clearly recalled horses. But these were not sketches for the film, whether in style or in meaning. They can be defined as 'graphic formulae' for the audiovisual combinations in the cinema: the blue standing for the image and the red for the music.

This was one of his life's paradoxes. In 1928 Eisenstein had welcomed the introduction of sound into the movies with a manifesto on the counterpoint of sound and vision – but ten years later, he still was not able to realize his ideas in practice. He had not been given the chance to make a new film, or even to give *The General Line* the soundtrack he wanted, either in Europe or in Hollywood. The film he had gone to Mexico to make did not reach the stage at which a soundtrack could be added. His work on *Bezhin Meadow* had been interrupted twice, so his devices in the preliminary cut of the images and the recorded soundtrack remained unknown to the viewer. In *Alexander Nevsky*, he had an opportunity to verify the possibilities of conveying meaning and emotion by way of different combinations of imagery with music.

Eisenstein tried to clarify the different forms of this combination in a diary entry, again from 12 April 1938:

> ***Gedanken zur Musik:***
>
> ***I. Illustrative music. Outwardly synchronized. The outline of the music follows the outline of the picture – effect: the acuteness of the plastic drawing is atrophied.***
>
> ***II. Inwardly synchronized in a formal way. Synchronous rhythms. The effect is doubled – with a static result. Structural lines are synchronous (with variations).***
>
> ***III. Inwardly synchronized in an imagistic way. The themes are synchronous: they do not coincide in linear fashion, but, being co-rhythmic, they are nonetheless independent. Effect: a heightened drama. The music is not pictorial and not depending on the subject.***
>
> ***IV. [Outwardly] synchronized in an imagistic way. The themes and the stories – the vehicles of the themes – are both synchronous. The musical equivalent of the imagery has also a pictorial side connected to the them, while being independent on the level of plot. Heightened drama.***[7]

We can guess from *Alexander Nevsky* that the fourth kind of combination refers to those drawings from the cycle where the red geometrical line becomes quasi-figurative, rather than purely abstract. In some of the sequences of the Battle on the Ice, Sergei Prokofiev's music clearly makes use (in rhythm and orchestration) of an 'equivalent that depicts' the action: the attack first by the Teutonic horsemen and then by the Russians. In other episodes, other kinds of synchrony or asynchrony were tried out ahead of the more complex forms of counterpoint in *Ivan the Terrible*.

Eisenstein gave the same title, 'Gedanken zur Musik', to another cycle, which he drew on 3 and 4 May and that had no direct connection to the cinema. It turned out to be exceptionally diverse thematically: dance and sport, hunters with dogs and a pair of lovers, a calm and distant St Sebastian transfixed with arrows and a triumphant Dionysus with a vine.... In the lightness and suppleness of the lines, and in the joyful condition of the characters and the artist, this cycle is striking reminiscent of Eisenstein's Mexican period. And each blue figure has its counterpoint of red geometrical lines – that imagined music, which could also be purely visual.

What had happened to Eisenstein? Had working on *Alexander Nevsky* really made him feel safe? Had it calmed his fearful apprehensions?

Partly – and only for a very short time. Soon the fear and despair would be driven in deep, and his drawings of 1939 bear witness to a mute cry for freedom that had again risen to the surface.

The cycle of 'musical ideas' was connected to quite another sphere – to be more precise, quite another level – of Eisenstein's experience and reflection. This became especially clear in the autumn of 1946, after the second part of *Ivan the Terrible* was banned. Working on *Non-Indifferent Nature* (his book on audiovisual counterpoint in the cinema and in other arts, based on his experience with *Ivan*), he also returned to the theme of 'Idée sur la musique' – titled this time in French, perhaps because of his encounter with the art of Matisse.

This return was preceded by reflections set out in his diary entry for 20 October 1946, written in the macaronic blend of languages that Eisenstein typically used when he was generalizing a torrent of ideas and hurrying to get them down on paper:

> ***Why is there music at all...***
> ***'In memory everything seems to happen to music...' – [says] Tom in* The Glass Menagerie *by Tennessee Williams.***
> ***With separation in time, nothing remains but the wave-like outline of the way the course of events oscillates.***
> ***And so we have the purely musical part of the process.***
> ***Art, quite apart from the fact that it too is in some sense always a 'memory' and develops according to memory's laws (and the laws of the unconscious: dream, recollection, etc.), needs music to give laws for the work's form and rhythm. In this sense, inward music is inwardly present in the development of art, and 'accompaniment music' only makes manifest the music that was already present in the laws of the construction.***
> ***So, with me, structure becomes immediately graspable as constructive law as soon as it is 'transcribed' in the music of S. S. [Prokofiev]. Then it becomes apparent at once how strictly (musically) my whole [scenes] and all the divisions within them are constructed [....]*** [8]

There, in the depths of his subconscious, among dreams, memories and sensual desires, Eisenstein felt not the abyss of Hell but a lost (primordial? infantile?) paradise, one that he could regain, or at least return to anyone who could be permitted to engage with music. One might call it 'Heavenly Music', 'the Geometry of the Spheres' or 'the Divine Harmony of the Universe'. And it was here that he saw both the task and the method of art: to help people to look without fear at once into the depths and into the height. He spent many years writing about just this, in his book *Method*, which he had begun in Mexico at the same time as he had returned to drawing, and without which, perhaps, he would not have understood either his theory or his own path as a film-maker.

Drawing, for him, was the most natural means of expressing – impulsively, and 'all the way' (with maximum clarity) – profound feelings that had not yet received a verbal formulation, or highly general ideas that could not be directly observed in reality.

On 17 April 1921, when he was hard at work on the Proletkult staging of *The Mexican*, Eisenstein recalled the 'formula' he had drawn up in August 1920 in Minsk: 'the beautiful is anything that is expressed to the limit'. He took the concept of 'the limit' into a new dimension – one whose importance for Eisenstein's future poetics, and more broadly for his artistic cosmogony, would be fundamental.

> ***Any rhythmically-constructed theatrical spectacle is a mystery-play: a representation of a universal law of harmony, to which all that gallops 'its own way' must come....*** [9]

After all the shocks, disappointments and losses, did Eisenstein – who always 'galloped his own way', and was punished for it – retain his faith in the 'harmony of the universe', through all the catastrophic turns of the first half of the 20th century? 'Gedanken zur Musik', the search for a rhythmic harmonization of the audio-visual spectacle in the spirit of Johann Sebastian Bach's harmonic polyphony, came not because of the time but in spite of it, in the most tragic circumstances for Eisenstein, as a secret oath of loyalty to art and its mission: reminding the viewer to uphold this faith in harmony as Law.

We do not yet know whether it was in 1938 or in 1946 that Eisenstein wrote out a quotation from the poet Aleksandr Blok's 1919 essay on 'The Collapse of Humanism':

> ***There are as it were two times and two spaces: one of history and the calendar, the other incalculable and musical. Great movements arise out of the spirit of music, and are penetrated by it as they act....***

Above the quotation, he wrote: 'Gedanken zur Musik'.

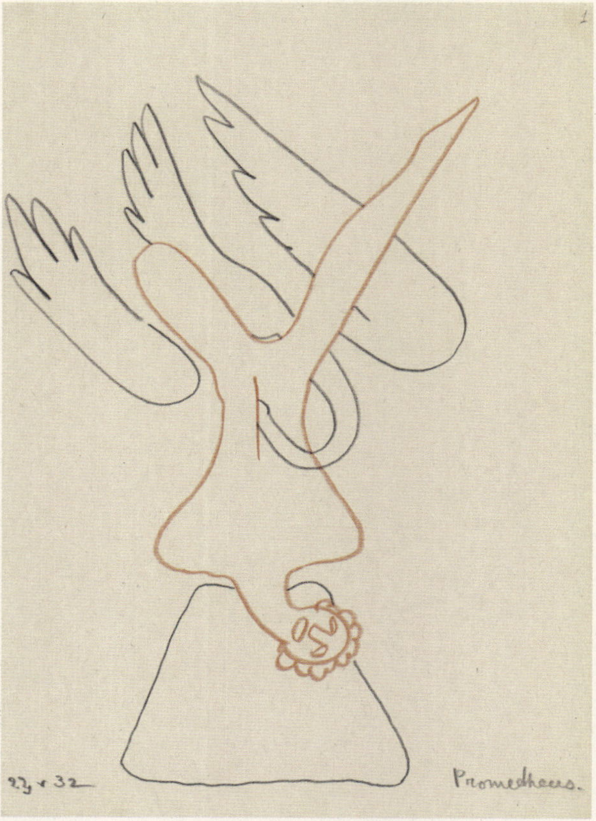
1
23 v 32
Promotheus.

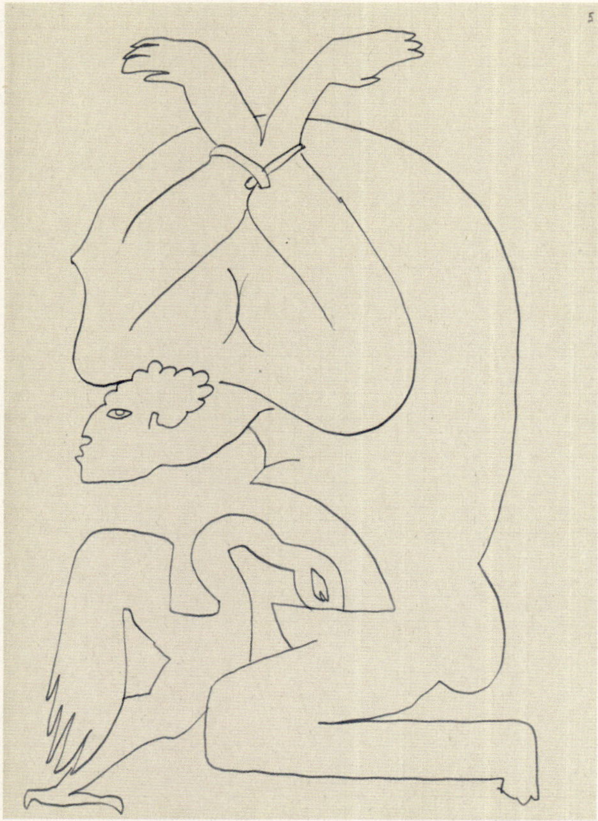
5

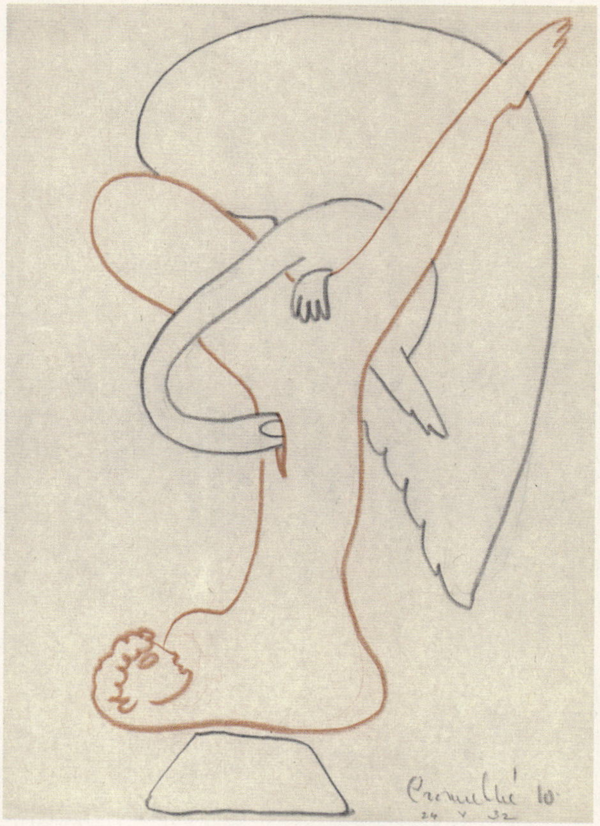
Prométhé 10
24 V 32

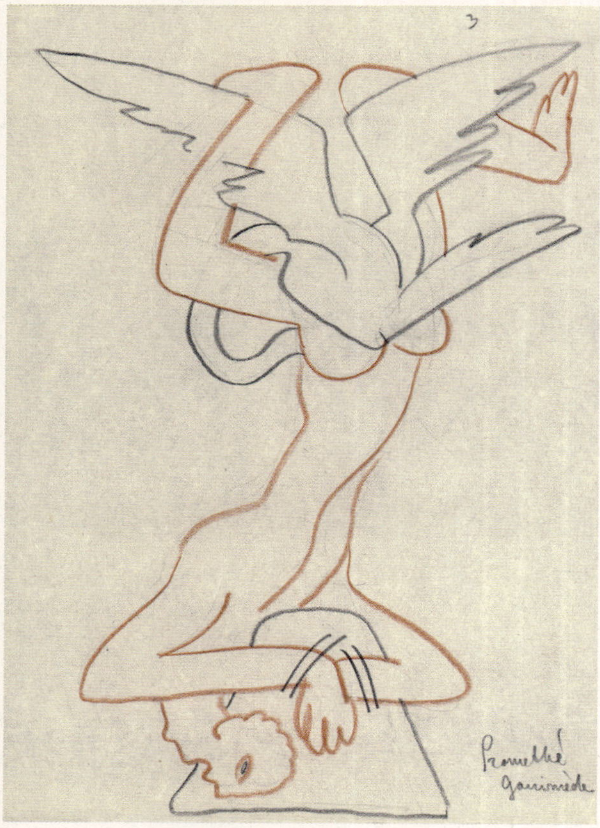
3
Prométhé
Ganimède

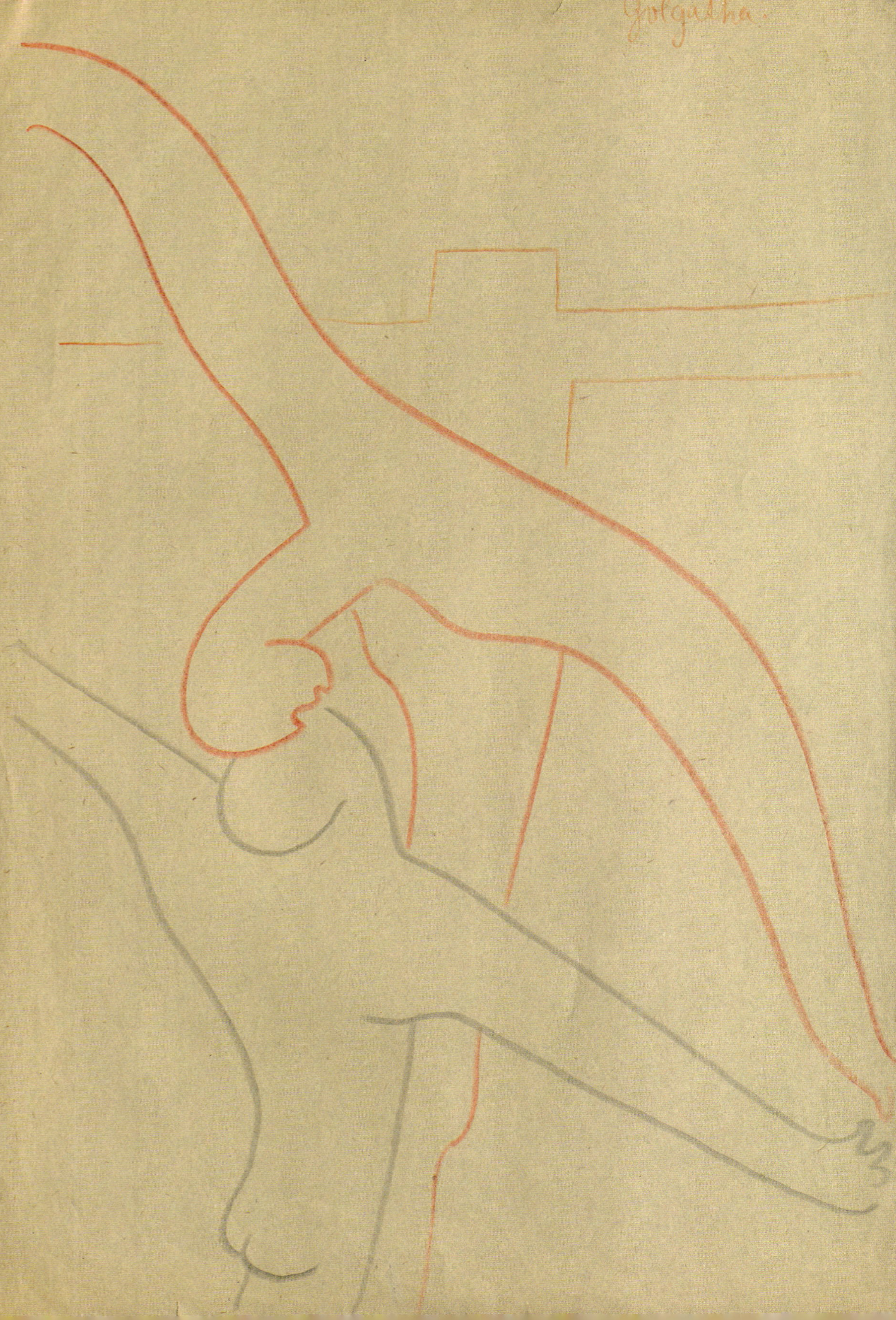
Golgotha.

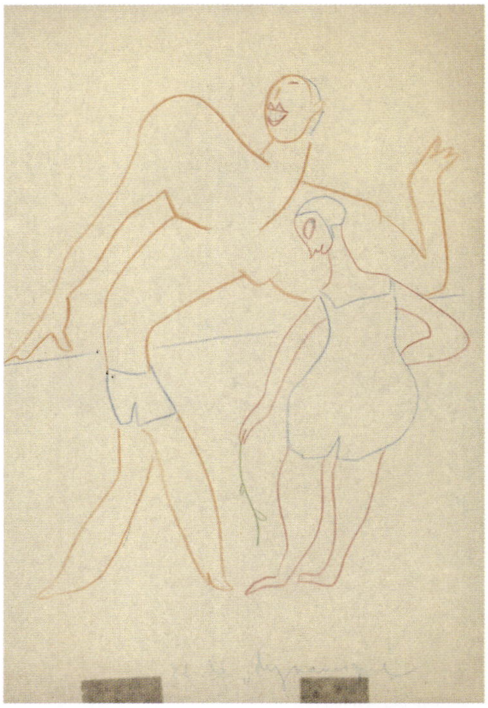

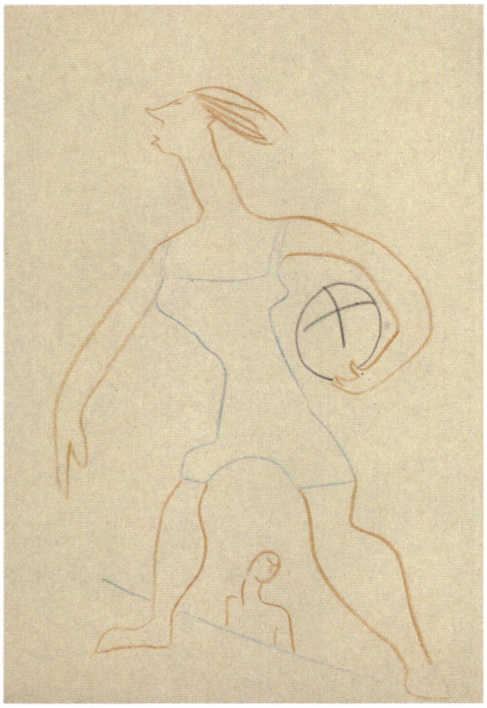

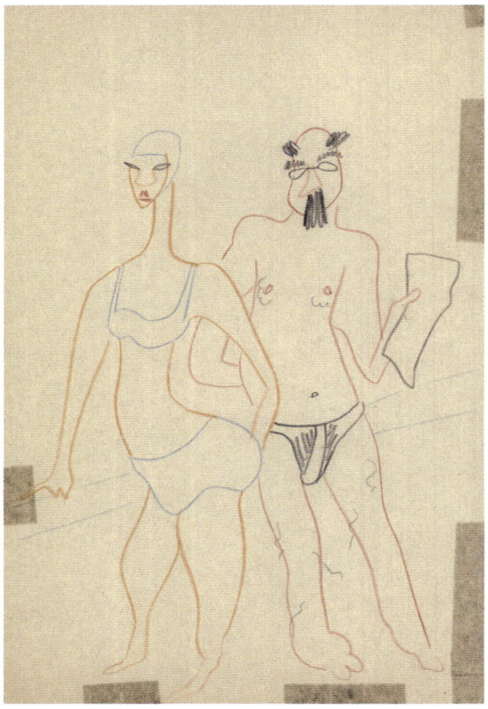

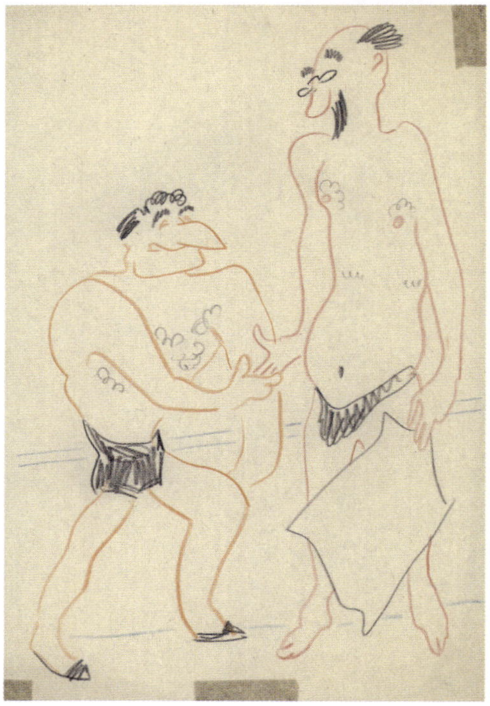

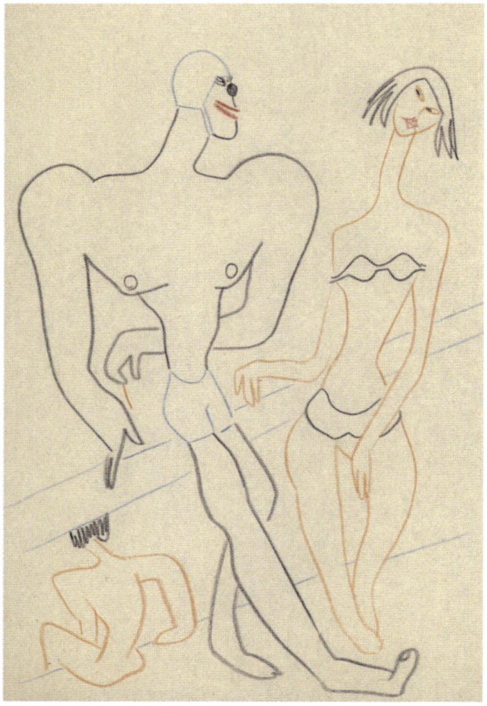

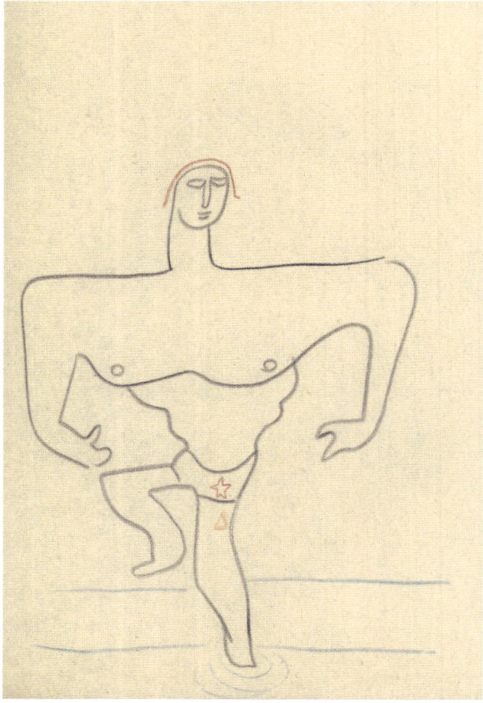

—PREVIOUS LEFT PAGE

TOP AND BOTTOM LEFT
From the cycle 'Prometheus' (Moscow, 1932)

BOTTOM RIGHT
Prométhée-Ganymède (1932)

—PREVIOUS RIGHT PAGE

From the cycle 'Golgotha' (Moscow, 1933)

THIS PAGE AND OPPOSITE

From the cycle 'Soviet holidaymakers' (1932)

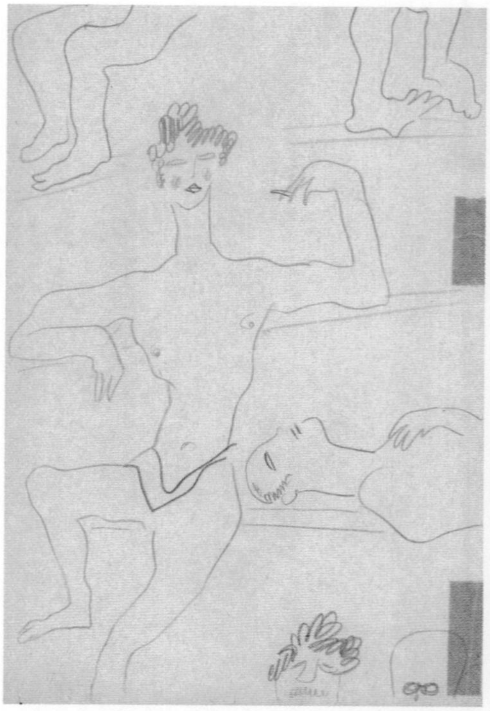

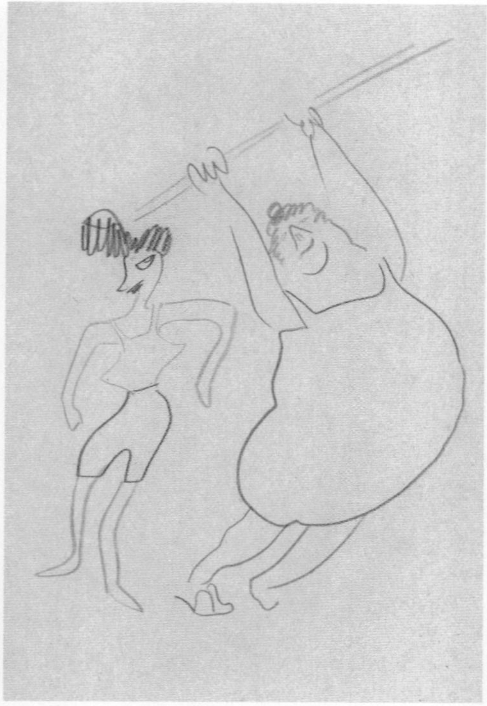

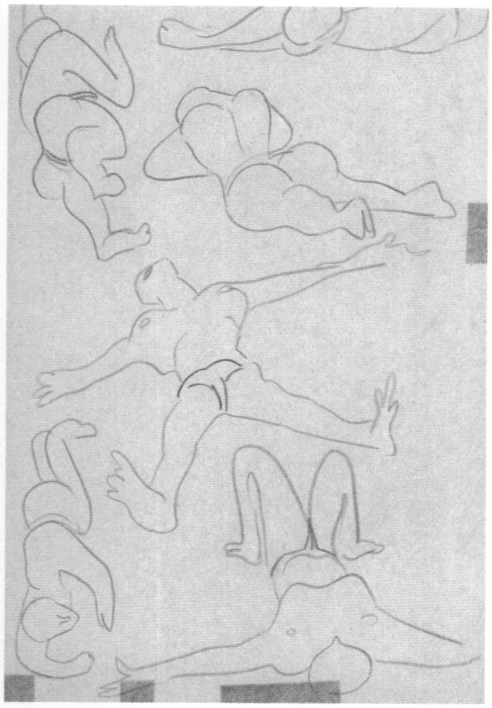

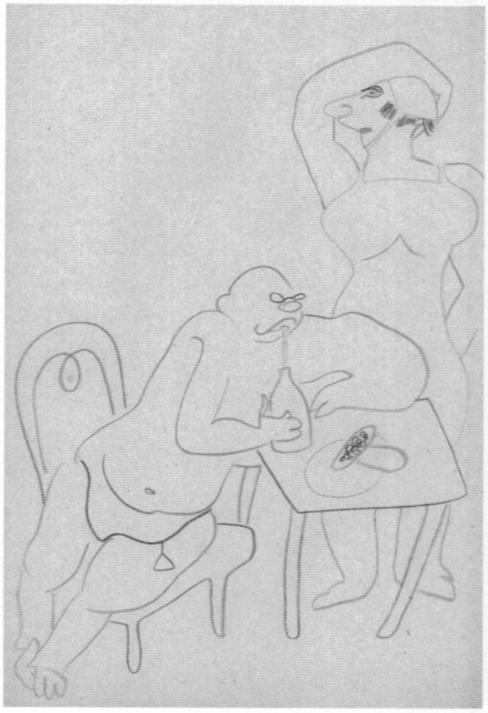

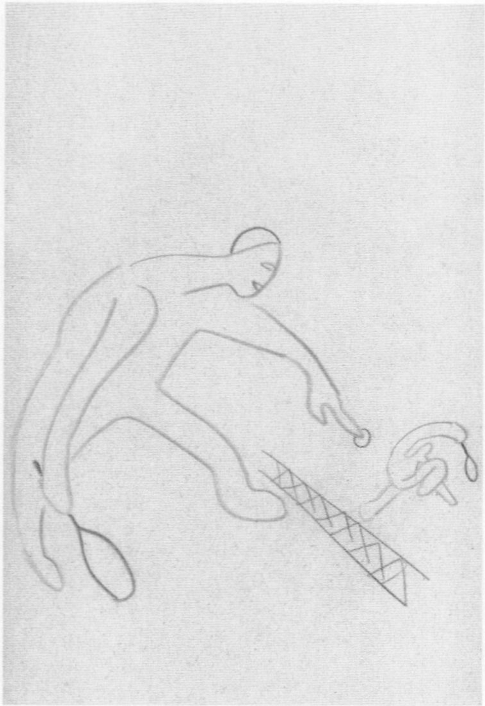

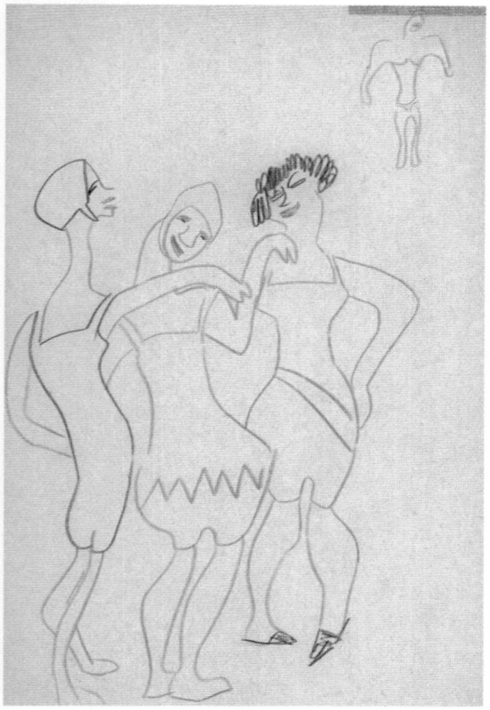

THIS PAGE AND OPPOSITE
From the cycle 'The revanchists'
(Moscow, 1933)

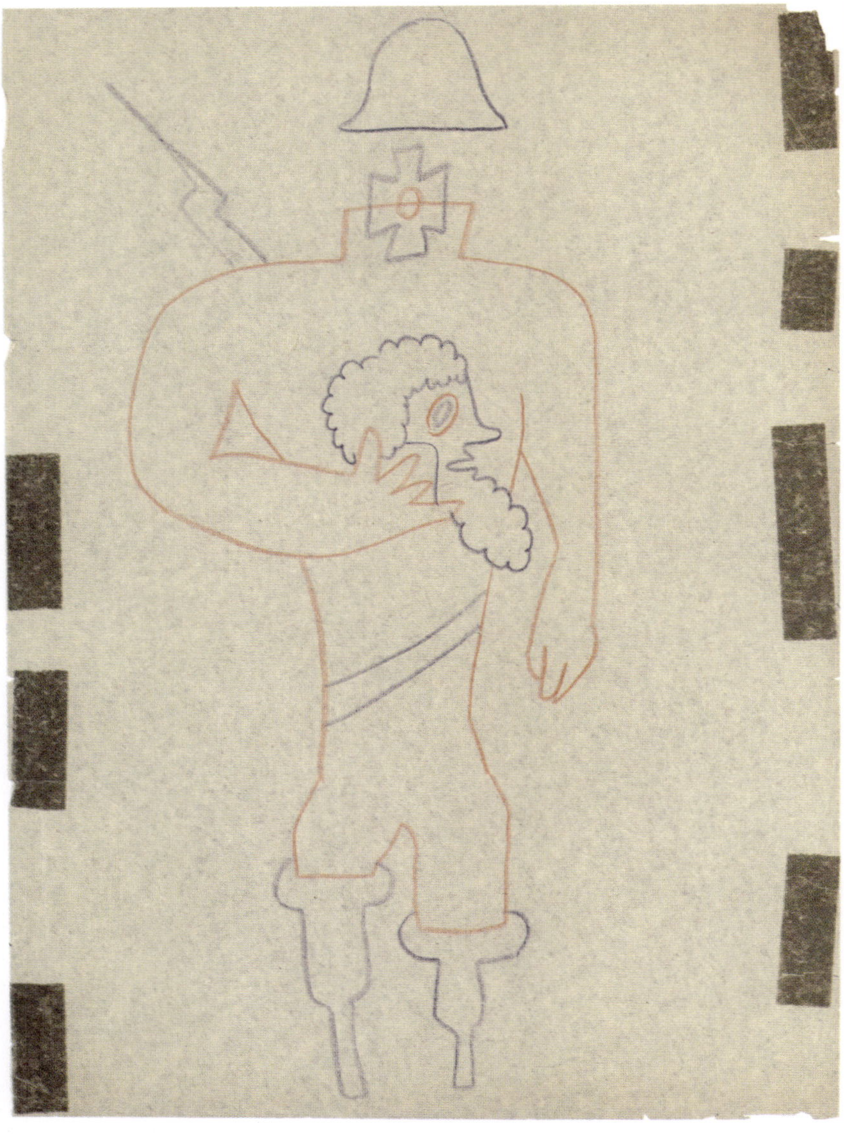

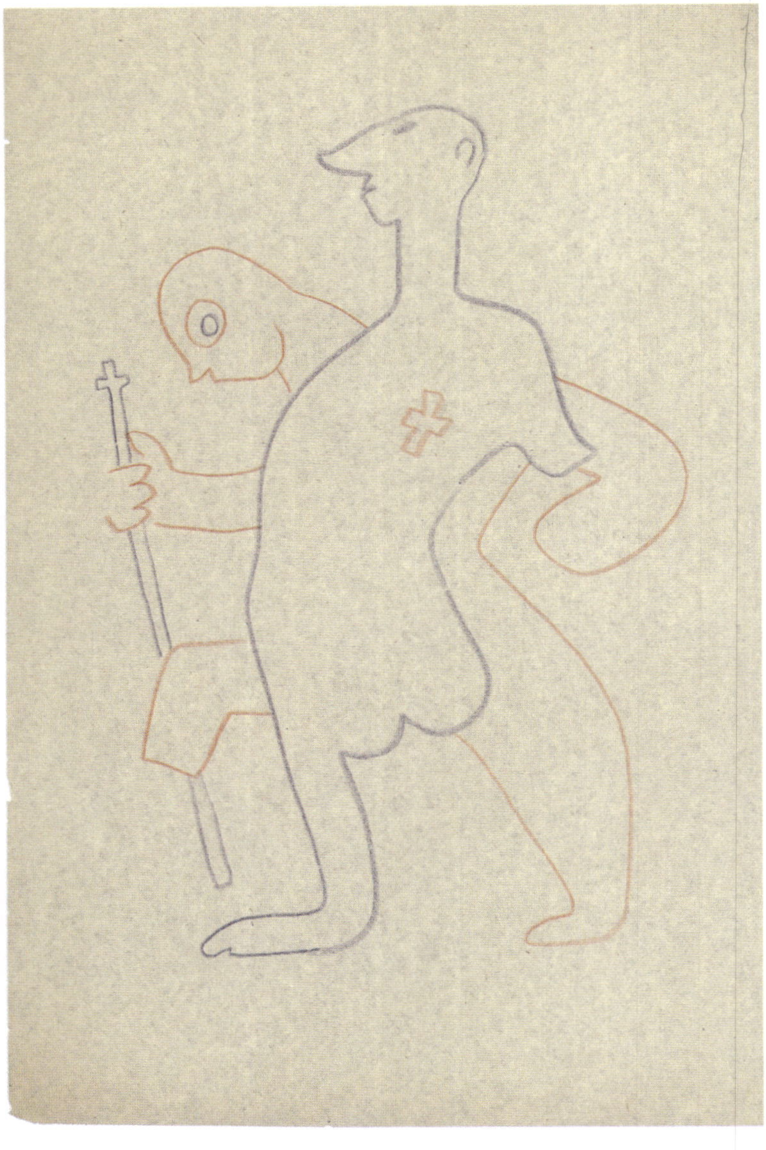

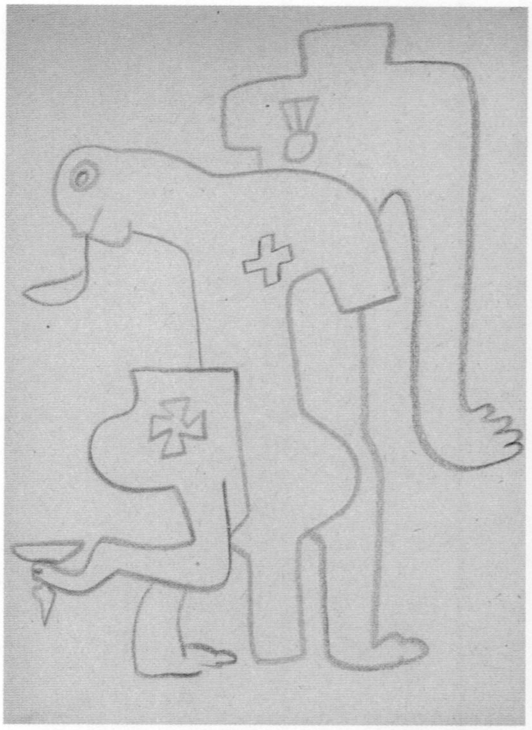

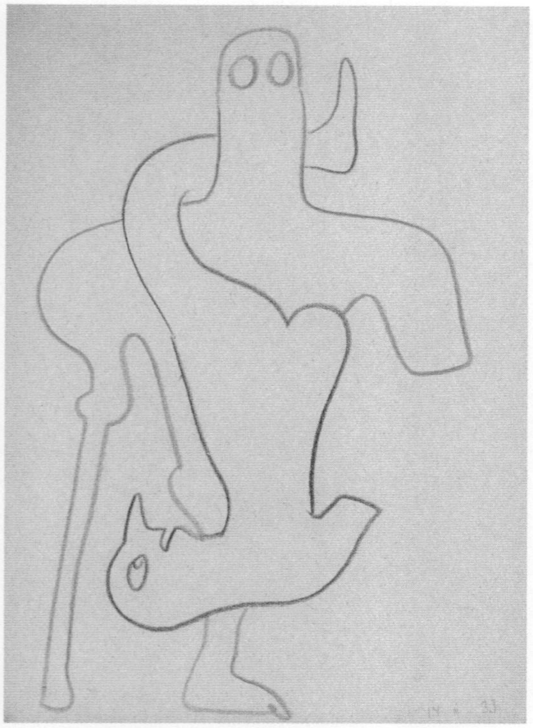

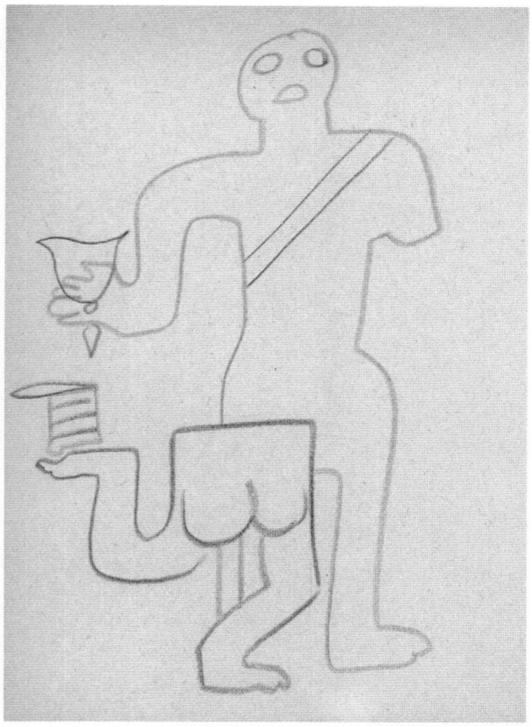

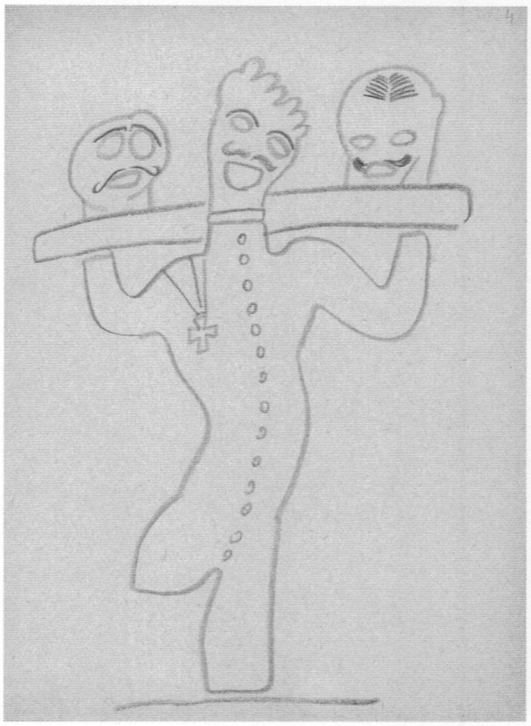

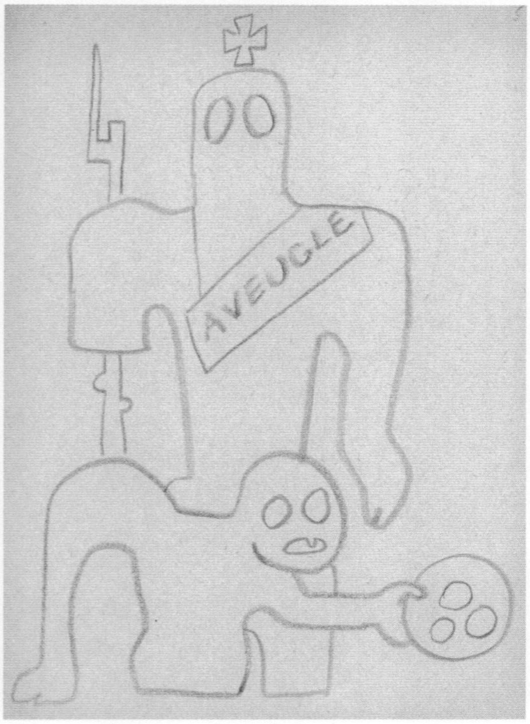
AVEUGLE

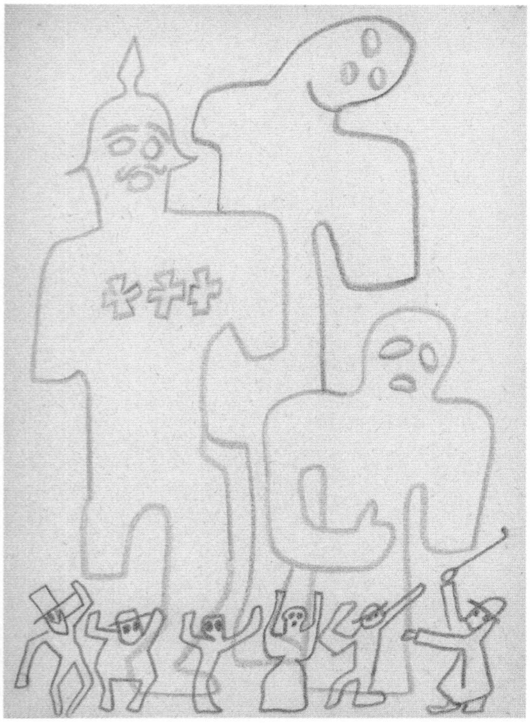

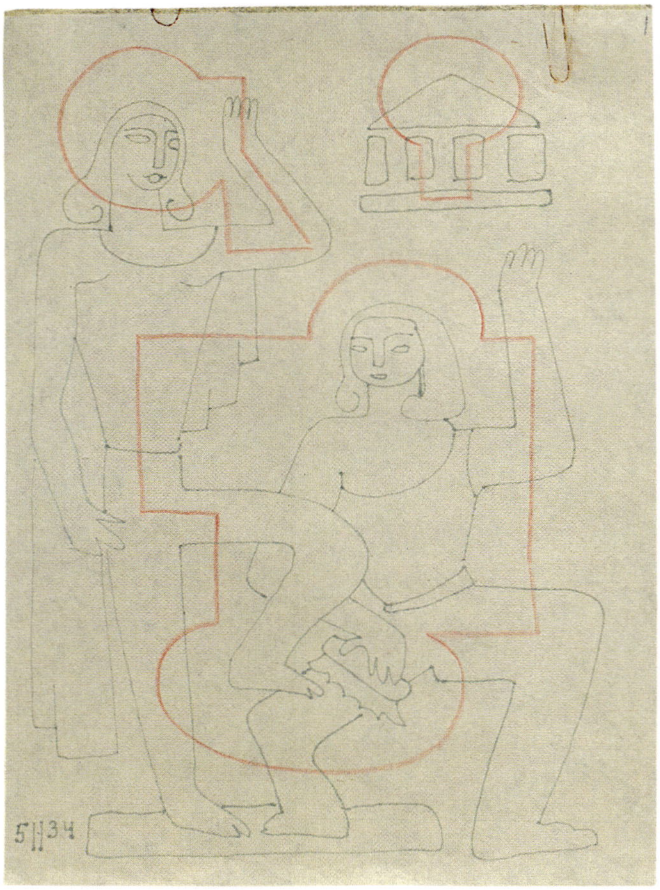
5 II 34

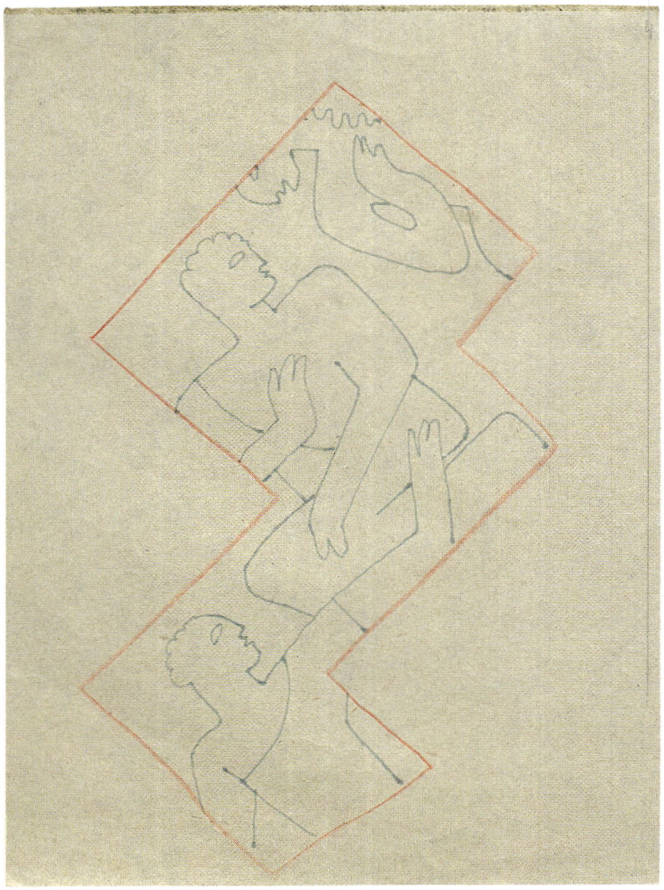

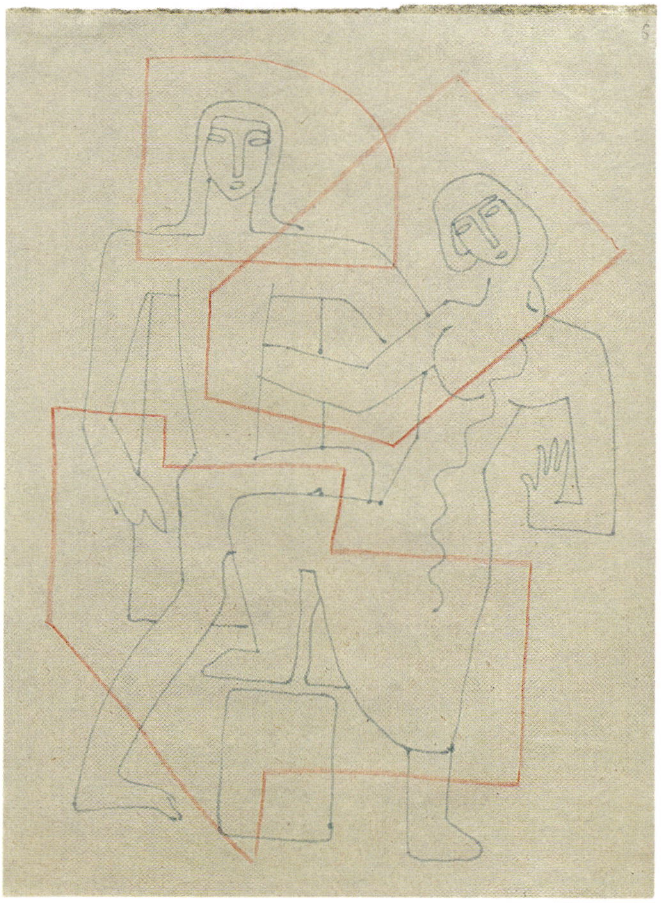

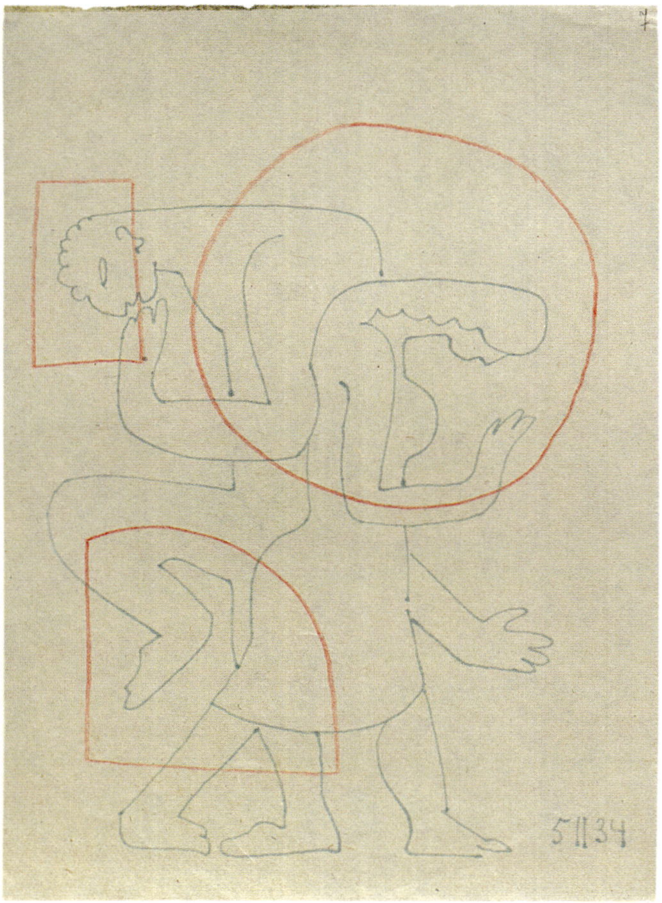
5 II 34

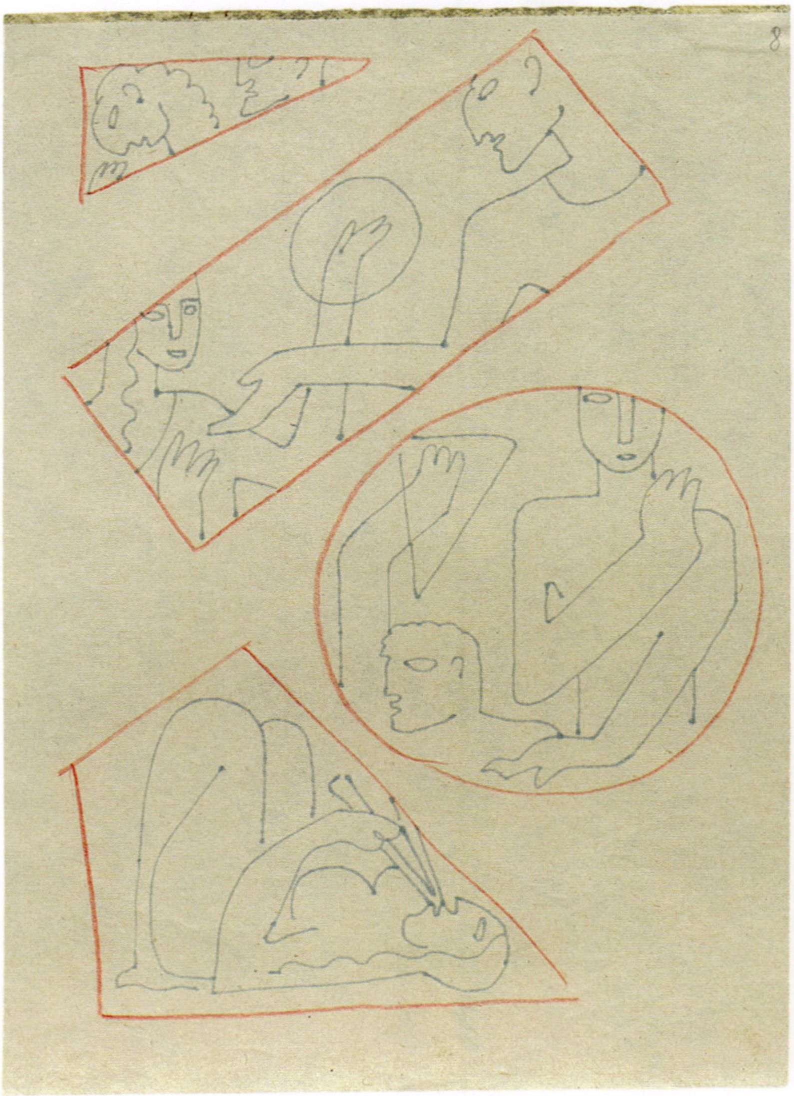

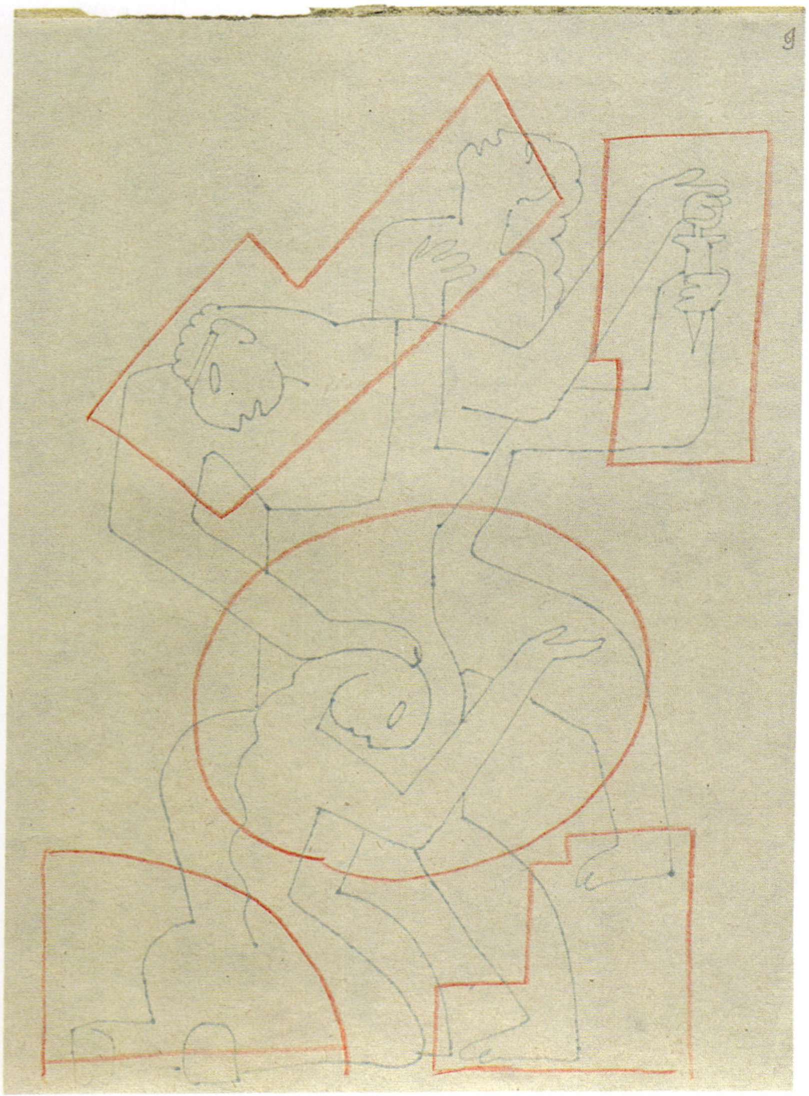

OPPOSITE AND THIS PAGE
From the cycle 'Stained-glass windows'
(Moscow, 1934)

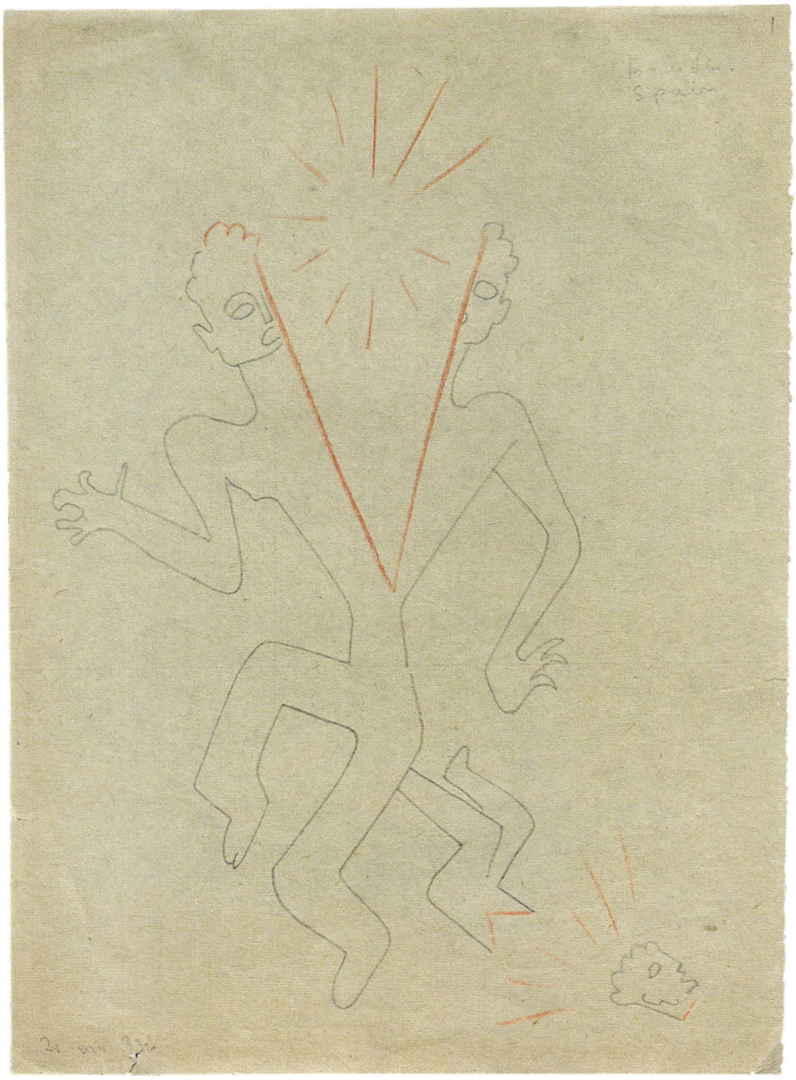

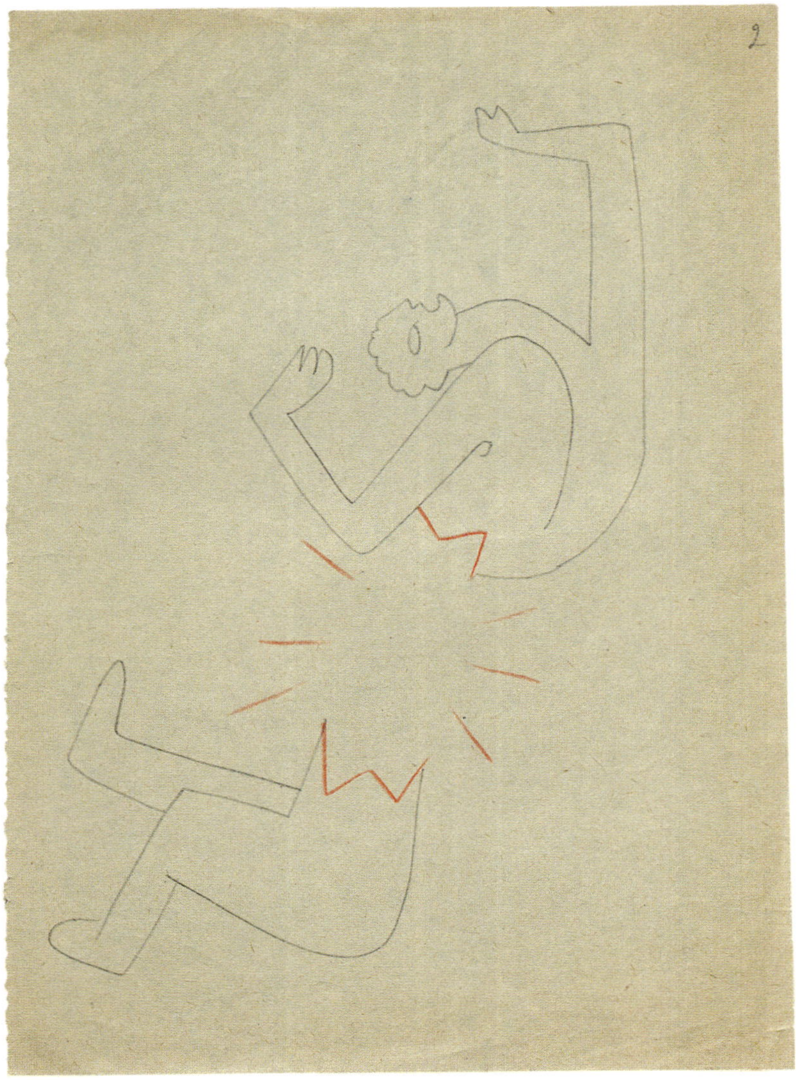

THIS PAGE
Bombs (Spain 1936)

OPPOSITE
La Garrotta (The garrotte)
(Moscow, 1937)

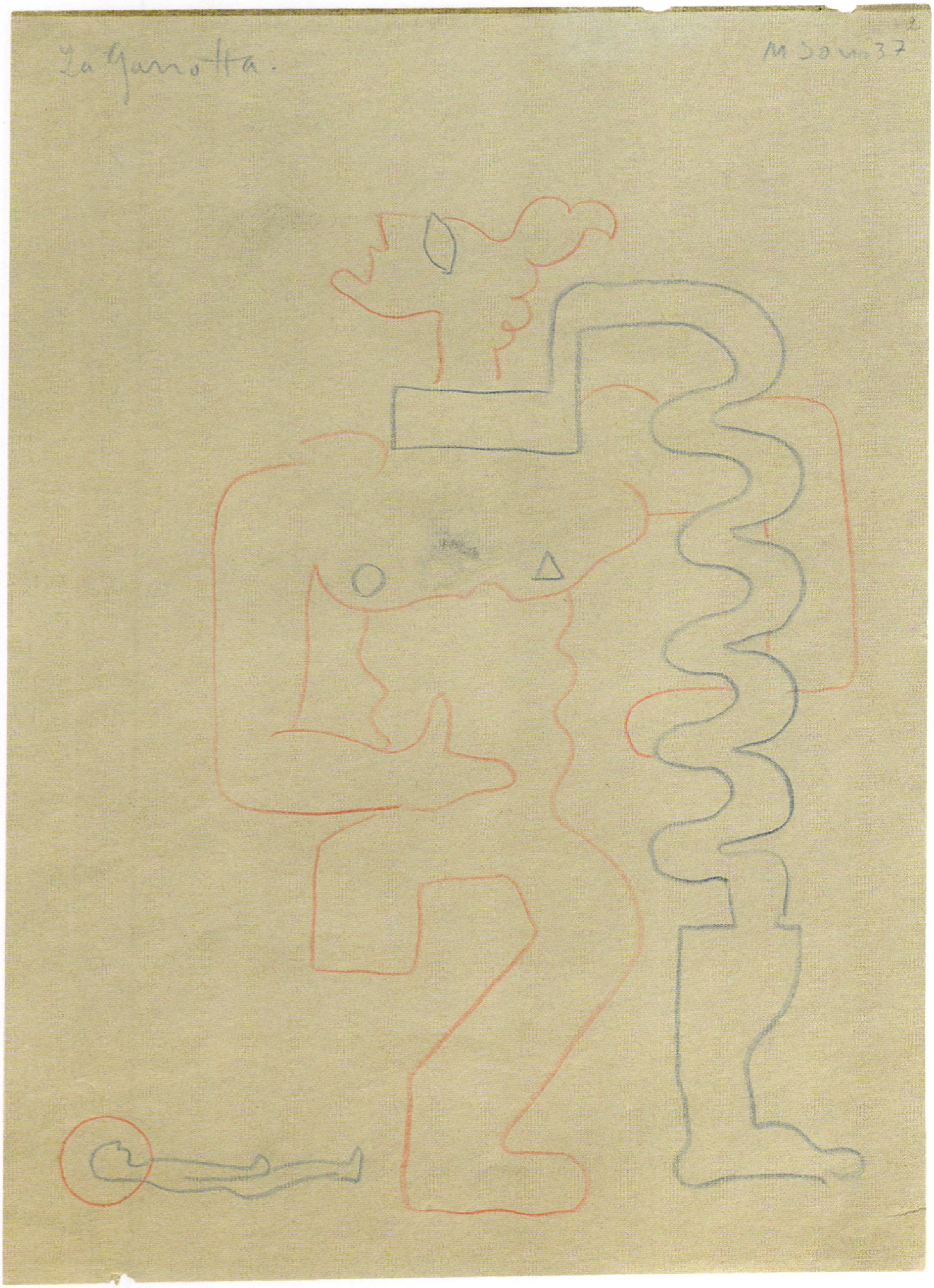
La Garrotta.

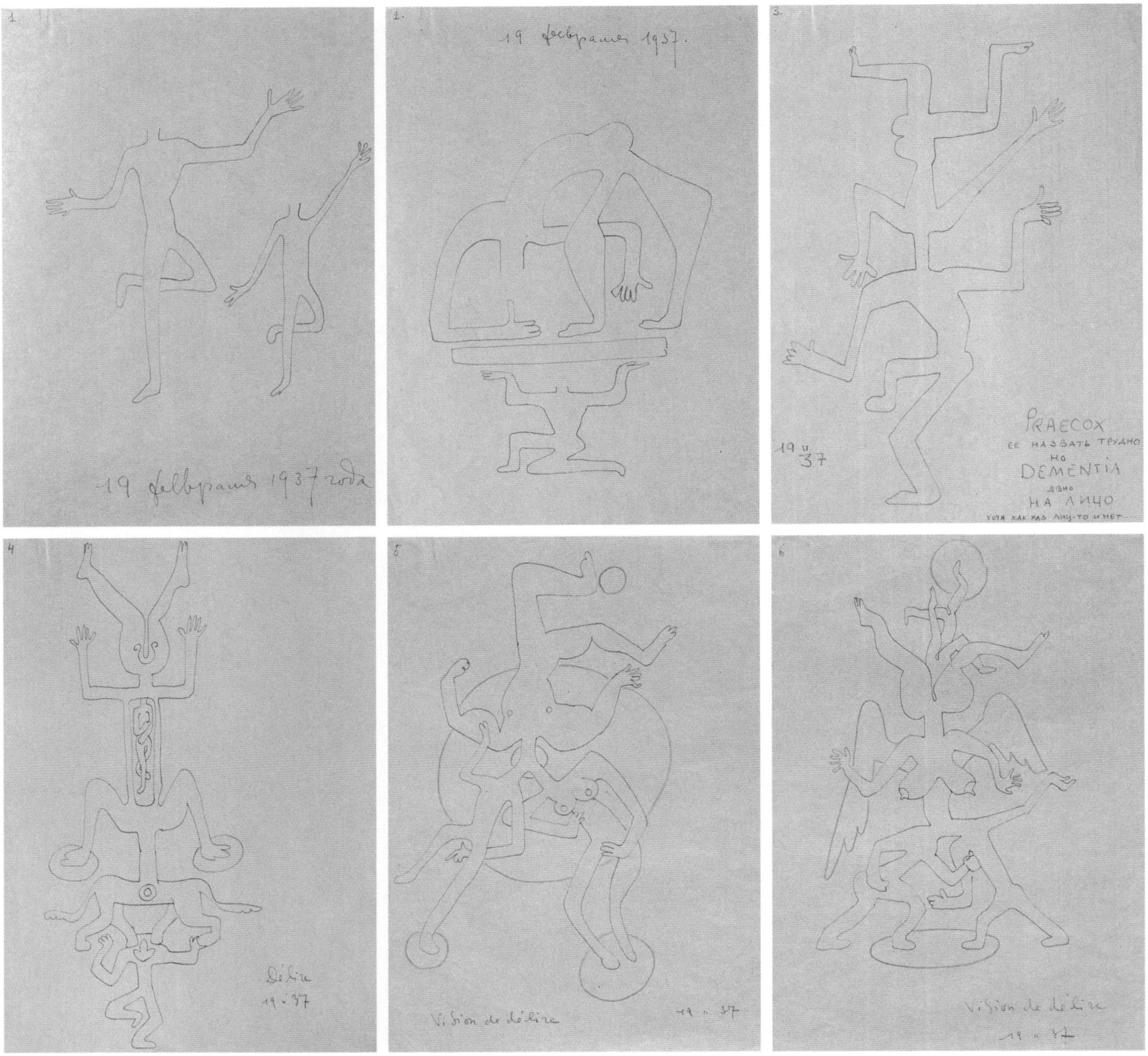

THIS PAGE

The cycle 'Vision de délire' (Vision of delirium) (Moscow, 1937)

Text on page 3: It is difficult to call that PRAECOX, but we are clearly facing DEMENTIA, although faces are absent…

OPPOSITE

Despair (Moscow, 1937)

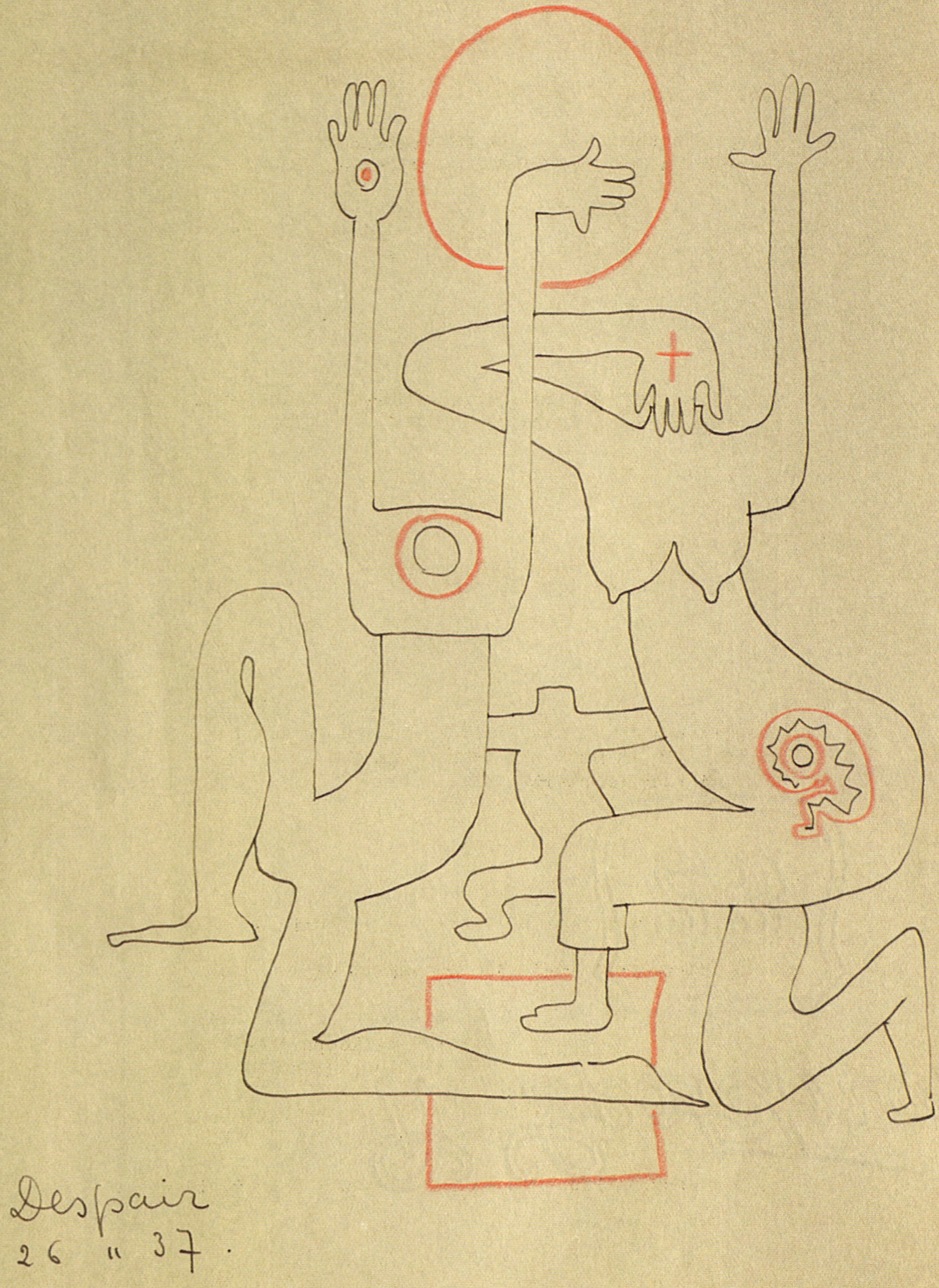
Despair
26 II 37.

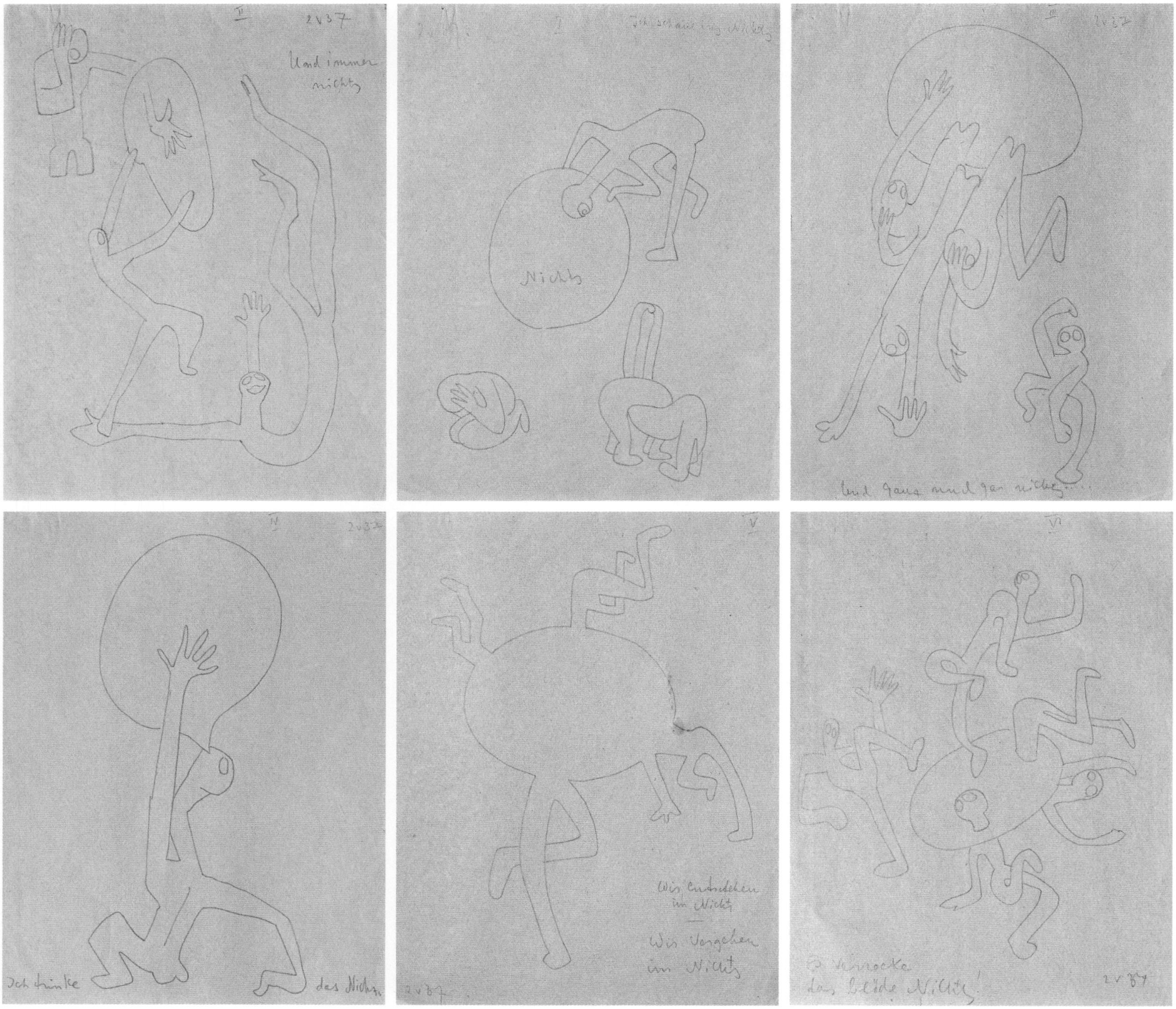

THIS PAGE AND OPPOSITE

From the cycle 'Nichts' (1937):

Text:

I. *Ich schaue ins Nichts.*

II. *Und immer nichts.*

III. *Und ganz und gar nichts.*

IV. *Ich trinke das Nichts.*

V. *Wir entstehen im Nichts. Wir vergehen im Nichts.*

VI. *Es verrecke das blöde Nichts!*

VII. *Sechs Blätter vom Ich und vom Nichts.*

(From the cycle 'Nothing' (1937):

Text:

I. I look into Nothing.

II. And still nothing.

III. And overall nothing.

IV. I drink the Nothing.

V. We arise in Nothing. We pass away in Nothing.

VI. It's dead, the stupid Nothing!

VII. Six leaves of Myself and of Nothing.)

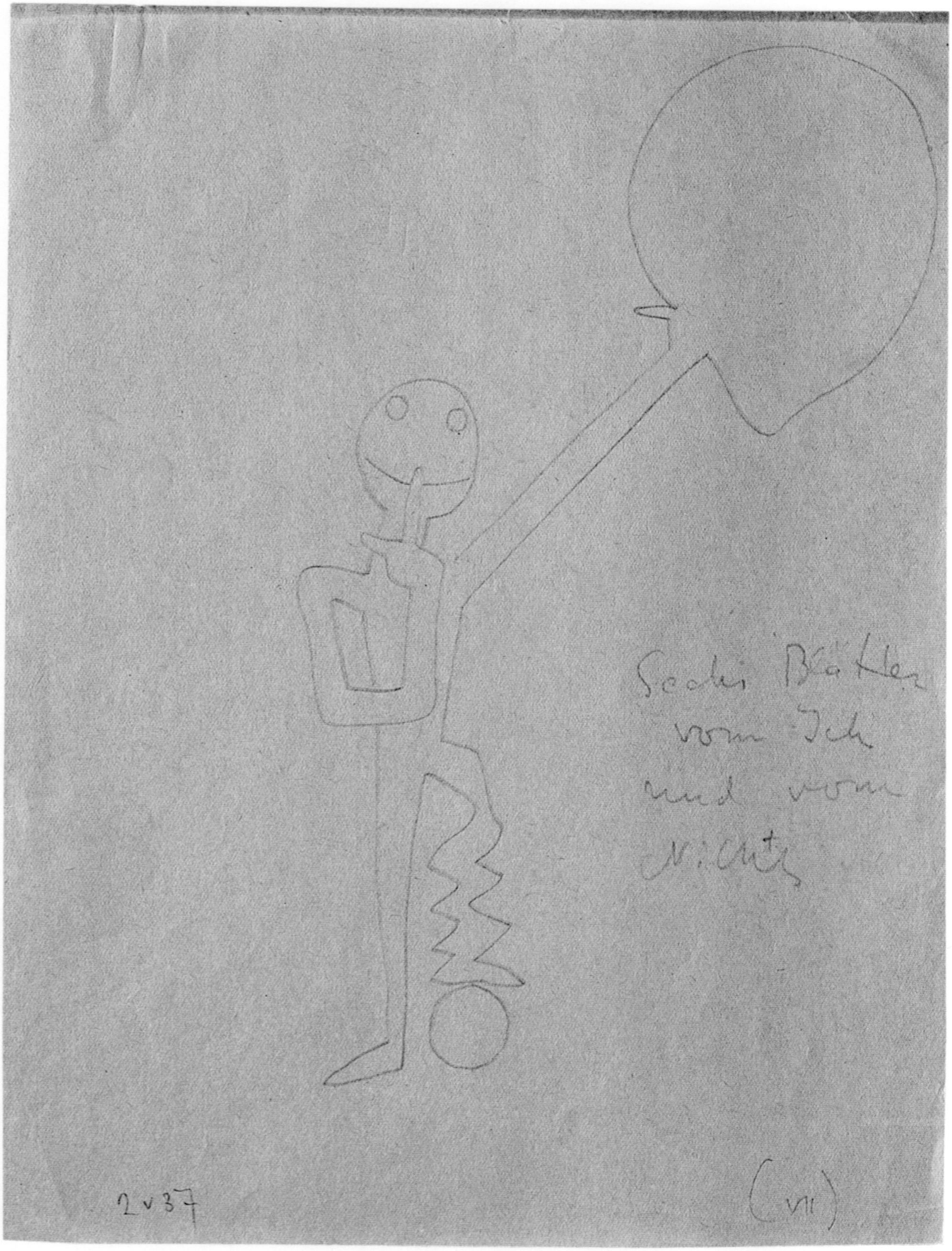
Sechs Blätter
vom Ich
und vom
Nichts
2 v 37
(VII)

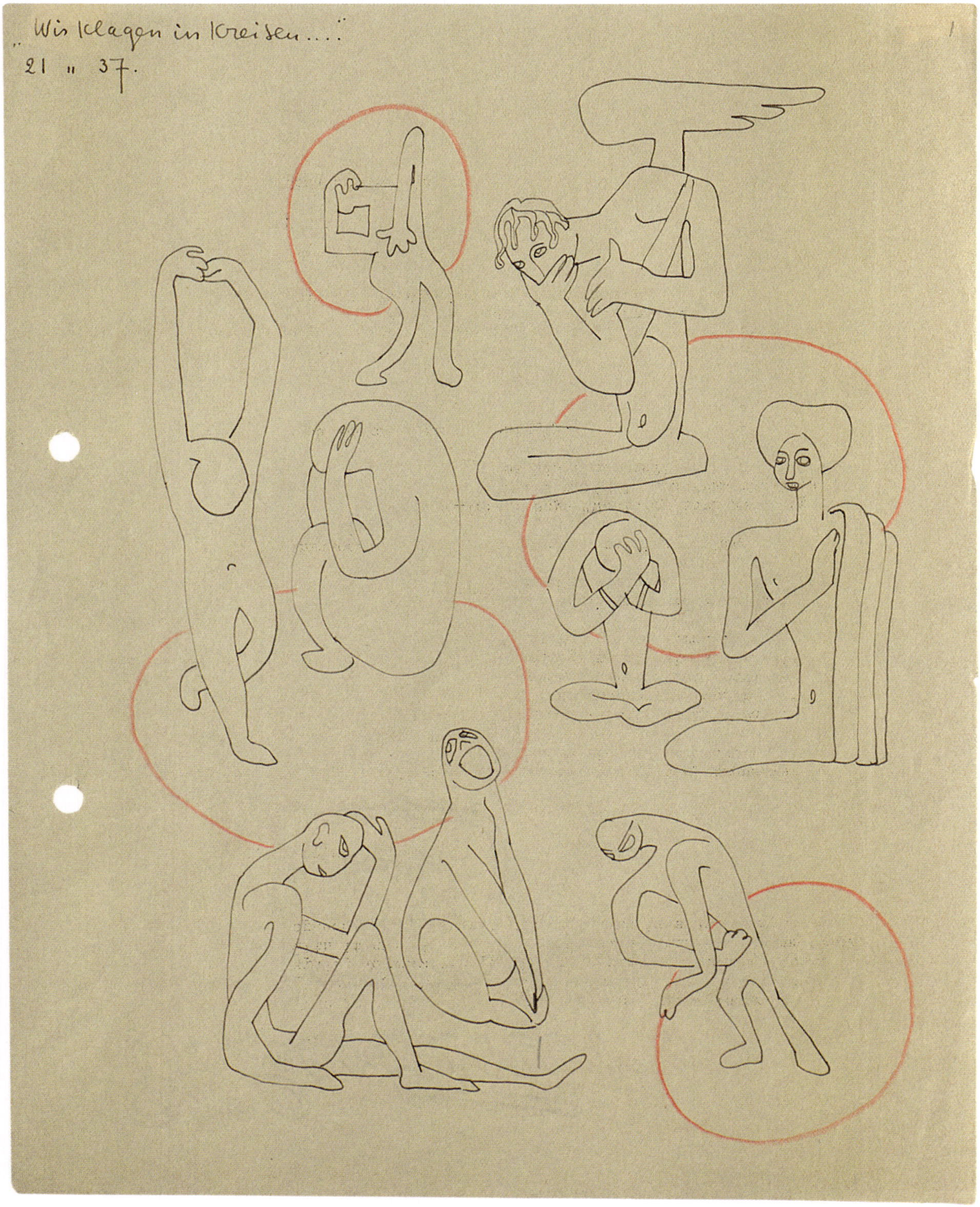

—THIS PAGE
Wir klagen in Kreisen (1937)
(We complain in circles)

—OPPOSITE
From the cycle 'Idolatry'
(Kratovo, 1937):

TOP LEFT
Espérance et Désespoir
(Hope and despair)

TOP CENTRE
Les Transporteurs de Momies
(Carriers of mummies)

TOP RIGHT
On Est en Train [de] Faire des Chemins (Making roads)

BOTTOM LEFT
L'Esclave Châtié
(Scourged slave)

BOTTOM CENTRE
Transportation de l'Idôle
(Transportation of the idol)

BOTTOM RIGHT
Histoire de Petits Chemins
(The history of little roads)

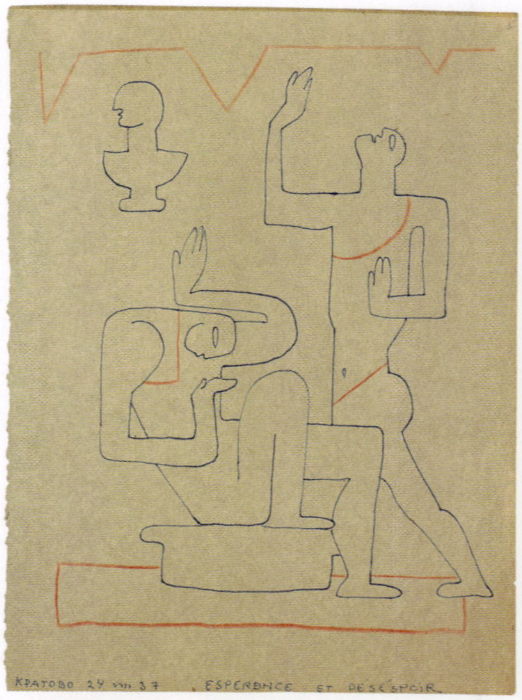
КРАТОВО 24 VIII 37 ESPERENCE ET DESESPOIR

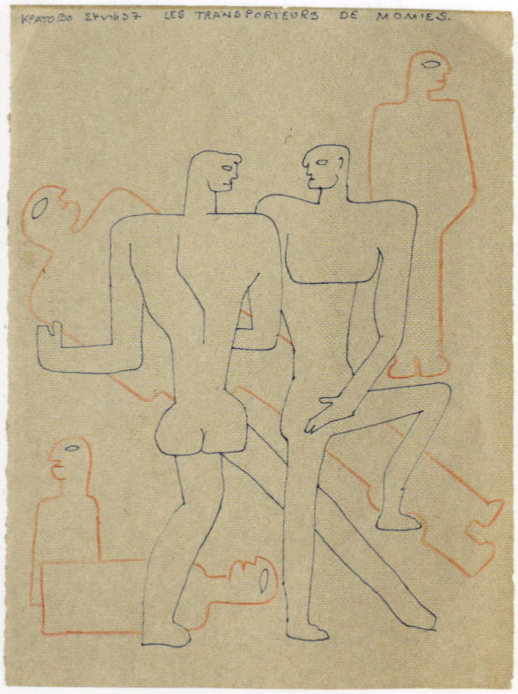
КРАТОВО 24 VIII 37 LES TRANSPORTEURS DE MOMIES.

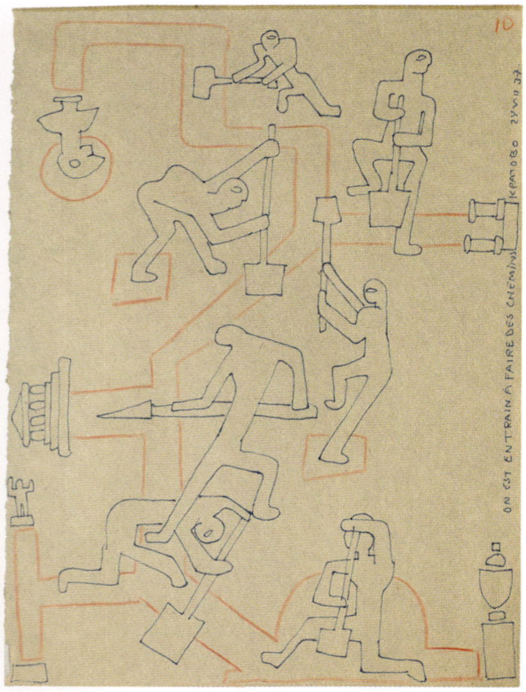
10
КРАТОВО 24 VII 37
ON EST EN TRAIN A FAIRE DES CHEMINS

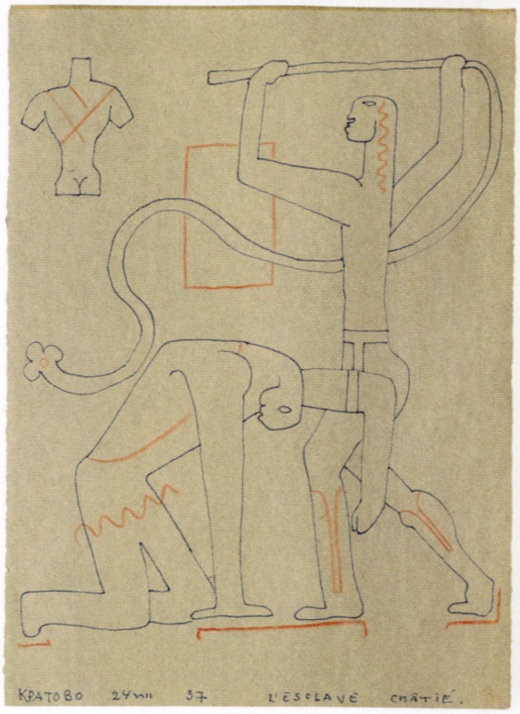
КРАТОВО 24 VIII 37 L'ESCLAVE CHATIÉ.

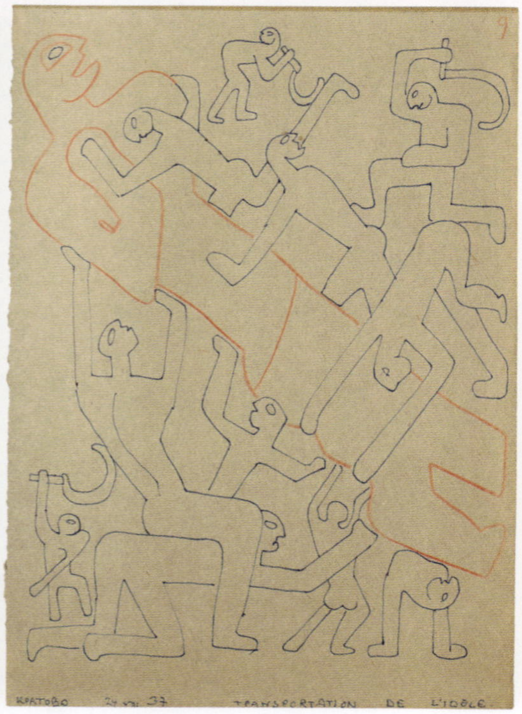
9
КРАТОВО 24 VII 37 TRANSPORTATION DE L'IDOLE

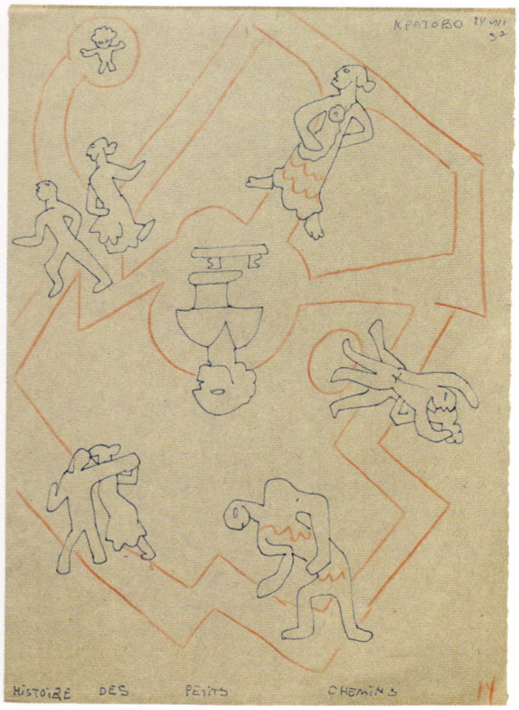
КРАТОВО 24 VII 37
HISTOIRE DES PETITS CHEMINS
14

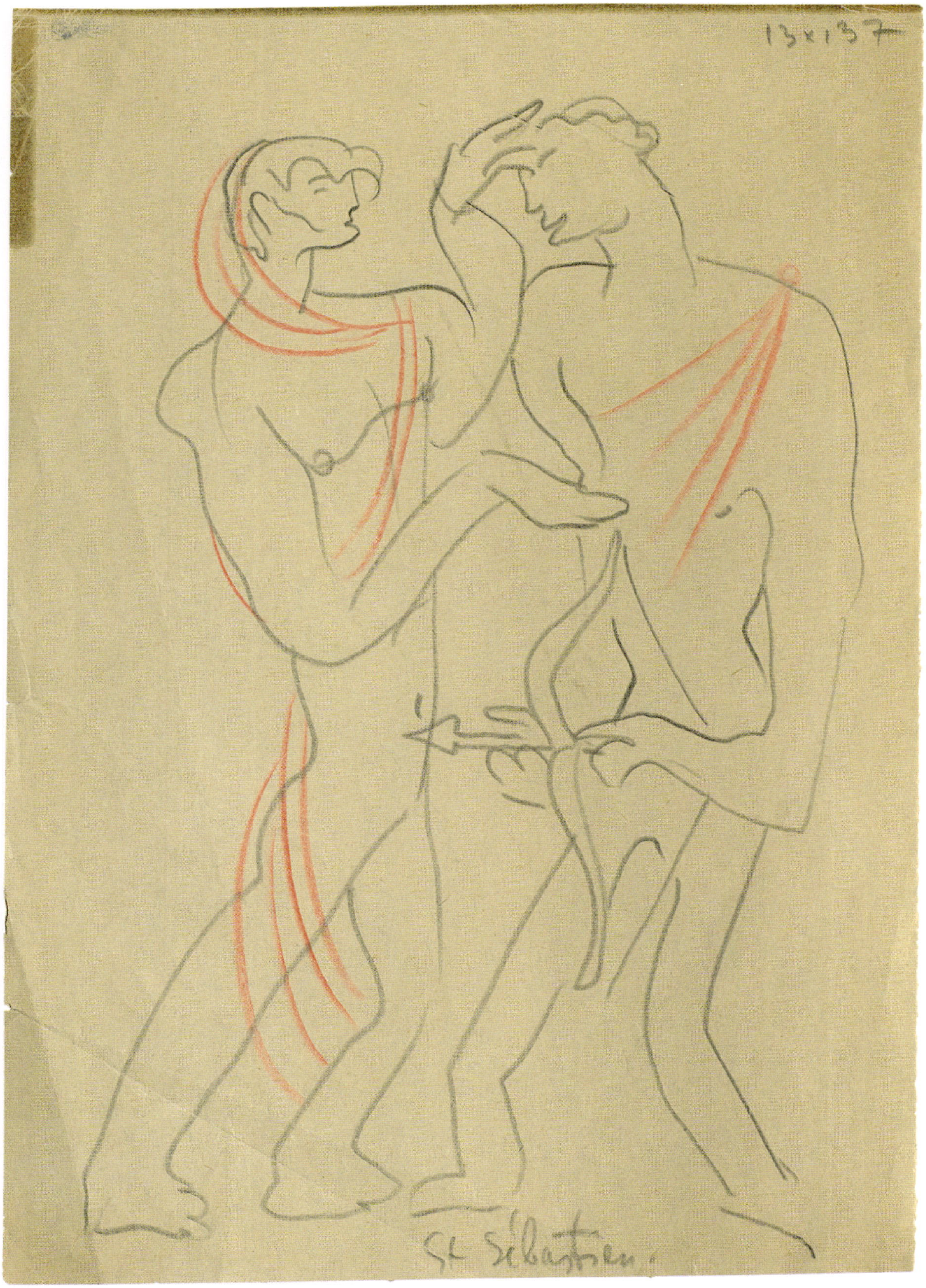
13x137
St Sébastien.

OPPOSITE AND THIS PAGE
From the cycle 'St Sebastian'
(Moscow, 1937)

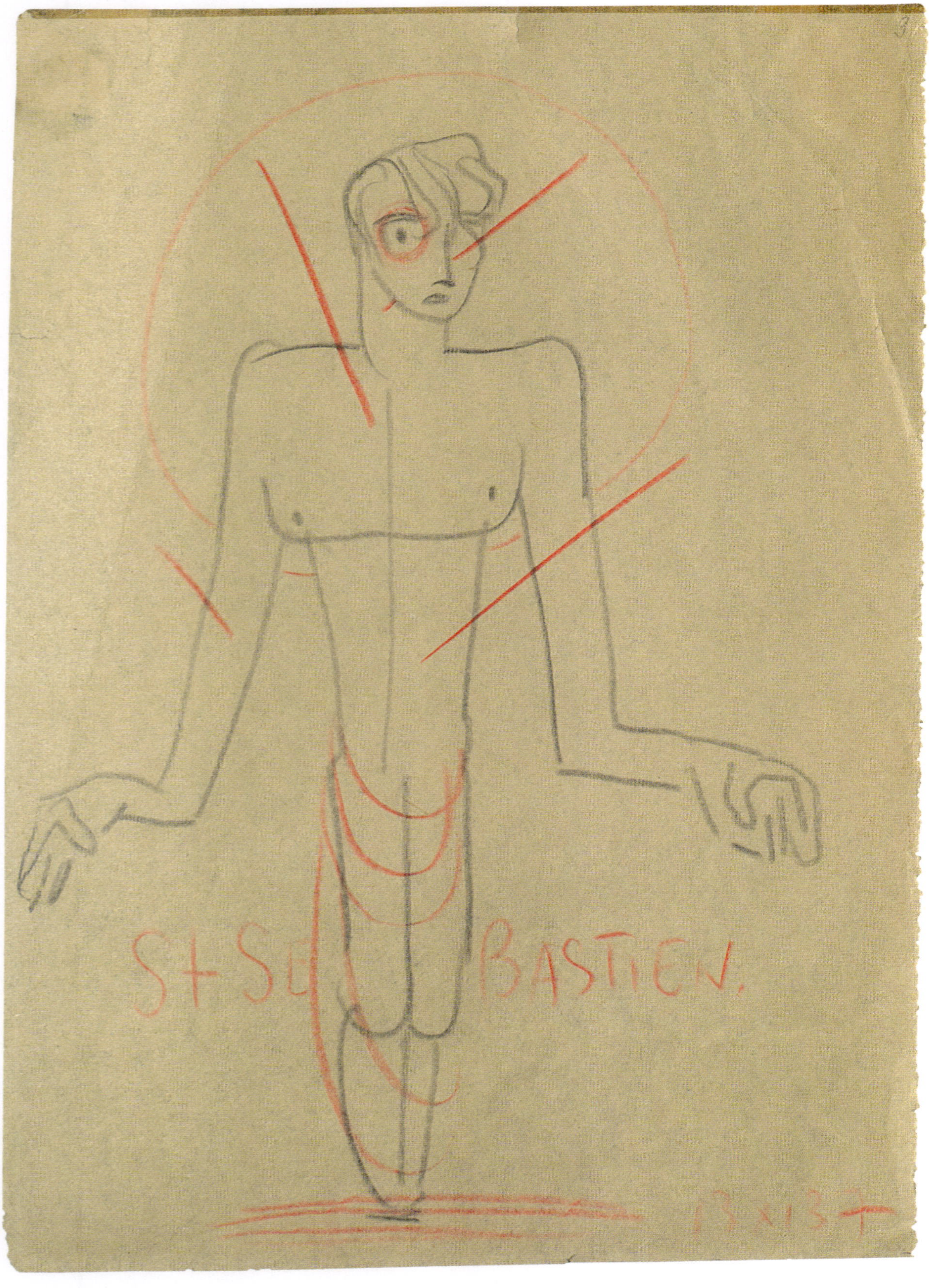

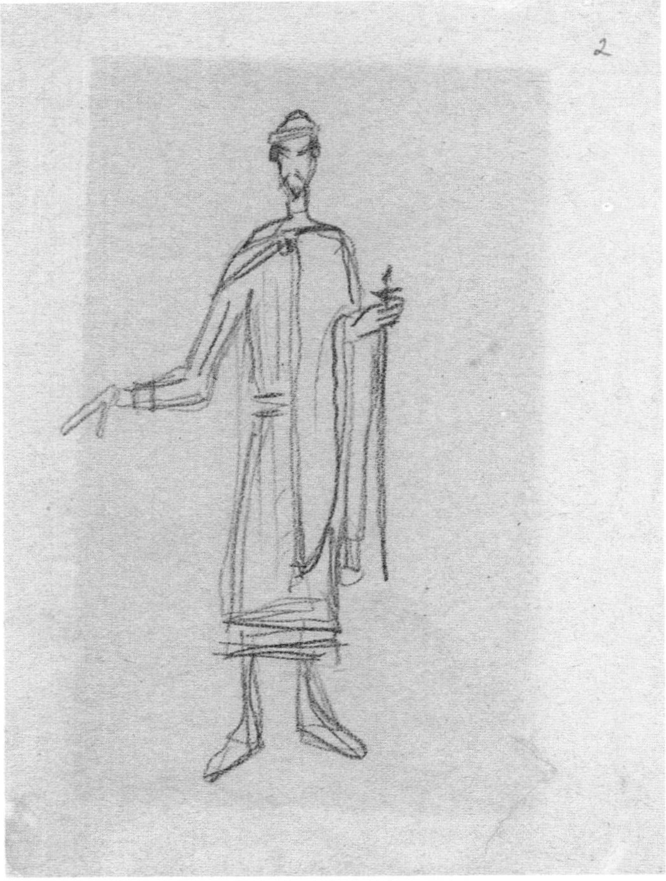
2

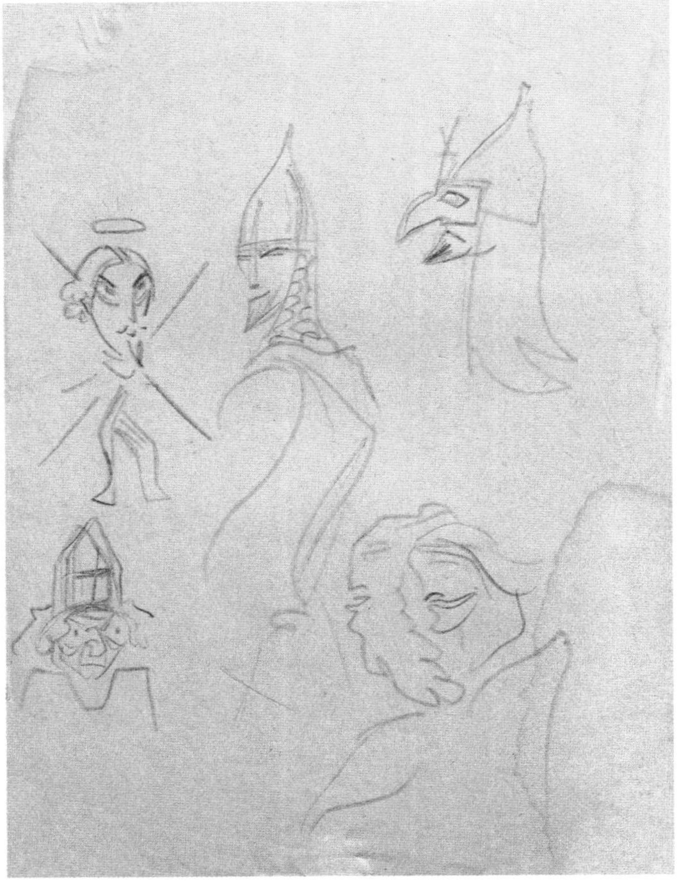

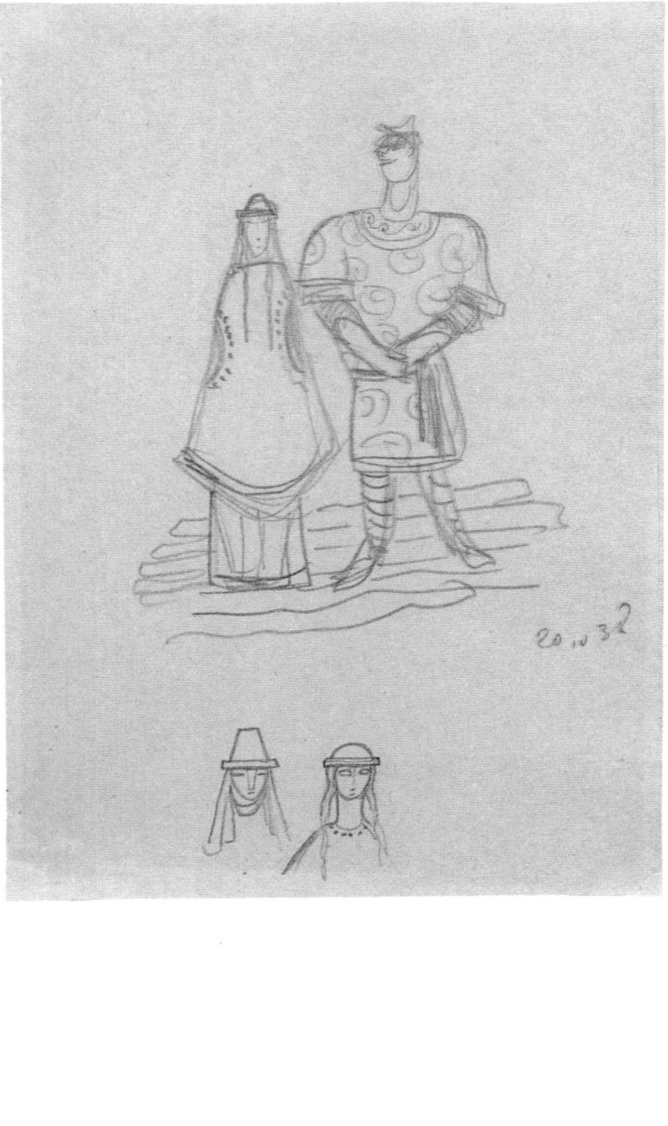

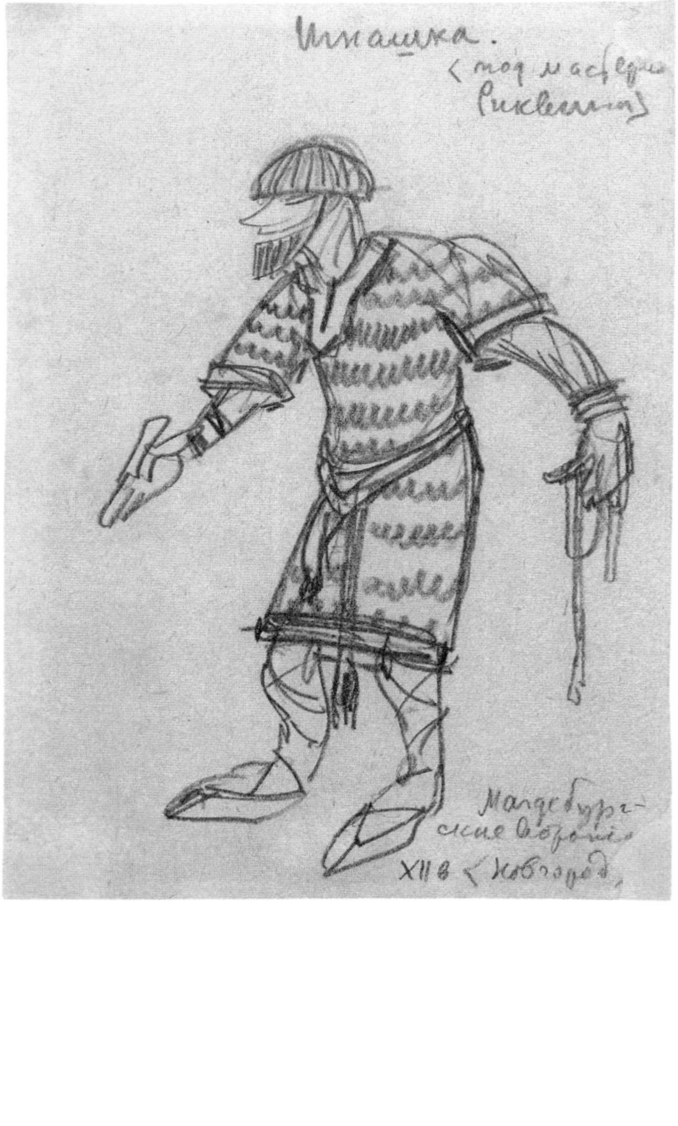
Магдебург-
ские ворота
XII в < Новгород,

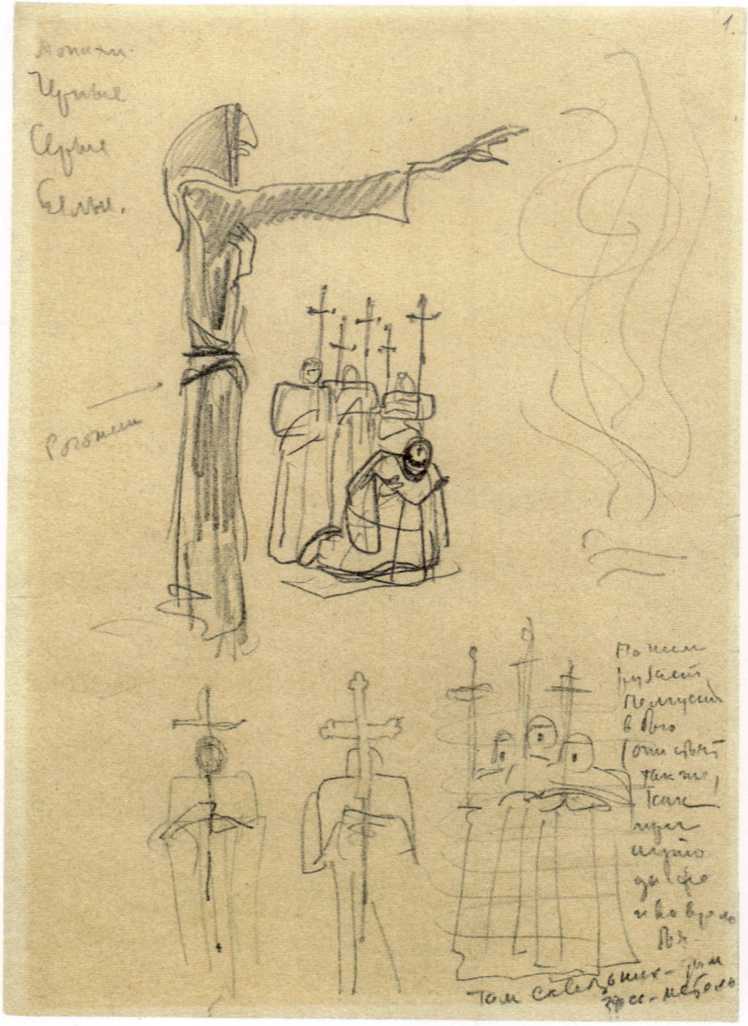

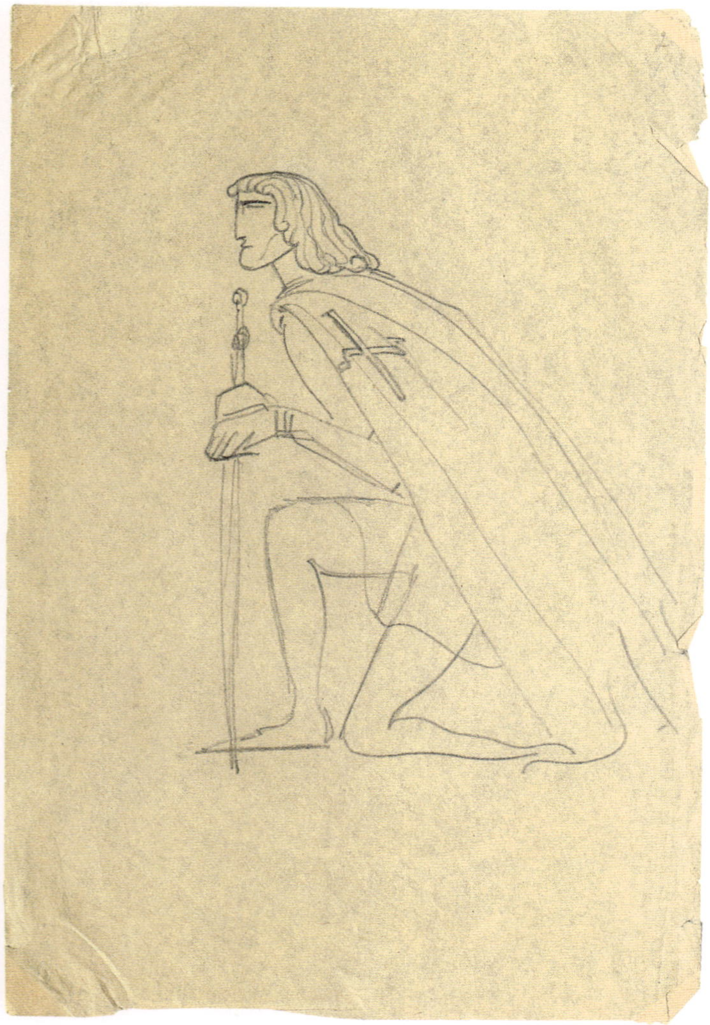

—OPPOSITE

Sketches for the film *Alexander Nevsky* (Moscow, 1937–38)

TOP LEFT

'Appearance of Prince Alexander'

TOP RIGHT

'Alexander as a saint and as a warrior'

BOTTOM LEFT

'Olga and Buslay, citizens of Novgorod' (1938)

BOTTOM RIGHT

'Ignat, the master of chain mails'

Text: Ignashka (after master Rikwin). Magdeburg gates, XII century (Novgorod)

—THIS PAGE

LEFT

'Teutonic monks'

Text: Monks. Black. Grey. White. [Actor] Rogozhin. Pelgusy is attacking them in battle as they stand [in prayer], as though undergoing public execution for their faith [in Pskov]. There [Pelgusy breaks] through them; here [is] a snowstorm.

RIGHT

'Teutonic knight'

—OVERLEAF

LEFT PAGE

'The costume and helmet of the Teutonic Master von Balk'

RIGHT PAGE

'Nobility of the Teutonic Order' (1937)

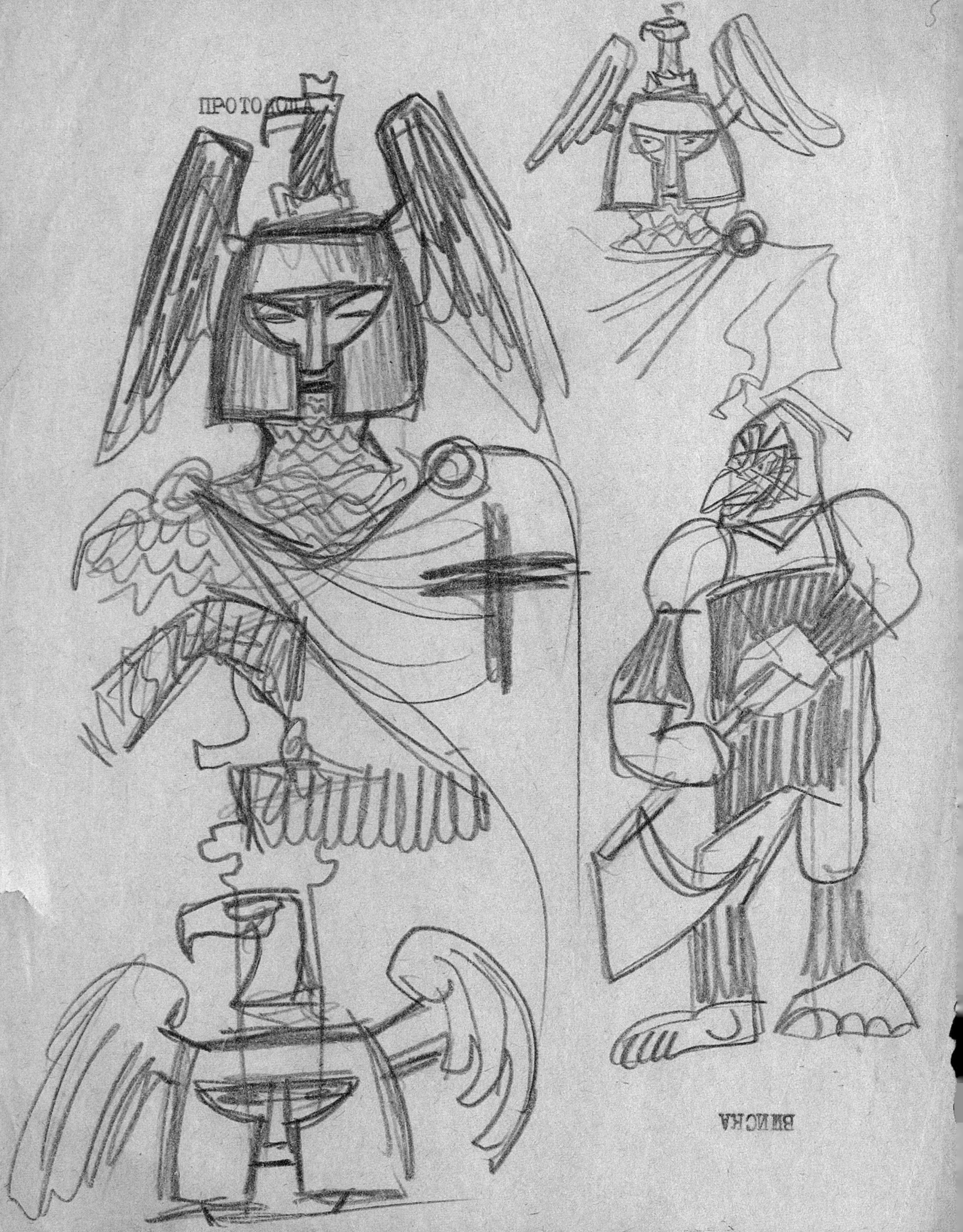
ПРОТО

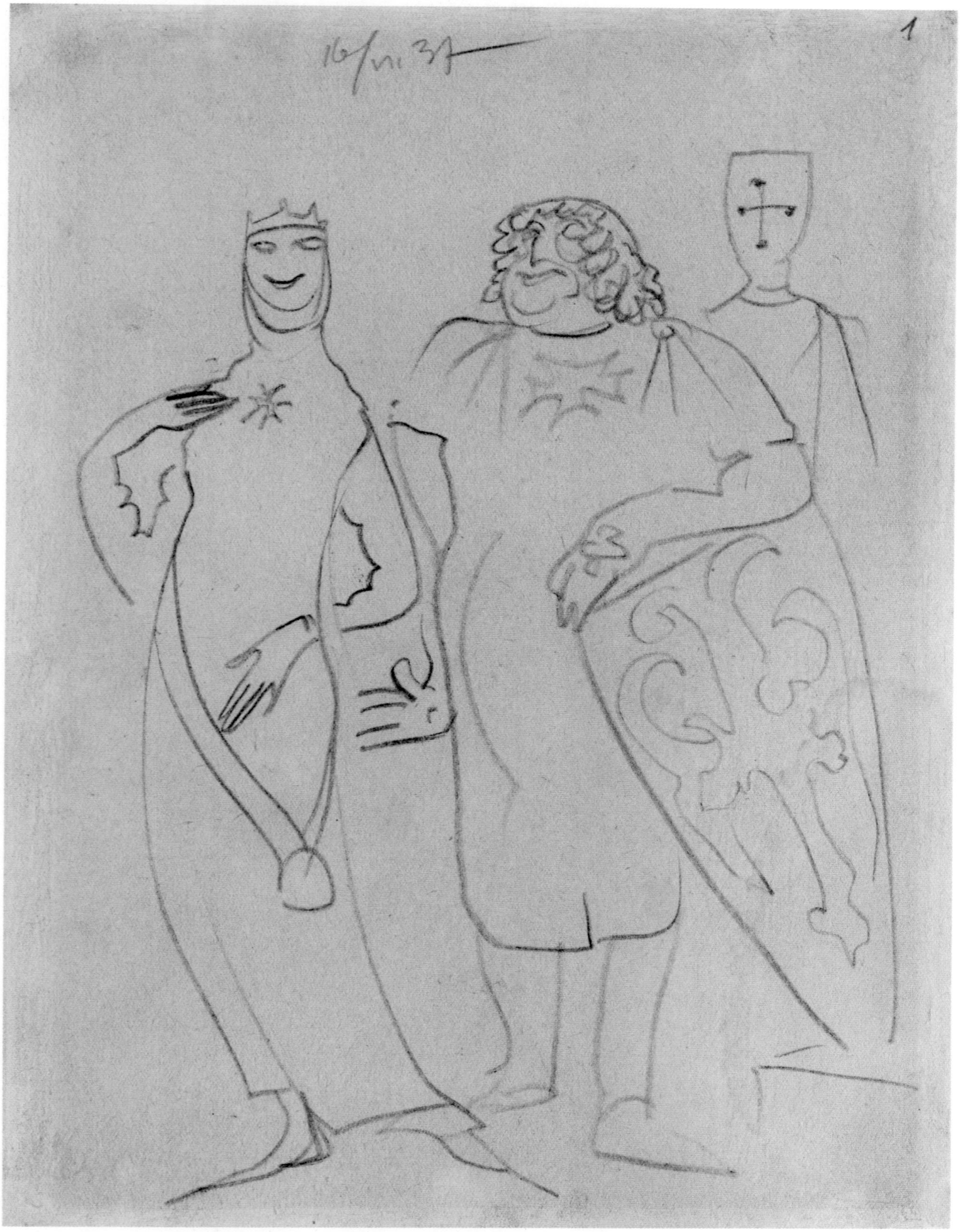

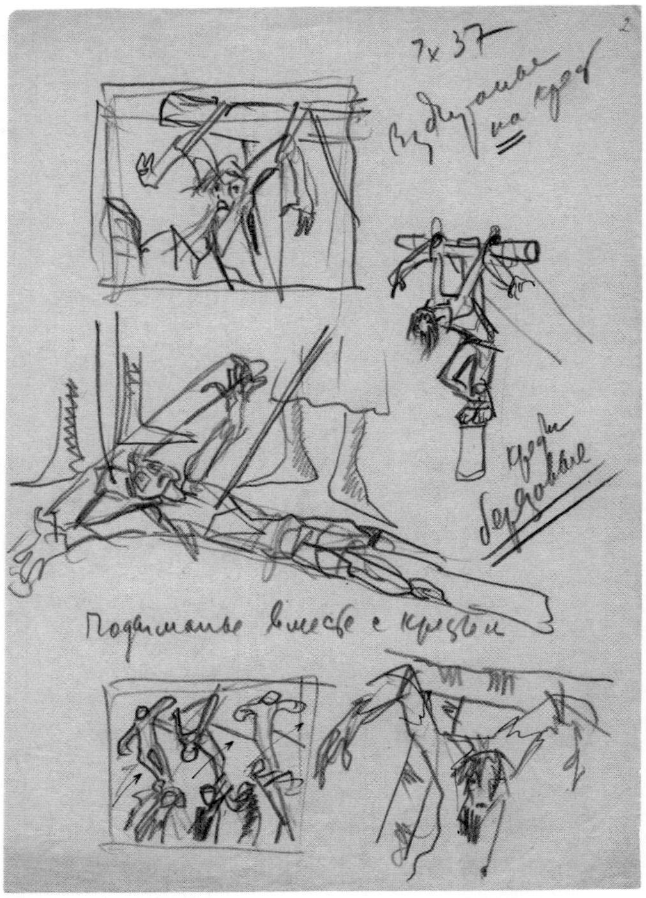

7 x 37

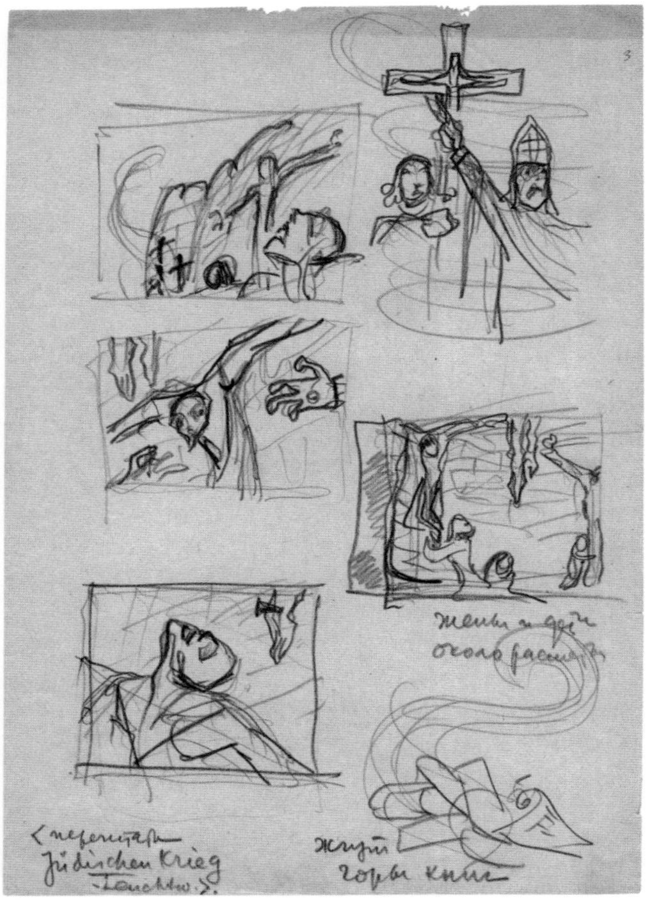

Jüdischen Krieg

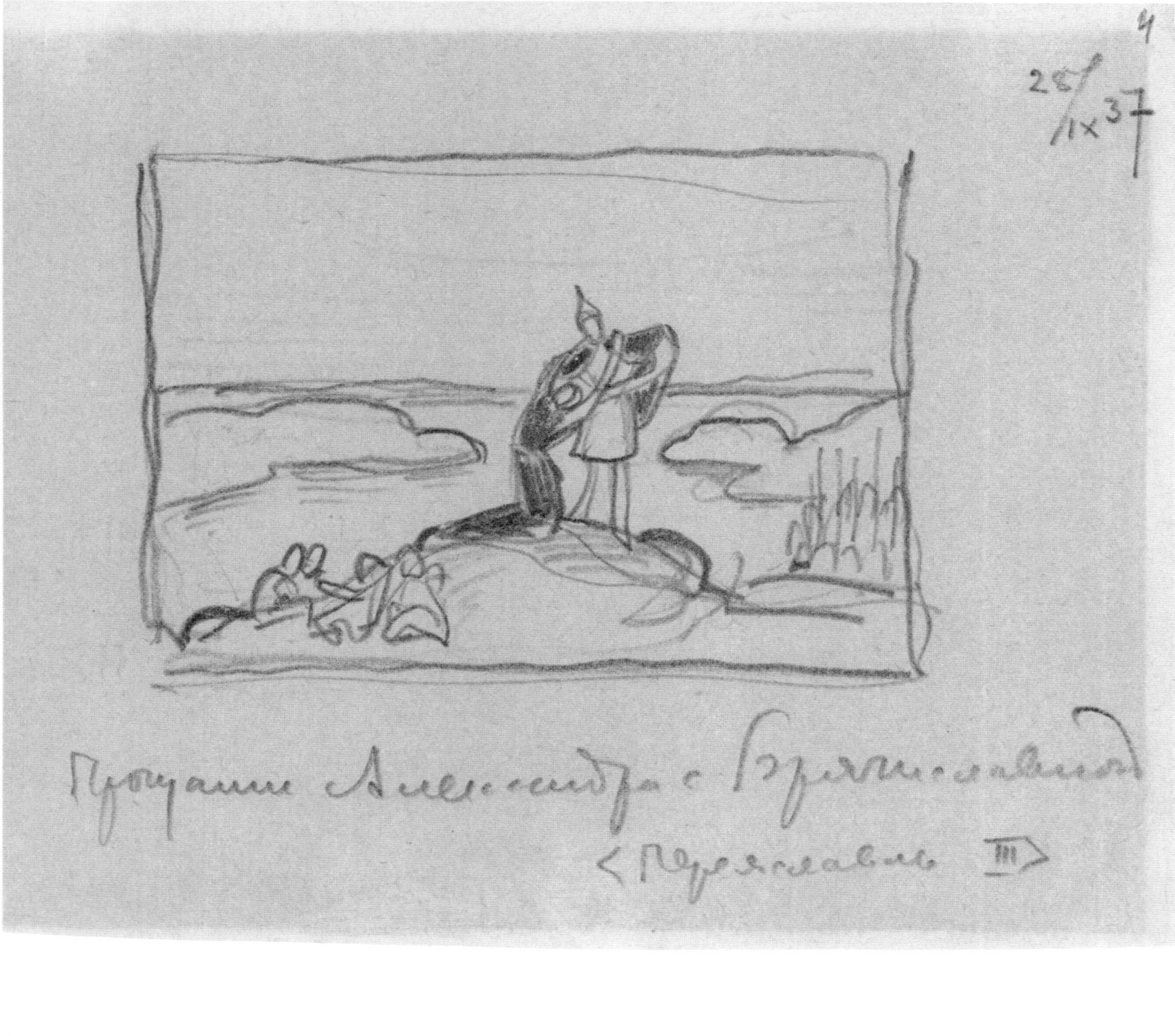

4
28/IX 37
<Переяславль III>

—OPPOSITE

TOP (LEFT AND RIGHT)
Sketches of the scene 'Martyrdom of the governor', from the episode 'Teutons at Pskov' (1937)
Text: They drag him up to the cross – The birch crosses – Lifting with the cross – Wives and children nearly crucified – They burn piles of books. (Reread *Der jüdische Krie* by Feuchtw[anger].)

BOTTOM
Farewell of Alexander and (his wife) Bryacheslavna (Pereyaslavl III) (1937)

—THIS PAGE

TOP
'Novgorod veche (highest legislature of the city). A rich merchant from Novgorod'

BOTTOM (LEFT AND RIGHT)
Sketches of the decorations of medieval Novgorod in the town of Zvenigorod near Moscow (1938)

Text on left page: First version of Zvenigorod. Here, backlighting can be used to create a good late evening entry to the Novgorod veche by Alexander and the guards. The bridge can be built in parts with gaps in between. For the cathedral and the upper shops, small models on a platform. The forest on the horizon confuses me; all hope for the (wide-angle) lens with 28mm (focal length).

Text on right page: For Alexander to move down from the bridge (part of the bridge, the river backlit, evening).

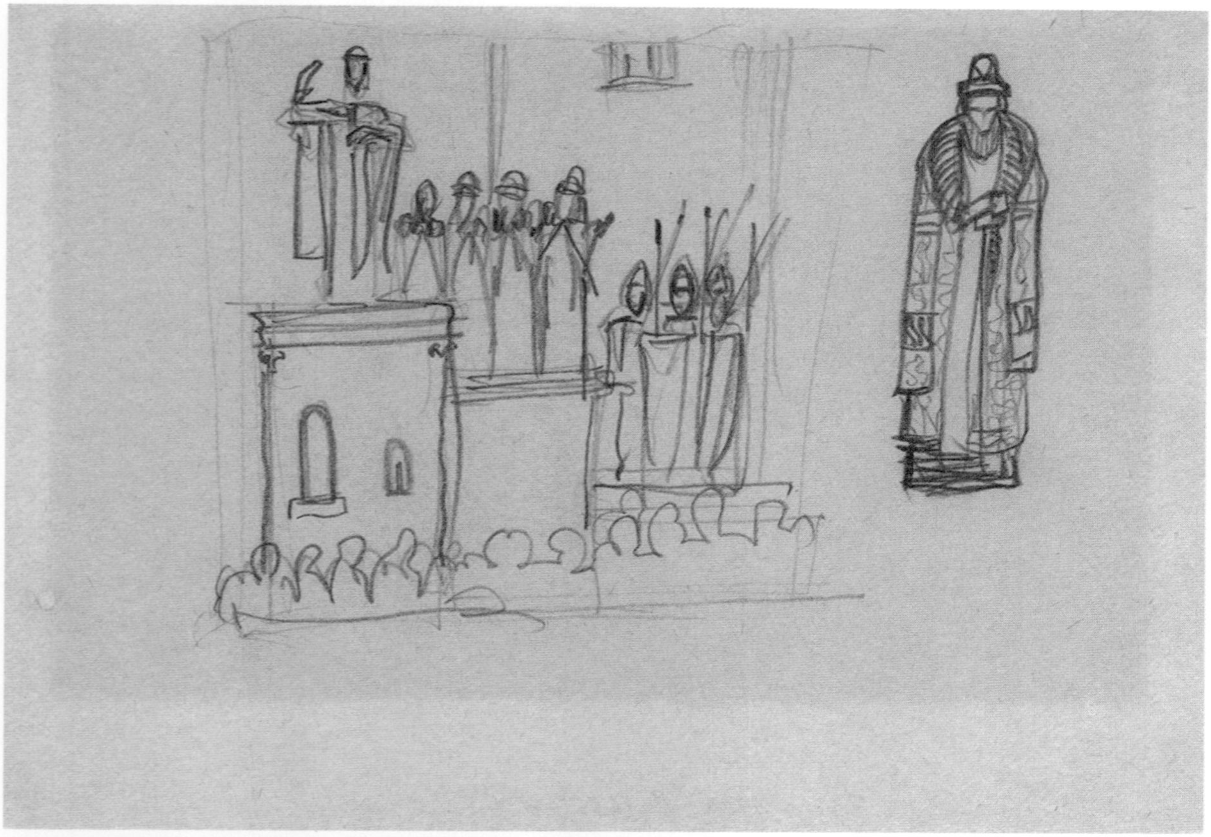

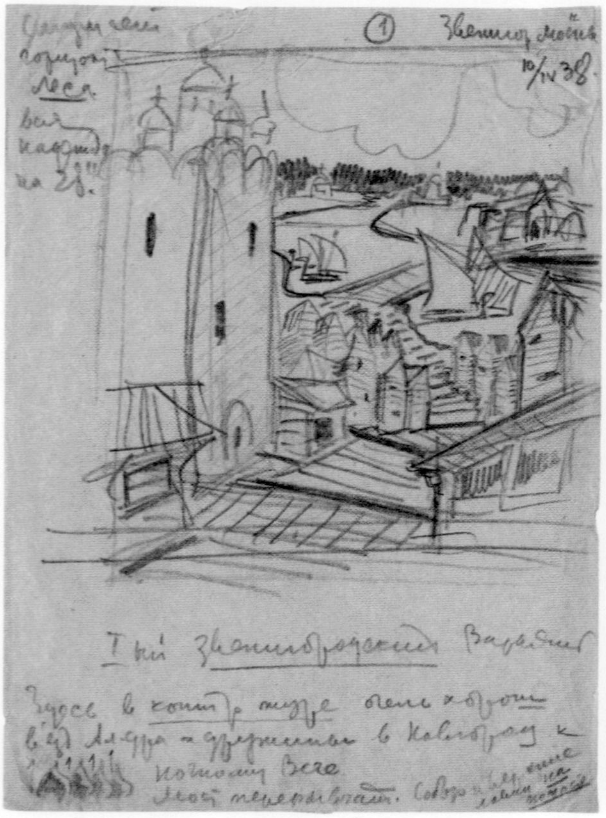

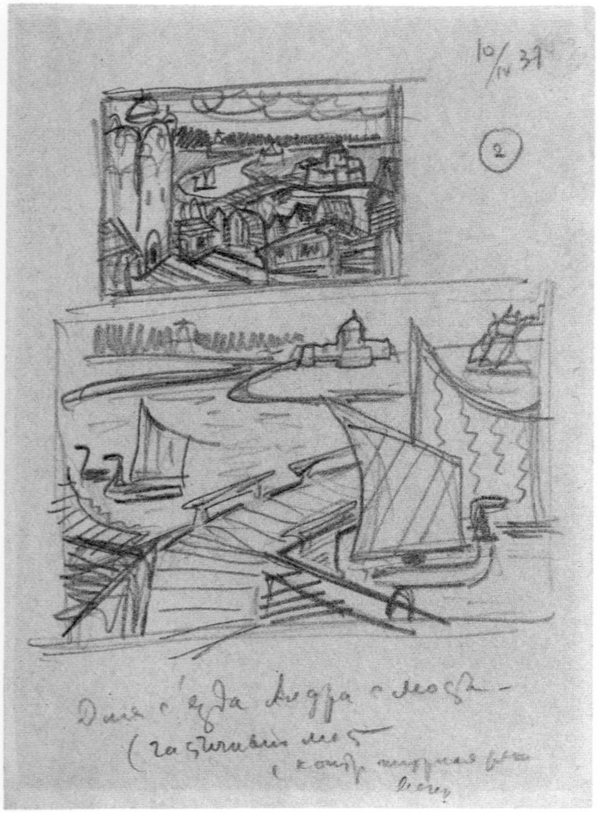

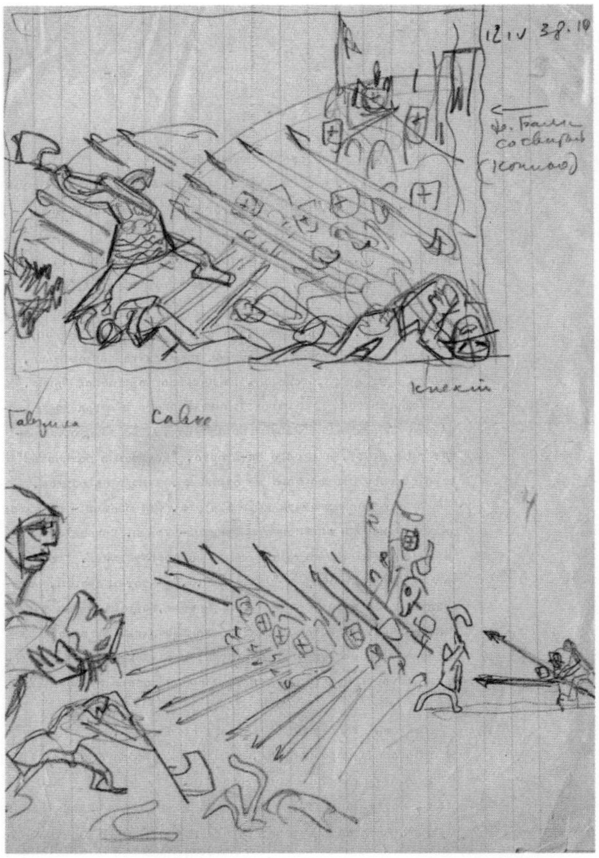

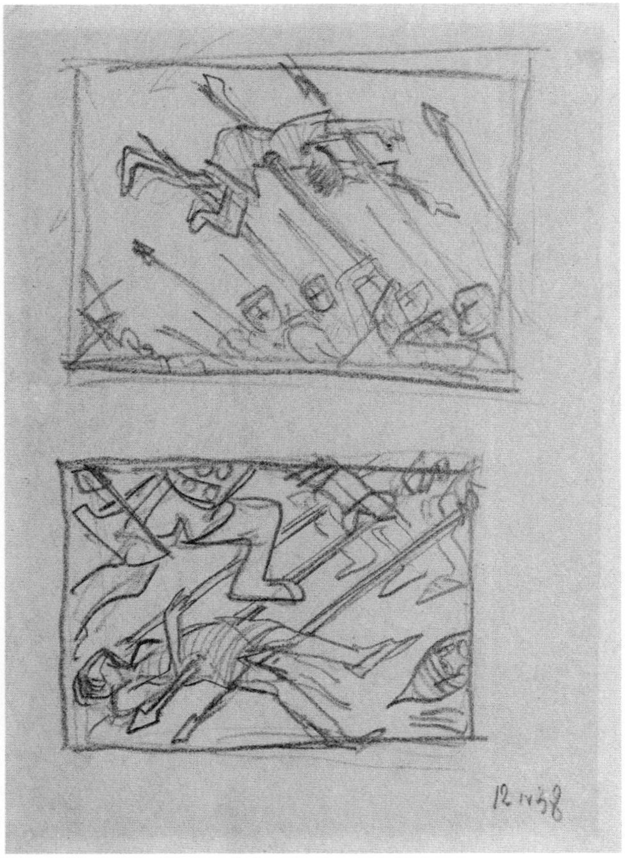

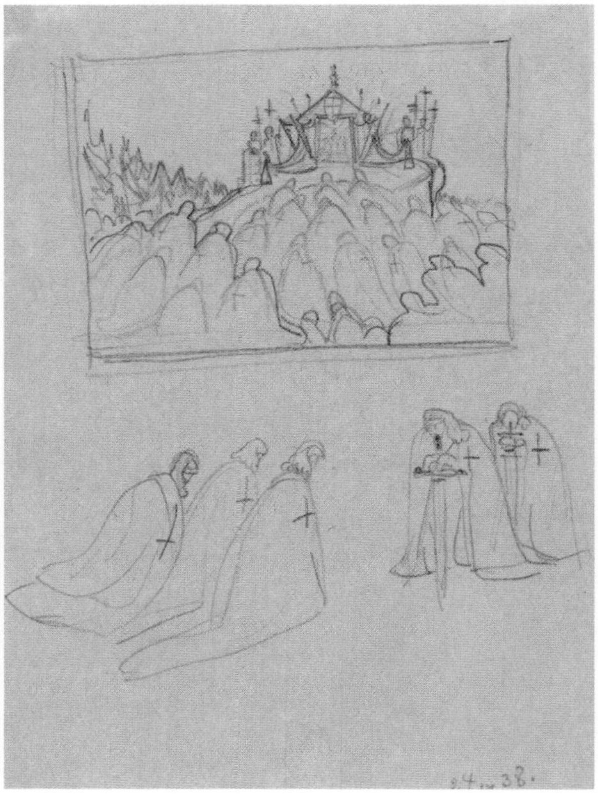

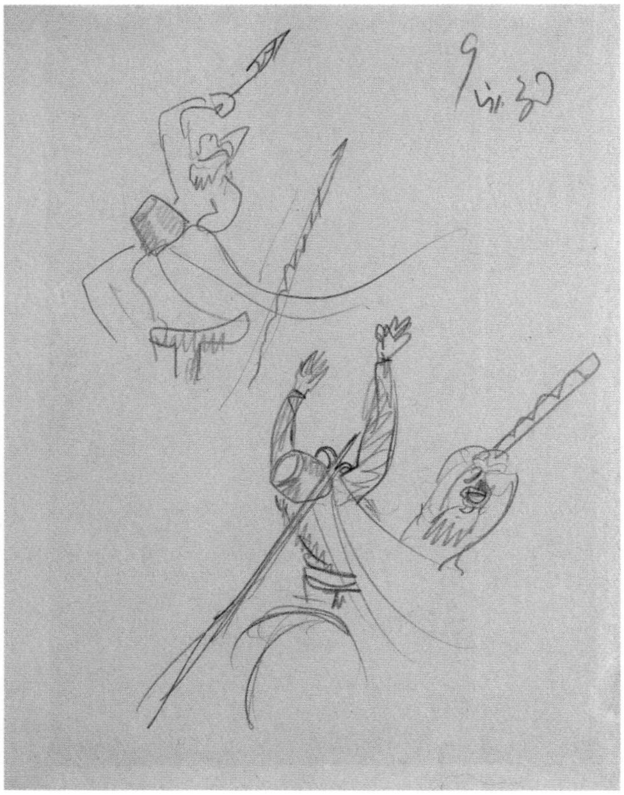

—THIS PAGE
Sketches for the episode 'The Battle on the Ice':

TOP LEFT
'Death of Savka' (1938)
Text: Gavrila – Savka – Knecht – Von Balk and his retinue (on horses).

TOP RIGHT
'Gavrila against the Teutons' (1938)

BOTTOM LEFT
'Prayer of the Teutons' (1938)

BOTTOM RIGHT
'Russian swords and spears against the Teutons' (1938)

—OPPOSITE
Prince Alexander in the Battle on the Ice (1938)
Text: The proportions of the group of knights are not correct. They are more distant and smaller. Frosty (white) trees. The fracture, of course, must go crosswise while preserving the view from Alexander to the knights. Part A is pulled from part B – the fracture spreads, and then the floe breaks. But, maybe, cut the crowd with the crack? (Cheluskin).

по горизонту
группы всадников
← всё не вверх
они дальше
и меньше - 10 / IV 38

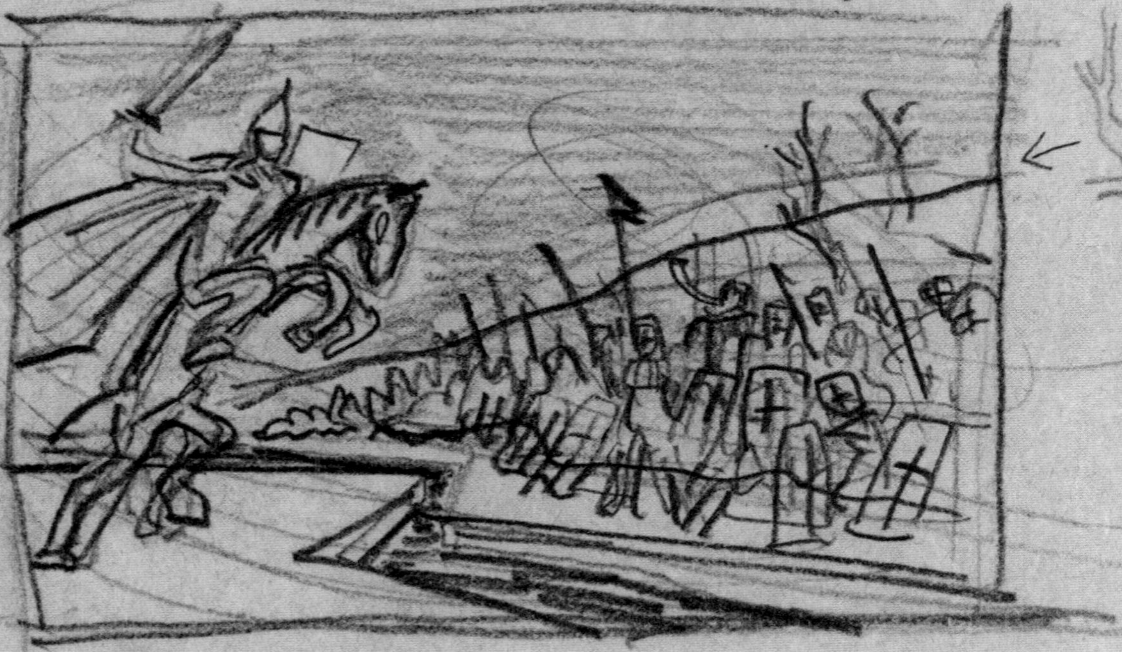

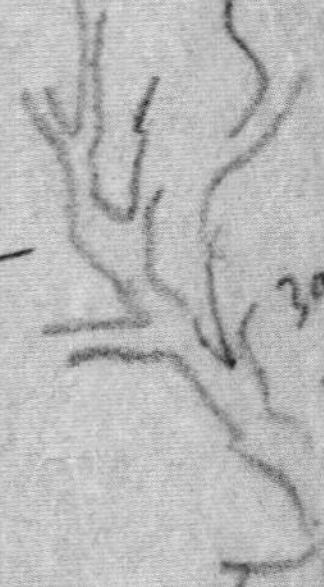

за ними деревья
(больше деревья)

Трещина конечно поперек
все же
~~не~~ с сохранением направления
от Александра к Рыцарям

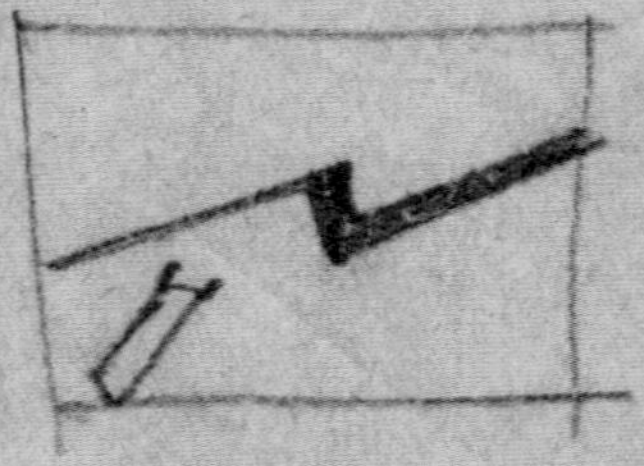

Часть А оттягивается
от В — трещина
ширится и зав…
уже льдина ло-
мается.

А м. б.
разрезать
массовку
трещиной?
(Чесноков)

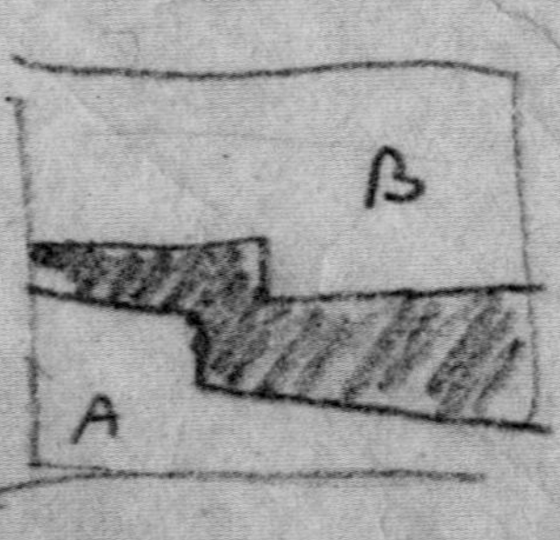

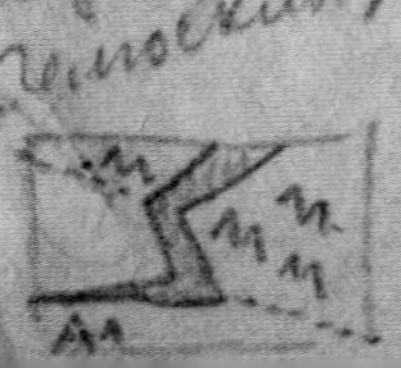

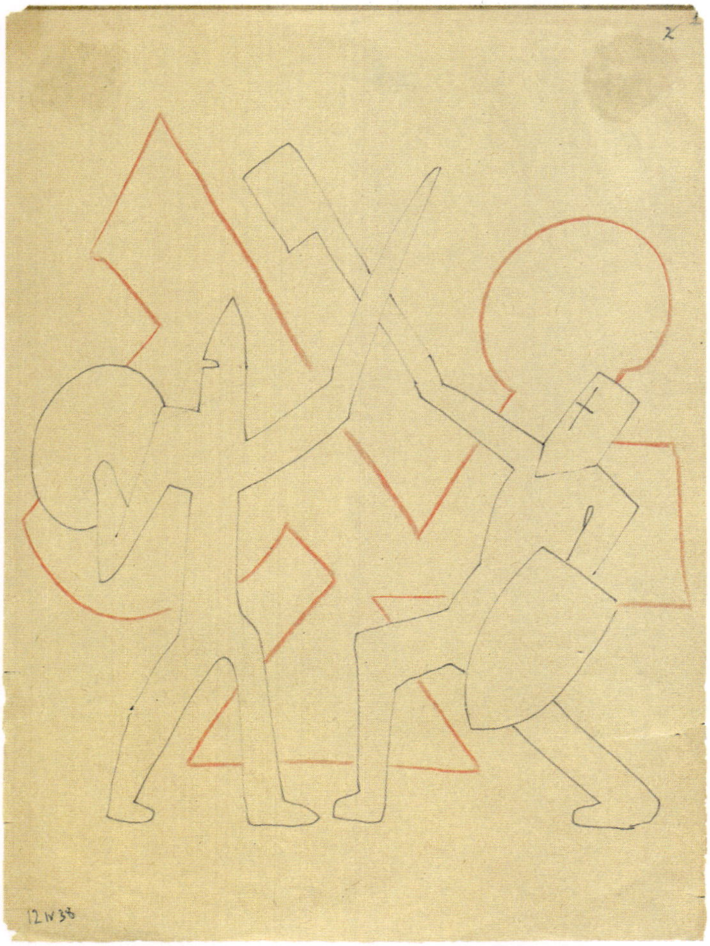
2
12 IV 38

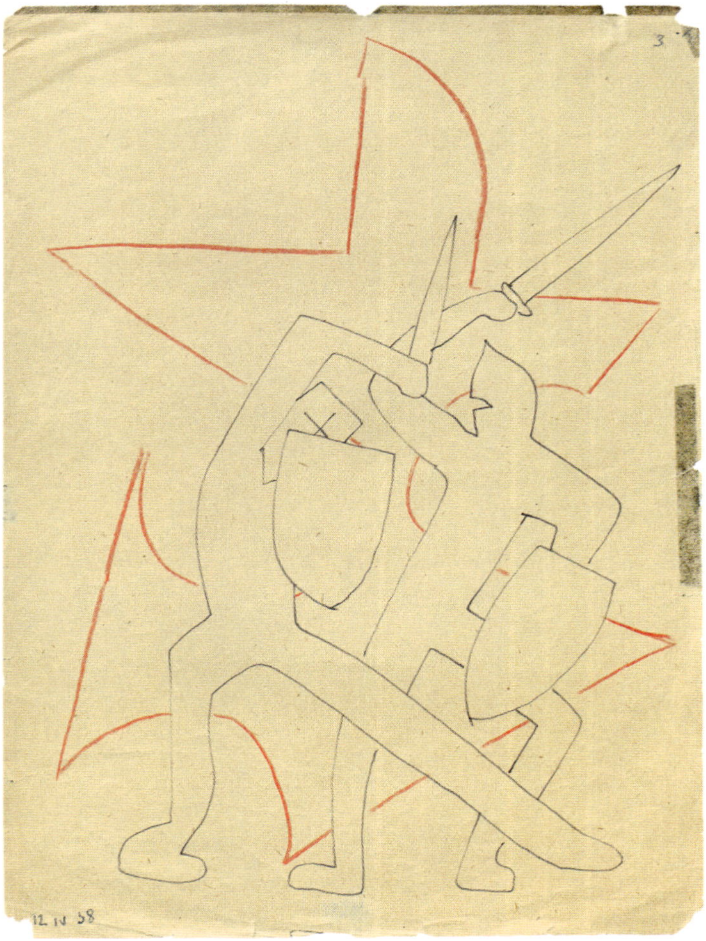
3
12 IV 38

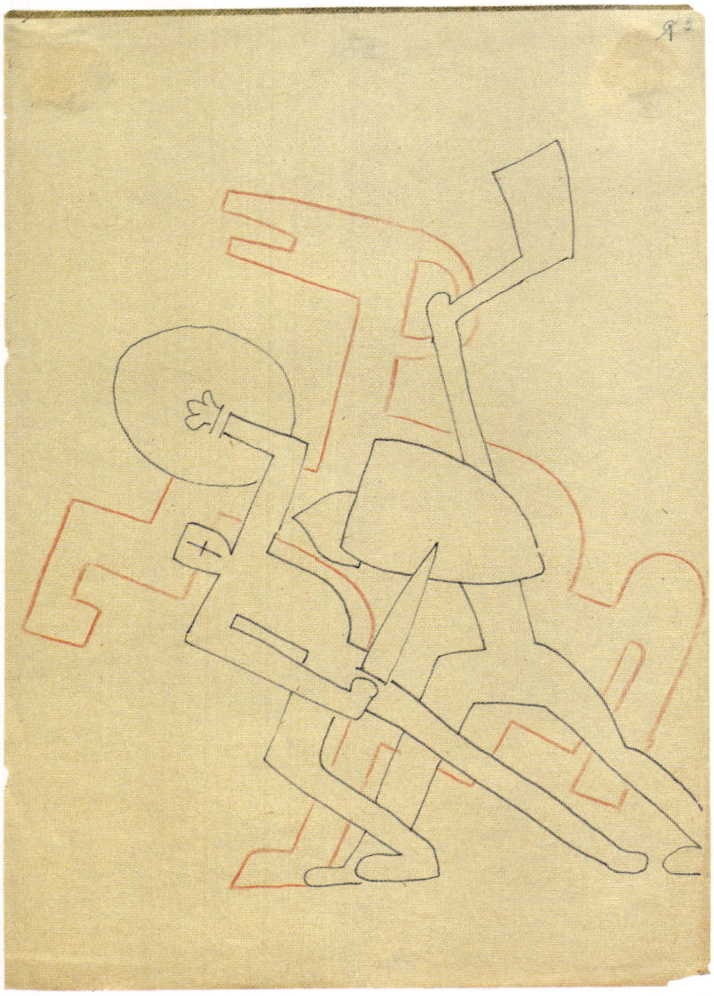
9

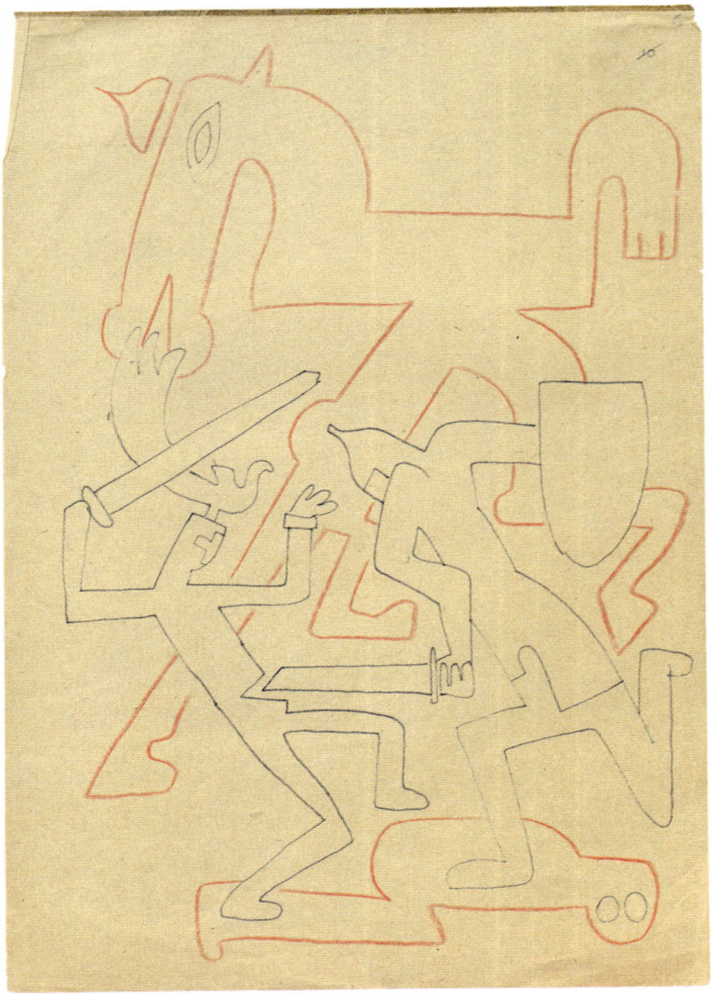
10

OPPOSITE
From the first cycle 'Gedanken zur Musik', with the motif of 'The Battle on the Ice' from *Alexander Nevsky* (1938)

THIS PAGE
From the cycle 'Gedanken zur Musik' (1938)

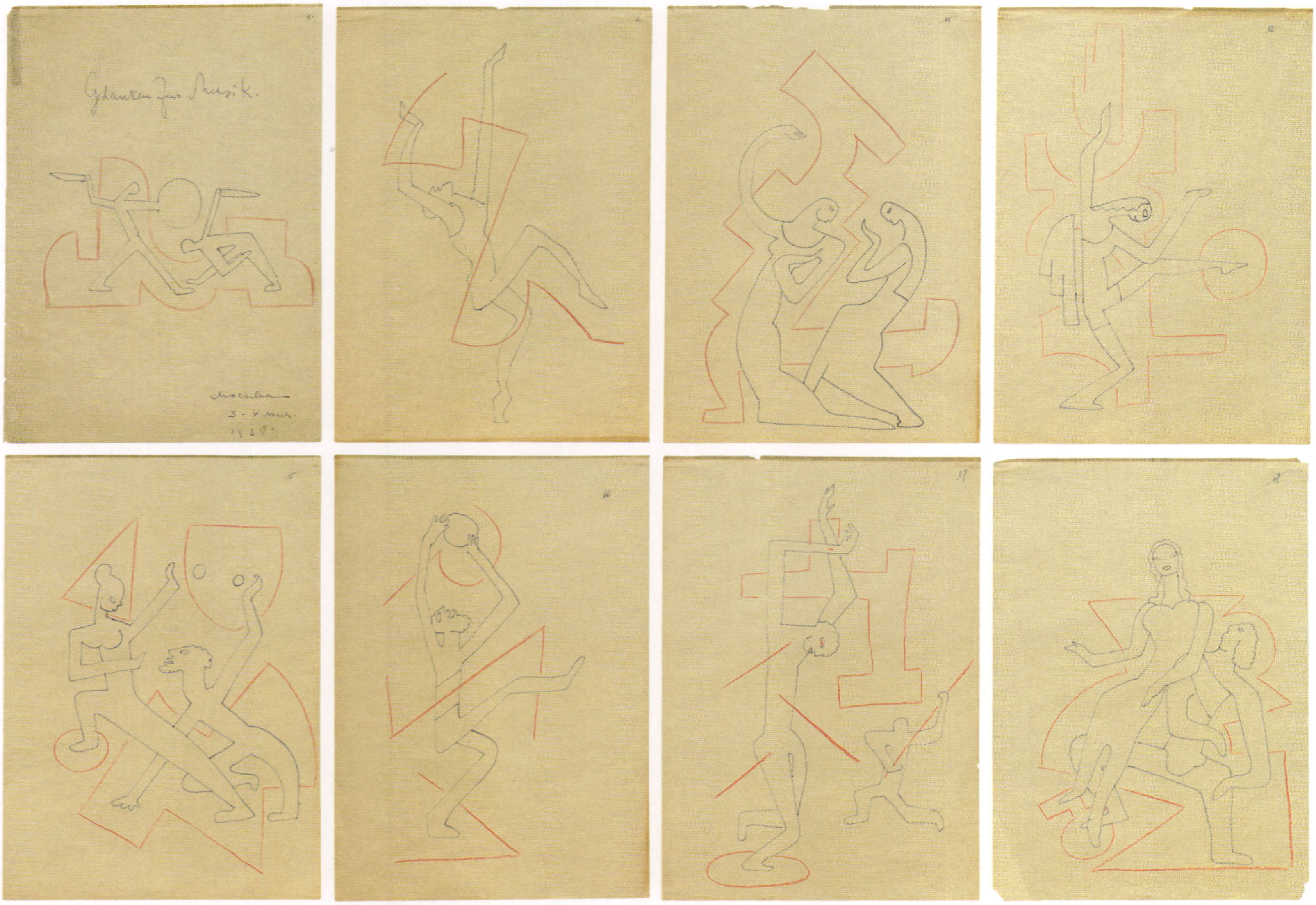

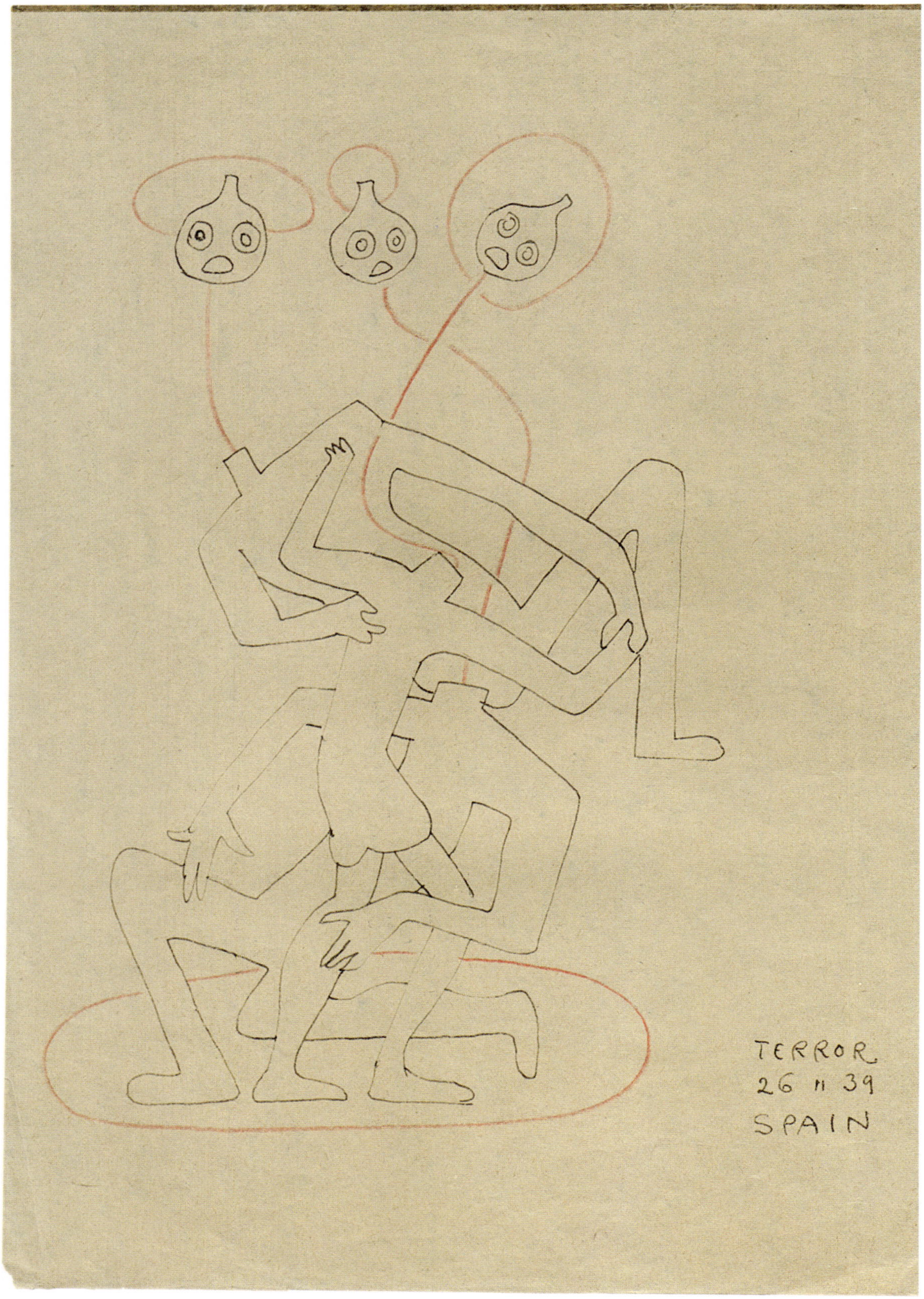

THIS PAGE
Terror (Spain, 1939)

OPPOSITE
Give Freedom! (1939)

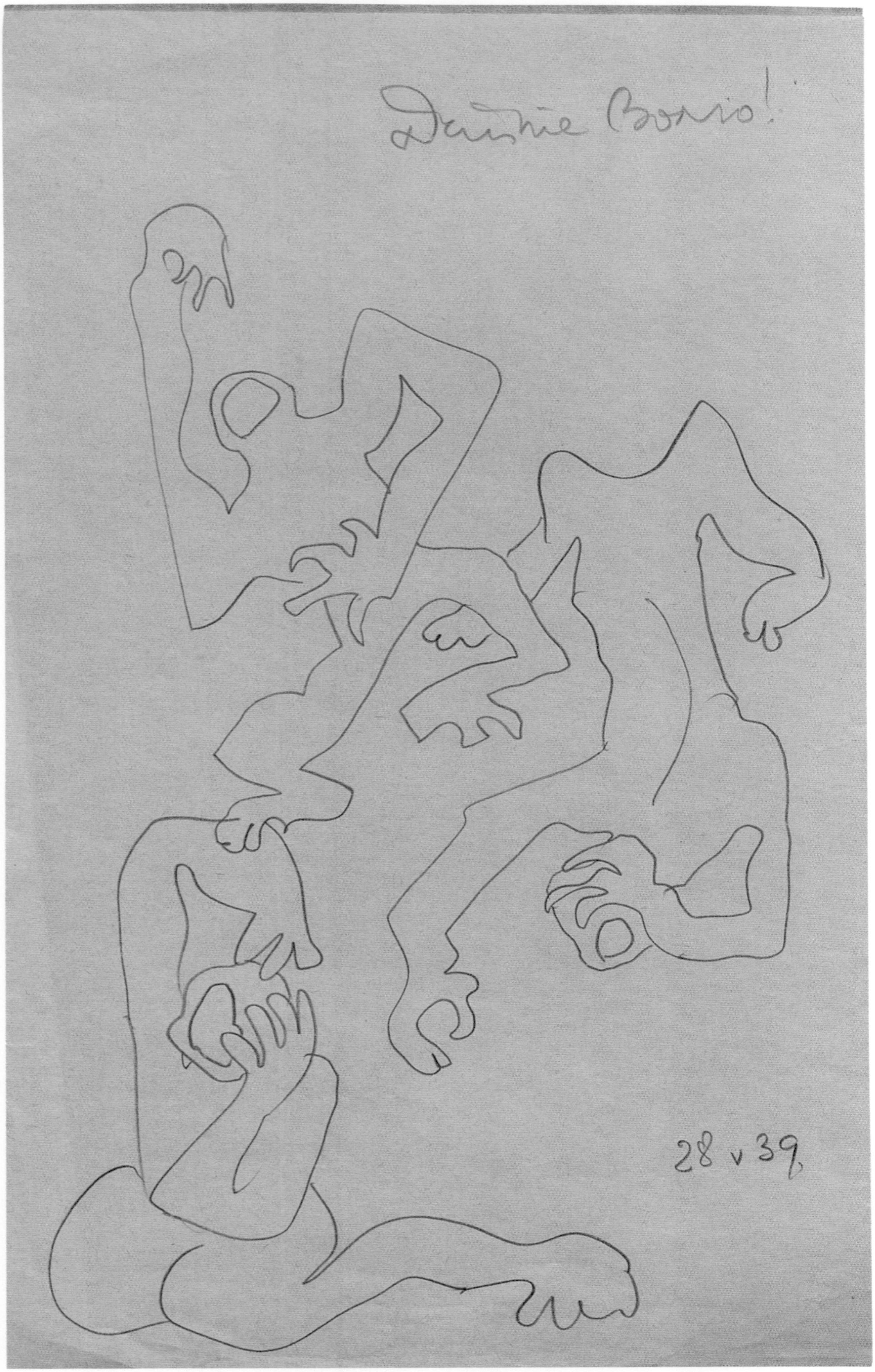
28 v 39

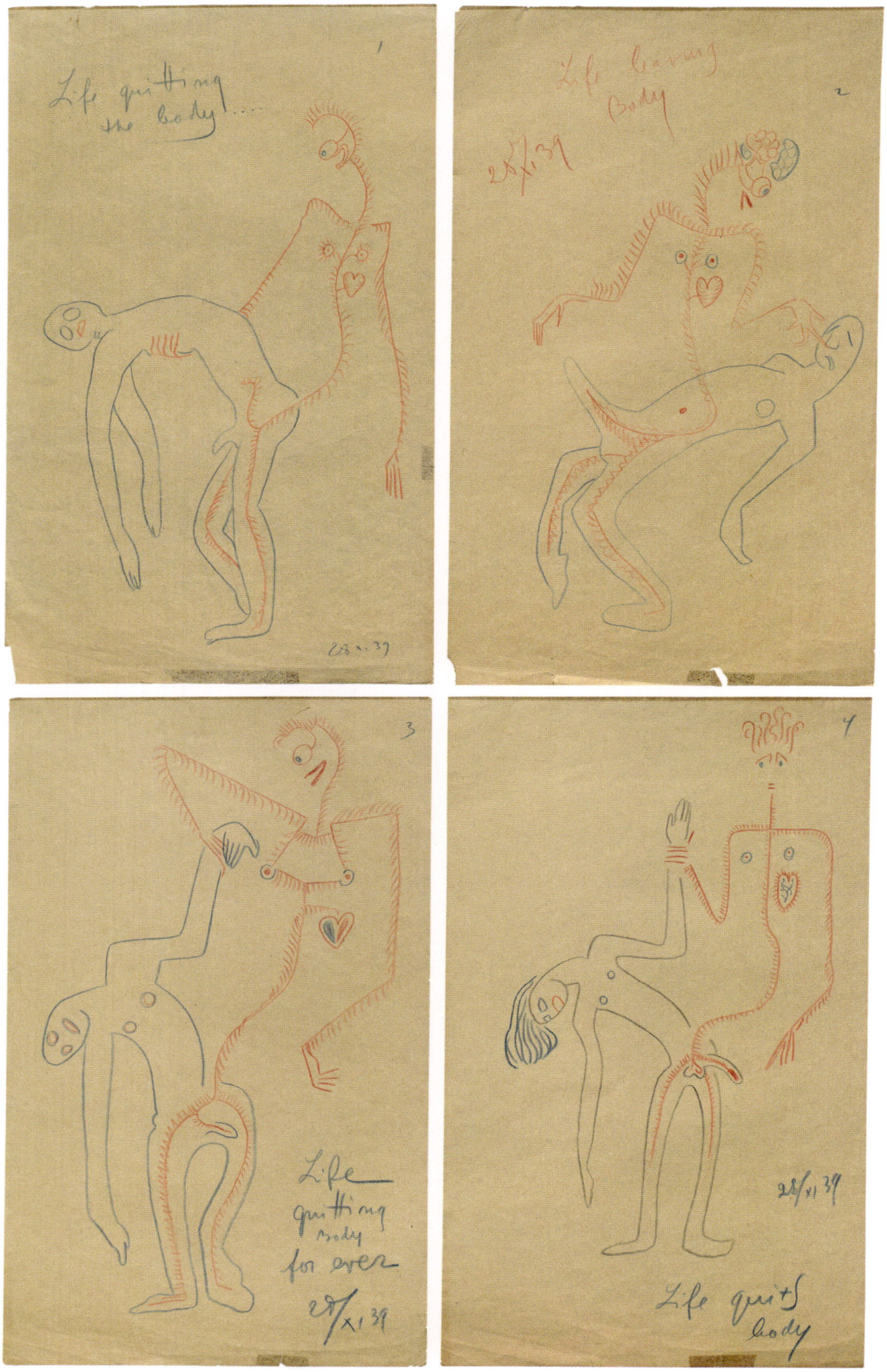

THIS PAGE
From the cycle 'Life quitting the body...' (1939)

OPPOSITE
From the cycle 'Sandino', based on the book *Sailing South American Skies* (1936) by James Saxon Childers (1941)

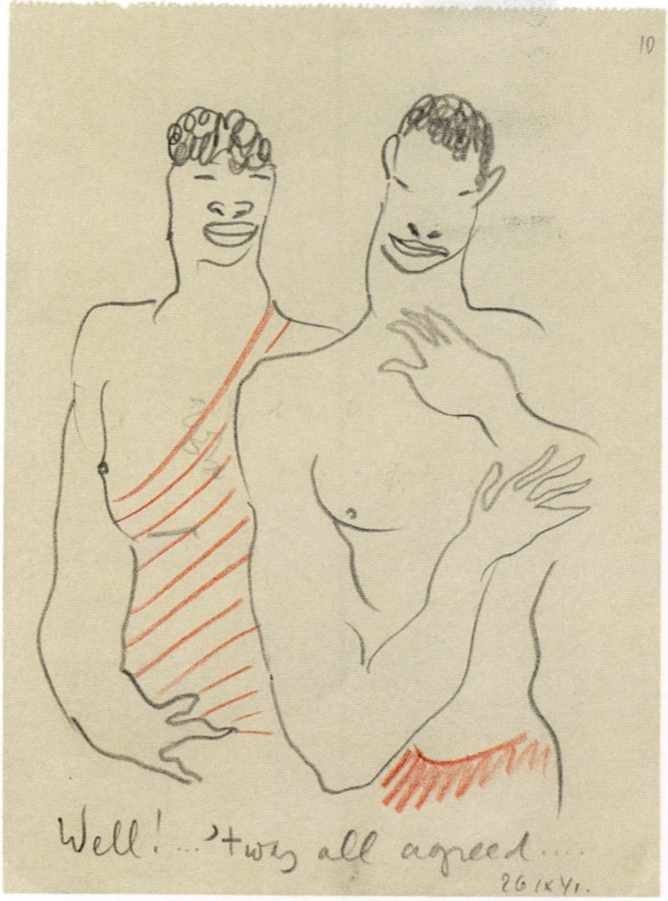
10
Well! ... 'twas all agreed ....
26 IX 41.

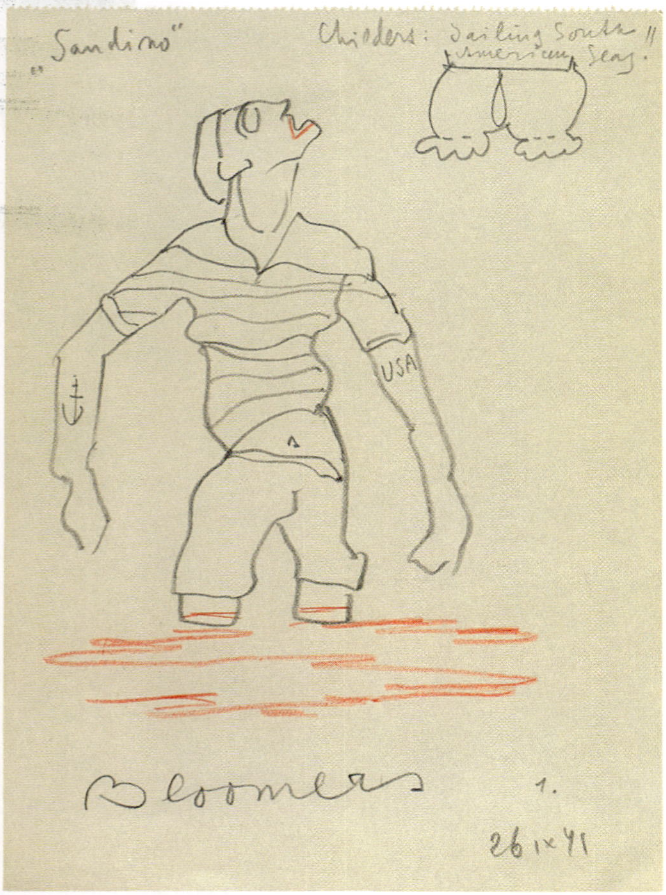
„Sandino"
Childers: Sailing South American Seas!
11
USA
Bloomers
1.
26 IX 41

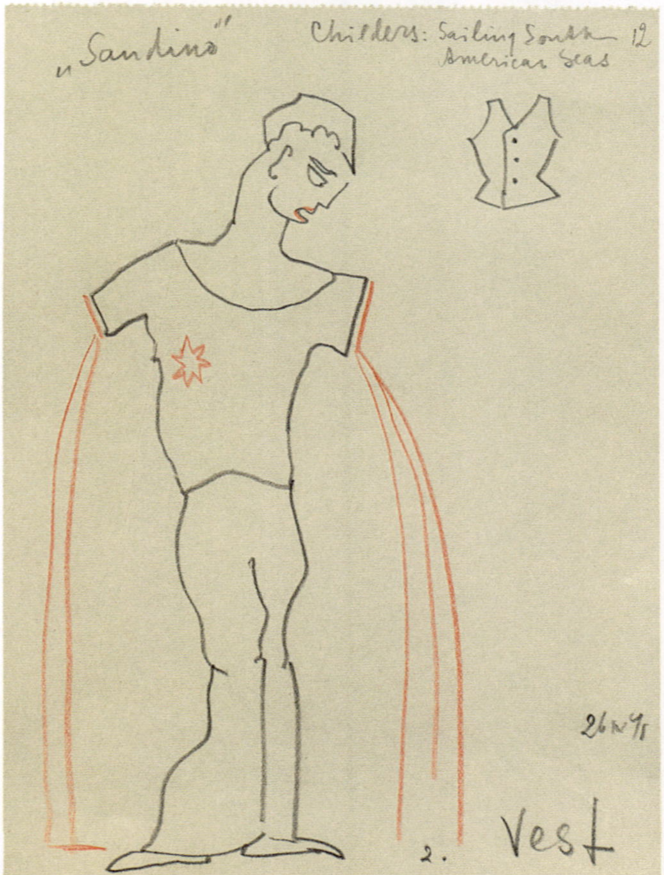
„Sandino"
Childers: Sailing South American Seas
12
26 IX 41
2.
Vest

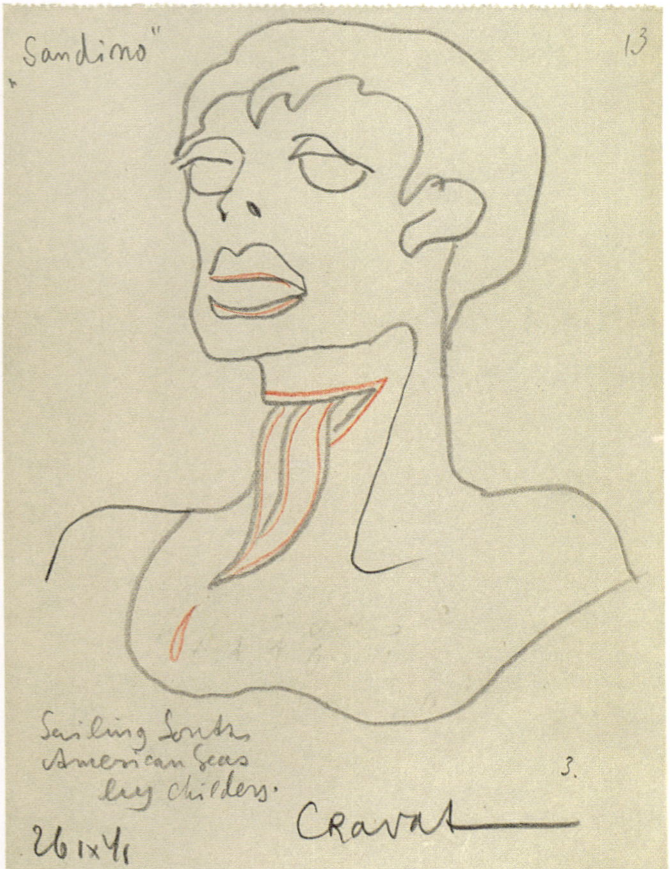
„Sandino"
13
Sailing South American Seas by Childers.
3.
CRAVAT
26 IX 41

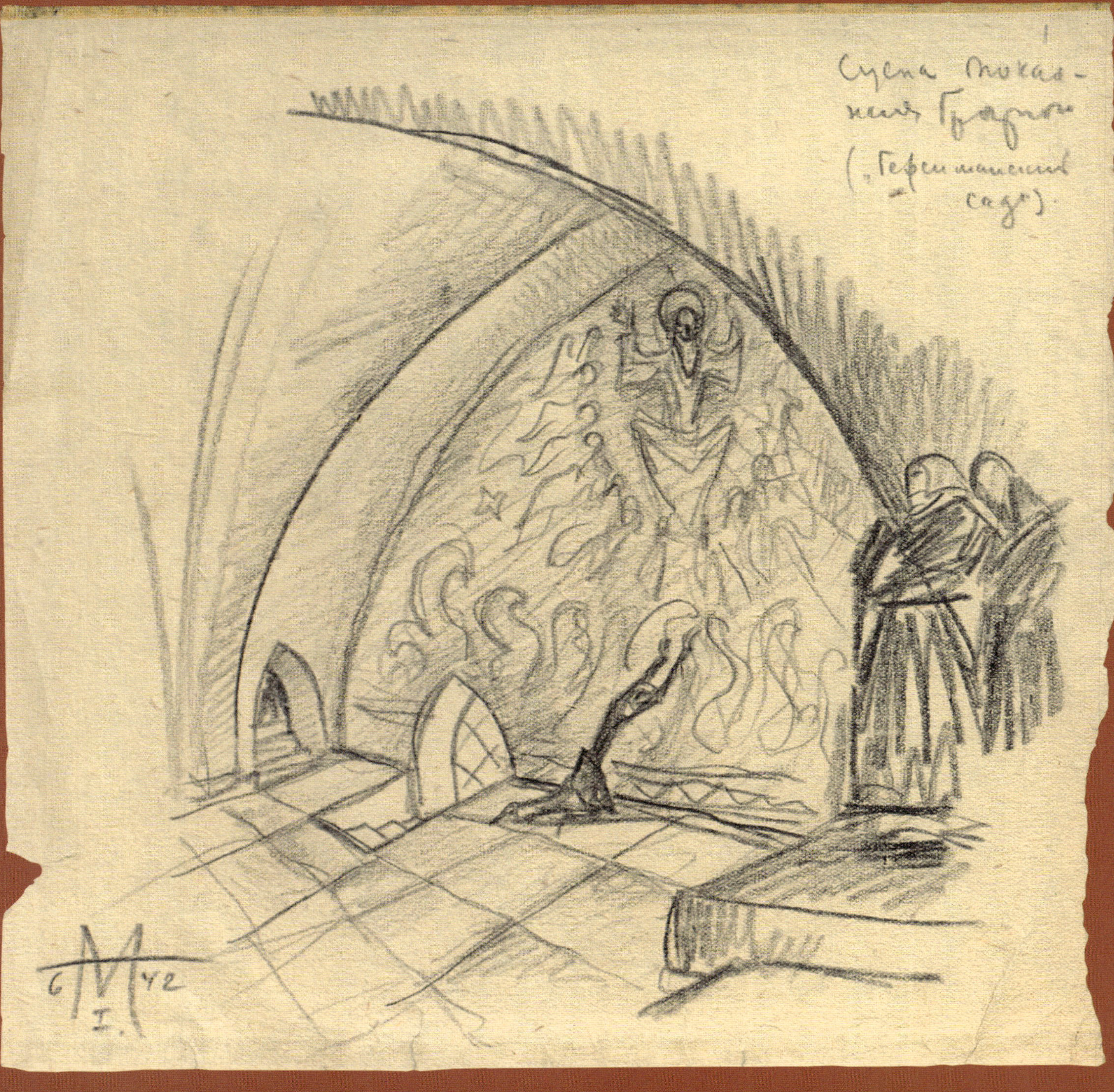
1
Сцена покаяния Грязного
(„Гефсиманский сад").
6 M 42
I.

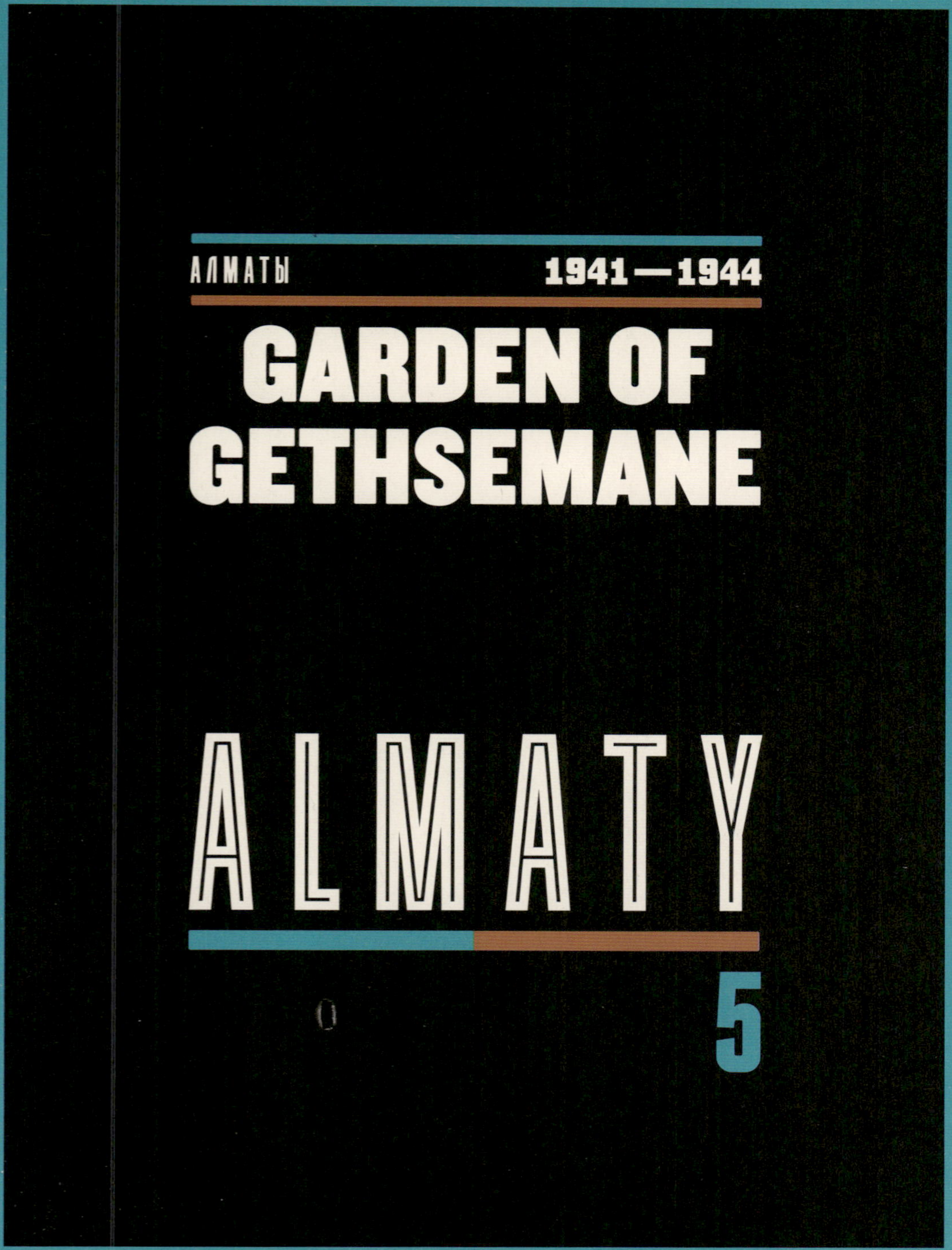
АЛМАТЫ
1941—1944
GARDEN OF GETHSEMANE
ALMATY
5

The scene took shape before Eisenstein's eyes in January 1941, more or less immediately after Andrei Zhdanov – Stalin's right-hand man when it came to agitation and propaganda – had passed on the wishes of the leader: a new image of Tsar Ivan IV was to be created on the screen (as, indeed, it was on the stage, and in literature and in painting). The first Russian autocrat, nicknamed 'the Terrible' or 'the Dread', was no longer to be considered a cruel tyrant: now he was a progressive statesman, the first to create a united Russia, a forerunner of Peter the Great. In his imagination, Eisenstein saw the dark corner of the Kremlin cathedral, where the all-powerful worldly sovereign would shudder before the fresco of the *Last Judgment*, his conscience tormenting him, as he prayed the heavenly sovereign to forgive his mass executions: 'It was not for my own sake – it was for the sake of the great Russian kingdom....'

Was it not natural to assume that Stalin's decision to justify the actions and methods of Ivan the Terrible, contrary to the documents and to the works of the most eminent Russian historians, came because he too was troubled by his conscience? That he wanted to ground his own monstrous purges on the historical precedent of the tsar who was proclaimed as the creator of a great and powerful state?

The theme of the repentant tsar had been in Eisenstein's mind as early as May 1940, but at that time it referred to a different monarch: Boris Godunov, who was crowned tsar after the death of Ivan the Terrible's weak-minded son, Tsar Feodor, and the mysterious stabbing of Feodor's younger brother, Dmitry. Popular rumour linked the death of Dmitry, the lawful heir to the throne, with the name of lord Boris himself.

In fast broken strokes of black, red and blue pencil, quite unlike the resonant 'mathematical' lines of his usual style, Eisenstein blocked out the infanticidal tsar's monologue from Aleksandr Pushkin's tragedy *Boris Godunov*: 'I've gained a royal crown....And yet my soul is joyless.'

The deathly moonlight in the Cathedral of the Dormition. The shadow of the crowned sinner twisting on the red carpet. The flames of the memorial candles. The hell fire on the fresco of the *Last Judgment*. The cry of horror, 'in my eyes are boys, covered in blood'. The fear for the future: 'I seem to see thunder and grief before me.' And the despairing admission that 'It's pitiful to have an impure conscience!'

It seems that Eisenstein abandoned the idea of filming the whole tragedy. It meant a great deal to him. In his youth, in St Petersburg, he had seen Feodor Chaliapin's inspired performance in the title role of the Mussorgsky opera, *Boris Godunov*, which Vsevolod Meyerhold – Eisenstein's future teacher – had directed at the Imperial Mariinsky Theatre. Meyerhold had tried twice, during the Soviet period, to stage the Pushkin tragedy itself, and both times the authorities had blocked it.

Eisenstein sketched the episode of Tsar Boris's repentance exactly three months after Meyerhold was shot, following dreadful torture, in the dungeons of the NKVD. The Pupil would certainly not have known of his Teacher's execution. But his arrest, in June 1939, had been one of the most terrible shocks in Eisenstein's life. It was not, of course, by chance that Eisenstein turned to Pushkin's 'rebellious' tragedy as soon as the prospect of shooting a colour film appeared. But he quickly understood that putting it on in the cinema was unrealistic – and he wrote 'Much better for Pushkin', in English, in blue pencil across the first page of his drawings. The criminal king's repenting monologue would be hidden inside another film: *The Love of a Poet*. The plot's love adventures concealed Pushkin's clash with Tsar Nicholas I. The conflict of the Poet and Society, kneeling before the Autocrat. The achievement of the 'Prisoner of Honour', as another poet, Mikhail Lermontov, called Pushkin, challenging Dishonour in power.

The Autocrat's monologue of repentance from Pushkin's tragedy, sketched out only a year earlier, could not but come to mind when Eisenstein received Stalin's proposal (or command?) to make a film about Ivan the Terrible. Could he refuse? And if he agreed, was there any chance he could show how devastating a cruel despotism was, instead of justifying evil deeds done 'for the sake of the great kingdom'? By the end of January 1941, Eisenstein had read accounts of Ivan IV's reign, comparing historians' treatment of the tsar's acts, aims and character, and the customs of his acolytes. The parallels between the 16th century and the present day were terrifying. Eisenstein was particularly struck by one source, which stated that the tsar's confessor, Evstafy, had been among those who had condemned his viciousness – and had been remorselessly punished on the order of his 'spiritual son'.

On 2 February 1941, the first sketches for the film of *Ivan the Terrible* were made: a simultaneous description and depiction of the 'Confession' scene.[1] The scene with the sinful tsar's confession, turning into an inquisition – a 'second confession' – and ending with Evstafy's arrest, was to conclude the 'repentance in the cathedral' episode, which already existed in Eisenstein's imagination. The verbal record of the 'Repentance' would change several times over the course of 1941, as the screenplay was written and reworked. But even in the earliest versions, there was a dangerous counterpoint: while Ivan prayed on his knees before the stern Judge of Heaven, while he tried to use 'necessity of state' to justify his bloody vengeance on Novgorod (the last free city in the Russian lands), Aleksei Basmanov – the head of the Oprichnina, the tsar's guard – was behind one of the columns in the cathedral, ordering a retainer to transfer part of Novgorod's plundered wealth not to the state treasury but to his own private estate. The force that Ivan had summoned up, from the depths of society, against the rapacious and mercenary boyars, turned out to be no less self-serving – and considerably more cruel.

—PREVIOUS

The scene of repentance of Ivan the Terrible (Garden of Gethsemane) (Almaty, 1942)

—THIS PAGE

TOP (LEFT AND RIGHT)

Two pages from the storyboard of the tsar's penitential monologue from Aleksandr Pushkin's tragedy *Boris Godunov* (Moscow, May 1940)

Text on left page:
36. 'I…scattered gold among them, found labour for them'
Orange background, golden implements, chests etc.
37. 'Furious for my pains, they cursed me'
Golden throne, orange walls, golden implements
38. 'Next, a fire consumed their homes'
(Seeing red carpet, he remembers the fire)
39. 'I built new dwellings for them…'
The carpet. On the run.

Text on right page:
61. 'Terribly!' (*Wie im Fegefeuer!*) (As though in purgatory!) During the *caesura* (pause) he throws the fire of candles.
62, 63, 64. He runs, overturning candlesticks, through candles (13, 14, 19 – the distant ringing of large and small bells).
65. He falls into the red carpet. Recoils in horror.
66. Straightens – before him the fresco of the Last Judgment.
67. Wide shot. 'Yes, miserable is he whose conscience is not clear'. NB Perhaps, Hell in the fresco should appear to burn.
68. Medium shot. Tries to shut out the terrible vision by covering his eyes with his hands.

BOTTOM (LEFT AND RIGHT)

'First sketches for the script *Ivan the Terrible* – the scene of the tsar's confession' (Moscow, 1941)

Text: Some touches. Ivan comes, like a drunk staggering: Confession … confession … falling to his knees: Not worthy … not worthy … Almost up to his chest under the stole. The sweat on his forehead – bloody, cold. Confessor's cross dangles from the top in the frame. Suspicion: one eye that squints upward. Fingers take up the cross. Pull… They rope the confessor's head into the frame. Whispering in the ear: 'but how do you know?' And the hands tug on the chain of the cross. Almost garotting – this 'second confession'.

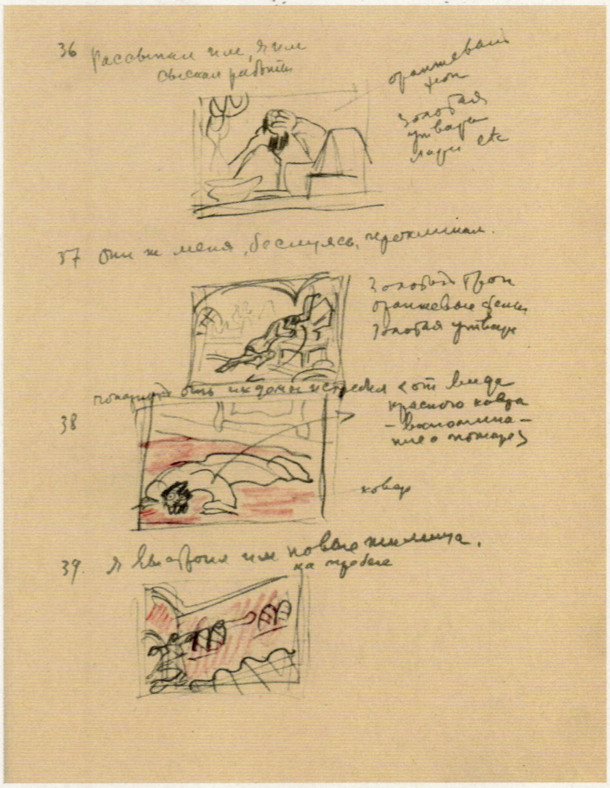

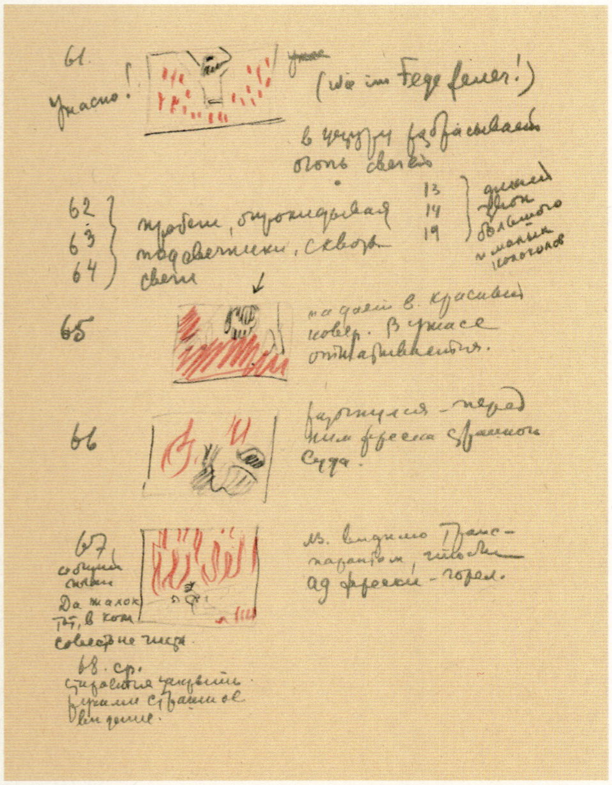

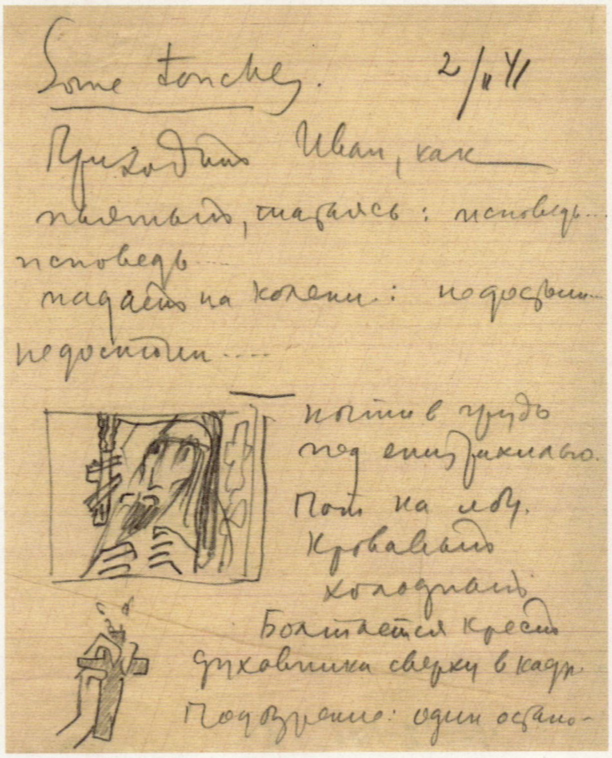

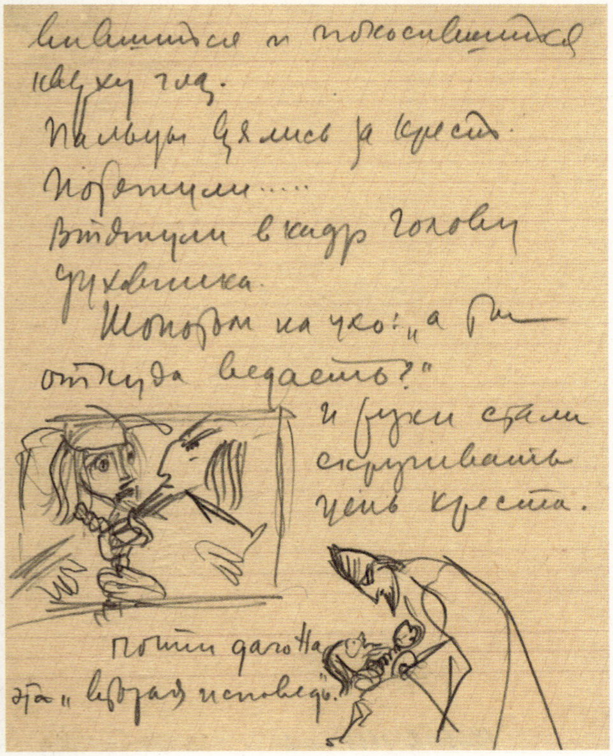

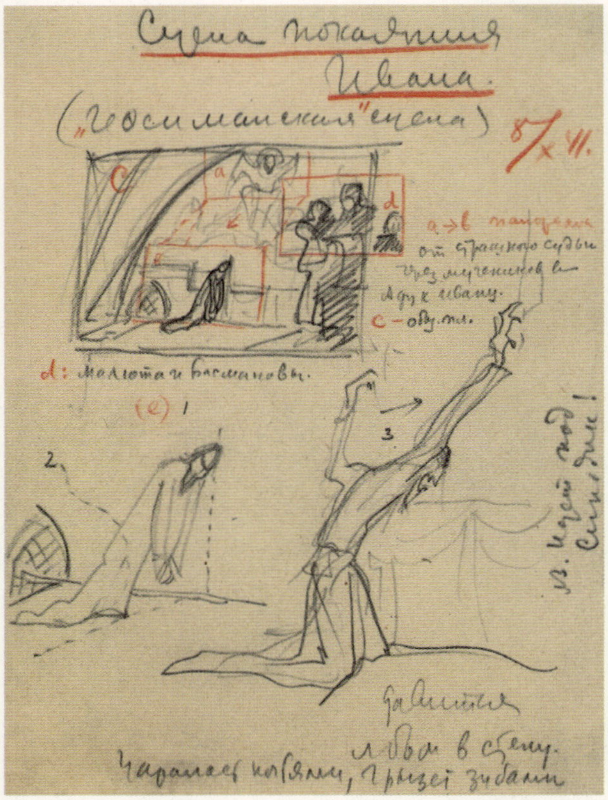

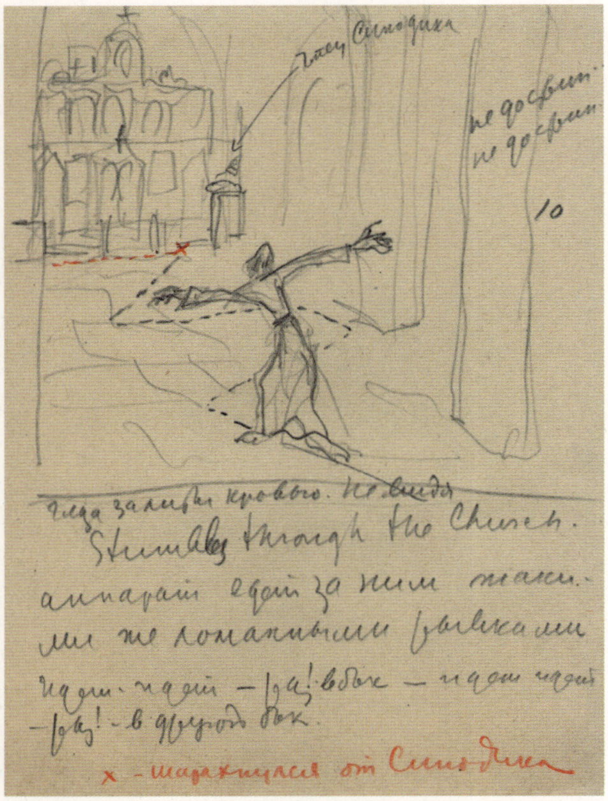

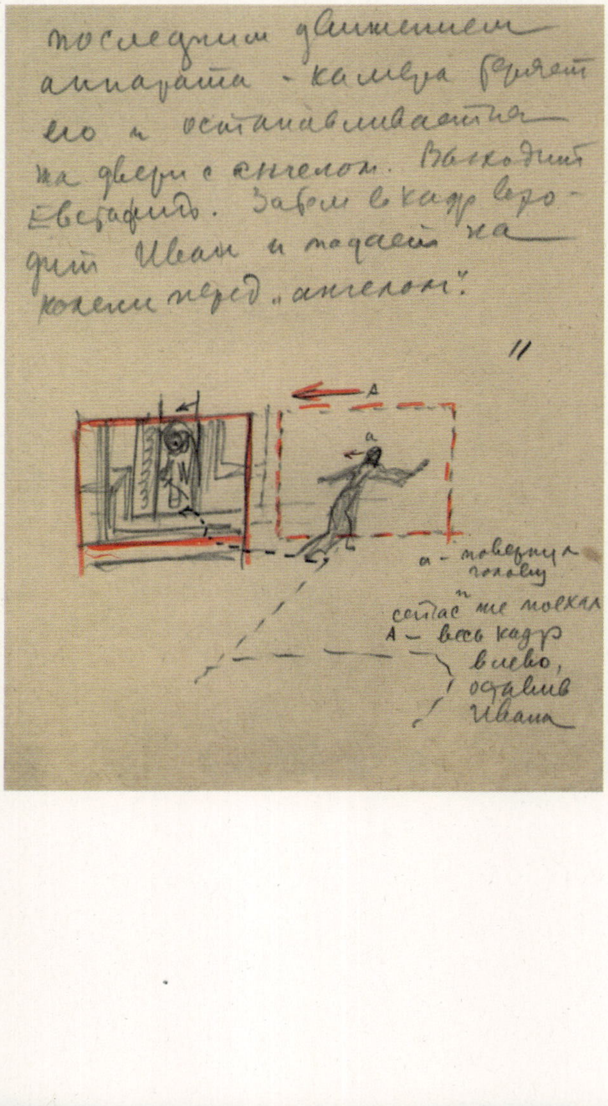

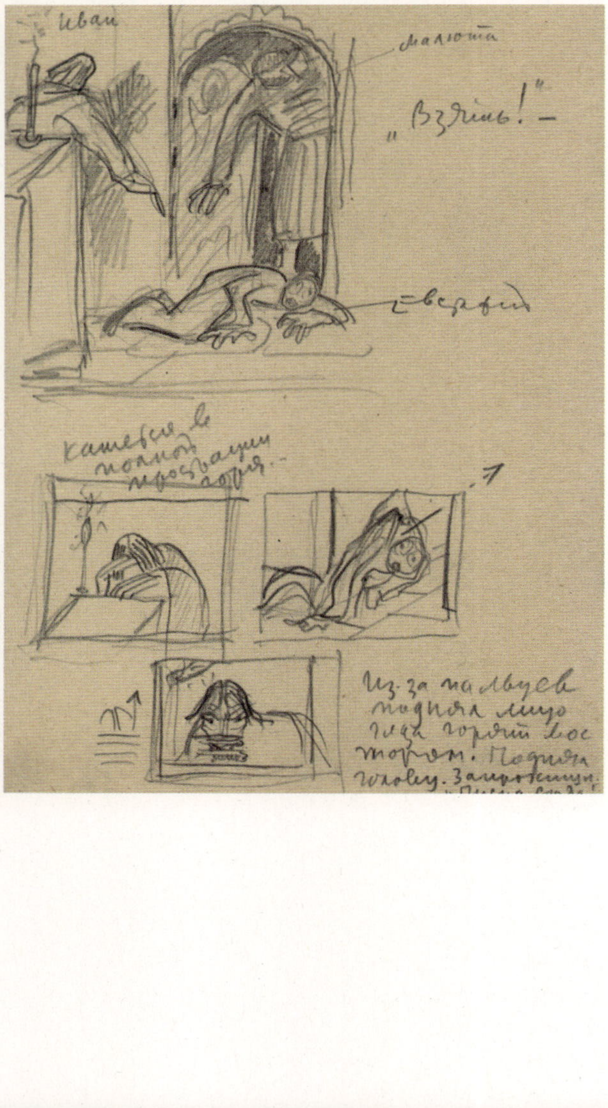

—THIS PAGE

'Scene of Ivan's repentance' (The scene of Gethsemane) (Moscow, 1941)

TOP LEFT

Text: (a – b) Panorama from the Last Judgment through the martyrs in Hell to Ivan. c – Long shot. d – Malyuta and Basmanovs. (e: 1, 2, 3) – Beats forehead against the wall, scrapes his nails, grinds his teeth. NB He goes during the reading of the memorial list of victims. 1– 2 – 3 – Presses down his forehead into the wall. He scratches it with his fingernails, with his teeth.

TOP RIGHT

Text: The monk who reads the memorial list of victims. He recoils from the list. His eyes are covered with blood. He doesn't see. Stumbles through the Church. The camera follows him with the same broken jerks. He goes, he goes – sideways! – goes, goes – to another side.

BOTTOM LEFT

Text: With the last movement – camera loses him and stops at the door with an angel. Evstafy comes out. Then, Ivan comes into the frame and falls to his knees before the 'angel'. 11 – a – He turns his head and immediately A – the entire frame moves to the left, leaving Ivan.

BOTTOM RIGHT

Text: Ivan. Malyuta. Evstafy. 'Take him!' It appears that Ivan is completely prostrate with grief. He lifts his face from under his fingers. Rapture in his eyes. Lifts his head up. Tilts it. 'Call the scrivener!'

Each successive re-editing of the episode brought further complexities in the form of allusions and subtexts. In his early drafts of the screenplay, Eisenstein had only mentioned once that 'the monk reads the synodicon of those killed at Novgorod'. And indeed, after each wave of repression Ivan did donate large sums to monasteries 'to pray for the souls of the departed', lists of whom he drew up in his own hand. But as Eisenstein worked on the screenplay, the voice of the monk grew more and more prominent, becoming one of the leitmotifs of the episode. The names of the victims crop up in the list that the monk reads, including people we know from the plot (the tsar's aunt Euphrosina and her son Vladimir, Archbishop Pimen, Metropolitan Filipp): some of the 1,500 dead are named, but many are unknown even to their executioners, and then we hear the refrain 'But thou, O Lord, knowest all their names.' At one point Eisenstein started to include in the synodicon the names of people close to him who had fallen victim to Stalin: Isaak (Babel, the writer, who had been killed in an NKVD prison), Litvin Maxim (the former foreign minister Maksim Litvinov, who had been removed from his post and was living in the expectation of being arrested). He tried to mention Tretyak (the poet and playwright Sergei Tretyakov, who had worked with Eisenstein in the theatre and had died in the Lubyanka) and 'Vsevolod Big Nest' (using the name of a 12th-century prince to refer to Vsevolod Meyerhold, whose 'nest' had seen many directors and actors fledged), too. But he crossed these names out: they would blatantly 'never get through'.

Eisenstein clearly understood that in Russia's logocentric culture it was customary to scrutinize all the nuances, subtexts and ambiguities of the verbal text. Before Stalin read the screenplay for *Ivan the Terrible* (and there was no doubt he would), it would be sniffed through by careful colleagues, officials and censors. That meant the words had to include the things they wanted to hear. But besides the text, there were also the drawings. Their function was broader than that of the sketches for *Alexander Nevsky*, where the objective had been to find a 'look' for the characters and a style for the costumes and sets, as well as the composition of the shots. In the case of *Ivan the Terrible*, the written screenplay was accompanied by a parallel, graphic screenplay – and what could be seen in the latter did not always coincide with what was written in the former.

Eisenstein hoped that the outbreak of war with Germany, in June 1941, would lead to the commission being cancelled, but it did not. By October, the Nazi armies were approaching Moscow in force. On 8 October, just before the Mosfilm studio was evacuated to Kazakhstan, the scene of Ivan's repentance before the fresco of the *Last Judgment* appeared in the drawings.

The eight pages of drawings that Eisenstein produced during October reveal the graphic manner and the type of sketches he was using for the new film. As in the sketches for *Alexander Nevsky*, he tried to capture the theme of the on-screen action, the relations in space between the figures and their surroundings, the personalities of the characters. But if his drawings for the earlier film, a 'screen hagiography', had been made using light strokes, the preliminary sketches for his 'cinematic tragedy' were now obliged to resemble – in the characters' look and movements – the expressive manner of his graphic cycles from 1937 to 1939.

The visual conception of the repentance begins with the tsar in front of the fresco and his followers behind the column (c), and the system of *mise-en-cadres* develops out of that: the panorama from the face of Christ Pantocrator to that of the tsar (a–b) is drawn out of (c), as are the mid-range view of the group of oprichniks (d) and the larger shots of Ivan (e). And it is here, in (e), that we notice phases in Ivan's movement and gestures, which would be acted out by Nikolai Cherkasov (1, 2, 3). The sculptural character of the tsar's repentant bows (4–9), against the backdrop of the sinners in Hell, is developed in the next two sheets. Thus, in the visual screenplay, the director draws on his principle of 'theme and variations', beloved to him ever since his childhood: it finds its development in the following versions. The staging of Ivan's path to the altar repeats Boris Godunov's zigzagging route through the cathedral in the staging of the monologue, but it is more laconic and intense, and it is underlined by the movement of the camera. Finally, the last three sheets ('The tsar's confession') pin down and develop the episode that had been first sketched out back in February 1941.

The sketches show important innovations in graphic style. The cross-hatching above the outline gives the figures weight and body, introduces a play of light and shade, emphasizes perspective in space, reveals the masses and surfaces of the decor and creates relationships of scale and mass among the architecture, the props and the people.

Eisenstein's graphic style for the *Ivan the Terrible* screenplay took definitive shape in Almaty. Among the first sketches he drew after being evacuated we find, once again, the 'scene of Ivan the Terrible's repentance'. From now on in his drawings for the film, Eisenstein usually does not restrict it to the rectangle of the shot: he develops the action in open space. He would later develop these visual motifs in series of sketches, refining the characters' looks and actions (makeup, costume, gestures or psychological state) or varying the sets and set-paintings and then drawing what he sometimes called 'a shot-take'.

He transcribed Leonardo's advice about rough sketches of historical figures as an epigraph, just in case his drawings for *Ivan the Terrible* should be published along with the screenplay: 'Let the sketches for historical subjects be rapid, and the working of the limbs not too much finished. Content yourself with merely giving the positions of these limbs, which you will then be able at your leisure to finish *as you please...*'[2] Eisenstein understood that his drawings would take their final shape in the form of shots on film. They would be brought to completion by actors, cameramen and set designers.

The visual screenplay's most important theme is the play of the fresco. What Eisenstein sketches on the paper is no longer, as it was in *¡Que viva México!*, film shots constructed according to the compositional laws of the fresco. Nor is it an image of the hero translated into the terms of mythic generality in the spirit and in the style of saints on columns in Orthodox churches, as in *Alexander Nevsky*.

Neither are the frescos in *Ivan the Terrible* just interior decor 'in the spirit of the age', as is customary in so-called 'historical films'. They are a kind of character, whose playing is almost a film within the film. The paintings come to life, their themes are directly related to the plot, and they are a fully fledged voice in the audio-visual counterpoint made up of the dialogue and the music, the actors' movements, the costumes and the makeup, the play of light and shade.

The step from playing with the fresco to the play of the fresco – a step forward in realizing his own conception – was one that Eisenstein took at the end of March 1942. On 31 March, he wrote himself a note:

> ***All the frescos (in the whole picture), without too much insisting, should nonetheless be thematic: they should echo the scene that is taking place, more or less closely. Like a 'development' (in the musical sense) of what is happening around them. [...] And the plastic development is actually extremely interesting in the transition from action in front of the fresco to the fresco itself. The play with the fresco (Last Judgment): immediately, or as a psychological backdrop.***
>
> ***Thus: little Ivan squeezed between the St George and the Dragon (right underneath – Andrei Shuisky coming out of Glinskaya's doors!) and the fresco of the Coronation. Then: on the throne beneath the Angel of the Revelation, judging with scales, devouring the sun. The fresco stories probably even had a historical influence on Ivan's imagination, no less than did the verbose readings from legends, the Scriptures, etc.)***[3]

On 30 and 31 March, Eisenstein drew scenes from the prologue ('Ivan's childhood') – the beginning of the future film. One showed the senior boyar Andrei Shuisky under the fresco of St George, in the scene where Princess Helena Glinskaya, Ivan's mother, is poisoned. The other depicted little Ivan and the Boyar Duma (assembly of nobles) receiving foreign ambassadors in the Golden Chamber in the Kremlin, with the Angel of the Revelation painted on the ceiling holding scales and a flaming sword.

Back in January, he had imagined the Golden Chamber with a cruciform ceiling, as was typical of Russian 16th-century architecture. But by 30 March, the cruciform design had been replaced by a semi-circular ceiling. The Angel with the scales and the sword now stretched along the whole length of its arc, taking up the wall behind Ivan's child-size throne and the arch in the centre of the Golden Chamber. Now the eyes of the timid youth on the throne would always meet the terrible stare of the Herald of the *Last Judgment*. Behind the boy's back, the Angel's feet were planted firmly on the doomed sun, while the legs of the young Grand Duke of Muscovy dangled from the throne and did not reach the ground.

Almost no documentary evidence survives as to Ivan's childhood (he was left an orphan at a young age): there are only the vague complaints about the boyars who ruled in his name that the tsar himself made in letters to Prince Kurbsky, who began as his friend and became an opponent. Even before he agreed to make the film, Eisenstein realized that he would need to grasp – and to show the viewer – not only the political and ideological but also the personal and psychological conditions that gave rise to the terror Ivan the Terrible unleashed against his enemies, his former friends, the followers he himself had appointed and his entirely innocent subjects. Explaining his unprecedented cruelty as simple madness would mean abandoning the desire to understand – replacing historical explanation by a crude medical diagnosis.

Eisenstein remembered exactly when and where he had discovered the key to Ivan's childhood psychological trauma – a trauma that had turned into a fatal passion for torture and repression. The discovery happened on 21 January 1941, in the Bolshoi Theatre. Eisenstein had been invited to the theatre not as the director of *Battleship Potemkin*, whose voyage all around the world had begun there, but as the recent director of Richard Wagner's opera *Die Walküre*. Each year, the Bolshoi staged a solemn concert in memory of Lenin, who had died on that day. Eisenstein looked over the red velvet of his box to the stage, where the present leaders of the party and the government were sitting in the praesidium. Almost none of the people with whom Lenin had prepared and carried out the Russian Revolution were still there among them. They had fallen victim to the mounting terror since 1929, since Trotsky's exile. And Trotsky himself had been assassinated six months earlier.

During the banal speeches about Lenin's role in history, Eisenstein thought about the formation of the personality of the sovereign who had been proposed to him, on behalf of Stalin, as the hero of his film. And all at once he understood: it was the boyars themselves who had taught Ivan the things that had ultimately been turned against them. By their own behaviour, they had given him an education in cruelty, amorality, hypocrisy and the destruction of enemies without trial or investigation.

It was from the boyars that the future tsar had first heard the order 'Take him!' – words that would come to terrify all his subjects, the great and the unknown, the strong and the weak. As a young man, Ivan had seen and heard the senior boyar Shuisky use his magic formula of power to remove his rivals – and perhaps he had even used it himself, for the first time, against his hated guardian.

For the purposes of the film, a theme like that could be a second basis for the screenplay! The fear of divine retribution pursues Ivan from childhood. The sinful tsar approaches the gigantic fresco of the *Last Judgment* with the same childish fear of inescapable punishment. But then, with his first 'Take him!', the heavens are silent! No thunder! And the boyars are more frightened than the boy king is. So his old, familiar fear turns into a longing to be feared by others, if we are to believe in the exclusive status of absolute power, where everything is allowed and nothing is punished.

But can the feeling of fear, the anticipation of a judgment from above, disappear without leaving a trace?

On 3 November 1941, just after his arrival in Almaty, Eisenstein drew the shot for the Prologue: the boy Ivan has just ordered his dog-handlers to 'take' the all-powerful Shuisky. Ivan is left alone in his murdered mother's chamber: he falls to his knees and huddles himself against the bed, frightened, awaiting thunder from on high. Incidentally, this is just now the supposedly ailing tsar will kneel before his boyars, to test their loyalty, when he asks for their oath of allegiance to his infant heir. And this is how he will repent on his knees after the executions at Novgorod, and confess – in order to 'take' his confessor.

It was on 28 February 1942 that Eisenstein worked out the motifs for the *Last Judgment* fresco: God in wrath, the Angels, the Righteous on the path into Paradise, the sinners in Hell. And it was only on 30 March that he found the right way of combining painted and real figures in the same shot. The earthly king, for all his dread power, was infinitely small and weak next to the wrathful King of Heaven. The Autocrat of All the Russias was only the size of one of the flames of the hell fire where the lost souls burned.

The reflections that find their graphic expression in the sketch were given verbal form on the same day, in the form of a note Eisenstein wrote 'for himself' under the title 'The frescos in *Ivan the Terrible*':

> ***In the Prologue they are particularly excessive in scale. This must reflect the way little Ivan perceives them. In his imagination they are super-grand, colossal, and threatening. The same thing recurs in the Last Judgment scene, where Ivan's childhood fears assail him again...*** [4]

Here we see formulated the principle behind the paintings in the film. The frescos for the sets depicting the Cathedral of the Dormition and Kremlin palace would be painted not in accordance with Orthodox canons, but so as to resemble outward projections of Ivan the Terrible's ideas of Bible prophecies, God and the Kingdom of Heaven, projections onto the environment in which the tsar and his subjects find themselves.

Many prototypes for the frescos can be found in genuine paintings, stern in their style and their subject matter, in the cathedrals and monasteries of northern Russia. Eisenstein had seen some of them in his youth, during the Civil War. But, even when he took the theme and spirit of the frescos from historical sources, he subjected them to the transformation he required, and filmed them in such a way that they corresponded to Tsar Ivan the Terrible's vision.

The 'subjective' appearance of the frescos add new life to an idea Eisenstein had first had in 1930, in connection with the Hollywood project *An American Tragedy*. At that time, too, he had been looking for a way of bringing the hero's inner monologue onto the screen – not verbally, as in Joyce's *Ulysses*, but in auditory and visual images.

But the terrible tsar's image of God as ruthless, as an avenging judge, did not mean he was ready to overcome his sins – and nor did his repentance before Christ Pantocrator. These were manifestations of a conflict within Ivan's psyche: the unresolved clash between his fears and his passions, his words and his deeds. The lamenting voice of the monk reading the names of the dead, the businesslike report from the executioner Malyuta about the numbers killed at Novgorod, the thieves' whisper of the corrupt oprichniks: words are layered onto the shudders and groans of the tsar, provoking in Ivan (in reality) and objectifying for the viewer (through the structure of the film) the autocrat's awareness of his own guilt.

Alongside these diverse words, there would also be diverse music, as Eisenstein noted on 25 April 1942:

> ***<u>The frescos:</u>***
> ***Just as the fresco provides a backdrop, or a background thematic accompaniment to the main theme of the action, the selection of ornamental ecclesiastical chants, psalms, readings from the synodicon, funerary laments, etc., create <u>a thematically consonant</u> auditory backdrop for the words and speeches that are uttered.***
> ***Sometimes it is a song. Often it is music.*** [5]

The 'ornate braiding of words' is one of the means by which the text is melodically formatted, on the basis of traditional liturgical chant melodies in Medieval Russian culture.

The verbal polyphony is surrounded on the one hand by the prophecy of the frescos and on the other by the choral singing of King David's psalms of repentance, the mournful melody of the chant for the dead and the music of Sergei Prokofiev. Once again, as in the 'Gedanken zur Musik' cycles, visual and musical images are intertwined: not as a 'formula', this time, but as a way of directing the audio-visual counterpoint on screen.

Two days later, on 27 April, Eisenstein wrote down some ideas that were to prove of central importance for the meaning and the poetics of the film:

> ***This is already almost on the question of unity in* Ivan the Terrible:**
>
> ***The Daniel (one of the earliest ideas) as the backdrop for the clash between Ivan and Filipp – actually the fresco background, come to life! From the very beginning it had been conceived as a miracle-play in fresco style! And so Daniel belongs altogether to the problem of the fresco in this film.***
>
> ***The same register in the language and in the music (ecclesiastical chants, Prokofiev).***
>
> ***And the most remarkable, of course, is that Ivan himself rises up as a part of a similar, crying fresco of interwoven interests from the 'social background': sometimes entering into its tapestry, sometimes standing out in front of it as he does in front of the interwoven horrors of the fresco of the Last Judgment.***[6]

A Daniel play is a liturgical drama, presented in church, that depicts a miracle from biblical legend. According to the book of the prophet Daniel (Dan. 3:22–51), during the Babylonian captivity of the Jews, three young men – Hananiah, Azariah and Mishael – refused to worship a pagan idol. And so the emperor Nebuchadnezzar ordered that they be cast into a fiery furnace; but an angel appeared from heaven and led them unharmed from the flames.

Muscovy inherited a kind of miracle-play on this subject – a rare thing in Russian culture – from Byzantium. In the 16th and 17th centuries, it was performed a week before Christmas, in the Cathedral of the Dormition in the Kremlin and in cathedrals in other Russian cities. Eisenstein calls the Daniel episode 'one of the earliest ideas'. This means that the idea of filming the ecclesiastical drama about the 'miracle of the three youths' had arisen not long after he had found a third basis – mentioned here – for the screenplay.

This third basis, which helped persuade Eisenstein to agree to make the film, was the feat of Metropolitan Filipp of Moscow (the ecclesiastical name of Fedor Kolychev), one of the most popular and beloved Russian saints. On 22 March 1568, in the Cathedral of the Dormition, he publicly refused to bless the tsar, who had arrived for the service with his oprichniks in black 'monastic' garments and wearing pointed hats.

Eisenstein read Filipp's denunciatory speech in Nikolai Karamzin's *History of the Russian State*:

> ***In such wise, in such strange garb I know not the Orthodox tsar; neither do I know him in the doings of the kingdom....O Sovereign! Here we render sacrifice unto God, and upon our altar is poured out the guiltless blood of Christ. Since the sun has shone in the heavens, it has been neither seen nor heard of, that pious kings should offend thus horribly against their own kingdom! In the most infidel and heathen kingdoms there is yet law and justice, there is compassion, and in Russia they are not! The wealth and life of the citizens have no protection. Everywhere are robberies, everywhere are murders, and in the tsar's name! Thou art high on thy throne; but there is also the All-Highest, Who will judge us and thee. How wilt thou appear at His judgment? Scarlet with the blood of the guiltless, dumb with the wailing of their torments? For the very stones beneath thy feet cry out for vengeance!...Sovereign! I speak as a shepherd of souls. I fear none but the Lord!***[7]

After this fearless speech, Metropolitan Filipp was stripped of his ecclesiastical title, arrested, tortured and then exiled to a monastery. A year later, when he refused to bless the tsar's campaign against Novgorod (a whole city accused of treason), he was suffocated in his monastic cell by the wicked Malyuta. In 1648, under Tsar Aleksei Romanov, he was canonized.

Even before his public denunciation of the tsar in the cathedral, Filipp had spoken out against Ivan's crimes and those of his 'trusty hounds' among the oprichniks. This, indeed, was where Eisenstein began: on 9 February 1941, at the very start of his work on the screenplay, he sketched the clash between Filipp and the tsar, while the boyars looked on in servile obedience, and made on the drawing a very significant inscription about Ivan's duplicity:

> ***Include in this scene right from the (first) entry of the oprichniks into Moscow: like a black cloud, with***

> ***wolves' heads and brooms (first appearance). The Oprichnina; I[van] IV; the boyars; despues [from here] Filipp. The Oprichnina programme set out, and first meeting with Filipp and his first opposition to what John's doing (the first meeting: [Filipp] only just arrived, and [Ivan's] first call: 'be silent, my Lord Bishop' – Filipp not yet a metropolitan). Then they stay alone together – to sort things out. And behind the walls the oprichniks already take boyars headmen. The boyars.*** [8]

A year later, drawing the same situation in Almaty, he begins with the same setting for the conflict: a diagonal, with Ivan in his black furs and Filipp in his bright habit, forming a contrast with the black mass of the oprichniks and the boyars in their fine caftans. But on 30 March, when he had just thought up the fresco of the Angel of the Revelation for the Golden Chamber, he wrote in the same note concerning frescos:

> ***...and in the Filipp scene, which will happen in the same place (with the terrible angel whose face flames with fire). And in this very same scene, the Terrible will be seized by a 'childish' (!) fear of loneliness.*** [9]

And on the very next day, Eisenstein introduced the 'voice of the fresco' into the conflict between Filipp and Ivan, as a reminder of his 'childish' fear of the *Last Judgment* – embodied here by the Angel of the Revelation.

His inscription on this new resolution of the scene contains a hint of how the conflict will develop: Filipp's voice is 'like a bell sounding the anathema...'[10]

The anathema – the church's curse – is recited in church as part of the service. The Metropolitan (as Eisenstein had decided in Moscow) would arrange a performance of the Daniel play, to shame the tsar by comparing him to the pagan despot Nebuchadnezzar.

Against Ivan's Angel of the Revelation we would set his own Angel of Redemption. Eisenstein drew this 'symbol of the faith' using the clean 'mathematical' line of his intimate graphic work – just as he did the face of Filipp himself, making him resemble a saint in an icon.

Eisenstein was aware, of course, that the Daniel play was performed in church before Christmas – and not in March, when Filipp, the intercessor for the disgraced and for the wrongfully murdered, made his challenge to the autocrat. But, as in other instances, Eisenstein departed from the letter of events if the image could reveal their spirit and meaning. The miracle of the salvation of the youths out of the fire, as staged by Filipp, was to become a metaphor for intervention on behalf of the victims of an unjust government. A Christian sovereign was to be excluded, *de facto*, from the church, not just by means of a speech of condemnation but also by means of art.

In composing his Daniel play, Eisenstein undoubtedly remembered Hamlet's 'mousetrap' – a staging of a crime, by which the Prince of Denmark held up a revealing mirror to the fratricidal king. Eisenstein followed in Hamlet's footsteps, but he went further than the Elizabethan theatre. He descended into the depths of the past, to the miracle plays and mystery plays of the Middle Ages, which were performed in the church porch or in the church itself. Actors and audience merged in the spectacle. In the course of the play, the viewers became participants: they came to share the thoughts and feelings of the performers, and were themselves changed. A 'congregational art' had been proposed in early 20th-century Russia, too, by the Symbolists: the old theatre had been revived by Nikolai Evreinov, and the young architecture student Sergei Eisenstein had believed in it.

Ivan the Terrible gave Eisenstein the chance to realize the ideas and principles that had attracted him in his youth in Petrograd, and which he had transformed in Moscow into the bold innovations of his theatre projects and stagings. He could now show on the screen what was possible when you abolished the boundary between the stage and the stalls – the very thing he had planned to do in Meyerhold's school with Ludwig Tieck's *Puss in Boots* and Bernard Shaw's *Heartbreak House*.

And also what he had shown, in a rather vandalistic way, in Sergei Tretyakov's version of Aleksandr Ostrovsky's *Enough Stupidity in Every Wise Man*.

Eisenstein probably smiled when he thought of including the Daniel play in Metropolitan Filipp's heroic feat. His long-held dream of an art that would draw the spectators into the play and 'plough up' their consciousness (a phrase he repeated many times in his youth) would at last be realized, albeit only on the cinema screen. The Daniel play in his film would be addressed not only to the tsar, but also to the people surrounding the 'furnace': the cathedral's parishioners. For them it would be not a backdrop, but a part of the ritual of the anathema. And Ivan would 'rise up' out of the living fresco, 'sometimes entering into its tapestry, sometimes standing out in front of it'. And for a mind that had not lost its receptive innocence, both planes would flow into one: the little boyar boy would point his finger at the black figure standing by the furnace, and would ask loudly, laughing, so that the whole cathedral heard it: 'Mummy, is that the heathens' Terrible tsar?'

In the fairy-tale kingdom he created, Hans Christian Andersen does not report what happened to the boy who loudly said of the naked emperor that which the grown-ups had seen but were afraid to say. In the real land of the Soviets, *Ivan the Terrible* was to play the same role as the one that Metropolitan Filipp, within its own plot, gave to the Daniel play. And the episode of the Daniel play itself would be comparable to the artless question from the boy in Andersen's fable.

Eisenstein could not fail to understand this when he thought up the whole situation, then wrote out one version after another of the episode's screenplay and drew Metropolitan Filipp exclaiming: 'Repent, Ivan, before the end comes'. He probably shuddered when he imagined how the words sung by the youths in the Daniel play would sound in Stalin's Kremlin cinema:

> ***Wherefore, O shameless Chaldees,***
> ***do you serve a lawless king?***
> ***Wherefore, O demonic Chaldees,***
> ***do you rejoice at a Satanic king,***
> ***an abuser, a torturer?***[11]

Oddly, these words – and the whole episode – escaped the reefs of the High Censorship (which had perhaps been weakened by the tragic events on the front line of the war with Nazi Germany).

In its theme, the Daniel play was an ideal way to unite the church service, the canonical ritual of blessing the tsar and Filipp's denunciatory sermon. In style, it was a perfect link between the gospel paintings in the church, the biblical account of the Chaldees and the three youths, and the 'crying fresco' of social interests, the real behaviour of the Autocrat of All the Russias, the supreme hierarch of the Orthodox Church, and the parishioners – 'people'.

Unlike the apocalyptic frescos, drawn the way Ivan imagined them, Eisenstein had the 'fiery furnace' built just as it would have appeared in a wall painting that had been produced according to Byzantine canons. Its side walls did not 'recede' into the depth of the space, as artists have been taught to portray perspective ever since the Renaissance – instead, they 'rush out' towards the spectator.

Eisenstein had made use of the 'reverse perspective' developed by ancient Greek craftsmen for icons and frescos back when he was working on *Bezhin Meadow*. He had incorporated the biblical myth of Abraham and Isaac into his story of a tragedy in a modern Russian village, as a reminder of the ancient ban on human sacrifice. In some scenes he wanted to achieve on screen the effect of Byzantine reverse perspective, as used in Orthodox frescos and icons. For *Bezhin Meadow*, the cameraman Vladimir Nilsen was to shoot the actors against a screen on which something or someone that had already been filmed was projected larger (rear-projection), so that the combined image created an effect of reverse perspective. Why?

Eisenstein could have replied to that question by referring to his thoughts about the metaphysics of different kinds of perspective, reflecting different understandings not only of space, but also of the semantics of depiction – from the bas-reliefs of ancient Egypt onwards. Or else he could have pointed to the different relationships that are created between the spectacle and the spectator if different rules and conventions are employed. One set of relationships with the Chinese, another set with the Japanese, or in mediaeval Europe, or among the classicists of the 18th century, or the avant-garde of the 20th century.

He could have recalled the multiple perspectives in the 'mosaic' of cinematic editing, when shifts in the location of the camera and changes of lens allow the dream of the Cubists to be realized in the cutting room – but without the customary appearance of the world being shattered, as it is in their canvases. Or, he could simply have shown his drawings, in which the laws of gravity and of Renaissance perspective play such a minor role.

In *Ivan the Terrible*, the figures in the frescos – larger than the actors in front of them – made it possible to realize this reverse perspective. The space occupied by the actors therefore ceased to 'draw' the viewer's gaze into the screen: it seemed to propagate out from the screen into the cinema, 'covering' the people sitting looking at the screen.

Nor did Eisenstein limit himself only to the painted sets. With the help of Andrei Moskvin, a master-craftsman in the field of lighting, he deployed a play of enormous shadows.

Now the screen did not pretend to give a reliable 'eyewitness account', as in Eisenstein's silent movies. It did not balance on the boundary between documentary fact and statuesque fresco, as in his Mexican epic. It was not stylized to resemble a supposedly historical canvas, as in *Alexander Nevsky*. Instead, what was depicted in the shot became artificial to the utmost degree, overtly conventional – as with the German Expressionists whom Eisenstein had once criticized so bitterly. And at the same time, the spectacle on the screen had to retain its attractiveness: it must work on the viewer just as strongly as it had in his previous films.

On 8 May 1943, when the film was already being shot, Eisenstein wrote in his diary:

> ***Re the staging of Ivan. It's funny to speak of the makeup. I was a crusader against wigs, makeup, sets; a flag-bearer for immersion in reality – and now I'm using up poods [about 16 kg] of false noses, false beards, makeup, false eyelashes (!!!).***
>
> ***A reaction? I don't think so. It's more 'a kind of return' to the style that preceded my first work [in the cinema].***
>
> ***That is, it's an anticipation of a new layer, a new stage, a new style – romantic cinema, after a cinema that was middling and grey.***

A cinema of passion after a cinema of warmth.
It's in the way the situations are constructed and the movements are drawn.
It's in the way the characters are constructed, and it's in the staging.
It's in the way of speaking.
It's in the style of the text.
It's in the way constructions are disposed rhythmically in time.
It's in heightened pronunciations, in gestures, etc.... [12]

All the elements that are listed here needed to be united into a single whole, without disrupting the graphic character of the shot – one of the most important 'voices' in Eisenstein's polyphony. In particular, all the movements of the actors – from crossing the stage to hand gestures and the direction in which they were looking – had to be inscribed into the shot.

Eisenstein knew what some of his colleagues would say behind his back: 'Eisenstein is forcing his actors to copy a painting.' Sometimes he met with resistance from the actors themselves, who found it hard to follow the director's instructions about how they were to move within the strict composition of the shot.

Even the actor playing Ivan, the former comedian Nikolai Cherkasov, who was limitlessly devoted to Eisenstein and was a virtuoso when it came to physical acting, rebelled – during the very scene with the tsar's repentance in front of the fresco of the *Last Judgment* – against the complicated series of movements that were set down for him. But Eisenstein refused to simplify his sketch of these movements. Instead, he calmly told the actor, 'You'll do it!' Cherkasov did not know whether to take this as a compliment or as an order. He practised and practised, and he did it. Then the director made things still harder for him:

From a state of what seemed to be genuine repentance for his brutality at Novgorod, Ivan was to pass at once into the opposite state – rage against God, who remained silent and would not grant the tsar reply or pardon.

And the earthly king flings his jewel-encrusted wooden staff at the Heavenly King. The staff breaks against the wall. Fragments fly. Jewels are scattered. They fly towards Heaven in vain, just like Ivan's prayers....

In real history, it was Ivan's son whom he attacked with his staff, killing him. In Eisenstein's film, the terrible ruler is ascribed the sin not of infanticide but of a Luciferian revolt against God.

The theme of Ivan as Lucifer was not a new one in Russian historical writing. In the early 19th century, both the historian Nikolai Karamzin and the literary critic Vissarion Belinsky had called this tsar a 'fallen angel'. In art, however, Russia's greatest painters and sculptors (Vasnetsov, Repin, Antokolsky) had portrayed Ivan the Terrible as a suspicious, gloomy, crazed tyrant. But Eisenstein wanted to find visual forms for a metaphor that would explain the profound sinfulness of Ivan IV – and indeed of autocracy as a form of government. 'The tsar's fall from God' was expressed in the repentance scene, both in the way the actor was to move and in the composition of the shots, with their 'reverse perspective' – an image of the earthly king's vain opposition to the Heavenly King.

But Eisenstein would not have been Eisenstein if he had not also explored an opposite way of expressing the same theme. With the help of Eduard Tisse, a great master of location filming, he emphasized an extreme form of the optics of 'deep focus'.

His masterpiece in this style of cinematography is the deep shot from the final scene of Episode 1, 'The procession with the cross to Aleksandrovskaya Sloboda'. The episode was based on one of Ivan IV's most cunning and demagogical moves on his path to unlimited power – one that was outwardly successful, but which had fateful consequences for Russia. In December 1564, the tsar suddenly abandoned the Kremlin and took up residence not far from Moscow, in Aleksandrovskaya Sloboda, where he established a special military force: the feared Oprichnina. The oprichniks, who renounced their 'mother and father' to serve the sovereign, were empowered to sell off the property of disgraced subjects for the benefit of the state – and, it became clear, for their own profits. In the end, Ivan's policy led to the complete disorganization of the kingdom of Muscovy.

In the screenplay, Ivan provokes the Muscovites' procession. Feeling themselves 'orphaned', fearing anarchy and the former corruption of the boyars, they implore their 'father' to return to his capital. As Ivan, the crowned autocrat, says in the film, 'the appeal of the people' gives him a 'second anointing'. Now he has the right to conduct a Last Judgment on Earth, not waiting for the judgment of God.

Eisenstein did not immediately find a plastic form for Ivan's appearance in this episode. In one of his sketches, he counterposed two versions of the clothing to be worn by the tsar, who would dominate the procession. Fur robes would create a seemingly humble silhouette of a sovereign who appeared to be 'obedient to the people', while a black monastic habit with sharp sleeves would make him look like a bird of prey over his quarry. And the latter version was shot first. But soon Eisenstein, seeking a better relationship between the tsar and the people in the frame, reshot the episode, ending it with a close-up of Ivan's face looming above a long shot of the procession with crosses, icons and gonfalons (heraldic banners).

The composition of this shot recalls medieval depictions of the face of God the Father gazing down from heaven on the World of People, with their virtues and their sins. For Tsar Ivan the Terrible, who permitted himself to slay and to spare according to his own will – to conduct a Last Judgment on his subjects – had fallen into the greatest of sins, which the ancient Greeks called hubris. This sin is the excessive pride of human beings who make themselves equal with God, or even try to replace Him. This kind of pride, according to the ancients, leads to inescapable vengeance and a tragic downfall.

Eisenstein could not but wonder whether the viewer would grasp his implications. For many, the shot of the tsar dominating the people would mean Ivan's triumph. If they did not hear that at that moment, when the tsar bows to the people in seeking agreement to their appeal, the crowd's song 'Come back, our father!' is replaced by Sergei Prokofiev's musical theme 'A storm is coming'.... If they took the operatic roar of the orchestra seriously....

Ivan's 'obedience' to the people is an act, a manifestation of his demagogy. And so is the line 'I stand on the shoulders of the people!', which the historical Tsar Ivan would never have said. In fact, Eisenstein deliberately included lines such as this in the screenplay. As anticipated, the high personage who had commissioned the film reacted favourably to them. It seems he also took the deep shot with the tsar's profile above the procession literally, when he watched the first part of the trilogy at the end of 1944. Because he was happy with it, and with his own hand he wrote *Ivan the Terrible* onto the list of works that were to be awarded the Stalin Prize. It was only with Part 2 that he noticed what was implied – and he did not permit Part 3 to be completed.

Eisenstein himself was content with his experiment in 'reverse perspective' in the cinema, and also with the revival of the 'deep staging' that he had begun to use in *Strike!* and brought to a peak of acuity in *The General Line*, many frames of which were shot using the shortest-focus 28mm lenses that were then available. In constructing the shot with Ivan's profile and the procession, he would certainly have remembered the 'close-up' shots in his uncompleted films too – and reflected on the ambivalence of this kind of graphic composition.

In *¡Que viva México!*, the shot in which an Aztec woman in profile is juxtaposed with a whole pyramid had become an image of the immortality of a culture that the Spanish conquistadors had sought to kill – but also a metaphor for the unity of time, of history and of the present day.

In *Bezhin Meadow*, the profile of a young peasant and the figures of two other supporters of the patriarchal Russian rural order were combined with a column of villagers who had accepted the collectivization of their farms: the graphic structure of the shot reflects the catastrophically rapid break between the past and the present, and draws out the conflict between them. In *Ivan the Terrible*, the deep composition of the shot with the tsar and the procession was included in the context of the tragedy of absolute power: the very context whose meaning had been developed by the Daniel play and repentance scenes in the Cathedral of the Dormition, with their fresco-style 'reverse perspective'. In Eisenstein's cinema, the two systems did not so much contradict one another as form an organic unity.

From his youth, Eisenstein had favoured constructions that involved setting off the foreground and background sharply against each other, and he had looked attentively into the different ways in which great artists had used emphatic perspective. At the ends of the bookshelves in his Moscow apartment hung bold prints from Jacques Callot's album of etchings titled *Balli di Sfessania*: the grotesque characters of the *commedia dell'arte* in the foreground and the crowd far in the background. On the wall of his study was a large reproduction of Honoré Daumier's *Il était votre amant, Madame!* – a depiction of a bloody melodrama from the popular theatre, with the murder on the stage in the background and the heads of the audience in the foreground. And in his file of Japanese drawings, there was a copy of Ando Hirōshige's print depicting a gigantic eagle above a snowy valley, which had suggested the 'key' shot with the terrible tsar looming above the peaceful procession of his subjects.

Besides Velázquez, Adolph Menzel, Edgar Degas and other classics whom Eisenstein considered his teachers in the deep composition of the shot, there was another favourite artist of his: Doménikos Theotokópoulos, known as El Greco, to whom he had devoted a whole chapter in his 1937 book *Montage*. His essay on 'El Greco and the cinema' pointed to the painter's depiction of Christ's prayer in the Garden of Gethsemane – a spatial treatment of a subject that is also often called 'the Prayer of the Cup'.

Is it not strange that Eisenstein should have labelled his first version of the 'Ivan's repentance scene', on 5 October 1941, with the subtitle 'Gethsemane', and that he should have stubbornly repeated this association in later sketches too? What is there in common between the repentance of the sinful Tsar Ivan and the prayer of Jesus before his arrest and crucifixion?

In 'El Greco and the cinema', Eisenstein's commentary on the painting compares four vertical and two horizontal versions (one of which 'is thought to be a copy, not the work of El Greco himself'), and notes at once that:

> ***The vertical version is especially remarkable for its unusually powerful group of sleeping disciples in the foreground, taking up the whole lower half of the painting.***[13]

A little later, he explains the acute 'deep composition' in terms of a peculiarity of the artist's vision and his attitude to his subject:

> ***This is a very pure example of a sharply expressed ecstatic perspective, that is to say a perspective that goes beyond the normal state, or, if you like, a scene that is very obviously photographed in a way that is only possible with a 28mm lens. This is equally expressed both in the perspective foreshortening within the [group of] disciples themselves in the foreground and also in the perspective relations between the foreground figures and the figures of Christ and the angel in the background.***
>
> ***I think that this is the source of the matchless sense of being 'drawn into' the painting that everyone who looks at it experiences. The ecstatic perspective 'pulls' us into the canvas.***[14]

In the foreground are the apostles who have fallen asleep in the Garden of Gethsemane, even though Christ had asked them not to leave him alone in his hour of sorrow and grief. The artist uses the spiritual weakness of their powerful bodies to 'pull' the viewer's gaze into the depths of the painting, towards the shining figures of the Angel and of Christ, kneeling to receive the Cup of Fate. The emphatic perspective foreshortening makes the figures in the background comparable in size to those in the foreground, almost creating an effect of reverse perspective (which the Greek had known from his youth) – 'advancing' on the spectator above the treacherously sleeping disciples.

And here is Eisenstein's commentary on another version of El Greco's painting on the same subject:

> ***He gives the whole canvas of the 'horizontal' version over to the scene depicted in the top half of the 'vertical' one (Christ and the angel with the cup); he raises the angel a little higher; and inside the cloud (which carries him in the other version), as though seen through it... he draws a precise, small-scale reproduction of the group of sleeping disciples that had taken up the whole lower half of the 'vertical' version of the painting! And he makes no other changes to the group, not to the poses, or the positions, or the perspectives of the figures: he just reduces the size.***
>
> ***I think this is the clearest example of the way in which El Greco manifests a montage-hieroglyphical attitude to visual phenomena. What is important to him here is to retain the combination of signs that are necessary, first and foremost, to express a particular conception that is resolved by their conjunction. And it is not at all important to him that the real physical objects should occur together 'in front of the lens'.***[15]

Eisenstein understood that the 'montage-hieroglyphical approach' made it possible to combine two significant actions in space, each with its own perspective. El Greco moved the foreground group of sleeping apostles not merely into the depth of the painting, but into a 'cloud'; and he moved the Angel with the Cup of Destiny that Christ was to drink into the foreground. This spatial 're-editing' and combination of two perspectives somewhat changed the theme of the painting. Now the artist was asking: can we condemn the weakness of simple people, if Jesus himself, as we read in the Gospel (Matthew 26:39), in a moment of purely human mortal sorrow 'fell upon his face, and prayed, saying: 'O my Father, if it be possible, let this cup pass from me'?

Knowing all the profundity of the autocrat's moral fall, Eisenstein would never, of course, have compared Ivan to Jesus. His tsar also speaks the phrase about the Cup, but not in the cathedral when he repents – in the bedchamber of the poisoned queen. And in reply he hears a merciless: 'It shall not pass!'

But Eisenstein could not deny the protagonist of his film, or indeed the authority who had commissioned it, the possibility of mortal sorrow, since they were human beings despite everything. He could not but allow that even manifest sinners have moments of fear in the face of inevitable vengeance, moments of repentance for the evil they have done. He would have liked to believe that even in the soul of a tyrant, during a conversation with the Heavenly Father or just with himself, conscience could awaken: that, in fact, was where his reflections about *Ivan the Terrible* had begun.

And is this not why Eisenstein attached the name of Gethsemane to the scene in which Ivan repents before the fresco of the *Last Judgment*? Does this not explain why he wanted to begin with an El Greco-like deep composition, in the foreground of which would be the oprichniks (the tsar's 'disciples'), who are betraying their oath of loyalty at the very moment when Ivan is praying God for forgiveness?

The longer Eisenstein worked on the screenplay – the more he drew, and then actually shot the film – the less he found himself believing in the sincerity of the tsar's repentance. At the height of the filming, on 6 December 1943, Eisenstein wrote in his diary (in German, perhaps so it would not be immediately comprehensible to others):

> ***Haßzustände. Haß zu Ivan dem Schrecklichen.***[16]
> ***(A state of hatred. I hate Ivan the Terrible.)***

Eisenstein's intuition had not let him down when, in his first sketches for the repentance scene, he had noticed and drawn Ivan in the confessional, using the chain of the cross to strangle his own confessor – a situation that eventually led him to the idea of the scene with the staff of state hurled at God.

On 6 January 1942, when he had drawn 'Ivan the Terrible's repentance scene' and added 'The Garden of Gethsemane', in brackets and in quotation marks, Eisenstein already knew that the montage-hieroglyphical conjunction of two perspectives was the only thing his painting had in common with the El Greco painting.

In some ways, Eisenstein's own situation reflected aspects of the 'Garden of Gethsemane' story. Several times – before agreeing to make the film, while he was working on the screenplay, during the filming and editing, before each finished episode was shown to the political leadership – he must have remembered Christ's prayer in the garden: 'If it be possible, may this cup pass from me.'

And each time, Eisenstein must have repeated inwardly, and probably with a shrinking heart, the words that the autocrat could never have uttered, but that Jesus spoke at the end of the Prayer of the Cup: '... nevertheless not as I will, but as Thou wilt.'

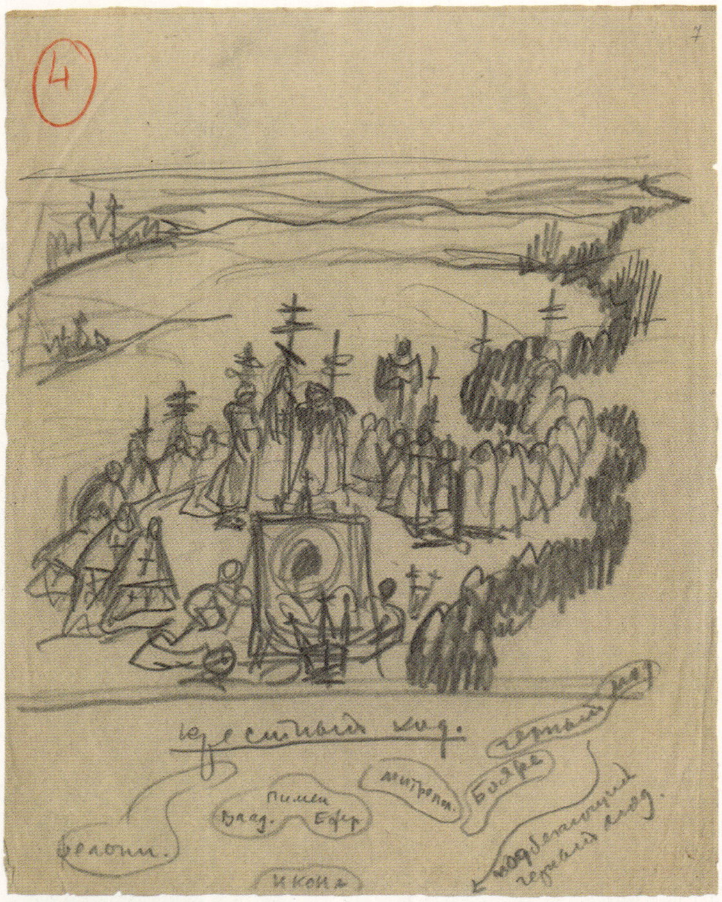

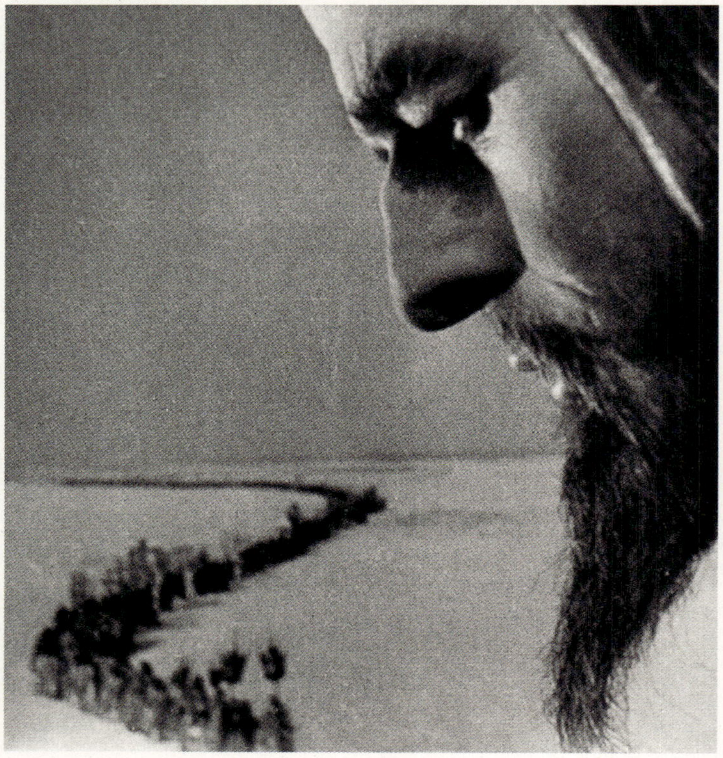

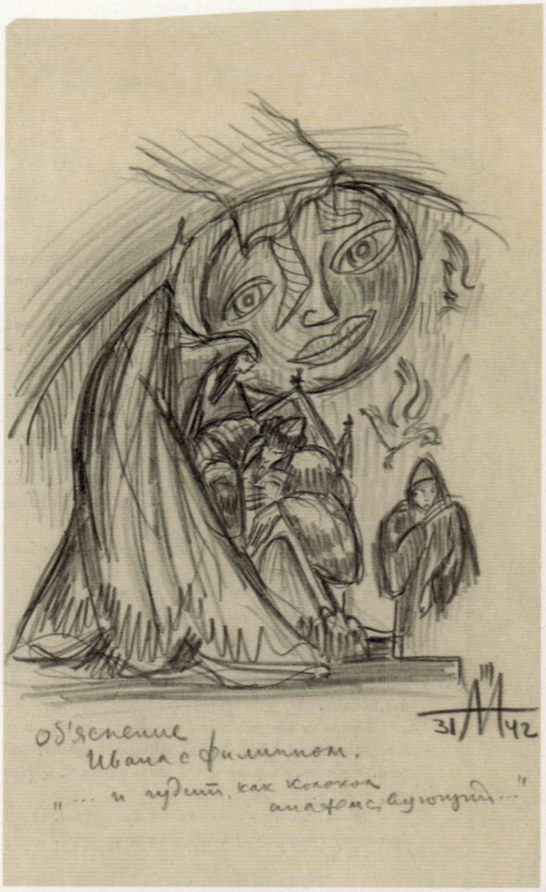

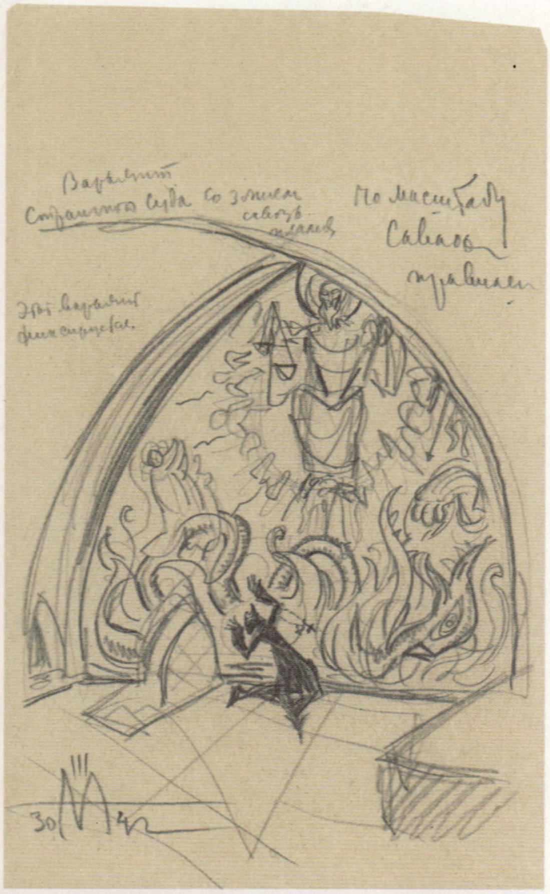

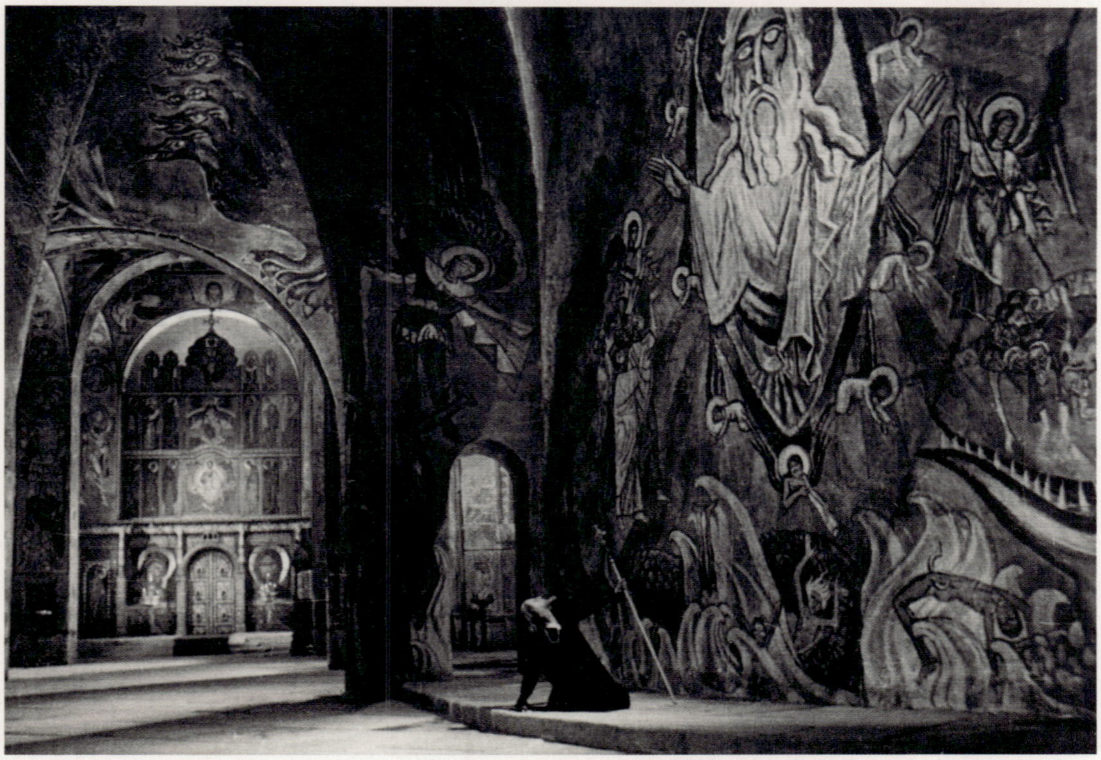

—OPPOSITE

TOP
The Procession: Phelonion, Pimen, Vladimir, Euphrosina, Icon, Metropolitans [monks], Boyars, Simple Folk, Running Simple Folk

BOTTOM
Tsar Ivan and the Procession From Moscow
Shot from *Ivan the Terrible Part 1*

—THIS PAGE

TOP LEFT
Ivan's Repentance (Almaty, 1942)
Text: The version of the Last Judgment with the Serpent through the flames. Sabaoth is correct in scale. This version is fixed.

TOP RIGHT
Face-to-Face Meeting of Ivan and Filipp (1942)
Text: ...and he hums like a bell that denounces....

BOTTOM
Ivan's Repentance
Scene from the third part of the film
Photograph by Victor Dombrovsky

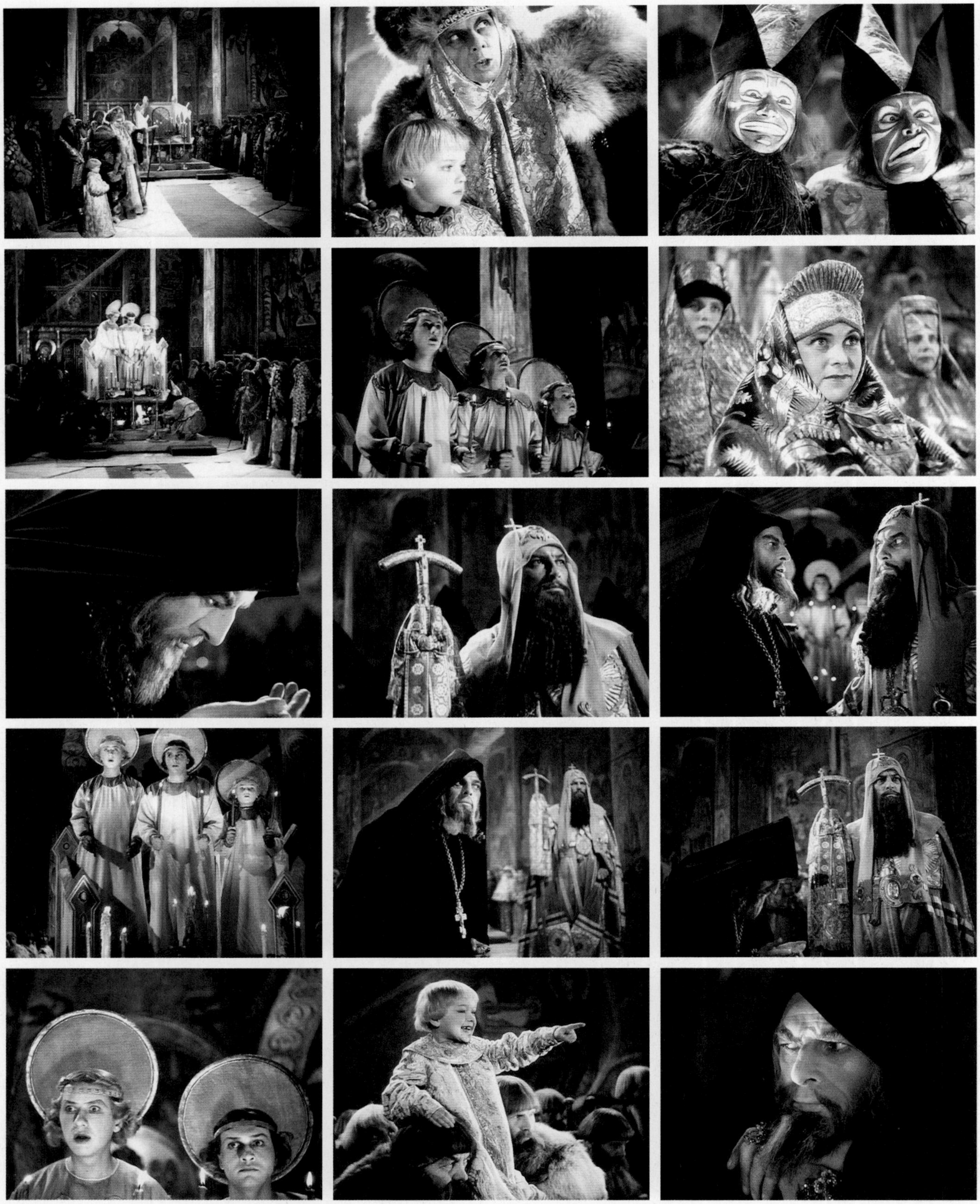

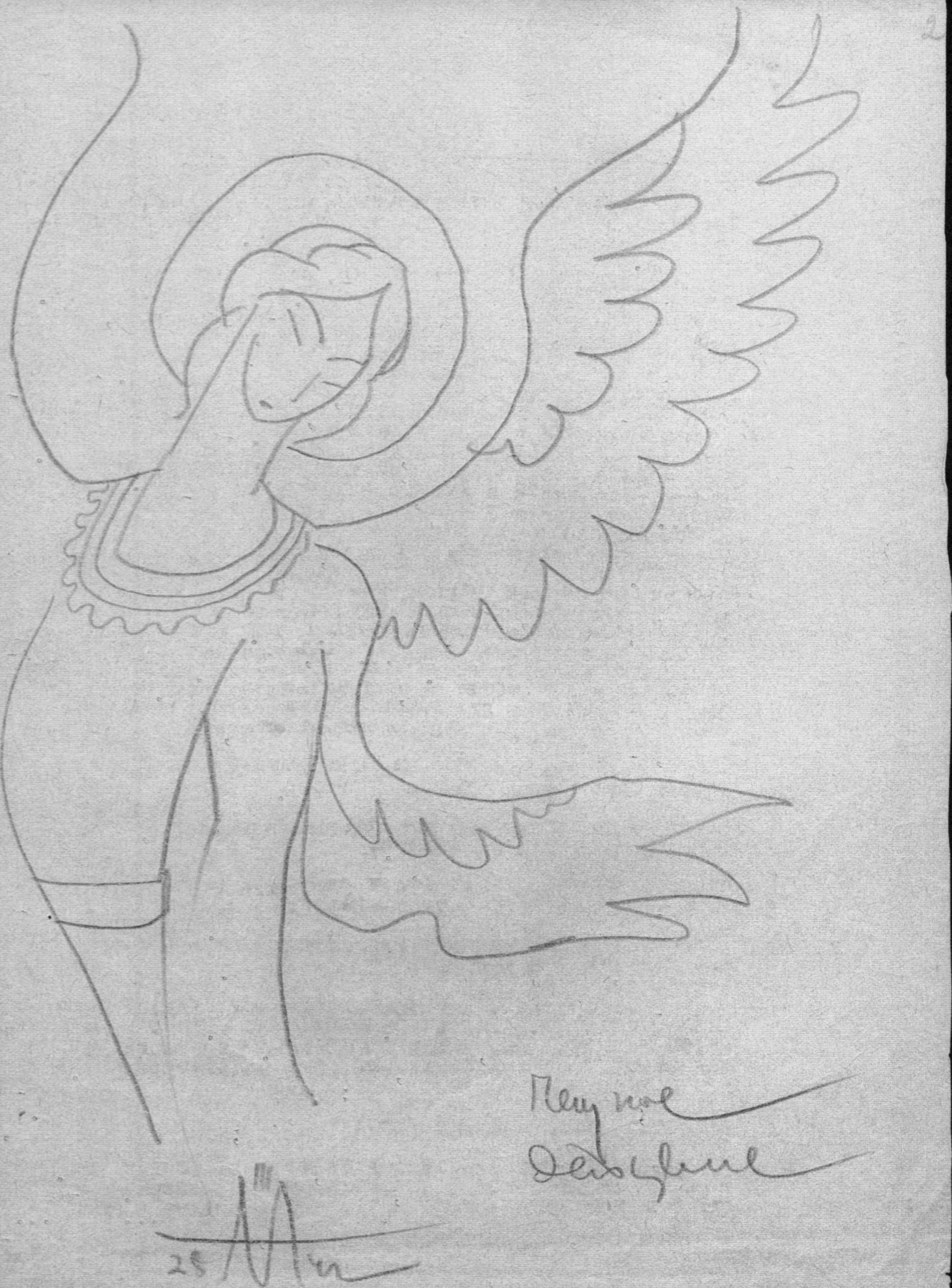

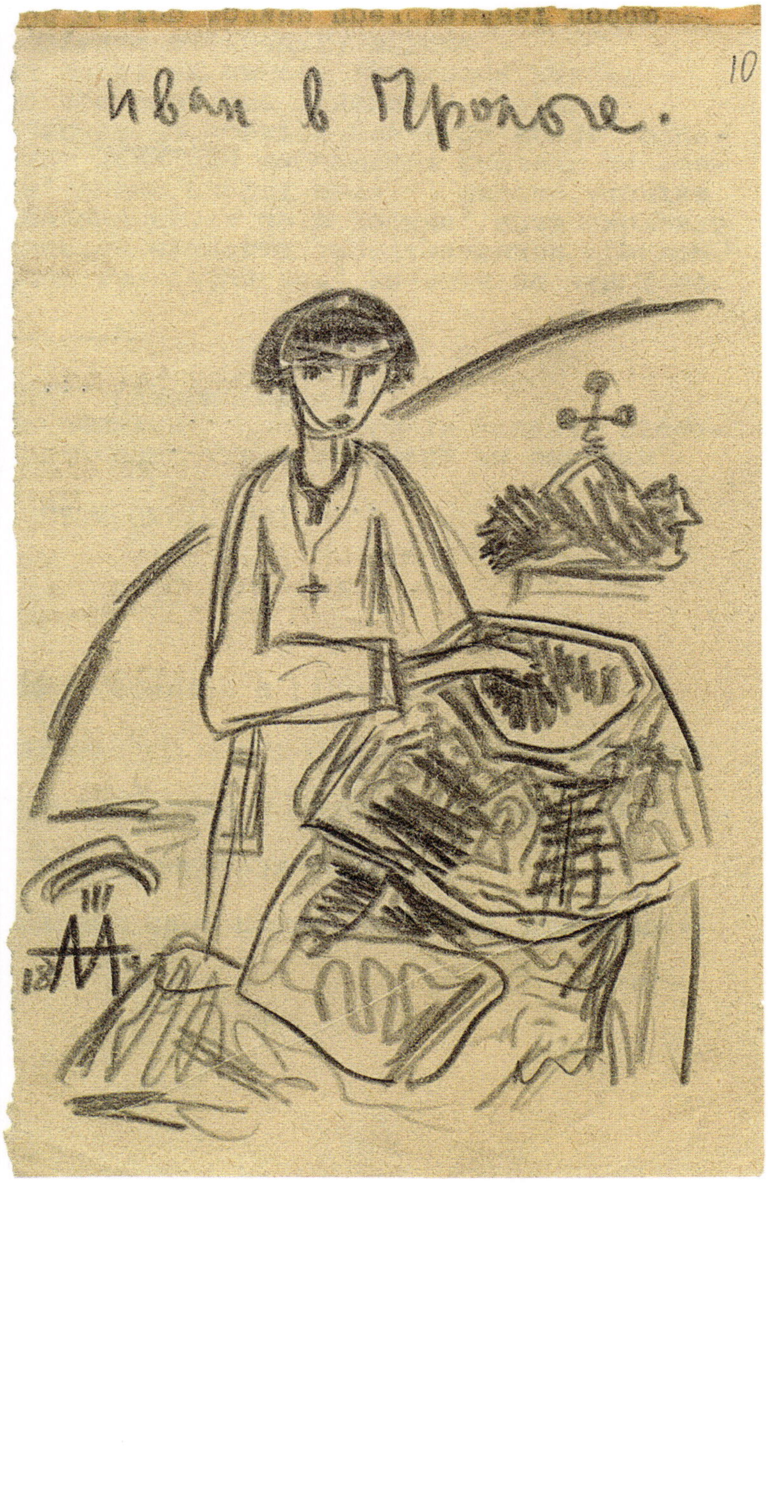
Иван в Прологе.
10

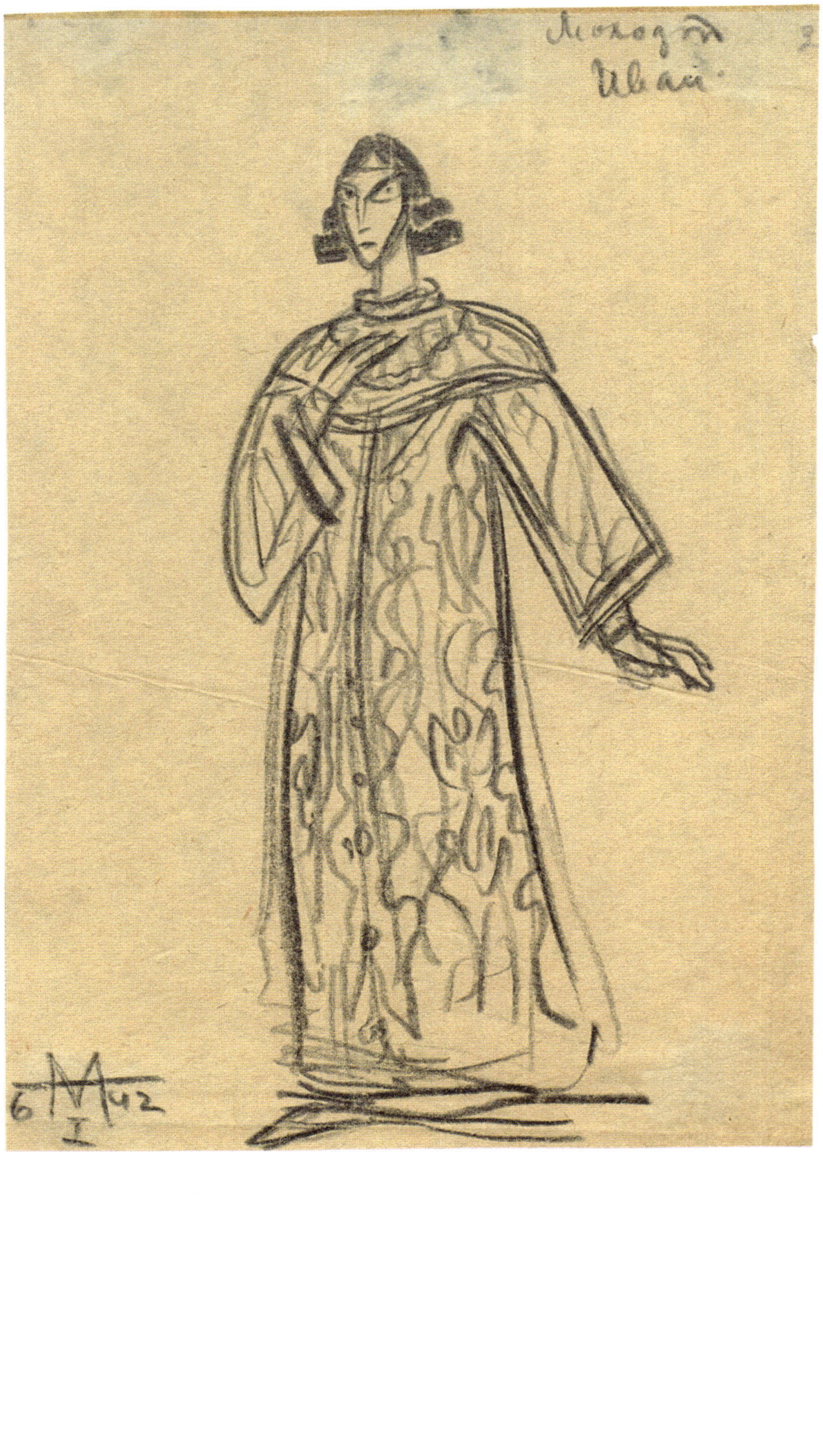
Молодой
Иван
6 I 42

—PREVIOUS

LEFT PAGE
Shots of *The Fiery Furnace* play from *Ivan the Terrible Part 2*

RIGHT PAGE
'Filipp's Angel-Savior from *The Fiery Furnace* play' (Almaty, 1942)

—OPPOSITE

LEFT
Ivan in Prologue (Almaty, 1942)

RIGHT
Young Ivan (Almaty, 1942)

—THIS PAGE

TOP LEFT
'Ivan's costume for the scene with Nepea, the ambassador to Queen Elizabeth of England' First part of the film (1942)
Text: For sending off Nepea. Black satin with scattered flowers (silver). Very dispersed.

TOP RIGHT
'Ivan in a fur coat and military armour' (1942)

BOTTOM LEFT
'Tsar (Ivan in monastic robe)' (1944)

BOTTOM RIGHT
'Ivan in the scene of repentance' (1942)
Text: To look from here, *en raccourci* (foreshortened)

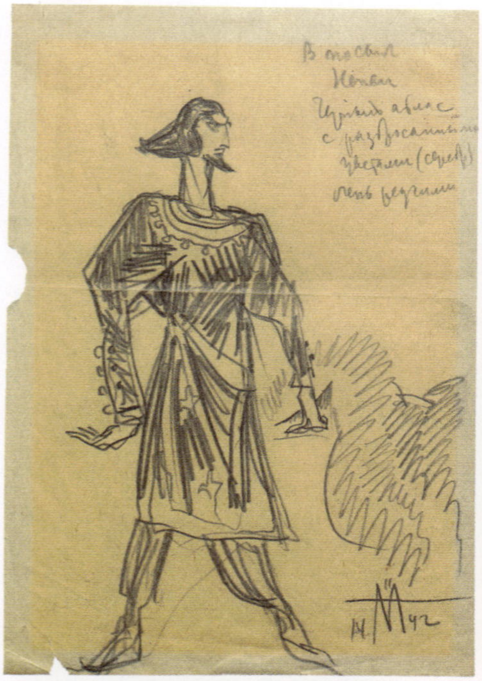

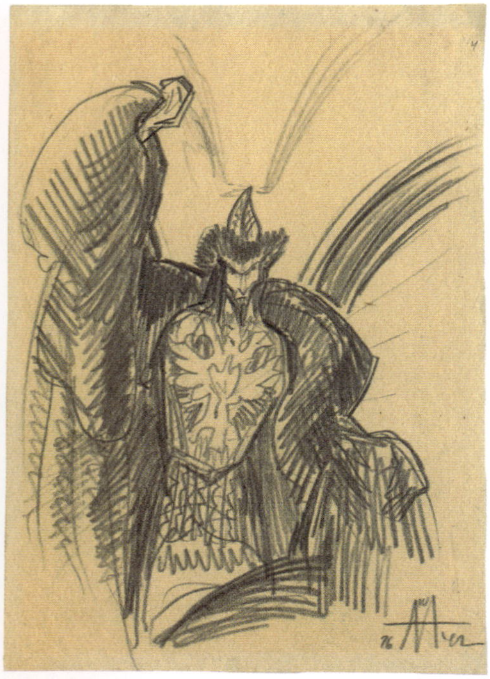

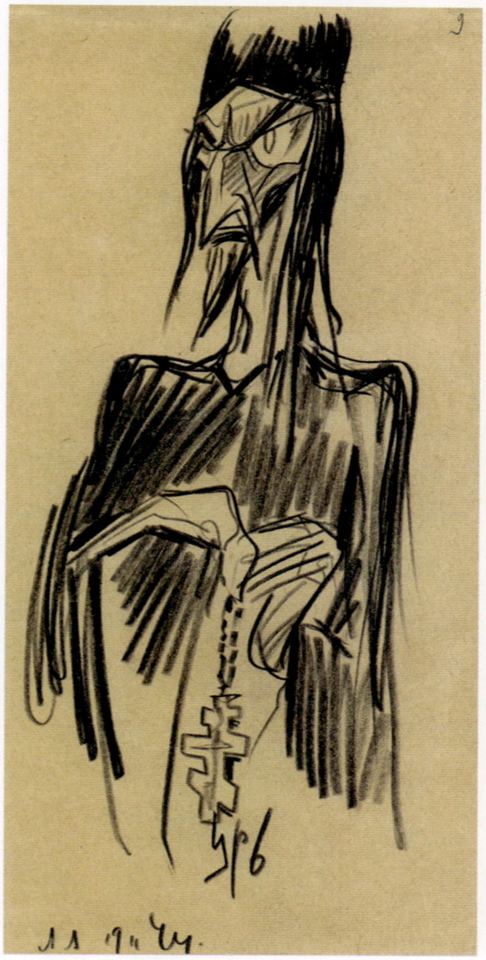

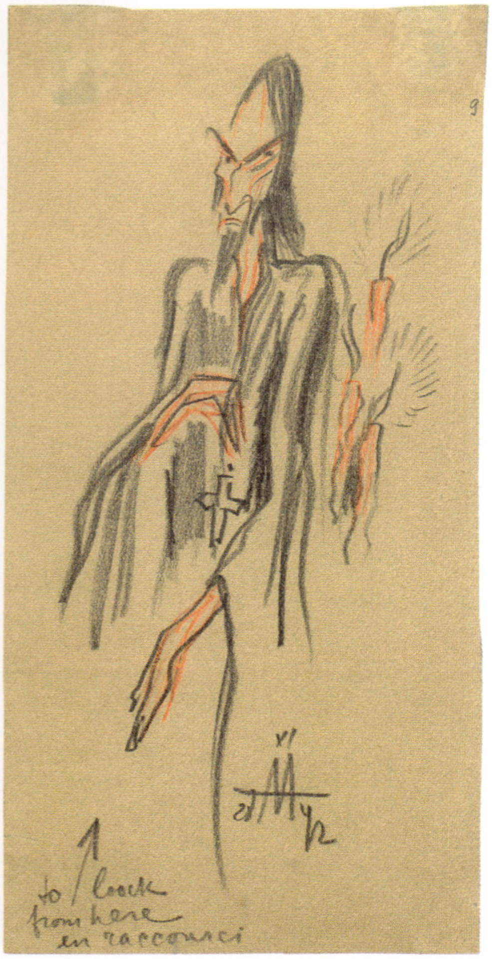

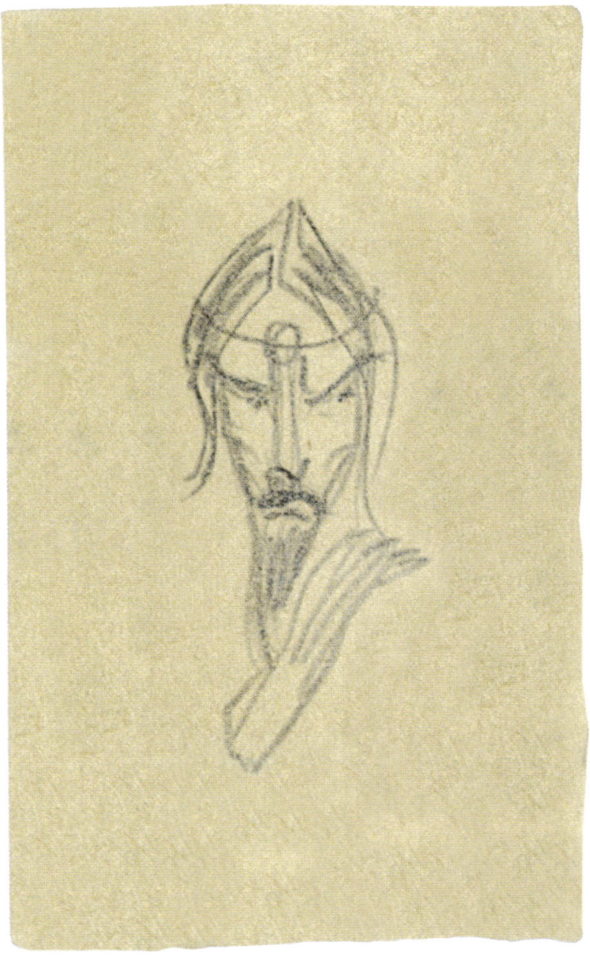

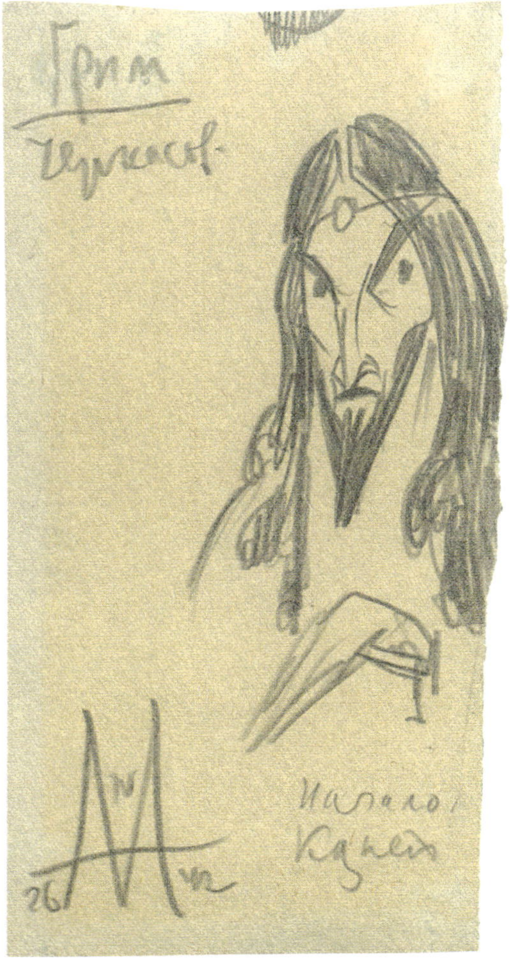

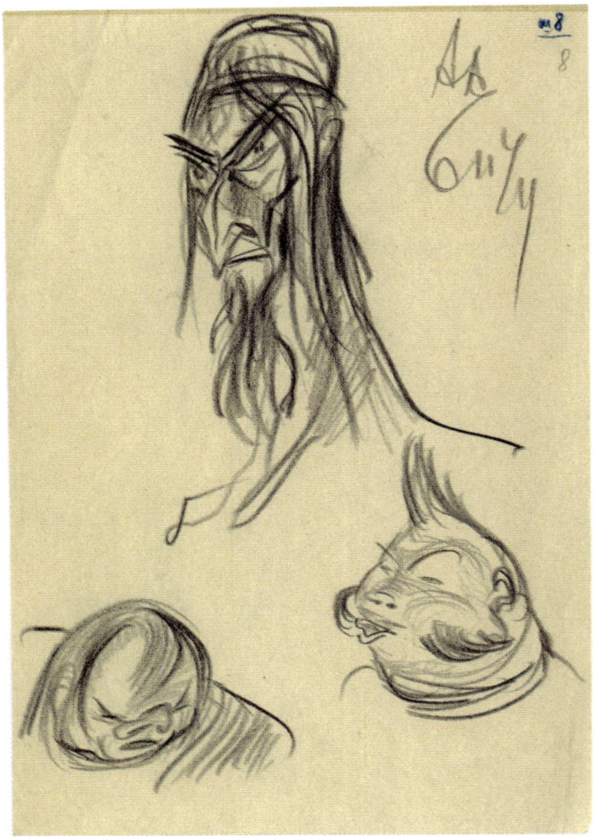

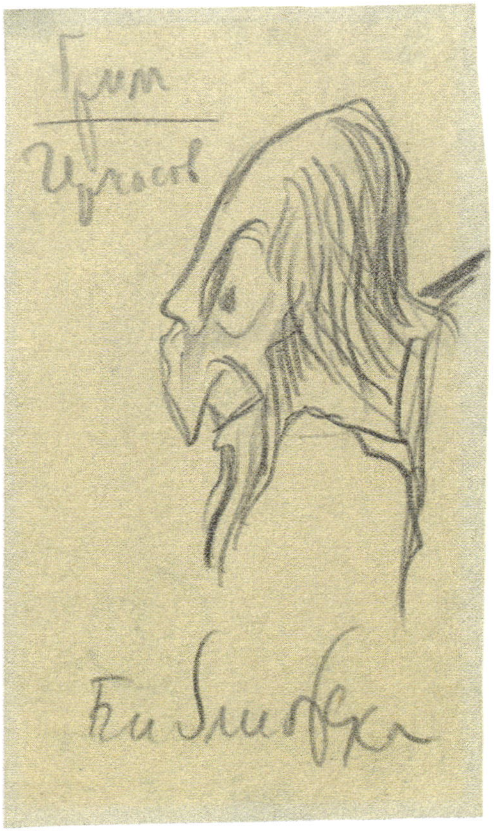

—THIS PAGE

TOP LEFT
'Ivan the warrior. Battle of Kazan'
First part of the film

TOP RIGHT
Greasepaint. Cherkasov.
The Beginning of the Executions
Second part of the film (1942)

BOTTOM LEFT
'Ivan and clerks'
Third part of the film (1944)

BOTTOM RIGHT
Greasepaint. Cherkasov. The Library
Third part of the film

—OPPOSITE
Tsar Ivan in a Soundless March
[against Novgorod] (1942)

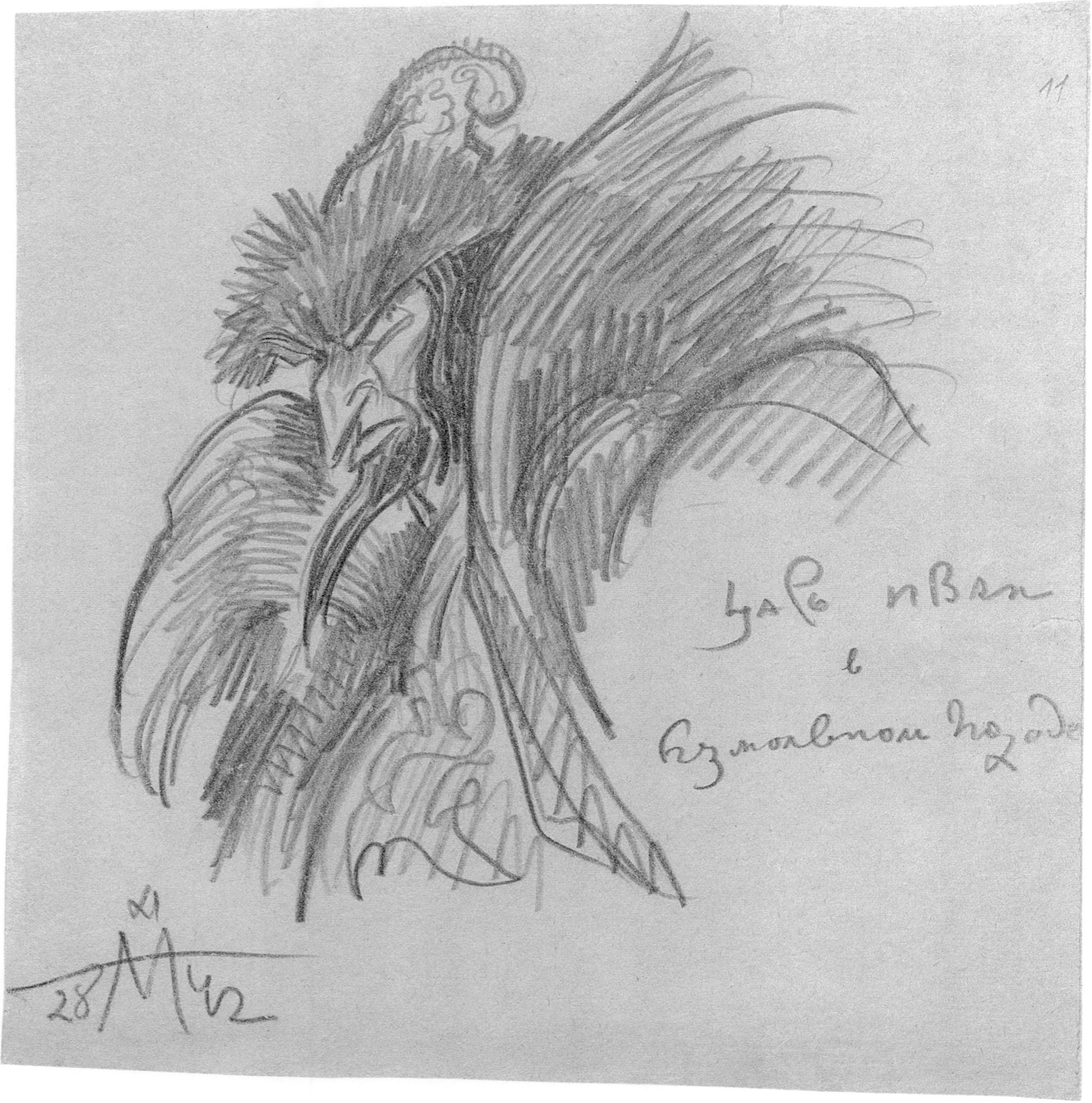

—THIS PAGE
Metropolitan Filipp (1942)

—OPPOSITE

TOP LEFT
Archbishop Pimen. The Scheme of Greasepaint for Pudovkin (1942)

TOP RIGHT
Aleksei Dikij. Basmanov-Father (1942)

BOTTOM
Greasepaint (Abrikosov). Metropolitan Filipp (1942)
Text: In the Golden Chamber. Filipp.
Tver Otroch monastery

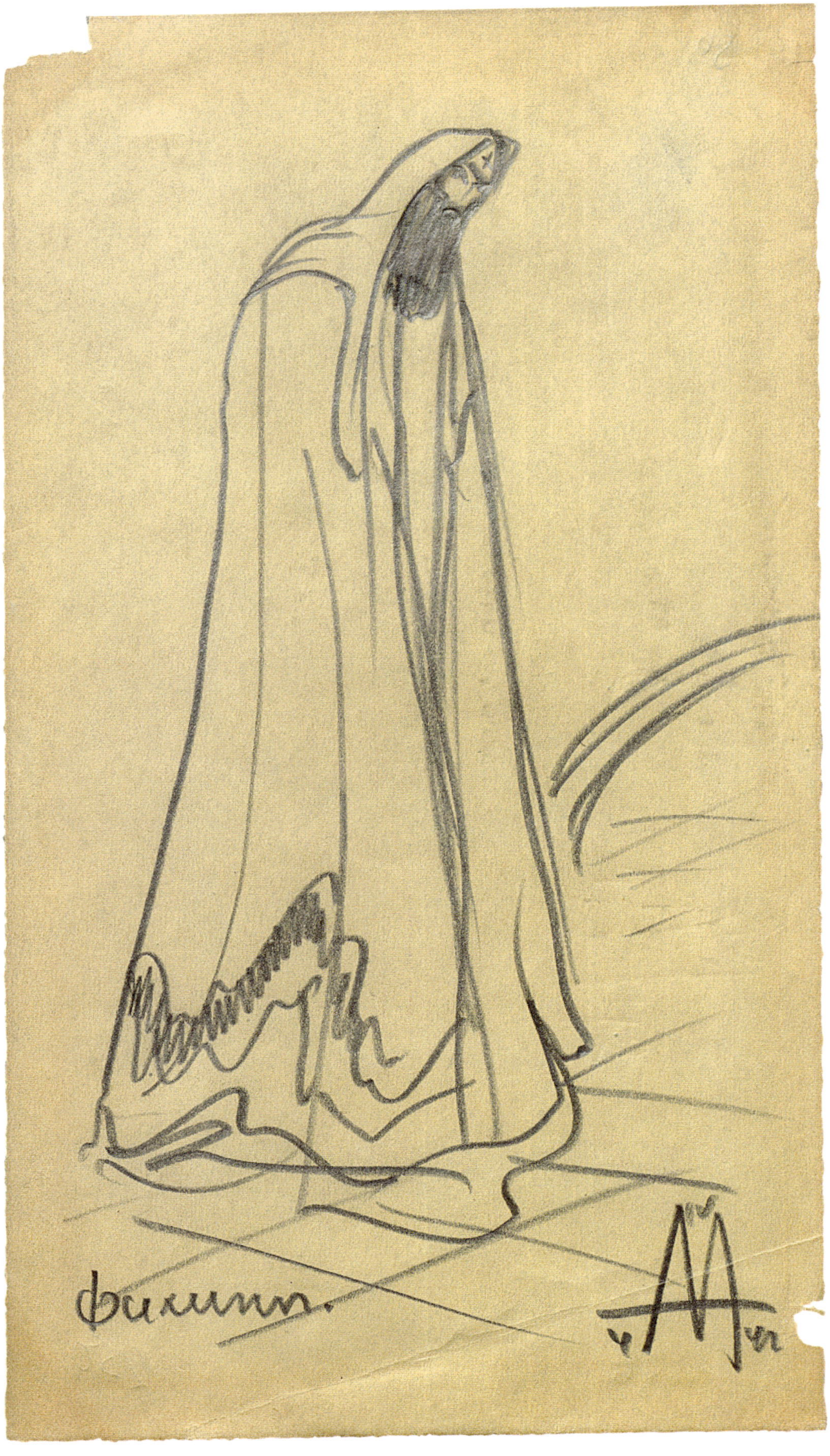

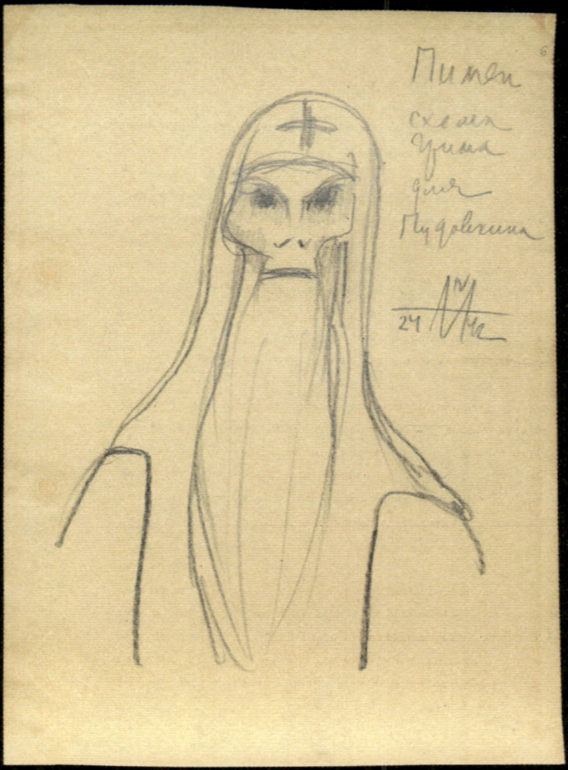
Пимен
24 IV 42

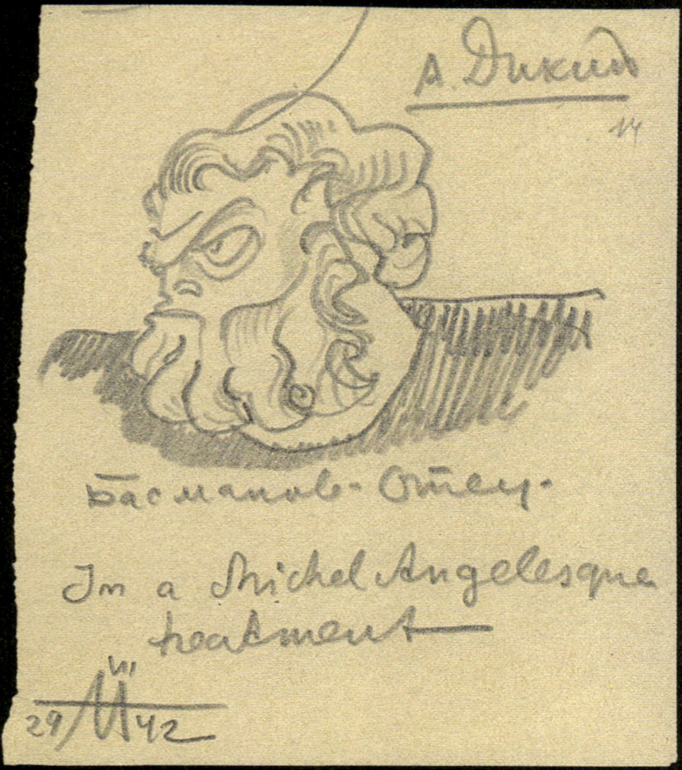
А. Дикий
Басманов-Отец
In a Michel Angelesque treatment
29 IV 42

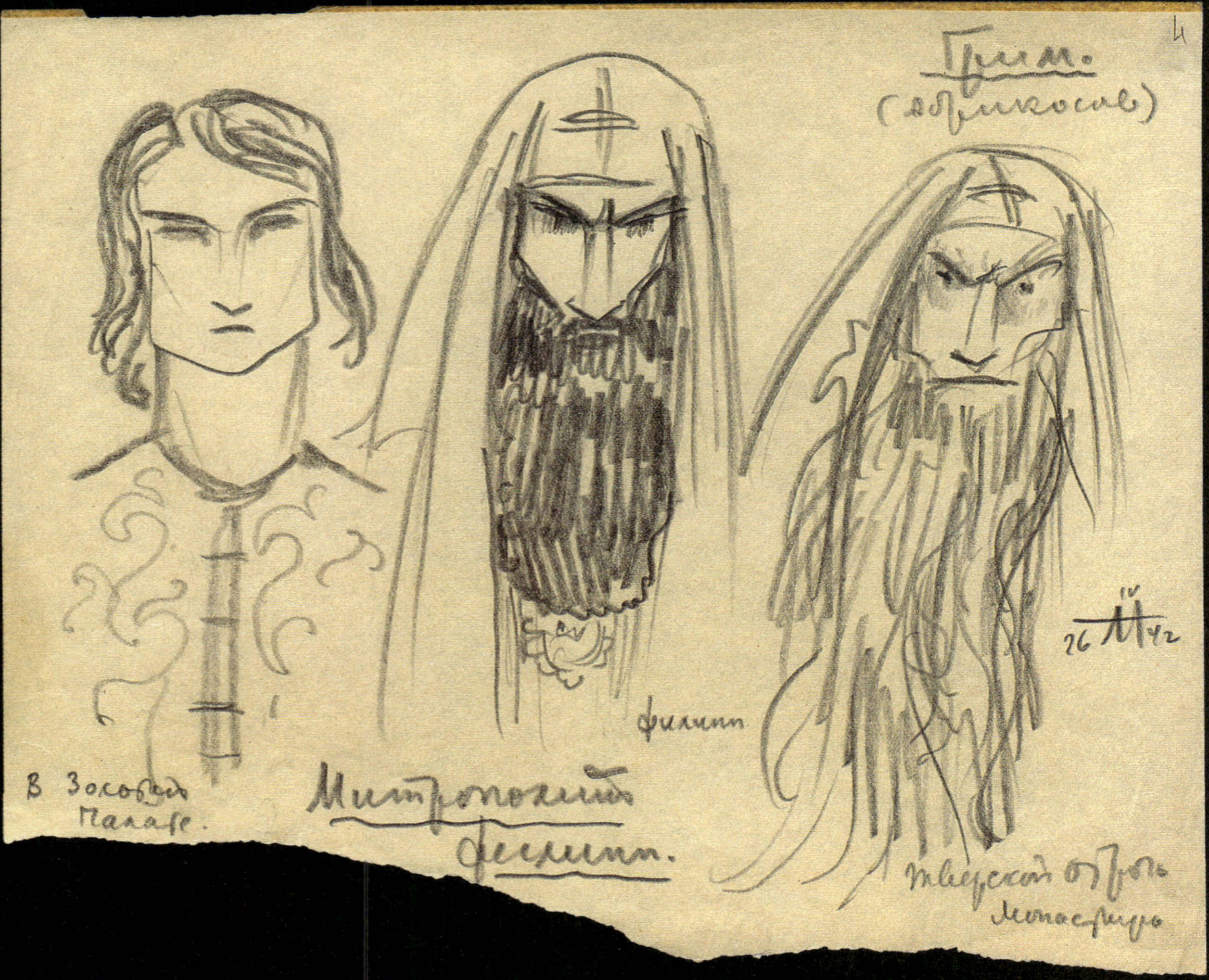
Грим.
(Абрикосов)
26 IV 42
Филипп
Митрополит Филипп.

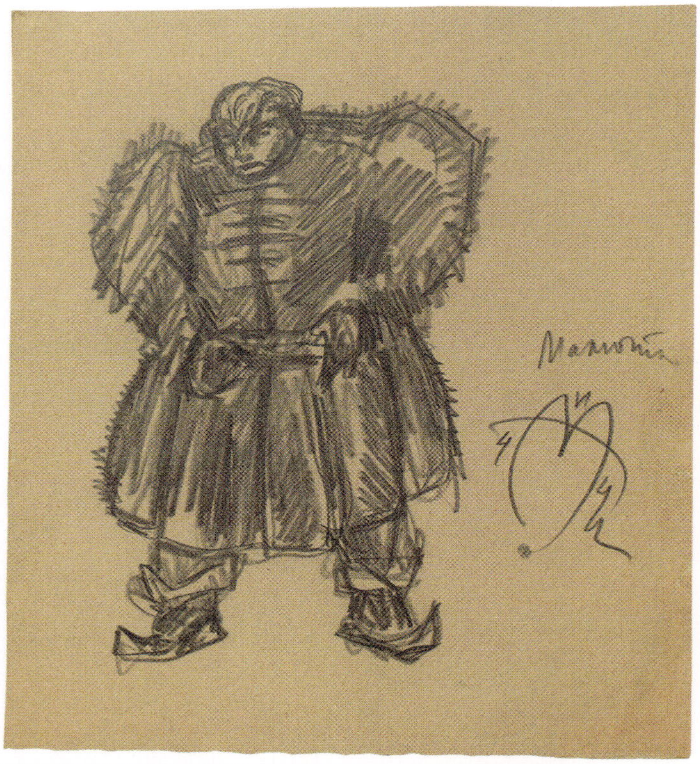

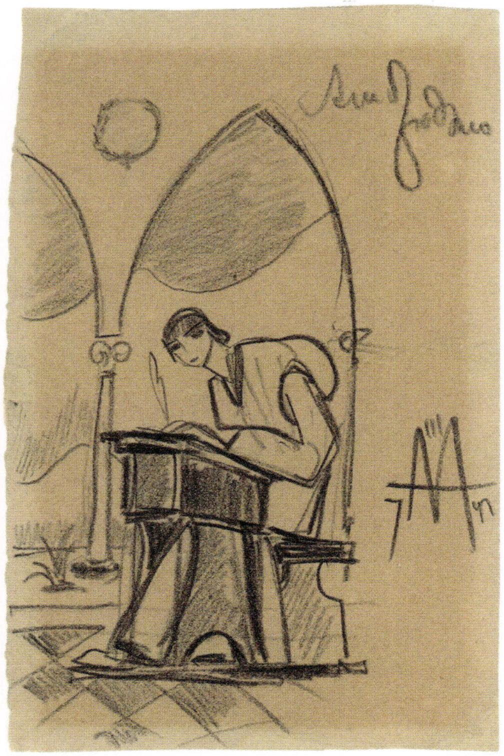

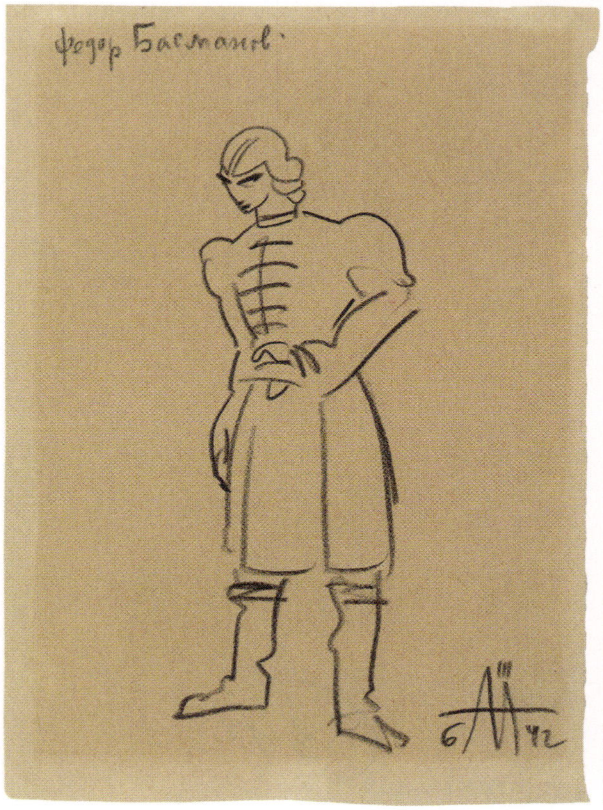

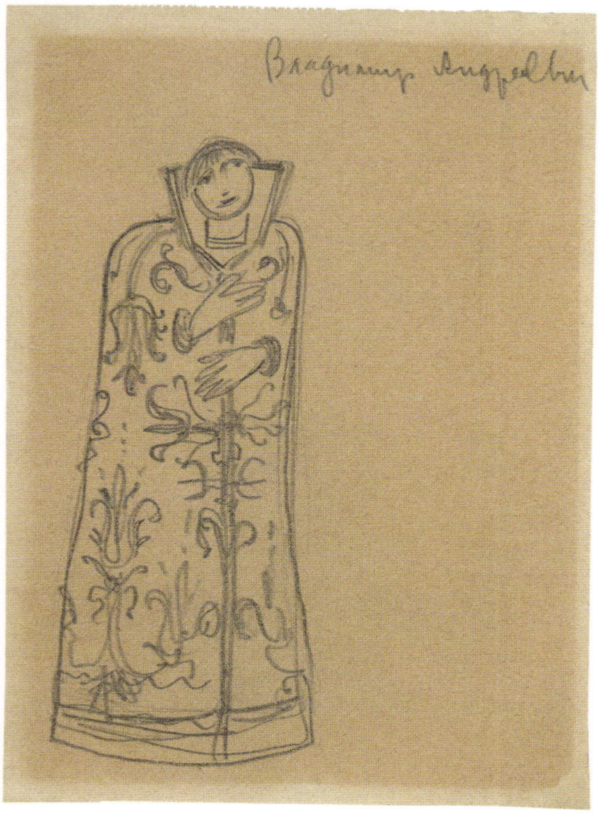

—THIS PAGE

TOP LEFT
Malyuta (Oprichnik Executioner) (1942)

TOP RIGHT
Ambroggio (Secretary of Prince Kurbsky in Exile) (1942)

BOTTOM LEFT
Feodor Basmanov (Oprichnik, Ivan's Favourite) (1942)

BOTTOM RIGHT
Vladimir Andreevich (Prince Staritsky, the Tsar's Cousin)

—OPPOSITE
Queen Elizabeth and Youth Blount (1942)
Text: ...Learn diplomacy, dear boy!

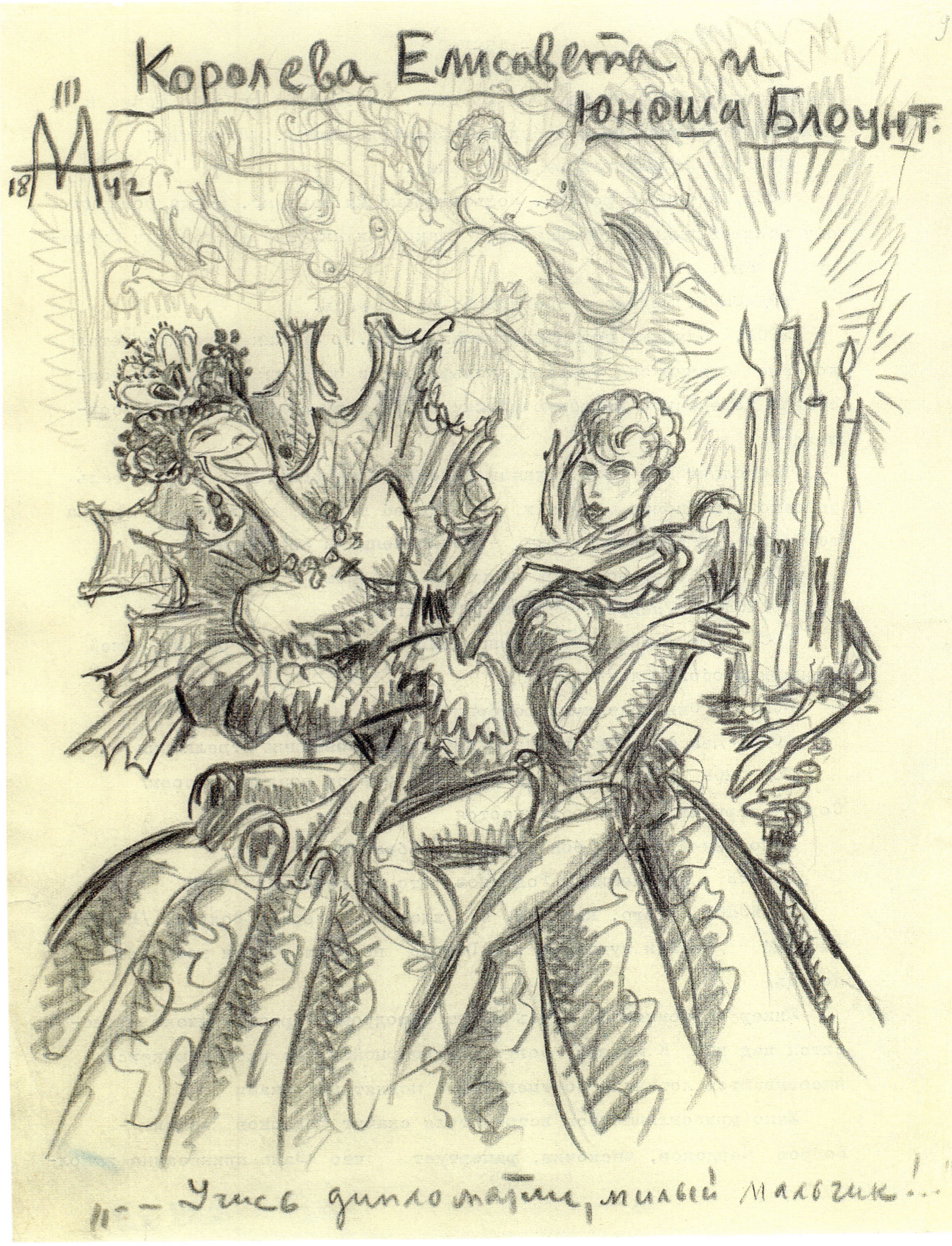

Королева Елисавета и юноша Блоунт.
18 III 42
"— Учись дипломатии, милый мальчик!..."

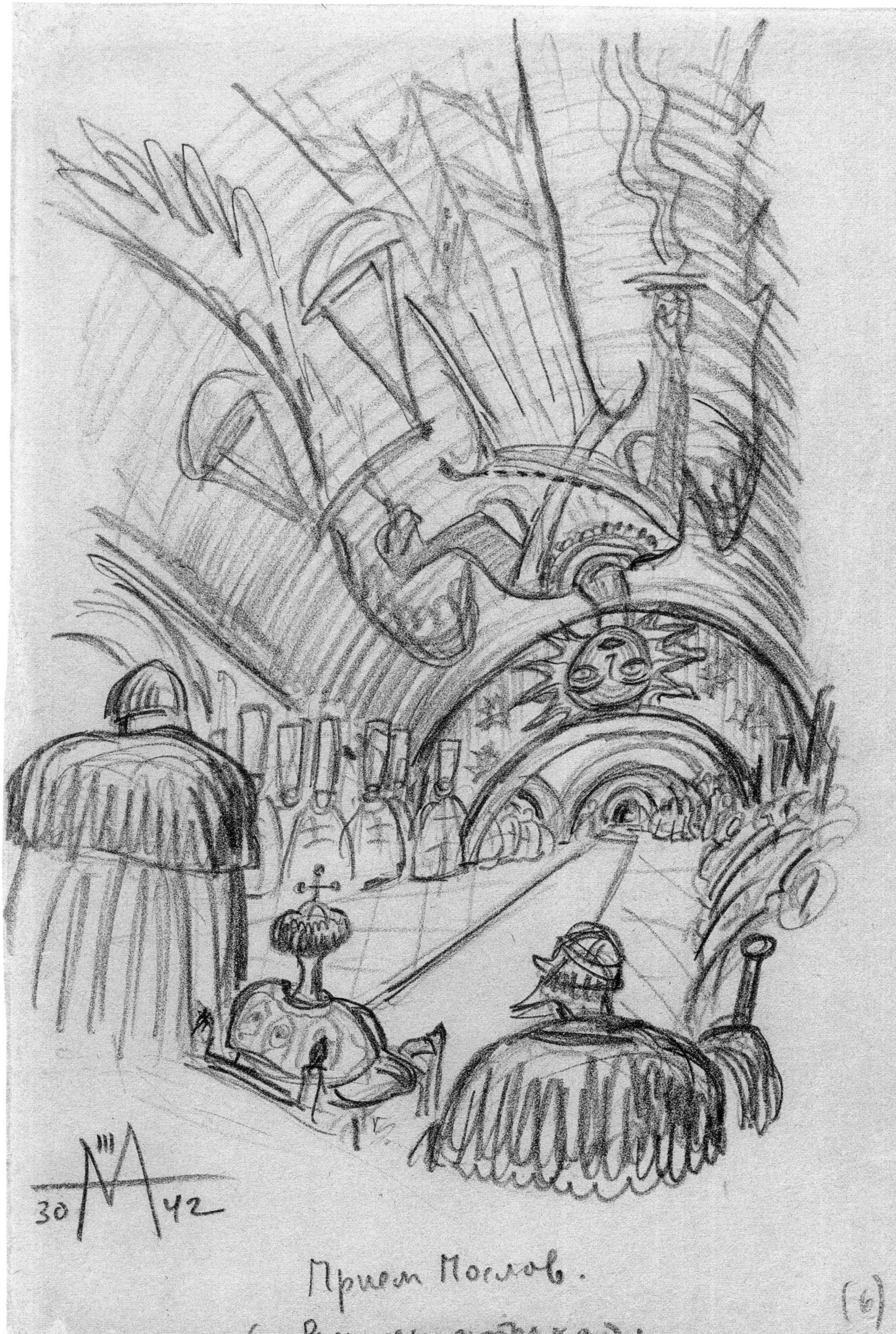
30 III 42
Прием Послов.
(Роспись потолка).
(6)

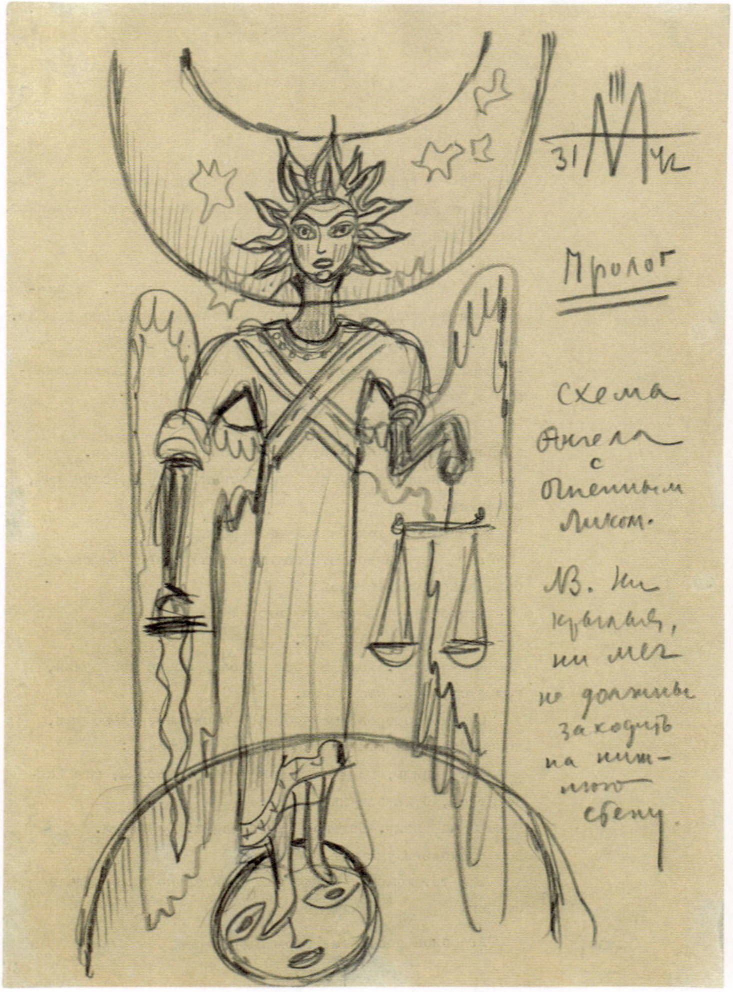

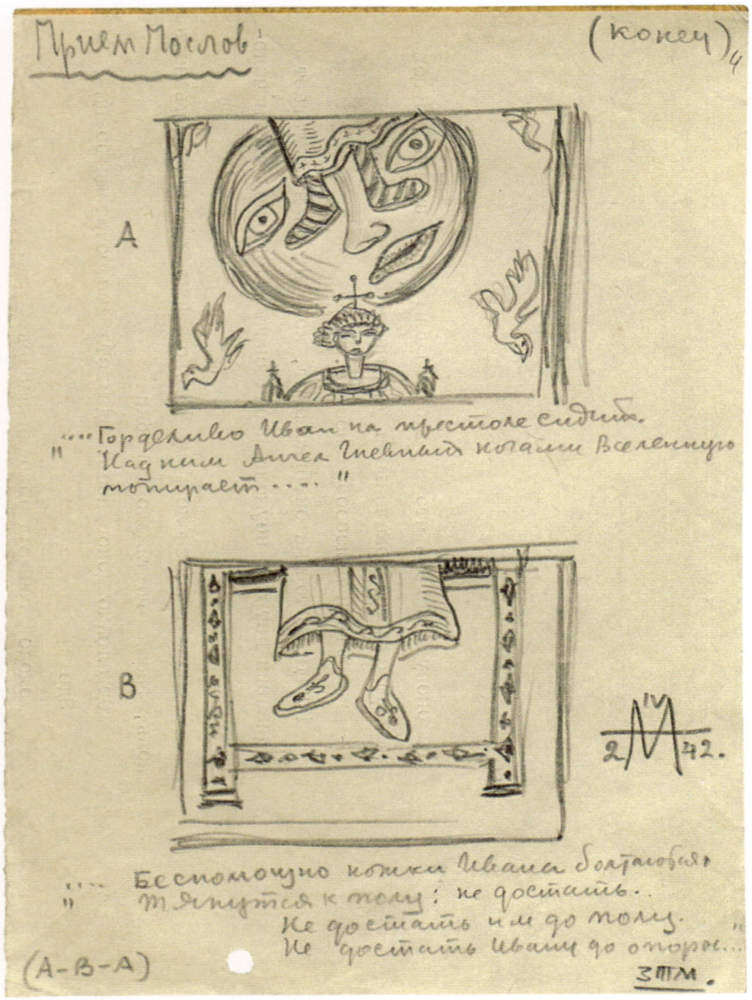

—OPPOSITE
Receiving Ambassadors (Fresco on Ceiling) (1942)

—THIS PAGE

LEFT
Prologue. The Scheme of the Angel with Fiery Face. NB Wings and sword must not reach the bottom of the wall (1942)

RIGHT
Receiving Ambassadors (The Ending) (1942)
Text: ...Proudly Ivan sits on the throne. Above him the Angel of Wrath – from the Apocalypse – tramples the Universe underfoot... The legs of Ivan dangle helplessly from the throne. They swing about: they cannot reach the floor. They cannot reach the support... (translated by Ivor Montagu and Herbert Marshall).

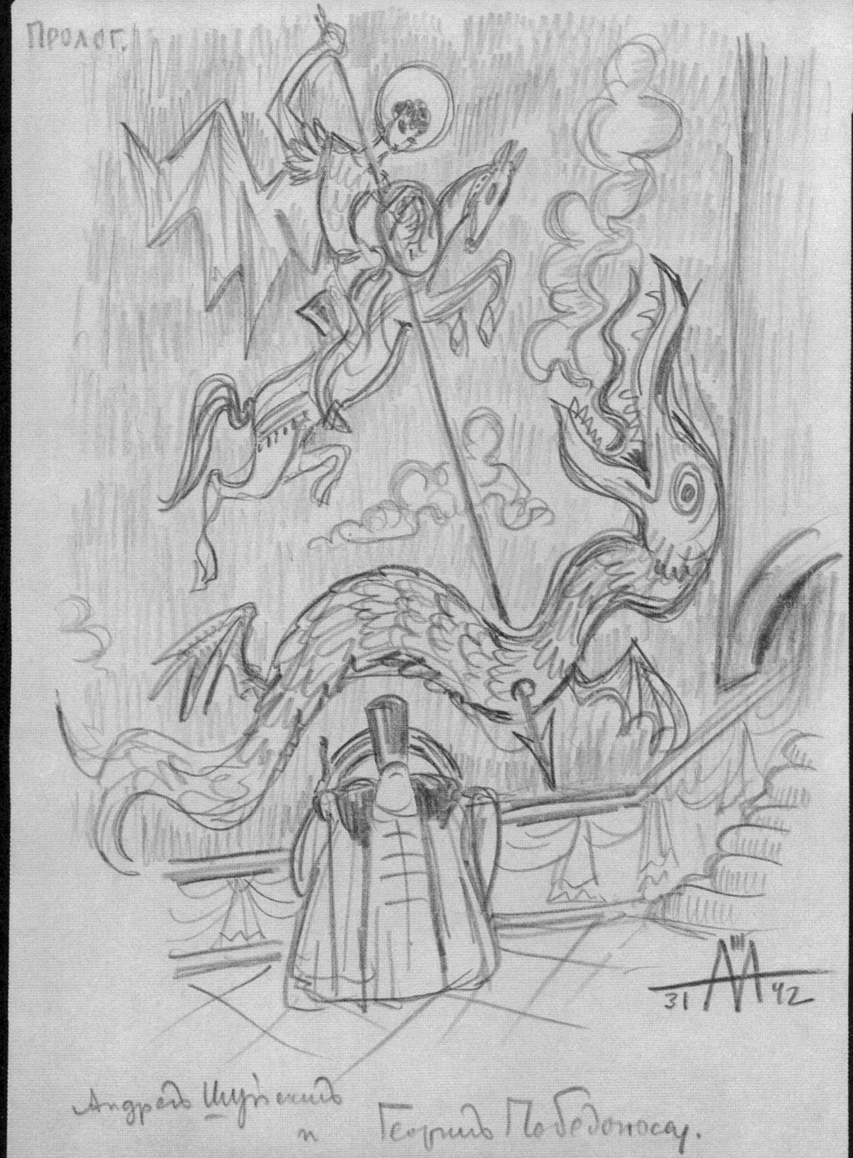
ПРОЛОГ.
Андрей Шуйский и Георгий Победоносец.

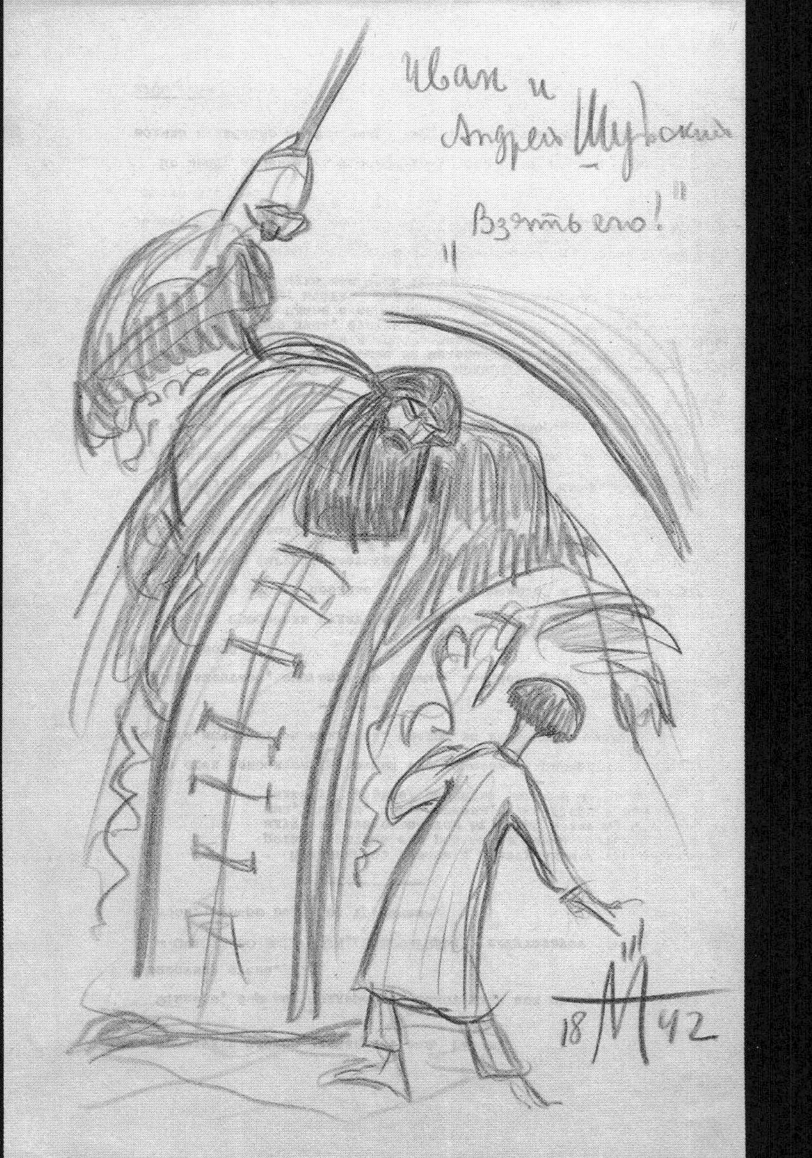
Иван и Андрей Шуйский
„Взять его!"

—OPPOSITE

LEFT
Prologue: Andrei Shuisky and St George (1942)

RIGHT
Ivan and Andrei Shuisky (1942)
Text: 'Take Him!'

—THIS PAGE
Kazan: Ivan and Kurbsky (1942)
Text: The collision on the earthworks

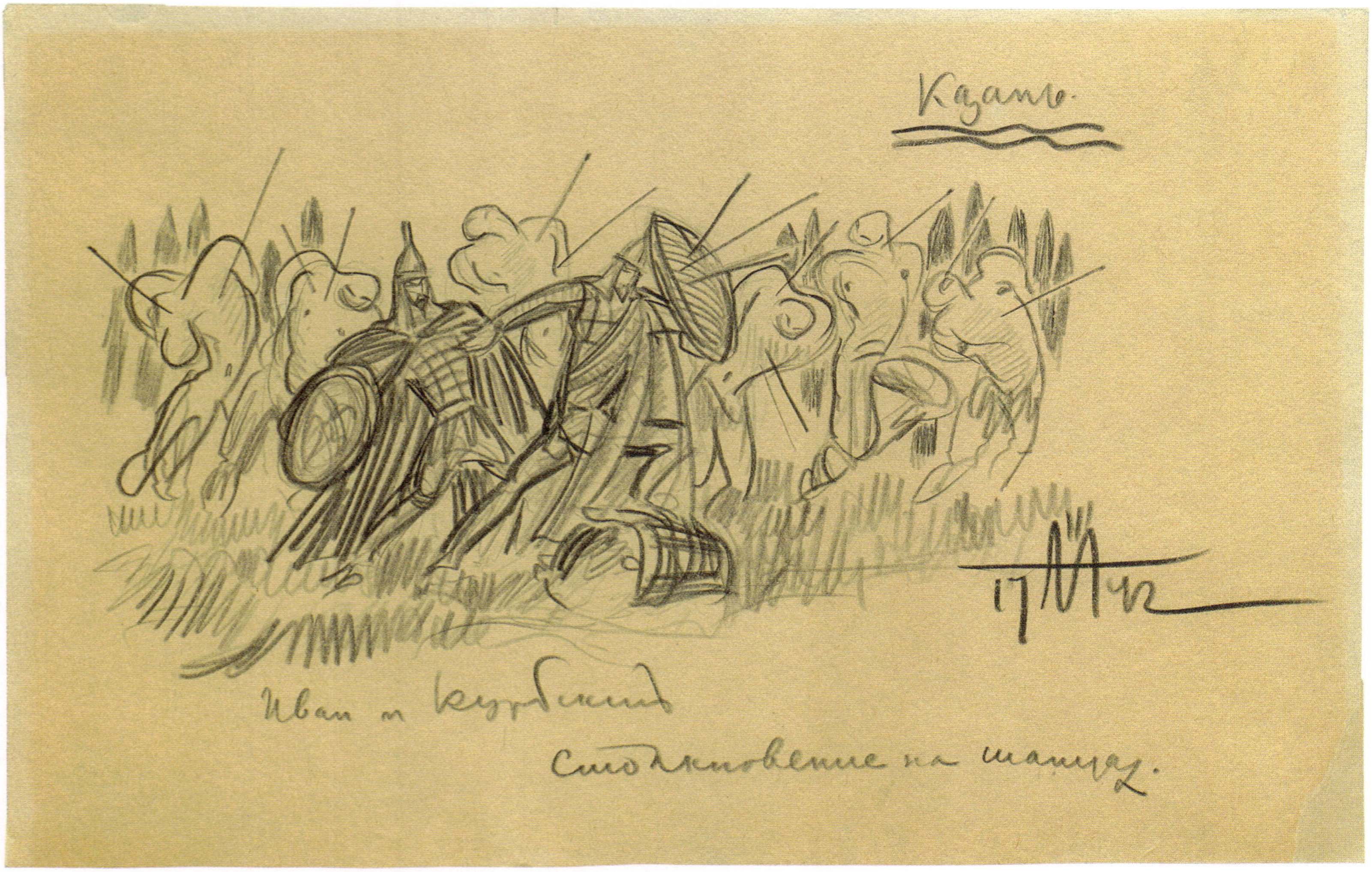

—THIS PAGE

LEFT

'Archbishop Pimen, Princess Euphrosina Staritsky and her son Vladimir in the procession with the cross' (1942)

RIGHT

Tsar Ivan in the Procession with the Cross to Aleksandrovskaya Sloboda (1942)

Text: 'Saddle the horses to gallop to Moscow….' NB But Ivan is not in a fur coat.

—OPPOSITE

Majolica Christ for the Chambers of Staritsky (1942)

Text: White with ochre and gold.

Cf. A. I. Nekrasov (*Old Russian Art*: Moscow, 1937), pp. 308–9.

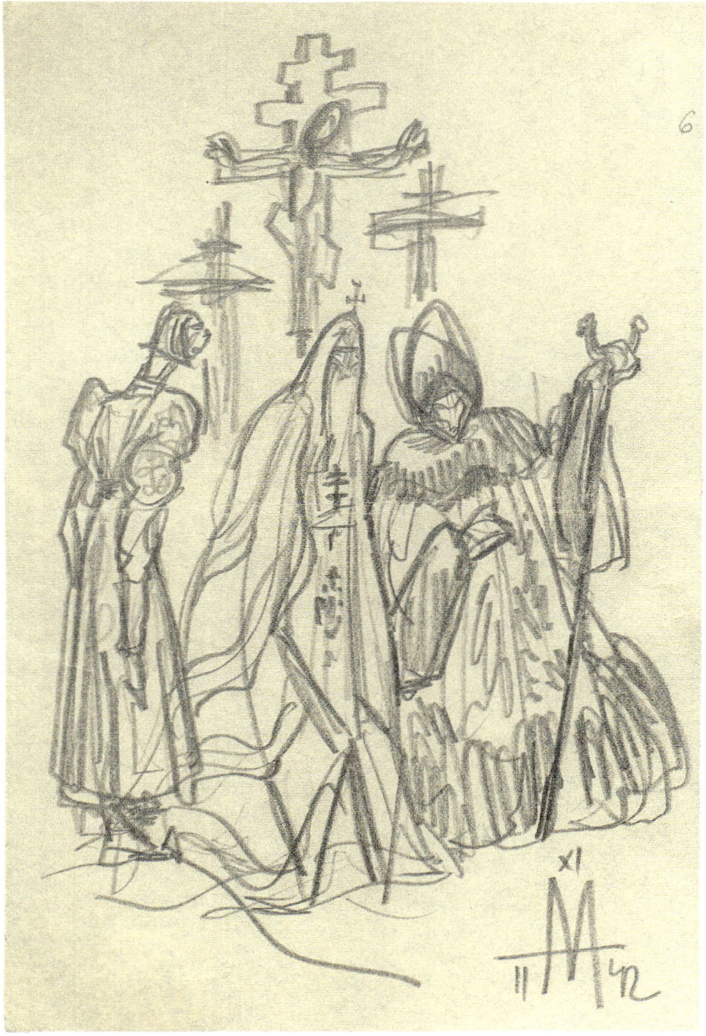

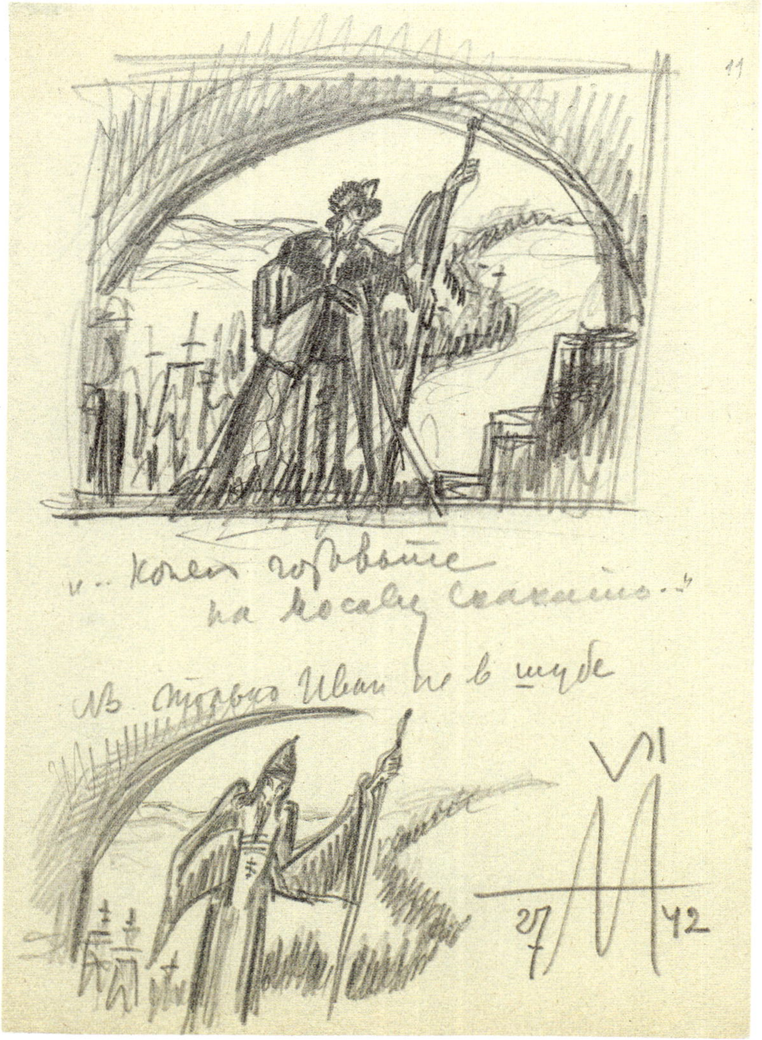

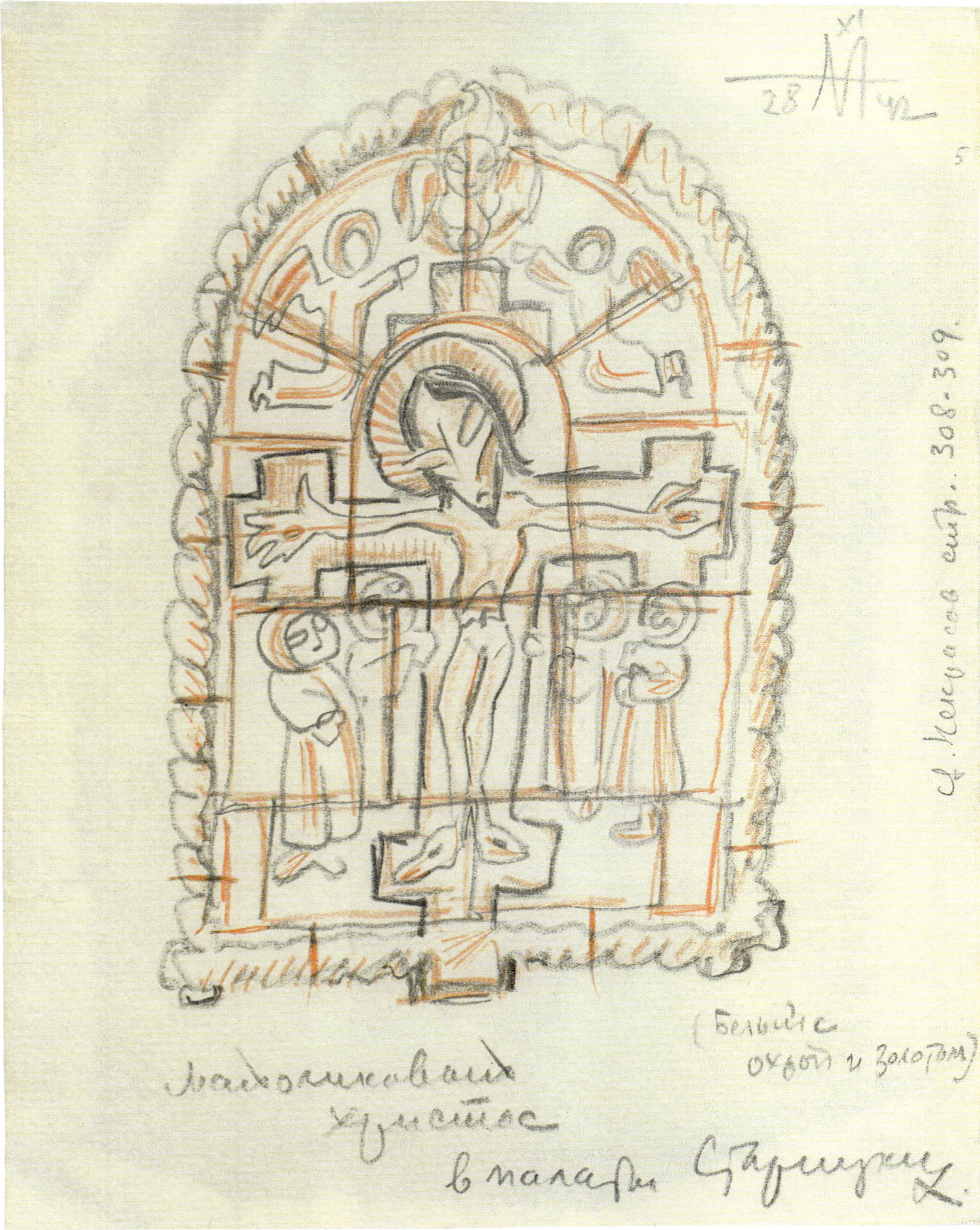
(Белый с охрой и золотом)
Христос

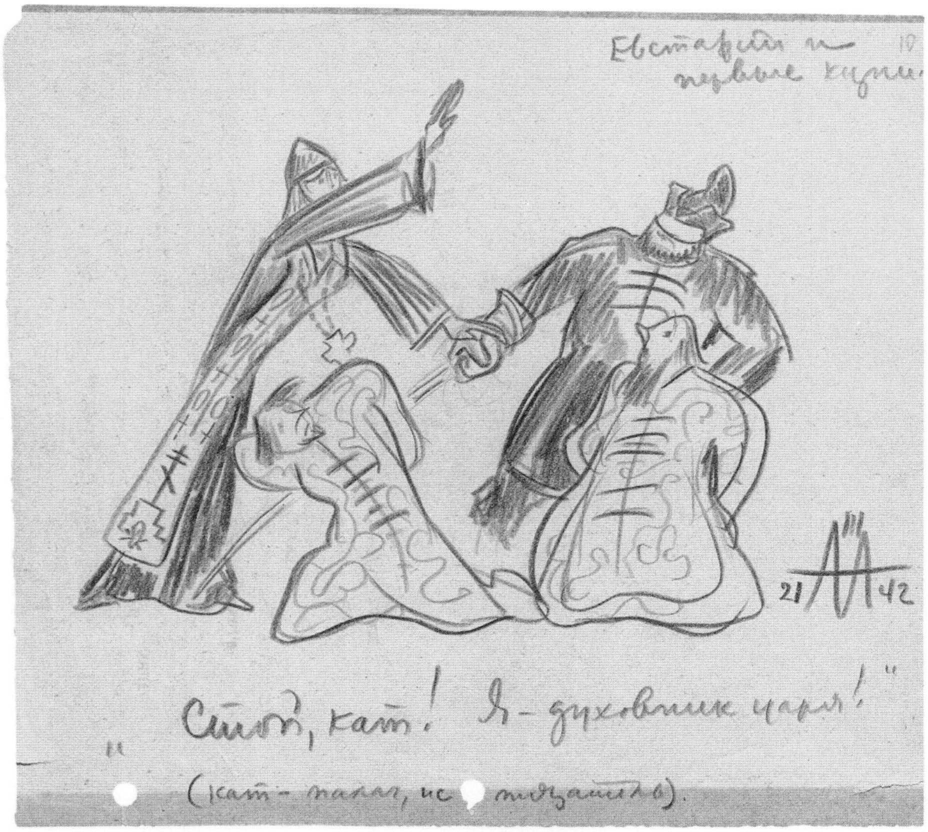

Евстафий и первые казни
21 III 42
«Стой, кат! Я — духовник царя!»
(кат — палач, не мучитель).

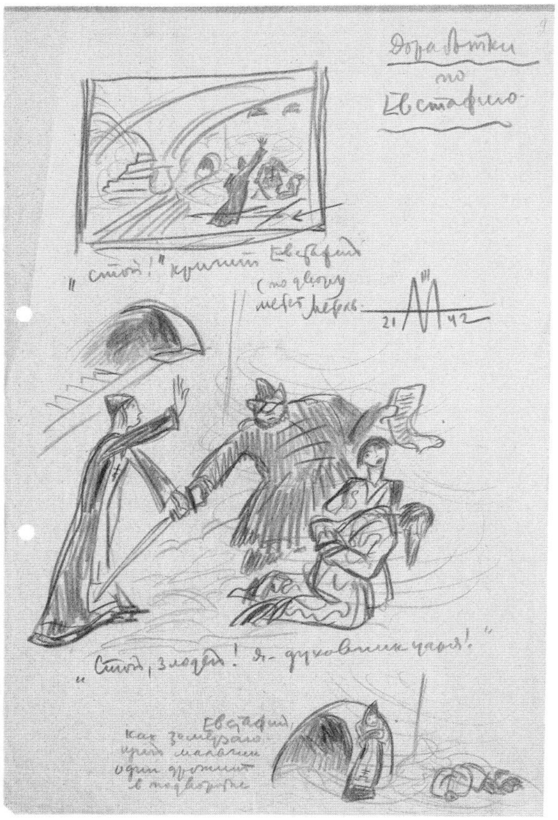

Доработки по Евстафию
«Стой!» кричит Евстафий
21 III 42
«Стой, злодей! Я — духовник царя!»
Евстафий

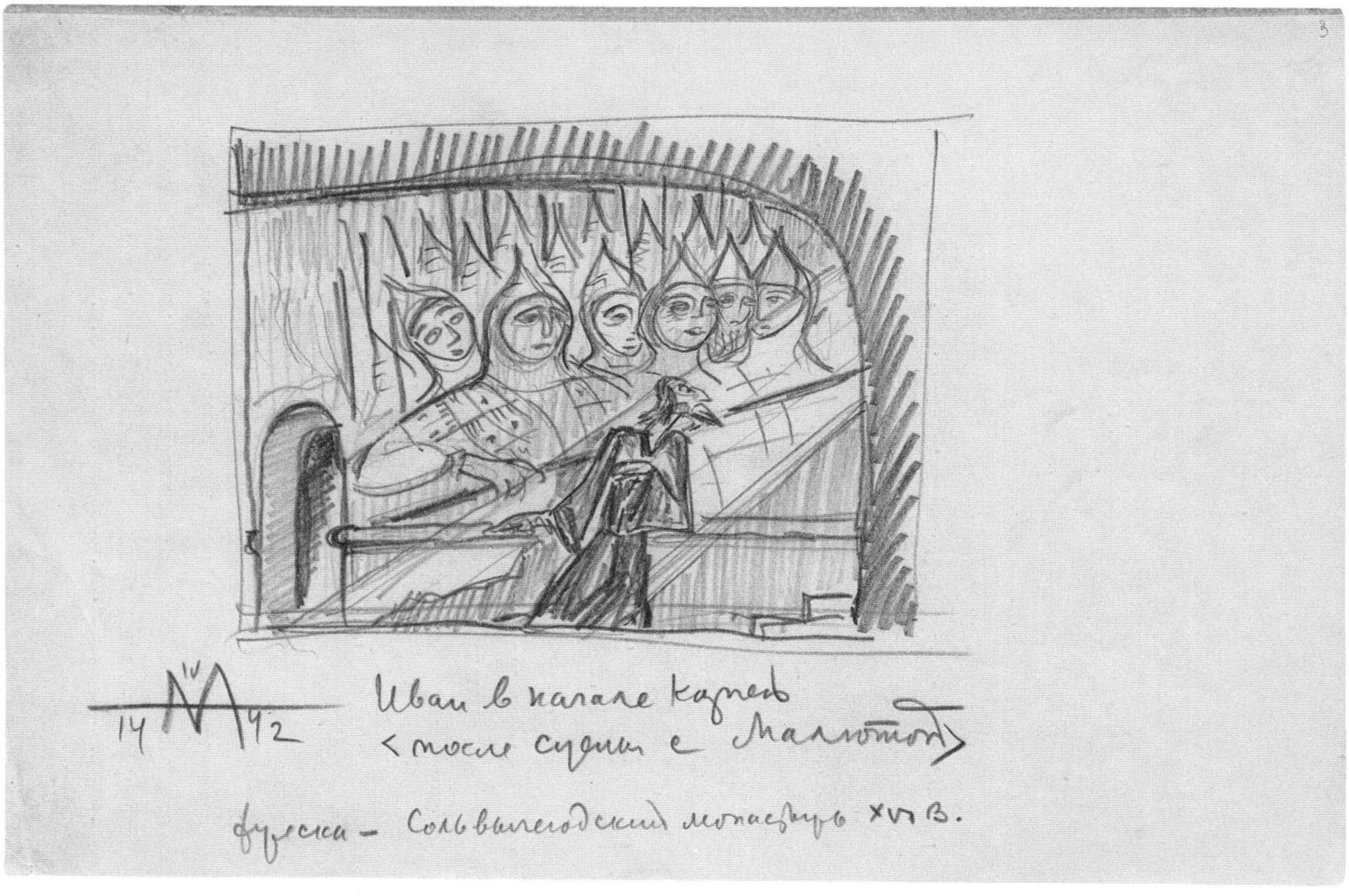

14 IV 42
Иван в начале казней
<после сцены с Малютой>
фреска — Сольвычегодский монастырь XVI в.

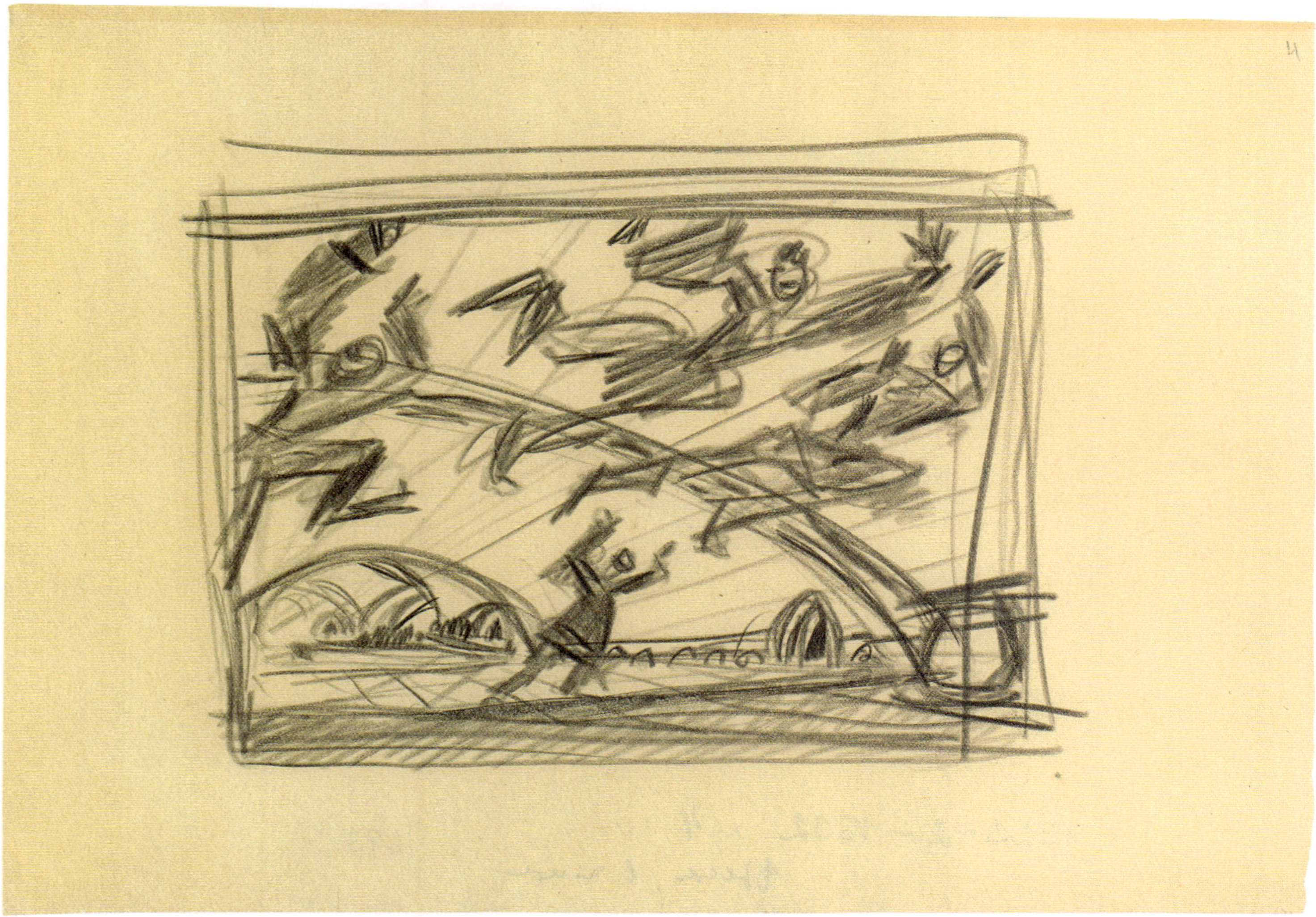

—OPPOSITE

TOP LEFT
Evstafy and the First Executions (1942)
Text: 'Stop, you butcher! I am the tsar's confessor!' (butcher – executioner, torturer).

TOP RIGHT
Perfection of Evstafy (1942)
Text: 'Stop!' cries Evstafy (a snowstorm sweeps across the yard). 'Stop, you villain! I am the tsar's confessor!'
Evstafy, like a freezing boy, shivers in the doorway.

BOTTOM
Ivan at the Beginning of the Executions (After the Scene with Malyuta). Fresco from the Monastery of Solvychegodsk XVI Century (1942)

—THIS PAGE
'The first executions. The version with shadows'

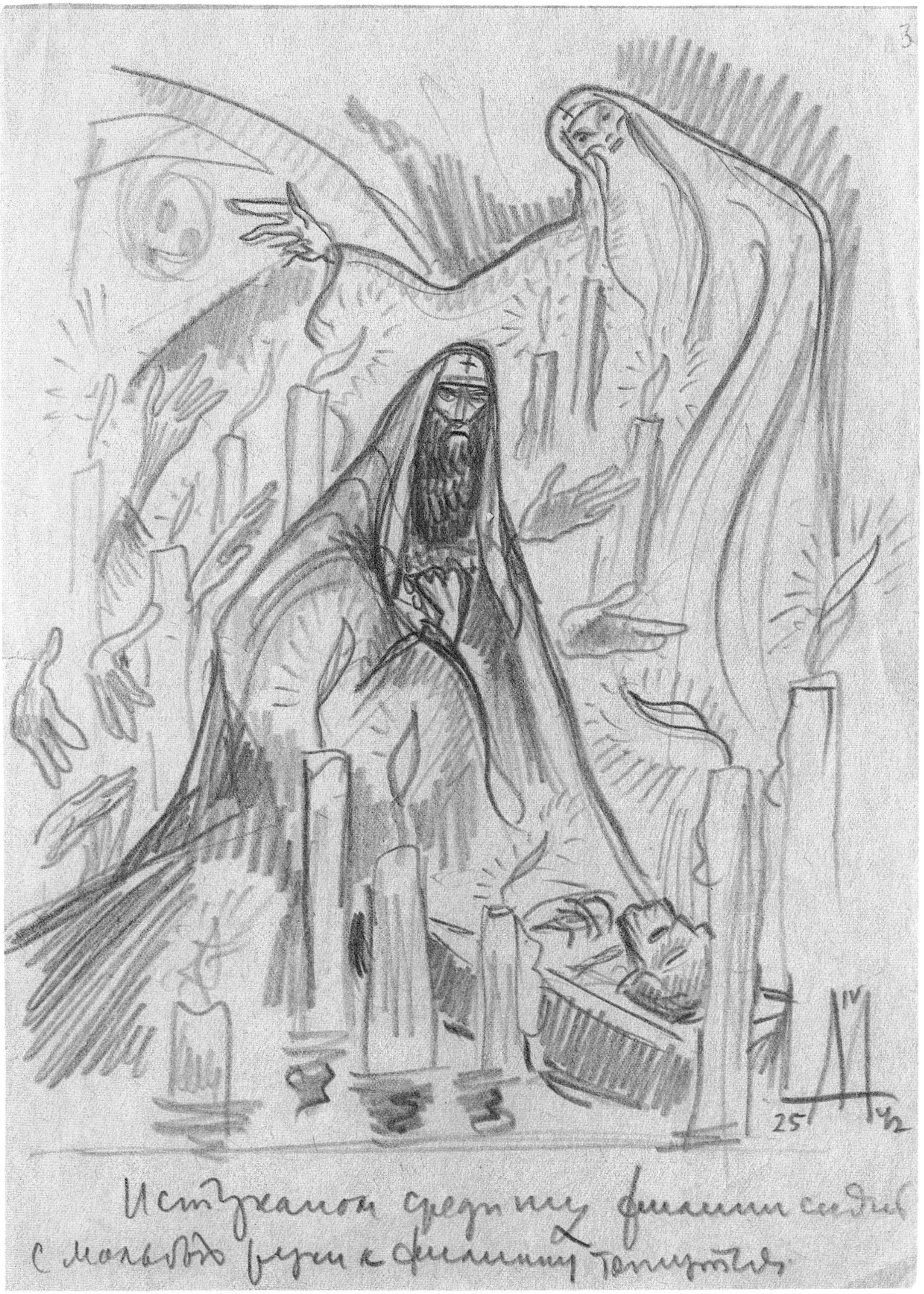

—OPPOSITE

'Metropolitan Filipp and Archbishop Pimen in the crypt' (1942)

Text: Filipp sits like a stone statue. The hands are stretched out imploringly to Filipp.

—THIS PAGE

LEFT

'*The Fiery Furnace* play in Uspensky Cathedral' (1942)

Text: 'Repent, Ivan, before the last hour has passed!'

RIGHT

'The Staritskaya group in the cathedral during *The Fiery Furnace* play' (1942)

Text: 'Mummy! Is that the terrible tsar of the heathens?!'

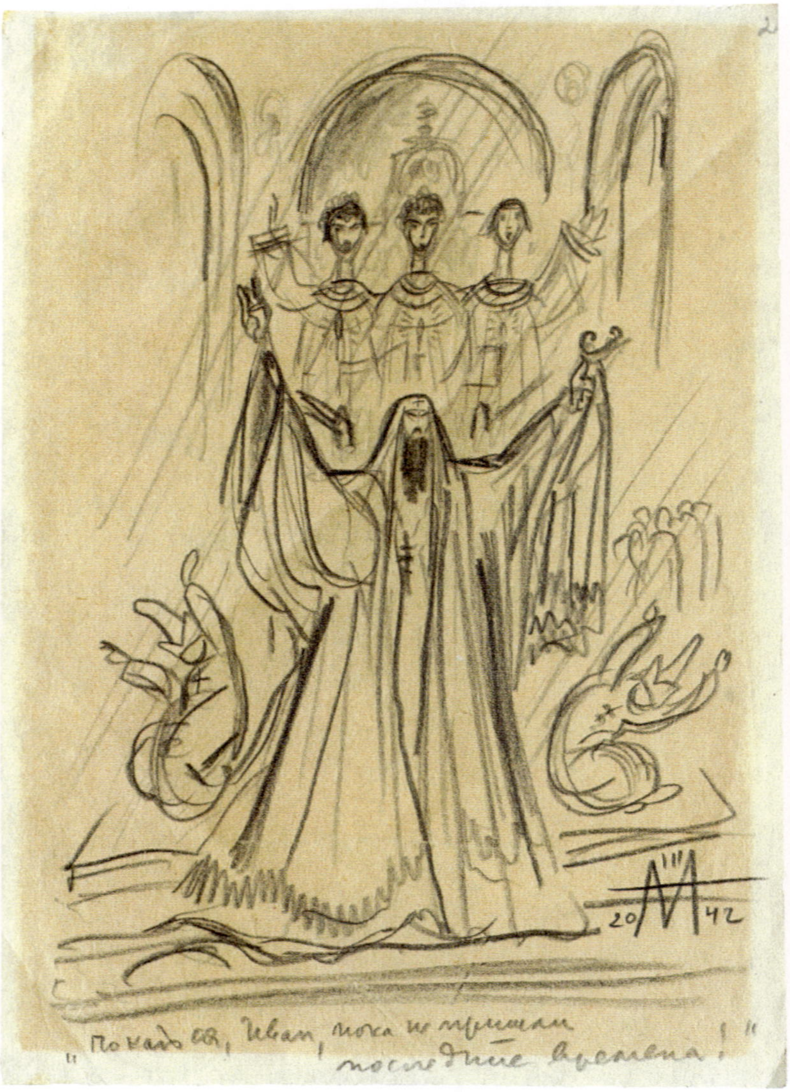

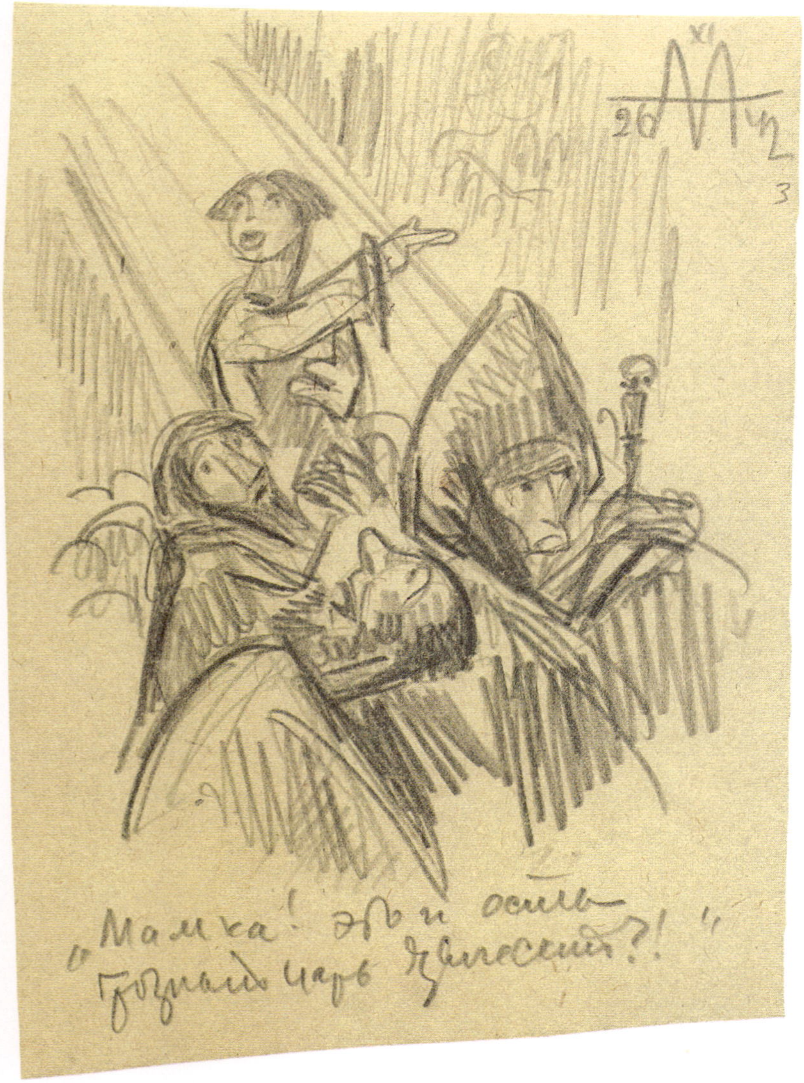

RIGHT

Why Vladimir Spilled the Beans (1942)

Text: The complete analogy of the placement and play (playing with Vladimir Andreyevich's hair). Euphrosina's lullaby about the tsar of the boyars. The conversation with Ivan at the feast in Aleksandrova Sloboda. NB Vladimir is, of course, more stupid and more loutish.

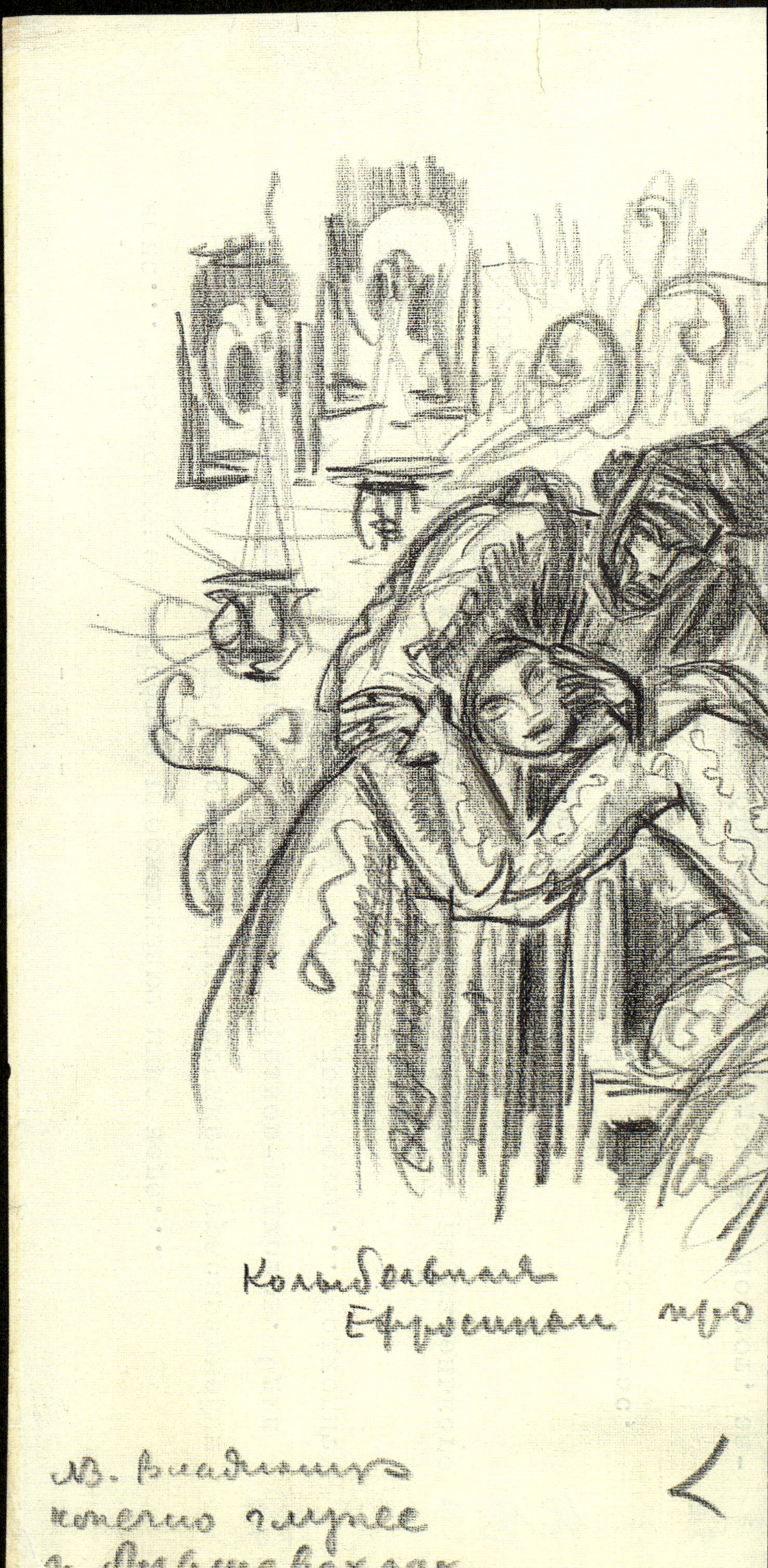

Порыв апатии (игра с волосами В.Л.)
разочарования
и игры.

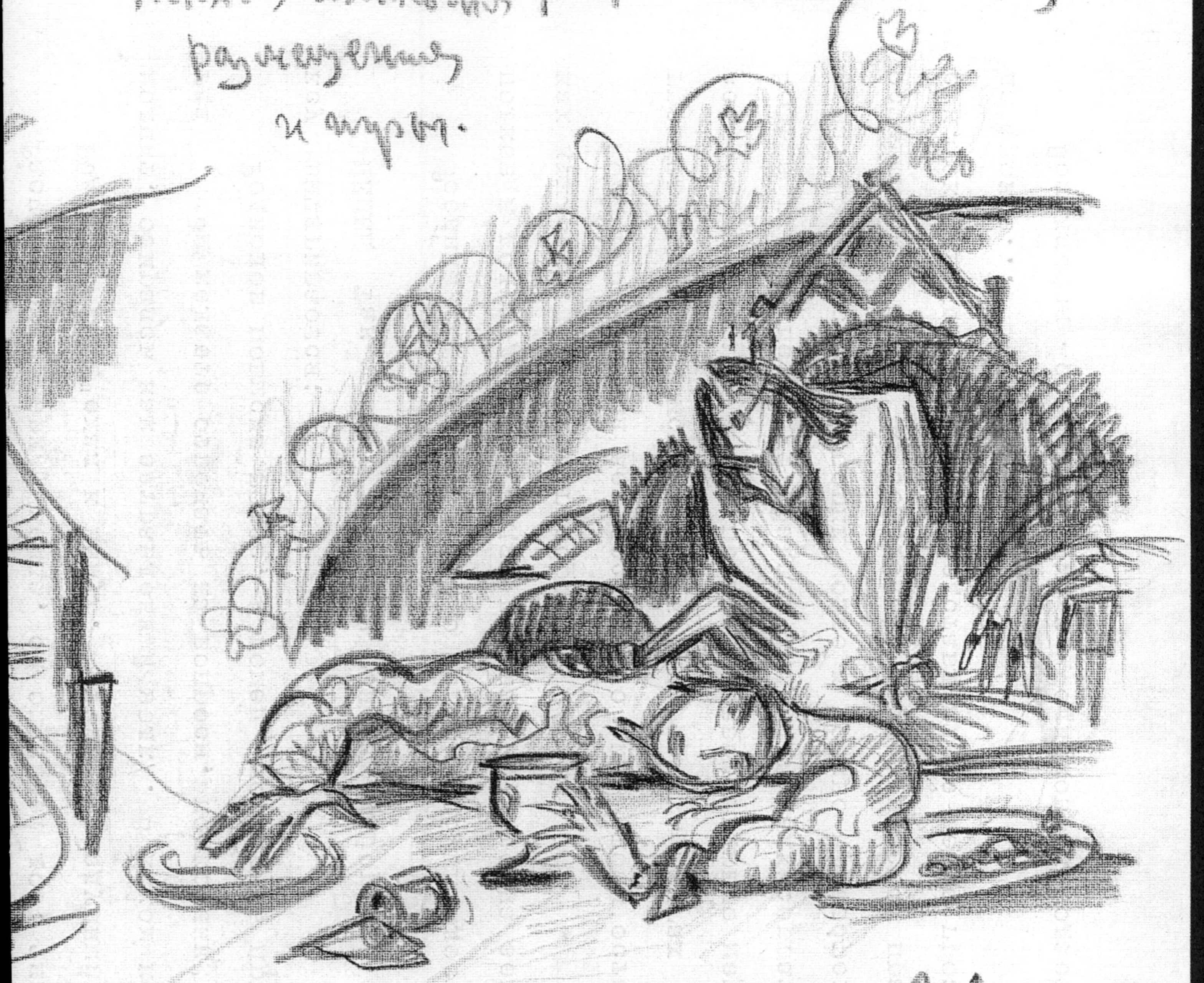

Разговор с Иваном
на пиру в Алекс. Слободе.

...а Боярского.

...олиц пробовался
Владимир>.

18 M 42.

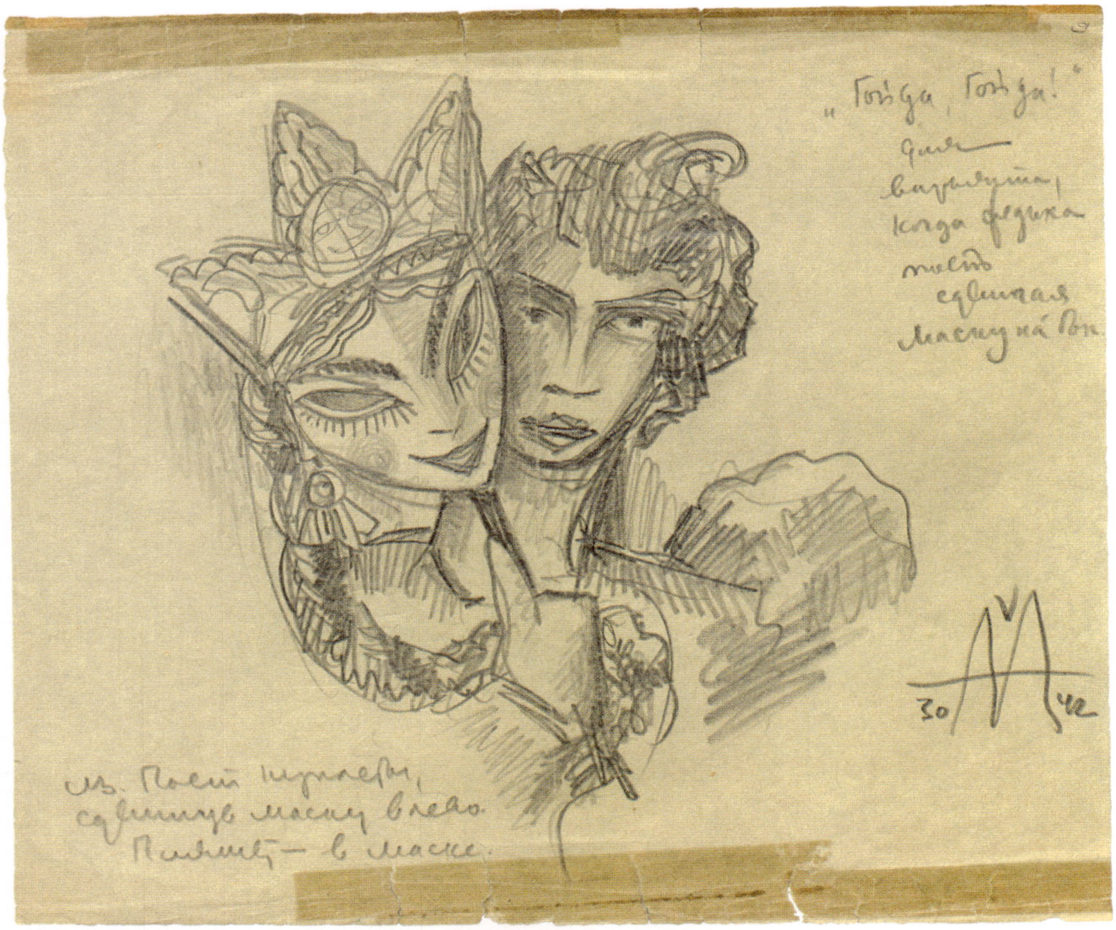

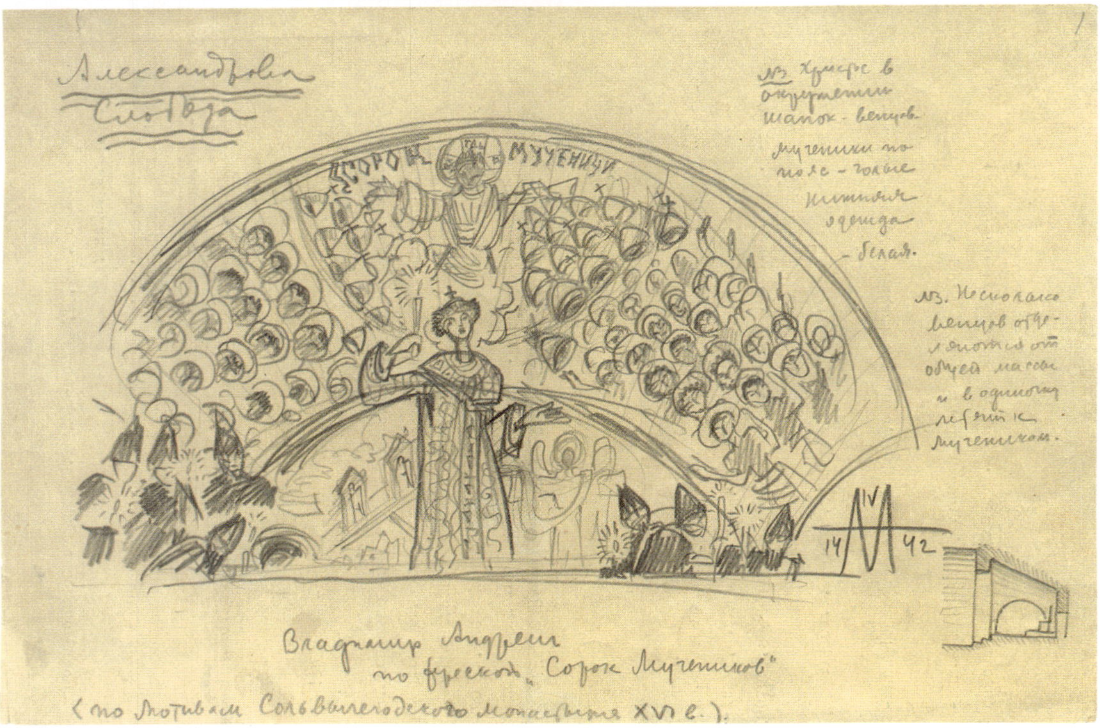

—THIS PAGE

TOP

'Feodor Basmanov with the mask at the feast in Aleksandrova Sloboda' (1942)

Text: 'Holla, holla!' For the version when Fed'ka sings, shifting the mask on the side. NB He sings his couplets, moving the mask to the left. He dances in the mask.

BOTTOM

Aleksandrova Sloboda (1942)

Text: Vladimir Andreyevich under the fresco *Forty Martyrs* (after the motifs of the fresco in the Monastery of Solvychegodsk, XVI Century). NB Christ is surrounded by mitres. The martyrs are naked to the waist. Their clothes are white. NB Several mitres are separated from the general mass and fly separately to the martyrs.

—OPPOSITE

Vladimir Andreyevich in the Cathedral (1942)

Text: The shot, but not the light, of course!

—OVERLEAF LEFT PAGE

The Stone Cross Near Tver Otroch Monastery (1942)

—OVERLEAF RIGHT PAGE

TOP LEFT

The Killed Novgorod Sentinels. Under Them Glide, Like Ghosts, the Black Shadows of Oprichniks (1942)

TOP RIGHT

The Soundless March Against Novgorod (1942)

BOTTOM LEFT

The Bows Were Thrown Up After the Fugitive (1942)

BOTTOM RIGHT

Behind Them in the Snow... Next to Them Glide the Black Shadows.... (1942)

Владимир Андреевич
в Соборе.

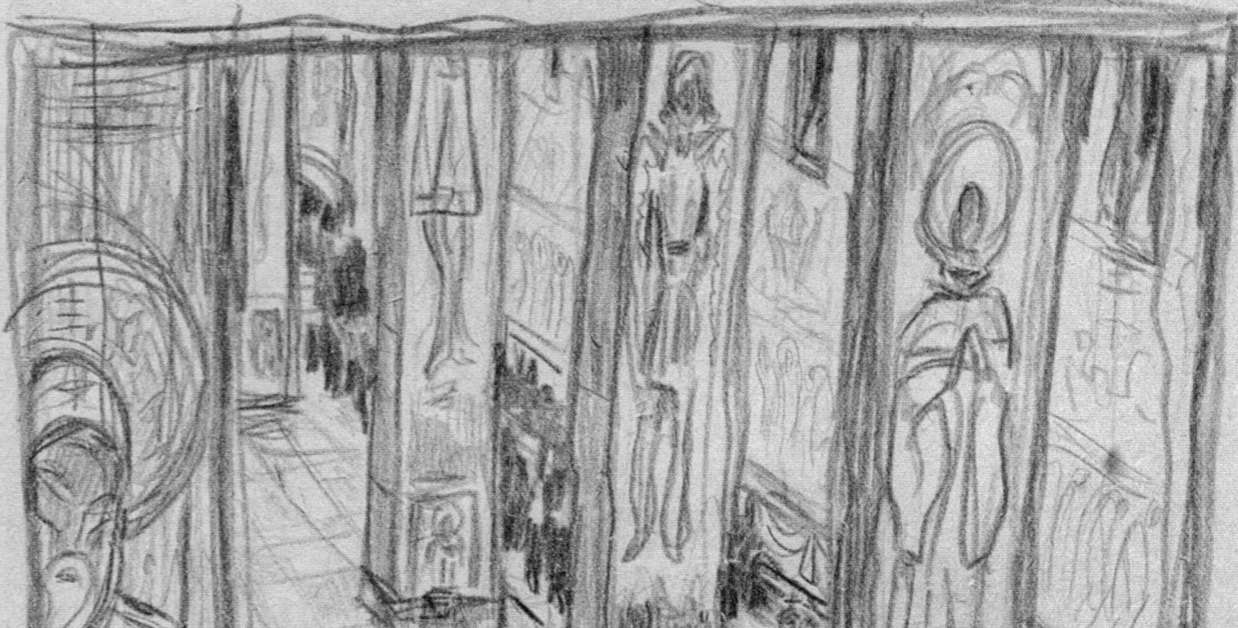

20 VI 42

Кадр, но не свет
конечно!

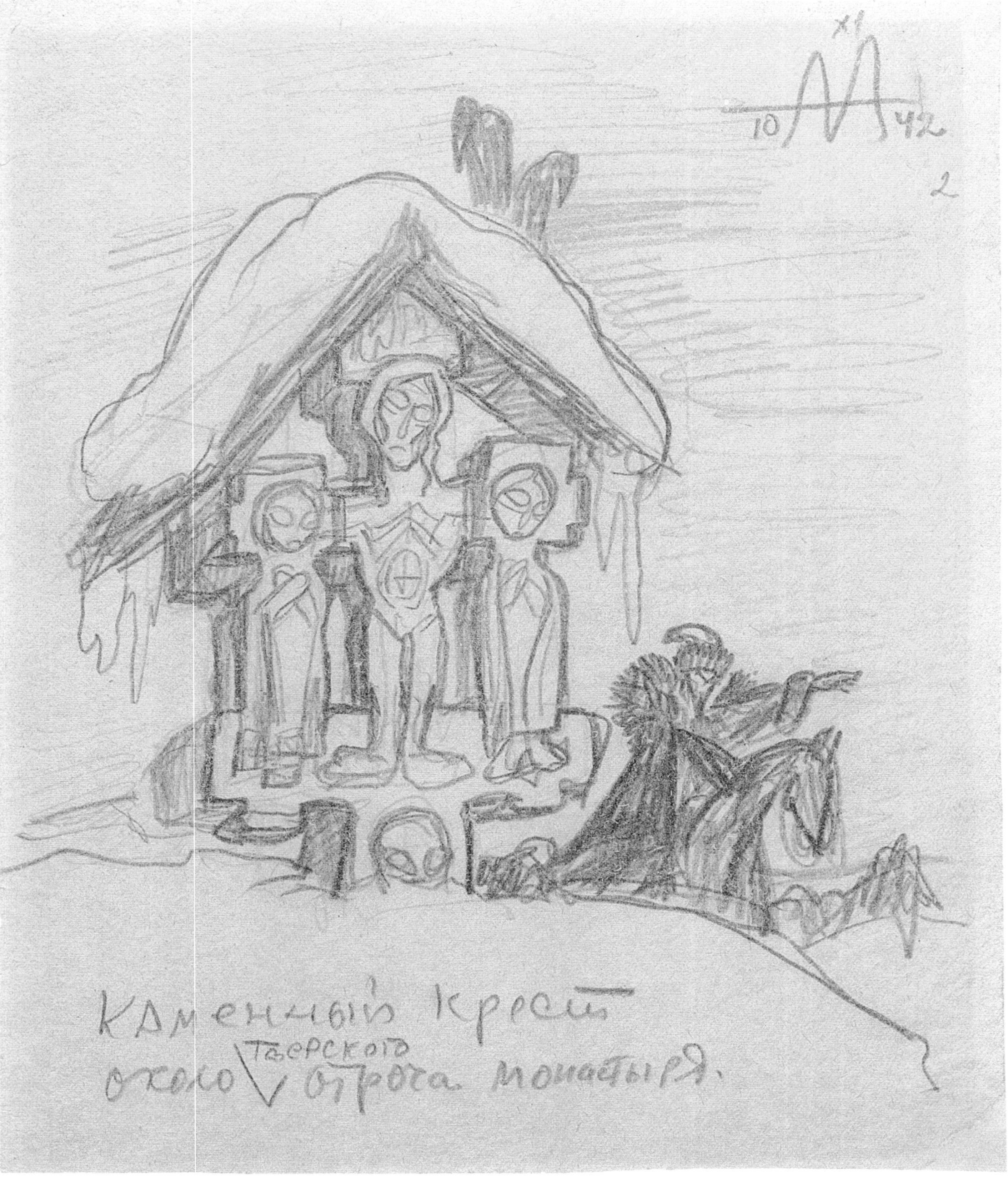
XI
10 42
2
Каменный крест
тверского
около Отроча монастыря.

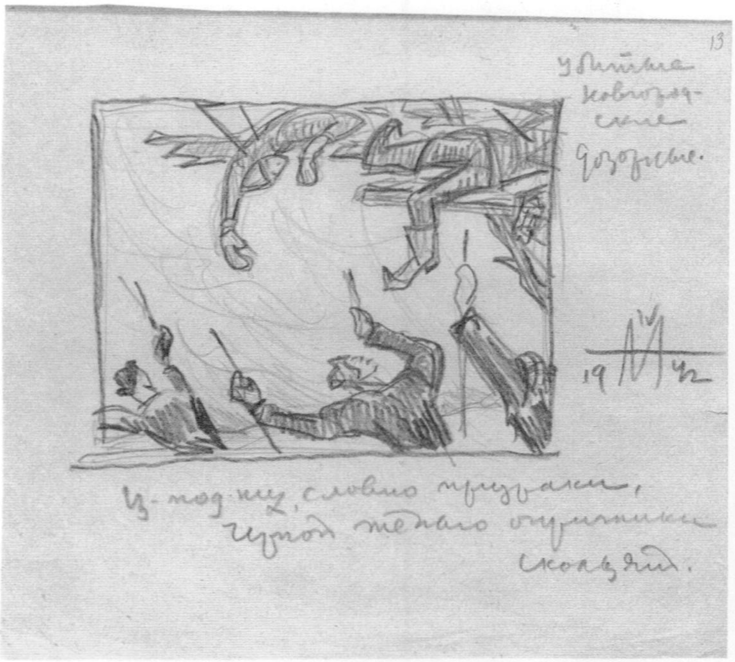

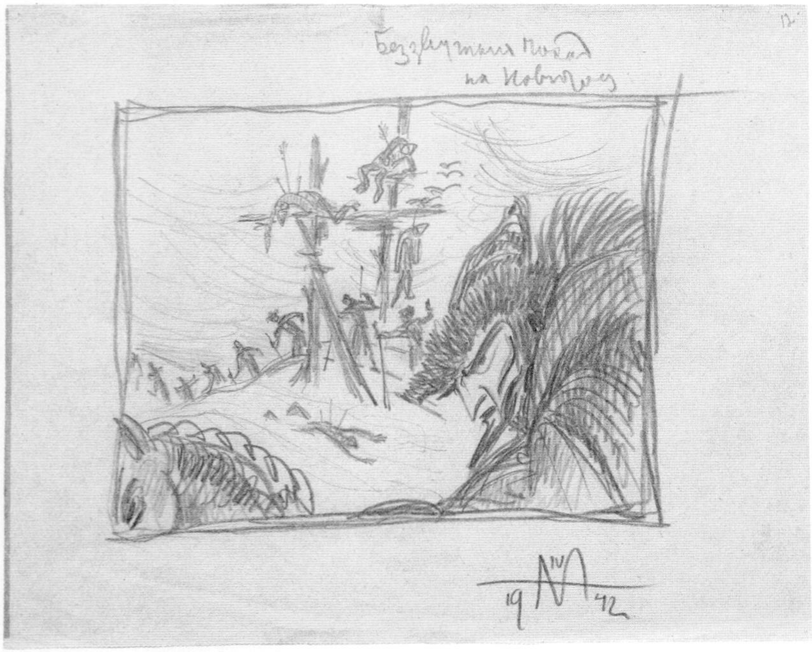

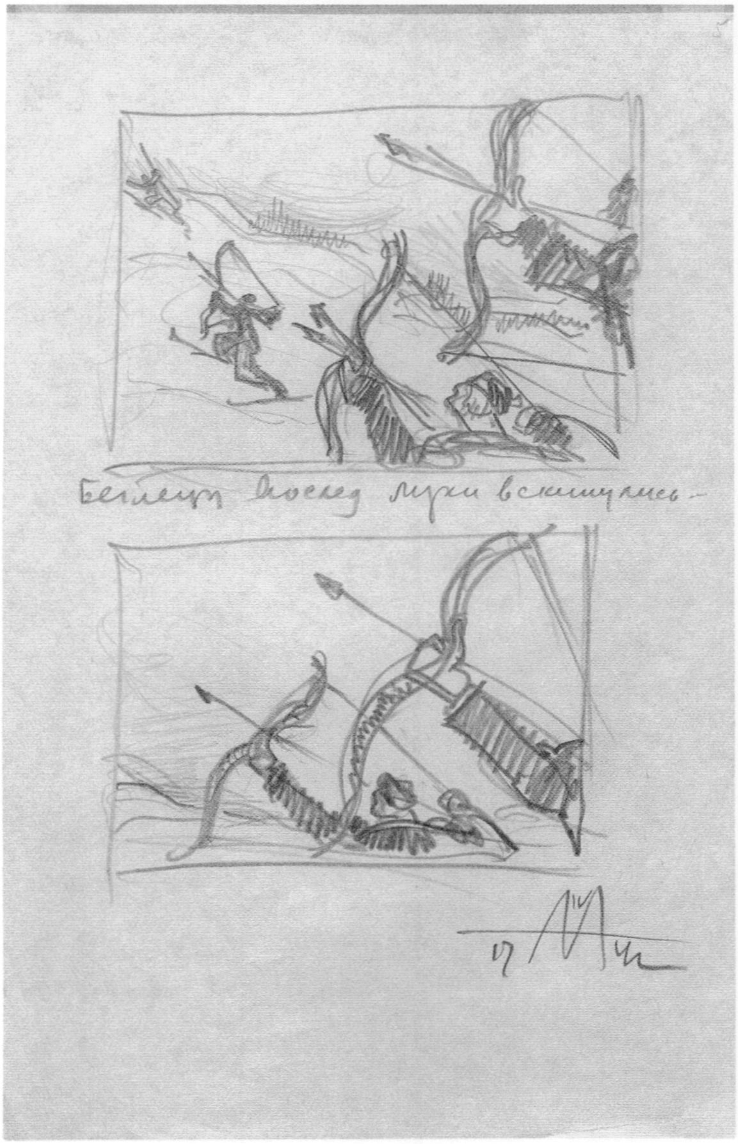

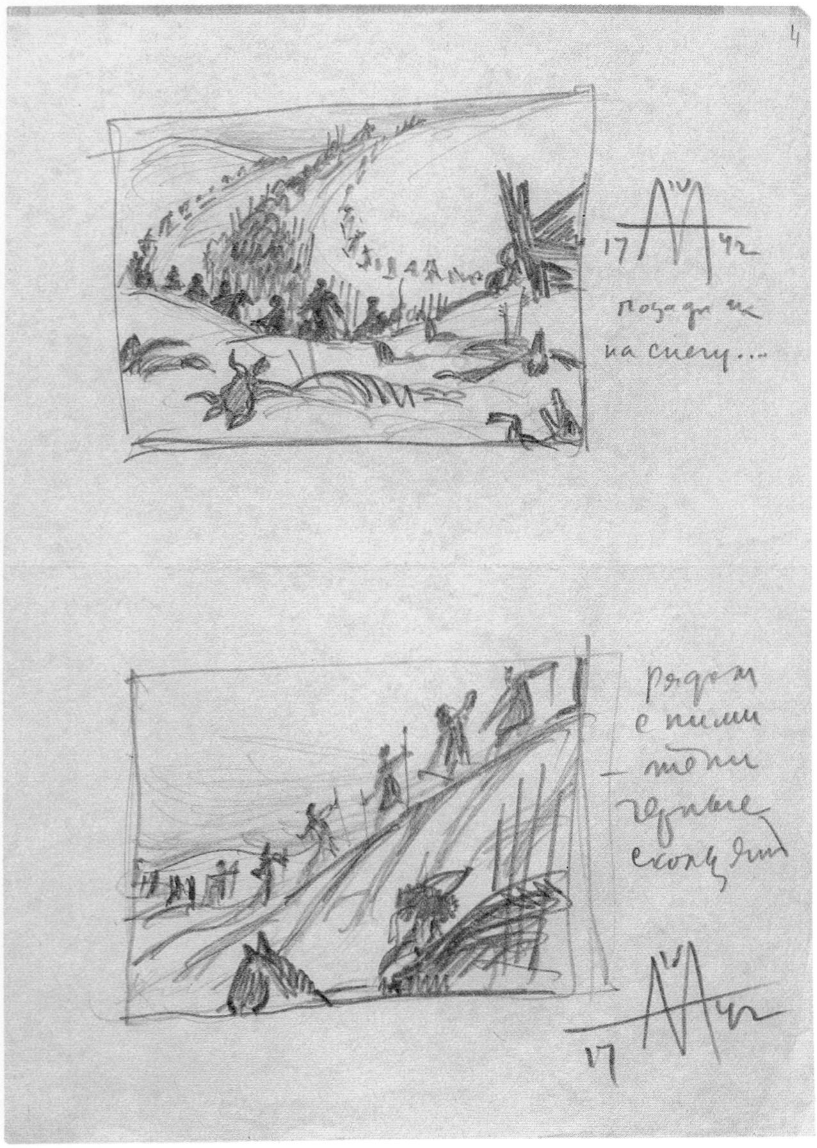

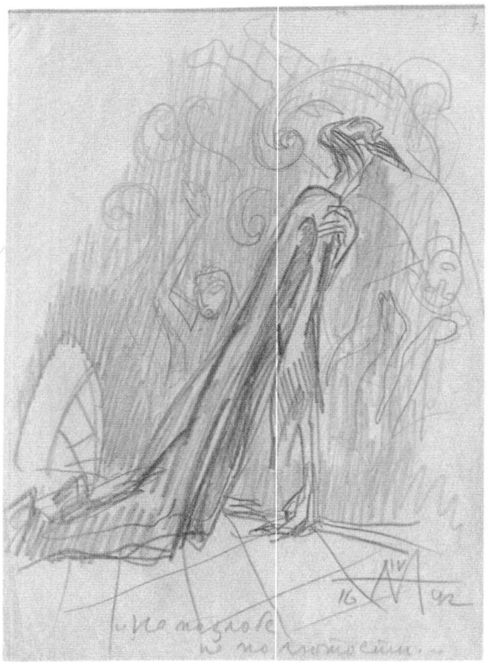

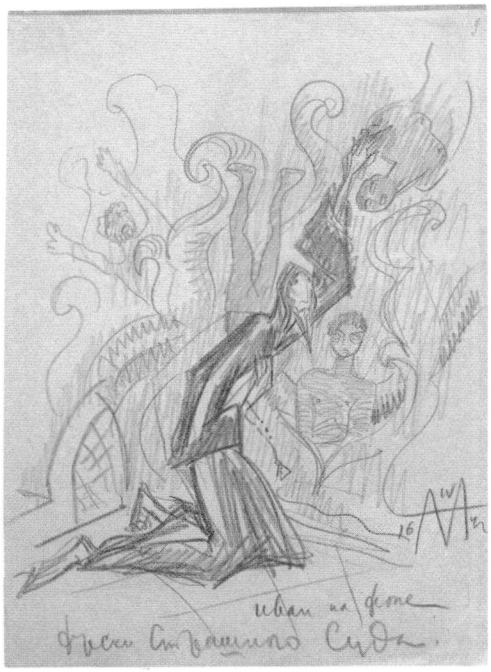

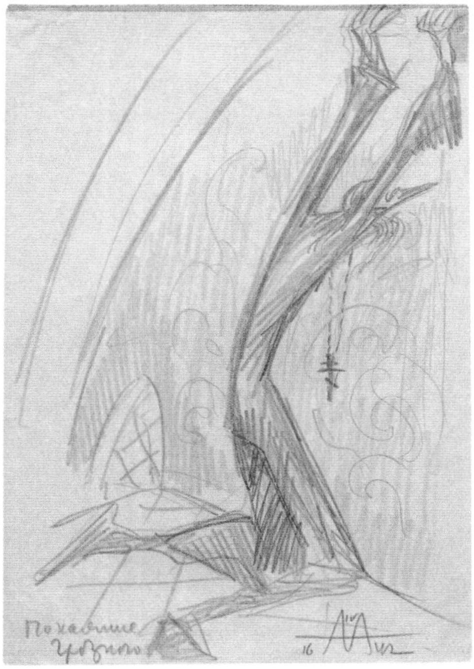

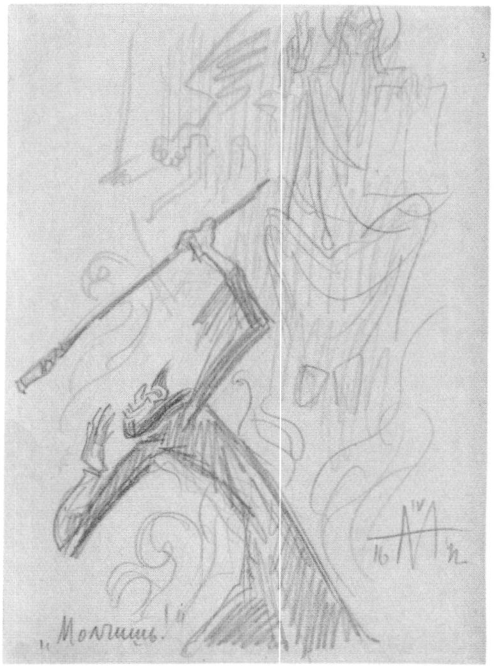

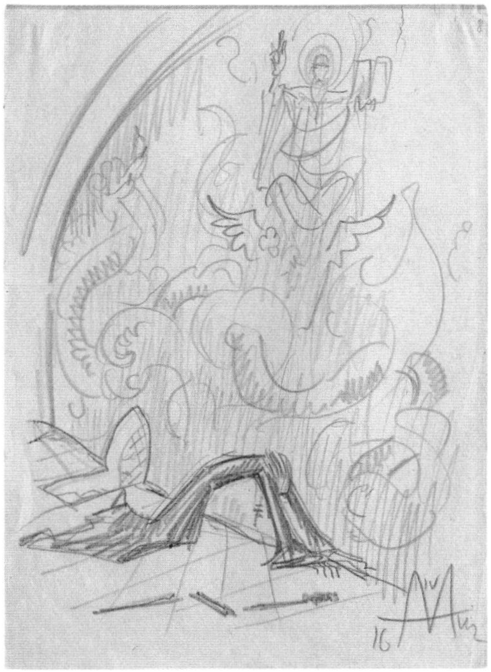

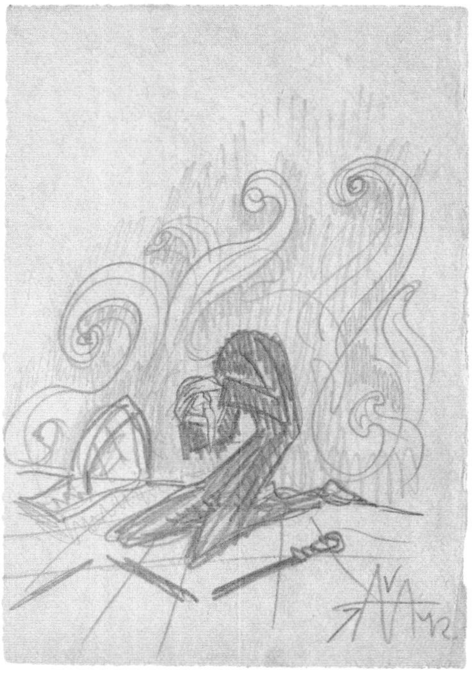

—THIS PAGE
'Tsar Ivan's repentance' (1942):

TOP LEFT
Not from Malice. Not from Wrath...

TOP CENTRE
Ivan and the Fresco of the Last Judgment in the Background

TOP RIGHT
Ivan's Repentance

BOTTOM LEFT
Thou Art Silent!

BOTTOM CENTRE
The Staff Shatters on the Smooth Wall

BOTTOM RIGHT
And the Earthly Tsar Sinks Down, Crushed by the Inexorability of the Tsar of Heaven

—OPPOSITE
'Ivan's confession' (1942)
Text: 'Who calls upon the Lord?'

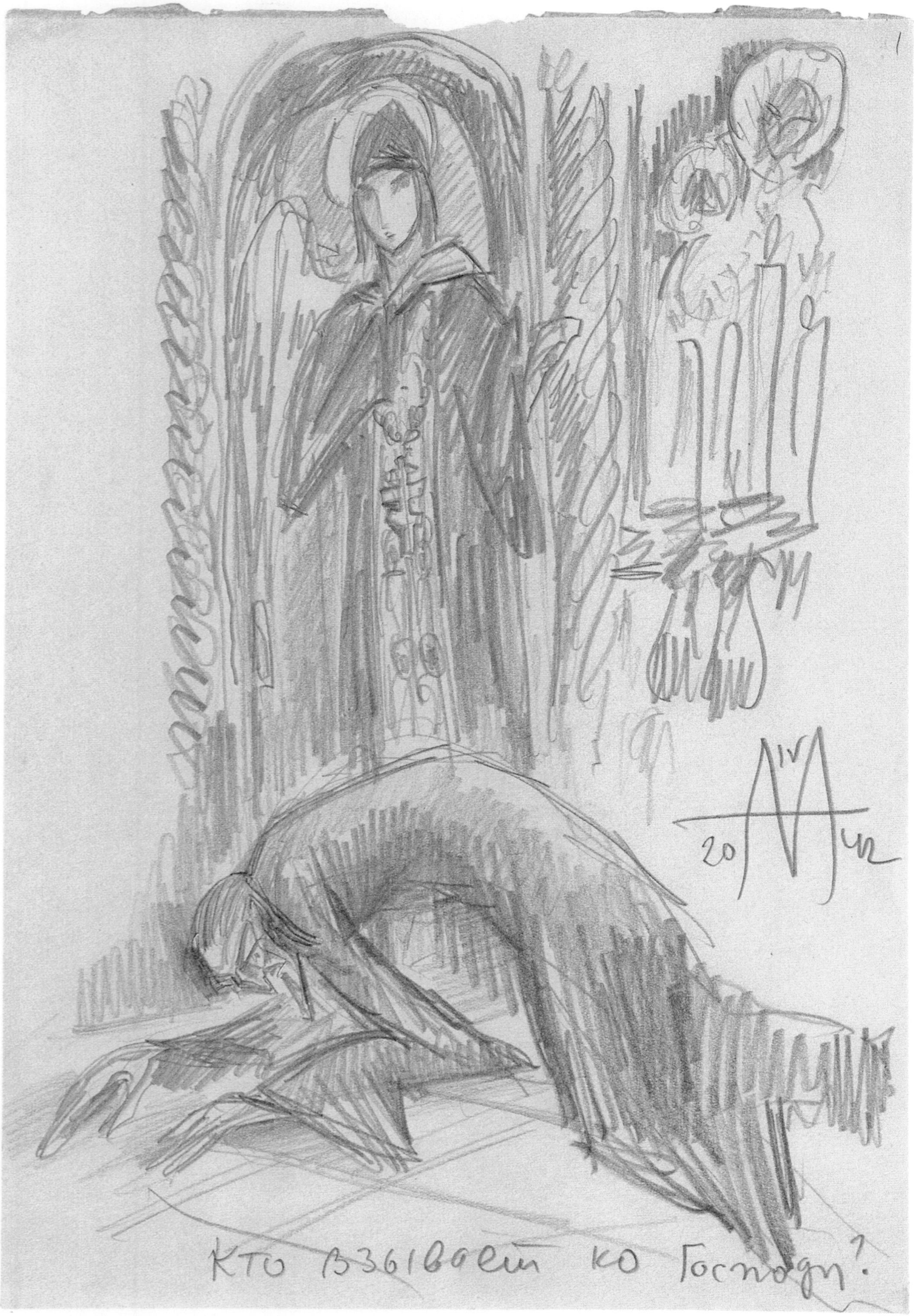
20 12
Кто взывает ко Господи?

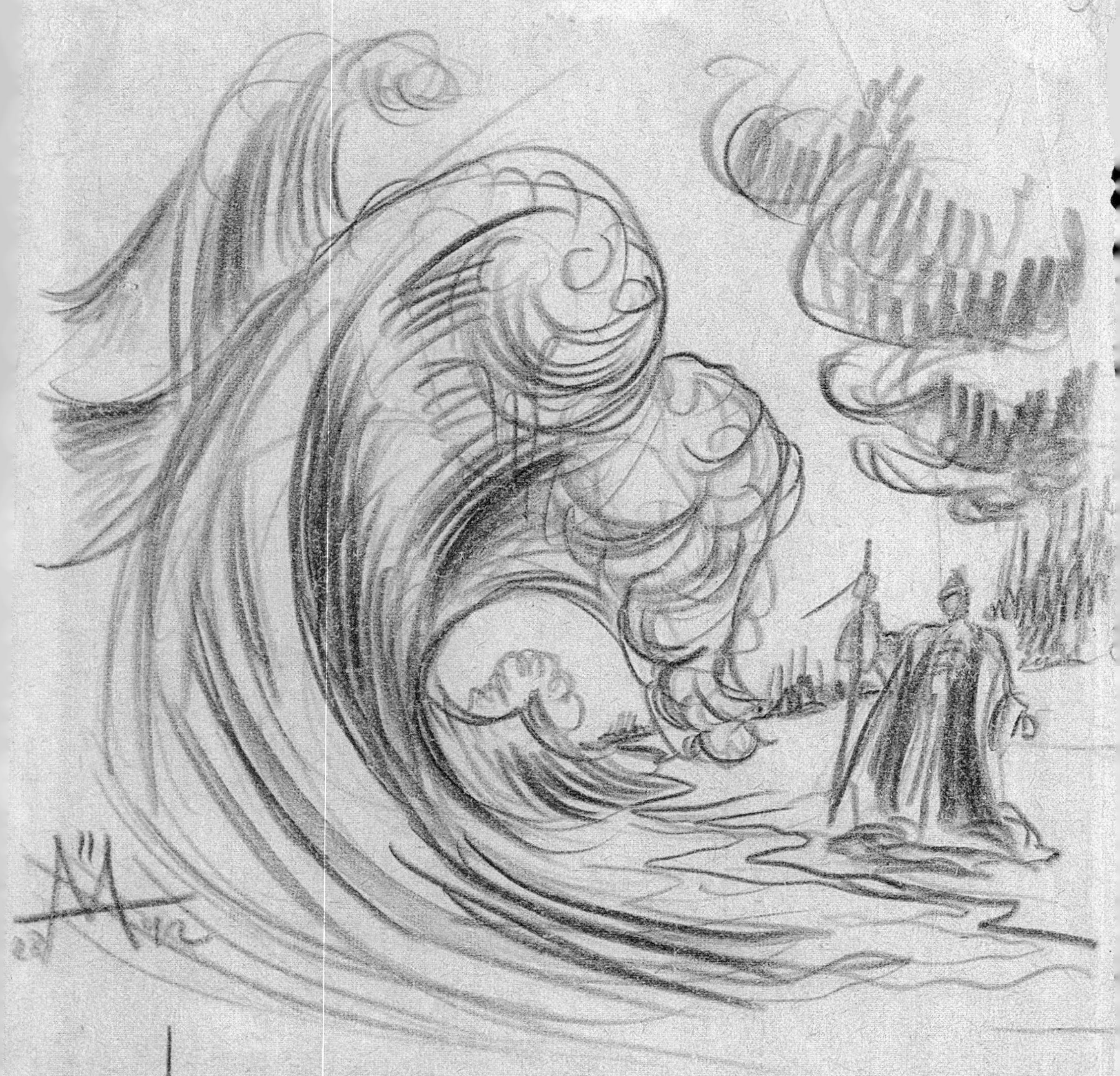

Финал: белая пена и чуткие дымы.

—OPPOSITE

'Ivan reaches the Baltic Sea' (1942)

Text: Finale: White foam and black smoke.

—THIS PAGE

TOP

'Ivan reaches the Baltic Sea' (1942)

Text: And he descends to the sea on the prostrate banners of the Order. (Petr with a banner). 'Alone?'

BOTTOM

'Alone?' (1942)

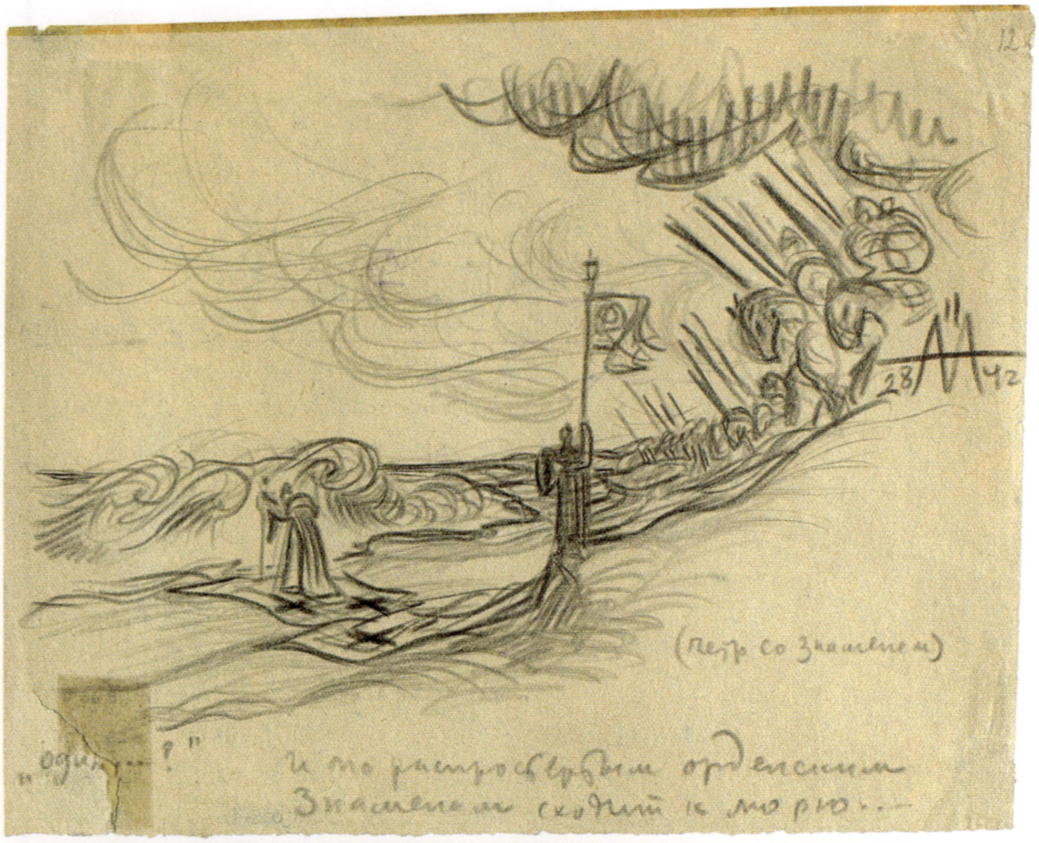

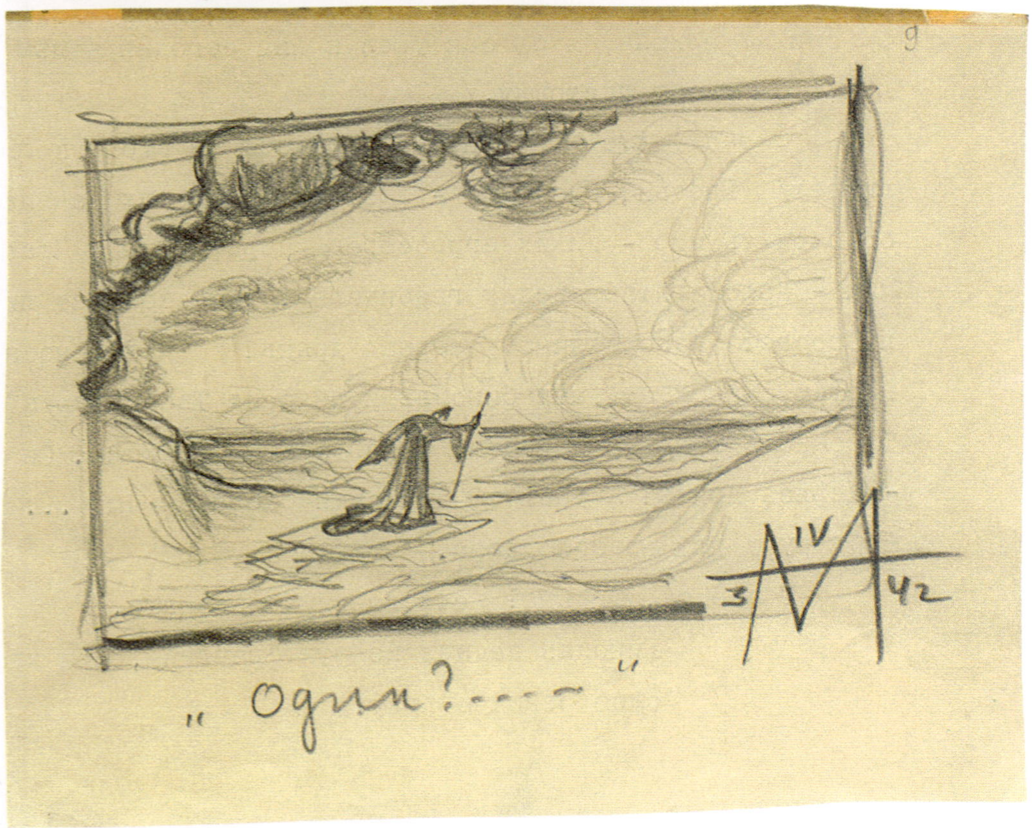

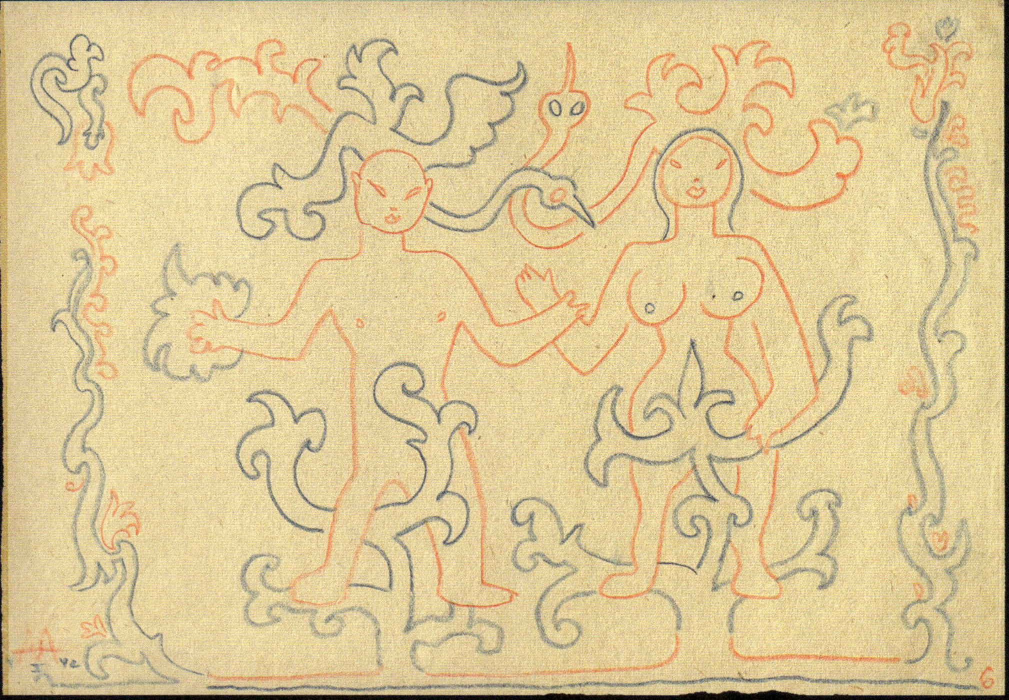

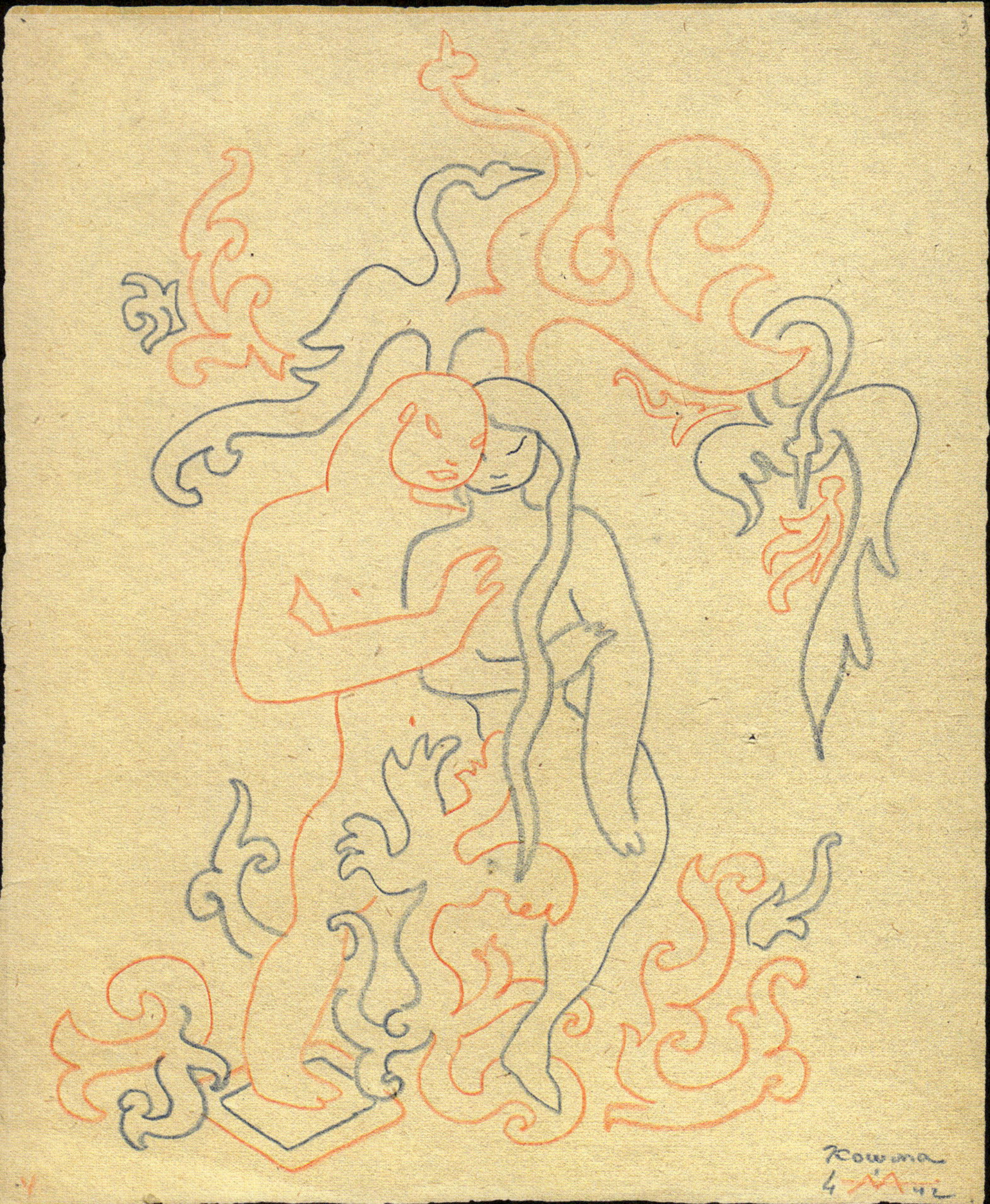

—THIS PAGE
'Variants of koshma patterns (felt carpet) with the theme of the ancient Kazakh legend "Kozı Körpeş and Bayan Sulu"' (Almalty, 1941)

—OPPOSITE

TOP LEFT
Totem (1941)

TOP RIGHT
In Memoriam of Hunters of the Mountain Goats (1941)

BOTTOM LEFT
At the Doctor's (1941)

BOTTOM RIGHT
The Family (1941)

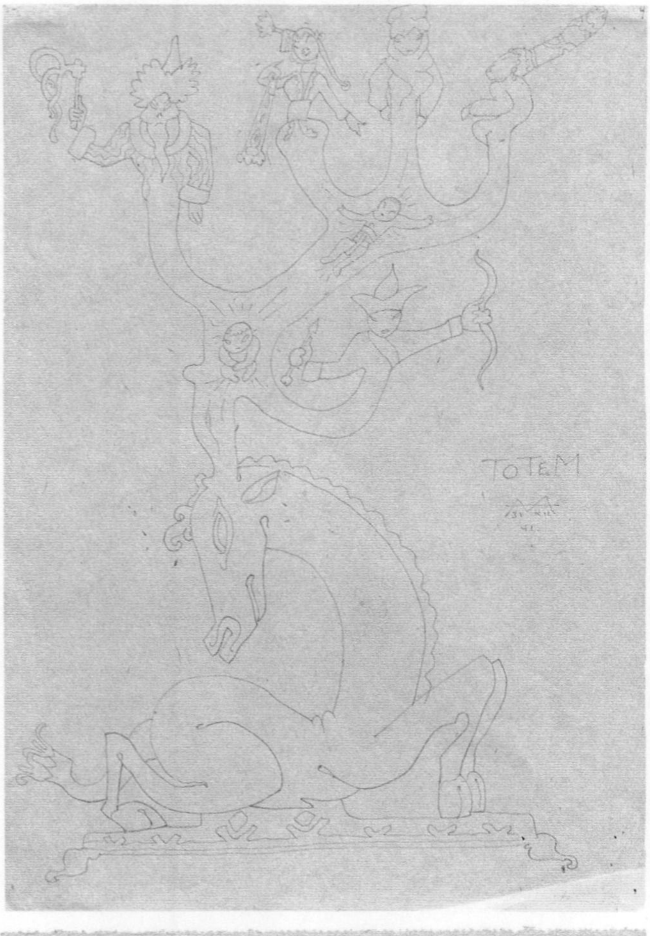
ТОТЕМ

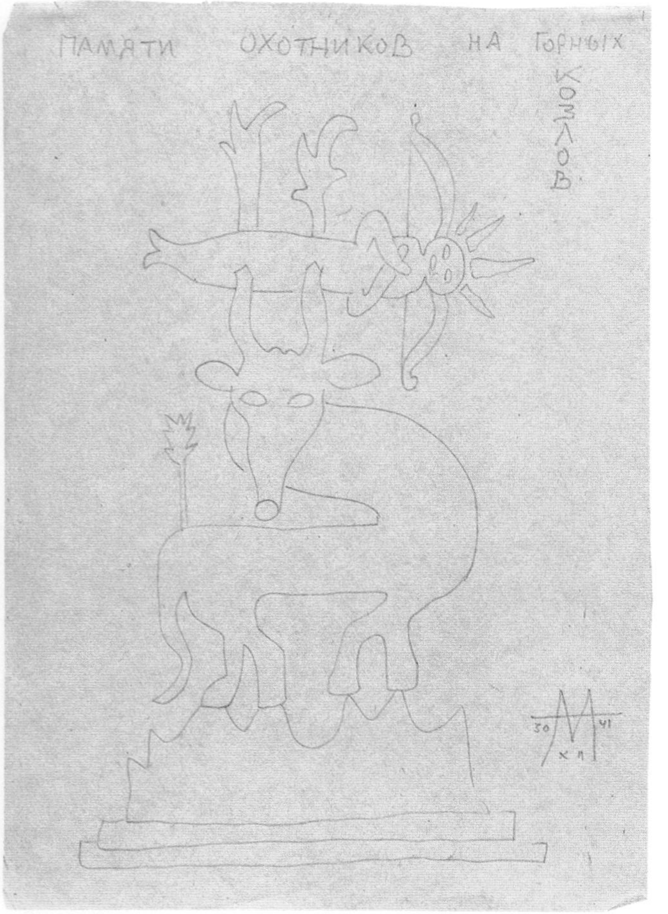
ПАМЯТИ ОХОТНИКОВ НА ГОРНЫХ КОЗЛОВ

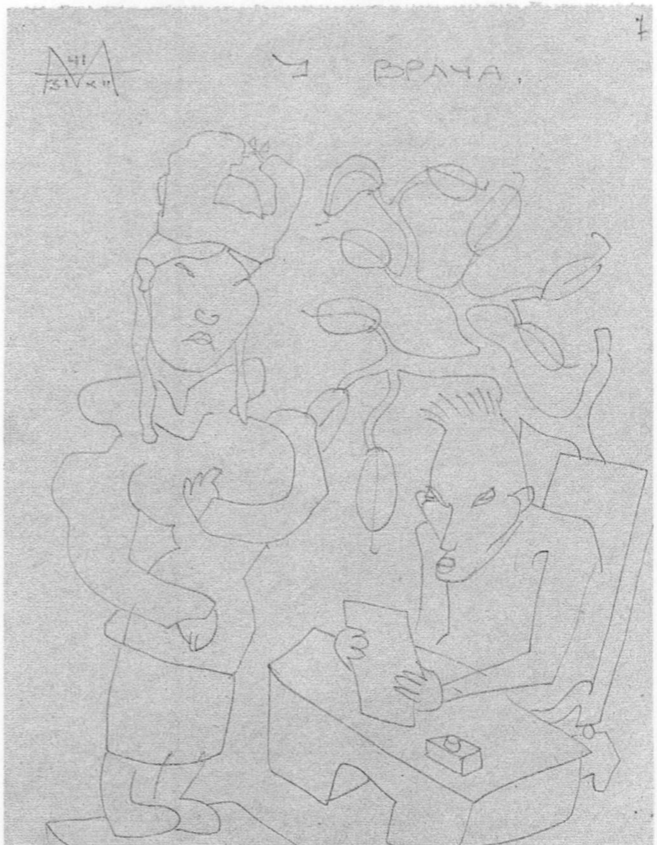
У ВРАЧА.

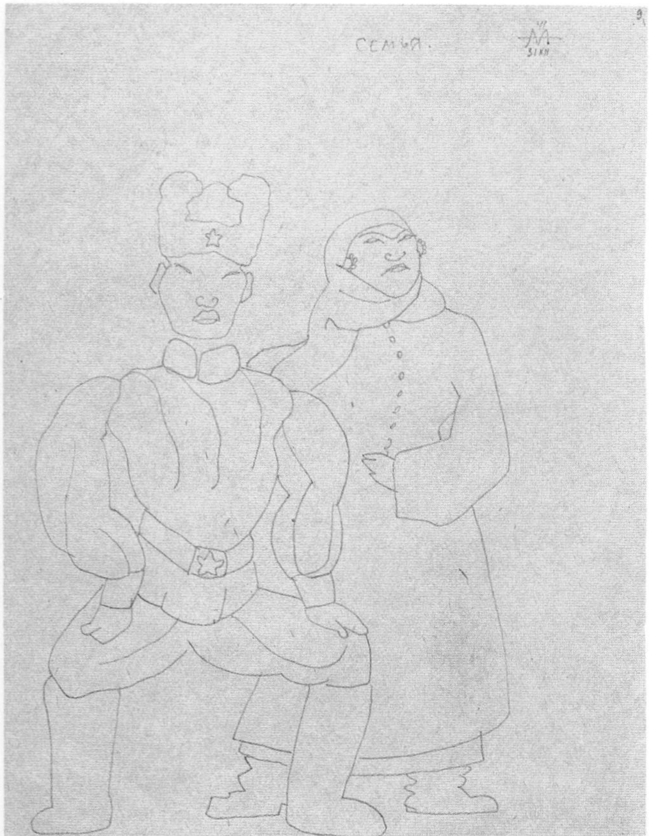
СЕМЬЯ.

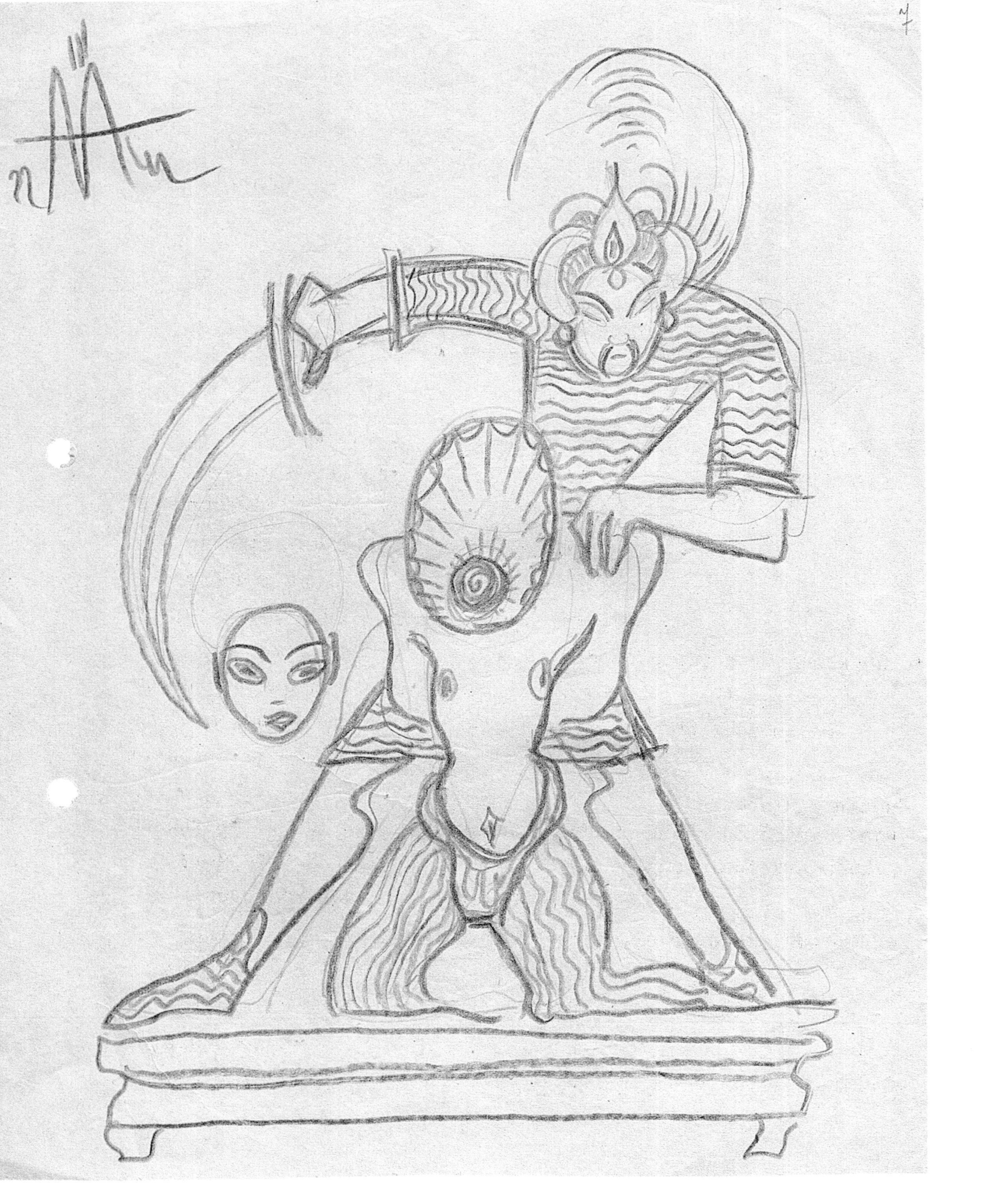

OPPOSITE
'Making faceless' (1942)

THIS PAGE
Drawings nos. 1, 3, 9 and 12, from the cycle 'Nero's suicide' (1942)

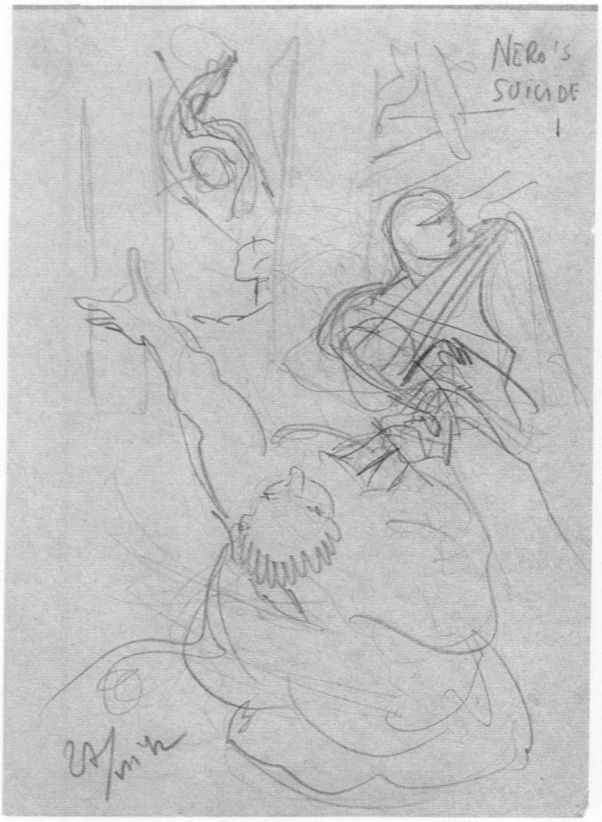

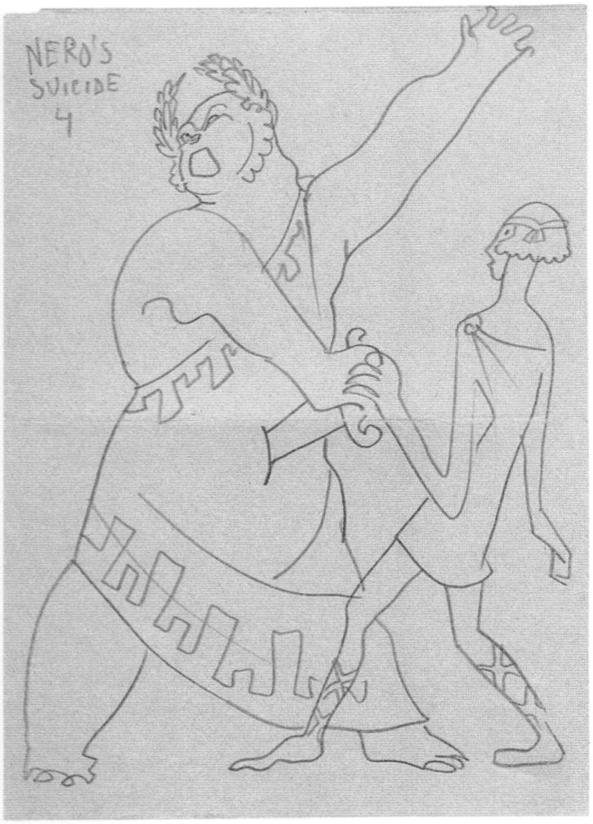

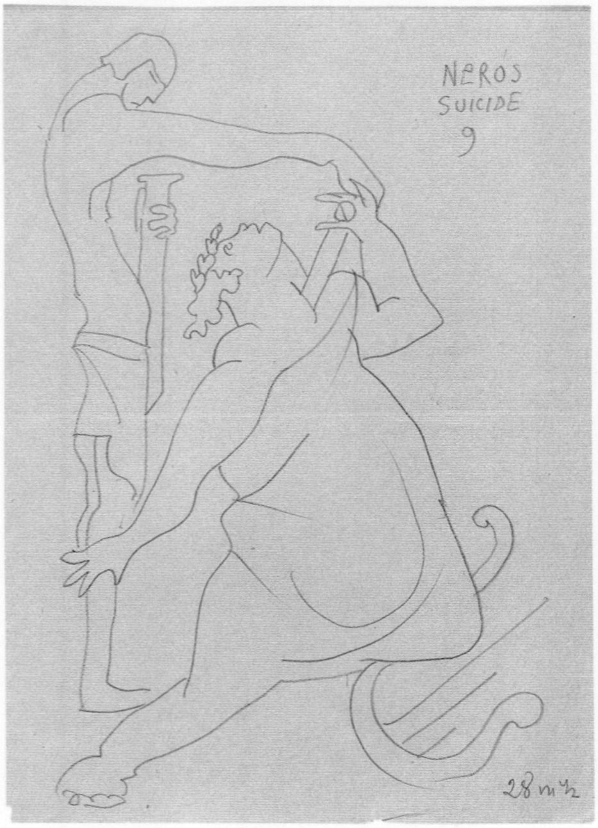

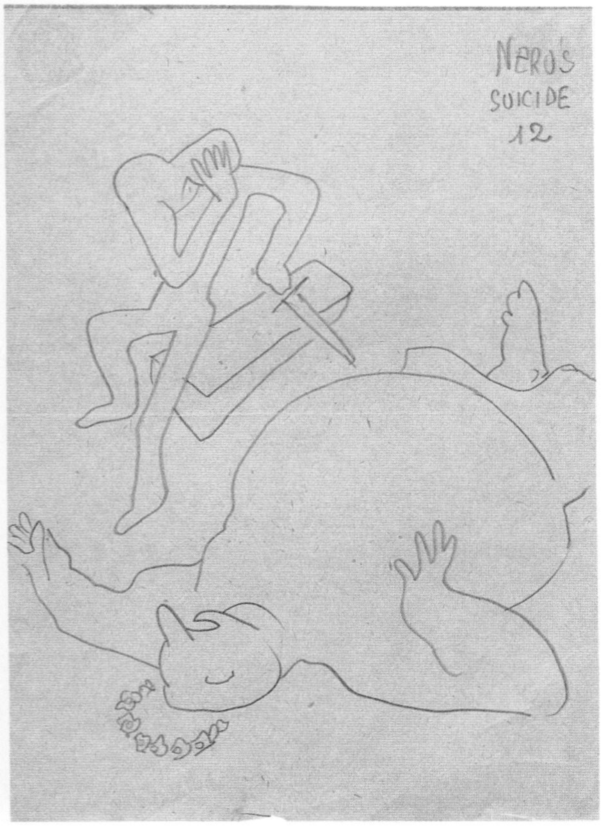

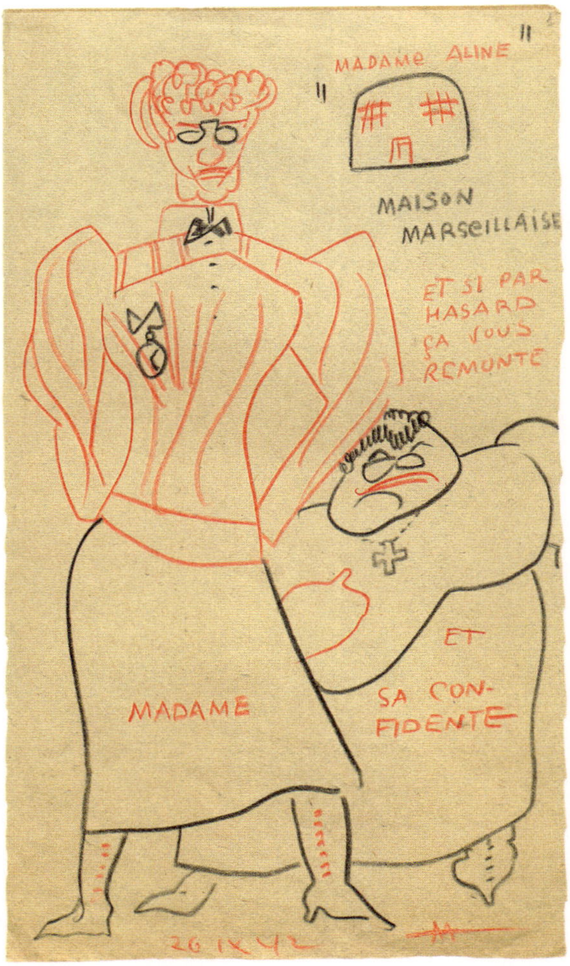

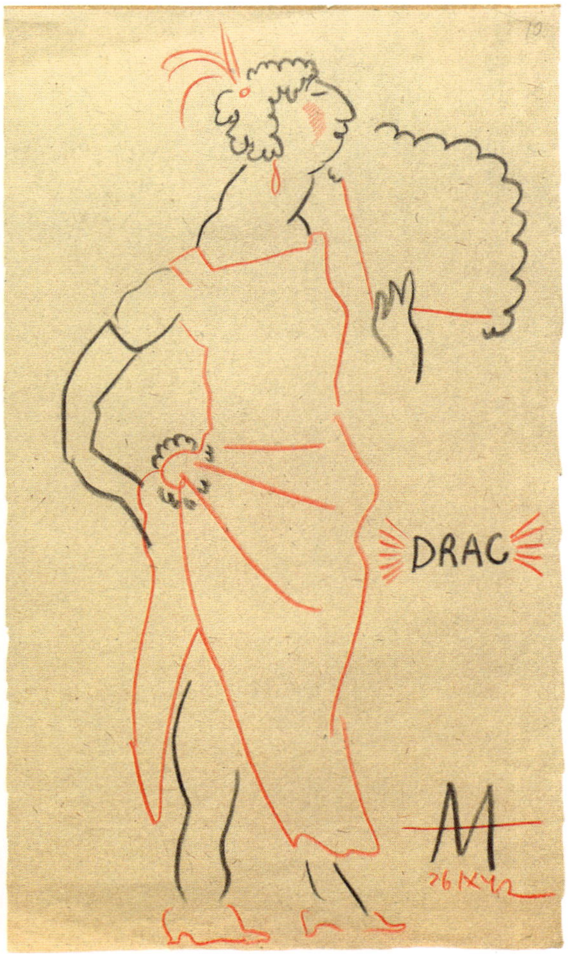

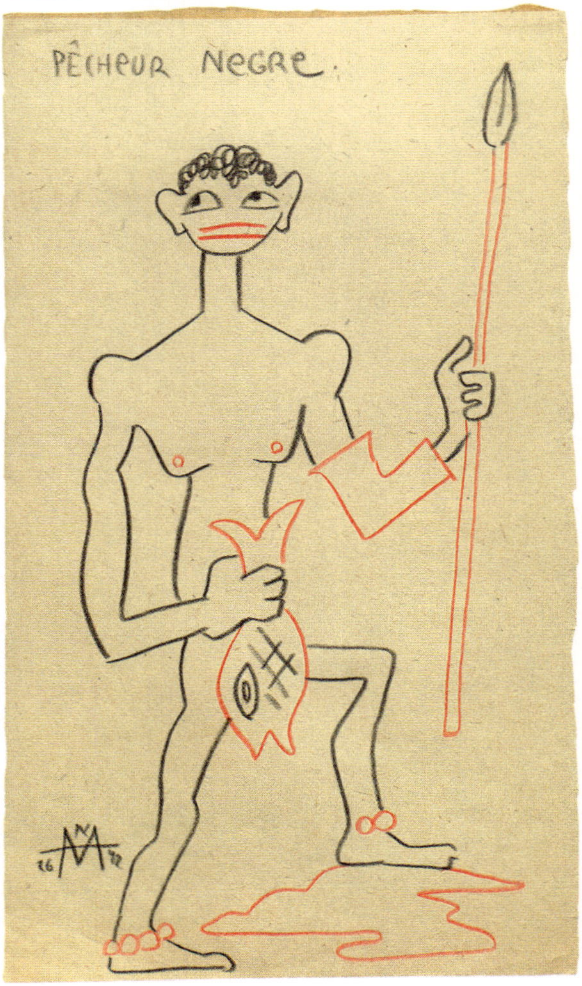

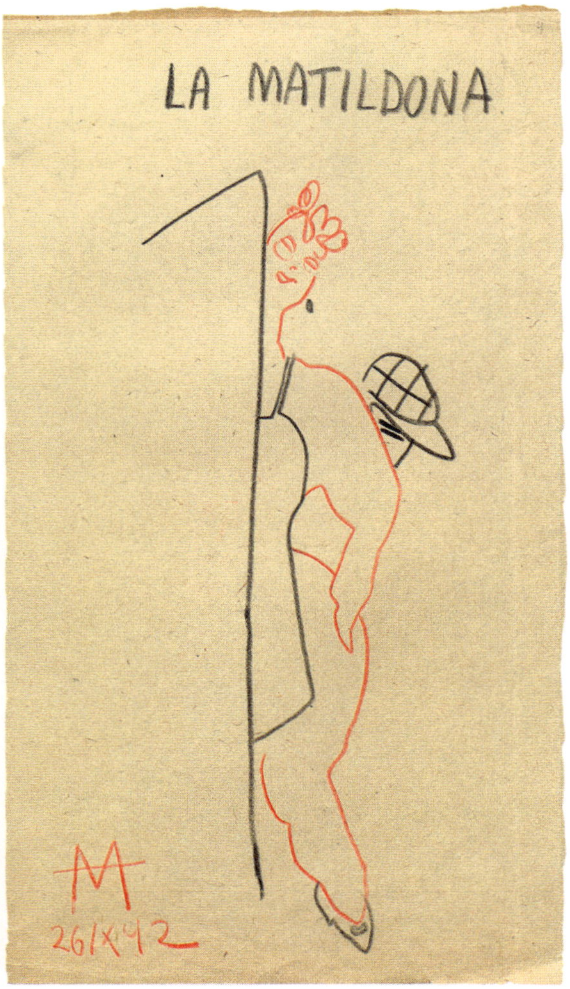

—THIS PAGE
From the cycle 'Memories of travels' (1942):

TOP LEFT
Madame et Sa Confidente (Madame and her confessor)
Text: *'Madame Aline'. Maison Marseillaise. Et si par hasard ça vous remonte.*
(And if by chance it gets you up.)

TOP RIGHT
Drag

BOTTOM LEFT
Pêcheur Negre
(Black fisherman)

BOTTOM RIGHT
La Matildona
(Matilda)

—OPPOSITE
From the cycle 'Memories of travels' (1942):

TOP
Berlin 1926
Text: *Wir brauchen keine Männer mehr,*
Wir lieben uns ja selbst so sehr.
(We do not need any more men,
we love ourselves and each other so much.)

CENTRE
Drag, New York

BOTTOM
Mexique? Du tout: Polotzk 1920
(Mexico? Not at all: Polotzk, 1920)

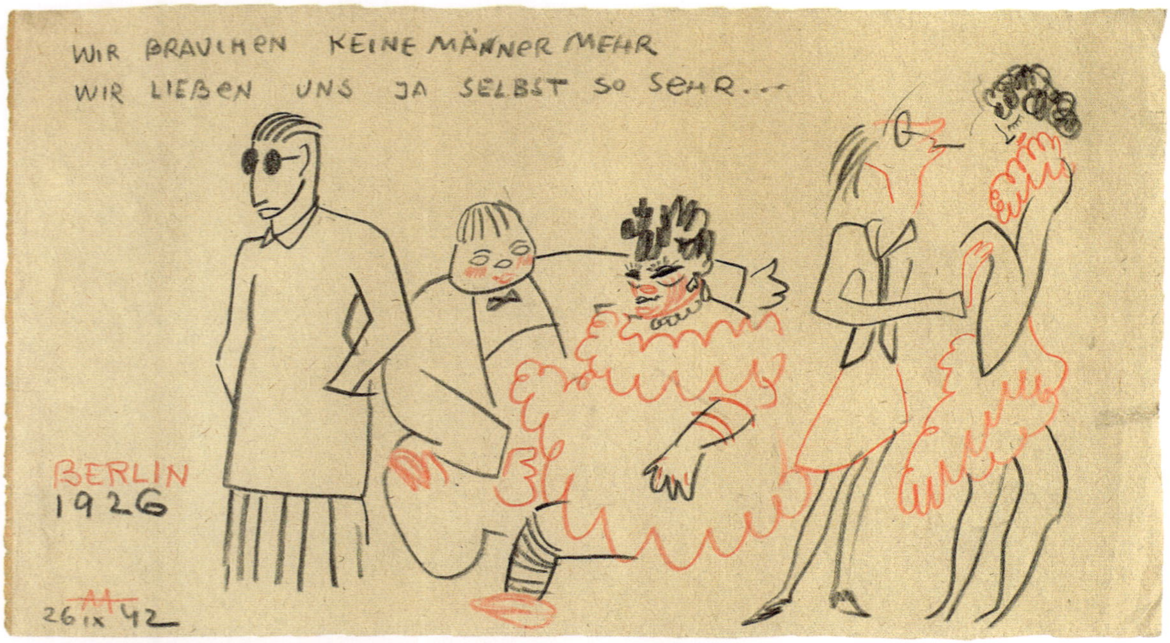
WIR BRAUCHEN KEINE MÄNNER MEHR
WIR LIEBEN UNS JA SELBST SO SEHR...
BERLIN
1926
26 IX 42

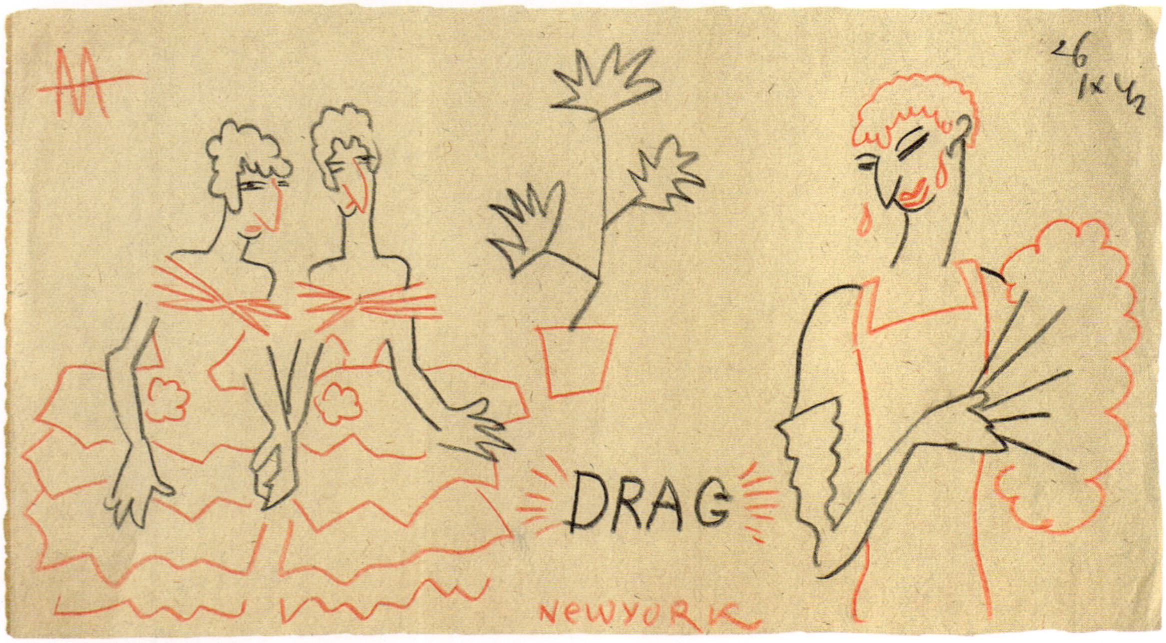
26 IX 42
DRAG
NEWYORK

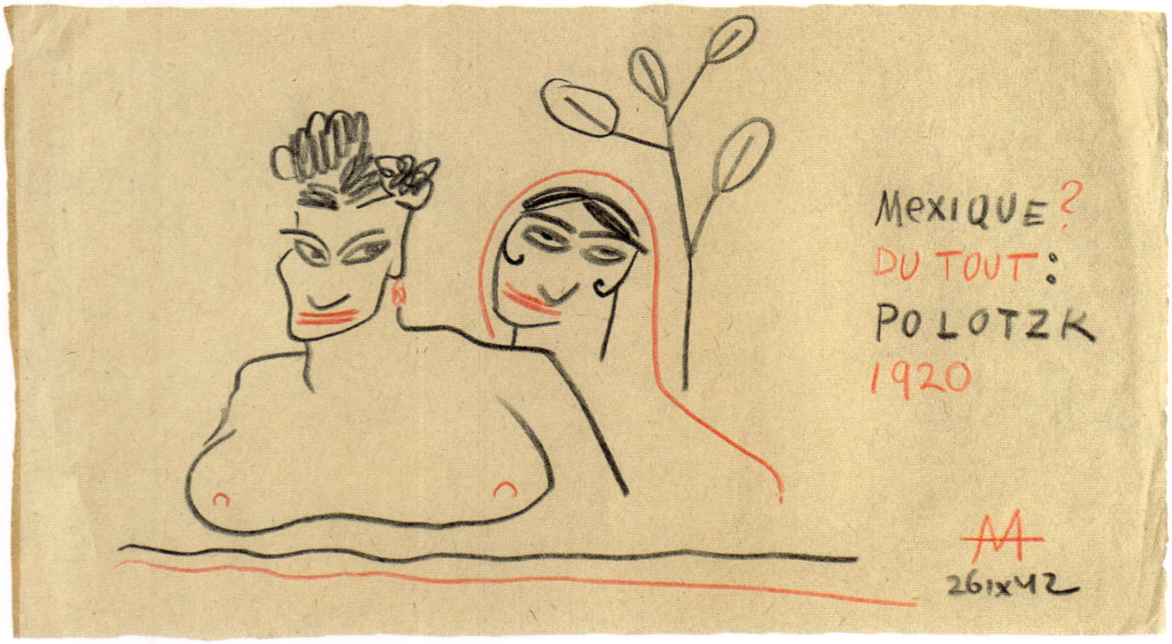
MEXIQUE?
DU TOUT:
POLOTZK
1920
26 IX 42

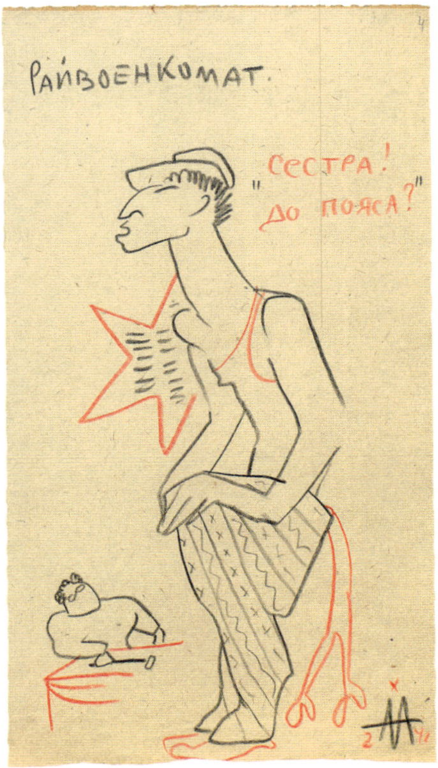
РАЙВОЕНКОМАТ.
„Сестра! До пояса?"

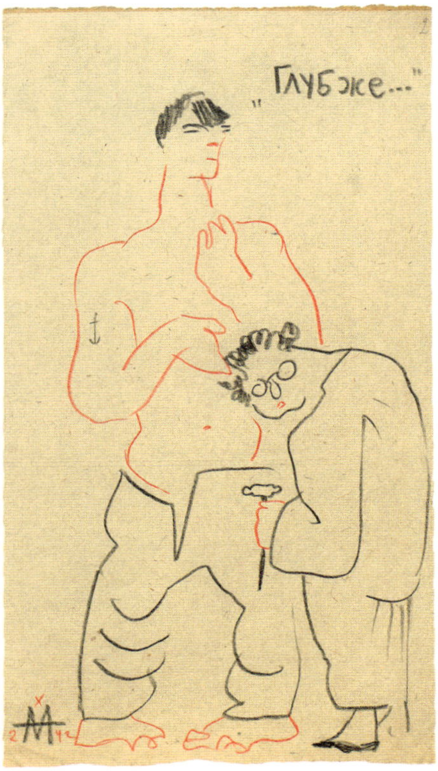
„Глубже..."

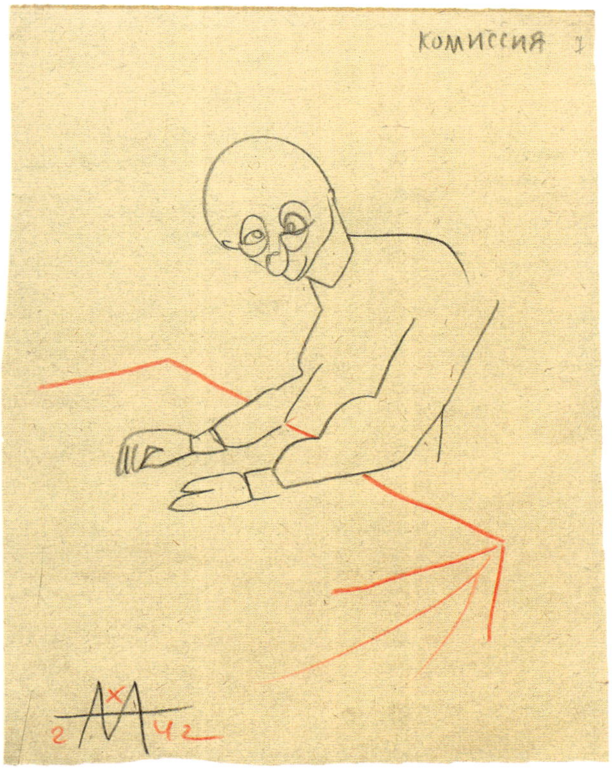
Комиссия

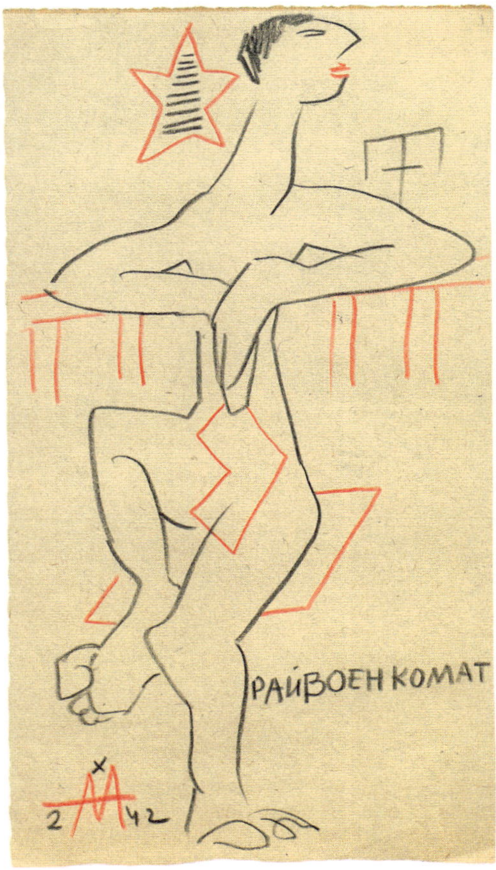
РАЙВОЕНКОМАТ

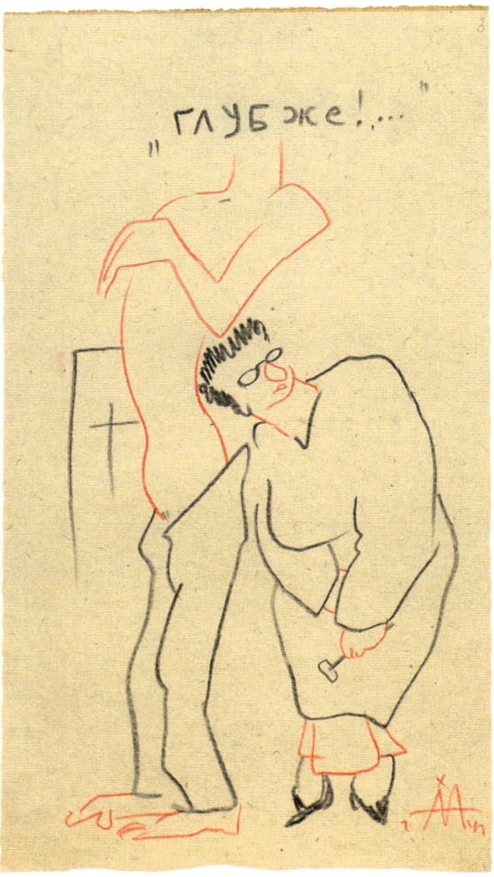
„Глубже!..."

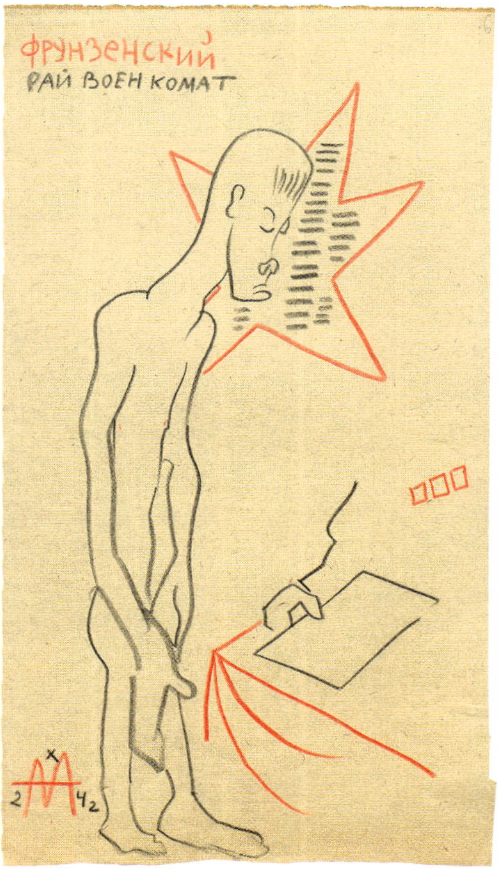
Фрунзенский
РАЙ ВОЕН КОМАТ

—OPPOSITE
From the cycle 'Regional recruitment office' (1942):

TOP LEFT
'Sister! To the Waist?'

TOP CENTRE
'Deeper...'

TOP RIGHT
Commission

BOTTOM LEFT
Regional Recruitment Office

BOTTOM CENTRE
'Deeper...'

BOTTOM RIGHT
Frunze Regional Recruitment Office

—THIS PAGE
From the cycle 'Regional recruitment office' (1942)
St Sebastian in the Recruitment Office
'Able!'

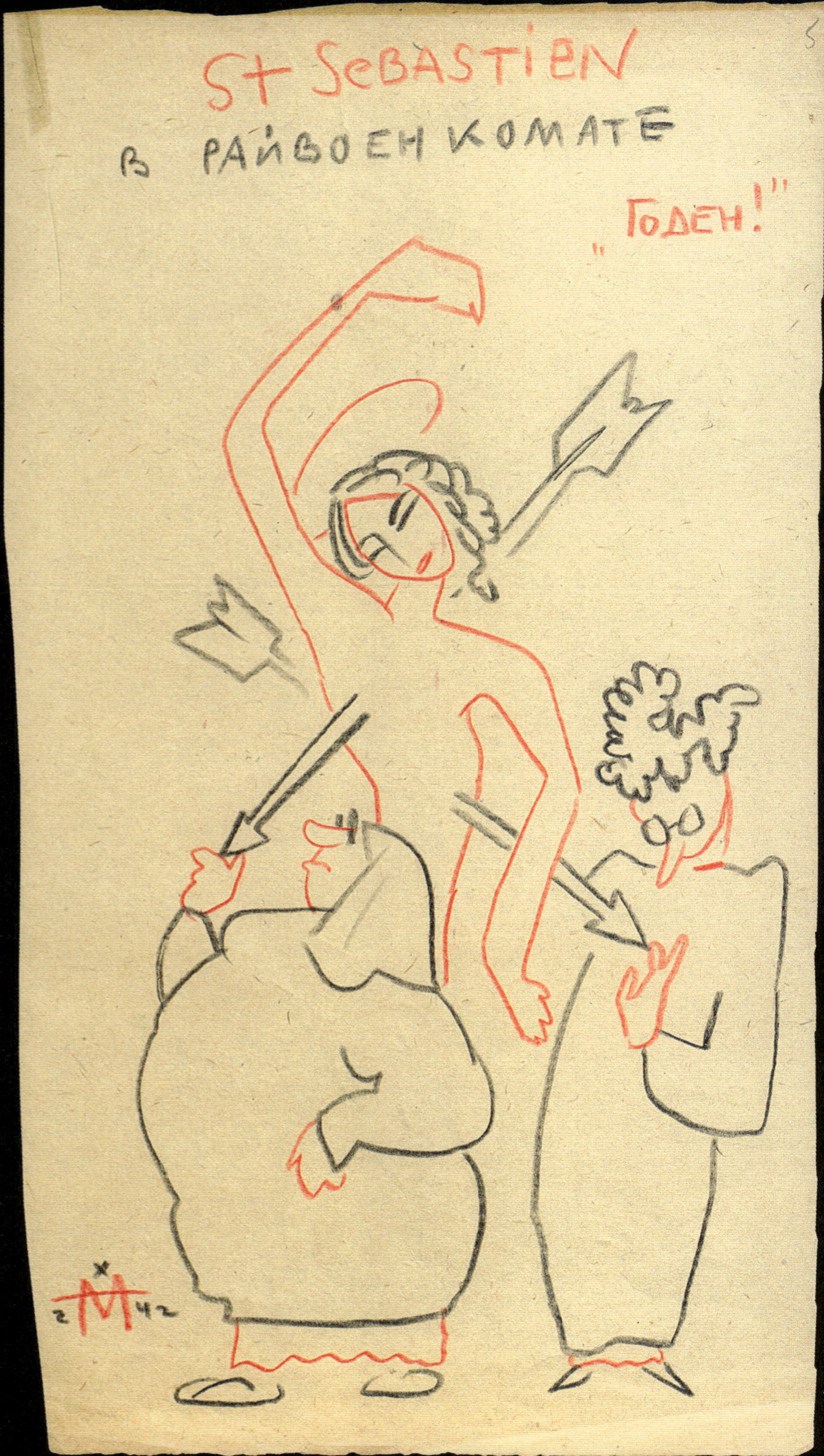

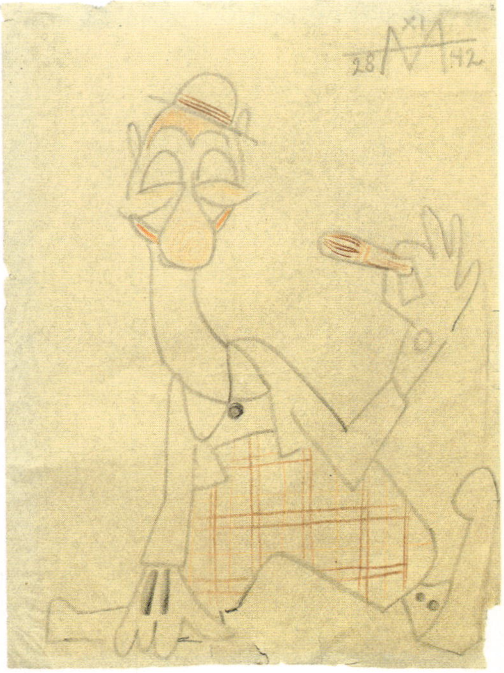
28 XI 42

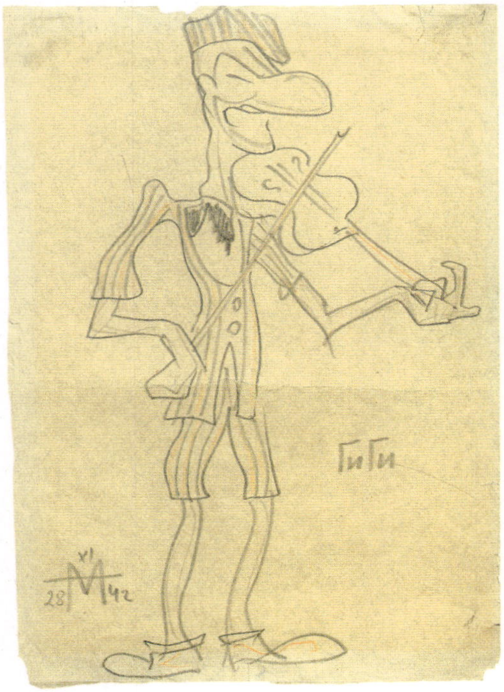
Гиги
28 XI 42

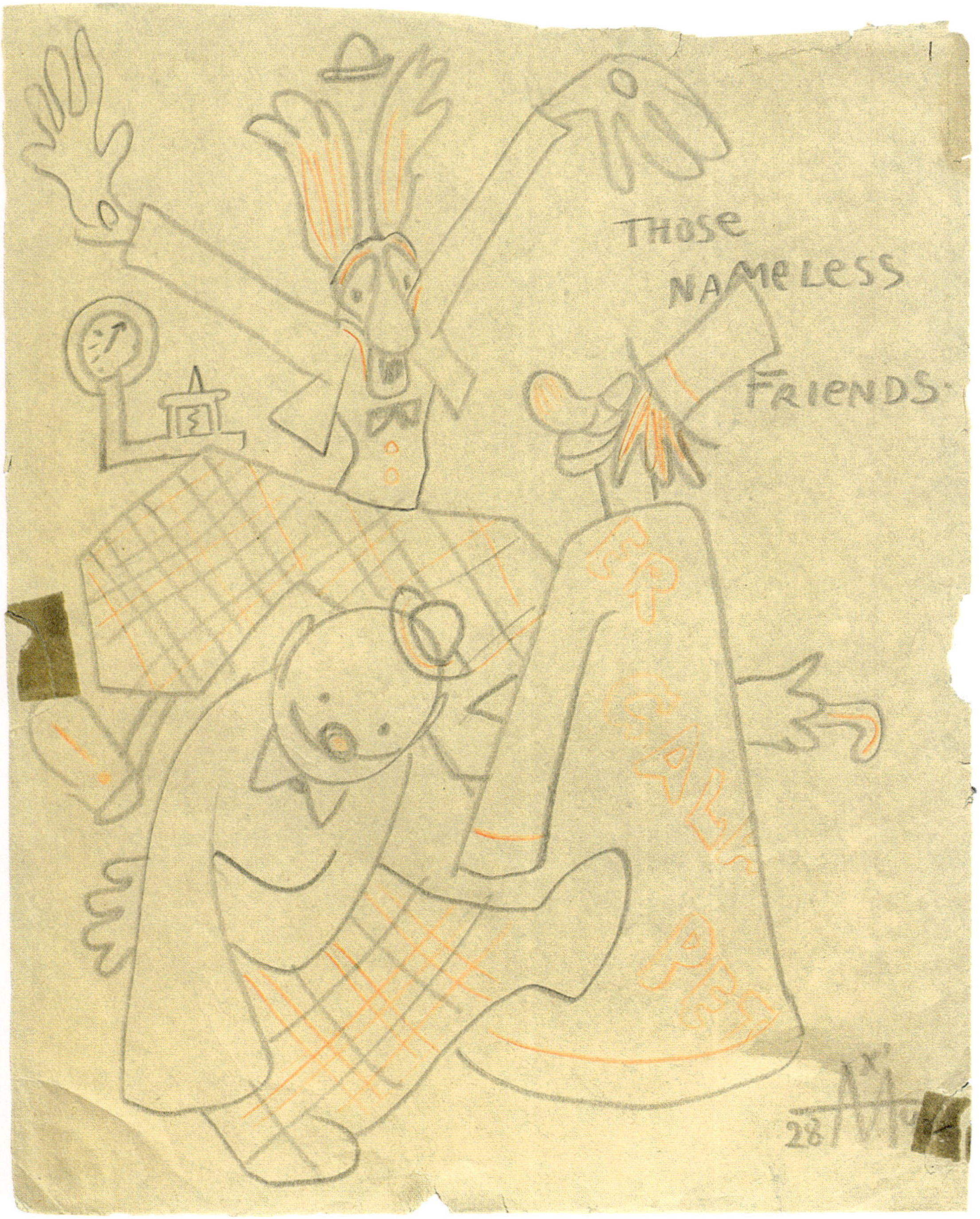
THOSE
NAMELESS
FRIENDS.
28

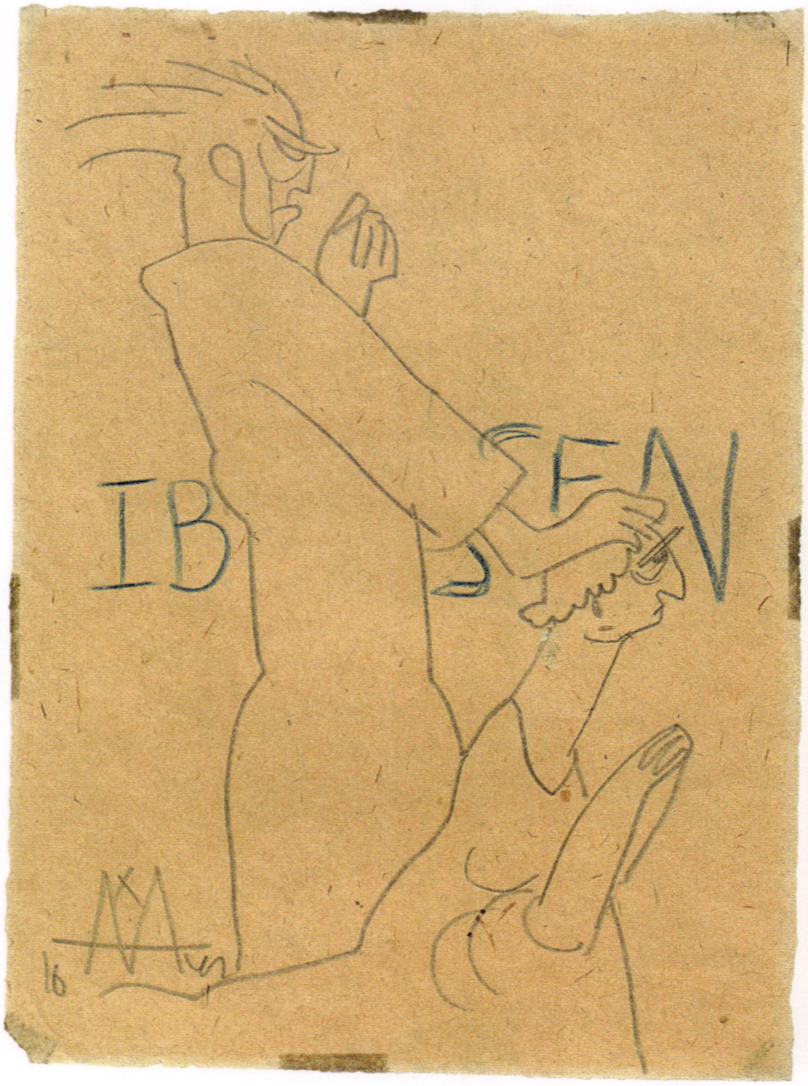

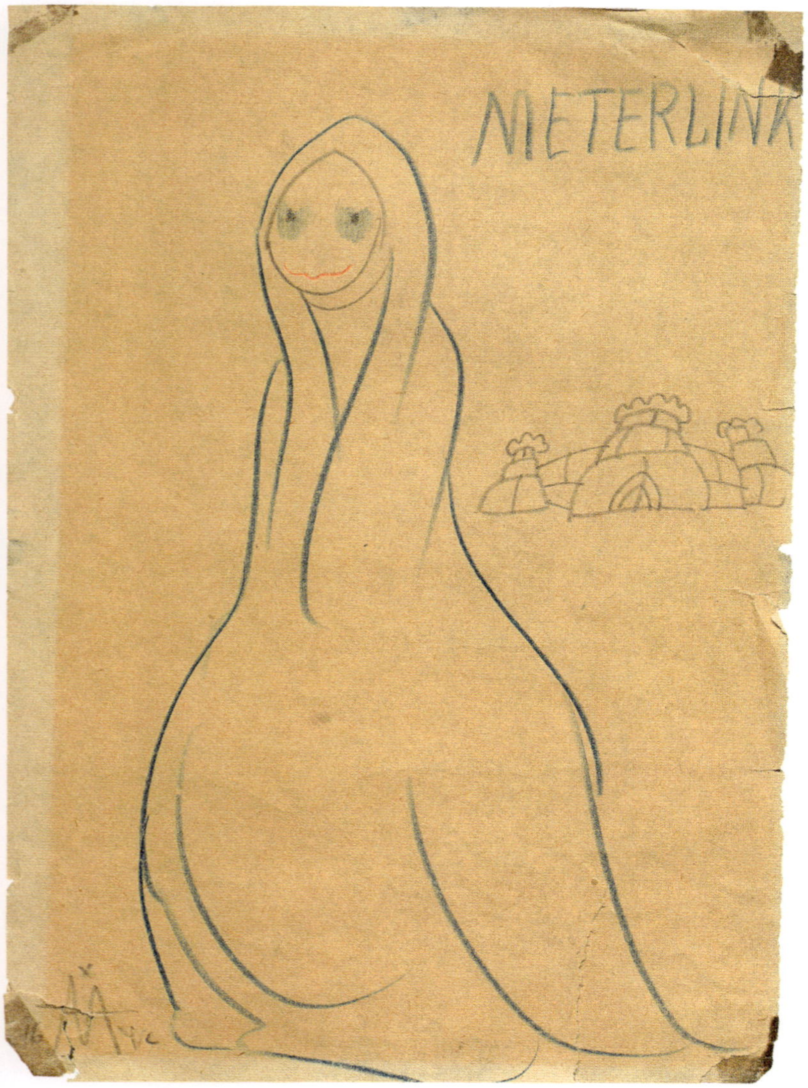

—OPPOSITE

From the cycle 'Souvenirs d'enfance' (Childhood memories) (1942):

TOP LEFT

Clown

BOTTOM LEFT

GeeGee

RIGHT

Those Nameless Friends

—THIS PAGE

LEFT

Ibsen (1942)

RIGHT

Meterlink (Maeterlinck) (1942)

—OVERLEAF

From the cycle 'The story of the prodigal son' (1942):

Text, left page, bottom right: False friends flattered him by palmistry

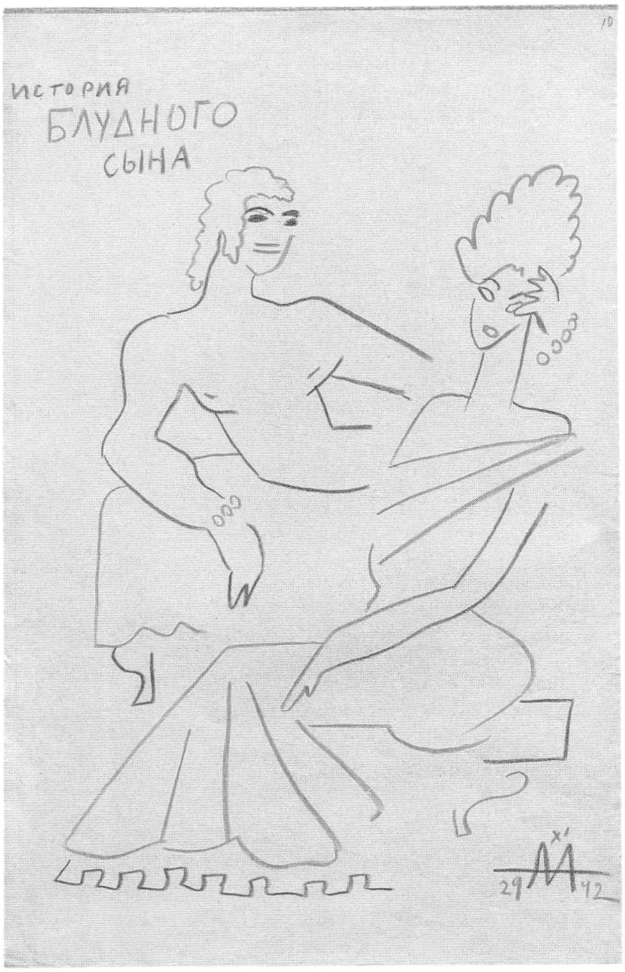
ИСТОРИЯ
БЛУДНОГО
СЫНА

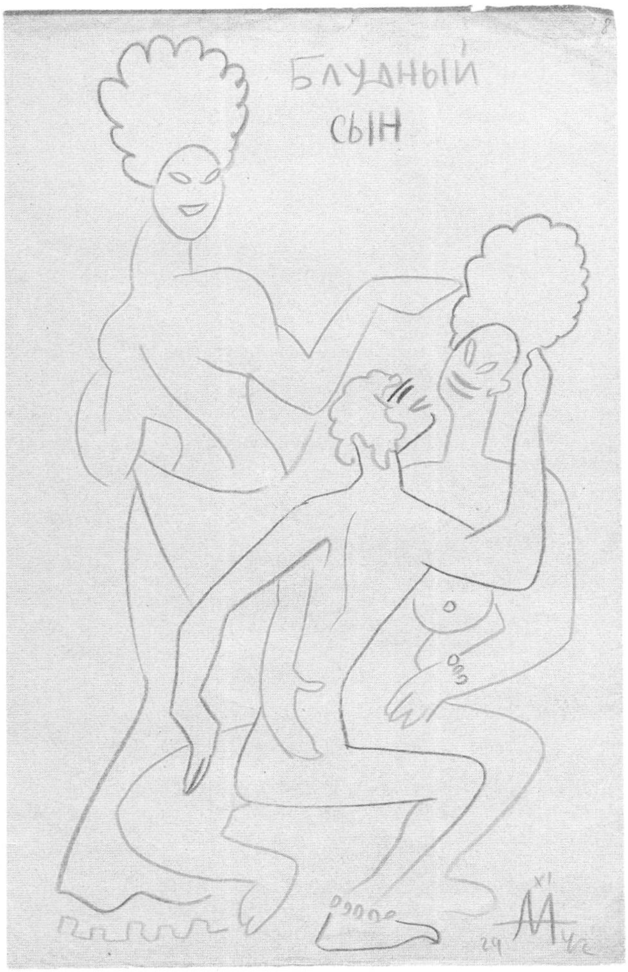
БЛУДНЫЙ
СЫН

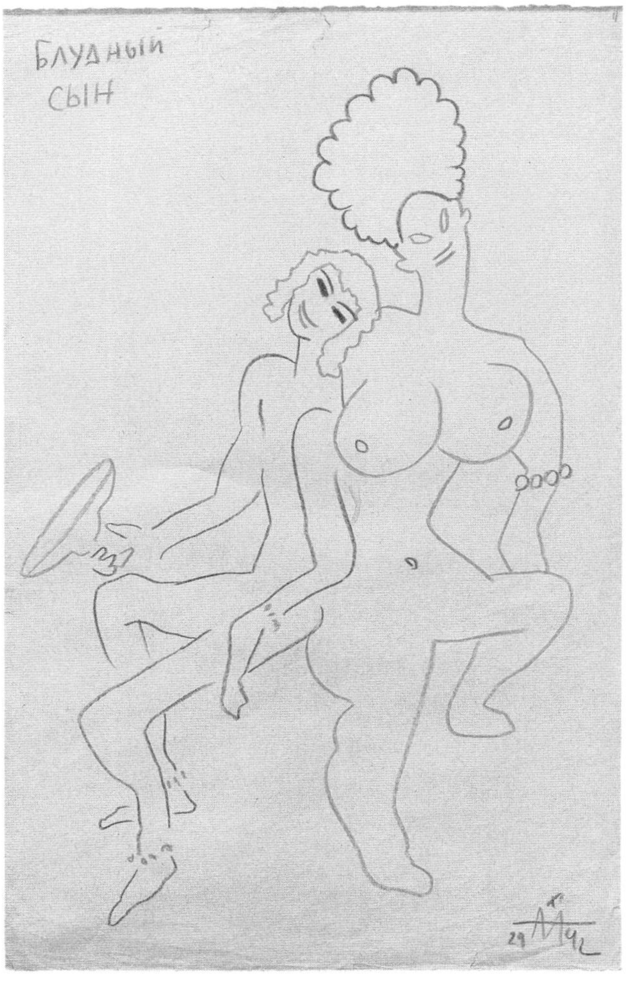
БЛУДНЫЙ
СЫН

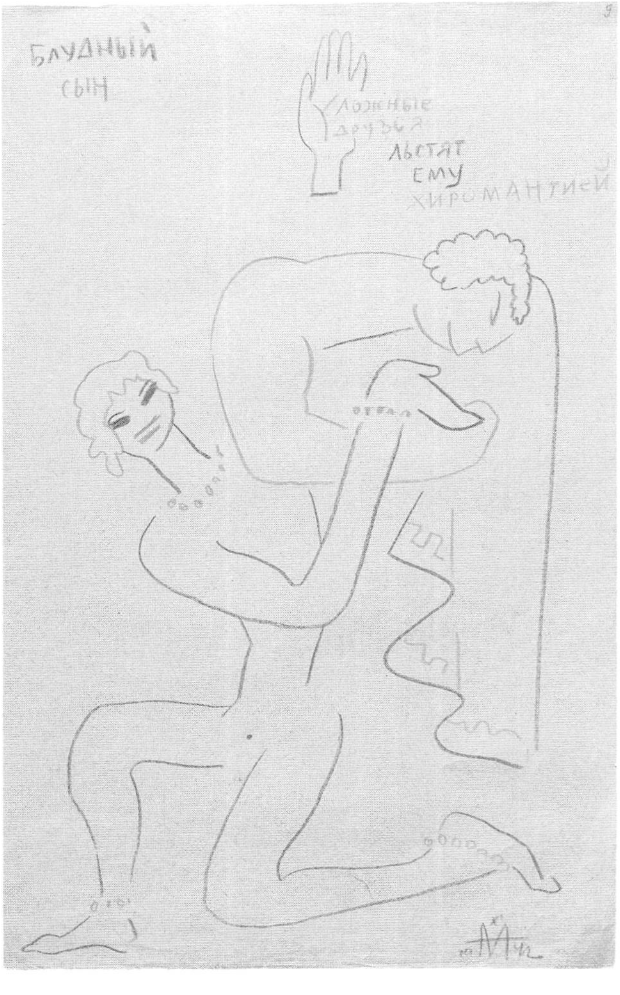
БЛУДНЫЙ
СЫН
ЛОЖНЫЕ
ДРУЗЬЯ
ЛЬСТЯТ
ЕМУ
ХИРОМАНТИЕЙ

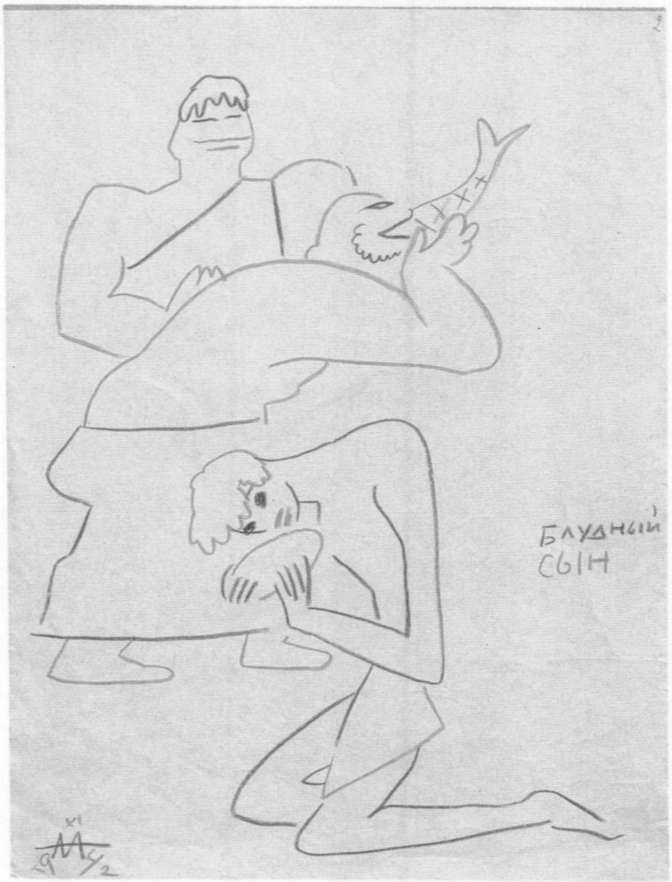
БЛУДНЫЙ
СЫН

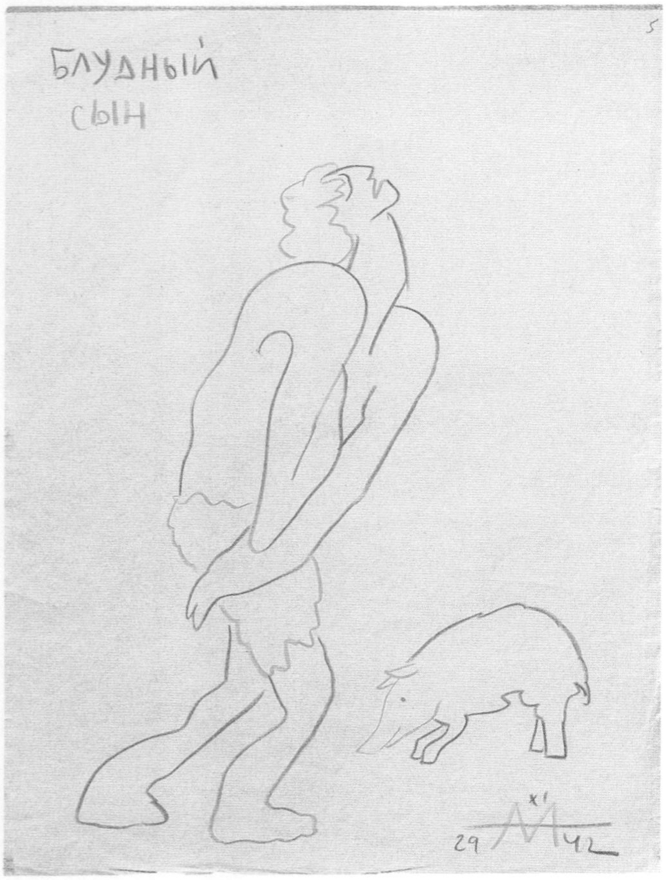
БЛУДНЫЙ
СЫН

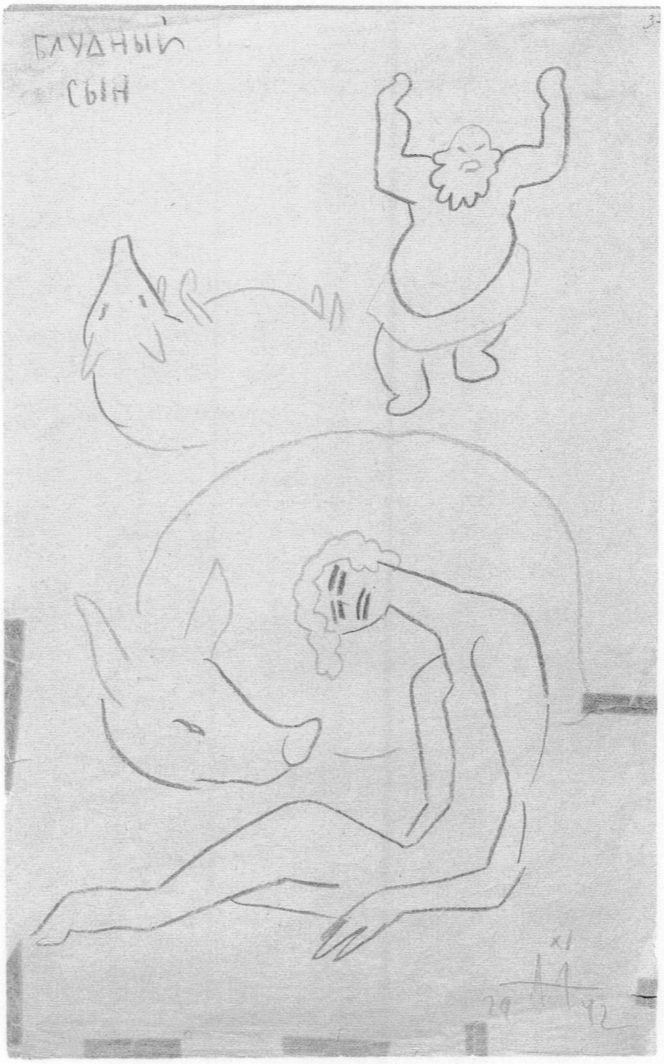
БЛУДНЫЙ
СЫН

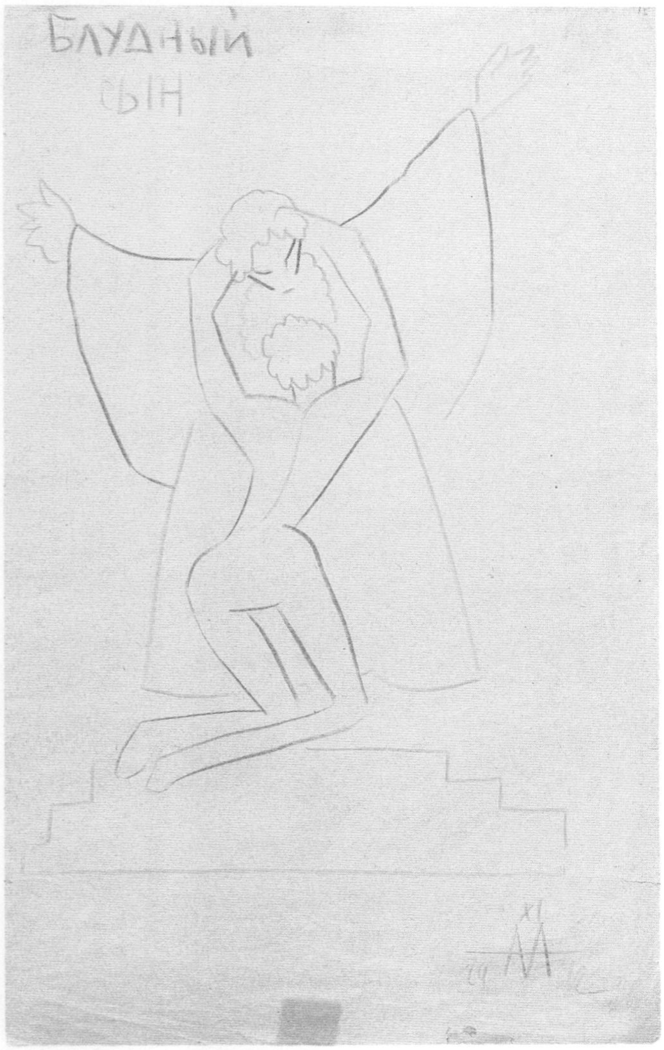
БЛУДНЫЙ
СЫН

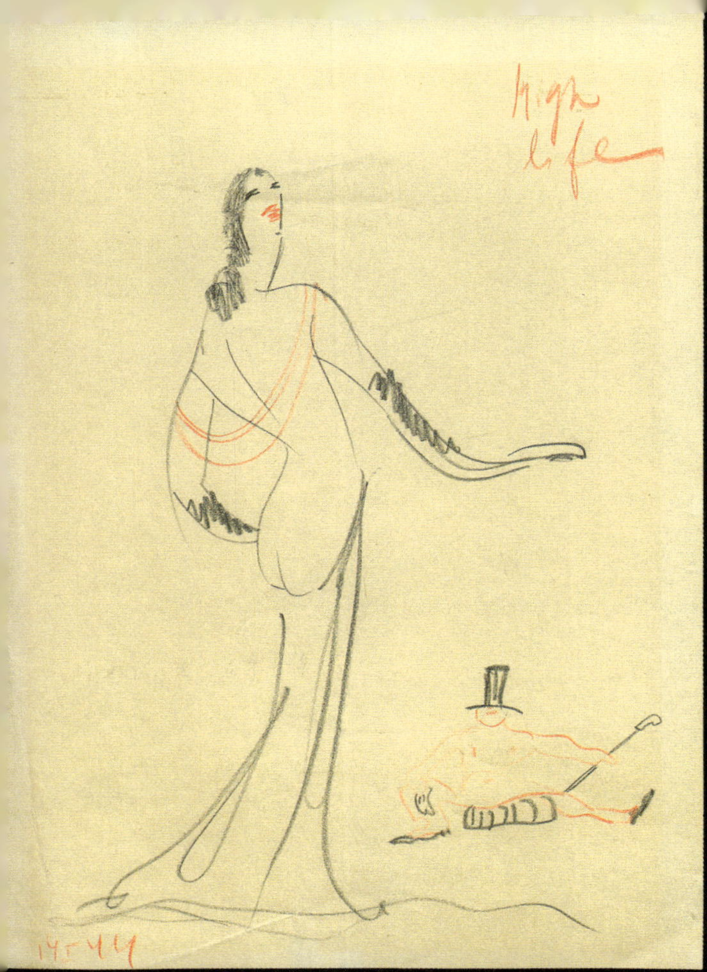
High life
14 I 44

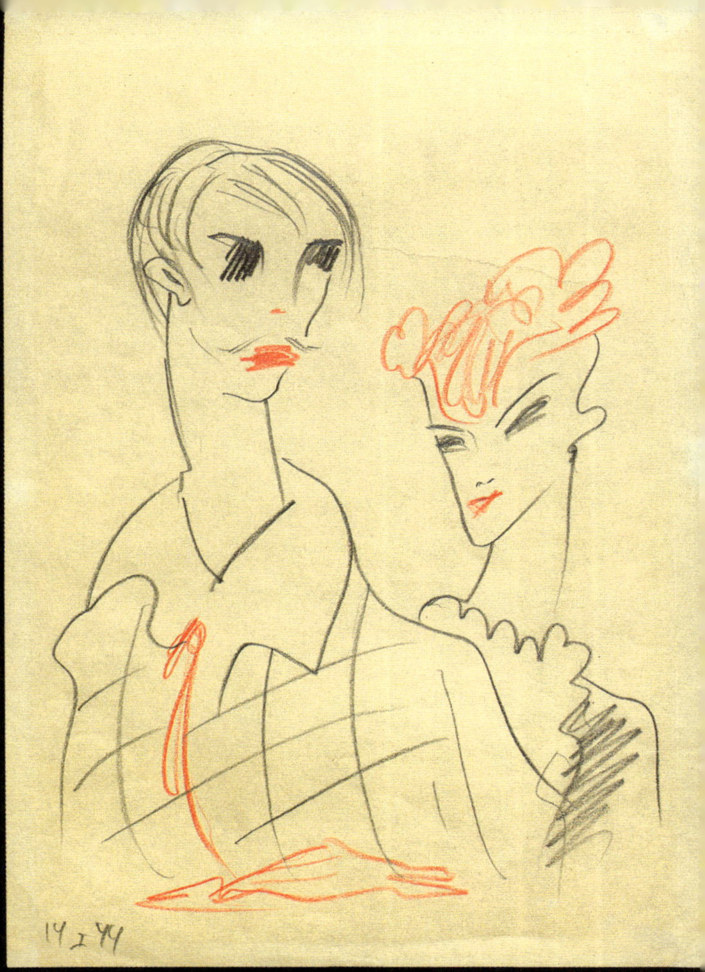
14 I 44

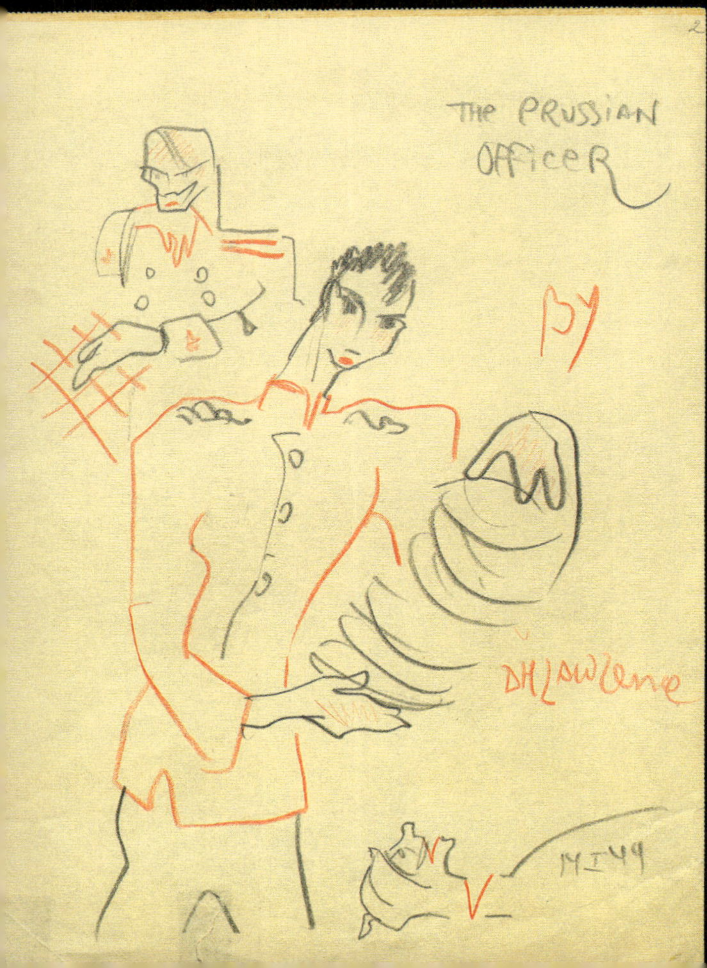
THE PRUSSIAN OFFICER
BY
DH Lawrence
14 I 44

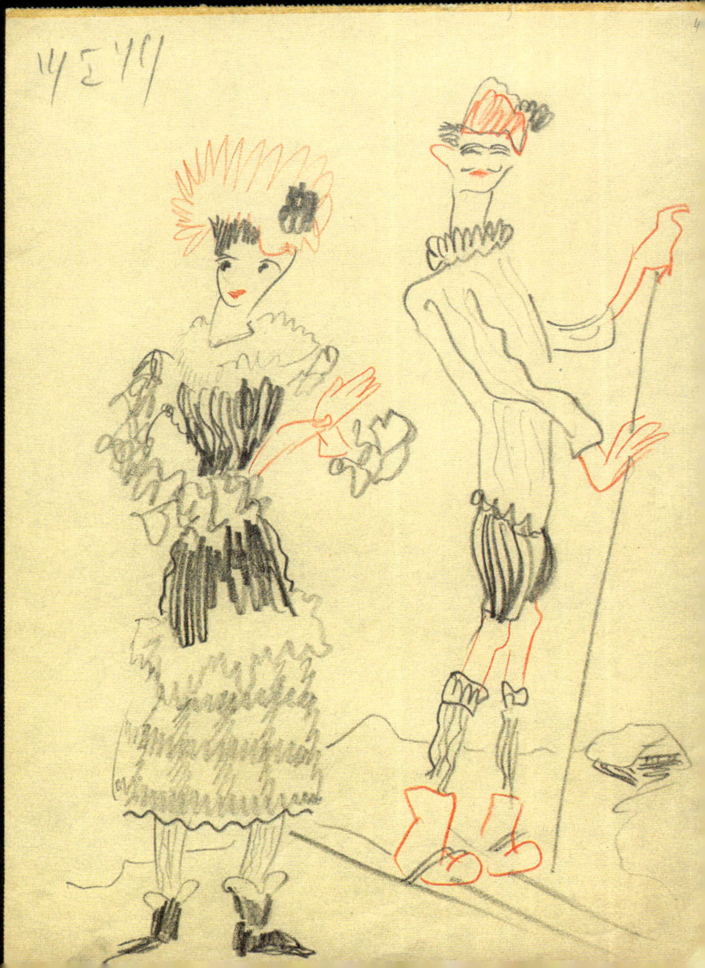
14 I 44

—OPPOSITE

From the cycle 'The themes of D. H. Lawrence' (1944):

TOP LEFT
High Life

TOP RIGHT
Lady Chatterley's Lover

BOTTOM LEFT
The Prussian Officer by D. H. Lawrence

BOTTOM RIGHT
Women in Love

—THIS PAGE
St John the Baptiste [sic] (1944)

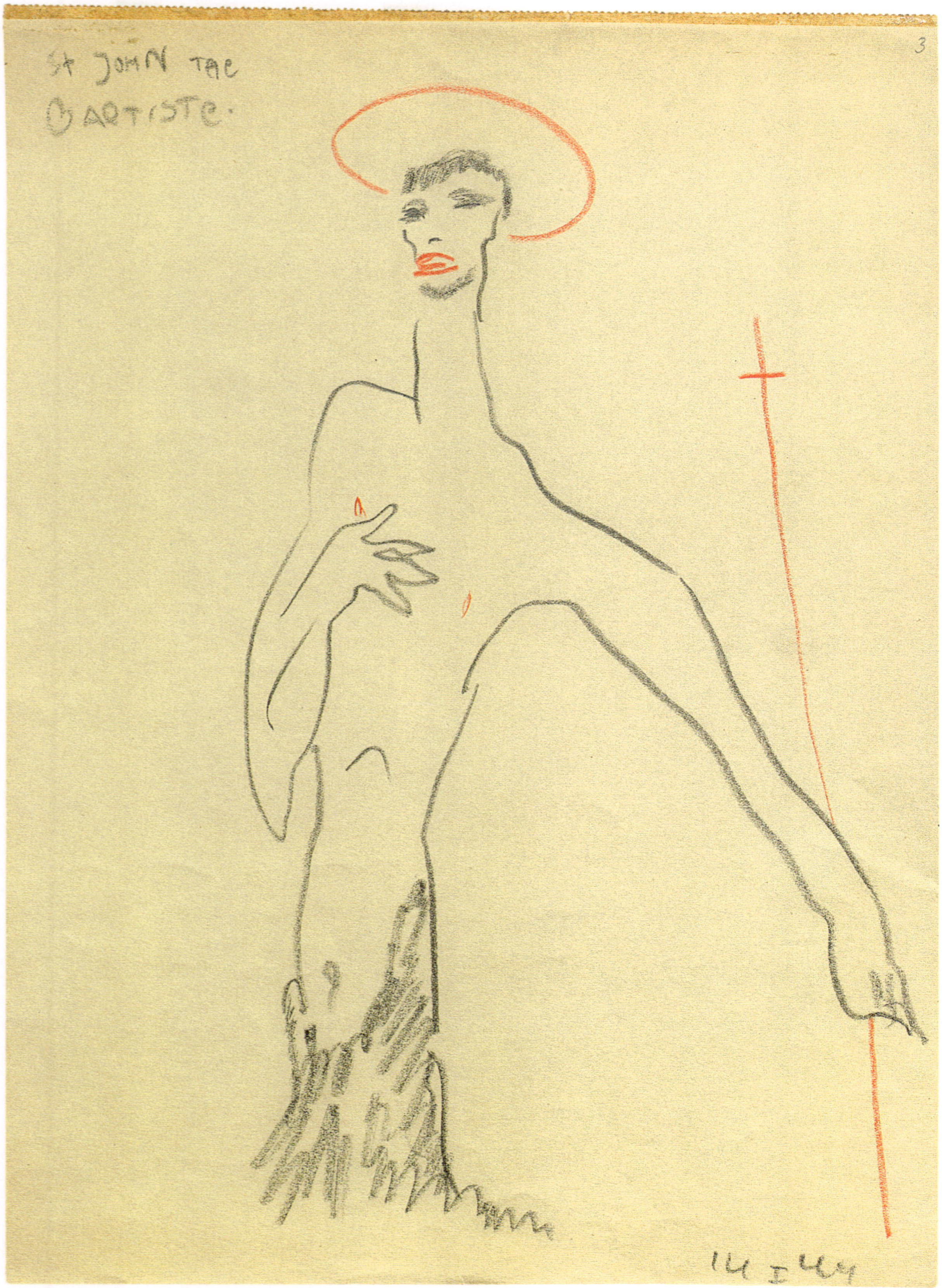

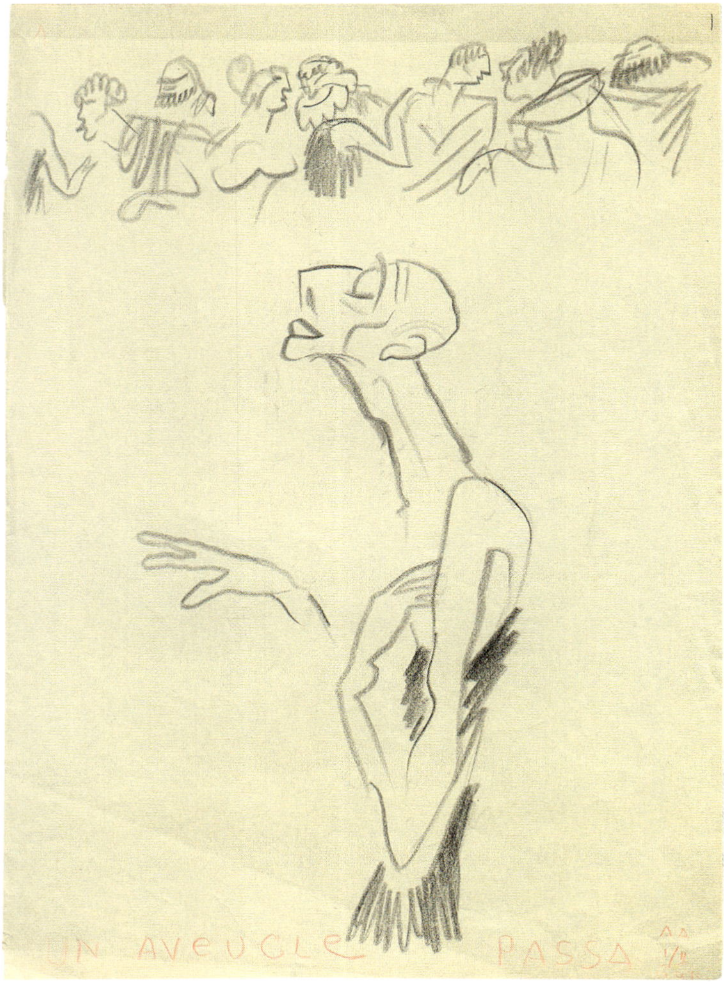
UN AVEUGLE PASSA
AA

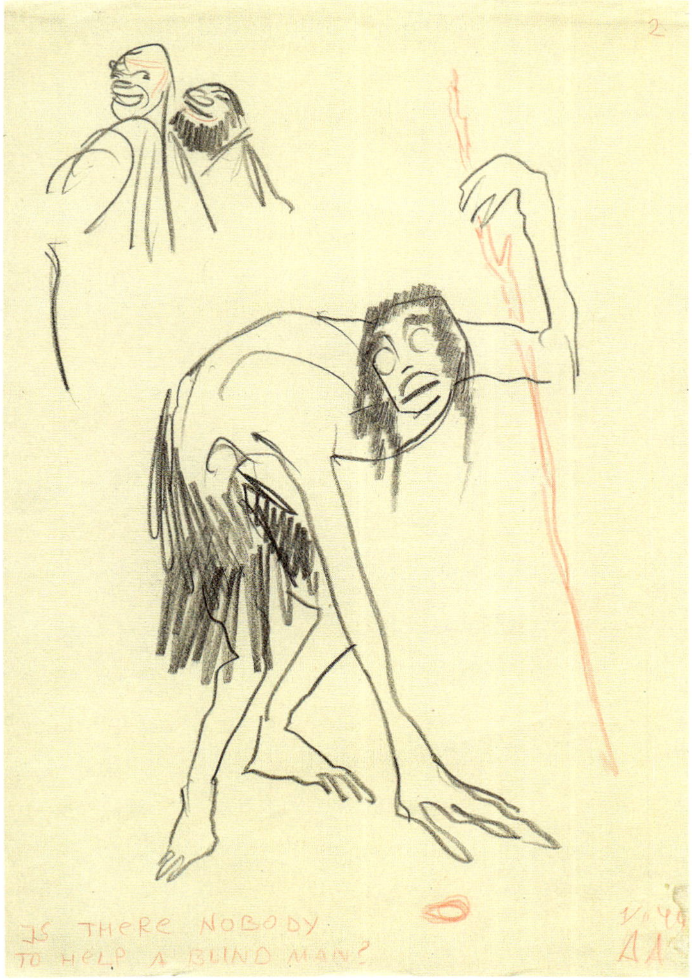
IS THERE NOBODY
TO HELP A BLIND MAN?
AA

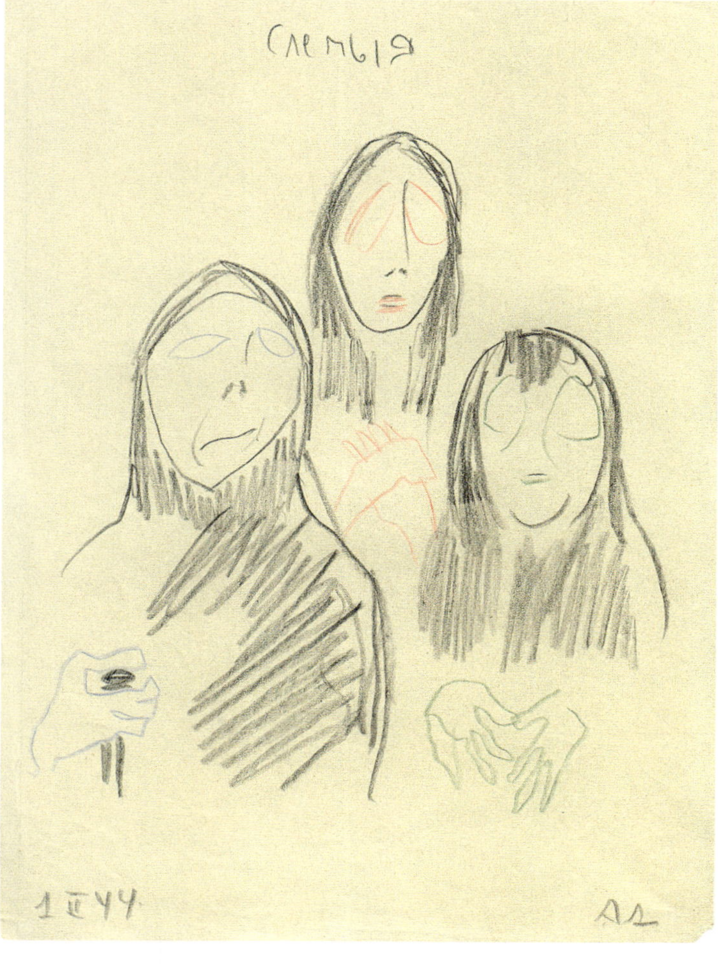
Слепыя
1 II 44
AA

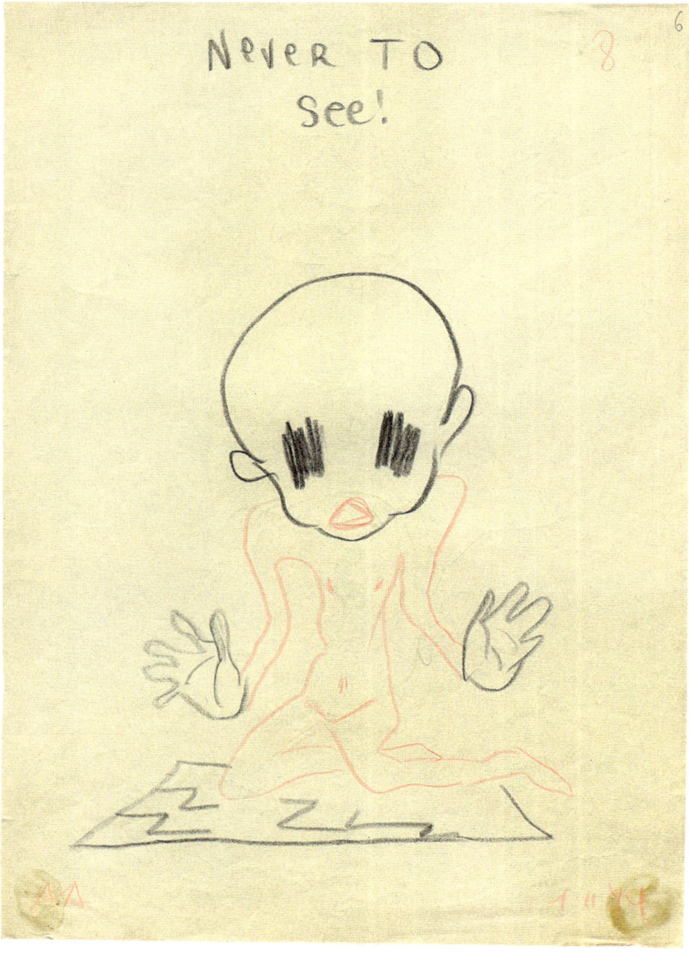
Never TO
See!
8
AA

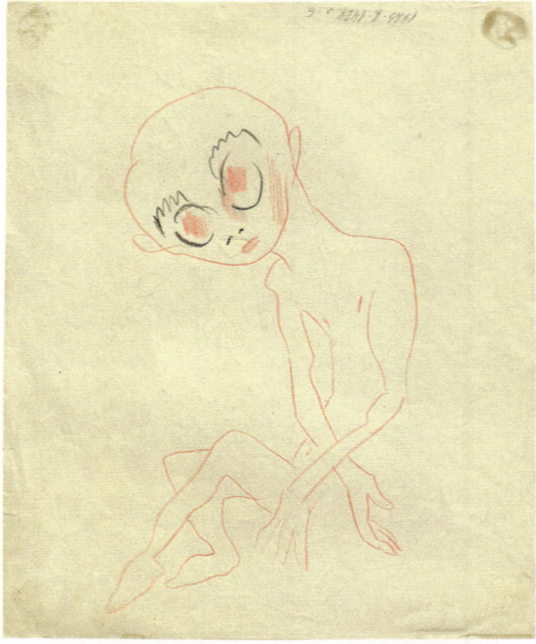

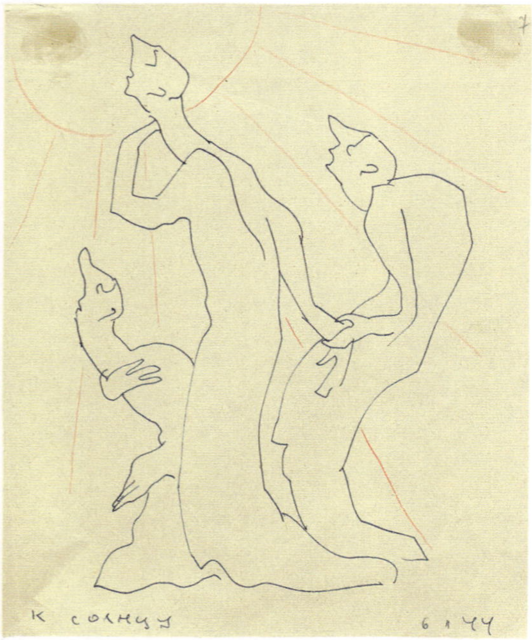

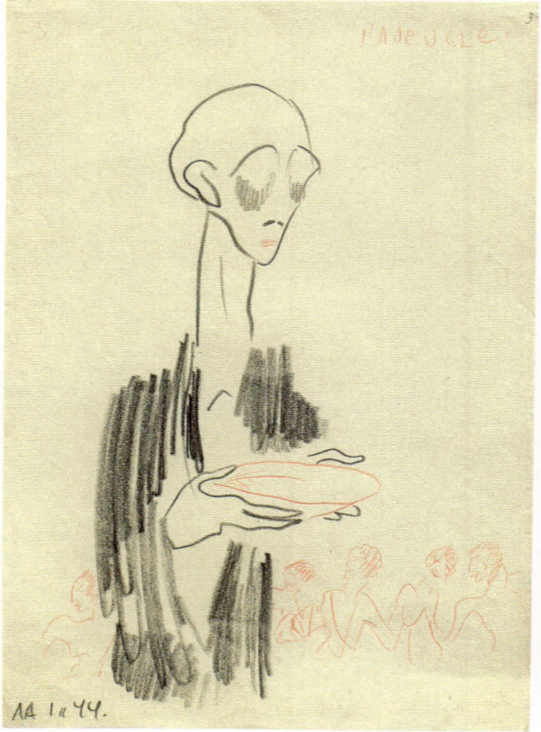

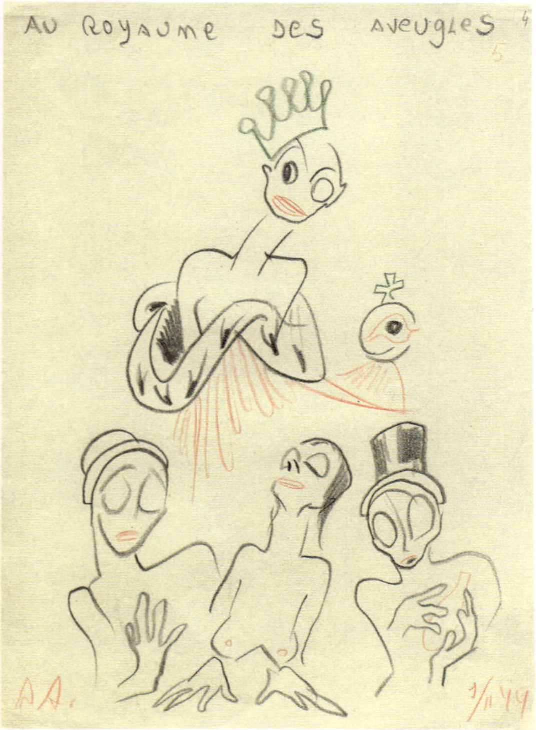

—OPPOSITE

From the cycle 'Au royaume des aveugles' (In the kingdom of the blind) (1944):

TOP LEFT
Un Aveugle Passa (A blind man passes)

TOP RIGHT
Is There Nobody to Help a Blind Man?

BOTTOM LEFT
Blind

BOTTOM RIGHT
Never to See

—THIS PAGE

From the cycle 'Au royaume des aveugles' (1944):

TOP LEFT
Untitled

TOP RIGHT
To the Sun

BOTTOM LEFT
L'Aveugle (The blind man)

BOTTOM RIGHT
Au Royaume des Aveugles

—OVERLEAF

LEFT PAGE
'Richard III at the beginning of Shakespeare's tragedy' (1944)

RIGHT PAGE
'Richard III at the end of Shakespeare's tragedy' (1944)

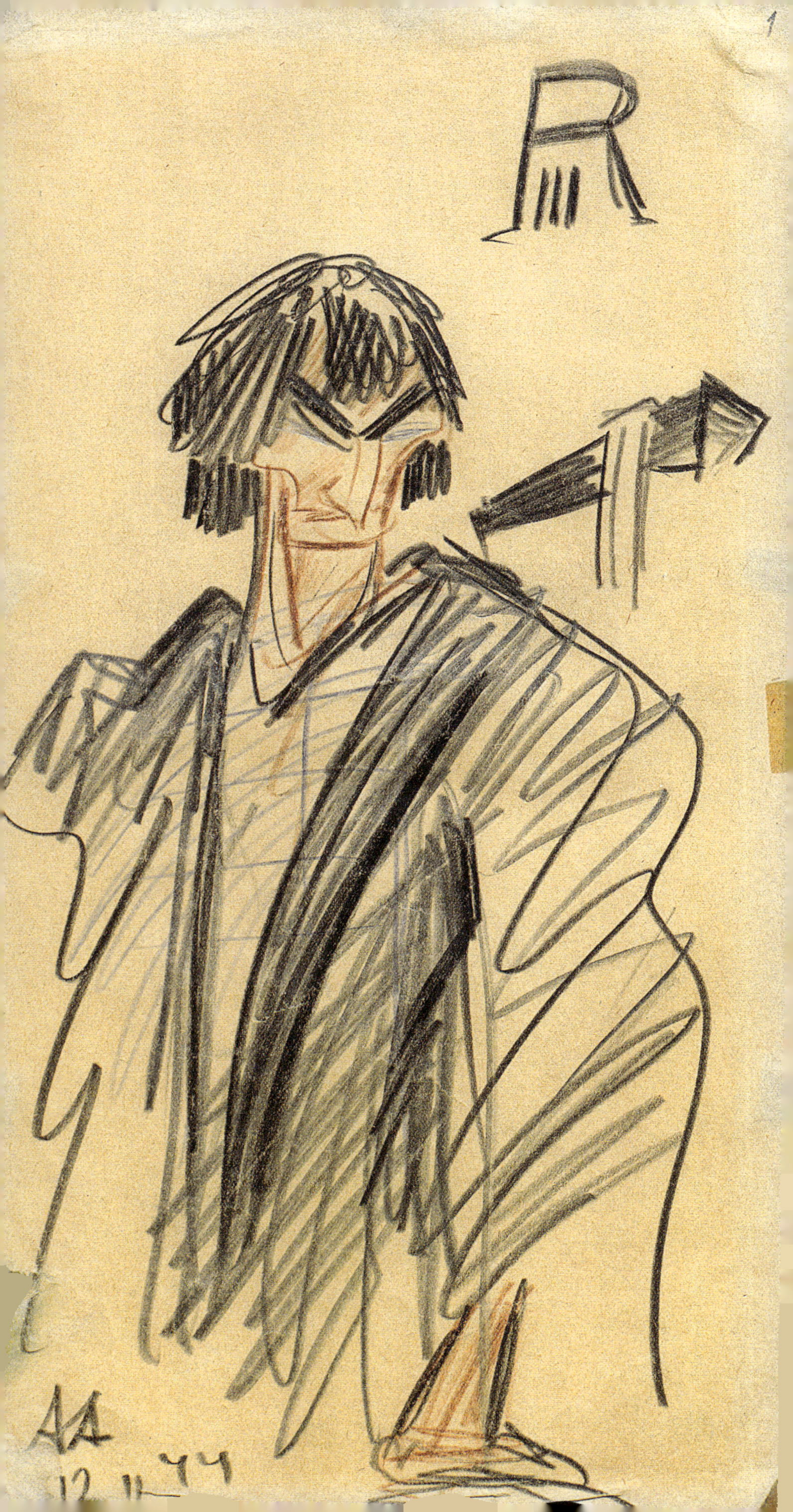
1
AA
12 11 44

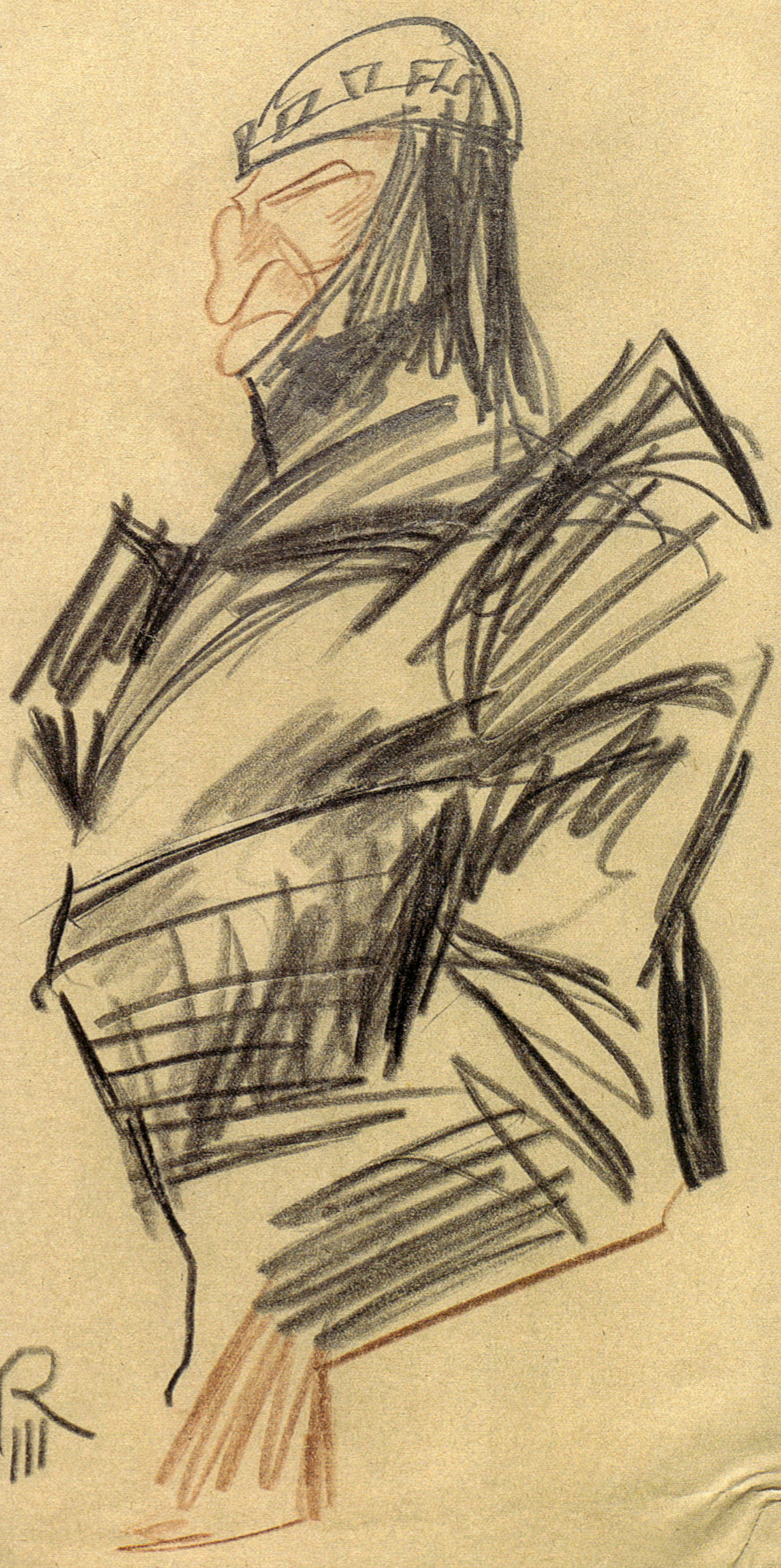

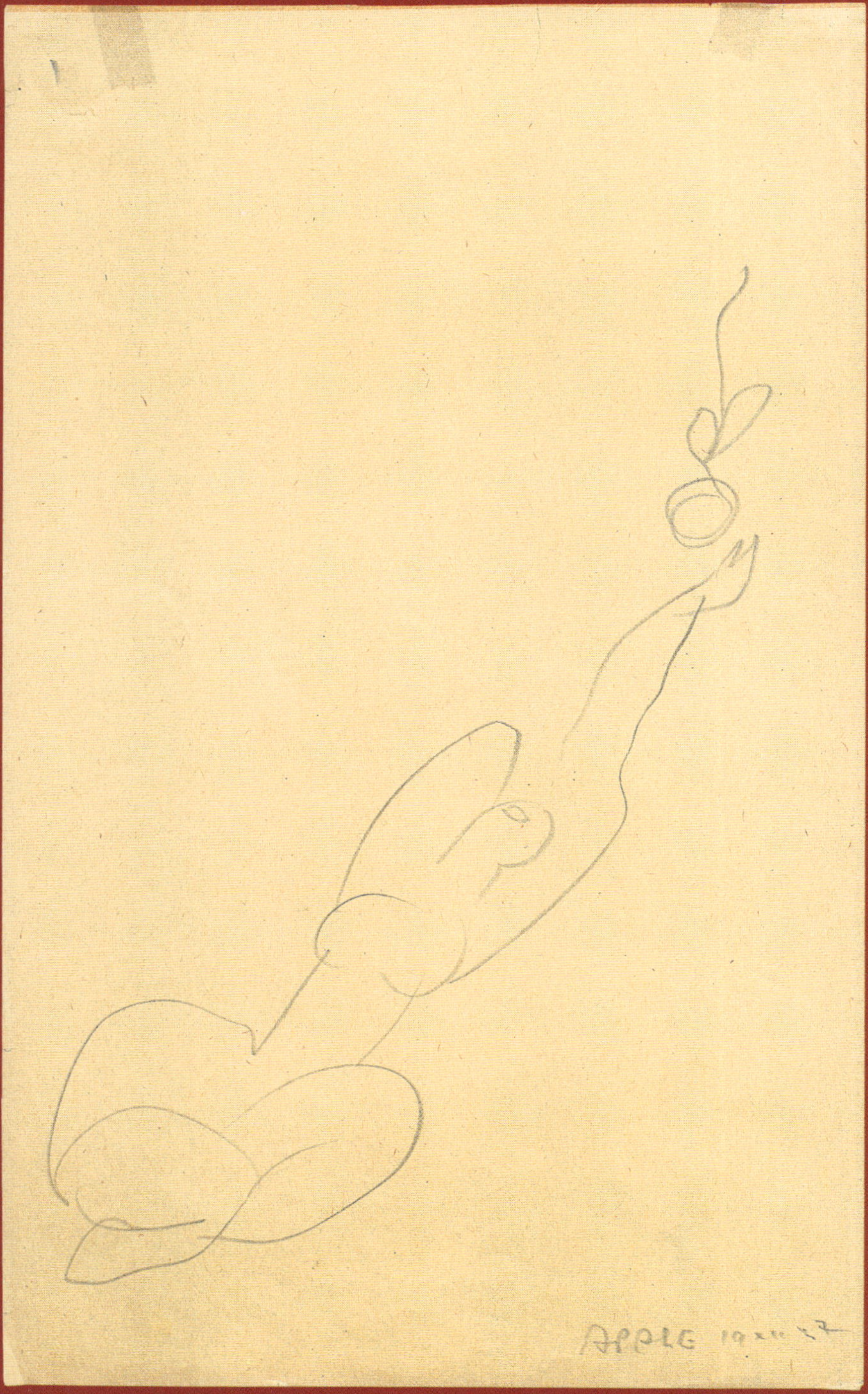
APPEL 19 XII 47

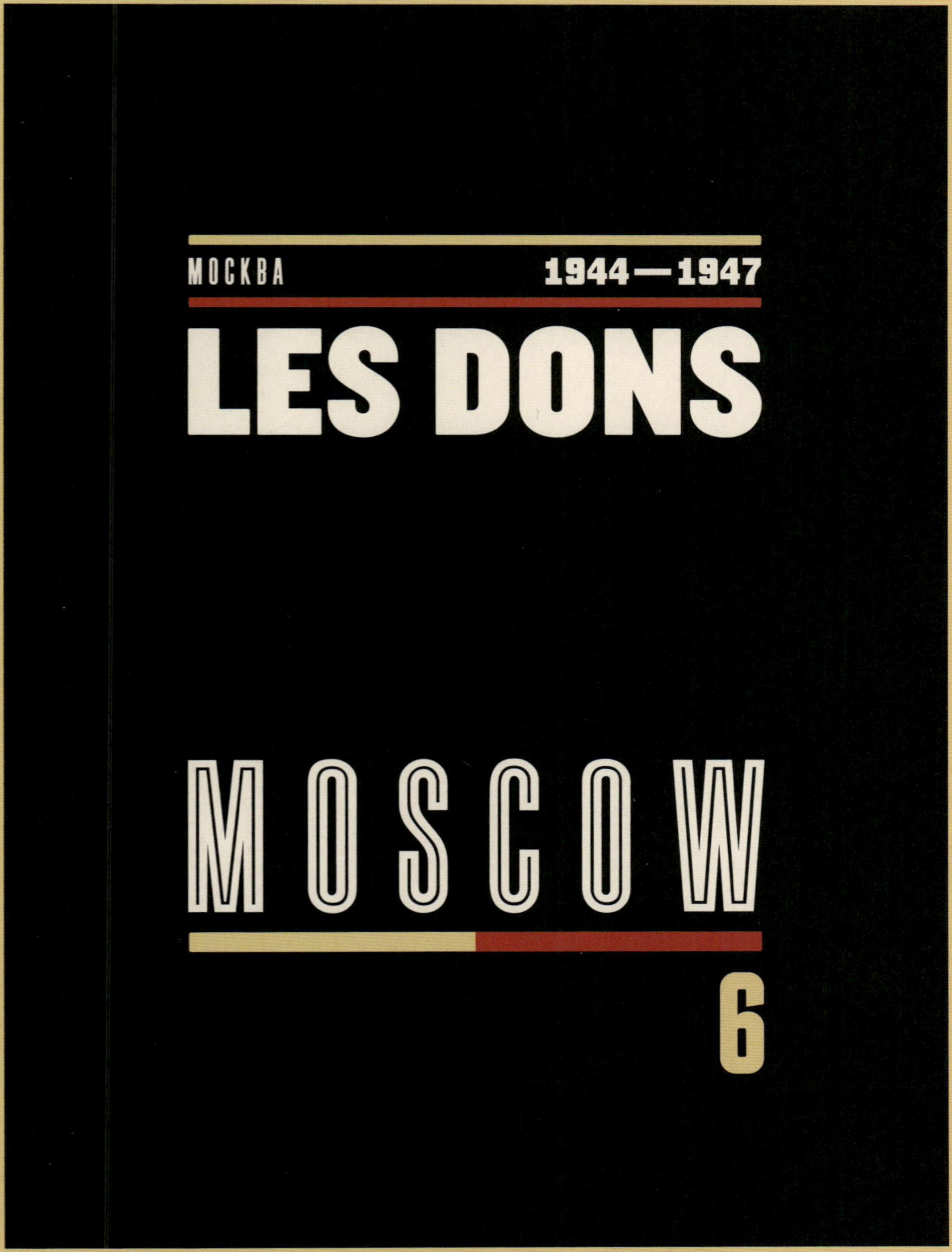
МОСКВА 1944—1947

LES DONS

MOSCOW

6

Seven drawings belonging to the cycle 'Les dons' (Gifts) came into existence on 19 December 1947.

What strange stories Eisenstein had dreamt up, amid Moscow's December frosts! It is as though he were remembering the nymphs of ancient Greece. But not their amatory sufferings and delights, sung in the old myths and passing thence into European culture. No, rather the peaceable joys of their everyday life.

A nude dryad sits on the ground and reaches for an apple on a branch. A Nereid dives into the sea in search of an oyster shell. An Oread, dressed in a light chiton, jumps after a butterfly. A Naiad stands in a stream and tries to catch a dragonfly.

Two more dryads. One hangs from a branch by her foot, joining the tree and the grass. The other, bold and acrobatic, stretches out her foot towards a squirrel that has slipped from her grasp.

But look: there is something wrong with the theme. There is a blatant anachronism: this nameless nymph going away into the distance...has a lighted cigarette! The tobacco smoke – unknown to the ancient Greeks – curls on the coarse brownish-yellow paper, all the more intriguing because Eisenstein himself was never a smoker.

He did not know, of course, that this would be the last cycle of drawings he would ever make. But he certainly remembered a prediction that had been made about him back in October 1930, in Hollywood, by a famous palm-reader known as Cheiro – a pseudonym used in his practice and in his writings by the self-styled Count Louis Hamon, who was in fact an Irishman by the name of William John Warner. Cheiro had predicted of Eisenstein that:

> ***With regard to health, although he has physically a strong vital constitution, I fear he will not live to any great age. The mental strain appears to affect the nervous system, and through it, the heart. His thirty-second year is not a favourable year for his health, neither is his forty-first; his fiftieth year appears to be extremely critical.***[1]

Eisenstein was to turn fifty in January 1948. And whenever people suggested a birthday party, he always replied: 'Come to the wake.' Those who did not know about the prediction, but remembered the myocardial infarction he had suffered two years previously, tried to reassure both themselves and Eisenstein: 'Fifty is no age, you have years and years left to live.' A few who knew about Cheiro's prophecy were bitter: 'How can you believe in palmistry! It's your superstition that'll be the end of you.' But Eisenstein only smiled: he was convinced that palmistry and its predictions were credible.

The first four characters in the 'Gifts' cycle are given the same gesture: the nymphs cannot quite reach some object, they can only reach out for the apple, the oyster, the butterfly and the dragonfly. The dryads have better luck: the first catches a blade of grass in her mouth, and the second manages to touch the squirrel's tail with her foot. Complete possession of the cigarette turns into smoke – like life departing from the nymph herself.

In the preface to his memoirs – which he had begun in hospital after his heart attack – Eisenstein had admitted that he felt life slipping away, and suddenly realized that he had largely failed to make contact with its simple joys:

> ***In February '46 I was struck down by a heart attack.***
> ***And for a few months, for the first time in my whole life, I was forcibly stopped, I was confined to my bed.***
> ***My blood circulated sluggishly.***
> ***My thoughts moved slowly.***
> ***Ahead of me were several months when I couldn't move about at all.***
> ***I was actually glad. I thought, at last I'll have a chance to look around, to have a think.***
> ***And then I'll understand myself, life, the forty-eight years I've lived.***
> ***Let me say right off: I didn't understand a thing.***
> ***Not a thing about life. Not a thing about myself. And not a thing about those forty-eight years I'd lived.***
> ***Nothing. Except maybe one thing.***
> ***Which was that I'd lived my life at a gallop, without looking around, as though I were always changing trains, rushing from one to catch the next.***
> ***With my attention always fixed firmly on the second hand.***
> ***Getting somewhere.***
> ***Not being late.***
> ***Making it to something.***
> ***Getting away again.***
> ***Fragments of childhood, a chunk of adolescence, layers of adulthood all flash past, as if seen through a carriage window.***
> ***Vivid, varied, shifting, colourful.***
> ***And suddenly the horrible realization!***
> ***That I haven't held onto any of it, haven't grasped it, have only sipped at it.***
> ***Never drunk it to the bottom.***
> ***Occasionally gulped it down, but mostly just bitten at it.***
> ***On the way up somewhere, I feel I've been living thinking about coming down.***

Unpacking my suitcase and already thinking about packing it.

Putting my books on the shelves and wondering who would take them down after my death.

And kissing new, still-unfamiliar lips for the first time, already thinking about their farewell kiss.[2]

The last sentence of this passage from his memoirs was written on a separate sheet of paper. Why not in the main text? Was it added later? Picked out from the mass of everyday cares and business? Or was Eisenstein still unsure how open his memoirs could be – memoirs that he also did not know when he would be able to publish?

He wrote the foreword to his memoirs in May 1946. A whole year later, his alarm grew – not only for himself and for the fate of his unfinished film, but also for the general state of the world, which more and more resembled the preparations for another war.

His colleagues suggested that the failure of his heart muscle had been caused by the back-breaking tension of filming the three episodes of *Ivan the Terrible* at once, or by a premonition that the second episode, just completed and still not shown to Stalin, would be banned. His devoted friend, Pera Atasheva – to whom Eisenstein, after his time in Mexico, gave the nickname 'soldadera' (she was at his side in all troubles and battles) – worried that 'Old Man' spent the few hours he had free from filming and teaching with his manuscripts – his only breaks were the minutes he spent drawing. The actress Vera Maretskaya blamed herself for dancing too wildly with Eisenstein at a Cinema House ball on 2 February: perhaps their eccentric foxtrot had damaged his heart....

Nobody knew that there had been another blow, straight at Eisenstein's heart, only a week before the ball. It was more than six months after his heart attack before he could put the experience down on paper. Twice he tried to write about it, once in his diary and once in his memoirs, and twice he retreated. Finally, on 8 August, he sketched out a drama in words about a film-maker and a rich girl – using for the latter a nickname (the Dollar Princess), after the title of an operetta that had been popular in his childhood.

First Eisenstein introduced the main characters of the tale, in English, French and Russian, as though he were making it up before our eyes:

We will try to fictionalize one's tragic romantic experience.

Let's see how the symbolizing machinery works.

Millionaire's daughter made...Princess (*NB:* Die Dollar-Prinzessin*).*

The movie director builder of 'Canvases' made – Cathedral Builder.

His inability to talk and to make conversation we transform [into] a literally swallowed tongue.

He swallowed his tongue and talked through his cathedrals.

Now elaborating this image we set:

The pillars of his cathedrals became his consonants.

The rose windows, his vowels.

The beating of his heart, the roll of the organ.

The reach of his thought, the dome that covers the nave.

The ringing of the bells, the voice of his message.

And, hidden somewhere in the cellar crypts of the cathedrals he was building, he placed mounting arches, gallery after gallery, and vaults, enfilade after enfilade...He spoke through the coloured patterns of his glass windows.

He invited people up to the very heights of thought, with the spires of his bell-towers.

He drew them into the greatness of feelings, with the organ.

Himself he was wordless and without a tongue.

And so he became the keeper of his own creations, which spoke for him.

As dancers can be the slaves of their own feet, and the girls who sing to the lute can be slaves to their own voices.

As those whose skill it is to pluck the strings of the harp can be slaves to their own hands.

Himself he remained in the shadows, whispering to himself or writing in the dust with a quivering finger:

'What am I, if not an assistant to my own thoughts, an obedient servant to the things I create...

A vessel through which the people, my brethren, speak. In myself, however: nothing...'

And one day, into his newest cathedral, there walked the Little Princess.

She went past the vaulted galleries.

And through the multicoloured radiance of the windows.

And she gazed into his underground crypt.

And took him by the hand and led him to a great celebration.[3]

Here, the introduction to the fairy tale breaks off. But, on the same day, Eisenstein returned to it and began again – this time in English. In the second excerpt, he presents the Princess and the Cathedral Builder quite differently: he surrounds them with mysterious characters, touches only lightly on the initial dramatic situation and finishes with a surprise ending:

> ***The Little Princess and the Great Cathedral Builder who swallowed his tongue.***
> ***Once upon a time there lived the richest Little Princess in the world.***
> ***Never married,***
> ***afraid,***
> ***and so she whored around and especially with a red headed lad of the lowest grade,***
> ***famous for his voice that carried over the oceans, and by his force that could overturn anything in the world.***
> ***On the other end of the great big world there lived the famous Cathedral Builder who swallowed his tongue and talked through the edifices he built.***
> ***At high table were the greatest Grands of the world at that time.***
> ***The Chinese Prince besides her Father, Earl Venceslas renown[ed] [in] one sixth of the world with his fair-haired spouse – Pearl of the East.***
> ***Sir Archibald, native of Scotland.***
> ***They drank the health of the Builder, but he couldn't say a word and had no Arches, Pillars and Counterforts.***
> ***So he was mute.***
> ***Then the Princess asked him to deliver her of a drunken beastly Baron trying to seduce her by his love proposals.***
> ***Asking her to dance with him.***
> ***So he delivered her and explained that there remains no need for dancing.***
> ***'Let us drink for springtime in the Great Builder's heart.'***
> ***Said her Father, the King, but being a Magician and not being it enough he couldn't break at once the spell resting on the poor little Great Builder.***
> ***But time went on and the Magician's words like seeds began to flourish.***
> ***And the poor little Builder saw that his spell and the spell of the Little Princess were nearly the same.***
> ***When somebody looked at him, he thought they looked at his Cathedrals.***
> ***When somebody looked at her, she thought they were hunting for her millions.***
> ***So he ran to her and wanted to tell her – sister don't we suffer of the same, and shouldn't we go together?***
> ***Aren't we really worth nothing at all, you for yourself, and me for mine?***
> ***But never, never could he get in touch with her. – Fate was against them. And so she went away with her Fatum. And he remained muter than ever.***[4]

Even if we suspect that this fairy tale is no more than an exercise in the metaphorical treatment of events and persons – just one more of the writing tasks Eisenstein invented for his students – we must nonetheless admit that it conceals real events and real persons. The fairy-tale pseudonyms are quite transparent, and the prototypes are not altogether hidden by their masks.

The reference to 'Earl Venceslas renowned in one sixth of the world' clearly represents Vyacheslav (i.e. Wenceslas) Molotov, the Soviet premier from 1930 to 1941 and foreign minister of the USSR from 1939 to 1949. His 'fair-haired spouse' with the fairy-tale name 'Pearl of the East' really was called Pearl: she was Polina Zhemchuzhina (*zhemchuzhina* meaning 'pearl' in Russian) born *Perl* Semyonovna Karpovskaya.'Sir Archibald, native of Scotland' is Archibald John Kerr Clark, 1st Baron Inverchapel, the British ambassador to the USSR from 1942 to 1946 – a man known for his immoderate behaviour and fondness for excessive libations. The 'Chinese Prince' represents T. V. Soong, the foreign minister in the Kuomintang's Wuhan government. He had arrived in Moscow on 30 June 1945 for talks with Stalin that led to the signing of the Treaty of Friendship and Alliance between the USSR and China on 14 August.

Thus, the 'fairy tale' is set in the summer of 1945. And the setting is also clear: it is Spaso House, the residence of the United States' ambassador to the USSR, where the 'King' – at that time Averell Harriman, a millionaire banker and industrialist turned diplomat – gave a reception in honour of the distinguished Chinese guest.

In charge of receptions in Spasopeskovsky Lane, in the Arbat district, was the ambassador's assistant: his daughter Kathleen, one of the wealthiest heiresses in the United States. She organized the screenings of new Hollywood films at the US embassy, to which she invited – alongside diplomats and selected representatives of Soviet culture – Sergei Mikhailovich Eisenstein. It seems that on several occasions Kathleen had brought him American books he needed, and had given him copies of *Time* magazine – featuring information that Soviet citizens were not supposed to know.

Did Miss Harriman guess what emotions she evoked in the Russian director?

After the defeat of Nazi Germany, Averell Harriman's relationship with 'Uncle Joe' became more and more tense; and he knew that the Soviet leader was unhappy with him as US ambassador. On 24 January 1946, the King's mission in Moscow came to an end and the 'Little Princess' departed with him. The first time Eisenstein wrote down her name was on 4 July 1946: not in a fairy tale, but at the head of a draft chapter of his memoirs that he had just begun in English. And her name appeared in mysteriously Russianized form: 'From Katrinka to Kathleenka'.

The English text of the draft is preceded by a Russian epigraph: a quatrain by the Symbolist poet Aleksandr Blok.

All that fades, that is not forever,
You've buried deep in the past.
Like a baby you sleep, Ravenna,
In dozing eternity's arms.

Well, it took some 17 years to make this transition from an 'r' to an 'l', 'R' to 'L'...

These four lines – all that's left from the 'R'...

And even less from the 'L'...

There are chapters unpublishable, like human wear...unmentionable.[5]

Who was this mysterious 'Katherine', to whom Eisenstein had been emotionally attracted ('not forever'? And when? In 1927 or 1929? Seventeen years before 1944, or 1946?) and from whom he draws a line straight to Kathleen? What was the link between this Katherine and the poetry of Blok? And Ravenna? Or is the verse epigraph just a poetic metaphor for passing love, against the backdrop of eternity?

The transformation of feelings, including love, into images – metaphor, metonymy, synecdoche – was a phenomenon that Eisenstein saw as characteristic of his emotional life. He could have added: the transformation into a drawing.

Was there a real K.? In 1922, Eisenstein had a brief liaison with Agniya Kasatkina, a student at Meyerhold's school: he referred to her (in English) as 'the first, I slept with'.

The same mysterious K. occurs in another text, too, devoted to the very topic of drawing: 'Some Personal Reflections on a Taboo':

I liked the maiden K. The two of us became close, by a very slow and difficult process. It's surprising: I'm drawing rather briskly. In my drawing I achieve a reflex-quick translation of a thought or idea straight into the drawing. That's how A. N. Ostrovsky taught the art of acting, using the actual term 'reflex'!

Reducing the translation phase to a minimum. I'm trying to think in lines. So I've driven the rubber and the preliminary sketch for future treatment out of my presence.

I spent a long time trying to capture K. on paper, from memory. I was just as unsuccessful as I had been on the other side of the page. In the end I got it. And I got what was characteristic about her appearance when...well, you know when. But not as a result of that, not at all. No! Just the two lines of knowledge, developing uniformly, reached completion at one and the same moment. The model submitted on paper – and in the psychology of consent.[6]

How can we understand this confession? Did Eisenstein and 'maiden K.' have a love affair after all? Or is the confession a mystification – a mere desire to reach her, to touch her?

The continuation of the same note reveals important psychological connections between drawing and the artist's feelings:

It seems almost like a magical operation. And up to that moment, success – in terms of achieving a likeness on paper – just wouldn't come!

That's a curious, spooky thing!

But in this case I think the drawing echoed the gradual way I'd come to know the features of the model. Merged with the model. Psychologically, at first. If we love someone, we come to resemble them. Do we not catch ourselves sometimes reproducing the one we love in our gestures and intimations, our movements, our manner of thinking?

And has the English language not retained the term 'like' to denote the first stage of love, the stage before fusion ('love'): and does 'like' not mean both 'feel affection for' (to a lesser degree than 'love') and... 'resembling'?! Is this not glaringly obvious in women who are in love?

Do they not think our thoughts, speak in our accustomed phrases, use our words?

[...] For a man, it seems, this [objectivization] takes place externally. In material. In the environment. Into the heroine of a novel. Into the figure of a woman on the screen. Into drama. Into an elegy. Into... a drawing.

But complete objectivization is only possible if one completely enters (psychologically) into the image

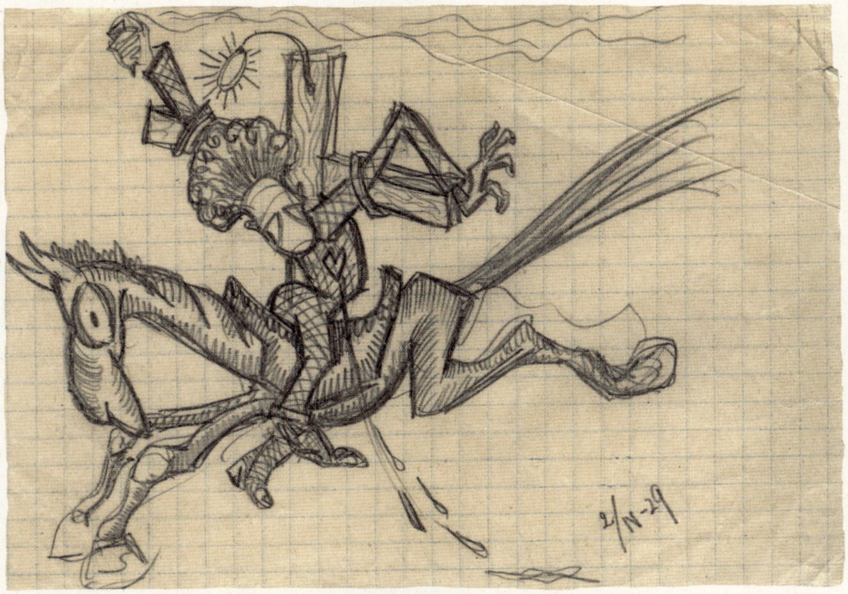

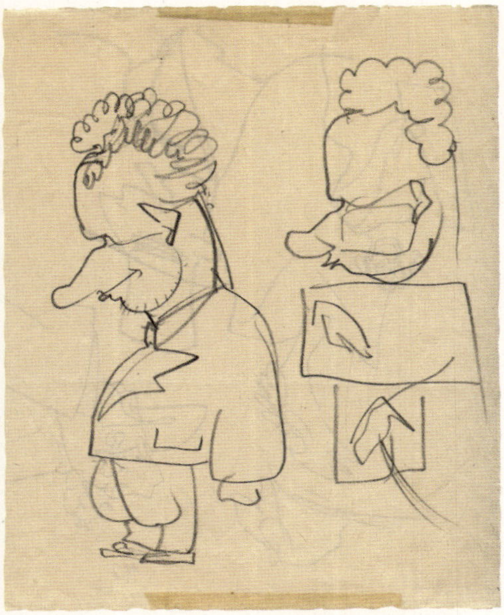

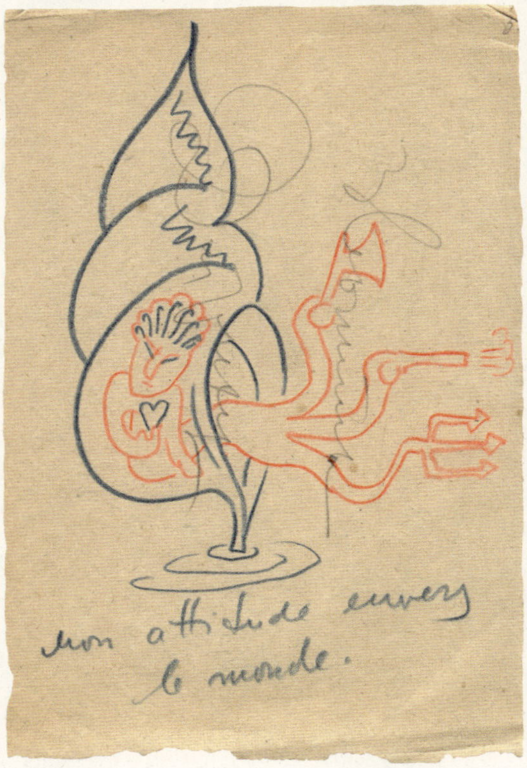

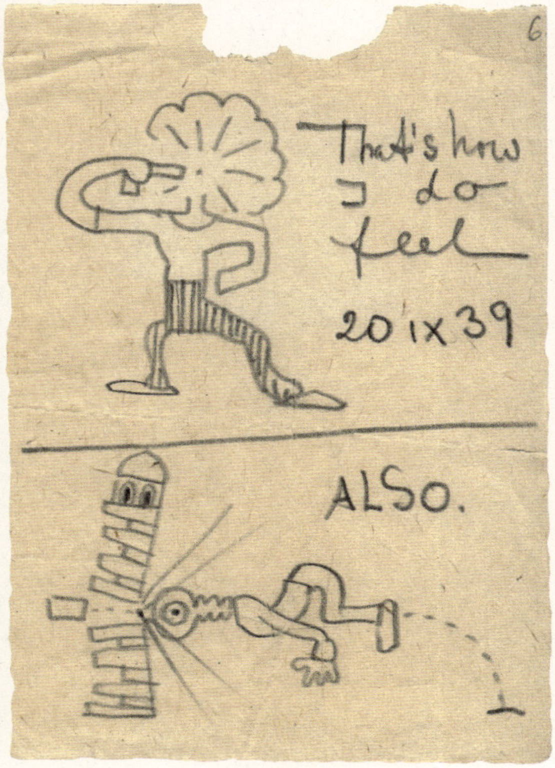

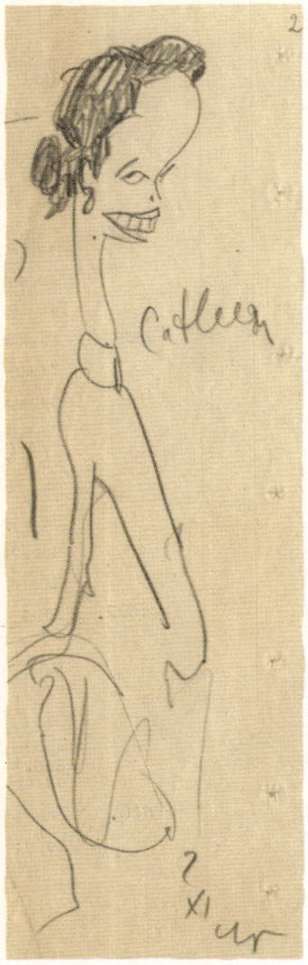

—PAGE 264

From the cycle 'Les dons: Apple' (1947)

—THIS PAGE

TOP LEFT

'Self-caricature' (1929)

TOP RIGHT

'Self-caricature' (1940s)

BOTTOM LEFT

Mon Attitude Envers le Monde (1930)
(My attitude towards the world)

BOTTOM CENTRE

That's How I Do Feel. Also (1939)

BOTTOM RIGHT

Kathleen (1945)

of one's model. This is the moment at which one simultaneously accepts her into oneself. This is fusion. This is where complete knowledge comes from.

But we remember what 'knowing' a woman means in the biblical sense. It does not only mean fusing with her, but mastering her – as a suitor.

You can only depict the other person in the second stage. After the first, when you first start imitating the model.

You reproduce her subjectively in yourself, taking her into yourself in order then to return her to objectivity as an image on paper.

Before this process of interpenetration – entering into the model and accepting her into yourself – is complete, no successful image will appear on the sheet of paper.

Image, specifically. I mean a combination of features that will make you recreate the original in your perception, not a likeness – a proper and correct dead depiction of what is given as existing.

So an image on paper is a faithful indicator that this interpenetration, with the accent on the active male, this mental mastery and taking-possession, has already happened.

The drawing is not a magic key to the deed, it is an indicator of how far the relationship has 'crystallized'.[7]

Eisenstein wrote this note in his diary in January 1943, a year-and-a-half before he met Kathleen Harriman. But it contains the explanation of the feelings he was experiencing when, in 1945, he drew his jokey but very lifelike portraits of the Dollar Princess. There was, of course, no love story. But after his heightened observation and 'imitation' of his model came the second stage: that of taking her image into himself, of 'mental mastery and taking-possession'. Unattainable and 'unmentionable', but sufficiently 'crystallized' that Kathleen 'submitted' on paper. Both cartoons are very good likenesses.

Despite the lifetime rumours, the posthumous smears, and the speculations about Eisenstein's exclusive homosexuality or complete asexuality, in no way did he banish women from his emotional life. Their presence in it, however problematic, had been read in the lines on his palm by the fortune-teller Cheiro:

In his love nature he will be difficult to understand. By nature he will be courteous and kind to all women – but very independent of them. They have no distinct hold over him. In spite of this he will have some unusual 'affaires' with women – the advances coming more from their side than his. There will be three very marked 'liaisons' in his life, but they appear to be with married women or under circumstances which prevent marriage.

Eisenstein's biographers know the names of several women who deeply and seriously attracted him, and at least two of them were indeed married. The German dancer and actress Valeska Gert, whom Eisenstein met in Moscow in 1928 and again in Berlin a year later, wrote openly of their mutual passion in her memoirs (published under the title *Ich bin eine Hexe*). Her eccentric dancing was recorded by Eisenstein's pencil, but the drawings – together with his letters to her – were lost in 1933 when Nazi stormtroopers raided the apartment belonging to Valeska and her husband. Another, concealed by the initials 'L. A. D.', is mentioned in Eisenstein's wartime diaries.

In Almaty, something – perhaps people's suffering, and his sympathy for them – changed Eisenstein's drawing. He seemed to become warmer and kinder towards many of the individuals he drew. Eisenstein did not lose the precision of his graphic characterization. Alongside the sarcastic cartoons of local and evacuated 'types' and of 'persons' he remembered meeting in his European and American travels, there are also sketched images shot through with sympathy, fellow feeling and even tenderness. The same applies to his drawings of literary characters.

As soon as he had established himself in Almaty, Eisenstein tried to capture the Kazakh style in his drawings and to penetrate the pre-Islamic belief systems of these descendants of Mongolian herders and hunters. With humour, but essentially seriously, he depicted their totems, and he drew the 10th- to 11th-century legend of Kozı Körpeş and Bayan Sulu (the Kazakh Romeo and Juliet) as a series of sketches for a felt carpet. Eisenstein interwove plant and animal motifs into the ornamentation around the human figures: in the ancient epics of any people, human feelings and human destinies are inseparable from the forces of nature.

In one of his drafts for the carpet, the embrace between the youth and the girl is represented as their fusion into a single being. This is also an ancient motif, one that had been in his imagination ever since Mexico.

Eisenstein had discovered a depiction of the 'primordial human being', from the ancient Chinese dictionary the *Yun Lüe*, in the French symbolist and mystic Joséphin Péladan's book *De l'androgyne* (Paris, from the series *Les idées et les formes*, 1910). This mythical being, two-headed and two-legged (two-gendered), coincided both in idea and in form with the graphic 'formula for love' in Eisenstein's drawings.

It is not just that it embodied the unity of the two fundamental principles, Yin and Yang, in their hypostases as the Male and the Female According to Péladan, the Chinese androgyne could be a prototype for the idea of primordial people known to Europeans through Aristophanes' 'tale' in Plato's *Symposium*. It could even be the source for the biblical myth of the creation of Eve from Adam's rib.

'Somewhere at the foundation of the system of Yin and Yang, just like at the foundation of these myths about the creation of the first people by binary fission, there probably glimmer the biological prerequisites for the historical formation of the genders, now quite well-known,' wrote Eisenstein in his essay on 'The Division of the One into Two', meant for *Method*.[8]

The same thoughts, themes and myths took possession of him when he devoted a whole cycle of chapters in his *Memoirs* to the same problem – not, now, in the context of 'the method of the creative process', but in that of hypotheses about the depths of personal memory. Contemplating the nature of ecstasy, including erotic ecstasy, Eisenstein boldly suggested that each person's unconscious memory retains the trace of a momentary fusion of male and female in the mother's womb:

> ***Rank writes wonderfully of 'coming into the world' in*** **Das Trauma der Geburt.**
>
> ***But I can somehow remember nothing of the divinity of the first spark.***
>
> ***And yet 'enlightenment', a moment within personal experience, is certainly here. Here, in one instant, in the moment: monsieur, madame et bébé.***
>
> ***In Hegelian language, monsieur et madame annihilate 'their selfhood' and fuse the two opposites into a unity.***
>
> ***And at that moment there appears the physical bearer of that unity: bébé.***
>
> ***The question of 'enlightenment' (and all ecstatics do speak of remembering a blinding light) is explained with elegant simplicity.***
>
> ***This very first trauma inevitably fuses in consciousness (pre-consciousness?), in perception (pre-perception?), and in memory (pre-memory?) with the second major trauma: the trauma or birth, the trauma of coming into the world. (For this trauma see Rank's exhaustive treatment.)***
>
> ***The two traumas are fused into one: after all, during the nine months in the womb there is as yet no conception of time!***
>
> ***And the point of beginning coincides with the point of ending!***[9]

In fact, what Eisenstein expressed in words in 1946 was something he had embodied in drawings as early as 1932, in his cycle 'Ex-Stasis' in Mexico. The 'Monsieur, Madame et Bébé' chapter of his memoirs closes with a confession:

> ***It sometimes seems to me that I am all three of them at once: monsieur, madame and bébé.***
>
> ***Not, alas, only in the moment of pathetic upsurge. But also on rare days of hard-working productivity, when, like a curious child, I break into the difficult layers of what we do with the decisive hand of a master, and then with the hands of a busy mistress I try to gather and collect the remnants of the broken seam to build them as blocks into a conception.***
>
> ***Blocks, or bricks?***
>
> ***Something serious, or a childish toy?***
>
> ***But more often I am sad for the infantilism of the overgrown child, awkward and helpless, pitiful and insignificant when he comes into contact with life. Eternally fastened to his father and mother (who are again me myself), a married couple who are deadly bored of each other, who have outlived each other, to whom 'no saviour from on high' can give freedom and liberation from each other – who cannot even kill each other, and who must eternally pay with their drab everyday lives for the triple portrait of monsieur, madame et bébé, that fairground-mirror reflection of the divine moment when the triple nature of humanity fuses in a momentary spark of ecstasy....***[10]

Eisenstein's learnt reflections on the nature of ecstasy or the roots of the creative impulse barely hide his admission of innate bisexuality, an admission that was not without dangers in the USSR. At the same time, he bitterly confirmed that he was poorly adapted for ordinary life – describing his problem as a manifestation of prolonged infantilism.

The other side of Eisenstein's boyishness, and of his speculations 'about the divinity of the first spark', was his erotic drawing – outwardly cynical but in fact full of humour. Now widely known, exhibited and published, in Eisenstein's lifetime it was familiar only to his close friends and to a few colleagues he could trust. Even at home he kept these drawings separate from the others. He did not, however, make an absolute secret of them. Several people have left reminiscences of times when Eisenstein would open some private chest and bring out drawings that would initially take his guest's breath away: the scenes and figures were so erotic, even – to be blunt – pornographic. In the sternly puritanical atmosphere of the Stalin period, they were shocking. But if the people to whom Eisenstein showed his bolder drawings – or for whom he drew them specially – did not have an entirely atrophied sense of humour, they would not be afraid: they would start to giggle. These 'dirty pictures' displayed such a witty imagination, such irrepressible irony. If anybody was offended, Eisenstein would know he had caught an inveterate bigot.

Eisenstein's graphic escapades, like his virtuosic mastery of obscene vocabulary, contained a good deal of provocation. Olga Shepeleva, who worked as the director's assistant on *Ivan the Terrible*, recounts one case of this kind of 'testing'. She was an architecture student, evacuated in 1942 from besieged Leningrad to Almaty. She visited the film studio in search of work, at the very beginning of the preparation period for Eisenstein's new production:

> ***Sergei Mikhailovich glanced at my little white dress (the only outfit I had) and my naive girl-from-a-good-family face, asked whether I really did want to work in the cinema, and suddenly addressed to the cinema itself a torrent of multi-storey profanity of a kind I'd never heard in my life. I went cold inside, but my musical ear detected a note of irony in his 'edifice' and so I collected myself and said, as calmly as I could, 'So what?!' Eisen burst out laughing, and said to someone who was standing nearby and also laughing (it turned out to be Andrei Moskvin, the cameraman), 'Yup, we'll take her. I've just set her an exam: would she faint when she heard the language used by the lighting technicians and the ordinary workers....' After that, through all the years I knew him, Sergei Mikhailovich invariably spoke to me in the most courteous 18th-century language, sometimes in French, which I understood.***[11]

An honoured place in Eisenstein's library was occupied by dictionaries of argot and slang: he knew 'vulgar' expressions in English, French and German as coarse as in Russian, and he called them the most genuine and, for him, the only interesting kind of folklore. In his memoirs, Eisenstein devotes a whole chapter – 'On Folklore' – to the reasons for his love of the expressiveness of 'low language':

> ***The creation of slang expressions, images, and turns of phrases is just as much a collective, nameless, and popular act of creativity as any other kinds of folklore were in the past, which were also nameless, collective, popular, and from the masses.***
>
> ***Every individual witticism makes its anonymous contribution to the common stock, and the expression that touches the deep wellsprings of feeling more than others lives on, enters into circulation, and will not pass out of usage for a long time. [...] In 'argot' and 'slang', as in the highest manifestations of poetry, an abstract concept and idea is restored afresh to the primordial sensory pleasure of an immediately created and uttered image.***[12]

Eisenstein gives an example:

> ***The first word that struck my imagination was* la veuve *'the widow', applied to the guillotine. I'm not sure I immediately grasped just how amazingly precise and 'generalized' this expression is, how ruthlessly it depicts the eternal hunger of the abandoned female.***
>
> ***It's hard to find a more colourful description for the yawning, ever-hungry hole at the base of the guillotine, the whole into which the convict must stick his head...***
>
> ***Many years later, this was probably what made me respond so sharply to Sadger's conception that all linguistic formations arose similarly from erotic and symbolic images – a conception that I accepted unconditionally, for a time!***
>
> ***This was in* The Significance of Psychoanalysis for the Mental Sciences, *a little book by Rank and Hanns Sachs.***[13]

Eisenstein's erotic drawings were the product of broadly the same feelings and ideas. Actually, he was not interested only in the origins of images, but also in the goal or at least the direction of the energy extracted from an emotional reservoir.

In June 1942, he drew for Nikolai Cherkasov a 'phallic parody' of the main situations involved in the screenplay for his tragedy about Tsar Ivan. The actor decided to show these drawings – very funny, but 'for your eyes only' – to his wife, with whom he always shared his thoughts about his work. Nina Nikolaevna, a clever and insightful woman, not only was not offended – to her own surprise – by such 'smut': she understood it and approved of it, as a witty and effective means of 'non-Stanislavskian directing'. She explained: 'Sergei Mikhailovich wanted to make sure Cherkasov wouldn't bow down before the image of the 'progressive autocrat'. In addition, these pictures helped my Nikolai overcome his artistically unnecessary anxiety about how complex the part was.' She felt that both the director and the actor achieved the result they needed.[14] But it was, of course, for himself that Eisenstein mostly improvised his erotic sketches.

Judging by the excited tone of his Mexican 'crib' for Anita Brenner, Eisenstein seriously thought that his erotic drawings were not only a Freudian sublimation of the libido, and not just an important instrument of self-knowledge. Drawing was a way of achieving a 'mystical', 'atavistic' world perception by way of ecstasy, with its paneroticism, its phallic cults and its orgiastic rituals.

Quite quickly, Eisenstein's investigative attention shifted from the stormy, ecstatic discoveries of the 'erotomaniac monk' to their graphic embodiment – the process and results of the creative process. On 8 December 1931, he added to his diary an observation based on his experience of almost a year drawing in Mexico:

It's funny: even here I owe my partial achievement in drawing to 'emotion': I started from 'erotic' croquis, and then I came to be interested not in the eroticism of the croquis, but in the eroticism of the croquis.[15]

The very line of the drawing, tense and rapid, bore witness to the state of his secret sensibility. But this was not all: through visualizing his private, subjective experience Eisenstein hoped to attain, if not knowledge and understanding of, at least a feel for much wider spheres, beyond the boundaries of the erotic.

Exactly sixteen years later there appeared the 'Les dons' cycle: seven drawings whose themes and lines are entirely without ecstatic eroticism. They are like seven sighs over what fades and is not forever, but belongs to the absolute joys of the real visible world. An apple...a butterfly...a blade of grass....Metaphors for the generally accessible gifts of life, which he had not managed even to touch. It was as if Eisenstein were repeating again the question that has pursued him in the first days following his heart attack: but was it a life?

In his tale about the Dollar Princess, Eisenstein calls himself 'an assistant to his thoughts' and 'an obedient servant to the things he creates', adding at the end that he himself is –

Nothing.

What does this self-characterization mean? Disappointment with himself? Or is this the self-belittlement that is 'worse than pride'? Cheiro, back in Hollywood, had warned him but also encouraged him:

The greatest weakness for the subject to guard against is loss of self-confidence owing to the opposition and interference of others. In this case it is unnecessary as the hands indicate sufficient mental strength and superiority of intellect to carry through to a successful conclusion whatever plans or artistic visions are originated by the subject.

The right hand indicates what amounts to self-made greatness with possibility of further strengthening of courage and character. Cheiro advises the subject in this case to cultivate personal power and independence of the opinions and wishes of others by deliberate exercise of his considerable will power, as the artistic genius is great enough to justify taking a solitary course.

Eisenstein wrote more than once about his 'lack of self-confidence' complex, despite his worldwide fame and his authority with his colleagues. It was not only in the tale of the Dollar Princess that he admitted he had 'swallowed his tongue'. The insightful palm-reader could scarcely have known how difficult his recommendations would be to carry out in the stern homeland to which Eisenstein – as Cheiro had predicted – did return.

In fact, it was not just under the 'dictatorship of the proletariat' – where film production depended on the zigzags of state policy, where private life was subjected to total surveillance – that retaining 'independence of the opinions and wishes of others took enormous effort. In Hollywood, too, Eisenstein had faced pressure (albeit of a different sort) from studio bosses opposed to the director's 'own course', the dependence of the project on the market and the press's unceremonious interference in celebrities' personal lives.

Neither was 'social life' easy either at home or abroad. On 3 September 1930, Eisenstein wrote from Hollywood to Pera Atasheva in Moscow:

I meet all kinds of people at all kinds of parties etc. and I feel as though I am made of quite different stuff. Something that doesn't mix. You'd think that would be very good: I'm not supposed to have anything in common with this crowd, I'm not supposed to mix. The 'respect mingled with some fear' that they mostly show me is the most correct, hereabouts. And my inability to engage with the things that interest them (bridge, golf, gossip, real estate, money) is also very correct. But this doesn't just characterize my relationship with Hollywood in particular: it is how things always are for me everywhere. I enclose a photograph of Moro Rock. I didn't climb it to the top today, because I thought the only logical thing would be to fling myself off it. I sat on the penultimate stage of the ascent and discussed it with myself very seriously. It probably would be the most reasonable thing to do. But don't be afraid for me: I'll never have

TOP LEFT
Autoritratto Realista (1944)
(Realist self-portrait)

TOP RIGHT
Idiotis Pelig[nus] (1942)
(Idiot magician)

BOTTOM LEFT
'Self-caricature from the cycle "Regional recruitment office", with the glued call-up paper' (1942)

BOTTOM CENTRE
From the cycle 'If I were working for the *New Yorker*' (1945)

BOTTOM RIGHT
[Kathleen]. Spaso [House] (1945)

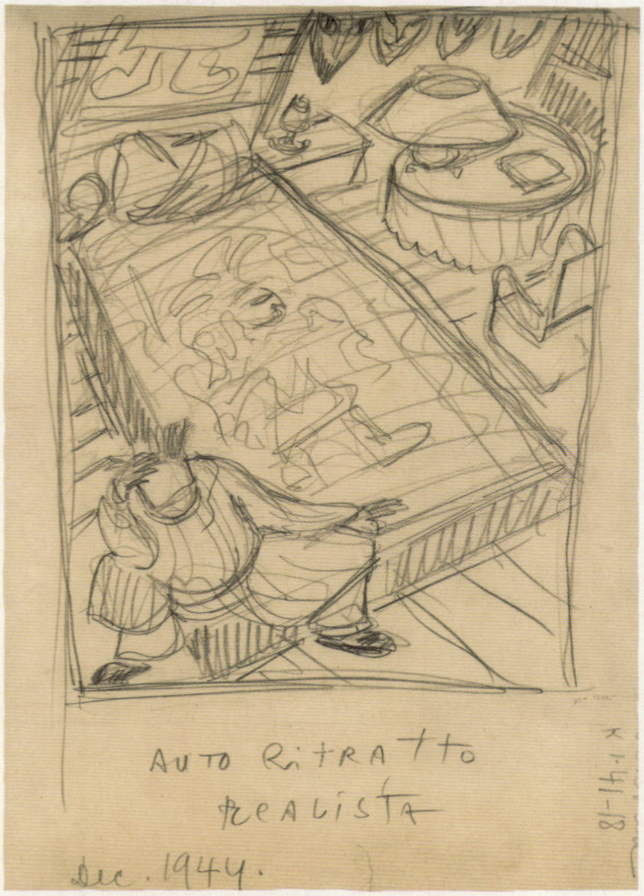

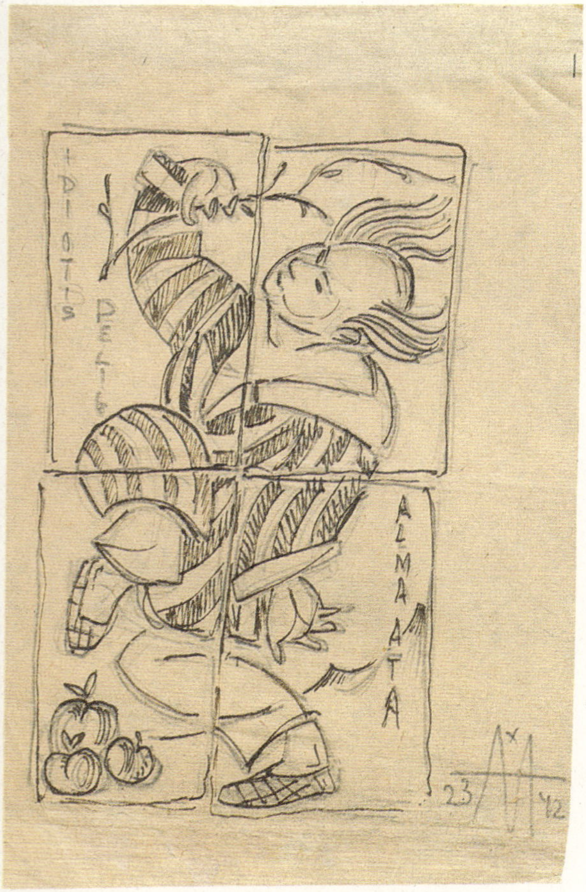

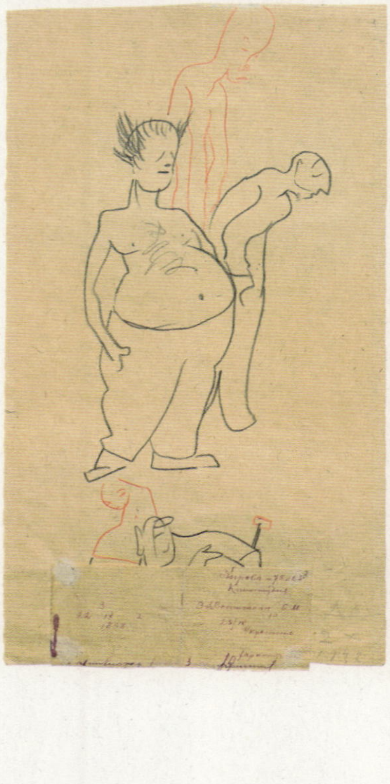

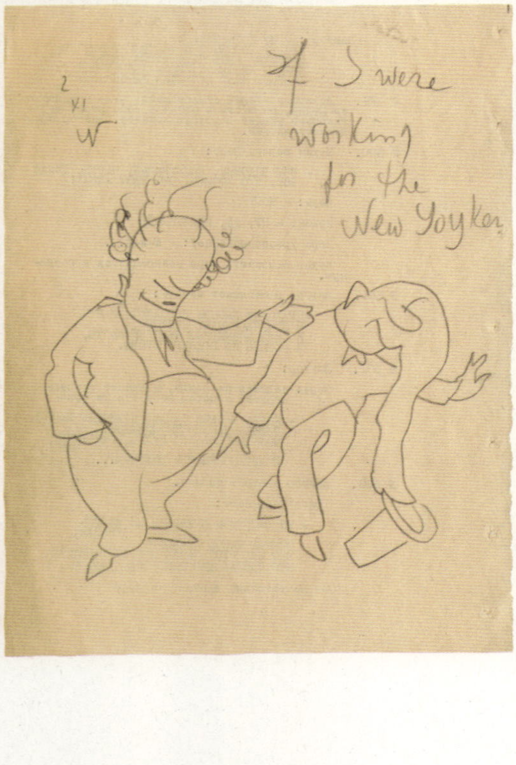

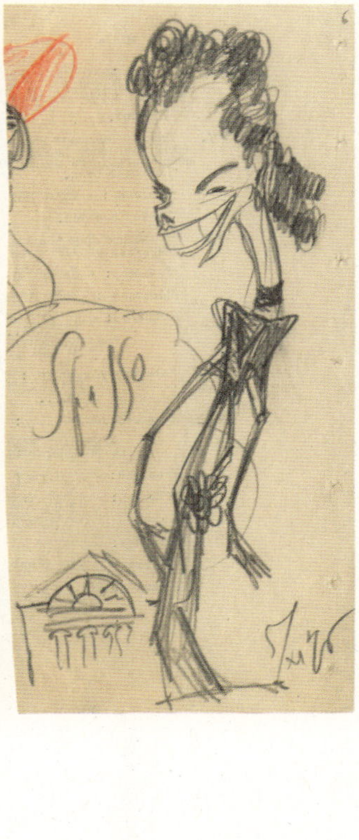

enough character to do anything like that. But human relations are absolutely crazy. I've even stopped getting to know people: you have no idea at all what to talk about.[16]

After his return to the USSR, he was on the edge of suicide three times. The first was on New Year's night 1932–33, when he realized he would not obtain the material he had filmed in Mexico for editing. The second, in May 1937, when *Bezhin Meadow* was banned and destroyed. And the last, in the autumn of 1939, when he foresaw that it would never be possible to film *The Great Ferghana Canal*, which he had just begun.

Comparing the lines on both hands, Cheiro saw this danger – but he also detected a probability that Eisenstein's attitude to himself would change:

It will be noticed that the Line of Head on the left hand has a long sloping branch line attached to it – one of its branches being extremely sloping towards the wrist. This denotes that in youth this subject suffered at times periods of deep melancholy – deep enough at times to drive him to contemplate ideas morbid enough for suicide.

On the right the branches at the end of the Line of Head are totally different, showing that the older he gets the more he will conquer and destroy the influence of melancholy in his life, and will adjust himself to see things from a brighter and happier standpoint. [...]

There is also shown a very decided idealism he will always have of sacrificing himself to others. There are indications that he has helped not only members of his own family, but also those of the larger human family in every way possible. This, taken with other indications shown on the hands clearly denotes that in his character he has little or no regard for the value of money.

The large outward stretch of the thumb with its second joint supple, alone indicates this 'giving' quality of his nature. He will make large sums of money at various stages of his career, but this money will in every case be either given to others or for some large-minded service to humanity.

Perhaps these flattering and encouraging predictions helped balance Eisenstein's oppressive lack of self-confidence. They may even have helped overcome his suicidal thoughts. But they could hardly remove the feeling of loneliness that had pursued Eisenstein since his youth. It broke through in his letters and journals, it is recorded in his drawing, and it found reflection in his self-caricatures.

In December 1944, Eisenstein drew *Autoritratto Realista* (his realist self-portrait). He depicted himself in the bedroom of his Moscow apartment, where he had been so delighted to return after Almaty. He succeeded in conveying his loneliness by placing his own figure towards the bottom left corner, sitting on the edge of a bed covered with a Mexican rug; by showing the preoccupied gesture of his hand as it smooths his thinning hair; by drawing himself from above, making him look small; by drawing a thoughtful expression of his look, though his eyes are hidden by the line of his brow.

But the 'Chinese sage's pose' in which Eisenstein drew himself, and his 'gaze into nothing', gives a particular colour of meaning to his anchorite loneliness – a paradoxical ambivalence.

Autoritratto Realista was drawn just when the USSR Committee on Cinematographic Affairs had accepted the first episode of *Ivan the Terrible*. This made it possible to continue with filming the second part of the film – the last 'cathedral', as Eisenstein suspected, that he would make in his life.

Eisenstein had probably already visited Spaso House more than once to attend screenings of new American films – professionally strong 'talkies', mostly. And at this time, without having managed to finish *Method*, he was beginning a new study: *Non-Indifferent Nature*, subtitled 'The music of landscape and the fate of counterpoint editing at a new level.' It was based on his work on *Ivan the Terrible*, as yet unfinished. But here is the paradox: there are hardly any landscapes in that film. There is, however, Sergei Prokofiev's music: it plays the part of the 'landscape', creating the emotional atmosphere within which the action of the tragedy develops.

The 'vertical montage' of imagery and music, noted in practice in *Alexander Nevsky* and then theoretically formulated in Eisenstein's articles and given a 'visual formula' in his cycle of drawings 'Gedanken zur Musik', was radically reconceptualized in this film.

The guide in Eisenstein's new efforts was no longer Richard Wagner and his *Gesamtkunstwerk*, no longer Scriabin with his *Poem of Ecstasy* and his *Prometheus*, but the ancient Chinese, with their remarkable landscape drawings that were at once graphic art, music, poetry and philosophy.

In *Non-Indifferent Nature*, Eisenstein refers to one tradition that reveals the artistic starting point for the Chinese landscape painters:

Around 750, the emperor was seized by nostalgia and by the desire to see the neighbourhood of the river Jialingjiang in Sichuan province, and he sent Wu Daozi to create a likeness in a picture. Wu Daozi

returned without a single sketch. When the emperor demanded an explanation, Wu replied: 'Everything is drawn in my heart.' Then he went into one of the chambers in the palace and in one day he painted a hundred miles of landscape. That is how H. A. Giles, in An Introduction to the History of Chinese Pictorial Art *(Shanghai, 1905), recounts the moment of transition from the old kind of painting as dossier – chiefly conveying information and narrative – to the new poetical and musical kind, the emergence of which is associated with the name of Wu Daozi.*

The absence of drafts and sketches, so striking to the emperor, speaks clearly of the fact that the painter had been attracted above all to the emotional resonance and the changing moods of the riverine landscape, rather than to an attempt at documenting the river's banks.[17]

What also excited Eisenstein about ancient Chinese landscape was the invariable presence within it of a hermit or a traveller contemplating nature:

If you mentally follow the gaze of one of these sages, you will see that it always passes through vague deliberations of plants, valleys, and mountain crags, and ends up directed towards the 'Nothing' – the white background of the picture, in fact, which is free of any hint at objects or their likenesses! These pictures a redolent of a particular kind of cosmic calm. Alongside the dozing smile of sculpted or painted Buddhas, this kind of landscape painting is probably the nearest approach to the experience of that submersion in 'Nothing' that India knows as 'nirvana'...

[...] In Chinese philosophy, this 'Nothing' is not a simple 'absence': it is simultaneously the 'origin that gives birth to all things', in which 'All' is potentially contained...

[...] This characterization of the power of that 'Nothing' in which 'All' is potentially contained is set out very poetically by Lao Tzu (sixth and fifth centuries BC):

Thirty spokes unite in one hub [forming a wheel], using the wheel depends on the spaces between [the spokes]. Vessels are made from clay, but using the vessels depends on the emptiness within them. We pierce doors and windows, but using the house depends on the emptiness within it. This is why the usefulness of [a thing that] exists depends on emptiness.'

But the end result still remains complete nirvana, complete immersion in the limitless infinite – the Nothing.[18]

Alongside the expressive, passionate, extravert ecstasy of the West, Eisenstein also discovers the East's introverted and profoundly contemplative type of ecstasy. And not only India with the Buddha's escape to a timeless nirvana, but also the calm wisdom of Lao Tzu and his Tao: the Way to grasping the Oneness of the World.

In the autumn of 1942, in Almaty, Eisenstein depicted himself as a Chinese man dancing 'idiotically' with a branch in his hand. The caricature is drawn as though it had been torn into quarters. Each quarter has its own theme: the powerful, balding head; the right arm holding the apple branch; the balletic leg and the big Kazakh apples (the Russian name for Almaty – 'Alma-Ata' – means 'Father of Apples'); the left leg twisting in the dance, and behind it the Tianshan mountain range, the boundary with neighbouring China.

Eisenstein had long noticed an interest in China gradually taking the place of his youthful attraction to Japan. He compared China to ancient Greece, and Japan to ancient Rome. Without rejecting the lessons he had learnt from ukiyo-e prints and the Kabuki theatre, Eisenstein was taking possession of the most ancient sources of Far Eastern culture on behalf of the new art.

Back in the spring of 1935, when the Peking Opera was due to visit Moscow on tour, Eisenstein had written an article about the complex system underpinning this spectacle, which included images created through dance, singing, gesture, makeup and props. The doyen of the Chinese theatre, Mei Lanfang, had made an even stronger impression than he had anticipated. Honoured with the lofty title of 'Sorcerer of the Pear Orchard', Dr Mei had played not women but Femininity itself – and, more than that, on stage he had been the harmonious embodiment of an aesthetic, rather than erotic, fusion between Male and Female, Yin and Yang.

Even on 23 January 1935, before the Peking Opera had arrived, Eisenstein had received for his birthday two books by Marcel Granet: *La pensée chinoise*, which had just come out in Paris, and an earlier work (now reprinted), *La civilisation chinoise*. The whole system of ideas and categories in Chinese thought and in the Chinese world perception turned out to be not just comprehensible to him, but necessary – for his practice as a director, for his theory of artistic creativity, for his analysis of works belonging to various art forms (including his own films) and even for his interpretation of his own drawings. In particular, he was attracted by the *visual poetry* of Chinese landscapes.

Non-Indifferent Nature is full of quotations from the most authoritative sinologists about the mutual transitions from poetry to visual art and from visual art to poetry:

> ***We should not be surprised that it is China where we find the most perfect models of this.***
>
> ***For it is in China that there exists, even in literature, a poetry that is not of sounds but of brushstrokes alone!***
>
> ***'The distinctive nature of the Chinese language, a unique phenomenon, forces us to distinguish poetry that is spoken aloud from written poetry, the words that make up a poetic work from the characters with which they are depicted. Everyone should be aware that in the Chinese writing system the strokes that make up a given word have no relation to the sound of that word' (V. Markov, foreword to* The Flute of China*, 1914).***
>
> ***Hans Bethge writes still more markedly of this aspect of poetry, in the afterword to this collection of translations from Chinese lyric (Hans Bethge,* Die chinesische Flöte*, Leipzig, 1919):***
>
> ***'Chinese prosody is extremely complex. A unique rhythmic system emerges from the combination of the highly complex pictorial nature of Chinese writing and the unusual phonetic structure of spoken Chinese, a rhythmic system that is dictated as much by visual as by musical considerations.***
>
> ***'The result has nothing common with European poetry, apart from the external characteristic that both feature rhyme.***
>
> ***[...] This poetry is addressed to the ear and the eye in equal measure.'[19]***

And vice versa: Eisenstein was also attracted by the poetic forms in Chinese visual art:

> ***[...] by means of their 'plastic pronunciation' – the graphical means by which they are drawn – two differently formed objects can be made to correspond in linear fashion, to echo one another, to relate to one another in what one might call 'plastic rhyme'.***
>
> ***Thus, the line of a rockfall in the mountains echoes the line of an old man's stooped back, the hem of a dress echoes the lines of a river's course, flying curls echo racing clouds, etc. But this is not all: the same hair, drawn differently, will 'rhyme' with the stream of a waterfall as it plunges vertically down, the old man's bent back will echo the lines of a weeping willow, and the course of the river will rhyme with the silhouette of a group of warriors galloping in the distance. And this 'rhyming' of lines is very characteristic of Chinese and Japanese drawing.[20]***

Did Eisenstein in 1947 recall the Chinese artworks he had written about two years previously, when he drew his 'Gifts' cycle?

Four sheets (I. Apple, II. Oyster, III. Butterfly and V. Blade of Grass) are linked by 'plastic rhymes' in the form of the nymphs' diagonal movement. And in I and III, the figures are moving from the bottom left to the top right corner of the page, while in II and V the movement is from top right to bottom left.

In VI. Squirrel, the opposite diagonal is used for contrast: from top left to bottom right. In IV. Dragonfly and VII. Cigarette, the figures are placed in the centre of the page, but the nymph who catches the dragonfly is leaning backwards, while the one who is smoking a cigarette is slouching to the other side.

And even the way Eisenstein draws the nymphs' bodies strikingly recalls Lin Yutang's description of the Chinese artistic tradition in *My Country and My People*, quoted in *Non-Indifferent Nature*:

> ***But in the portrayal of human forms, the Chinese are deplorably backward. For the human form is made subservient to the forms of nature. If there is any appreciation of the female human form as such, we see no traces of it in painting. Ku K'aichih's and Ch'iu Shihchou's female forms suggest, not the beauty of their bodies but the lines of the winds and the waves. For this worship of the human body, seems to me to be the most singular characteristic of Western art. The most singular contrast between Chinese and Western art is the difference in the source of inspiration, which is nature itself for the East and the female form for the West.[21]***

But are not Eisenstein's nymphs, reaching so abstractedly for their 'gifts', just as inseparable from nature as the Chinese figures? Does the body of the Nereid who stretches out for the oyster not turn into the ocean wave? Does the dryad hanging from the trees not seem to be a group of branches that have come to life?

The 'Gifts' cycle represents all five of the Chinese elements (wu xing) that define the world: Earth, Water, Wood, Fire and Metal. Perhaps it was for the benefit of these last two primordial elements that Eisenstein came up with the anachronistic drawing VII, with the metallic curve of a gas lamp by whose light the paradoxically nameless nymph smokes her cigarette.

And there is another paradox in the cycle: drawings III and IV introduce a sixth element: Air. It does not feature in the doctrines of the ancient Chinese, but it was known to the ancient Greeks (along with Earth, Water and Fire) and it was one of ancient India's five elements or tattvas (Earth, Water, Fire, Air and Aether).

This blending of times and countries, mythological beliefs and scientific insights, can be considered a typical instance of Eisenstein's eclecticism. He himself was not troubled in the least by accusations of this kind. As the years went by, he became all the more convinced that the deep, basic laws governing the creative method of different artists, in different cultures and working in different art forms, were one and the same. And when he was trying to understand what the cinema resembled, he looked not for what was 'specific to it' but for its 'genetic code' – for the way the general laws of the perception of the world in terms of images came through in it. He was embittered by his colleagues' lack of attentiveness and sensitivity to the problems that troubled him – especially when even his friends and pupils called for 'stripping the robe with Chinese glyphs', paying attention to 'the real values of life' and shooting films that would be 'comprehensible to the masses'.

Eisenstein would reply, smiling politely, that he was consciously forgoing public success and the joys of life so that his pupils could make films with a fluent mastery of the skills necessarily for bringing their projects to life. But inwardly, however, he suffered from the fact that his ideas were not understood when he managed to set them out even partially in his articles, his speeches and his courses at the Film Institute. As a counterweight to the scepticism of his contemporaries, he could have recalled Cheiro's conclusion:

> ***He has however, a very noble type of nature, very advanced and radical in his ideas, but absolutely sincere and honest. He is a natural philosopher and humanitarian, fond of research into occult or metaphysical subjects, with a keen sense of intuition and power of observation.***

Did Eisenstein need compliments from a Hollywood palm-reader? It is not quite impossible: judging from the worn condition of the envelope that contained his hand prints and Cheiro's comments, he referred to them more than once.

But how he missed any well-meaning and serious, even if critical, discussion of the concepts laid out in his unpublished books! In December 1946 he wrote in his diary an entry with the title 'Old Man':

> ***I look at my own activities and I think: it's not for nothing that my favourite image has long been that of a tigress in a cage, dragging a newborn cub [...] by the scruff of the neck for hours and hours. And imagining she hasn't been carrying it for long, but she will carry it...a long way.***
>
> ***All my storms, realizations, discoveries, polemics, corrections to things I have never written down, references to things I have never published, priorities, and imaginary applause for my brilliant insights, are just like that.***
>
> ***And in the meanwhile the paper is yellowing under my pencil jottings.***
>
> ***Cracking along the folds.***
>
> ***Drowning in cobwebs and dust.***
>
> ***And you do catch yourself thinking that you've spent years looking for material that would confirm some thought, some 'position', and suddenly and delightedly you'll find it – and at once you'll realize you've absolutely forgotten why you were looking for it...***[22]

Before he had managed to finish one fundamental work, Eisenstein would begin another: it was not so much that they interrupted each other as that they were built into each other as extensions, forming an expanding 'spherical' book to which he kept inserting new aspects and new examples. He mobilized the whole might of his intellect and the whole acuity of his intuition to justify his ideas, together with his boundless erudition and his strength of observation, his imaginative freedom and his boldness as an experimenter. But Eisenstein knew that spontaneous drawing – that precise diagnosis of his emotional state – was also a true path by which he could access the deep layers of his mind, and also a visible test of his theoretical propositions.

And his visual poem 'Les dons' became just such a Goethean incarnation of the ideas (*Verköperung der Ideen*) that he had expressed in *Method* and *Non-Indifferent Nature*, and at the same time a graphic lament over the missed joys of life.

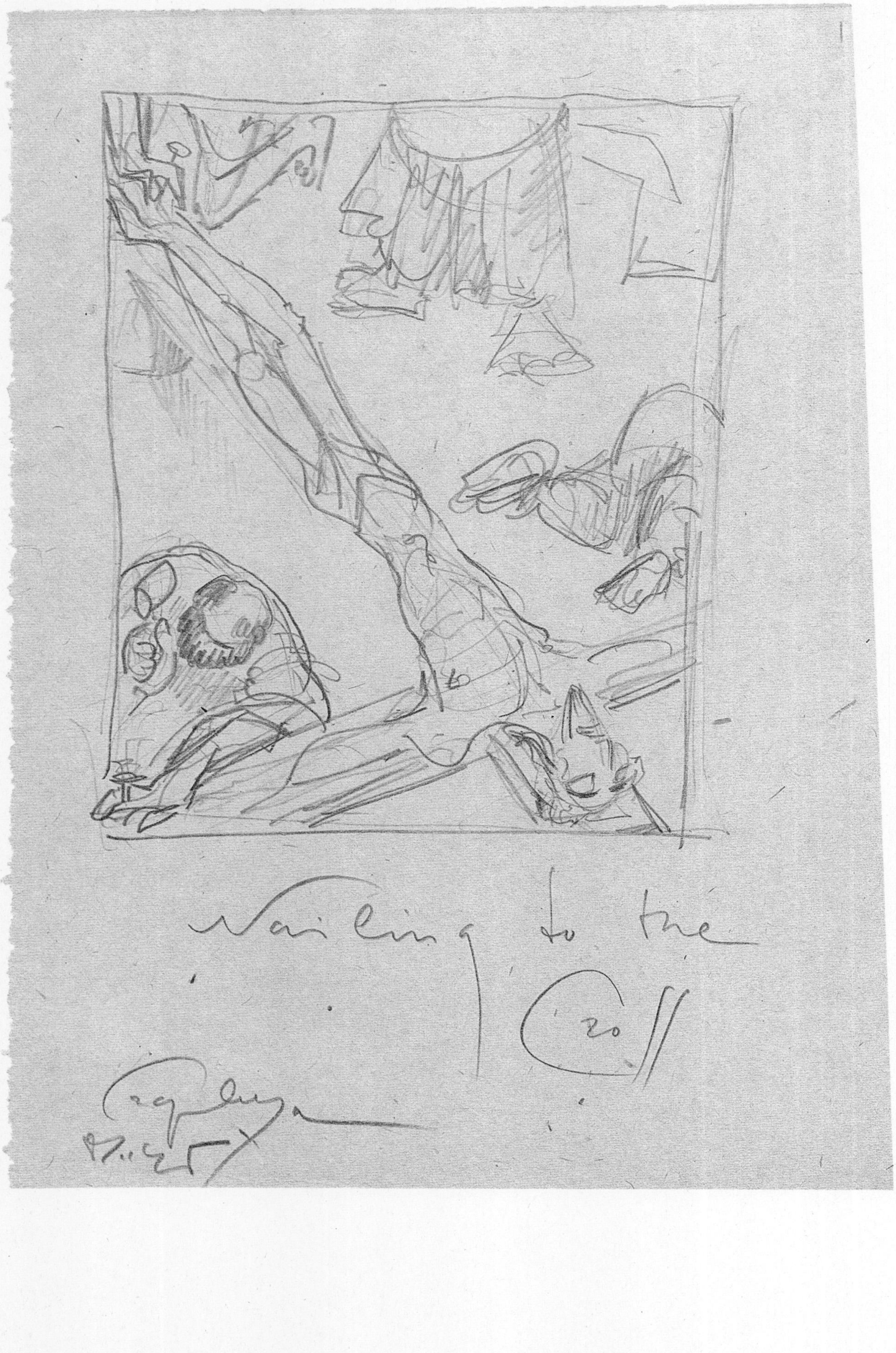
Nailing to the

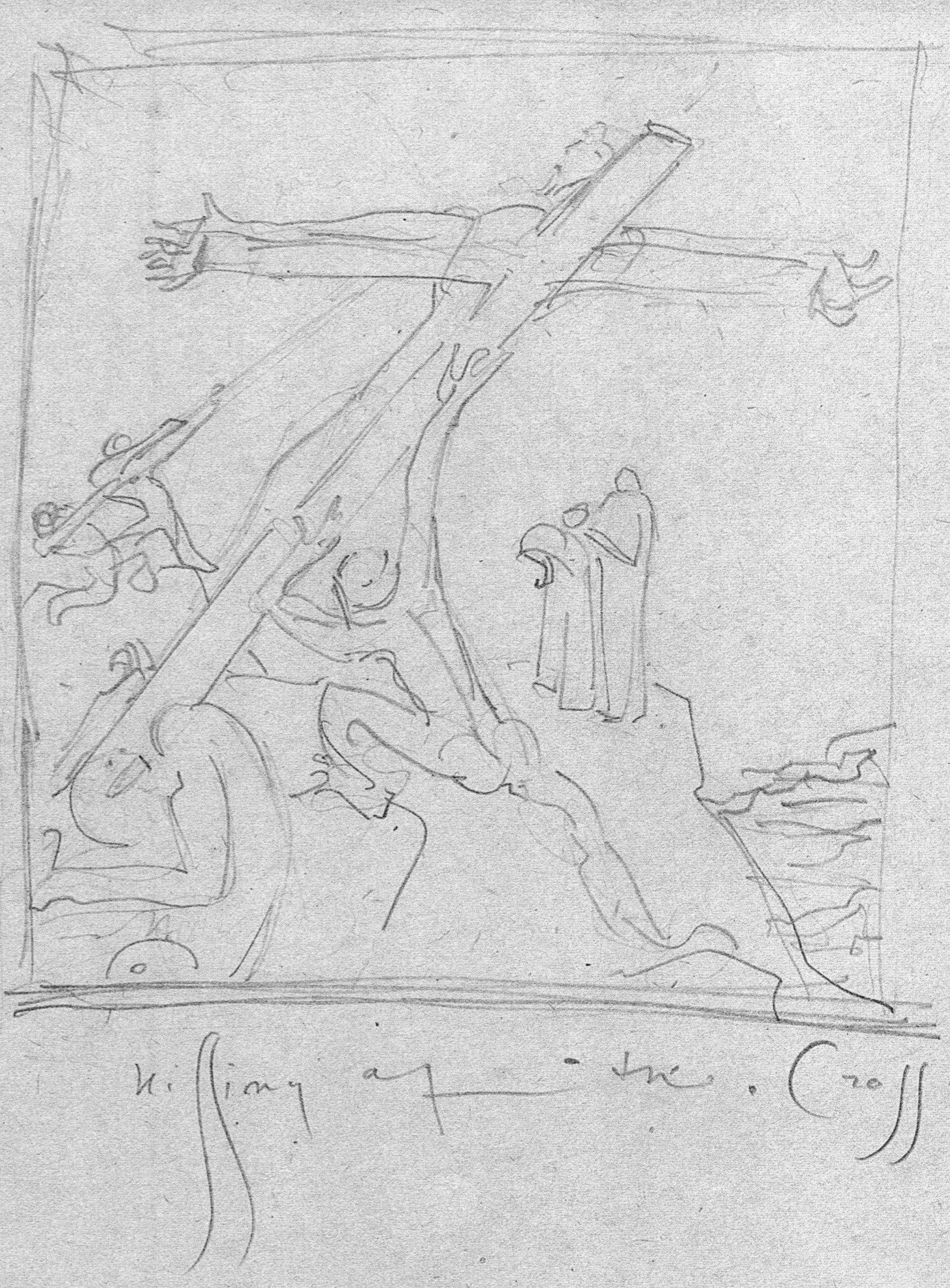

Lifting up the Cross.

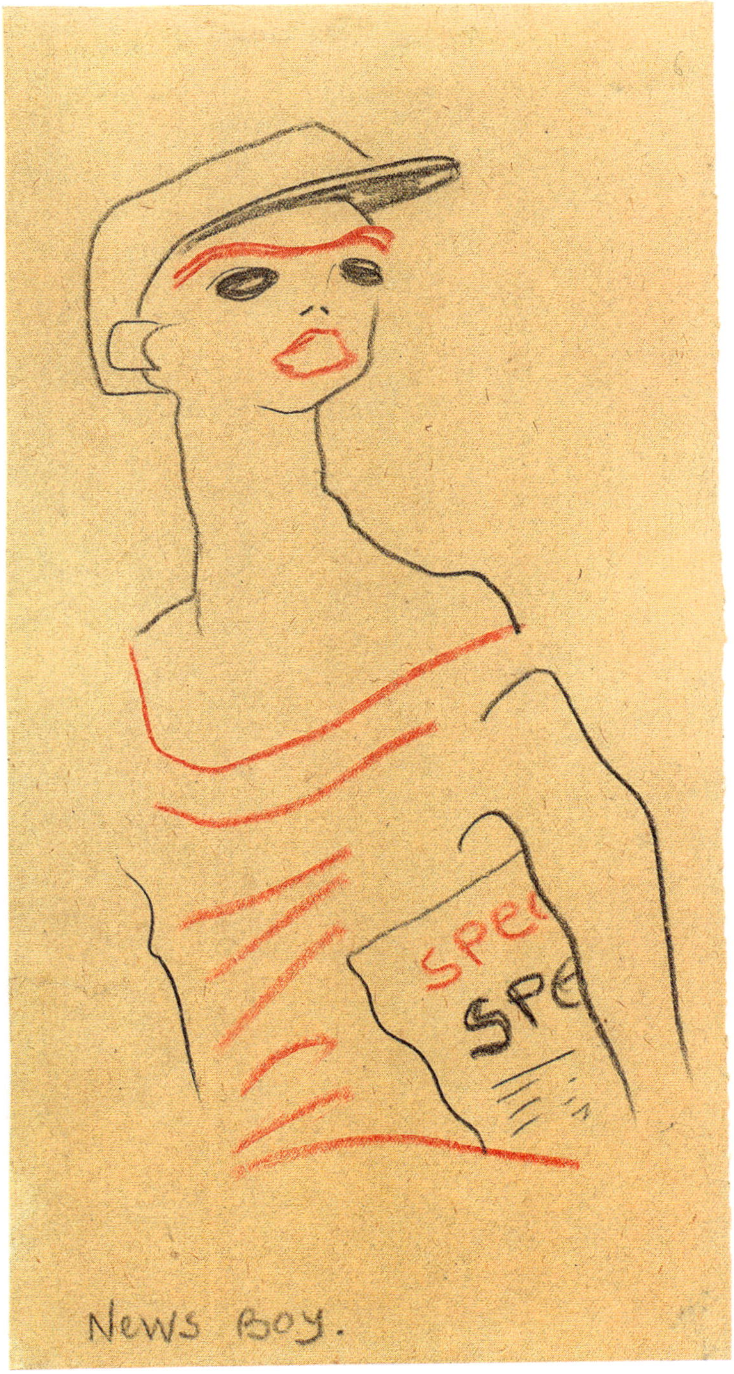
spe
SPE
News Boy.

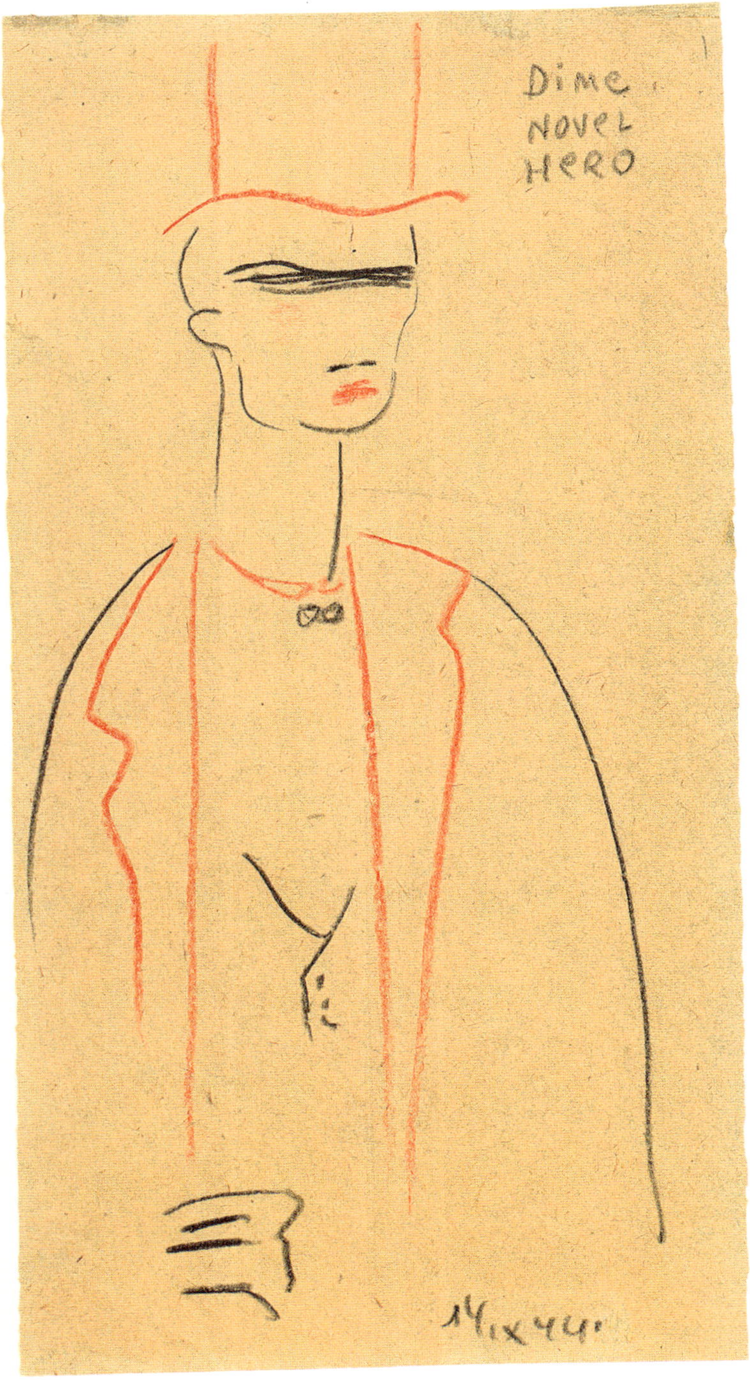
Dime
Novel
Hero
14ix44.

—PREVIOUS

LEFT PAGE
Nailing to the Cross (Barvikha, 1945)

RIGHT PAGE
[Exaltation] of the Cross
(Barvikha, 1945)

—OPPOSITE

LEFT
News Boy (1944)

RIGHT
Dime Novel Hero (1944)

—THIS PAGE

LEFT
Jane (1944)

RIGHT
'Chevalier de Légion d'Honneur'
(Knight of the Legion of Honour)
(1944)

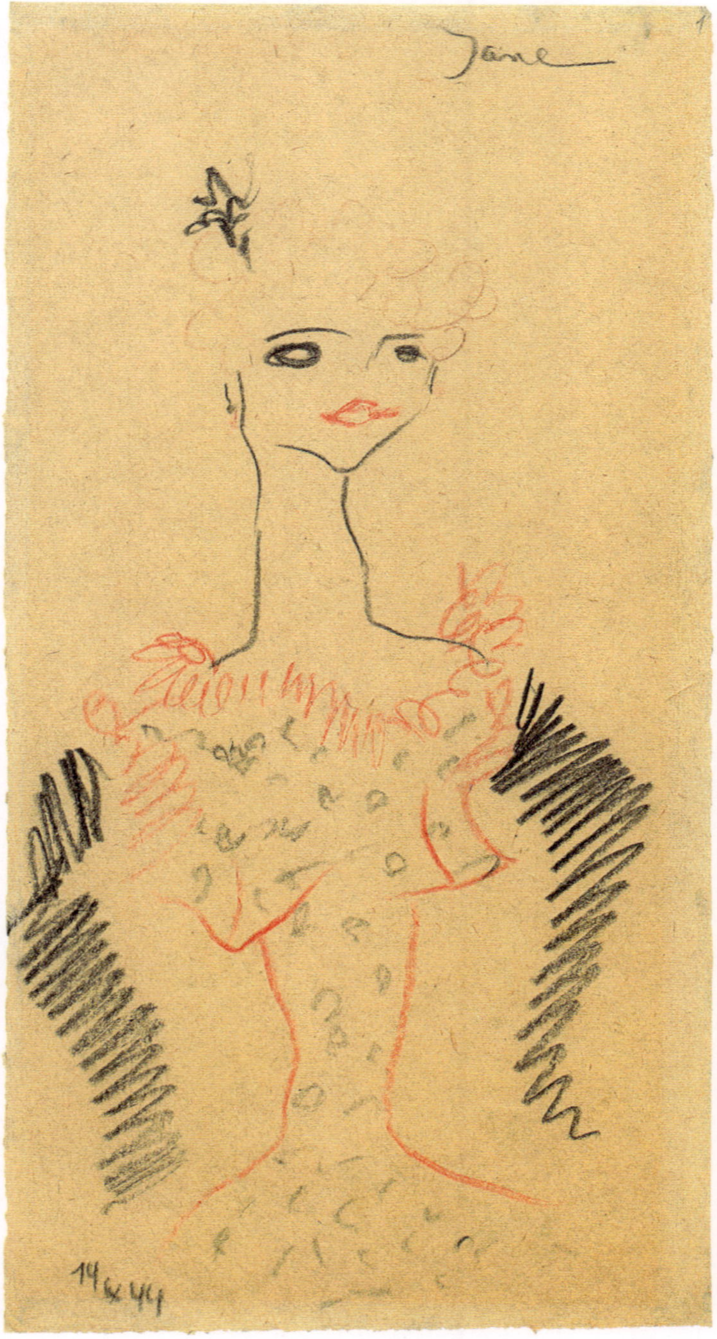

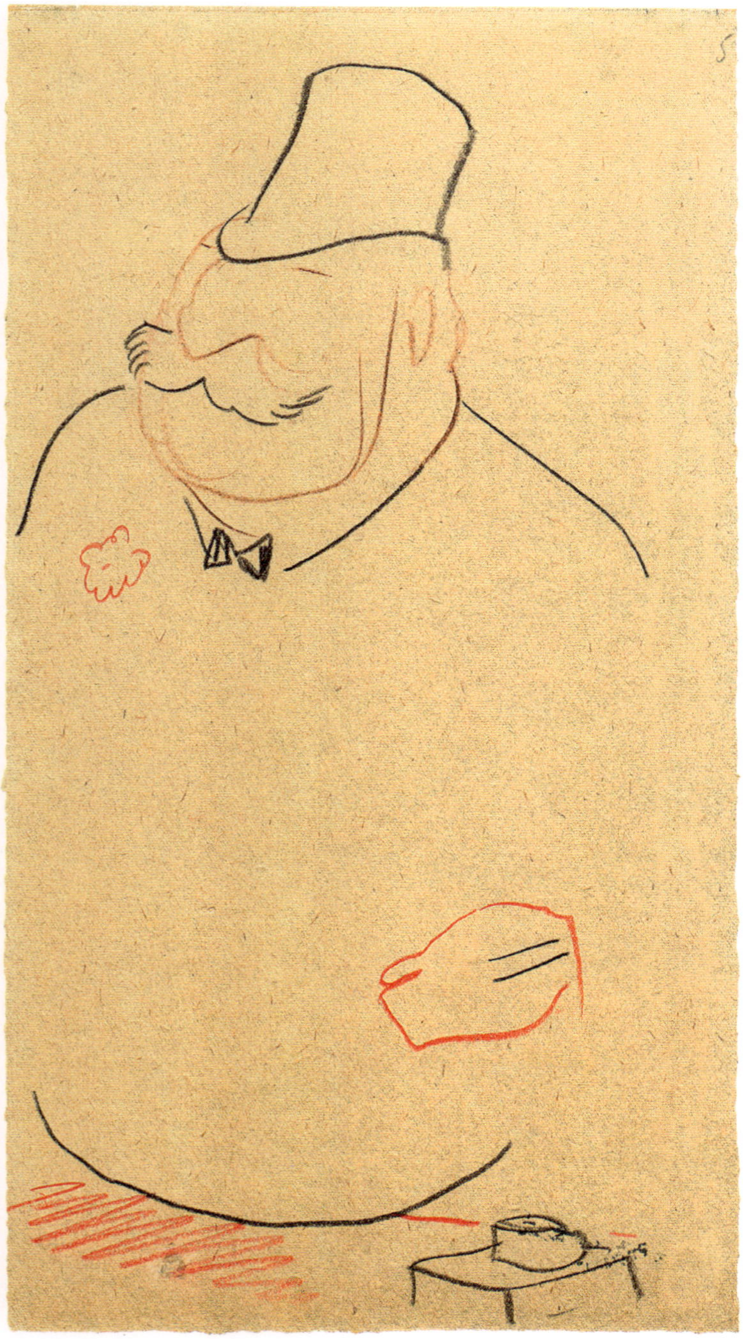

—THIS PAGE
The Tailor (1944)

—OPPOSITE
En Filature (Shadowing)
(1944)

—OVERLEAF

LEFT PAGE
The Perfect Tragedy. Evocation of Nijinsky (1944)

RIGHT PAGE
Diaghilev. Croque Voyou (Biting scoundrel) (1944)

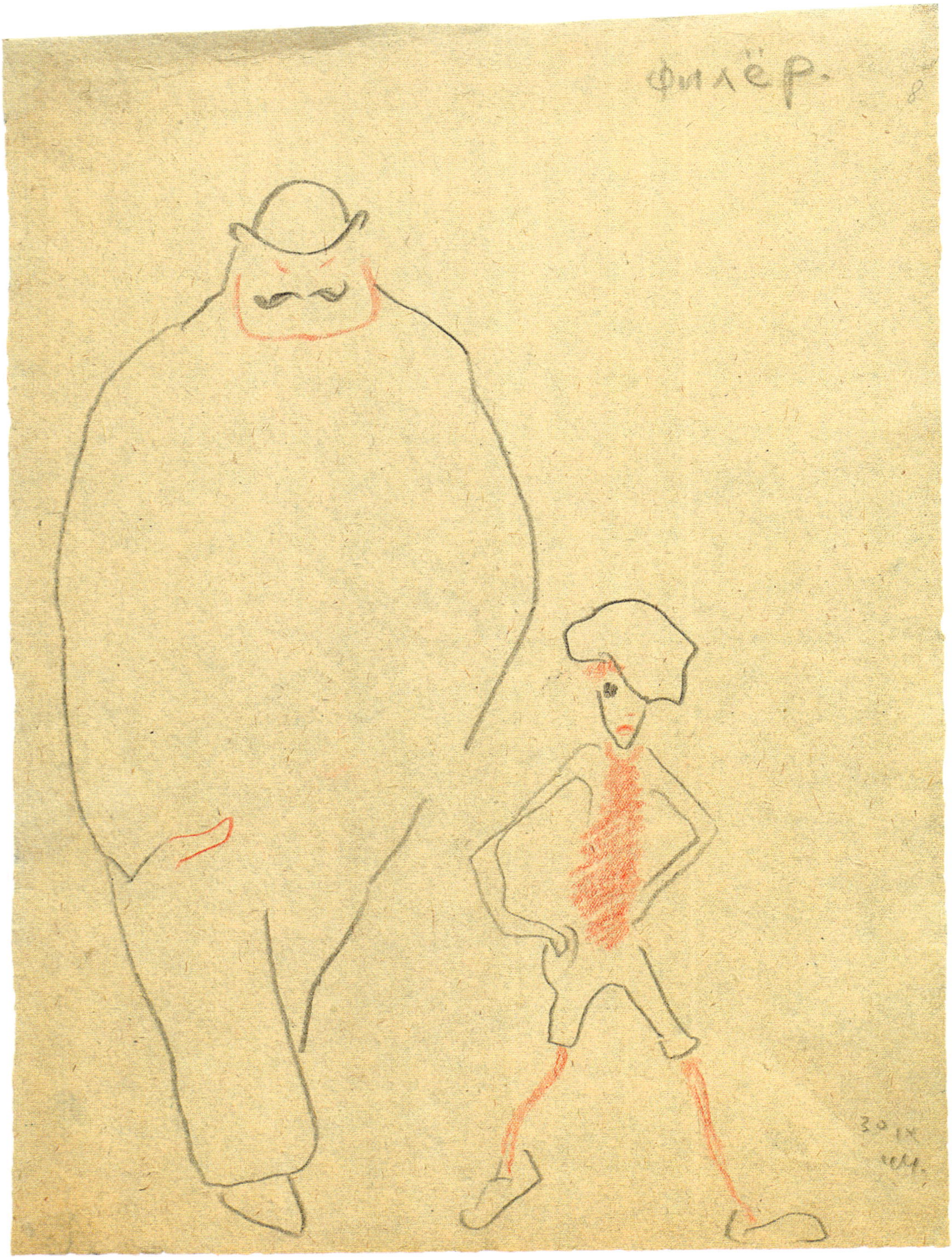

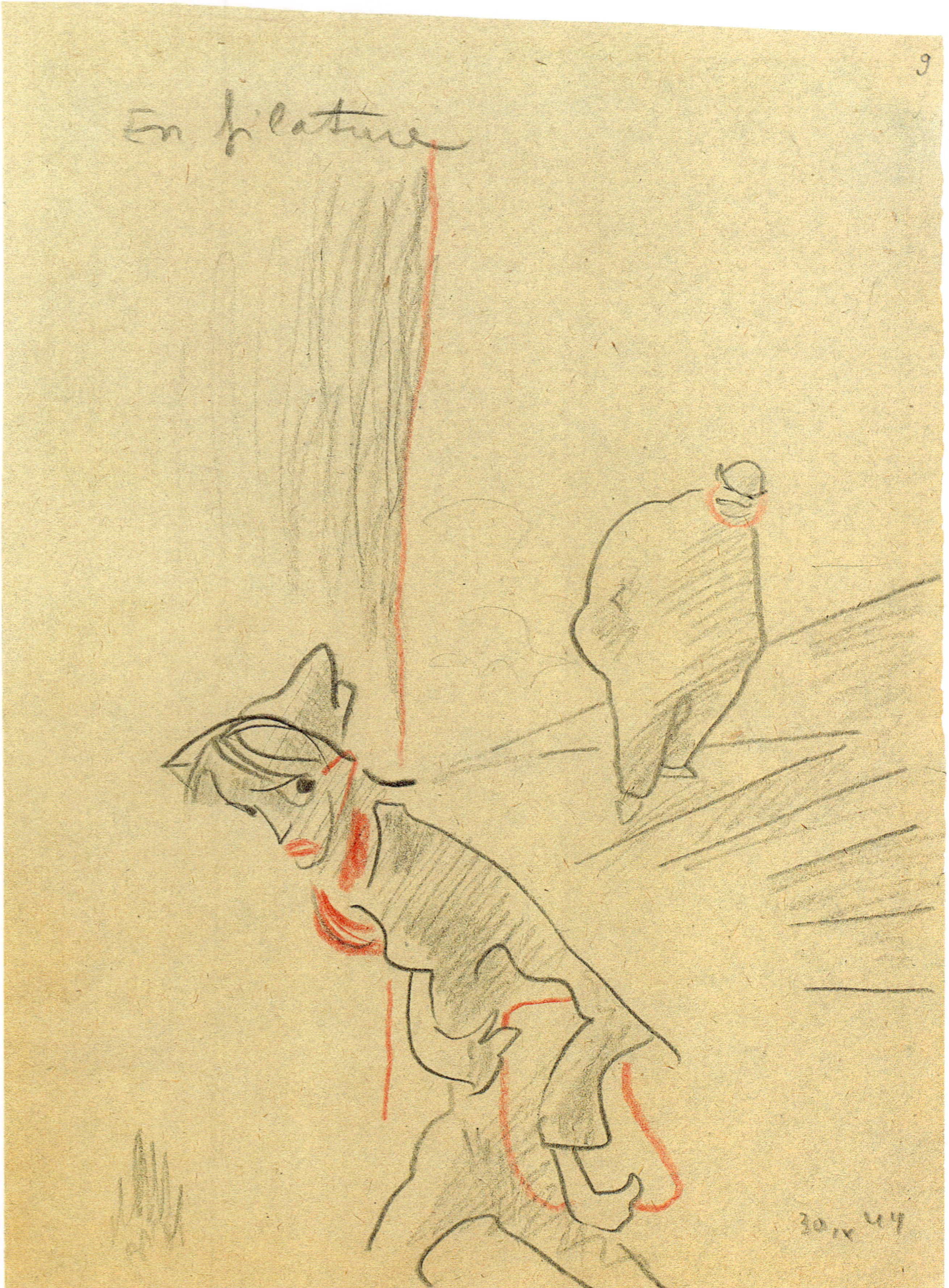
9
En filature
30.IX.44

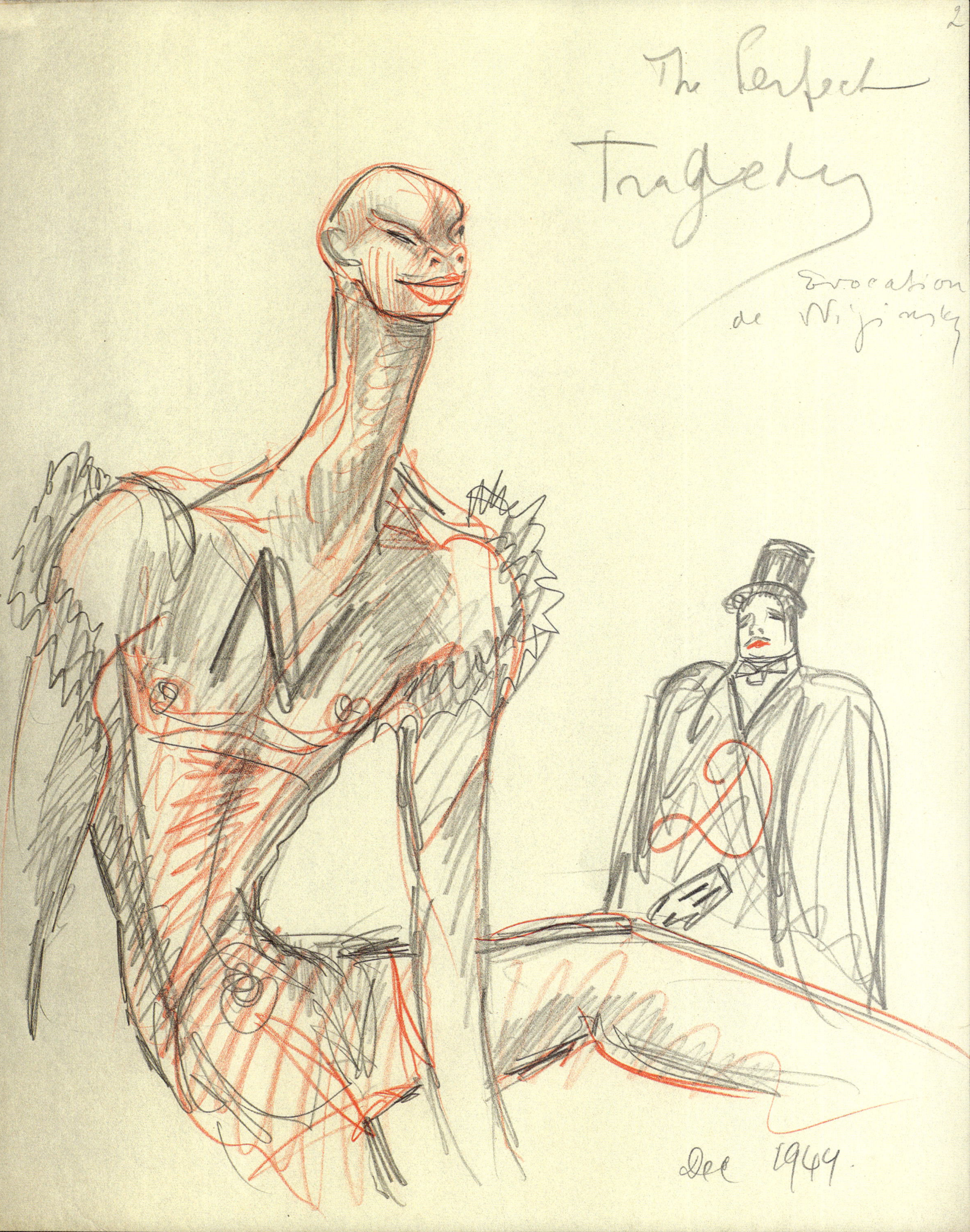
2
The Perfect
Tragedy
Evocation
de Nijinsky
Dec 1944.

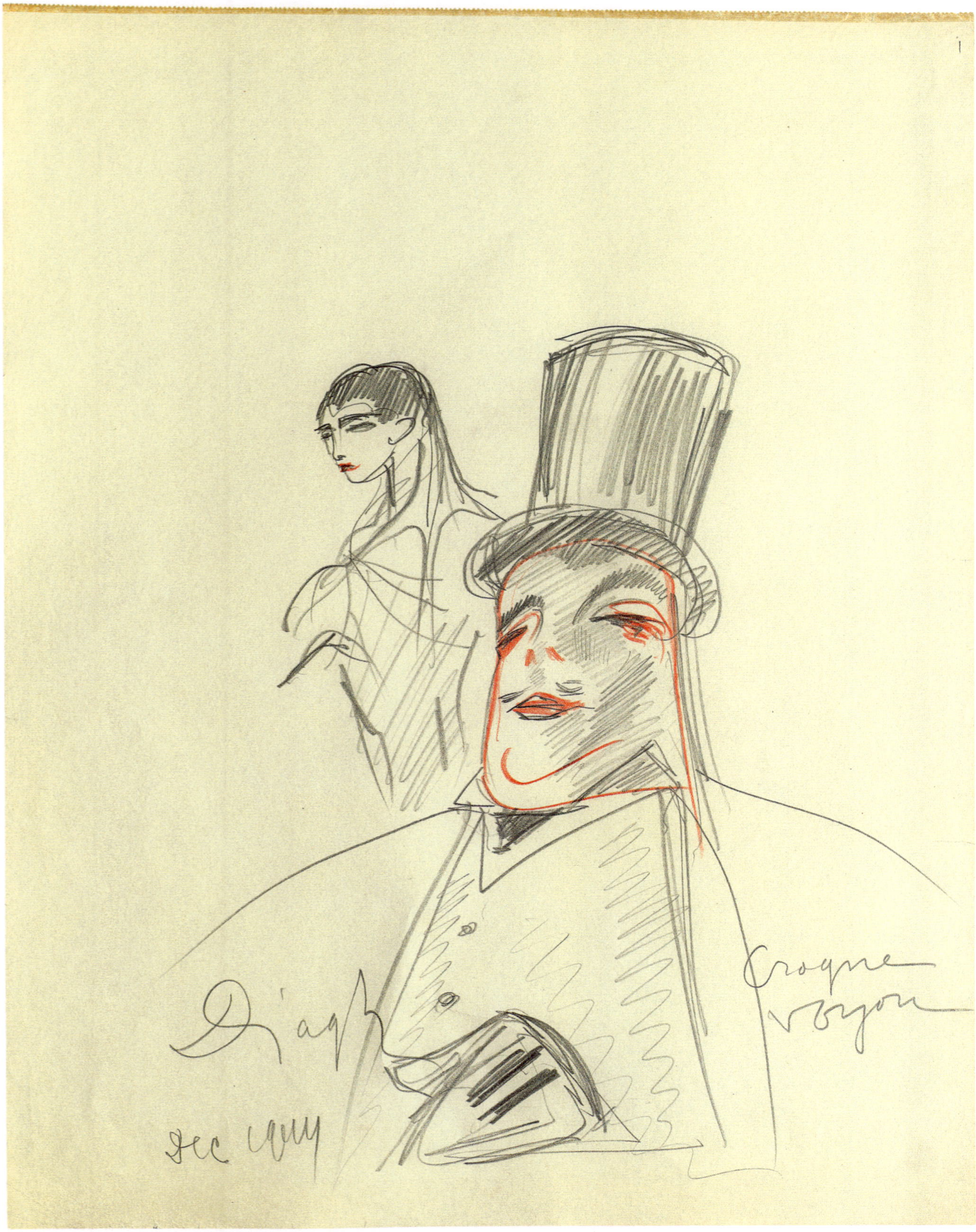

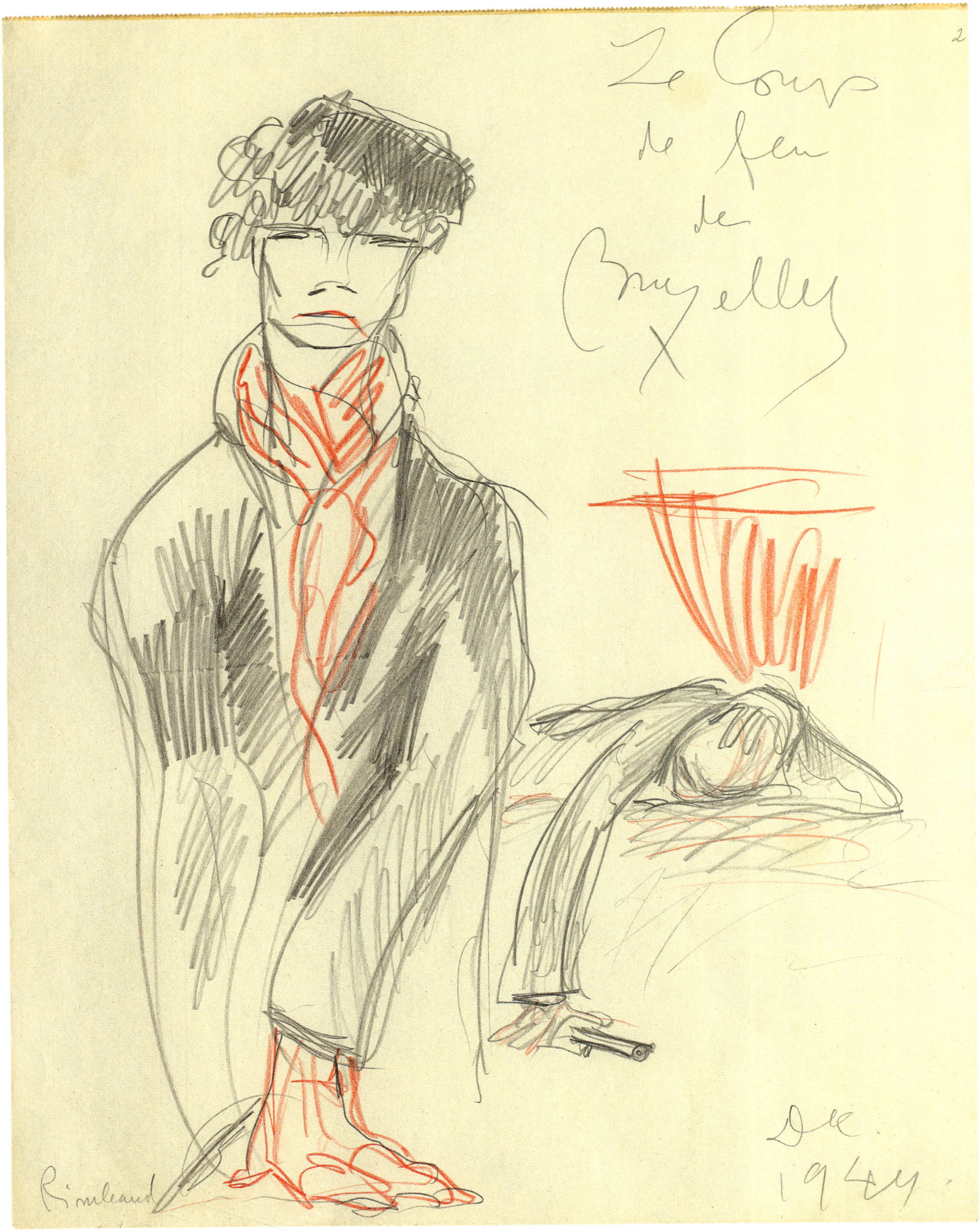
Le Coup de feu de Bruxelles
Déc. 1944
Rimbaud

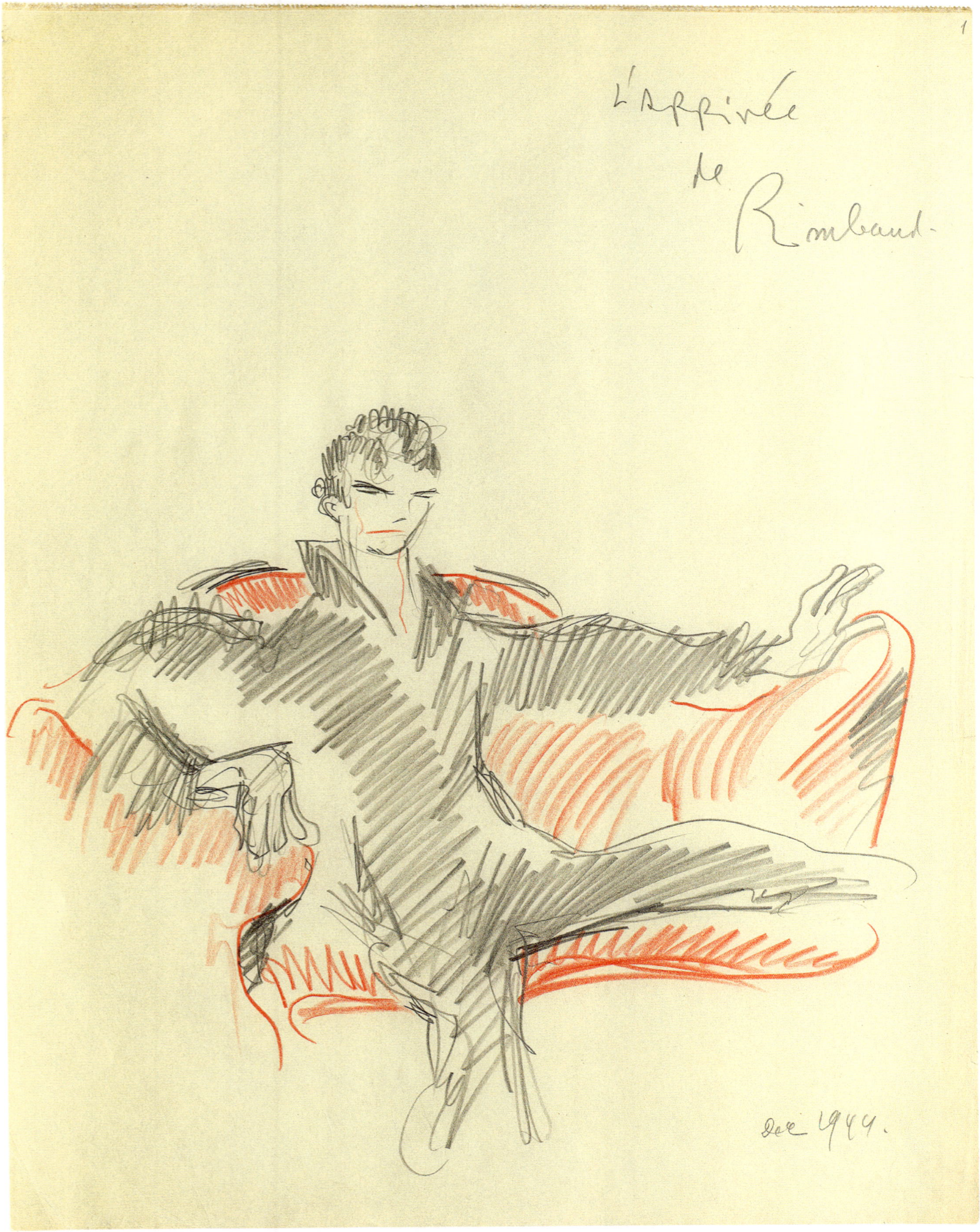
1
L'arrivée
de
Rimbaud.
déc 1944.

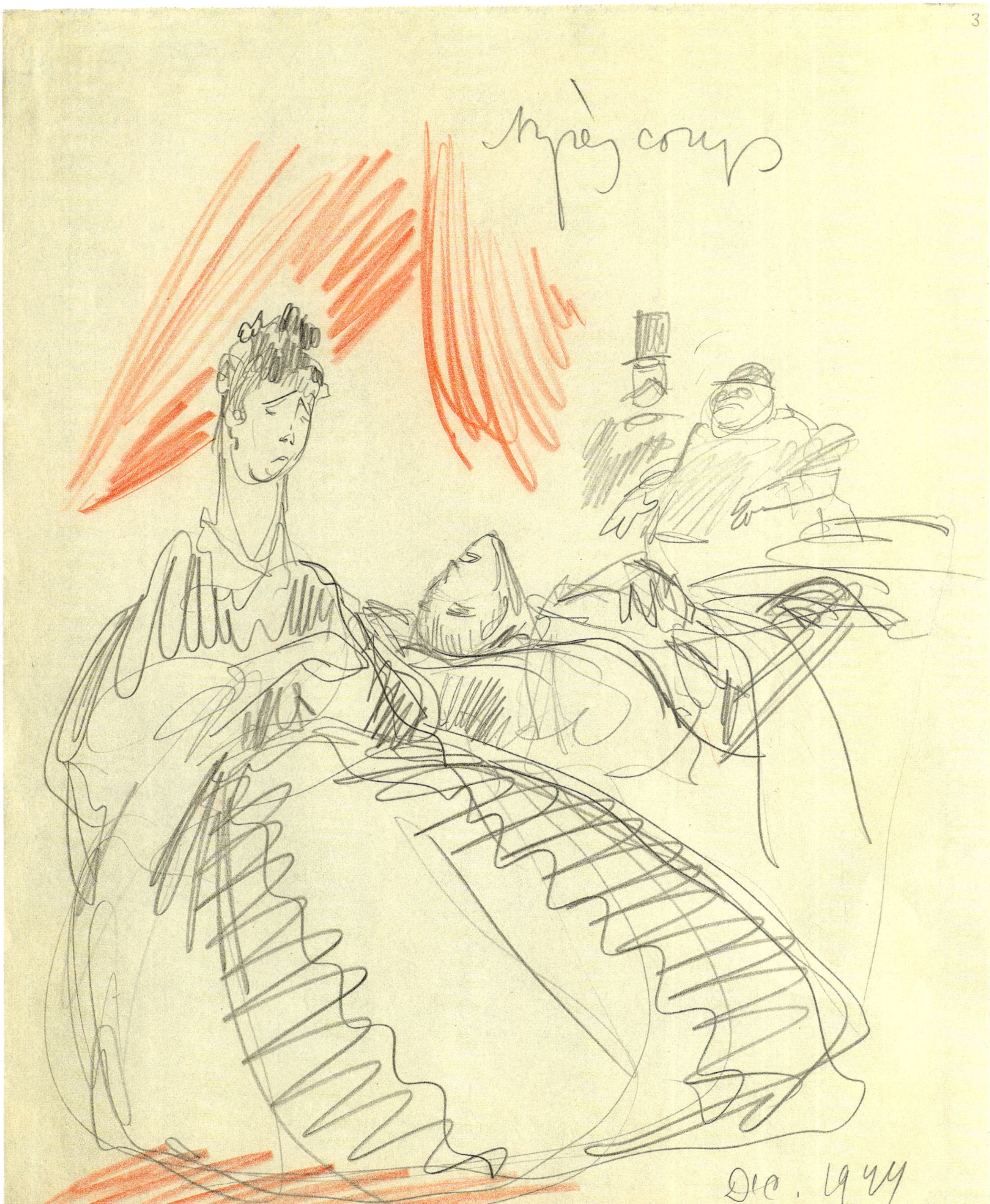
Après coup
Dec. 1944

—PREVIOUS
From the cycle 'Rimbaud et Verlaine' (1944):

LEFT PAGE
Le Coup de Feu de Bruxelles
(The gunshot in Brussels)

RIGHT PAGE
L'Arrivée de Rimbaud
(Rimbaud's arrival)

—OPPOSITE
Après Coup
(Afterwards)

—THIS PAGE
Departure of Rimbaud

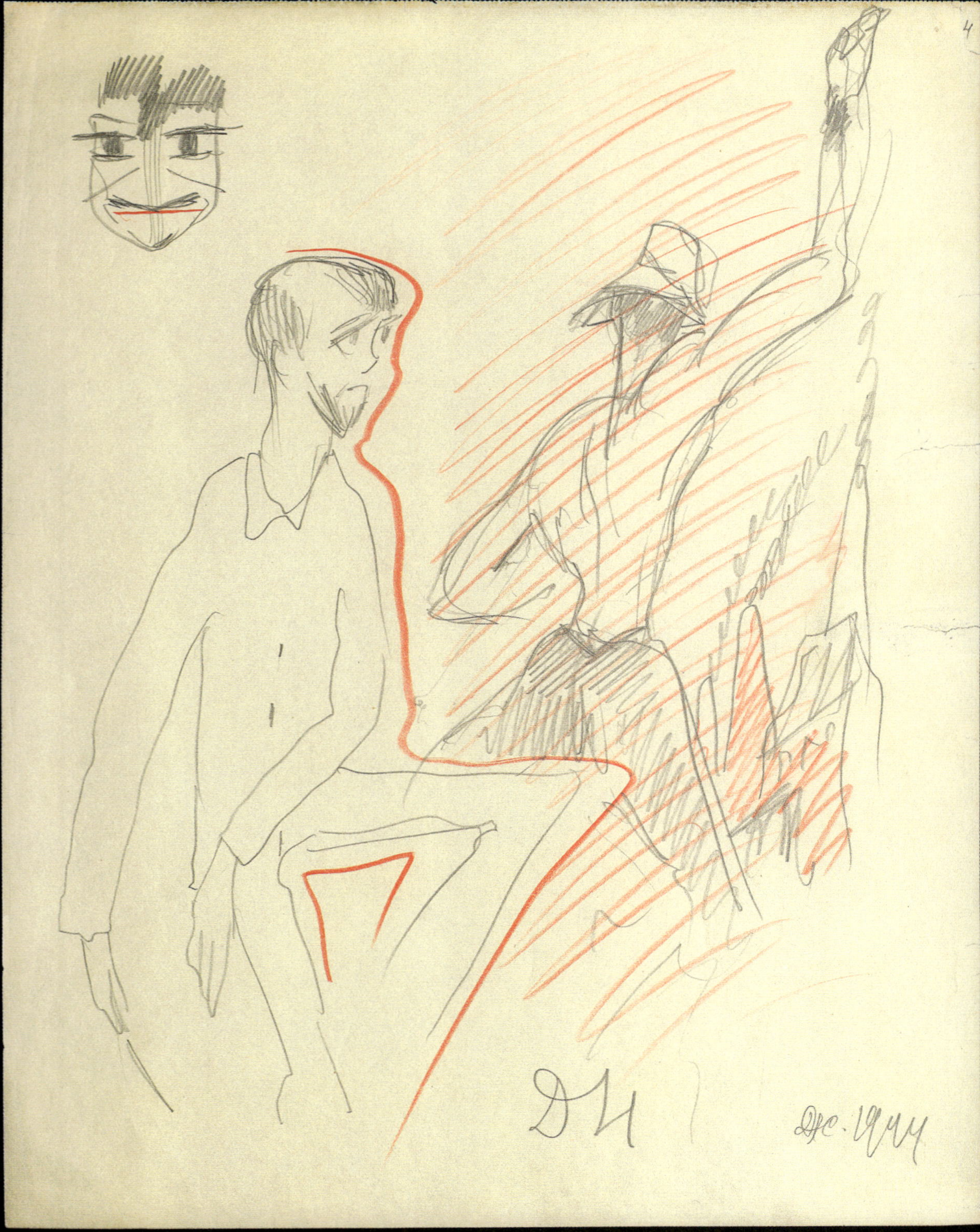

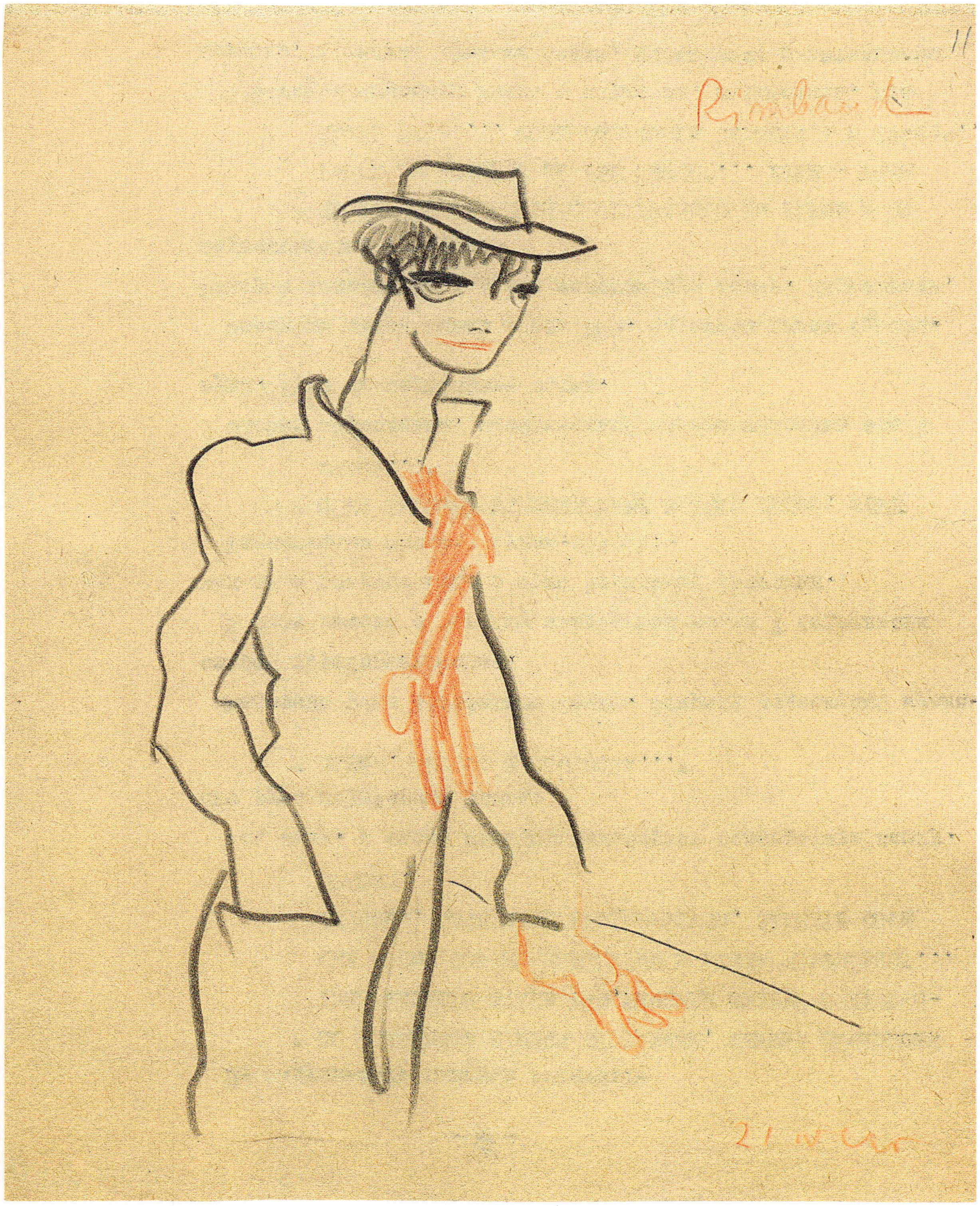

THIS PAGE AND OPPOSITE
From the cycle 'Rimbaud à Londres' (1945)

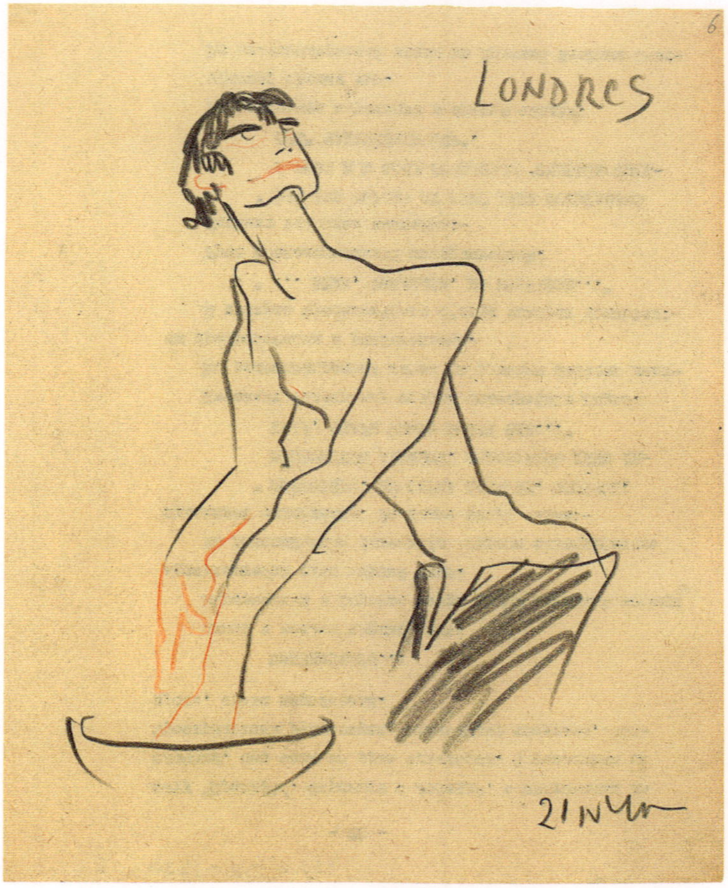
6
LONDRES

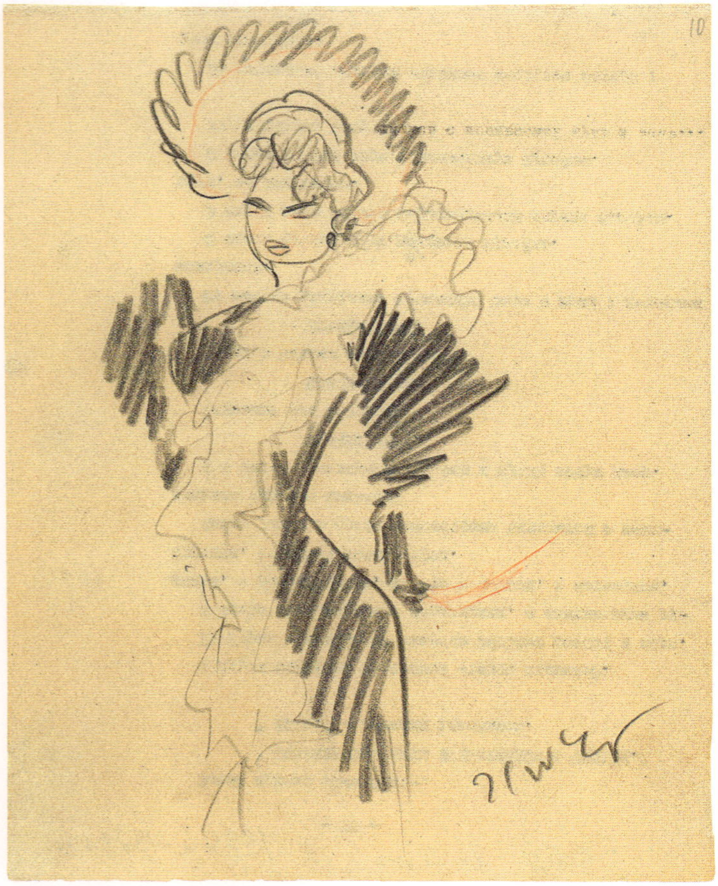
10

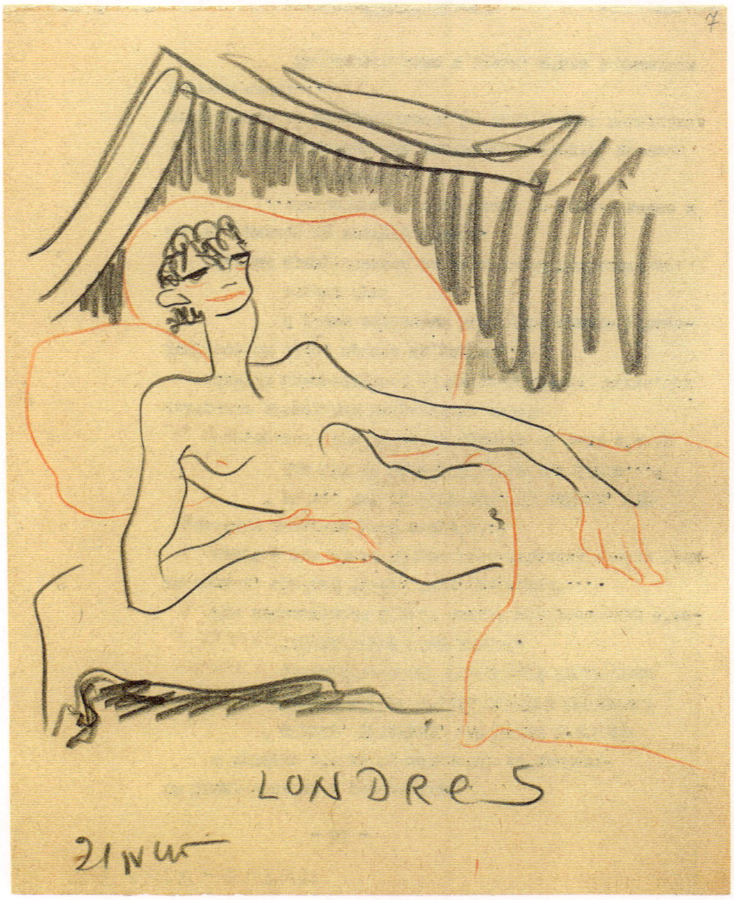
7
LONDRES

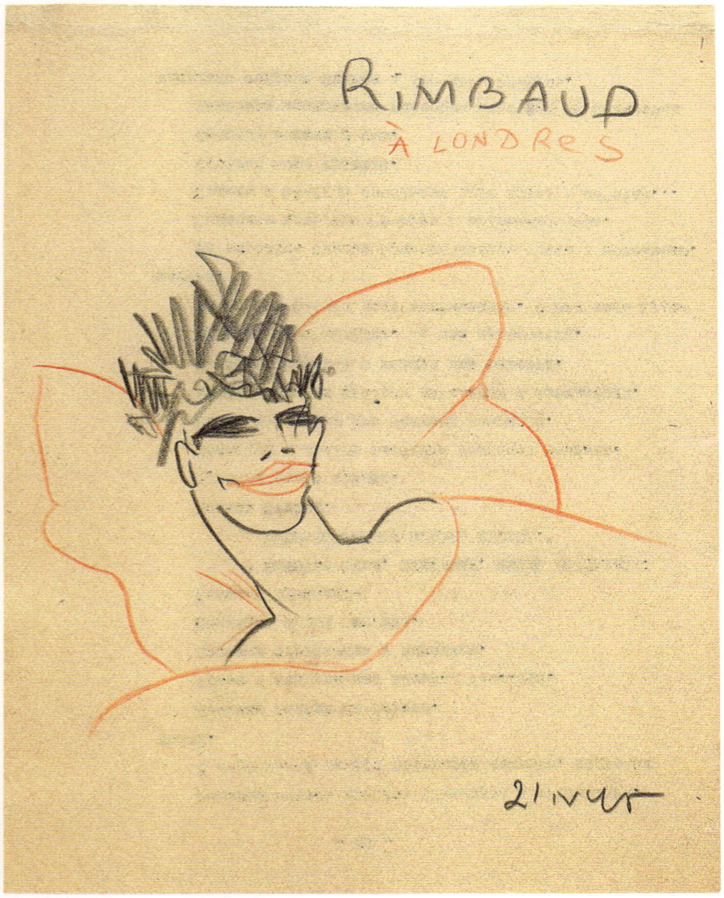
RIMBAUD
À LONDRES

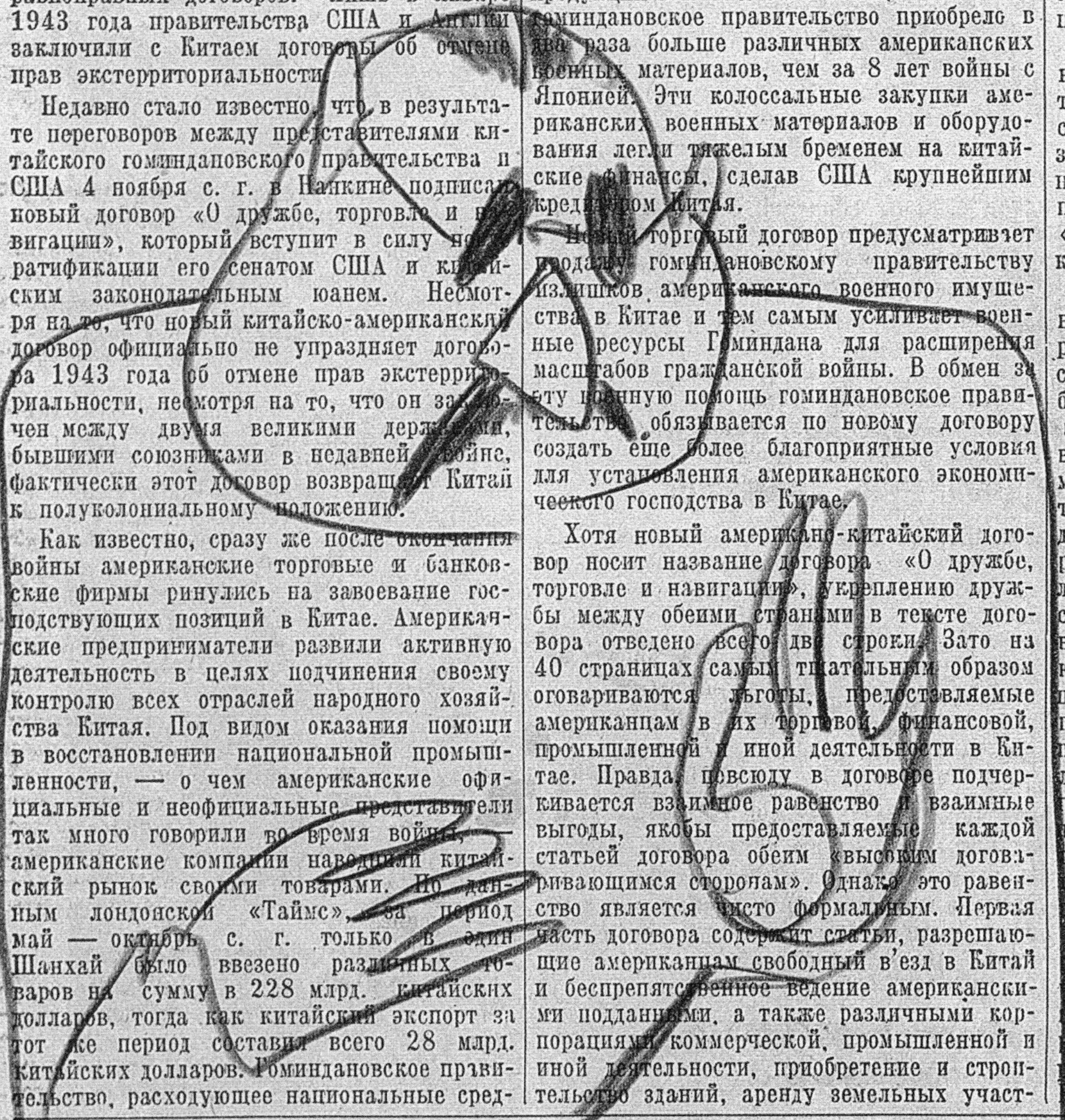

Китаю капиталистическими державами неравноправных договоров. Лишь в январе 1943 года правительства США и Англии заключили с Китаем договоры об отмене прав экстерриториальности.

Недавно стало известно, что в результате переговоров между представителями китайского гоминдановского правительства и США 4 ноября с. г. в Нанкине подписан новый договор «О дружбе, торговле и навигации», который вступит в силу по ратификации его сенатом США и китайским законодательным юанем. Несмотря на то, что новый китайско-американский договор официально не упраздняет договора 1943 года об отмене прав экстерриториальности, несмотря на то, что он заключен между двумя великими державами, бывшими союзниками в недавней войне, фактически этот договор возвращает Китай к полуколониальному положению.

Как известно, сразу же после окончания войны американские торговые и банковские фирмы ринулись на завоевание господствующих позиций в Китае. Американские предприниматели развили активную деятельность в целях подчинения своему контролю всех отраслей народного хозяйства Китая. Под видом оказания помощи в восстановлении национальной промышленности, — о чем американские официальные и неофициальные представители так много говорили во время войны, — американские компании наводнили китайский рынок своими товарами. По данным лондонской «Таймс», за период май — октябрь с. г. только в один Шанхай было ввезено различных товаров на сумму в 228 млрд. китайских долларов, тогда как китайский экспорт за тот же период составил всего 28 млрд. китайских долларов. Гоминдановское правительство, расходующее национальные сред-

... промышленни-кам новые возможности для сбыта своей продукции в Китае. За 7 месяцев этого года гоминдановское правительство приобрело в два раза больше различных американских военных материалов, чем за 8 лет войны с Японией. Эти колоссальные закупки американских военных материалов и оборудования легли тяжелым бременем на китайские финансы, сделав США крупнейшим кредитором Китая.

Новый торговый договор предусматривает продажу гоминдановскому правительству излишков американского военного имущества в Китае и тем самым усиливает военные ресурсы Гоминдана для расширения масштабов гражданской войны. В обмен за эту военную помощь гоминдановское правительство обязывается по новому договору создать еще более благоприятные условия для установления американского экономического господства в Китае.

Хотя новый американо-китайский договор носит название договора «О дружбе, торговле и навигации», укреплению дружбы между обеими странами в тексте договора отведено всего две строки. Зато на 40 страницах самым тщательным образом оговариваются льготы, предоставляемые американцам в их торговой, финансовой, промышленной и иной деятельности в Китае. Правда, повсюду в договоре подчеркивается взаимное равенство и взаимные выгоды, якобы предоставляемые каждой статьей договора обеим «высоким договаривающимся сторонам». Однако это равенство является чисто формальным. Первая часть договора содержит статьи, разрешающие американцам свободный в'езд в Китай и беспрепятственное ведение американскими подданными, а также различными корпорациями коммерческой, промышленной и иной деятельности, приобретение и строительство зданий, аренду земельных участ-

2

...ви, движение капита
мерческие и промышл
осуществление контр
приятиями.
Вполне понятно, чт
ностей Китая и США
таловложений в про
страны не может бы
зить, что Китай будет
ные капиталы в Со
пишет по этому пов
«Синьминьбао», —
ком большой шутник
Столь же призрачн
ная выгодность» стат
рая гласит, что «ме
соких договаривающ
быть установлена св
вигации». Вполне
всерьез говорить н
между Китаем, не и
торгового флота, и
державой — Соедине
рики. Особенно много
лено статьям, освобо
ских предпринимател
вояжеров, американс
какими-либо налогам
шающими налоги, в
предпринимателей и
шается возможности
либо защитительные
протекционистских
поддержания своей
тайские националь
предприятия не смо
американскими фирм
Китайская печать
цев тому назад сооб
таях закрытия кита
ых компаний из-за
ировать с дешевым
ами, заполонившим
Новый договор созда

АДРЕС РЕДАКЦИИ и ИЗДАТЕЛЬСТВА: Москва, 40, Ленинградское шоссе, улица «Правды», д. 24. ТЕЛЕФОНЫ ОТД... Д 3-36-82; Транспортного — Д 3-10-82; Иностранного — Д 3-37-50; Писем — Д 3-15-69; Местной сети — Д 3-15-47; Инфор... Д 3-10-81; Науки и техники — Д 3-35-33; Критики и библиографии — ...

Б 08136. Тип...

—OPPOSITE
'Soviet official' (1946)

—THIS PAGE
From the cycle 'Jewish family' (1945)

TOP LEFT
Genius

TOP RIGHT
Pianist

BOTTOM LEFT
Young and Bashful Jewish Boy

BOTTOM RIGHT
Wonder Kid

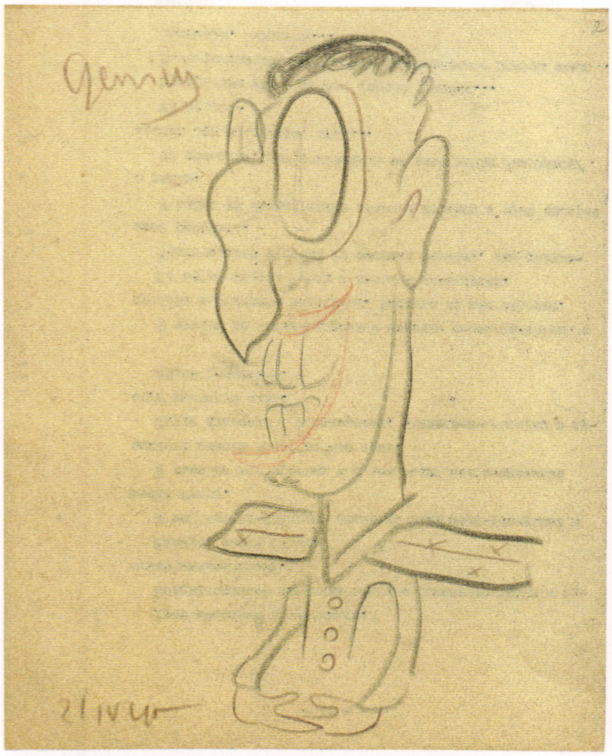

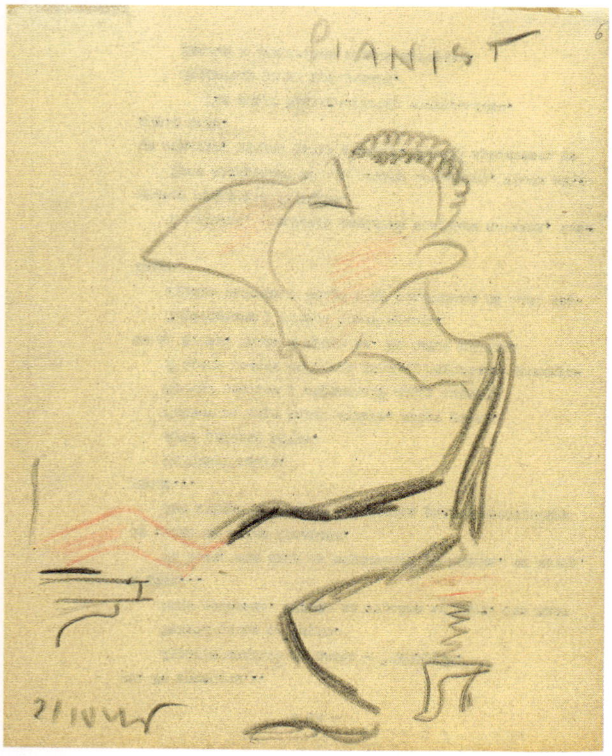

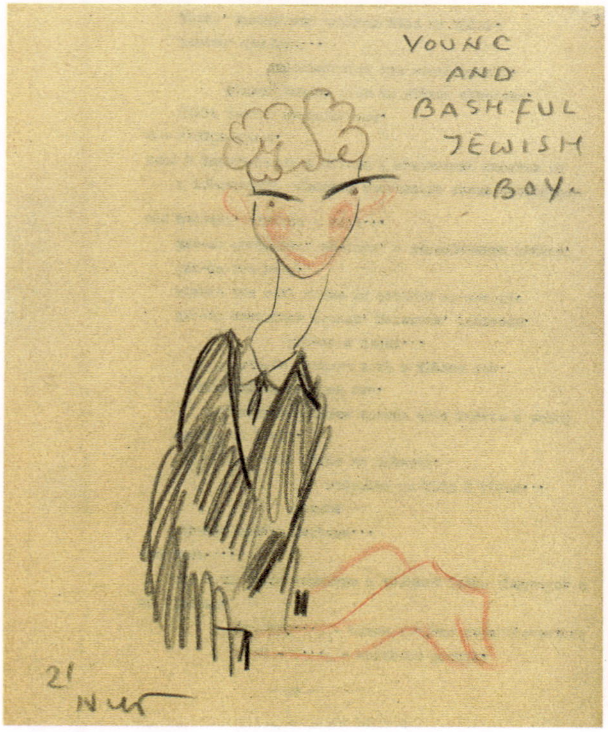

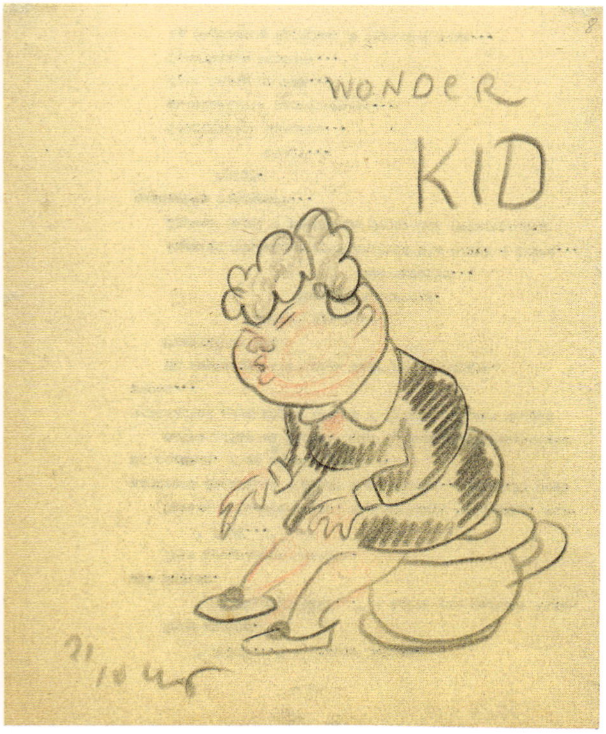

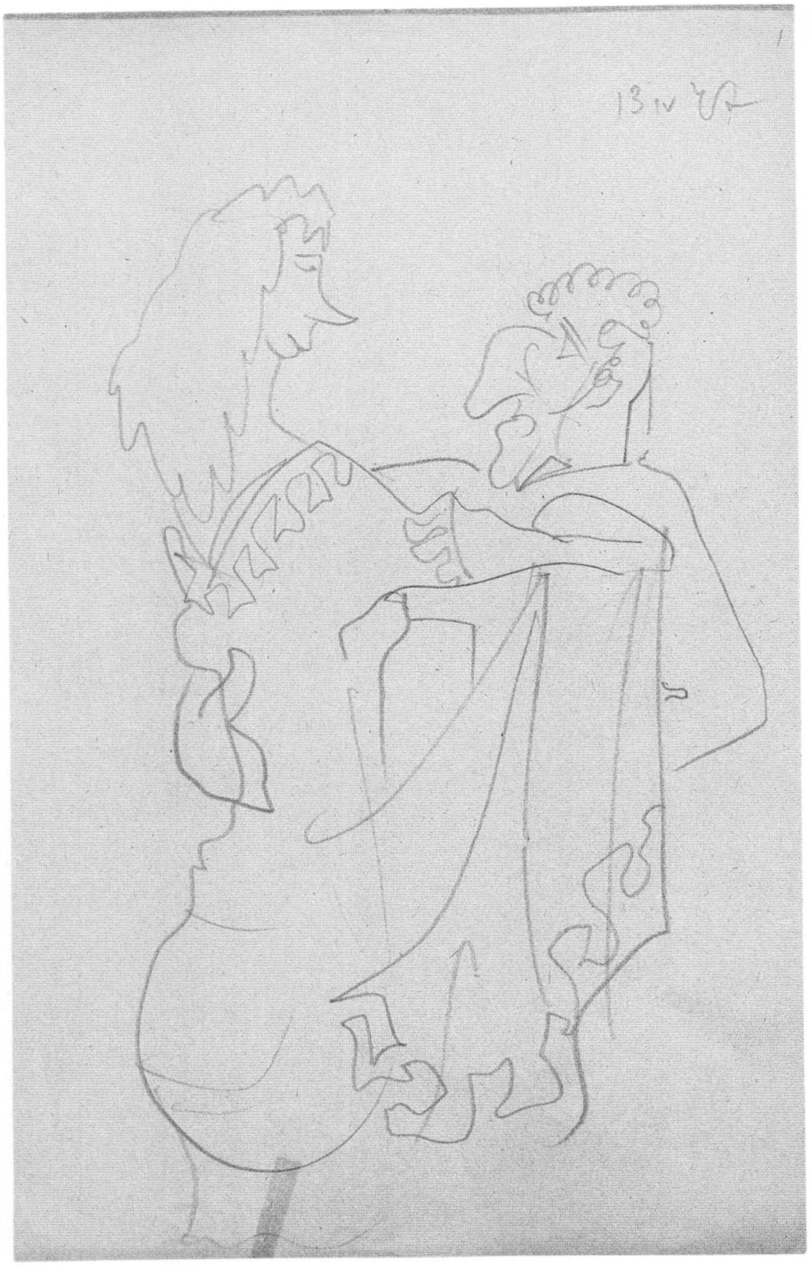

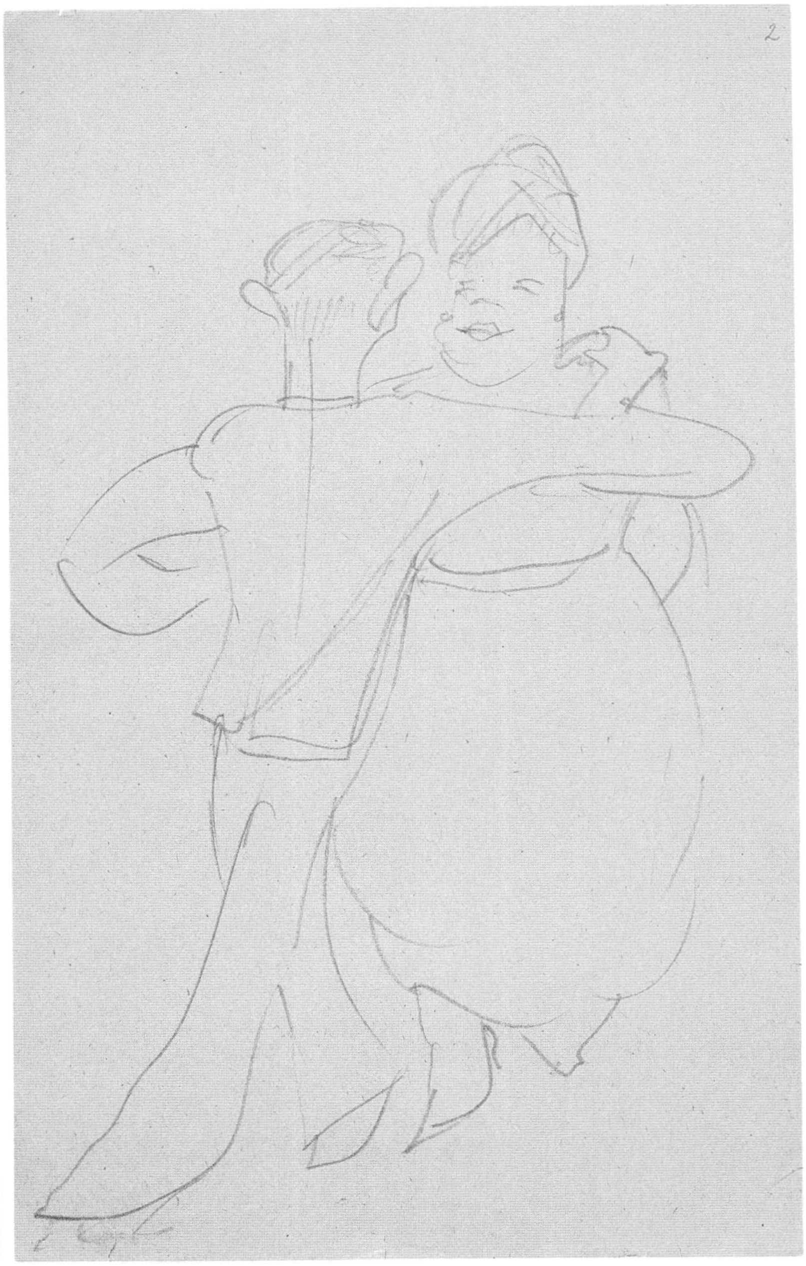

THIS PAGE AND OPPOSITE
From the cycle 'Dances' (1947)

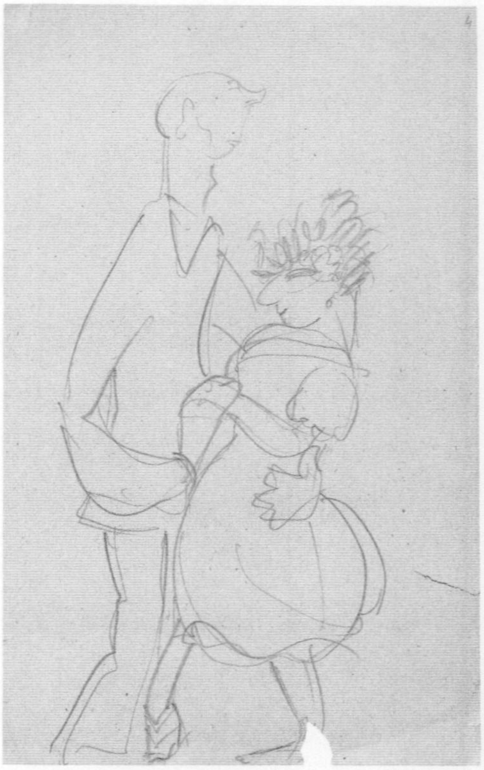

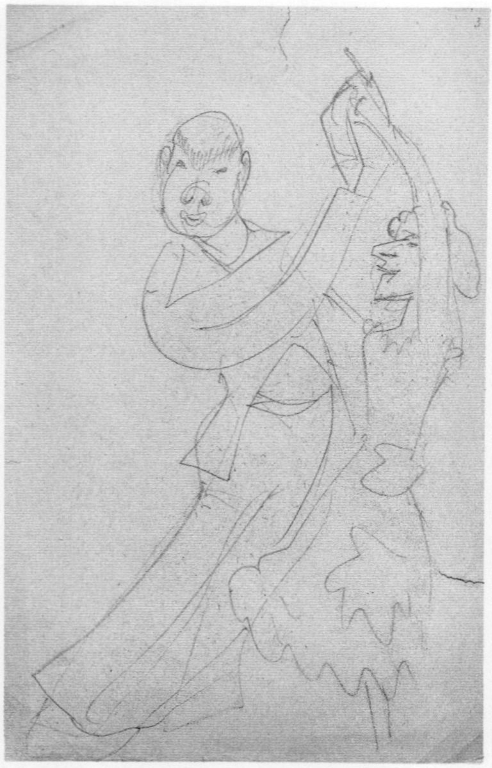

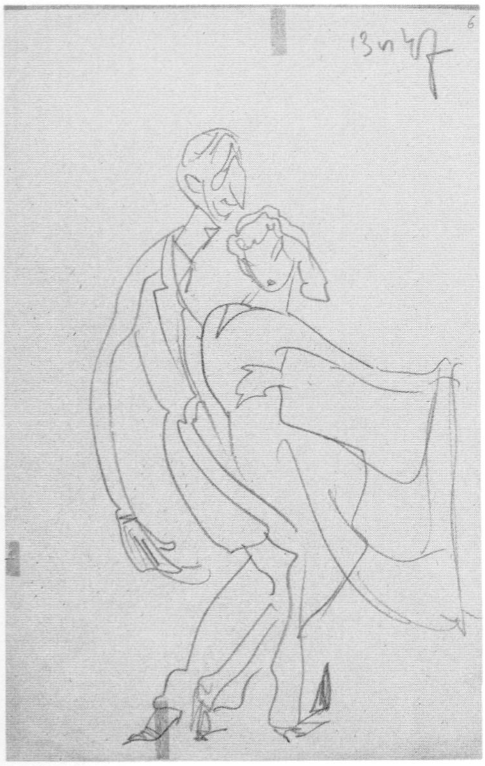

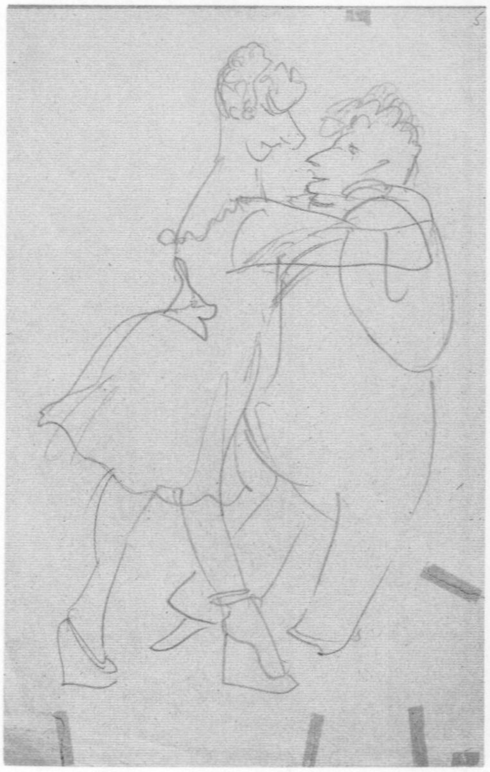

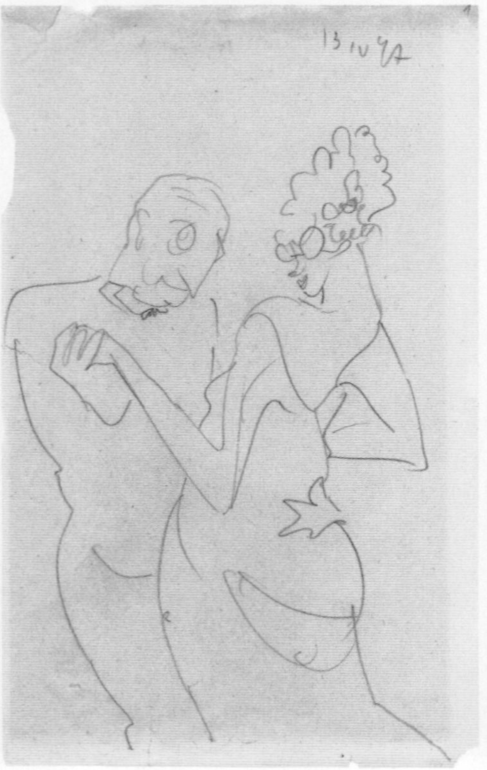

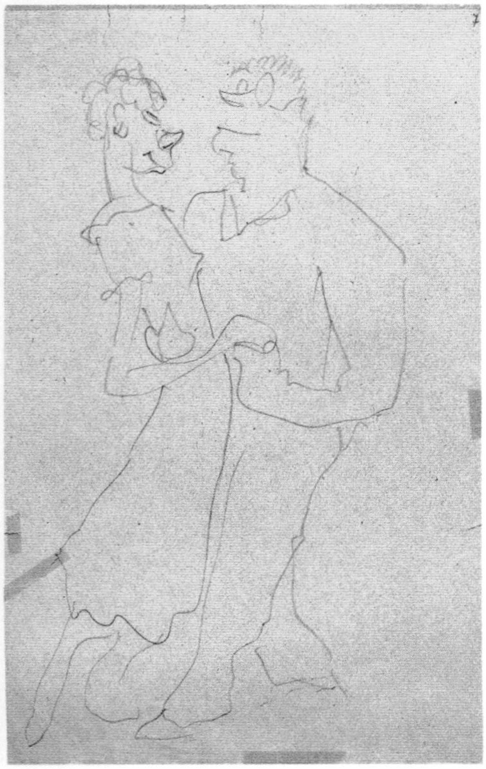

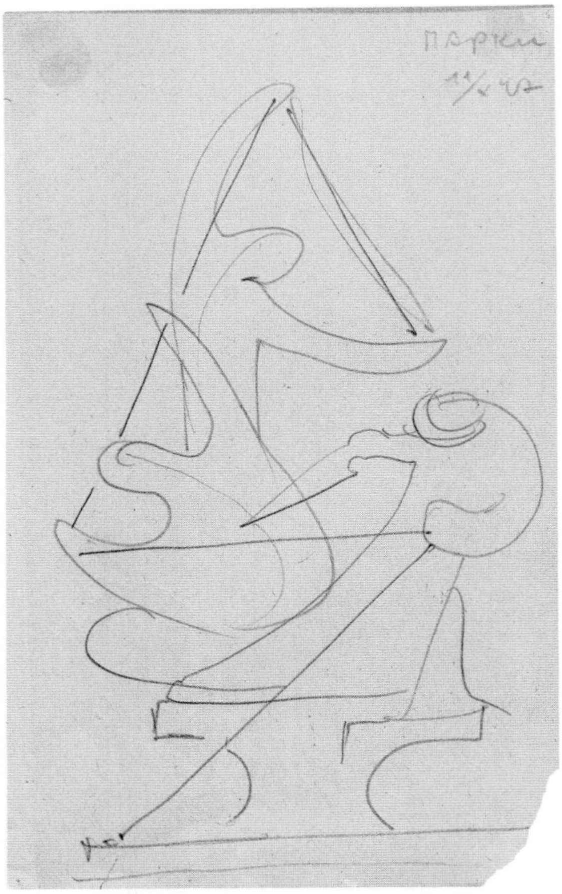
Парки
11/x 47

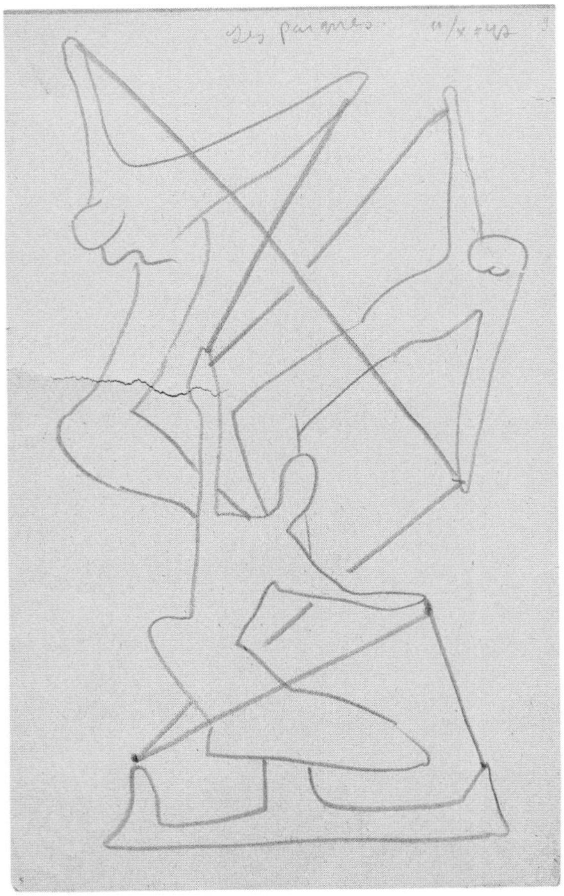
Les Parques 11/x 47

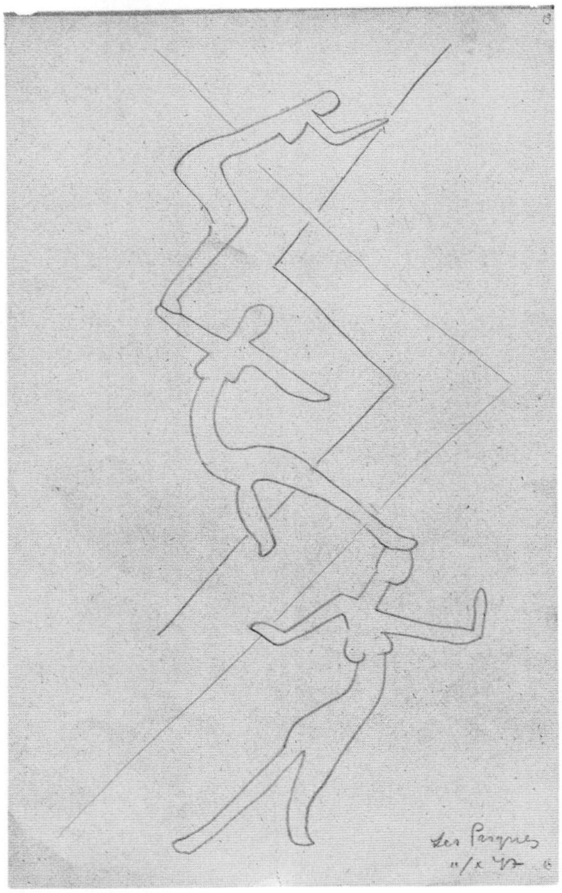
Les Parques
11/x 47

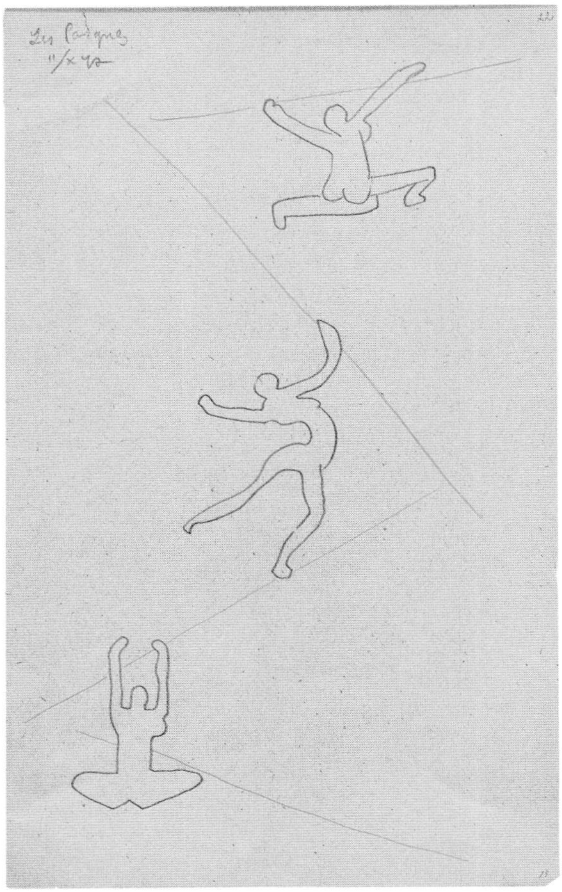
Les Parques
11/x 47

—OPPOSITE AND THIS PAGE

From the cycle 'Les parques' (The Fates) (1947)

—OVERLEAF

LEFT PAGE

3x3 Parques (1947)

RIGHT PAGE

Les Parques Sentimentales (The Sentimental Fates) (1947)

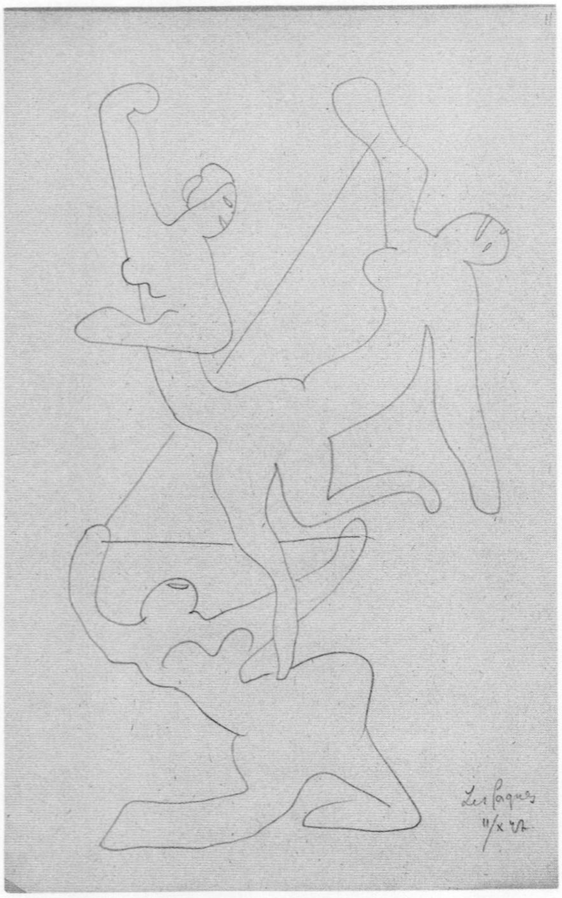

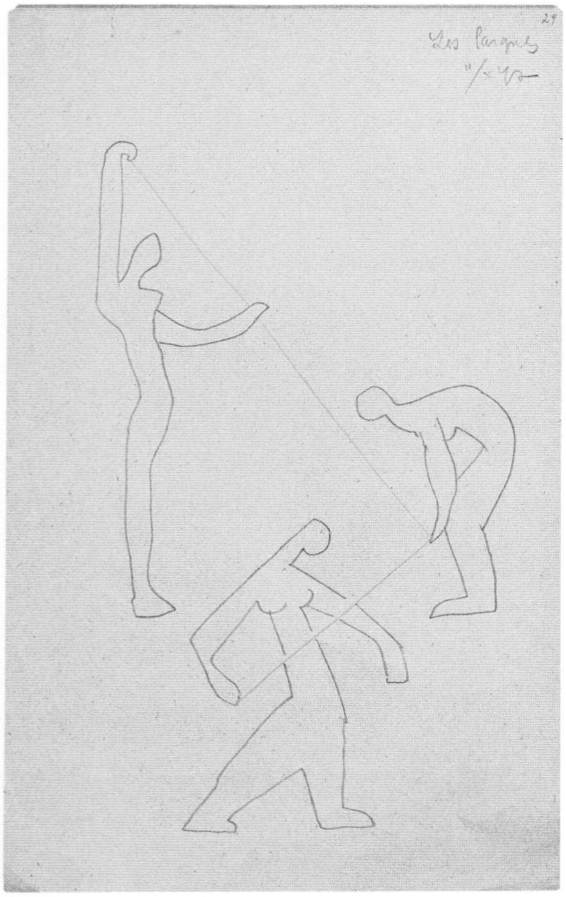

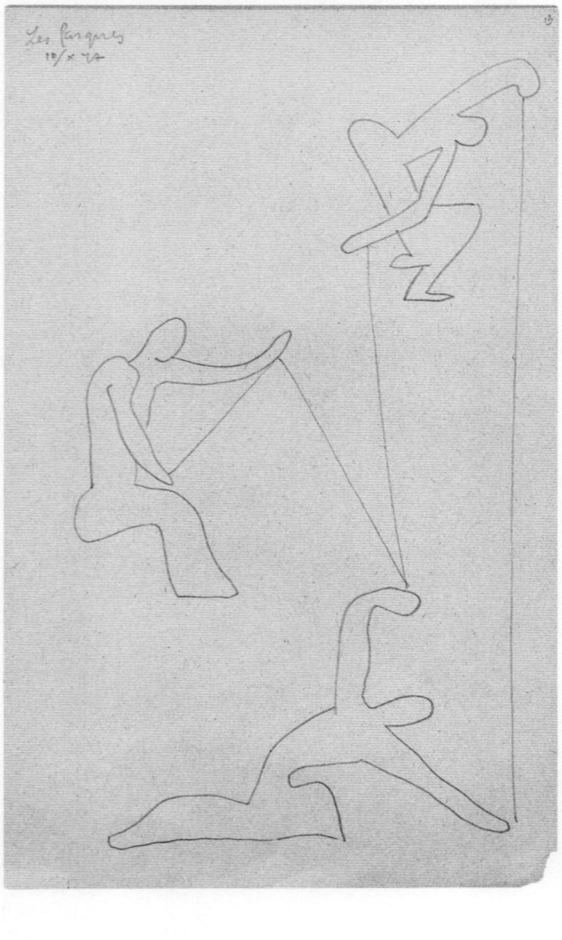

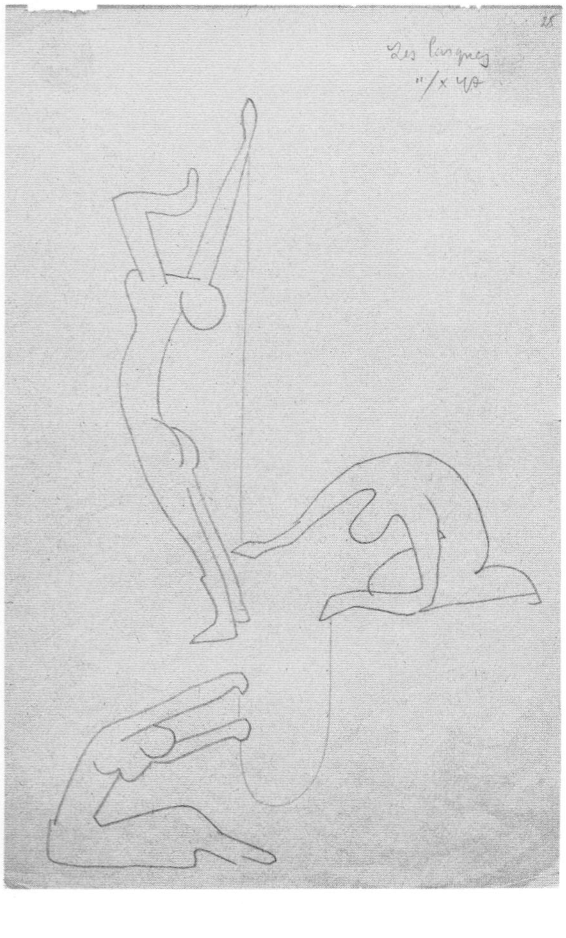

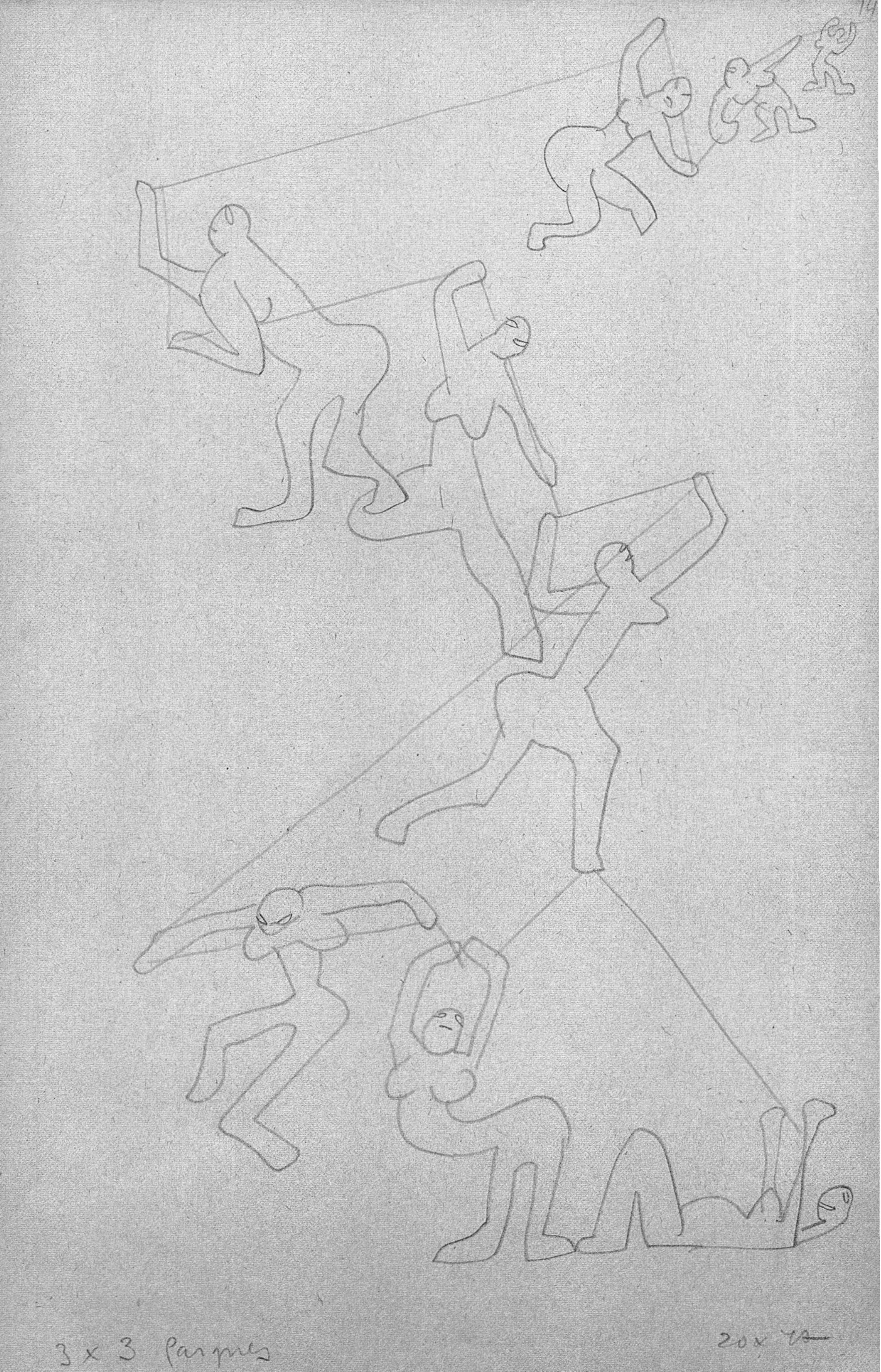
14
3 x 3

Les Parques
sentimentales
20 X 47

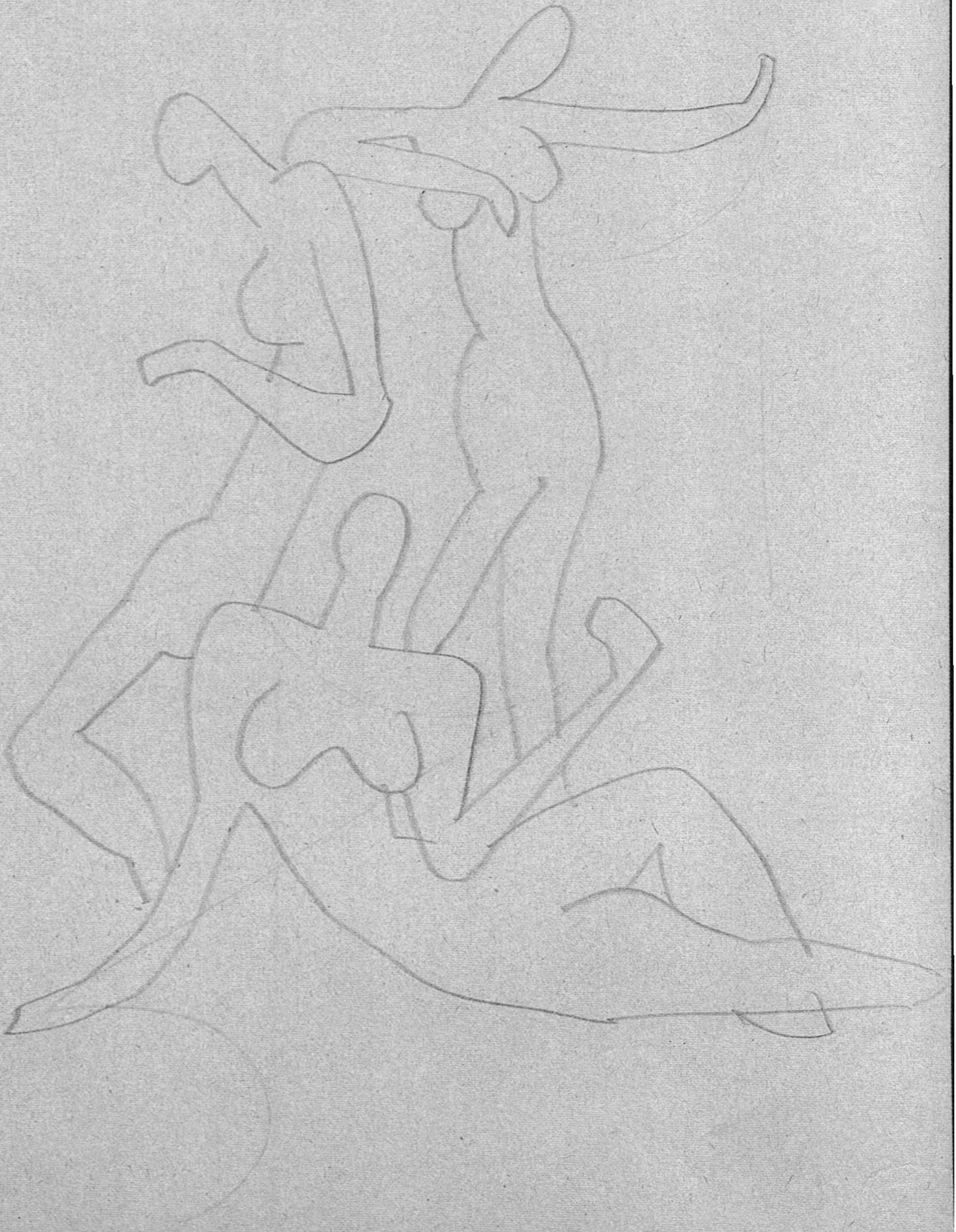

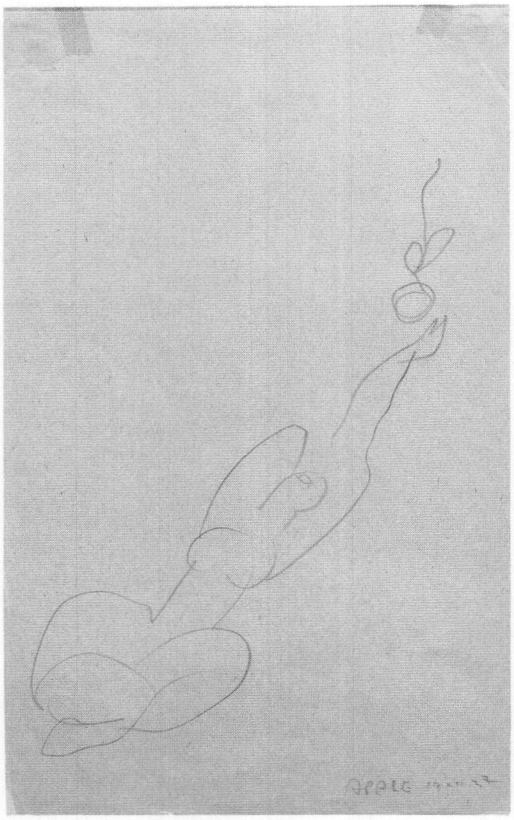
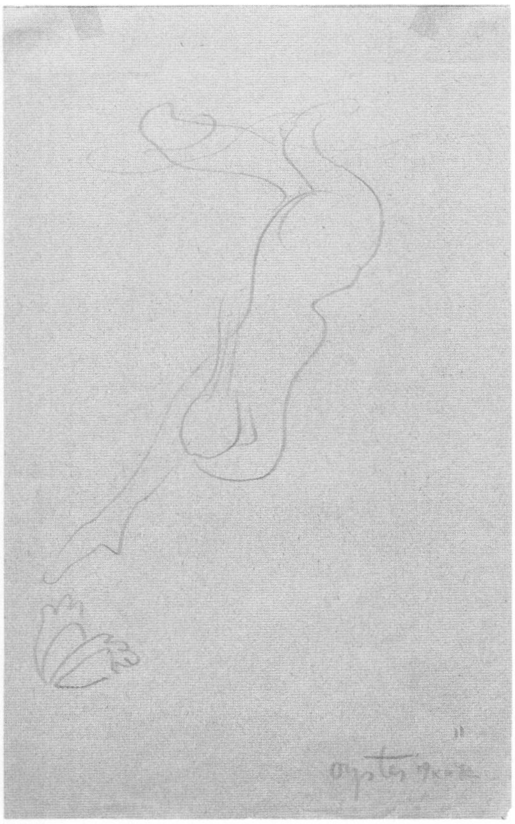
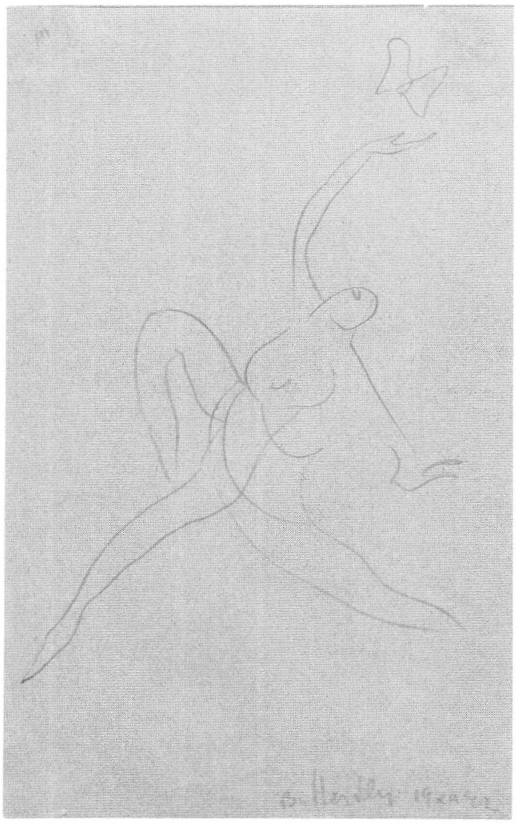
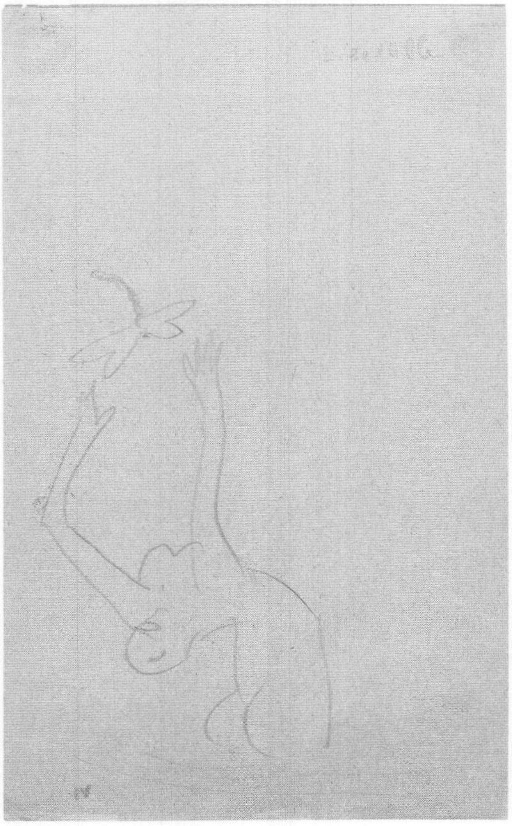
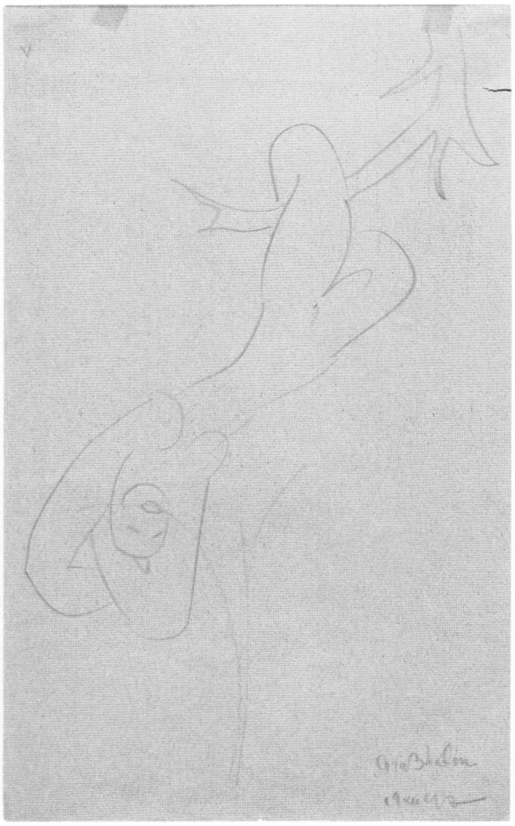
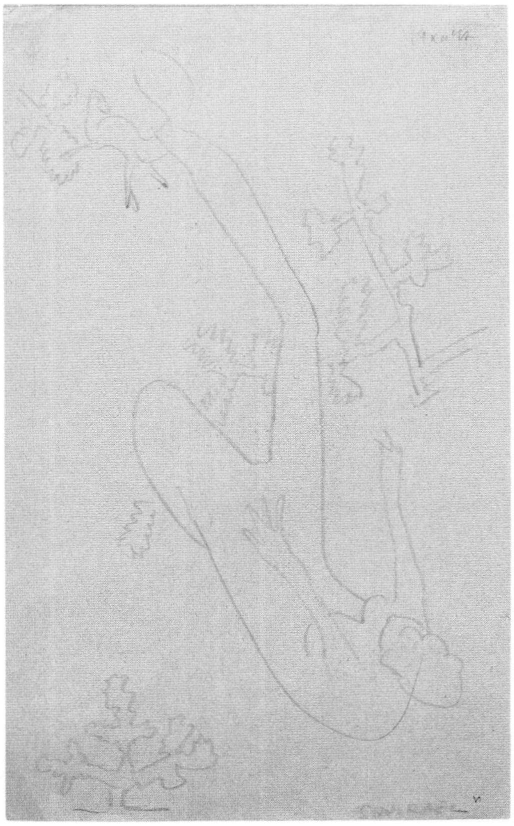

From the cycle 'Les dons' (1947):

—OPPOSITE

TOP LEFT
'I. Apple'

TOP CENTRE
'II. Oyster'

TOP RIGHT
'III. Butterfly'

BOTTOM LEFT
'IV. Libellule (Dragonfly)'

BOTTOM CENTRE
'V. Grasshalm (Blade of grass)'

BOTTOM RIGHT
'VI. Squirrel'

—THIS PAGE
'VII. Cigarette'

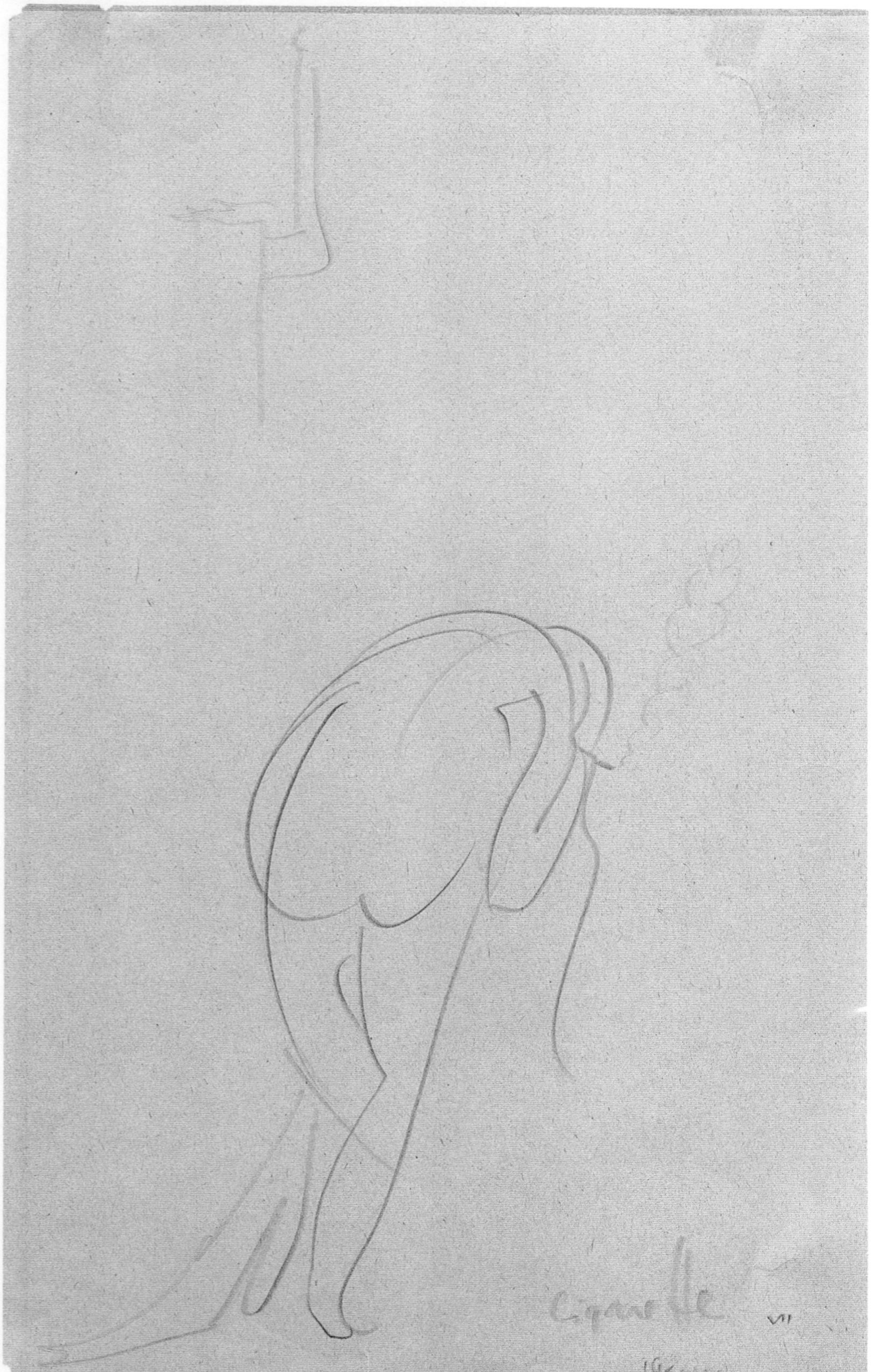

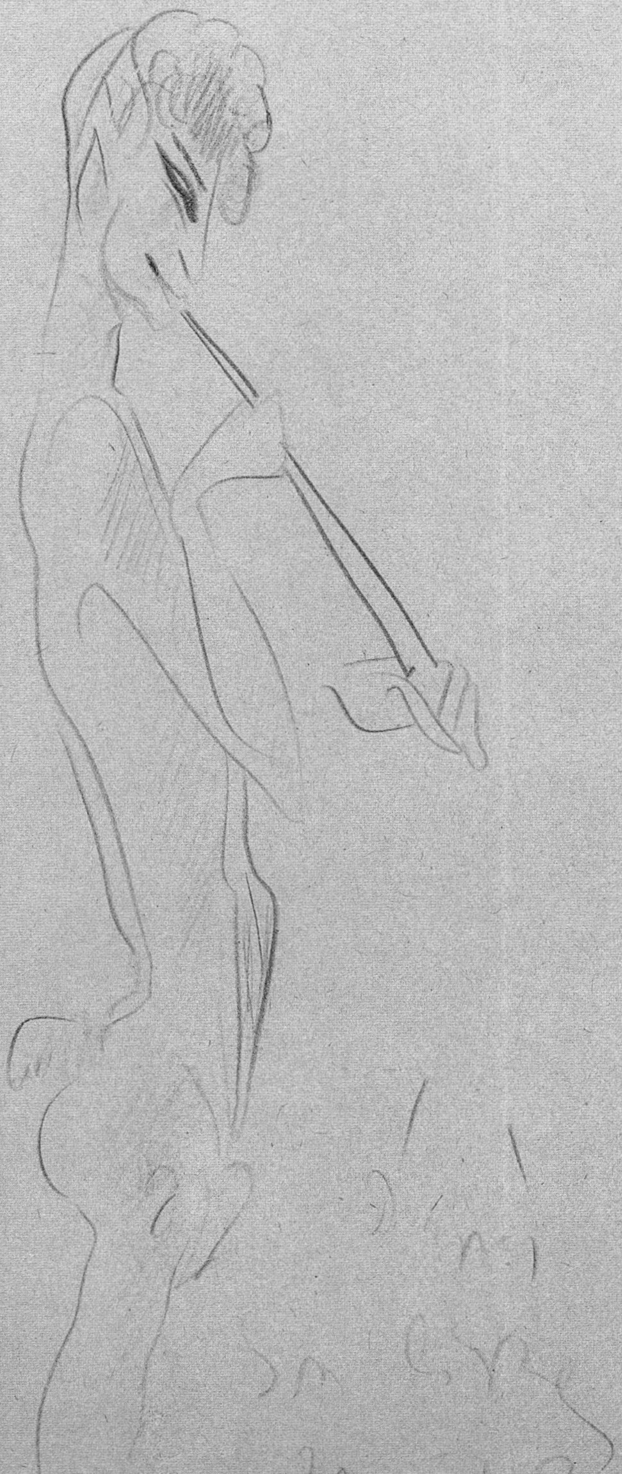

AFTERWORD

'LE POINT DU JOUR D'UN FAUNE'

The faun with a whistle was born on 23 January 1948, when Eisenstein was celebrating his fiftieth birthday.

Perhaps it was drawn in the morning. But it is more likely that Eisenstein's day did not begin with drawing. Most probably, as soon as he had woken up he grabbed a piece of paper and without thinking – automatically, as the Freudians, Surrealists and graphologists put it – wrote in Russian and in English:

It was a graphological test of the state of his heart, and also of his spirit, on this date that the Hollywood palm-reader Cheiro had identified as fateful for Eisenstein.

In his library, on a shelf whose unofficial name was 'The Inexact Sciences', Eisenstein kept books not only on palmistry but also on graphology. Originally, back in the 1920s, he had become interested in handwriting as a trace of the micro-gestures that he observed making up the process of writing. If ordinary gestures combined personal manifestations of emotion with national and social traditions, if the 'expressive' gestures of the stage provided an outward sketch of the character's inner state, then there was no reason why the lines of the handwriting could not bear witness to the writer's current state and individual character traits.

Eisenstein looked for confirmation in the works of Ludwig Klages, Sigmund Freud, Carl Gustav Jung and Alfred Adler, and in the interpretations put forward by the Russian graphologist Dmitry Zuyev-Insarov. He was especially convinced by his meeting in 1929 in Berlin with Rafael Schermann, who had just predicted the death by heart attack of Germany's foreign minister, Gustav Stresemann, based on his handwriting. Eisenstein asked the graphologist how he had made his prediction, and learnt that many of the loops in letters and figures that Schermann had seen in a note written by the minister ('o', 'a', 'b', 'd', 'o', '6', '8', '9') had been broken: it was as though the heart was signalling the impending myocardial rupture to the unconscious, by way of the handwriting.

In the Russian writing test that Eisenstein carried out on his birthday, the 'o' of the word 'Moscow' is broken and the top of the '8' does not close. In the English test the same is true of the 'a' in 'today', the first 'o' in 'Moscow', and once again the '8'.

Then he resolved to try it in German:

The German text is longer – 'A test of my handwriting on my fiftieth birthday' – and so it gave more opportunities for analysis.

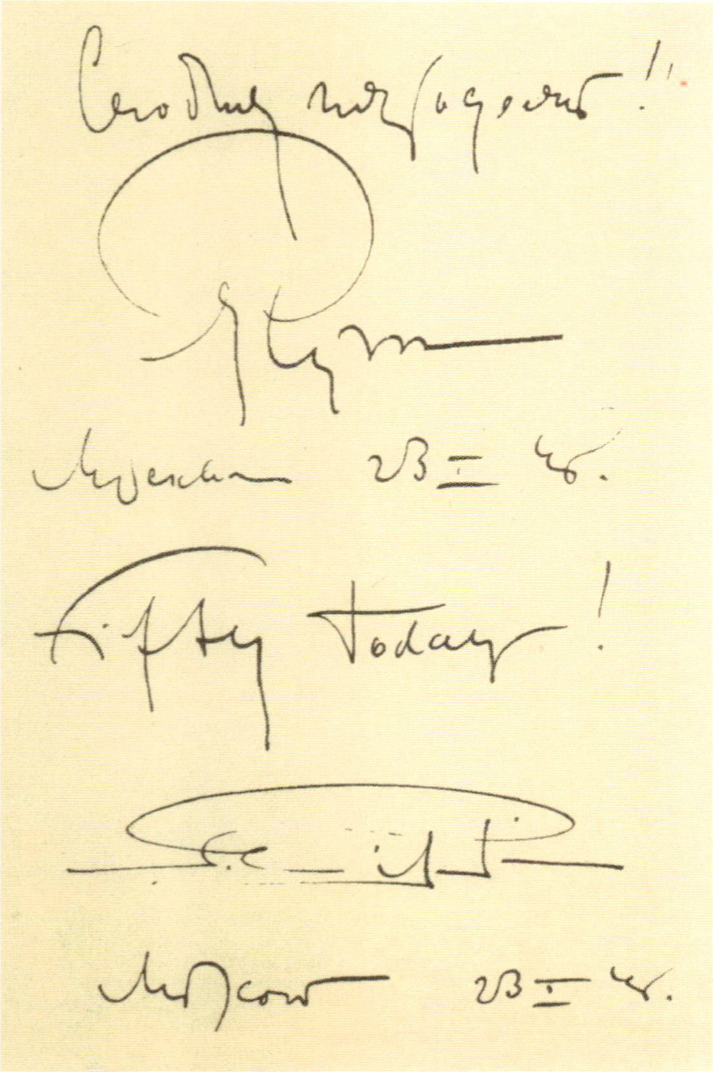

OPPOSITE
The Faun (1948)
Text: *D'après son livre*
(After his book)

THIS PAGE
The graphological test, in Russian and English, written by Eisenstein on his last birthday – 23 January 1948

But here it is only the '8' in the date that inspires worry: the number of breaks in letters with loops does not exceed the normal ratio for Eisenstein's handwriting on any other day.

Perhaps this second graphological test calmed Eisenstein: perhaps he took the German text as a sign that Fate would graciously extend the 'postscript' that his life had been granted.

Two years earlier, in December 1946, he had written a confession to himself – neither exactly a diary entry nor a passage for his unfinished book of memoirs – under the heading 'P.S.':

P.S. P.S. P.S.
Of course P.S.!
On the second of [February] this year I experienced a rupture of the heart muscle with internal bleeding. (A heart attack.)
And by an incomprehensible – awkward – pointless miracle I survived.
By all the data of science, I should have died.
But for some reason I lived.
So I consider everything that happens to be a postscript to my actual biography...
A P.S. ...
And in fact, who gets to read of himself at age 48 that he is '...un des plus fameux metteurs en scène de son temps...'
(Critique des critiques, in the monthly of the Institut des hautes études cinématographiques, Paris, 1946, referring to* Ivan the Terrible*)
or
("La revue du cinéma" I. X 1946):
'...The showing of a new film by Eisenstein provokes the same astonishment that would meet a new play by Corneille. So much effort was used to invest cinema with a history, that it seems as if directors, proclaimed as classics, come from a different age.
One could readily forgive Eisenstein for still being alive, if he were content with remaking* Potemkin *or* The General Line*. But* Ivan the Terrible *has just overturned all the healthy, simple truths that criticism had easily drawn from studying the experience of the great* auteurs *of silent film....'

I imagined they might write that way about me by my seventies, at best; and I thought I just wouldn't live to see it!
And here it is, by the time I'm 48...P.S., P.S., P.S....[1]

The two years of the 'postscript' were filled to bursting – against his doctor's advice – with work. Writing books and articles, reading literature on the most varied questions, lectures at the Cinematographic Institute, setting up the Cinema Section at the USSR Academy of Sciences' Institute of the History of the Arts, and...creating ballets!

Yes, choreography was the latest incarnation of Eisenstein's drawings. His turn to dance does not seem surprising after *Ivan the Terrible*. The dance of the oprichniks at the feast in the Alexandrov Kremlin only appears to be a balletic divertissement in this 'opera without singing'. The characters' movements in other scenes too are close if not to dance then, perhaps, to a pantomime, rhythmically coordinated with the music.

Eisenstein lived to hear many critics, in anger or in bewilderment, accuse his last works of being operatic or balletic. *Alexander Nevsky* and *Ivan the Terrible* were counterposed to his own early films, most frequently to a vital and purely cinematic film like *Battleship*. Could they really not have noticed that *Potemkin* is, in its way, no less 'balletic'?

Around 1935, Eisenstein was preparing the illustrations for his textbook *Directing. The Art of the Mise-en-Scène*. With his students' participation, he sketched out the lines of movement of the groups of sailors and officers across the deck, in the successive shots of *Potemkin*'s Act Two: the beginning of the sailors' protest against the wormy food they are given to eat, the commander's attempt to suppress the protest with gunfire, the mutiny by the crew. The staging of the 'death of Aba' scene. Camera locations around the Odessa steps... The plans for these scenes produced an elegant, 'choreographic' drawing! But the staging, the 'dance steps' for the actors and extras, would only be the beginning of the cinematic choreography of *Potemkin*. These movements of people across the set were supplemented with the movement of the camera from one point to another, delineating shots of different scales from different angles – the process that Eisenstein wanted to call '*mise-en-cadres*'. The selection of these was aided by a third stage: the reshuffling of the phases of various simultaneous actions extracted with the aid of the cutting-room scissors from the film that had been shot. Only this triple choreography, with its all-subjugating rhythm, could create a convincing movement of ideas and emotions in the cinematic spectacle.

And if we take another couple of steps backward through Eisenstein's biography: did the actors' movements in the *Heartbreak House* project, determined by the 'machine for playing', not aspire to the acrobatics of avant-garde ballet?

If the project had been completed, it could have used Sergei Prokofiev's ballet music as an accompaniment. It was not by chance, five years later, that Diaghilev – prophetic and paradoxical as usual – had wanted to entrust the choreography for *Le Pas d'acier* to none other than the film director Sergei Eisenstein!

In the end, were his youthful drawings in Riga not a compensation for his lack of success when it came to dance lessons? But in 1947, Eisenstein took up the ballet in a literal, not a figurative, sense. His debut in his new capacity had already taken place: Susanna Zvyagina and Konstantin Rikhter, of the Bolshoi ballet, had appeared in *The Last Conversation*, a dance number invented and staged by Eisenstein, when they were on tour in the Caucasus.

(In the 'feast in the Alexandrov Palace' scene in *Ivan the Terrible*, Rikhter had performed the dance of the tsar's favourite, Feodor Basmanov, in a gold sarafan and a mask with a Mona Lisa smile. He also appears in other scenes without the mask.)

The ballerina Susanna Zvyagina recalls: 'Once, they showed some material and there was a shot like this: Mikhail Kuznetsov in the middle, his face in close-up, and on either side the two faces of the Oprichnina – K. Rikhter and V. Kudryashov. Then Sergei Mikhailovich bellowed at Rikhter: "What are you doing acting a Spaniard for me! I need an oprichnik! What's that: Rudolf Valentino?!..." And then, after a few days' filming, he said: "Listen! If you're such a Spaniard, we'd better make a number for the stage. And you have an appropriate partner! Bring her to see me, I've wanted to meet her for ages!" [...]

'When he saw the Bolshoi ballet production of *Don Quixote* (the Minkus version), where Rikhter played Espado and I was Mercedes, he got a new idea: "Kids! What about if we made it *Carmen*?! Eh?!..." And he clapped each of us on the shoulder, adding: "Well then, now I've got something new to work on: pouring some of Mercedes and Espado into Carmen and José..."

'In the finale, Sergei Mikhailovich demanded that I rush so quickly to Escamillo (when his leitmotif was played) that I would literally fly over José, who was standing in the middle and blocking my path... Down on one knee, on José's shoulder, with my arms flung sharply forward, I was struck in the back with a *navaja* and crept very slowly, winding myself around the gently swaying figure of my partner...' [2]

Eisenstein 'poured' more into the choreography for *The Last Conversation* than only the dance from *Don Quixote*, more than just his favourite 'leap to the breast then knife stroke' exercise from Meyerhold's biomechanics. The musical theme of the toreador Escamillo and José's fatal blow with the *navaja* to his deathless Carmen – his temptress Eve – his conqueror Europa – represented a transformation into dance or the motifs from Eisenstein's Mexican cycle of *corrida* drawings: the *torero*'s blade stabbing the bull, and the bull's horn striking the *torero*.

And Eisenstein created two more ballet numbers for the duo of Zvyagina and Rikhter. He created a series of sketches and a libretto for the tragic ballet *The Queen of Spades*, based on Aleksandr Pushkin's novella – maybe using music from the Tchaikovsky opera, maybe musical themes by Sergei Prokofiev written in 1937 for the film that Mikhail Romm was unable to complete.

The second number is a comedy: Eisenstein threw together an outline libretto based on Chekhov's short play *The Wedding*. The main attraction of the choreography was tap dance: the telegraph opera Yat, smitten with Mme Zmeyukina, was to use both heels to tap out a passionate confession of love – in Morse code. Rikhter was already learning the translation of the Chekhov text into the telegraph's language of dots and dashes.

Zvyagina affirms that, after *Ivan the Terrible*, Eisenstein would have liked to make a ballet for the cinema. Not to record a stage dance on film, but to use all the resources of choreography and film-making to create an on-screen ballet. The only doubtful question is whether he would have been allowed back into a film studio, after the second part of his film was banned and the suggestion of reworking it was refused.

If Eisenstein had lived to see 1949–1952, the period of the 'struggle against formalism and cosmopolitanism', the ballet stage would have been the place where his work as a director might have been able to continue.

Perhaps, alongside *The Last Conversation* (*Carmen*), *The Queen of Spades* and *The Wedding*, his cycles of drawings would have been turned into ballets? The 'Prodigal son' cycle from Almaty could have become a dance to the music of Sergei Prokofiev's 'corresponding' ballet. And, as a pendant to another staging by the old Diaghilev man George Balanchine, the 'Les parques' cycle from Moscow could easily have become a 'plotless' ballet.

It is indicative that at that time when no one could speak, Sergei Mikhailovich Eisenstein was thinking about the choreography of the Russian Parisian Serge (Sergei Mikhailovich!) Lifar. On 24 March 1947, he drew Lifar as the 'Emperor with No Clothes', based on a description of the 1936 Paris production inspired by Andersen's fairy tale. Eisenstein had probably read Lifar's books *Diaghilev* and *With Diaghilev*, both published in 1939: for them to reach Moscow after the war would have taken a miracle, but was not impossible.

It was probably the second of these, in which Lifar touches on his productions and roles at the Grand Opera in Paris, that Eisenstein drew upon for a series of six pages on 23 January 1948. Some of them he labelled in French: 'D'après son livre' (after his book). According to the book, written by the dancer himself, he would imagine the look and movement of the characters in a Lifar ballet even though he doubt not see them on the stage.

The striking thing about this series – which makes no claim to be a fully fledged cycle of drawings (it has neither a developing plot nor variations on a specific theme) – is the contrast between the first five drawings, which are ironic, even grotesque, and the sixth, touchingly lyrical in mood and radically different from the others in its graphic style and therefore also in Eisenstein's attitude to the image.

The youth with a whistle is, of course, the Faun, Vaslav Nijinsky's creation for the Diaghilev company's 'Russian seasons' in Europe, first presented – to uproar in the theatre – on 29 May 1912 at the Théâtre du Châtelet in Paris. He is the hero of the ballet *Prélude à l'après-midi d'un faune*, with music by Claude Debussy inspired by a poem by Stéphane Mallarmé.

Lifar had also danced the 'Prelude to the Afternoon of a Faun', in a careful and not unsuccessful copy of Nijinsky's masterpiece. Above all, however, he had performed it at a time when this 'number' – bold in its open emotionality, upending all the canons of classical dance – had itself already gained recognition as a classic.

The faun that Eisenstein draws – with pointed ears of modelling clay and gilded horns peeking out through his curls, with his tail sticking naïvely up and markings on his hips, with high cheekbones and eyes raised towards his brows and temples – is, of course, closer to Nijinsky's faun than Lifar's. Not all the details correspond to Nijinsky's appearance, to Léon Bakst's costume or to elements of the dance, though. Eisenstein's faun is younger than the original and simple-hearted: he does not cover his loins with a vine. Even his manner of blowing his whistle is quite unlike Nijinsky's. The ballet opened with Nijinsky half-reclining by a hillside lake in the heat of the afternoon, half human and half animal, thoughtlessly producing long notes on a reed pipe that he would cast aside when the nymphs awoke instincts in the goat-footed youth that were unclear even to him. But this faun stands thoughtfully with his pipe, immersed in its sounds, or in himself, mastering the music or being mastered by it, a composer, performer and audience all at once: a young man awakening to art.

But perhaps this 'imprecise echo' of the ballet is not a reconstruction at all: perhaps it is Eisenstein's own interpretation of images from Mallarmé, Debussy and Nijinsky? He was well aware of how Nijinsky had looked, and even of the outlines of the choreography, from numerous descriptions and photographs. More than that: he had once reproduced quite accurately, on paper, the faun's manipulations with the Nymph's lost garment, repeating on paper the erotic motifs – at the outer edge of what was once acceptable – that had caused such a scandal on the Paris stage.

On 4 December 1944, in Moscow, Eisenstein had produced a cycle of drawings called 'L'après-midi d'un faune', just as he was completing the edit for the second part of *Ivan the Terrible.* Had the idea of a future in choreography already occurred to him? Or was this December 'faun' cycle a testimony to quite different experiences and plans? It is possible that his recollection of Nijinsky's Faun was an ironic (the irony being directed at himself) prelude to the 'Tale of the Dollar Princess', or a sarcastic comment on *Autoritratto realista* – something like an *Autoritratto sarcastico.*

For it was not long before his forty-seventh birthday that the Cathedral Builder suddenly started to feel an adolescent excitement, and he would hardly, of course, have failed to mock himself by comparing himself not just to the half-goat of ancient Greece but also to the greater dancer, doomed to madness, who had honestly revealed to the whole world how a spontaneously awakening emotionality manifests itself.

But there was another reason – profound, and not personal in the least – for his interest in Nijinsky's scandalous and prophetic choreographic debut. It is reflected in a book from Eisenstein's library: *Diaghileff. His Artistic and Private Life*, by Arnold Haskell.

Eisenstein had received the book from London on 22 November 1936; as was his habit whenever he acquired a book, he wrote the date in the front. Tucked inside the front cover is a receipt from A. Zwemmer, the London second-hand book dealer, who had dispatched two more books to 'Serge Eisenstein, Esq.' on 11 November of the same year: *Du temps que j'avais faim*, by Serge Lifar, and *Essai sur la formation de la pensée grecque*, by Pierre-Maxime Schuhl. It seems that at the end of 1936, while he was re-shooting the ill-fated *Bezhin Meadow*, Eisenstein was collecting and reading literary works that appeared to have no connection either to that film or to the reality that surrounded the director!

It is clear why Eisenstein needed Schuhl's essay on the formation of the ancient Greek world picture: the author writes about the attempt in Plato's dialogues to synthesize rational and mythological (mystical) thought, which Eisenstein used to call the *Grundproblem* (basic problem) of the creative process. At that time he was generally reading a lot about antiquity, and he often drew ancient gods, mythical heroes and real ancient Greeks. In his new apartment (the first home he had had in his life) he had hung, along with portraits of people from 'his circle', a photograph of a head of Socrates, whom he regarded as the best teacher in history, since Socrates had led his interlocutors towards the truth by way of dialogue: questions and the search for an answer, rather than forcing things. He called his own method of teaching at the Cinematographic Institute a 'Socratic' one.

On one occasion, he drew a caricature of Socrates, cheerful and slightly drunk, still crowned with laurel, before Athens had sentenced him to drink hemlock. The drawing surprised one student, not particularly well-educated, who asked: 'Sergei Mikhailovich, is it you as an old man?' He had noticed that the old man in the picture had a forehead like Eisenstein's: what he didn't know was that Eisenstein's forehead was actually Socratic.

Eisenstein, involved with the problem of ecstasy, might also have welcomed Schuhl's observation that 'Dionysian music' on the pipes 'made a secret string in the Hellenic soul vibrate'.

But what had interested Eisenstein, at that time, in an early book of Serge Lifar's? The key to his interest in it, and in Nijinsky's *Faun*, can be found in a note:

> ***Nijinsky's* L'après-midi d'un faune.**
> ***The flowing Debussy and the chopped staccato of the 'change of poses' and of Lifar's Icarus (after Mme Safonova).***

The testimony Eisenstein gathered from people who experienced Nijinsky's historic debut as a choreographer and from people who pondered subsequently on *Faun*'s innovations helps to clarify what the 'chopped staccato of the "change of poses"' meant for the ballet.

Auguste Rodin published a glowing review in *Le Matin*:

> ***Not one of Nijinsky's roles is as worthy of surprise and excitement as his role in* L'après-midi d'un faune. *No jumps, no leaps, nothing but the poses and gestures of the semi-conscious animal being. He stretches, bends, stops, drops to the earth, straightens up, goes forward and back, moving now slowly, now abruptly, nervy, angular: his eyes track, his arms stretch out, his palms open and close, his head turns away and turns back again.***[3]

The great sculptor understood the place of sudden and jerky movements in dance. Their staccato does not even need any outside music to link the dancer's positions, poses and gestures into the unbroken framework of the dance.

The opinion of Cyril W. Beaumont, the notable British historian and theorist of dance, also attracted Eisenstein's attention:

> ***His first effort was the* Prelude to the Afternoon of a Faun, *in which he employed straight lines and angles, contradicting the ideas of curvilinearity that still largely dominated in the ballet [...]***
> ***Perhaps the combination of static poses hinting at movement with actual movement sometimes failed to harmonize, and, from the standpoint of the pedant, turned out to be an artistic mistake: but, as a spectacle, the ballet possessed both novelty and charm, supported by the silvery music of Debussy and the delightful costumes of Bakst, which foreshadowed the dancers' movements even in the sketches. In this ballet, the music was used purely as accompaniment, and it accompanied it brilliantly, with its sweet piping and its evocation of rusting leaves and singing streams....'***[4]

The politely sceptical connoisseur saw the formal novelty of combining static poses with movement, elegantly alluded to the way they 'sometimes failed to harmonize', deflected any suspicion of pedantry, and re-addressed the choreographer's success to Léon Bakst's sketches and Debussy's music – even though the latter did not dominate the ballet, but merely 'accompanied' the dance.

It is clear from Eisenstein's notes, however, that he, like Rodin, understood and even felt an affinity for Nijinsky's choreographic innovations in *Faun*, where the music was not at all an 'accompaniment' to the dance, where its fluidity was an auditory image of the movement, combining as equals with the 'broken staccato' of the dance, for the true music is the flow that runs all through the 'change of poses'.

Eisenstein's early films (*Battleship Potemkin*, for example, and especially *October*) were also accused of 'intransitive play' within the shot – of reducing the movement of people and things to stasis; they too were criticized for their 'staccato' editing. Even those who admired the energy of the editing rhythm in his films did not always sense the movement of the 'unheard music' that flowed through his shots. In fact, in his essays on editing he himself initially emphasized rather too firmly the need for a collision of different shots – in opposition to Pudovkin, who preferred to link shots together.

From the early 1930s onwards, however, Eisenstein paid ever more attention to the lines that penetrated and linked his shots: lines of images and themes, plastic lines, musical lines. The editorial and sound composition of his pictures was determined not but illustrativeness, but by an audiovisual counterpoint.

The first time he tested his hypotheses in practice was in 1935, in his first sound film: *Bezhin Meadow*. Judging from the recollections of people who saw the film before it was destroyed, Eisenstein achieved a powerful emotional effect in the episodes he manages to combine with Gavriil Popov's music.

In the same year, Lifar, the rightful heir to Sergei Diaghilev's innovations and to the revelations of Nijinsky's *Faun*, published his 'Manifesto of a Choreographer'. One of its basic propositions was that dance must be independent, and in a certain sense autonomous from the music: in ballet, a counterpoint between the audible and the visible was both possible and necessary. This was the slogan for his balletic manifesto *Icarus*, the latest mutiny of the Dance demanding a full partnership with Music, genuine equality between the visual and the auditory, movement and statics, orderliness and spontaneity, freedom and the law by which the artist acknowledged he was bound. At the end of the day, this was what Vaslav Nijinsky had had in mind when he had flung down his bold challenge – the broken outline of the dance, against the piping fluidity of Debussy's music – to the audience at the Théâtre du Châtelet and to international ballet as a whole.

Eisenstein could not but notice how his own experiments in the cinema, and the thoughts about them that would eventually find graphic expression in his 'Gedanken zur Musik' cycles, resonated with these tendencies in ballet. Rodin, in his wisdom, had pointed out the sources for the choreographic revolution Vaslav Nijinsky accomplished in *Faun*:

> ***In dance, as in sculpture and painting, progress and flight are held back by routine laziness and by the inability to be young. We admire Loïe Fuller, Isadora Duncan, and Nijinsky, because they have again bared the soul of a tradition founded on respect and love for nature. That is why they can express all the emotions of the human heart.***[5]

And Eisenstein's own evolution as a director and as a theorist of art went in the same direction: from the exaggerated rationalism and technicism of his youth towards an understanding of nature and the organic. He found the solution to his *Grundproblem* in the double 'movement' of the creative process, rising to the heights of scientific knowledge about the world and at the same time sinking into the depths of an emotional world perception. He was convinced that of the need for a united movement both forwards and back, both 'progress' and 'regress'.

Returning to the depiction of the faun, it makes sense to turn our attention to the orientation of the profile: the youth with the whistle is turned from the left towards the right.

The left/right opposition has no political overtones here, whatever might be the opinion of some dogmatist who wanted to attach the label 'left' to the early *Potemkin* and the label 'right' to the late *Ivan the Terrible*. Here, left and right are to be understood in their Eisensteinian sense, as synonyms for 'earlier' and 'later'.

Eisenstein, the theorist and teacher, would often explain the connections between the stages of some phenomenon by using spatial terms as metaphors for time or for levels of development.

> ***On the left, antiquity; towards the right, the Middle Ages; all the way over to the right, the future.***
>
> ***On the left, the gesture; towards the right, staging (movement across the stage); still further to the right, montage. On the left, the Dionysian dithyramb; on the right, the tragedy; in the left field, emotional instincts; further to the right, the integral (as yet undifferentiated) perception of the world; then rational (analytical) thought; and then dialectical thought and thinking in images.***
>
> ***On the left, whatever is earlier; on the right, whatever is later.***
>
> ***On the left; whatever is less developed (but more primordial and impulsive). On the right, whatever is more developed and more complex, which arises out of the less developed (although it has often been transformed a great many times along the way).***

Eisenstein, of course, understood – and pointed out to his students – that this spatial metaphor was relative and not absolute. It is natural for someone reared with the European tradition of writing from left to right, and it 'doesn't work' with the Near Eastern tradition of writing from right to left, or indeed with the Japanese characters and their movement from top to bottom. Eisenstein sometimes used below/above as a replacement for left/right.

Is it a coincidence that the faun he sketched automatically is turned away from the past to face the future?

For an experienced draughtsman it is no problem to turn a figure or to change its orientation or position. But when the drawing is done automatically, even professionals prefer either one orientation or the other when they are drawing heads and profiles. And profiles facing from left to right are instinctively drawn by left-handers. The first time the artist and animator Francesca Yarbusova, Yury Norstein's wife and collaborator, saw Eisenstein's faun, she asked whether he had drawn it with his left hand.

An analogous question was raised in 1975 by Professor Alexander Luria, the distinguished neuropsychologist, who had been Eisenstein's lifelong friend from 1923 onwards. It was Luria who was given Eisenstein's brain to study after the director's death. The scientist was struck by a glaring asymmetry in Eisenstein's enormous brain, which was quite untouched by sclerosis: the right hemisphere was bigger than the left. In 1948, no one yet knew what was discovered in the 1970s: Eisenstein had been gifted by nature with an advantage in the visual and musical spheres, and he should have been left-handed as well. The professor could not remember which hand his friend had used to write and draw, and he wondered whether, if it had been the right, that had been the cause of the psychological discomfort Eisenstein had always observed in himself.

Yes: in a diary entry Eisenstein does indeed mention a strange feeling when he drew, and proposes that perhaps he was born left-handed and then taught to use his right hand in early childhood (a common practice in the 19th century).

Among his drawings from 1946 there is a sheet on which figures of peoples and animals are confidently drawn, with an inscription in a slightly unsteady handwriting that reads 'My first left-hand drawing'. And it is true: the profiles of almost all the characters are turned from left to right. Only one, in the bottom left corner, is looking the other way.

How tempting it would be to suggest that Eisenstein, on his last birthday, had overcome the habit of right-handedness imposed on him in childhood, had liberated his innate instinct and had taken the pencil in his left hand!

There is also the possibility of a less radical interpretation: perhaps the faun's turn from left to right is simply the subconscious preference of a 'right-hemisphere man' who retained the impulse of his nature while still being right-handed.

But there is another possibility too: perhaps the turn from left to right is a visual metaphor for Eisenstein's perception of time and history. In that case, his mythical youth would be turned from the past to face the future. Does this metaphor not express Eisenstein's cherished hope of cutting through the limit of the fateful date that the palm-reader had once named?

Or again, perhaps the metaphor here does not refer to time at all, but to space, in accordance with the norms of European geographical orientation: left is the west and right is the east. In that case, the faun would be turned towards the sunrise. And then it would become clear why he is not lying, like Nijinsky, under the hot rays of the afternoon sun, playing lazily on his whistle, but is instead standing with his flute and intently waiting for dawn to break. In which case, we would have to understand the drawing not as 'L'après-midi d'un faune' but as 'Le point du jour d'un faune': faun before sunrise.

So, what was this drawing dated 23 January 1948 for Eisenstein?

Was it a seed that might have grown if Cheiro's prediction had not come true: a sketch for a future production of a ballet number? The Nijinsky original? Or Lifar's version? Or his own choreography? Or was it just another test, graphic rather than graphological, to diagnose his emotional and physical condition on his birthday?

The faun is not drawn with Eisenstein's usual ascetic (mathematical) line, not with an enclosed (protoplasmatic) outline, but as a system of free gestures arising and breaking off whenever and wherever they choose. The series of light, dense zigzags intersects with the figure itself: this is not classical cross-hatching, of course, but rather a hint at the three-dimensionality and even the 'texture' of the body. The base colour is brown, slightly darker than ancient terracotta or the reddish clay soil of the Moscow region. Yellow is twice applied on top of it – either a trace of gilt, or a reflection from the first day of the rising sun, or the straw colour of a shepherdess's hair in a mid-Russian village. A stern black creates a rhyme between the oriental eyes (not the blank, blind eyes of a sculpture, but the shaded eyes of a musician absorbed in sound) and the corner of the slightly open mouth on the face of the youth with the pipe, who has put music in the place of sight. And the faun's lips are delicately marked with red: the tenderness of his smile, the joy of his playing, the pulse of his life.

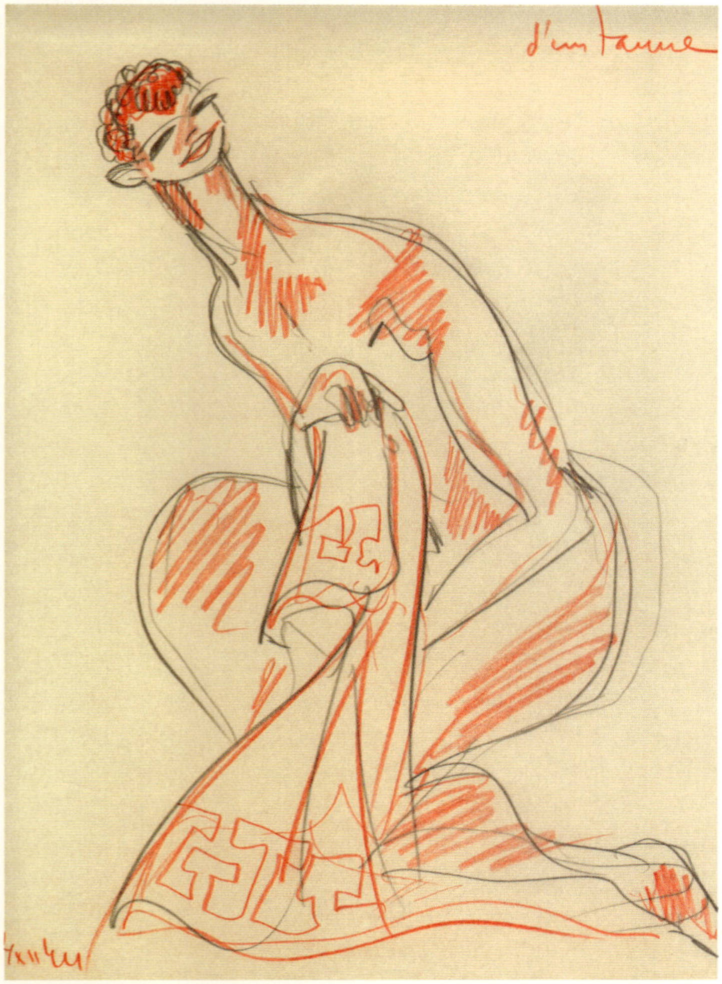

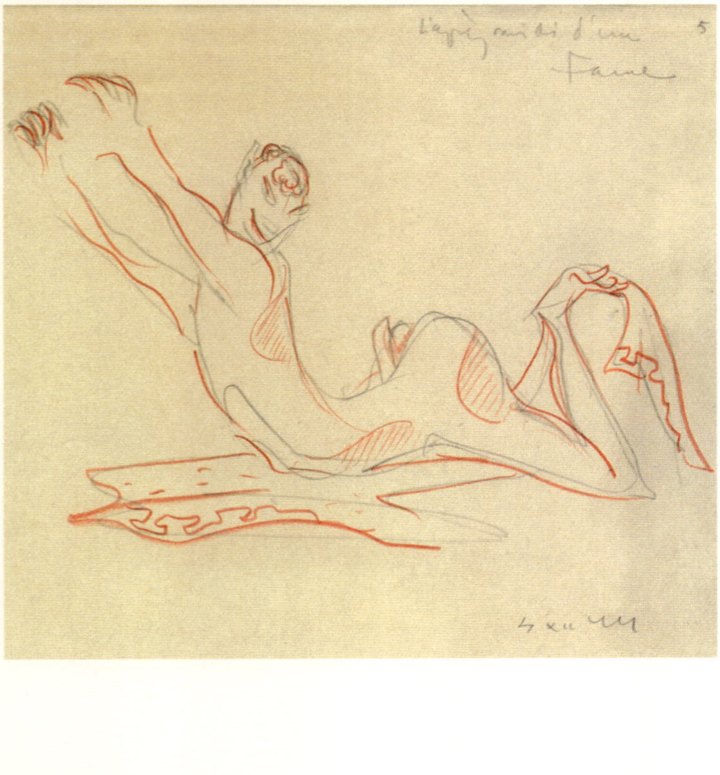

What was Eisenstein thinking about when he sketched this vision of a faun onto the oblong piece of paper, using four coloured pencils of the kind that children usually draw with?

He probably drew without taking thought, rapidly and impulsively, as he once had in Mexico, where the same kind of pencils (he had not used them as a child) that helped him to extract frightening and attractive confessions from the depths of his subconscious or his proto-memory. The visual images of the *corrida*, of Golgotha, Old Testament myths, erotic fantasies had seemed to come of their own accord, and it was only later that he had tried to understand the meaning of these unexpected visual metaphors and spontaneous associations. What could this drawing tell him, when Eisenstein had finished drawing it, had added the date of his last birthday and then looked questioningly at his newborn faun?

This modest drawing of a single figure only seems to be simple, like the melody of a reed pipe playing a single voice.

The very first time Eisenstein's future friend, the African-American actor and singer Paul Robeson, met him, just after watching *The General Line*, he impulsively burst out: 'Oh, how polyphonic you are, Mr Eisenstein!' And the film-maker did not pretend not to be flattered.

Perhaps the initial impulse is not so important: whether it was a memory of Nijinsky's ballet, or an inspiration from Lifar's book, or a preparation for his own ballet, which he was never to bring to fruition.

This drawing of Eisenstein's was born in the depths of his imagination, channelled on the one hand through the labyrinths of his ever-active memory, his colossal erudition and his free associations, and on the other, through his mental state at that precise moment – his grim forebodings and secret hopes. The sketch, projected onto the paper and danced out first with one pencil and then with another, the pencils gripped in a pinch using all five fingers, became an illustrated image of everything Eisenstein had ever thought, read, hunted down in books, written, directed in the cinema or the theatre, or said to his colleagues and pupils.

And if we recall the themes and voices we have heard in his films, texts, lectures and marginalia, then we will understand why the stream flowing through the image of Eisenstein's faun is not the liquid prelude of the impressionist Debussy but a paradoxical fugue for a fife – forefather of the organ.

To describe the interweaving of themes and voices in the spirit of Bach's harmonic polyphony (as we remember, S. M. was dreaming to build such a cathedral), we would need a whole book:

on the ancient Roman Faun, the favourable god of the fields, woods and hills, the protector of the herds;

on the Fourth Eclogue of Virgil, in which a Shepherd Oracle foretells the coming birth of a boy who is called to save and reorder life on Earth in accordance with the divine law of the Brotherhood (the echo of this prediction passed through the Russian film about a mutinous battleship);

on the Pastors of the western Middle Ages, who accepted the Roman poet as a prophet – alas, being a pagan, he was placed not in paradise but in purgatory, and even the first man of the New Age, Dante Alighieri, had to accept it when he left his Guide 'at the very gates of Salvation', shedding 'tears like black rain', but by his Divine Comedy *he helped Virgil stay alive in humanity's memory;*

on the pastorals of the Renaissance and the Age of Gallantry, an attempt to restore the lost 'Golden Age' at the dawn of the Age of Steel (this utopia would be transformed, in the 20th century, into bloody social projects);

on the terrifying thunderbolts at the end of the century of Reason and the Encyclopaedia, *sounding, alas, not without the influence of the fluid refrains of Jean-Jacques Rousseau of Geneva (his honest name had been on the lips of Gavroche – the idol of a well-brought-up 'boy from Riga' – when this Paris* gamin *fell on the barricades in 1832);*

on the bucolics and epigrams of André Chénier, the singer of freedom and honour, who tried to defend the victims of the Jacobinic terror and was one of the last to mount the guillotine before Robespierre (this poet was chosen by Aleksandr Pushkin as his High Ideal – and later, Pushkin himself became an Ideal for Eisenstein);

on Mallarmé's 'Faun's Monologue' of 1865, eleven years later reworked by the author into an eclogue that would turn into Debussy's Prelude *some eighteen years after that, and, after another eighteen years, would cry out in the ballet of Nijinsky, only to find an echo after thirty-six more years in a drawing of Eisenstein's.*

And it would also be good to remember:

that the benevolent Roman Faun's relatives were the goat-footed satyrs of Greece, the acolytes of the dying and rising god Dionysus, the Asian god of Night and the Abyss, the giver of catharsis by way of frenzy and ecstasy;

that the brother and conqueror of Dionysus, the god of women, is solar Apollo, the god of men, the protector of the Muses, the uniter of the peoples, the giver of purification after ecstasy and catharsis;

that there were the strange dual cults of Crete, Dionysus the Bull or Zeus the Bull in the labyrinth, the god of orgiastic victims, and that the 'bright thinking of the Greeks' synthesized even Zeus and Dionysus and Bacchus and the Bull into the

God of omophagy, of tearing the victims to death and ritually consuming the meat raw;

that there was the feat of Theseus, the conqueror of the Minotaur with the aid of Ariadne, who betrayed her father the king for the sake of her lover and was then abandoned by him, after which she became the lover of Dionysus himself;

that the Pyrenean corrida, *heir to the Cretan minotauromachy, the duel between the Bull God and the God-Fighting Torero, takes place no longer in the darkness of the labyrinth but in an arena drenched with sunlight, the descendant of the Roman circus and before that of the amphitheatres of Hellas.*

And we will see:

how Eisenstein, in his Mexican drawings, showed the fusion of the torero and the bull in death, adjoining the element of ecstasy that he managed to tame later, at the end of his life, and created this peaceable goat-footed hybrid, after the example of the ancient Greeks, who knew of the metamorphosis of the Bull into the Steed and the Goat – mutations that are incredible in scientific genetics but that were accepted in archaic mythology, which proclaimed the horse god Silenus the leader of the half-goat satyrs;

how Silenus brought up both the hero Heracles and the singer Arion, the mythical father of tragedy, a play that also derives from 'tragos', the ordinary Greek goat, who was as well at the sources of comedy, and this secret connection gave birth to European theatre as a whole, with its pastorals and Grand Guignols, its satire and its ballet (the source of Eisenstein's path in art);

how tragedy was born also from the spirit of music, in the formula of Nietzsche, who muddled some things in the interpretation of the myths, including those of Dionysus and Apollo (so that Eisenstein found it necessary to quarrel with him about Dionysian ecstasies and their meaning);

how Helios Apollo became the embodiment of rhythm and of the spirit of music as well as Zeus Dionysus, worshipped also as Tree-God (Endēndros), who is also linked with the splitting into male and female hypostases and who is symbolized by the reed, the plant of orgiasm and purification, and how the Asiatic Dionysus' wild flute was pacified by the soothing harp of Apollo Citharoedus in the name of the future polyphonic music of Bach (the ideal for the polyphonic cinema of Eisenstein);

how the jealous Sun God, in his divine cruelty, skinned Marsyas alive after this satyr virtuoso had beaten him in a pipe-playing contest (this legend was transformed by Eisenstein, in his Mexican drawings, into the earthly cruelty of Macbeth skinning legitimate King Duncan, and was again used in Moscow as a metaphor for the attitude of a pagan tyrant towards the saints and artists);

how the centuries-long mutations of the image of the Greek reed, through the Reed as Measure of the New Universe found by John the Evangelist on Patmos via Blaise Pascal's metaphor of Human as the 'thinking Reed' came to the image of the harmless Reed, more resilient in the face of the storm than the arrogant Oak, in Pushkin's poem 'Aquilonis' (a lesson for Russians on how to survive under the hostile winds of the history);

how the single-voiced shepherd's pipe became a symbol of the pastor, called to lead the straying flock from the Abyss of Perdition, a pipe that might, alas, turn out to be a hysterical flute, fatally leading the obedient sheep to their doom, or that might become a stupefying whistle and lure the children of sinful Hamelin away.

And we will be able to hear:

an elegiac echo of the ancient passionate pipe that became the sad whistle of Meyerhold the White Pierrot in Blok's Balaganchik *(in 1922, in the finale of the unfinished* Heartbreak House, *Eisenstein planned to introduce the clarinet of the eccentric Randall as a parody of it, but in 1948 the Faun's fife was playing an apology for the executed Teacher);*

a naïve tune of a whistle that broadens at the end and was called a 'pity-pipe' (zhaleika) *in the Russian countryside, not just for its mournful sound, but also because in demotic Russian the verb 'to pity'* (zhalet) *also means 'to love';*

a tender melody of the whistle of Lel, the Shepherd God, between Faun and Cupid, whom the pastoral authors and pan-Slavist pedants synthesized after the model of the gods of old Olympus, searching at once for Russia's originality and for its kinship with the culture of the Mediterranean (but ideologists don't understand that the historical route from Hellas through Byzantium to Russia came alive not in the imperial policy of Catherine the Great and of her descendants, but in the great creations of Rublev and Pushkin, Eisenstein's predecessors and mentors, and in the inspiration of Malevich and Mandelstam, his contemporaries);

the magical sounds of the Far East, to which Eisenstein increasingly looked: the Indian transverse flute or Bansuri – played by the giver of the happiness of Love and the joy of Contemplation, the God Krishna (the wooden statuette of whom could be seen next to a porcelain Buddha in Eisenstein's Moscow apartment) – and the Chinese flute Xiao, whose sound, like smoke, can reach the world of the Gods, and sink people into a blessed Peace, like the classical landscapes of the Celestial Empire – an image of non-indifferent nature....

In fact, you do not have to remember any of these cultural and historical landscapes that form the background against which the Faun is depicted. You can just agree that he is facing east and waiting for the light.

This interpretation of the drawing is hidden in a text written by Eisenstein himself, back in 1942, as a foreword to the London edition of *The Film Sense*, the only book he published in his lifetime. The text never reached the publishers, Dennis Dobson – because of the Nazi blockade of the British Isles, according to what they told the author, but perhaps also because some of his remarks sounded very ambiguous in the USSR. Maybe the foreword was simply never sent.

It was very important to Eisenstein to get this foreword to the reader, and he included its entire text in his book *Non-Indifferent Nature.*

The possibility exists that the image of the faun with the pipe waiting for daybreak, drawn six years later, belongs to these metaphors:

Art is the most accurate seismograph there is.

And the tragic dead end it has been in in recent years has merely reflected the level of tension the world has been plunged into as a result of the contradictions that are tearing it apart.

These contradictions have erupted in a worldwide slaughter on an unprecedented scale.

No mind can grasp either the paradoxicality of what is happening, or the scale of what has already been, or the prospect of what the world still has to endure.

We are firmly aware that victory over the darkness lies ahead.

Ahead there is light.

But we cannot yet grow accustomed to its rays, make out the new life in these new rays, move along the new roads that they light up.

We foresee it, sense it, anticipate it.

But the light is still being forged, in the truly apocalyptic madness that now flames through the Universe.

Humanity is striving for it, for that new, unknown light of the future.

[...] And just as the very face of the future is impossible for us to guess at, so too the future appearance of the arts renewed must slip away from any speculations and conclusions that we might think to make.

Three things are left for us:
to wait for it,
to speed it along,
to be ready for it.

To wait for this new era.

To hasten its approach, giving all our powers, all our life, making any sacrifice, to speed up its coming.

And to be ready, armed with the experience of the past, so that we are worthy to apprehend and move further along the things that this unprecedented future will bring us.

There is something delightful in this wait for the forthcoming fructification of art by a new phase, a new page of life.

In the awareness of our entrancement until the moment of its arrival.

Thus, entranced, young brides wait for the moment when they submit themselves to the love of the yet-unknown bridegrooms; thus, entranced, the earth spreads out in tremulous anticipation of the time when the spring shoots will be fertilized.

There is something dizzy not only in the awareness of the spiritual freedom, but also in the sense of the historical limit set for the waning phase of life, before life's ascent ordains us into the new stage in the development of art. In moments like this one can experience first-hand the historical movement of the Universe.

As we wait for the light, may the lamps in our hands be pure and ready for the hour in which our arts will meet the necessity to express life's new word.[6]

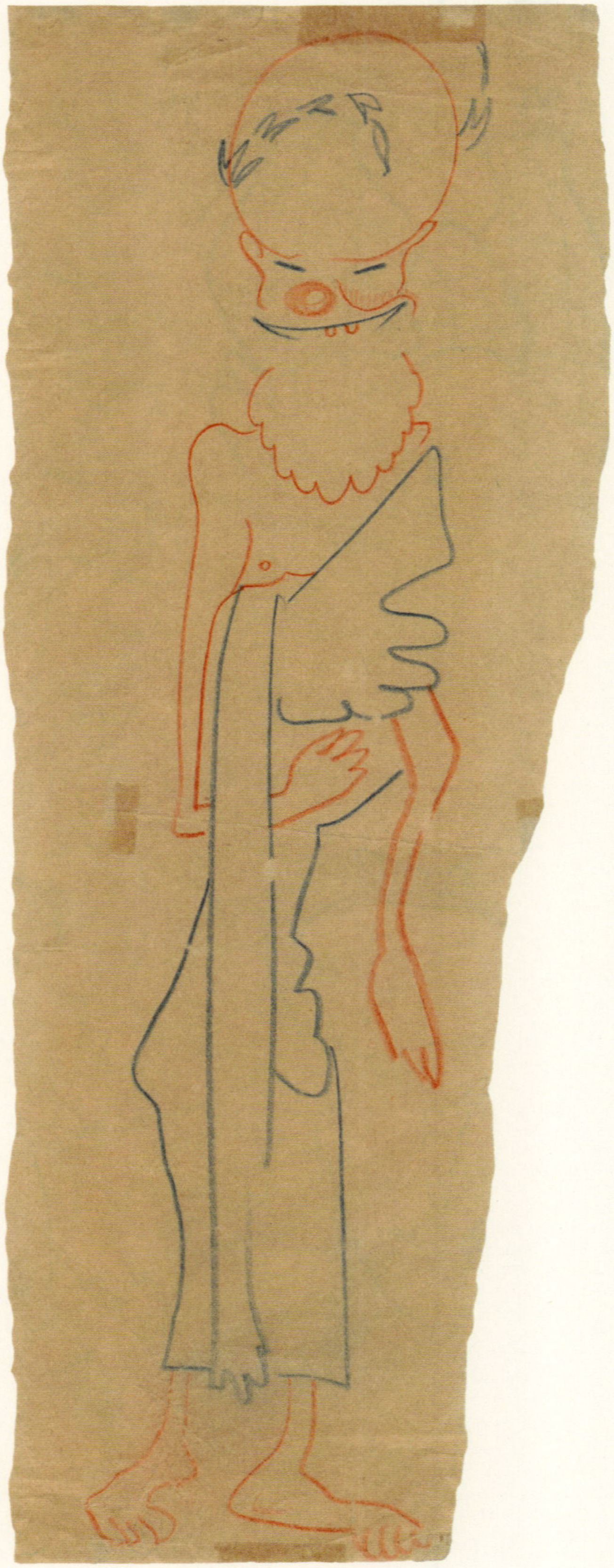

PAGE 311
From the cycle 'L'après-midi d'un faune. Nijinsky' (Afternoon of a faun) (Moscow, 1944)

THIS PAGE
'Old man Socrates'

NOTES

INTRODUCTION BY IAN CHRISTIE

1. Nikolai Cherkasov's and Eisenstein's transcript was first published during the perestroika period, in *Moskovskie novosti*, 7 August 1988, and translated in *Moscow News* no.32, 14–21 August 1988, pp.8–9.

2. Eisenstein's own Foreword begins: 'I must warn you. These notes are completely amoral.' He goes on to explain that they will lack salacious details, but are amoral in the sense that 'they do not moralise'. This and later quotations are from the edition *Beyond the Stars: The Memoirs of Sergei Eisenstein*, ed. by Richard Taylor, trans. by William Powell (London: BFI, Calcutta: Seagull Books, 1995), p.4.

3. The 'cosmopolitanism' campaign began in January 1948, with a lead article in *Pravda* denouncing all 'foreign influence'. Jews, such as Eisenstein, were the main targets, and he wrote in his diary: 'The battle against those who bow to the west is developing with a crescendo. No mercy is shown to either the living or the dead' (quoted in Oksana Bulgakowa, *Sergei Eisenstein: A Biography* [Potemkin Press, 2001; German edition 1998]), p.231.

4. Although *The Strike* won a prize at the Paris *Exposition Des Arts Décoratifs* in 1925, it effectively disappeared from view until the late 1950s, when it was revived by the Belgian cinémathèque. It was first shown in London in 1962.

5. For an up-to-date history of Eisenstein's ill-fated Mexican film, see Gabrielle Murray, 'Knowing Icons and Transforming Experience: Sergei Eisenstein's *¡Que Viva México!'* (1932): http://sensesofcinema.com/2009/feature-articles/knowing-icons-and-transforming-experience-sergei-eisensteins-que-viva-mexico-1932/. Accessed 30 September 2016.

6. S. M. Eizenstein, *Izbrannye proizvedeniya v shesti tomakh* ('Selected Works in Six Volumes') (Moscow: 1964–71).

7. Wollen's essay formed a chapter in his immensely influential *Signs and Meaning in the Cinema*, which appeared in at least three editions between 1969 and its most recent, in 2014.

8. From an 'interview' that Peter Wollen wrote in 1997, conducted by his earlier alias 'Lee Russell', and included in the 2014 edition of *Signs and Meaning*. Full text at: http://www.bfi.org.uk/news-opinion/news-bfi/interviews/looking-signs-meaning-cinema. Accessed 30 September 2016.

9. André Bazin, 'The Evolution of the Language of Cinema', in Hugh Gray (ed. and trans.), *What is Cinema?* (Berkeley and Los Angeles: University of California Press, 1967), p.25.

10. S. M. Eisenstein, *Oeuvres*, vols 1–6 (Paris: Union Générale d'Editions, 10:18, 1975–79).

11. V. F. Perkins, *Film as Film*, Harmondsworth: Penguin Books, 1972. J. Dudley Andrew, *The Major Film Theories* (New York: Oxford University Press, 1976). Both of these books are still in print and remain widely used. The current publisher's blurb for Perkins's book promises that 'Readers will learn why a scene from the humbler movie *Carmen Jones* is a deeper realization of filmmaking than the bravura lion sequence in the classic *Battleship Potemkin*.'

12. Jay Leyda assembled various drafts of Eisenstein's essays on Disney in 1986 for a series of previously uncollected writings, translated by Alan Upchurch and published by Seagull Books (Calcutta). A fuller edition of his writings on Disney has been edited by Oksana Bulgakowa and Dietmar Hochmuth as *Disney* (San Francisco: Potemkin Press, 2012).

13. Bulgakowa recounts Eisenstein 'discovering' Sigmund Freud's *Leonardo* in 1917 (Bulgakowa, p.11). Seton had already prefaced her biography with a quotation from Leonardo, and used further mottos as epigraphs throughout the book, stating that 'the more he read [of Freud on Leonardo] the more he felt there was some inner connection between Da Vinci and himself' (Marie Seton, *Sergei M. Eisenstein: a Biography* [London: The Bodley Head, 1952]. p.30).

14. See, for instance, Martin J. Kemp, *Leonardo da Vinci: The Marvellous Works of Nature and Man* (Oxford: Oxford University Press, 2006).

15. Bulgakowa, *Sergei Eisenstein: A Biography*.

16. S. Eisenstein, 'Through Theatre to Cinema' (1934), in *Film Form: Essays in Film Theory*, ed. and trans. by Jay Leyda (New York: Harcourt, Brace and World, 1949), p.3.

17. This treatise on aesthetics was planned and largely written by Eisenstein in 1945–6, and published in English translation by Herbert Marshall in 1987.

18. Bulgakowa notes that during its first weeks' showing in Moscow, *Potemkin* beat Douglas Fairbanks's spectacular *Robin Hood* in two cinemas, but that not enough prints were available to satisfy provincial demand (*Biography*, pp.61–2).

19. *Close Up*, vol.3 no.3, 1928, p.13.

20. Beckett's letter was never answered, probably because Eisenstein was ill at the time and embattled with the production of *Bezhin Meadow*.

21. Bulgakowa, p.75.

22. Trotsky had played a leading part in the Bolshevik organization of the October Revolution. But after Lenin's death, he clashed with Stalin, who had him expelled from the Communist Party late in 1927, then exiled and eventually assassinated in Mexico in 1940.

23. See selection from the conference proceedings in *The Film Factory: Russian and Soviet Cinema in Documents 1896–1939*, ed. by Richard Taylor and Ian Christie (London: Routledge, 1988), pp.348–70.

24. *The Film Sense*, edited by Jay Leyda, appeared in 1942, and included an analysis of sound-image relations in *Alexander Nevsky*, with a chart that brought the precision of Eisenstein's analytic thinking to a new generation, unaware of his earlier essays published in the 1920s.

25. Ivor Montagu wrote to Eisenstein in 1945 to tell him about the clear debt that *Henry V* owed to *Alexander Nevsky*, and the enthusiasm of Dallas Bower, who had already commissioned a radio play of *Nevsky* from Louis MacNeice in 1941, before promoting the idea of Olivier's film. See IC, 'Censorship, Culture, and Codpieces', in *Eisenstein at 100: A Reconsideration*, ed. by Barry Scherr and Al LaValley (New Brunswick: Rutgers University Press, 2001), pp.113–16.

26. In a 'P.S.' chapter of the *Memoirs*, he wrote that, after a surviving a heart attack from which he 'should' have died: 'I therefore consider that everything is a postscript to my own life' (*Beyond the Stars*, p.797).

27. 'Inversions', written in July 1946 (*Beyond the Stars*, p.630).

28. The remainder of this quotation is taken from a different source: the essay 'Judit', which has a much longer discussion of *A Guy Named Joe* and its implications, and appeared in French translation in *Memoires* 2, vol.5 of *Oeuvres* (1979), pp.227–8.

29. From the chapter titled 'Inversions' in *Beyond the Stars*, written in July 1946, p.630.

30. Quoted in Bulgakowa, p.229.

31. Ian Christie, 'Eisenstein's Third Text: the Drawings and their Ancestors', in *The Body of the Line: Eisenstein's Drawings*, Drawing Papers 4 (New York: The Drawing Center, 2000), pp.29–33.

32. A selection of these was published in France by Jean-Claude Marcadé and Galia Ackerman in *Sergueï Eisenstein. Dessins secrets* (Paris: Seuil, 1999).

33. Eisenstein chaired an evening held in Bely's honour in 1933, a year before the writer's death. His lasting enthusiasm for Bely's insights on Gogol formed a chapter in *Beyond the Stars*, pp.639–46.

34. *Zhiznetvorchestvo*, or 'life creation', has been viewed as the creed of the Russian intelligentsia that was shaped by the philosophy of Nietzsche and Kant, and by the Russian mystical thinkers Nikolai Fedorov and Vladimir Soloviev. See for instance G. S. Smith, *D. S. Mirsky: A Russian-English Life 1890–1939* (Oxford University Press, 2000) and *Creating Life: the Aesthetic Utopia of Russian Modernism*, ed. by Irina Paperno (Stanford University Press, 1994).

PREFACE: RULES OF THE GAME

1. Anita (born Hanna) Brenner (1905–74) – American-Mexican anthropologist, writer and art critic of the magazine *Creative Art*. Her *Idols Behind Altars* (New York: Harcourt, Brace and Company, 1929), the first book on Mexican art and customs from Precolumbian epochs through the 1920s, influenced Eisenstein's conception of *¡Que viva México!*. Anita, daughter of immigrants from Latvia, the region of Russia where Eisenstein was born, was the friend of many Mexican muralists, and sympathized with the Soviet film director. The full text of 'Notes for Anita Brenner's Article on my Drawings for *Creative Art*' has been published in Eisenstein, Sergei M., *Method* (Moscow: Eisenstein-Centre, Cinema Museum, 2002), vol.2, pp.494–7. For the translation, see pp. 122–4.

2. Many drawings from the cycles 'Murder of King Duncan' were exhibited and published in different countries. The 1934 commentary, with some examples of the drawings, appeared for the first time only in 1998 in *Kinovedcheskie zapiski* 36/37, and then was published in Eisenstein, Sergei M., *Neravnodushnaja Priroda / Non-Indifferent Nature* (Moscow: Cinema Museum, Eisenstein-Centre, 2004), vol.1, pp.477–84.

3. This essay was first published in Eisenstein, Sergei M., *Drawings* (Moscow: Iskusstvo, 1961), pp.191–93. It was translated into English by Ivor Montagu and published under the title *My Drawings in Ivan the Terrible, A screenplay by Sergei M. Eisenstein* (New York: Simon and Shuster, 1962), pp.301–4. Another translation, with the title *A Few Words about my Drawings*, was made by William Powell – see *Sergei Eisenstein: Selected Works. Volume 3: Writings 1934–1947*, ed. by Richard Taylor (London, New York: I. B. Tauris, 2010), pp.240–2.

4. See the English translation of the chapter 'How I Learned to Draw: A Chapter about my Dancing Lessons' in *Beyond the Stars: The Memoirs of Sergei Eisenstein*, ed. by Richard Taylor, trans. by Willam Powell (Calcutta: Seagull Books, 1995), pp.567–91.

5. Eisenstein, *Drawings*, p.7.

6. Eisenstein's collection at Russian State Archive of Literature and Art (RGALI) has the number 1923. This notebook is in the archival list 2, folder number 1125. Henceforth, these archival sources will be referred to as: RGALI, 1923-2-1125.

7. RGALI, 1923-2-1128.

8. *Ibid.*

9. Eisenstein, *Method*, vol.2, pp.430, 621.

10. RGALI, 1923-2-1173.

11. The article 'Perspectives' (1929), translated by Richard Taylor, was published in *S. M. Eisenstein, Selected Works. Volume I: Writings, 1924–34* (London: BFI; Bloomington and Indianapolis: Indiana University Press, 1987), pp.151–60.

12. This is how Eisenstein referred to his 1934 article 'The Middle of the Three'. It can be found in Eisenstein, Sergei M., *Film Form: Essays in Film Theory*, ed. and trans. by Jay Leyda (New York: Harcourt, Brace & World, 1949).

CHAPTER ONE: THE KING OF THE UNIVERSE?

1. The article 'It is Done!' ('Svershilios!') was written by Eisenstein on May 1945 on the occasion of the Victory over Nazism, but the newspaper *Izvestia* refused the text. It was published for the first time in *Sergei Eisenstein: Selected Works in Six Volumes*, vol.5 (Moscow: Iskusstvo, 1968), pp.284–5.

2. Eisenstein, Sergei M., *Neravnodushnaja Priroda / Non-Indifferent Nature*, vol.2, c. 409

3. English translation of the chapter 'To the Illustrious Memory of the Marquis' in *Beyond the Stars: The Memoirs of Sergei Eisenstein*, pp.510–57.

4. RGALI, 1923-1-1544.

5. English translation of the chapter 'The Boy from Riga (An Obedient Child)': in *Beyond the Stars: The Memoirs of Sergei Eisenstein*, pp.16–22.

6. Eisenstein didn't finish the work on this autobiography, written in 1939. It was published for the first time in *Sergei Eisenstein: Selected Works in Six Volumes*, vol.1, pp.72–4.

CHAPTER TWO: HEARTBREAK HOUSE

1. The rough cartoons that Eisenstein had drawn for the design of George Bernard Shaw's *Heartbreak House*, and the sketches of costumes and sets, and Eisenstein's explanatory note quoted here, and also character outlines by V. E. Meyerhold, are held at RGALI, 1923-1-811 and 1923-2-1630. The main collage of the stage design, reproduced here on p.64, and some important representational materials of the project, are held in the collection of the A. A. Bakhrushin State Central Theatre Museum in Moscow.

2. Published unsigned along with Eisenstein's sketches in the magazine *Ekho*, no.7, 1923, pp.15f.

3. RGALI, 1923-2-1178.

4. In the sketches for this fantastical play by Gozzi, created in late 1917 and early 1918, we clearly sense the influence of the scenography of the two *coryphaei* of Russian 'Silver Age' theatre, Aleksandr Golovin and Leon Bakst.

5. From 'Notes on the Theatre'. RGALI, 1923-1-891.

6. *Ibid.*, 22 October 1920. RGALI, 1923-1-744.

7. RGALI, Collection of Vsevolod Meyerhold. 998-1-984.

8. I. A. Aksenov, *Sergei Eisenstein. A Portrait of the Artist* (Moscow: Kinotsentr, 1991), p.27.

9. From 'Notes on the Theatre' 1922–1923, in RGALI, 1923-1-747.

10. The directing notes, scenario, sketches for costumes and decorations for *Columbia Girl's Garter* are held in RGALI, 1923-2-815, 816, 817 and 1923-2-1631.

11. RGALI, 1923-1-747.

12. *Ibid.*

13. Cit. V. M. Meyerhold, *Correspondence 1896–1939* (Moscow: Iskusstvo, 1976), p.214.

14. Eisenstein kept this note, but it is presently held in the Meyerhold archive.

15. I. A. Aksenov, *Sergei Eisenstein: A Portrait of the Artist* (Moscow: Kinotsentr, 1991), p.35.

16. Eisenstein's essay 'Why I Became a Director' (1944) was included in *Beyond the Stars: The Memoirs of Sergei Eisenstein*, pp.23–44.

17. A. I. Levshin, 'At the Rehearsals of *Wise Man*', in the book *Eisenstein Remembered By His Contemporaries* (Moscow: Iskusstvo, 1974), pp.148f.

CHAPTER THREE: YO AUTORITRATTO NUEVO LAREDO

1. Entry in Eisenstein's 'Nuevo Laredo' notebook #1, dated 19 February 1932. RGALI, 1923-2-1136.

2.. The manuscript of 'Notes for Anita Brenner's article about my drawings for *Creative Art*' is a part of the same 'Nuevo Laredo' notebook #1.

3. Enunciator – Eisenstein's coinage based on the French verb *énoncer*.

4. This sentence bears witness to the fact that Eisenstein, thinking about the nature of artistic creation while he was in Mexico, intended to devote an analytical work to the artistic methods and the lives of two writers, the poet Arthur Rimbaud (1854–91) and the prose writer Joris-Karl Huysmans (1848–1907), with whom he compared himself (very revealingly, even if the comparison took the form of a contrast).

5. Eisenstein added a footnote here: 'The comparison with a bad monk belongs to Anita Brenner, after looking at my drawings.'

6. Several cycles of Eisenstein's Mexican caricatures were directed against the commercial use of Christian symbols in banks, clubs, or in household equipment. Mrs Kate Crane Gartz (1865–1949) was a daughter and heiress of Richard Teller Crane of Chicago, the founder of Crane Plumbing. She was a philanthropist and an active member of the socialist movement in the USA. Mrs Crane Gartz was a friend of Mary Craig Sinclair, and Eisenstein may have met her in Upton Sinclair's house at Posadena at the time of the creation of the The Mexican Film Club.

7. The second part (reel) of Eisenstein's film *The General Line* (1926–29) contains two episodes: 'Drought. Crusade' and 'The Separator'.

8. From the chapter 'My Encounter with Mexico', published in *Beyond the Stars: The Memoirs of Sergei Eisenstein*, pp.411–22.

9. *Ibid.*

10. From the chapter 'Monsieur, madame et bébé'. *Ibid.*, pp.487–506

11. From 'How I Learned to Draw: A Chapter about my Dancing Lessons'. *Ibid.*, pp.567–91.

12. Entry in Eisenstein's 'Nuevo Laredo' notebook #2, dated 29 February 1932. RGALI, 1923-2-1137.

13. From 'How I Learned to Draw: A Chapter about my Dancing Lessons'. *Ibid.*

14. From the chapter 'Wie sag' ich's meinem Kinde?!' – see *Beyond the Stars: The Memoirs of Sergei Eisenstein*, pp.424–53.

15. See the chapter 'Le Bon Dieu'. *Ibid.*, pp.73–83.

16. Entry in Eisenstein's 'Nuevo Laredo' notebook #1. RGALI, 1923-2-1136.

CHAPTER FOUR: GEDANKEN ZUR MUSIK

1. RGALI, 1923-2-1141. This text and two following diary entries were published in Russian as an appendix to Eisenstein's essay 'Disney' (1940–42) in the collection *Problemy sinteza v khudozhestvennoj kul'ture* ('Problems in the Synthesis of artistic culture'), ed. by A. Prokhorov, B. Rauschenbakh and F. Khitruk (Moscow: Nauka, 1985), pp.269–72. They were translated by Alan Upchurch for *Eisenstein on Disney*, ed. by Jay Leyda (Calcutta: Seagull Books, 1986). We quote here this translation.

2. *Ibid.*

3. RGALI, 1923-2-1172

4. Diary entry: RGALI, 1923-2-1159.

5. The manuscript of this essay is held at RGALI, 1923-2-475. The quarterly 'Kinovedcheskie Zapiski' published for the first time the complete text in 1998, in the special issue (#36–37), dedicated to Eisenstein's centenary. *Neravnodushnaja Priroda [Non-Indifferent Nature]*, vol.1, 2004, p.477–84.

6. Will Durant, *The Story of Philosophy*, 2nd edition (New York: Simon & Schuster, 1927), p.38

7. Diary entry: RGALI, 1923-2-1158

8. Diary entry: RGALI, 1923-2-1176. *Translator's note*: The passage is written in German and Russian, with snippets of English and French. The English words appear as Eisenstein wrote them.

9. From '*Notes on the Theatre*' (1920–21). RGALI, 1923-1-891.

CHAPTER FIVE: GARDEN OF GETHSEMANE

1. Notes for the script for *Ivan the Terrible*. RGALI, 1923-2-1666.

2. Leonardo da Vinci. *Manuscript Ashburnham I*, Bibl. Nat. 20388v.

3. From the director's notes for *Ivan the Terrible*. RGALI, 1923-2-124.

4. *Ibid.*

5. From the director's notes for *Ivan the Terrible*. RGALI, 1923-1-565.

6. *Ibid.*

7. Karamzin, Nikolai Mikhailovich. *Istorija Gosudarstva Rossijskogo* ('History of the Russian State'), vol.9, chapter 2.

8. RGALI, 1923-2-1666.

9. RGALI, 1923-2-124.

10. RGALI, 1923-2-1695.

11. When writing the scene of the miracle play, Eisenstein used the biblical text of Daniel's book, but he made an important change: he turned the words of one of the youths incriminating Nebuchadnezzar in his prayer to God (Daniel, chapter 3, verse 32) into an appeal to the people in the temple.

12. Diary entry: RGALI, 1923-2-1169.

13. From the essay 'El Greco and Cinema' (1937): S. M. Eisenstein, *Montazh* (Moscow: Muzei Kino, 2000), pp.404–63. It was first published in French translation in the collection *Cinématisme: Peinture et cinéma*, ed. by F. Albera, trans. by A. Zouboff (Bruxelles: Édition Complexe, 1980).

14. *Ibid.*

15. *Ibid.*

16. Diary entry: RGALI, 1923-2-1171.

CHAPTER SIX: LES DONS

1. The original is stored in RGALI, 1923, list 4. The Russian translation was first published in 2013, in the quarterly *Kinovedcheskie Zapiski*, #102–03.

2. The complete text of this foreword is published in *Beyond the Stars: The Memoirs of Sergei Eisenstein*, pp.4–15.

3. Chapter Katerinki, written in English – *ibid.*, pp.709–11.

4. *Ibid.*

5. This draft note is stored at RGALI, 1923-2-1077.

6. The manuscript of this short essay is stored at RGALI, 1923-2-1176. It was published in 2002 in *Method*, vol.2, pp.501–5.

7. *Ibid.*

8. *Ibid.*, pp.178–191.

9. See the full text of the chapter in *Beyond the Stars: The Memoirs of Sergei Eisenstein*, pp.487–506.

10. *Ibid.*

11. From Olga Shepeleva's speech at the Scientific-Memorial Flat of S. M. Eisenstein in Moscow on June 1973.

12. See the complete text of the chapter 'On Folklore' in *Beyond the Stars: The Memoirs of Sergei Eisenstein*, pp.487–506.

13. *Ibid.*

14. From Naum Kleiman's and Leonid Kozlov's conversation with Nina Cherkasova during the preparation of the collection of articles and materials for *Nikolai Cherkasov*, ed. by N. N. Cherkasova, and S. Dreiden (Moscow: VTO, 1976).

15. Entry in Eisenstein's notebook. RGALI, 1923-2-1129.

16. RGALI, 1923-3-39.

17. From the chapter 'Aesthetic canons of the Far East Landscape' in *Non-Indifferent Nature*, vol.2, p.330.

18. From the chapter 'Landscape as an Embodiment of the Cosmic Conceptions' in *Non-Indifferent Nature*, vol.2, 19. p.460–1.

19. From the chapter 'Music for Eyes' in *Non-Indifferent Nature*, vol.2, p.330.

20. *Ibid.*, p.317.

21. Lin Yutang, *My Country and My People* (New York: Halcyon House, 1938), p.310.

22. Entry in Eisenstein's notebook. RGALI 1923-2-1177.

POSTSCRIPT: LE POINT DU JOUR D'UN FAUNE

1. *Beyond the Stars: The Memoirs of Sergei Eisenstein*, pp.797–8.

2. From the essay 'The Last Conversation' by Susanna Zvyagina in the magazine *Sovietskaya musyka* (Moscow: 1979), #9, pp.91–5.

3. From the article 'La rénovation de la danse. Loïe Fuller, Isadora Duncan, Nijinski', by August Rodin in the newspaper *Le Matin*, 31 May 1912.

4. From Cyril W. Beaumont, *Complete Book of Ballets* (London: Putnam, 1937), pp.793, 797.

5. From 'La rénovation de la danse', *ibid.*

6. From the foreword to the British edition of *The Film Sense* in *Non-Indifferent Nature*, vol.2, pp.400–1.

INDEX TO THE ILLUSTRATIONS

All page numbers refer to Eisenstein's drawings with the exception of those followed by a ▾, which refer to the film stills, and those followed by a ●, which refer to the biographical photographs.

ACKNOWLEDGMENTS

Thames & Hudson would like to thank:
Naum Kleiman for his engaging and illuminating text and for his patient explanations and guidance regarding the choice and placement of the illustrations.

Vera Kleiman for her invaluable assistance in structuring the book and interpreting the author's ideas.

Ian Christie for his crucial role in bringing this book into being with his introductions to Naum Kleiman, Justine Waddell at Kino Klassika Foundation. This book would not exist today had it not been for his initial support and enthusiasm for the project. We thank him too for his introduction to the book, 'Reconstructing Cinema's Renaissance Man', and for his careful review of the text.

Tatiana Goryaeva, Director RGALI, for providing the preface and for making it possible to reproduce so many of Eisenstein's previously unpublished drawings.

Martin Scorsese for writing the foreword and giving permission to feature his drawing of an image from *Ivan the Terrible* in the book.

Rosetta Translations for providing the English translation of the original Russian text.

The author would like to thank:
Tatiana Goryaeva, Natalia Strizhkova and all colleagues at RGALI for their consistently friendly help in my researches of Eisenstein's graphic art and their generosity in scanning the drawings.

Tristan de Lancey at Thames & Hudson Ltd for his trust and his enthusiastic support from the very beginning of this project.

Edmund Griffiths at Rosetta Translations for his talented workmanship in finding English equivalents to the Russian text, especially regarding the really complicated Eisenstein's notes, and Robert Dimery, our editor, for his thoughtfulness, delicacy and stylistic flair.

Jane Laing at Thames & Hudson Ltd for her wonderful work, full of benevolence and patience, at all stages of the preparation of this edition, and Tzortzis Rallis, designer of the book, for his talent, flexibility and generosity.

And, last but not least, Justine Waddell and Ian Christie for their recommendation to Thames & Hudson Ltd and their participation in the work, and Martin Scorsese for the honour of having his introduction to this book.

Additional illustrations:
Biographical photographs of Eisenstein on p.10 and Eisenstein film stills on pp.22, 25, 85, 123, 125, 126, 129, 130, 132, 214, 215, 216: courtesy Naum Kleiman
Photograph p.4: courtesy Private Collection/Archives Charmet/Bridgeman Images

Front cover:
From the cycle 'Murder of King Duncan' Drawing no.1, 1931 © RGALI

Back cover: From the cycle 'Ex-stasis', 1932 © RGALI

First published in the United Kingdom in 2017 by Thames & Hudson Ltd, 181A High Holborn, London WC1V 7QX

British Library Cataloguing-in-Publication Data
A catalogue record for this book is available from the British Library

ISBN 978-0-500-09393-1

Manufactured in China by Imago